PRECIS

VITALITY OF THOUGHT

DEPTH OF VISION

These are the qualities of French theater that have made its playwrights famed throughout the world as leaders in ideas and theatrical form.

This outstanding anthology pictures the dynamic course of French theater, from its inimitable farce, through romantic tragedy, to existential tragicomedy. Each play is presented in full and is preceded by an informative introduction and biographical notes on the author.

The collection is further enriched with enlightening essays on French theater and playwrights by André Gide, George Meredith, Algernon Swinburne, Eric Bentley, Joseph Chiari, and others. The volume ends with an essay by Francis Fergusson on "Sartre as Playwright," commenting on the French theater's present position with a glance toward its future direction.

MENTOR Books of Special Interest

THE GENIUS OF THE
FRENCH THEATER

EDITED AND WITH AN
INTRODUCTION BY ALBERT BERMEL

A   M E N T O R   B O O K

PUBLISHED BY THE NEW AMERICAN LIBRARY

CONTENTS

~

INTRODUCTION

The title of this book is not meant to assert the genius of a few selected French playwrights over all the others or even, as somebody interpreted it before publication, to refer to the late Louis Jouvet. I am not sure that "genius," when applied to a person, means anything, and the attempts of our society to pin it down to digits exceeding 160, or whatever the current number is, only confuse capacity with achievement. Defensive and offensive biographers alike tend to drop the word into their texts from time to time, if only to justify their writing the biography in the first place, and all the playwrights represented here have been called geniuses at least once in print and in some cases thousands of times.

The splendidly emotional word "genius" applies far more legitimately to the French theater as a whole—to its diversity and richness, the characters it has thrown into being, its amplitude of topics and rhythms and treatments, its vigor, its restless searching out of new forms and techniques. No dramatic literature has encompassed as many styles as has the French or had such noticeable influences on other literatures; and skilled pigeonholers can find for every category a French playwright who has been its outstanding exponent: for the drama-of-honor, Corneille; for satire on unnatural behavior, Molière; for classical tragedy, Racine; social comedy, Beaumarchais; romantic tragedy, Hugo (and de Vigny); the well-made play—sometimes almost the puppet show—Scribe (and Sardou); naturalism, Becque; vaudeville, Labiche; farce, Feydeau; the play "of language," Giraudoux; surrealism, Jarry; psychological exploration, Marcel; private fantasy, Cocteau; the existential "committed" play, Sartre; and so on. (English critics like to think that most of the other categories are associated with Shakespeare.) Even in the last ten years French dramatists have led the theater into new dramatic territory; and they have led it a wild dance. Over Montherlant's gritty hills and down Ionesco's bathetic slopes. Across Beckett's plains of melancholy and Anouilh's silk-disguised rockscapes. Through Adamov's dream forests and Audiberti's littered passes. In and about Genet's caverns with their clanging echoes and vermicular burrowings.

With all this variety of subjects and styles, is it possible to discern any over-all tradition in French playwriting? Yes, it is possible. Playwrights from Corneille to Montherlant, from Racine to Sartre, from Molière to Ionesco have been peculiarly adept at dramatizing abstract concepts; they have been concerned with ideas as these ideas moved people—such ideas as honor and dishonor, sin and innocence, loyalty and treachery, will and necessity, respect and contempt, authority and servility. By contrast, the theater-in-English deals with states of mind, with personality, with emotions. Naturally, there are hundreds of exceptions on either side: *Cyrano de Bergerac,* for example, is in many ways "English," while Dryden's *Aureng-Zebe* and *All for Love* are quite "French." But by and large there are not many great characters—characters who are what E. M. Forster has called "round"—in the French repertory; the plays are mostly tidy and rigidly bolted together; unlike us, the French do not delight in—to use an obnoxious term—human quirks and foibles; the characters are in the plays not for their own sakes, but to serve the ideas and to advance the plot and to make the situations "come off." Some English and American critics have not been happy about this. They have called French plays inhuman or bloodless or dry; they have not been able to reconcile themselves to this French theater dominated by intellect.

But it is not the differing traditions that have kept English-speaking audiences from French drama; it is the lack of decent translations. Up to now the bulk of French theater has remained as good as untranslated; the most classical of the classics, the "required reading" plays, have been mutilated into English many times by ladies and gentlemen of deadly sincerity; but the vast remainder of French drama lies unmauled and unknown. Such a statement prompts the question: What then makes a good translation? The answer is not as difficult as translators and critics have made it seem. For many years they have been divided over two hoary arguments: (a) whether a translation should hew to the words or to the spirit of the original; and (b) whether an old play, say *Andromache,* should read and perform like a recent work *or* be cast in an approximation to the English of 1667 (whatever that was) *or* be somehow bastardized between ancient and modern. We can glide around both these arguments; they are irrelevant and misleading, the first because in almost all writing words and spirit are inseparable; the second because a good translation, whether of drama, prose, or poetry, may become dated in some respects but it does not go out of date. Every few years somebody attempts a new version of the *Iliad*. Not one of these versions, even one as skilled as C. Day Lewis', has supplanted Pope's. Nobody has made a better translation of *Don Quixote* than Ozell.

There are two qualities in a good play translation. First, it is written in persuasive dialogue, that is, it is an *English* play in its own right. Second, it penetrates the meanings, and overtones of meaning, of the original. It hardly matters whether the play is translated word by word or freely adapted, although generally a so-called "faithful" translation, which runs its sentences back to front and reproduces every exclamation literally, even when the emotional values are glaringly wrong in English, is unreadable and, in both senses, unspeakable, while an adaptation may be so free that it liberates itself from the original and becomes a new play. Nor does it matter much whether or not the translator tries to stay close to the "style" of the original, for style is no more than a fluent or pleasing way of expressing meanings, and if the translator is true to the meanings in a play, sentence by sentence, speech by speech, act by act, he almost automatically finds an equivalent for its style—provided that he has a gift for dialogue.

A gift for dialogue—that suggests that plays should be translated only by playwrights. And so, ideally, they should. Not all playwrights, but selected playwrights, at any rate. It has been said with some reason that contemporary English dialogue is too soggy to support French drama, especially the precise classical mode of Corneille and Racine. Many playwrights are turning out scripts that consist of grunts and burps separated by slabs of stage direction that read like unscanned verse, or else they spin webs of prep-school psychology in the course of which the actors ask one another whether the hero can be a homosexual even though he plays football, or whether the girl who likes to sit on his lap has a furniture fixation. These playwrights have entered American and English drama more pervasively than is realized; during the 1960–61 season they occupied something like 60 per cent of Broadway's stages and a good proportion of Off-Broadway. When they are asked to make a French play over into English, as they sometimes are, they thin down the dialogue, sometimes change the setting to an American backwater, and simplify the ideas out of recognition and value.

I would like to suggest a standard to judge translations by: they should seem to have been written by the original playwright in English. This is a high standard and a presumptuous one; but it takes a presumptuous man to write a play in the first place, especially if it is a great play. It is a standard that only an extraordinary translator can meet and extraordinary translators are probably as rare as extraordinary playwrights. But it has been met. Robert Lowell and Richard Wilbur and Morris Bishop have shown that complex French drama can be brought into living English,[1] and one hopes that other translators will follow their leads—if they can.

The eight plays in this collection are not meant to stand for the brimming French theater as a whole, any more than one play can stand for a playwright's total output. What they amount to is a sampling of the best writing in eight French dramatic genres, plays that, with one exception, are not easy to get hold of elsewhere in readable, actable dialogue. And they happen to form the first conspective anthology of French theater to be published in English. Three of them were written in verse and have been translated into prose. This is not as grave as it seems, despite Dryden's misgivings about prose "as being too weak for the government of serious plays." Today, the boundary between prose and blank verse has as good as vanished. (Are Joyce, Lagerqvist, Mishima, Faulkner, and Nabokov novelists or long-distance poets? Are not poets like Eliot, Perse, Quasimodo, and Jiménez also essayists *in their poems?*) A careful prose translation of a play can be as dramatically affecting as a careful verse translation, and will sometimes "speak" better on stage.

Almost every published play translation claims the right to be performed, and not merely read. These eight make the same claim. The late Barrett H. Clark's translation of *The Romantics* has already had many productions, and Mr. Fry's translation of *The Lark* was successfully produced in London in 1956. Five of the other six plays were translated for this book, and the sixth, Mr. Raikes's version of *Song of Songs*, has not appeared in book form before. It is hoped that they will all serve the actor and the spectator, as well as the reader.

---

[1] In Mr. Lowell's translation of *Phaedra*, published by Farrar, Straus & Cudahy; Mr. Wilbur's translation of *The Misanthrope*, published by Harcourt, Brace (both of these translations are reprinted in *The Classic Theater*, Vol. 4, ed. Eric Bentley, published by Anchor Books); and Mr. Bishop's translations of *Eight Plays by Molière*, published as a Modern Library volume.

"THE IMAGINARY INVALID":
Molière and Oral Medicine

Five of Molière's thirty-three plays are concerned with doctors and impersonators of doctors, and of the five [2] *The Imaginary Invalid*, his final work, is the most bitter and, at the same time, the most farcical. For his plot and much of his technique Molière dipped again into the *commedia dell' arte* tradition which he had been instrumental in introducing to French drama and had followed in a number of his early plays. The tragic irony of this comedy is that the central character Argan is a hypochondriac but at the time when he wrote the play and performed this part, Molière was himself dangerously ill. During the fourth showing he was seized by convulsions onstage, but insisted on completing the performance; he died several hours later.

The main line of the plot is the familiar Italian theme of an unsuitable marriage: Argan's determination to marry his daughter to a doctor, so that he can enjoy free and continual medical consultations with his son-in-law. Argan—Molière makes it quite clear—is not suffering from anything but stupidity, which is conclusively demonstrated in the ballet-epilogue, during which Argan believes that he is being inducted into the medical profession when, in fact, he is on the wrong end of an elaborate joke planned by his brother-in-law.

In the course of the three acts and the comic interludes (which feature Polichinelle, a French version of the Italian puppet Punchinello), Molière takes one hard knock after another at doctors and medicine and padded fees: these attacks are by no means out of date when one considers the nature of the AMA and the plight of doctor-bound, psychiatry-awed Americans today. Thomas Diafoirus, the would-be son-in-law, is a near-idiot and his father, also a doctor, is a money-grabber, interested only in the size of the dowry. Another mercenary is Argan's second wife, Béline,[3] who wants to relegate her stepdaughters to a convent and induce her husband to think himself to death so that she will inherit his fortune. Béralde, Argan's brother-in-law, sounds echoes of other "sensible" characters in the Molière reper-

---

[2] The other four are *Le Médecin Volant* (*The Flying Doctor*), *L'Amour Médecin* (*Love, the Doctor*), *Le Médecin Malgré Lui* (*The Doctor in Spite of Himself*), and *Monsieur de Porceaugnac*.

[3] Accent marks have been omitted from this and certain other names in the translations printed in this book.

tory, notably Philinte (in *The Misanthrope*), Cléante (in *Tartuffe*), Chrysalde (in *The School for Wives*) and Anselme (in *The Miser*).

Argan, based like many of Molière's protagonists on the playwright's own fears and weaknesses, is not as fully developed and memorable a type as Tartuffe, Don Juan, George Dandin, or Jourdain the bourgeois gentleman. But this is less a play of character than a thesis comedy, and as such it makes its points gracefully, delivers a continuous flow of amusement, and sets up a succession of masterly scenes, from Argan's opening lament about his medical bills to his dialogue with the maid Toinette (disguised as a doctor) in Act III, and on to the final cabalistic episode.

"ANDROMACHE":
Racine's Tragedy on a Greek Theme

The Imaginary Invalid was Molière's final comic onslaught (written late in 1672) on ordinary people with exaggerated characteristics: greed, pretentiousness, hypocrisy. *Andromache,* written slightly earlier, was Racine's first effective tragedy of extraordinary people involved in great passions: love, hatred, jealousy, fealty. Molière, the practical and satirical moralist, ridiculed people who are still recognizable—give or take a few minor traits—as prototypes today. Racine, the man of letters, reached back into legend, and reconstructed Greek characters who hardly touch the outside world. Orestes, Hermione, Pyrrhus, and Andromache behave in a human chain reaction; they are circumscribed by Racine's meticulous plotting, and are so interdependent that they cannot be easily conceived *as those characters* in any other relationship. And this is not simply because two of them, Hermione and Pyrrhus, are dead by the end of the play, while Orestes has been used up by the tragedy. One of the most striking contrasts between Racine and his older fellow-dramatist Pierre Corneille (1606–1684) is that Corneille's drama is continually building and resolving, while Racine's is relentlessly destroying and dissolving.

In the preface to *Andromache* Racine gives his main sources, Euripides and Virgil, and tells briefly how he has modified the data taken from them. From these and other Greek and Roman authors Racine also borrowed, in adapted form, a dramatic philosophy—determinism. His characters are governed by "fate"; they are unwilling toys of the gods, and their tragedy is that they make the wrong choices be-

tween the alternatives available to them, choices which the
gods had callously prearranged.

In other words, like the heroes and heroines of Greek
tragedy, Racine's characters are fatally flawed and have, in
reality, no choice at all. In this respect they are at the opposite end of the psychological scale from the existential
heroes of Sartre and Camus, who are presented with a
genuine freedom of choice. Robert Kemp's review of *Andromache* in this book suggests that Racine's characters *are*
free to choose, but for every quotation he adduces to make
this point, four or five others could be found to contradict
it. Andromache may *think* she is making her own decisions;
that is an important, ironic element in the tragedy.

Racine's determinism has led one of his recent appraisers,
a French Marxist, Lucien Goldmann, to deduce a theory of
tragic extremes: the tragedy arises because the gods force
selected men and women to try to reconcile opposites. Thus
Andromache feels driven both to save her baby and to be
faithful to the memory of her husband, Hector; but in her
situation she cannot possibly do both; either her child or her
honor must be sacrificed. Here is a partial guide to the understanding of other Racine plays (*Phaedra, Britannicus*),
although it is by no means an inclusive theory of tragedy.
Even when he limits it to Racine, M. Goldmann goes too far.
He ends by claiming Racine as "one of the great representatives of a humanist tradition of which Marxist thought and
proletarian literature are the living expression and the con-
tinuation today."

Giraudoux, on the other hand, was preoccupied with Racine's style, and played down the philosophy and theology in
Racine's work. It is true that Racine was a conscious stylist,
but his style was only a fraction of his craftsmanship, and
Giraudoux's motive in laying emphasis on it was perhaps less
pure than he realized: he was trying, whether or not consciously, to point to himself as one of Racine's literary descendants, which he was not.

Most of the conventions in *Andromache* are artificial by
today's standards of playwriting, including the simplicity
and purity of the language, which is free of slang and applied
meanings; the infrequency of physical action onstage; the
lofty and similar speech patterns of all the characters; and
the confidants, who serve as consciences and are a vestigial
form of the Greek chorus leaders. Yet these "artificial" elements are not weaknesses in Racine's art; they are its discipline and strength. Using them with unequaled skill and
discretion, Racine evolved the finest expression of the classi-

cal drama: a series of meticulously painted and framed canvases which, even more than those of his contemporary, the painter Poussin—*The Bacchanalia, The Crucifixion, The Massacre of the Innocents*—depict raw and terrifying scenes.

"THE BARBER OF SEVILLE":
Beaumarchais Versus the Court

Racine's dramatic technique imposed itself so rigidly on the playwrights who followed him that nearly a century after the first performance of *Andromache* Voltaire (who wrote fifty-eight plays in the Racinian meter and tone, most of them now forgotten) could say categorically that French authors "had to" work in the rigid conventions of the rhymed alexandrine, a six-beat, twelve-syllable line. The alexandrine persisted, in fact, down through Hugo to Rostand, but one playwright who broke away from the tradition was Beaumarchais, who went back to the almost naturalistic dialogue and comic intrigues of Molière. Beaumarchais, snubbed as an upstart by the courtiers of Louis XV and Louis XVI (see biographical note), took his historic revenge by poking fun at nobility and high society and by making his hero a lowborn barber-valet. *The Barber of Seville* may be set in Spain but its references are French. Figaro (the name is thought to be taken from *fi*, the French word for "fie," and *Caron*, Beaumarchais' family name) is very likely Beaumarchais' interpretation of himself, a commoner, a jack of all trades and master of most of them, a man with the resources and agility to tiptoe around one sticky situation after another. Count Almaviva, for all that he is the "juvenile lead" in the play, is an aristocrat and therefore inept when he is not operating on Figaro's instructions.

Beaumarchais owed many ideas in his story to Molière's *L'Étourdi* (*The Blunderer*), in which there is a parallel situation between the master, Lélie, who continually wrecks his chances of winning the heroine, and Mascarille, the valet, who has to keep coping with the obstacles that Lélie stupidly sets up against himself.

Much of *The Barber* is broad comedy or satire. The few semiserious scenes, between the Count and Rosine, lean toward melodrama and must be frankly played as such. The "characters" in the play are Figaro and the doctor, whose name, Bartholo, comes from Pantaloon, the old cuckold of *commedia dell' arte*. The Count, a pretty stock figure, becomes much more interesting when he is pretending to be someone else, the horse doctor or the music teacher, and acquires something of Figaro's dimensions during those scenes, although there is no way of knowing if this was deliberate on Beaumarchais's part. Rosine is a traditionally harmless and colorless ingénue; evidently all that Beaumarchais expected from the actress was beauty, gasps, sighs, restrained coquettishness, and horrified asides. Bartholo's two servants, Puberty (*La Jeunesse*) and Lively (*L'Éveillé*) are pulled in and out for quick laughs, but another minor character, Don Bazile, is the center of one of the brightest comic scenes in French drama, which compares favorably with, say, Molière's Act II, Scene 6, in *Le Dépit Amoureux* (*Spiteful Love*) or Scenes 9 and 11 in *Les Précieuses Ridicules* (*The Precious Young Ladies*).

The plotting in *The Barber* is elegant, a model for playwrights and spectators who like every exit and entrance accounted for; the structure of each act is firm and the story gallops to its conclusion, hardly slowing up when it delivers a kick at hack playwrights here and at doctors there and at nobility most of the time.

"HERNANI":
Hugo, Censorship, Passion, and Honor

The plays of Beaumarchais may be said to have prefaced the French Revolution. Hugo's, coming after the revolutionaries had triumphed and then abused their power and finally given way to Napoleon and the restoration of the French monarchy, may equally be said to have prefaced the proletarian uprisings of 1848–1851, by reaffirming the dignity of "commoners" and the weaknesses of kings.

Apologizing to his readers in an introductory note to *Hernani* for the "changes I have had to submit to" in the script before it could be performed, Hugo called the censorship of the time "this little inquisition of the mind" with its "secret judges, its masked executioners, its tortures, its mutilations, and its death penalty." Today, the textual revisions that Hugo was forced to make do not seem startling.[4] Mostly they were softening of references to the king Don Carlos and to monarchy in general, and the play itself was less political in its implications than such later works as *Le roi s'amuse*, in which a French king, François I, was

---

[4] The differing versions can be compared in the 1880 edition (publisl ed by Hetzel and Quantin) of *Hugo's Complete Works: Drama*, Vol. II.

portrayed as an indecisive statesman and a libertine. François is also, incidentally, referred to in *Hernani*. What Hugo's supporters found most applause-worthy in *Hernani* was its bravura, an unstinting heroism, and a glorification of the concept of honor, which derive in large part from the drama of Corneille, and especially from *Le Cid*.

Hugo himself was less conscious of his debt to Corneille than to his readings of Byron and Shakespeare, Goethe and Schiller. He wanted to write French plays that would be as tragic as Racine's, but with a freedom and sweep of settings that were wholly outside the confining unities of place and time. There were many pairs of flooded eyes at the initial performances; to our age the suicides of Hernani, Doña Sol, and Don Ruy Gómez are less tragic than those of Andromache and Hermione, partly because they are "inserted," that is, tagged on and not absolutely called for by the story—they are something of an excuse for Act V—and partly because "honor" is today a scorned, inexplicable quality; it has been pushed aside in favor of pride. If the hero of a contemporary play were to take his life, as Hernani does, to fulfill a pledge of honor, the reviewers would come out of the theater asking each other, "Yes, but what was his *real* motive?"

Psychological subtlety does not belong in a playwright who aims at "grandeur," any more than it belongs in a politician like Charles de Gaulle. Thus we have Hugo offering this advice to "the actors who may be called on to perform the principal roles in this play . . . to take note in Hernani of the untamed harshness of a mountain-dweller combined with the native pride of a Spanish grandee; in the Don Carlos of the first three acts, the gaiety, the carelessness, the spirit of adventure and pleasure and behind all that, the firmness, the haughtiness, and the indefinable prudence in his daring—one already sees the budding of the Charles V of Act Four; in Don Ruy Gómez, the dignity, the sad and profound passion, the respect for ancestors, hospitality and pledges, in short, an homeric old man in the tradition of the middle ages. . . ." All of which is pretty obvious from the dialogue, if not from the accompanying stage directions. Still, if subtlety of observation and character go by the board in Hugo's work, if he depends to an outrageous extent on coincidence, if the excesses in his work have been repeated and imitated to the point of exhaustion by others, he does compensate us with tremendous theatrical qualities: the great, ironic confrontations, the play founded on a major theme, the all-out assault on an audience, and an unashamed adventuring through "the big emotions." The long speech of Don Carlos in Act IV is—apart from one or two passages in *The Song of Roland*—the finest monologue in the French language.

"POTS OF MONEY":
Labiche Along the Boulevards

Molière worked a few normal characters into his plays to offset the abnormal ones and to put his points over. Labiche, who had almost no points to put over, did not try to portray abnormal people. In *Pots of Money* he and his collaborator, Delacour, lifted a few stock types out of the sack labeled "funny people" and kneaded them in and out of one misunderstanding after another. Labiche's comic effects lie, as Bergson pointed out in his essay *Le rire* ("Laughter"), somewhere "between very rough and very refined amusement," veering now toward one extreme, now toward the other; toward broadness and shallowness in the characterization; and toward refinement in the situations, which are meticulously thought out and arranged in sequence. *Pots of Money* is, in short, a comedy of action, of situation, not of character. We can still laugh at Boursey, the honorary commandant of the Endives-Under-Glass fire brigade, who goes through life striking noble platitudes; at Danne the farmer, with his affection for dung; at Leonida and Corden in their quest for partners and "future happiness"; at Poche, the marriage merchant who caters to "some of the finest names in the country." But these are side effects, twitches set up by the major and pervasive movements of the play, which are the scenes and predicaments in which these characters find themselves.

Being a humorist, and therefore vicious, Labiche took pleasure in embarrassing each of his characters in turn. Being a good-natured man, he got them out of trouble by the end of Act Five. Being a realist, he did not attempt to slap a happy ending on all their lives. Modern theatergoers who are accustomed to a moral—even (or rather, especially) in the flimsiest comedies—are entitled to ask, after all the capers are over, what Labiche was getting at. The answer: his audiences, who saw themselves locked in jail with nothing to get them out but a pickax and a song, or mistaken for a gang of jewel thieves, or trapped in a restaurant after misreading the prices on the menu. And how did these audiences, who picked up the pith of this play from the first scene

onward, respond? With hatred? With indignation? No, just
the reverse. The more Labiche mocked them and punctured
their pretenses, by showing them caricatures of themselves
and their neighbors in ridiculous circumstances, the more
they cheered.

There is, then, social comment in Labiche, but it is subor-
dinated. The plays come over as almost pure comedy—phe-
nomenally, durably successful comedy. His career continued
at full strength until 1958, seventy years after his death,
when André Malraux, as Minister of Culture, put out a di-
rective against further productions of Labiche's and Feydeau's light or boulevard comedies at the Comédie-Française, where they were crowding out the French classics.

But they are now coming back. . . .

"THE ROMANTICS":
Rostand, the Light Heavyweight

Rostand's first produced play, The Romantics, gets under
way in the style of a good old-time bout of passion, with
secret meetings between young lovers across a garden wall,
and love poetry, and a family vendetta. The plot is as neatly
laid as a table. Then, in Scene 2, the author whips away the
tablecloth. The silverware is still there, but the whole thing
looks different. Is what follows more of the same sentimentality
or a spoof on it? At the end of Act I there is no way of telling;
we have reached a happy-ever-after, where most romances
end, and a new collection of circumstances is needed to set
the action in motion again. But by the final curtain the story
has turned out to be roughly what we thought it was at the
beginning: Rostand is a sentimentalist, after all, a voice in
favor of mystery and danger and insecurity in the cause of
happiness.

Rostand was better equipped than most other writers of
his time to lead the sentimental battalions. For one thing, he
had had a comfortable upbringing and was unfamiliar with
the social and material injustices that occupied the naturalistic authors of the late nineteenth century; for another and
bigger thing, he was a first-rank verse writer but not a first-
rank poet. Much of the verbal legerdemain and felicity have
tended to disappear in translations of Rostand; the cracks
begin to show and the plays keel over. Almost fifty years
ago Ludwig Lewisohn wrote that the then-current translations
"deliberately give up the poetry of Rostand and are there-

fore practically worthless." [5] Many of the translations were indeed practically worthless, but not because the translators deliberately gave up the poetry—no translator does that deliberately, though he may do it accidentally—nor because, as Mr. Lewisohn meant, they gave up the *poetic form*, i.e., the rhyming verse, but because Rostand could plaster over the cracks in French with a skill that could not be matched by his translators in English. In the 1920's, Henderson Dangerfield Norman, possibly spurred on by Mr. Lewisohn's words, made a gallant attempt to get the whole of Rostand into English rhyming verse; it was a labor of love and frustration. A French translator would face comparable agonies in putting W. S. Gilbert or Swinburne into French.

The Romantics is fortunately a lightweight play, and does not present so many or such acute difficulties to a translator as the succeeding plays. It is buoyed up by its comedy and impudence and even in an unpretentious version it comes across as an agile, minor tour de force.

"SONG OF SONGS":
Giraudoux on Love and the Age Barrier

No excuses are tendered to the reader of this volume for giving him a one-act of Giraudoux instead of a full-length play. *Song of Songs* is shorter and less known than *The Madwoman of Chaillot, Judith,* and *The Trojan War Will Not Take Place* (*Tiger at the Gates*), but in its own compact way it rivals these plays for completeness of dramatic idea and for the virtuosity of its writing. And in the girl Florence, Giraudoux realized one of his most persuasive and captivating heroines—a more interesting stage person, certainly, than Ondine, Tessa, or Agathe.

Song of Songs was written in 1938 at the invitation of the director of the Comédie-Française, where it was played under the direction of Jouvet and with a set by Vuillard. The theme is simple: the victory in love of youth over age. The President may be worldly, brilliant, considerate, influential, handsome; Jérôme [6] may be clumsy, unlettered, thoughtless, accident-prone, and negligible-looking. No matter. The young man wins the girl.

[5] *The Modern Drama,* 1915. In this book, Lewisohn's own translated extracts from Rostand are not exactly dazzling. They include such mock poetic Jacobeanisms as *'tis, o'er, ne'er, ween, shouldst,* and *'twill.*

[6] See note 3.

On this simple tissue Giraudoux grafted complex features and embellished them in turn with an elaborate tattooing of words and free association. Some of the decorations have to be viewed swiftly and then passed by. Giraudoux's most passionate admirers probably regard them as triumphs of style, but an author's most passionate admirers tend to do the greatest harm to his reputation, and some of the decorations amount to no more than language trying to give birth to ideas. Giraudoux, perhaps aware of his occasional over-embroidery, has artfully warned us in *The Improvisation in Paris* not to analyze his weaving and musing; the character called Jouvet says that "the word *understand* does not exist in the theater. . . ."

The language in *Song of Songs* may be forced, but there is no forcing of the theme. If it had been the work of an American playwright, the President in the play would very likely have flung blood-freezing insults at Jérôme; he would have shouted Florence down with rage; eventually, she would have alluded to an embarrassing or incriminating incident from his past. Giraudoux kept the dialogue on a cool, discursive level; the President's heartbreak is more obvious when he surrenders easily, and the play touches tragedy at several points, without ever straining for it. As Chris Marker points out,[7] Giraudoux did not resort to surprise tactics; he avoided the shock and the twist; he constructed a plot that was not plotted but merely happened; he presented, not a slice of life but, in Marker's words, "a slice of eternity."

Robert Kemp, in his "Thoughts on *Song of Songs*," noticed the resemblances to and the divergences from the Biblical poem, the original Song of Solomon. King Solomon is now the President, the young shepherd is Jérôme, and the Shula-mite Maiden is Florence. We also learn from Mr. LeSage[8] that Victor the waiter is probably based on a Victor who served in a café on the Boul' Mich' in Paris. Given the rudi-mentary Biblical outline, what does Giraudoux add to it, besides a modern setting and his own brand of dialogue? Principally, his mature sense of reality, almost of fatality, even during the most wildly fanciful speeches. One becomes more conscious of, and won over by, the elementally *real* qualities of this play with each reading of it. This may be why Louis Aragon, the poet, wrote: "I have changed. One fine day I realized that I had found a taste for Giraudoux. He no longer irritated me. . . . Yes, I'd begun to love it. All

[7] In *Giraudoux par lui-même.*

[8] In *Jean Giraudoux, His Life and Works.*

of it. . . . And—may I be forgiven!—I think that what I had begun to love in Giraudoux was France."

"THE LARK":
Anouilh and a Slicked-up Joan

Every age has its dramatic craftsmen who know what moves their contemporaries and can write effective dramas to a happy fare-thee-well. Their works do not necessarily live beyond their era—who is enthusiastic today over the plays of Dekker, Voltaire, Scribe?—but they may enjoy sweeping popularity during their authors' lifetimes. Jean Anouilh is the strongest candidate for the title "Dramatic Craftsman of the Mid-Twentieth Century." His themes and people are scrupulously planned; he does not seem to care much what he is saying as long as the scenes come off. His integrity, in other words, is not ideological but technical, his responsibility not to his material but to his technique. He rarely underestimates himself and produces an all-out failure. He never purposely overreaches himself to aim at a masterpiece. What, never? "Well," in the Lord High Admiral's words, "hardly ever."

One of M. Anouilh's rare overreachings is *The Lark.* (The only others I can think of are *Antigone* and *Becket.*) Here he has taken the historic saint-witch, peasant-leader and tried to reduce her to a theatrically acceptable tintype: an image of courage. He has not succeeded. Joan has outmaneuvered him; she has made his version of her bigger than her author intended. M. Anouilh, with the edges of his material slipping out of his hands for once, has accidentally put together a not-so-commercial play, with a fluidity in the early scenes—the masterly freedom of narration between present and past—and an assembly of characters that make one wish he could have sworn away the craftsmanship he is so proud of and assigned himself to a bold, untidy piece of writing—and carried it through.

Some critics prefer Anouilh's small plays—*The Waltz of the Toreadors, Thieves' Carnival, Eurydice.* They think that he should stick to his last and his well-cobbled pessimism. (It has also been pointed out, quite rightly, that in this play Anouilh has crept along in Bernard Shaw's footsteps.) Yet the very uncertainty in the handling of *The Lark,* particularly in the closing scenes, gives the play and the character a depth that is missing in Anouilh's other, confidently negative comedies with their episodes of Hollywoodish relief.

In his prefatory note, Anouilh states that he is not trying to "explain" Joan, only to present her. The play itself is a denial of that statement. Merely to write about a character like this is to attempt to explain her. And it is *because* he tries to explain her, whether consciously or not, that *The Lark* is an interesting work. What are the elusive qualities that make this obscure girl into a kingmaker and a willing martyr? Courage? Yes, of course, but also dialectical skill, violent patriotism, spiritual fervor, hatred (of the English), self-sufficiency, and other characteristics, all of which the author is forced to face up to, in spite of his intention not to explain. *The Lark* may have opened in Anouilh's mind as another variation on his favorite theme: corruption against innocence. It reaches the theater as a vigorous contest between a slick French playwright and a profound French story.

The eleven essays in this book have been reprinted for good and bad reasons.

George Saintsbury's article originally appeared as the introduction to a collection of the plays of Molière, published in 1925. In addition to making fairly detailed comments on Molière's art, Saintsbury sketched in some biographical material; I therefore thought it unnecessary to add a separate biographical section on this playwright.

Gide's short statement, written by a man who saw himself as "the best representative of classicism today," equated French classicism with understatement and classical art with "the French genius"; and in a succession of highly charged and convincing paradoxes, he differentiated classicism from romanticism, in which "the emotion ends with the word and is held within it."

The extract from George Meredith's "An Essay on Comedy" contains no reference to *The Imaginary Invalid*, but it does have interesting points to make about the humor in several other great plays by Molière, notably *Tartuffe, The Misanthrope,* and *The School for Wives,* and contrasts Elizabethan humor with that of seventeenth-century French playwriting.

Robert Kemp's two reviews were chosen for their immediacy; they appeared the morning after the productions described, in Kemp's theater column in *Le Monde,* and easily excel in breadth of learning, depth of insight, and descriptive power the material put out by any daily play reviewer today, French, American, or English. This may be because Kemp came to theater criticism as a practiced essayist, and not as a promoted sports writer, director *manqué*, or wielder-of-woolly-adjectives.[9]

Swinburne's excerpt from his book on Hugo is not reprinted as a joke, in spite of its almost laughable effusions, but to give some indication of the influence exerted by Hugo on writers inside and outside France, an influence that remained powerful from the third through the ninth decades of the nineteenth century.

"The Psychology of Farce," by Eric Bentley, is the most eclectic and sympathetic treatment of farce that I have read, recent or otherwise. It deals almost entirely with French plays and, like all first-rate essays on a general topic, it has considerable bearing on particular plays, in this case the Labiche printed here. Readers are also referred to "A Plea for Farce," the last chapter of Brander Matthews' *Studies of the Stage* (1894).

When *The Romantics* was first performed in this country in 1901, two representatives of *The Theatre*, a lavish periodical of the time—now defunct—went to Philadelphia to see it and wrote newsy pieces about the play and the playwright. They are reproduced here, slightly abridged but undefeated.

Joseph Chiari's brief survey of modern French drama is the final chapter of his book *The Contemporary French Theatre*, published in 1958 and subtitled "The Flight from Naturalism"; the book contains chapters on Rostand, Ghéon, Supervielle, Claudel, Copeau, Cocteau, Giraudoux, Sartre, Anouilh, and Montherlant. I do not agree personally with many of M. Chiari's verdicts on playwrights and plays, but his point of view demands respect and he draws attention to some of the ideas and ideals with which recent French dramatists have been outstandingly concerned.

I had wanted to include a play by Jean-Paul Sartre in this collection, but his American publisher, Alfred A. Knopf, Inc., would not permit any of his drama to appear in a competitive volume.[10] Sartre is one of the two most significant dramatic writers since World War II—the other being Brecht, whose early work was not widely known outside Germany until the late Forties and Fifties—and has the finest natural talent of our generation for creating inherently dramatic situations and sustaining them with terse, dialectical talk. His *Le Diable et le bon Dieu* (*Lucifer and the Lord*), written

[9] From a recent newspaper review of an Off-Broadway play: "Call it an evening of unabashed, unpretentious, heartfelt, occasionally touching and far from exhilarating sentimental willfulness, disarming but rather ineffective, and I think you will have it about right . . ."

[10] The plays of Albert Camus are similarly restricted.

in 1950 and translated by Lionel Abel, is the most ambitious play since Shaw's *Man and Superman*. Almost as powerful is Sartre's most recent (1959) play, *Les Séquestrés d'Altona*, translated as *The Condemned of Altona*. I am grateful to Mr. Francis Fergusson for allowing me to reprint his review of three famous Sartre plays; it was written shortly after they were first performed in the United States.

My warm thanks go to the contributors and publishers listed in the Acknowledgments; to Mrs. Linda Asher, Mrs. Mildred Marmur, and Mr. Lionel Abel for undertaking new translations; to Mr. Eric Bentley, Mr. Walter W. Wriggins, and my editor at the New American Library, Mr. E. L. Doctorow, for their fund of suggestions; to Mrs. Ann Elmo and Mr. T. W. Raines, valued friends and advisers; and to my wife Joyce for her translations of Robert Kemp's essays and Beaumarchais' introduction, and for more typing and reading chores, judgments, and warnings than I dare to remember.

ALBERT BERMEL

New York, 1961

PART ONE ❧ THE PLAYS

MOLIÈRE: The Imaginary Invalid

MOLIÈRE (1622-1673)

AN INTRODUCTION TO MOLIÈRE [1]

by George Saintsbury

The position of Molière in biography is somewhat like that of two very great English writers who had not a little in common with him in other ways—Shakespeare and Chaucer. That is to say, we have no inconsiderable number of documentary facts about him, but nothing, or next to nothing, of the real matter of biography—personal and private letters to and by him, minute and direct accounts of his character and manners from persons who knew him well, full details of incidents or conversations in which he took part. As his later date and different circumstances would lead us to expect, we have indeed a much larger amount of gossip about him, but the more this gossip is examined, the more untrustworthy it is seen to be. Through and behind his work there looms, of course, the mighty shadow of himself: but, as all critics of literature ought to know if they do not, this shadow is always the most treacherous thing in the world. Its features are sometimes created—are always shaped and coloured—by the eyes that see it: and, to vary Goethe's famous words, it may be like the Molière or the Shakespeare that the critic could understand, without being like the Shakespeare or the Molière of reality.

There is, however, this striking difference between our documentary facts about Molière and those which we possess about Chaucer and even about Shakespeare, that almost all the former, after Molière's early youth, are directly con-

[1] First published in 1925. *Ed.*

nected with his work. It is therefore most convenient, in
dealing with him, not to adopt the usual method of giving
the Life first and surveying the Works afterwards, but to
interweave the accounts and separate only the summings-up.
The period of his actual and finished production covered not
much more than a quarter of his life, for he was all but
thirty-seven when *L'Étourdi* was first played in Paris, and
he was not yet fifty-two when the "sick man of fancy" [2] left
the stage to become the dead man of fact in the same night.

As again with Shakespeare, so with Molière, we do not
know the day of his birth, but we do know that of his bap-
tism, January 15, 1622. He was probably born in the Rue
Saint-Honoré, Paris, where his father, Jean Poquelin, of an
old bourgeois family from Beauvais, was an upholsterer.
Nine years later this upholsterer became *valet tapissier* to
Louis XIII. A year later again, in 1632, Molière lost his
mother, whose maiden name was Marie Cressé. He went to
school at the Collège de Clermont, a Jesuit establishment,
where (though there are chronological difficulties) it is an
accepted fact that he had for schoolfellow the Prince de
Conti (younger brother of the great Condé), with whom he
was certainly connected in after-life. After leaving school he
studied philosophy and law, the former under Gassendi.[3]
Here also he had fellow-students, distinguished though in
another way, such as Cyrano de Bergerac and Chapelle. He
is said to have translated Lucretius, and the taint of Gassendi's epicureanism no doubt made itself suspicious to orthodoxy in subsequent controversies. As for law, it has been asserted, and never disproved, that he was actually called to
the bar. At any rate, there is no doubt that his education
was rather above than below the average of that of great
men of letters. He had earlier received the reversion of his
father's employment in the Royal Household, and perhaps
actually accompanied Louis XIII to Provence in 1642; in
fact, legend connects him with the tragedy of Cinq-Mars as
having endeavoured to save the unlucky Grand Écuyer.
But he had caught stage-fever; at the beginning of 1643 he
gave up his reversion, took the portion of his mother's goods
that fell to him, and later in the year is found—in conjunc-
tion with three members, Joseph, Madeleine, and Geneviève,
of the Béjard or Béjart family, with which he was ever afterwards connected, and others—as occupier of a tennis-

---

[2] Saintsbury is referring to the play title, *Le Malade Imaginaire*. Ed.

[3] Gassendi is not mentioned by the oldest authorities; but there is
little reason to doubt the fact.

court for theatrical purposes. The company called itself
L'Illustre Théâtre. He was still Jean Baptiste Poquelin simply—Molière was a stage-name which he assumed, we do
not know why, and we do not know exactly when.[4] According to frequent if not universal stage custom, he became M.
de Molière—the "de" even in ordinary life having none of
the exclusive and universal connection with nobility which
was afterwards assigned to it. And till long after he had
distinguished himself as an author the name was constantly
spelt *Mollier;* indeed, the pronunciation of the two forms is
said to have been at the time identical. In any case the name
was a real one, and had belonged to, or been assumed by, a
romance-writer years earlier. And there was even a third
Mollier or Molière who, as a dancer and musician, actually
performed in his great namesake's pieces during his lifetime.

But distinction was in no hurry, and in a year or two the
Illustrious Theatre discovered that "Paris" was a shorthand
form of "arrestment for debt." Molière himself seems to
have undergone this process. For a time they had the countenance of "Monsieur," the King's brother, Gaston d'Orléans, but the protection of Gaston never did good to any
human creature. At last—whether after previous essays or
not is a moot question, but from 1647 pretty certainly onwards—the company determined to take to that nomad life
of the player which seems to possess such a curious mixture
of inconvenience and fascination, and of which, as regards
this particular period, we have a direct picture of great talent
from Scarron in the *Roman Comique,* and a marvellous
recreation of genius from Gautier in *Le Capitaine Fracasse.*

The biographers have "extenuated themselves" upon the ten
years from 1648 to 1658. The *régistre* of La Grange the
actor (who, according to another Shakespearian coincidence, was Molière's comrade during his life, and his first
editor after his death) does not begin so early, but it has
some backward entries: and the *Preface* of the edition of
1682, with divers business entries of various kinds, pre-
served after the methodical habit of the French, supplies
dates which sometimes require harmonising, sometimes not.
Bordeaux, Nantes, Toulouse, Lyons almost as a headquarters, Montpellier, Rouen, and many lesser places had the advantage of welcoming, or the shame of not welcoming, the
Illustrious Ones. . . . .

It is disputed whether *L'Étourdi,* the first "number" of
Molière's recognised theatre, appeared in 1655 or earlier, in

4 It first appears in a legal document dated June 28, 1644.

1653; there seems to be no doubt that the next and still better one, the *Dépit Amoureux*, was produced at Béziers in 1656. Two years later the last provincial stage of the Illustrious Theatre at Rouen gave Molière an opportunity of negotiating for the protection of Louis XIV's brother Philippe, who constituted them his "servants"—"the Duke's House," as shortly afterwards it would have been called in England. This gave them a title no more burlesque; a re-entry to the capital, now settled and laying itself out seriously for pleasure and servitude; patronage which might mean anything or nothing, but was at any rate "a spring-board"—in fact, for the first time what is called an opening. As means for availing themselves of this opening they had fifteen years' practice; apparently (with no doubt plenty of petty jealousies and bickerings) a pretty solid *esprit de corps* and habit of working together; a considerable *répertoire* of stock pieces, Corneille's and others, with certain specialties of their own to supplement it; and one of the men of greatest genius then living in Europe for leader, chief actor, and chief author. . . .

As for this earliest *Maison de Molière*, the more important members were at first, as has been said, Molière himself, the three Béjarts (of whom the brother Joseph seems to have been particularly good at old women's parts, then generally acted by men), and Du Parc, who, according to a fashion still prevalent, though going out, was known as "Gros René." Between Madeleine Béjart and Molière scandal of a persistent and never-refuted kind has always asserted the existence of very close relations, though an atrocious exaggeration of it in reference to the youngest sister, Armande (Molière's future wife, and long afterwards a member of the troupe likewise), has no justification.[5] After a few years Du Parc married a wife with the extremely beautiful name of Marquise de Gorla, who also acted, and the troupe was further joined by a married couple named De Brie. Mlle. du Parc (the wives of actors were always called Mlle., not Mme.) and Mlle. de Brie are supposed by the same scandal to have succeeded or supplemented Madeleine Béjart in their manager's and comrade's affections. Both were beautiful: Isidore in *Le Sicilien*, with her blue eyes, her dimpled chin, and her *nez un peu trop gros* (like Madame de Sévigné's) is supposed to be a portrait of Mlle. de Brie, who apparently created the part. These two ladies, till Armande Béjart joined, took the chief female parts, Molière the

---

[5] Many modern French specialists on Molière take an exactly opposite point of view. *Ed.*

great male ones; and though all the forces of theatrical and literary jealousy combined to abuse him, there seems to be no doubt that, however inferior the kind of acting may be to the kind of writing, his right to these parts was not official or usurped, but natural. There are no two characters in which tradition assigns to him greater success than those of Alceste and of M. Jourdain: [6] and an actor who can play these two has very nearly "filled all numbers" as far as non-romantic comedy goes.

The arrangements of the actual theatre on which he and his company played were, even in the capital, an odd compound of splendour and shabbiness. Until after 1660 the buildings had rarely been intended for the purpose, but were converted tennis-courts or other makeshifts. The fittings-up were neither magnificent nor comfortable, most of the audience standing in the pit, though (as in England long before, though apparently the institution was more recent in France) you could sit on the stage, to the great inconvenience of the actors. There was very little regular scenery, and very few properties, these being of the simplest description. Candles were stuck about in sconces on the walls, and (not invariably) in rude, cross-shaped wooden chandeliers. Considerably more attention, however, seems to have been paid, when it was possible, to the wardrobe. In the early days of the Illustre Théâtre the Duke of Guise is said to have given it his cast-off clothes; but when success came nothing was spared on the costumes, and Molière himself seems, from the particulars that we have of those in which he played most of his celebrated parts, to have been by no means indifferent to splendour in this respect. Satin and velvet and gold figure largely, while many of the most famous pieces positively necessitated exemplifications of the elaborate fashions of the day, huge *canons* (knee-ruffles), buckles, plumed hats, wide-skirted coats, gaudily mounted swords, costly wigs, and the rest.

The disparity of the apparatus was not ill reflected in the character of the comedies (to confine ourselves to these) which were presented. The French comedy was of a much "truer" stock (to speak as the gardeners) than the French tragedy; it went right back to the early thirteenth century through a long and unbroken succession of work, inclining indeed to the farcical side of the kind, but not the less comedy for that. In the century before Molière, however, it had

---

[6] In, respectively, *The Misanthrope* and *The Bourgeois Gentleman*. Ed.

been strongly "crossed" from classical Italian and Spanish sources; and it cannot be said that, as yet, the various strains had resulted in a thoroughly satisfactory blend. In the earlier part of this century (the latter half of the sixteenth) the Pléiade dramatists and Larivey (from the last of whom Molière himself took something) had done not a little; and in the later part (the first half of the seventeenth) men of talent, sometimes running very close to genius, had done more. Had Corneille gone on with comedy after *Le Menteur,* and had his subsequent work been as much better than that as that was better than its forerunners, Molière would have been put to it to surpass him. And as it was, Scarron, Cyrano de Bergerac, Saint-Evremond, and, even later, Quinault, Boursault, Montfleury, did remarkable things . . . (the last three named dramatists were contemporaries of Molière's, and in some cases his rivals). . . .

The actual *répertoire* of his own work with which he started was, so far as we know, composed of the two first substantive plays, *L'Étourdi* and the *Dépit,* together with an uncertain number of smaller farcical sketches of the old type, but already shot with Molièresque humour. Two only of these—*La Jalousie du Barbouillé* and *Le Médecin Volant*—are extant; but we have the names of others, and one of these, as we shall see presently, played an important part at the critical moment.

In consequence of the negotiations with Monsieur [7] the company was formally presented to Louis XIV, and they played before him at the Louvre on October 24, 1658. The "some confounded play or other" (as Shadwell put it in one of his least dull moments some years later) was Corneille's *Nicomède*—not the worst but far from the happiest effort of that great dramatist, and not in all probability specially suited to bring out the illustriousness of Molière and his fellows. But Molière asked and obtained leave to follow it with one of his own farces of the type just referred to, and this, *Le Docteur Amoureux* (which has not survived, but the nature of which one can easily fancy), was played with complete success. Establishment in Paris was authorised; a hall in the Petit Bourbon—the old half-destroyed and soon-to-be-destroyed-utterly palace of the unlucky Constable—was assigned to the company on alternate days with an Italian troupe. And so the *Maison de Molière* was housed in the other sense. But it did not become the King's own troupe for another seven years; and the coalition which made it the

[7] The King's brother. *Ed.*

"Théâtre Français" did not take place till after Molière's own death. During the whole of his life there was much rivalry and jealousy with the older houses of the Marais and the Hôtel de Bourgogne—even occasional desertions between the hostile camps. The opposition actors were spiteful; the opposition playwrights were venomous and furious. But Molière had come to his own in place, and he held it. Before long he came to his own in genius likewise.

For the first year in Paris—November 1658 to November 1659—he depended, naturally and wisely, on his stock, the chief constituents of which, *L'Étourdi* and *Le Dépit Amoureux,* were quite new to Parisian audiences. *L'Étourdi* was very closely adapted from an Italian original, *L'Inavvertito,* and is itself reproduced in *Sir Martin Mar-all,* which, not many years afterwards, Dryden helped the Duke of Newcastle to write, or perhaps very mainly wrote for him. . . . If, however, any one cares to compare *L'Étourdi* and the comedy, he will, I think, discover what is meant by this "spirit of his own." You cannot define spirits, but you can be aware of their presence.

But if *L'Étourdi* had been mainly spirited adaptation, and the *Dépit* adaptation plus originality, originality (in the wide not the narrow sense) was to exert itself alone and triumphantly in the third important piece, now "new and original" in every sense, that was played in Paris—the immortal and delightful *Précieuses Ridicules.* . . . The piece is just the right length, its high-jinks are just not too high, and it is very important to observe that, severe as it is, the satire is not in the least cruel. The girls are quit for their folly by being made fools of—some dramatists would have carried their punishment much further. Gorgibus himself, whatever his annoyance, may, when he recovered his temper, have thought the lesson not too heavily paid for. There is no doubt that Mascarille and Jodelet, in one way or another, got compensation for their beatings and strippings. It is *la bonne comédie* —intensely ludicrous, but never in the least savage, engineered with perfect theatrical skill, and clothed with a perfectly literary garment of diction. There is only one point of pathos connected with it. Jodelet, one of the most famous if not the most famous of the older generation of actors, had "come over to help" the new company, and appears to have played the part that bears his name most brilliantly to Molière's Mascarille. But he died in the spring, and could do no more for his new comrades.

They only played one more piece, *Sganarelle ou Le Cocu Imaginaire* (which we may group with some others later) in the Petit Bourbon. This was pulled down in October 1660, and the company transferred to the Palais Royal, with its memories of Richelieu, and his Five Poets, and his dramatic ambitions. Molière was not lucky with his overture, *Don Garcie de Navarre*, one of the numerous, but not quite universal, instances of the tendency of the greatest men to mistake their vocation. It is a tragi-comedy, or rather a tragical comedy, of jealousy, exceedingly dull to read (Sainte-Beuve ingeniously called it an *essai pâle et noble*), and it is said that it was badly acted. It was withdrawn, and seems never to have reappeared, except in part during the *Année Terrible* in 1870–1—an odd juxtaposition of disasters. At midsummer appeared *L'École des Maris*, one of the numerous adjustments of the Terentian *Adelphi* with variations; and later in the summer, the very amusing *Les Fâcheux*, played before the King at Fouquet's fatal Fête of Vaux, and containing at least one scene suggested by Louis himself.

Next spring, on an uncertain day, Molière married Armande Béjart.[8] The arrangement, though we may put the worst scandal glanced at aside, was undoubtedly an "inconvenient" one, and it may have brought trouble with it; but the present writer, at any rate, has no doubt that this trouble has been immensely exaggerated. Or, to speak with almost legal exactness, he believes that there is very little evidence of it. We may not indeed attach very much weight to the laborious alibis which have been worked out for Mademoiselle Molière's supposed lovers, and to other maladroit defences of the kind. Here one may vary the Ariostian incredulity in a similar matter, and say, "Perhaps the defence is true, but it is not very convincing." If Armande Béjart was a *bourgeoise* Faustina or Messalina, no doubt she found plenty of opportunities to behave as such, even when this particular marquis was at Lons-le-Saulnier, and that particular viscount in Lithuania. If she was not actually first too jealous, and then too fond, of the young actor Baron, the temptations of her life would have been open to her in plenty of other instances. Far more really important facts are these, that the chief source of the aspersions on her character, the anonymous *La Fameuse Comédienne*, dates from 1688, long

8 Her full name was Armande-Grésinde-Claire-Elisabeth, and she seems generally to have used the first two members of it. There is perhaps less difficulty than has sometimes been thought in identifying her with "a little unbaptized sister" of the Béjarts, who appears in a document of March 1643; but more in another identification with a child called Mlle. Menou, who is mentioned in 1653 as having pleased Molière by reciting verses. [Recent evidence indicates that "Menou" was a nickname for Armande. *Ed.*]

after Molière's death and her second marriage; secondly, that numerous and savage as were Molière's enemies during his life, none asserted that he was his own Sganarelle, less the "Imaginary," though they did say that he was jealous, which is exceedingly probable. Jealousy is, if not the invariable, the usual seamy side of love; and all parties are agreed that Molière loved his wife, if only too well. Nor does it seem at all unlikely that she was a considerable flirt. For she appears to have been, if not regularly beautiful (her eyes were too small), extremely attractive; she had been born and brought up in Bohemian society; and she was on the stage. . . .

Whatever bad effect Molière's marriage may have had, it certainly did his genius no harm. At the end of the year appeared *L'École des Femmes,* perhaps the first of those plays which are generally accounted *majorum gentium* among Molière's. We may have something to say against the justness of this distinction later; but the consummate wit and nature of this piece are undeniable. Unfortunately it did, to a very small extent, lend itself to the accusation of what is called (in French of Stratford-atte-Bowe) *double entendre.* These accusations were multiplied and intensified absurdly and (though in this case with not even the same slight amount of justification) they were made to lend themselves to much more serious accusations of impiety. Molière had already enemies enough in rival actors, rival authors, and the *marquis* and others whom he satirised—enemies who were prepared to move Heaven, earth, and Acheron (besides the Queen-mother) against him. They had now, as they thought, an opportunity, if not of getting Heaven on their side, of putting themselves on the side of Heaven, and against Molière. And in a very short time *Tartuffe* and *Don Juan* gave them more. These latter accusations were far more serious for Molière than anything else. . . .

It may seem that no one but an absolute fool can have seen any real slight on religion in *L'École des Femmes.* It may be asked with wonder why Devotion, if real itself, should be offended at the condign punishment inflicted in *Tartuffe* on its counterfeit and worst enemy, Hypocrisy—the vice most hated of God and most noisome to men. *Don Juan,* though containing some things startling to weak brethren, can hardly be said to encourage either vice or impiety, seeing that the representative of both comes to an end which few persons would exactly court, and is loaded throughout with the disapproval of every one, from his respectable father to his rascally valet. But no doubt these considerations do not settle the matter. . . . In the first place, in order really to understand it, we must remember that the antipathy of Church to Stage—originating, for very good reasons, in the earliest ages of Christianity, and brought rather to a truce than to a peace during the mediæval period, when the Stage had in a manner become a department of the Church itself—had broken out once more when the Stage emancipated itself, and had been proof even against the fact that the Church's rebels—the extreme Protestant sects —partook, and even exaggerated, the dislike.

This antipathy had brought about in France all sorts of curious conventions and restrictions, such as (one which Molière himself generally though not invariably observes) that you must not so much as mention the word *église* in a play, though *temple*, as partly Pagan and partly Protestant, was permissible. And it might, of course, at any moment breed trouble in honest minds of various classes. For one class may stand Pierre Roullé, *curé* of the appropriate parish of Saint Barthélemy, who wrote, or rather screamed, on *Tartuffe* to the effect that Molière was a "demon, clad in flesh and blood," and distinctly wished him a flesh-and-blood experience of the element with which demons are supposed to be familiar. Roullé of course was merely a fool. But Bourdaloue was not a fool; and Bourdaloue called *Tartuffe* a "damnable invention." Baillet, the author of *Jugements des Savants,* may have been nearer to Roullé than to Bourdaloue in actual brains, but he was certainly a long way from the mental state of the Curate of Saint Bartholomew's, and yet he denounced Molière as one of the most dangerous enemies of the Church. As for Bossuet, his much later censure must be qualified by the remembrance that he was first of all a born rhetorician, and that Molière's death gave opportunities which no born rhetorician could resist. But still Bossuet is never negligible. The truth seems to be . . . that Molière hit several weak and sore places at once. Jansenists and Jesuits early identified each the other with Tartuffe; but there is no doubt that both secretly owed Molière a grudge for suggesting the identification. An odder thing, but certain in Baillet's case and probable in others, was that much of the resentment seems to have been directed against the *usurpation* by a mere player of the right of reproving sin. And it may be feared that we must add a less unreasonable but far more discreditable motive. The fact was that the *personnel* and *moral* of the French Church at this time was not in a state that would bear investigation or criticism. . . .

The year 1663 was chiefly occupied by the quarrels over *L'École des Femmes,* in which Molière's chief enemies were

the journalist and literary hack, Donneau de Visé (afterwards converted), and the rival dramatist Boursault, supported by a crowd of angry marquises, *précieuses*, *dévots*,
scribblers, players, etc. Their rage went to such a pitch that
the elder Montfleury formally accused Molière to the King
of having married his own daughter.[9] But in February 1664,
the King himself and his sister-in-law, Henrietta of England,
stood by proxy as godfather and godmother to the Molières'
first child.[10] And the royal favour further enabled Molière
to take still better vengeance in his own way, by two pieces—
irregular, almost Aristophanic, in their kind, but extraordi-
narily full of wit and vigour. These are the *Critique de
L'École des Femmes*, in which the common objections to the
piece are acted to more than the life, and the *Impromptu de
Versailles*, in which the joke in earnest is carried still farther
by the company appearing in their own persons as at a rehearsal, and discussing themselves and their enemies. There
is nothing quite like these two pieces in modern literature.[11] ...

The year which was opened, or nearly so, by the royal
sponsorship was again one of triumph and trouble. . . . The
King was particularly fond of *comédie-ballets*, things in
which a more or less slight and sometimes, though not always, quite separate drama of the lighter kind was intermixed
with all sorts of spectacle, musical interlude, and dancing in
which he himself and his courtiers could, if they chose, take
an actual part. In fact these things were very nearly masques
of the Jonsonian kind, with the purely dramatic part much
more developed. *Le Mariage Forcé*, the first of them in this
year, is slight. . . . *La Princesse d'Élide*, which followed, and
which contains some very pretty and some very amusing
touches, is actually unfinished—so largely was the comedy
in these cases a mere vehicle for the "entertainment." But
among the same princely pleasures of Versailles (*Les Plaisirs
de l'Île Enchantée*) appeared also . . . the first three acts of
Tartuffe. Strangely enough, in this time of endless private

---

[9] It has been suggested that Madeleine Béjart, who was twenty
years older than Armande, was not her sister, but her mother. And
that, since Madeleine was Molière's mistress for many years, Armande may have been his illegitimate child, without his having known
it. It is most likely, though not proved, that Armande was the daughter of Madeleine, but not of Molière. *Ed.*

[10] Molière and Armande had three children. Two boys died young;
the third, a girl, Esprit Madeleine, married, rather late, a M. de
Montalant, and died childless in 1723.

[11] Except Giraudoux's *L'Impromptu de Paris*, written thirteen
years after this essay. *Ed.*

gossip, and almost as endless official record about Court
amusements, we have not a single account, given at once and
before the storm broke, of the actual reception of the piece.
But a week later its production in public was forbidden;
though it was again played, as three acts only. . . .

Perhaps one of the strongest proofs . . . that Molière meant
no harm by *Tartuffe* is the nature of the piece that followed
it. This was most unlucky and not a little surprising in a man
of such shrewdness, who had had two warnings. . . . The
play is a very fine one, and while the tragic part of the wonderful and poetic legend is perfectly rendered, the comic
additions and contrasts are of the very best Molière. Nothing but the most "fugitive and cloistered" piety could honestly object to it; as for the dishonestly pious, it must have
been as much more unpleasant than *Tartuffe* as Don Juan's
final destination was than the "Impostor's" temporary one.
Anyhow, it was ferociously attacked, and the representation
stopped suddenly—no doubt by order, though we do not
know this as a fact.

But it took a good deal to suppress Molière. In the words
of one of the greatest efforts of the Muse of Parody:

> "He was more than three examiners
> Could plough from morn to night";

and pedants, and fribbles, and true or false bigots combined
could never quench his vein. Later, in 1665, he produced the
admirable *comédie-ballet* of *L'Amour Médecin* . . . ; he followed it in the summer of 1666 with *Le Misanthrope*, which
it is customary in French literary criticism to couple with
Tartuffe as the masterpieces not merely of his but of their
comic theatre. Perhaps a little of the *distinguo* is here necessary, but it may be better given later. This, in any case, capital
play was succeeded quickly by the delightful *Médecin Malgré
Lui*, one of his greatest eternisings of old *fabliau* motives. At
the close of this year and the beginning of the next there was
a series of fêtes at Versailles to which Molière contributed
three pieces—*Mélicerte*, of the kind of the *Princesse d'Élide*,
the unimportant *Pastorale Comique*, and one of his most
charming small things, *Le Sicilien*, or *L'Amour Peintre*, the
last of which became deservedly popular. Later, the King
went to Flanders, and it seems that he gave (when and how
is unknown) some sort of permission to set *Tartuffe* free. It
was actually represented, though with the title changed to
L'Imposteur, and the hero-villain's name changed to Panulphe,
in August. . . . But the Archbishop of Paris . . . struck in

with a formal threat of excommunication to all who played, read, or heard the piece—which settled the matter for the time. Molière, who had long been suffering from the lung disease which killed him later, seems now to have been overwhelmed for a time, and the theatre was even shut.

But he rallied. 1668 saw the admirable adaptation from Plautus of *Amphitryon*, the incomparable farce-tragedy of *George Dandin* and his marriage into the family of Sotenville, and the triumph (again adapted from the Latin and Italian, but made amply his own) of *L'Avare*, one of the most perfect things that even he had done. And this battle of heart against fate was rewarded by the setting free of *Tartuffe* in February 1669, with the immense success which its merits deserved, and which the tactics of its opponents had made certain. It was played twenty-eight days running— the first half of them with enormous receipts for the time— between the beginning of February and Easter, nineteen times in May and June, and again later. But Molière, before its first vogue was over, "tricked it up" with the admirable contrast of *M. de Pourceaugnac* in September. 1670 saw, in his two manners, the Court entertainment of *Les Amants Magnifiques* and the again incomparable *Bourgeois Gentilhomme*. Next year he joined Corneille, Quinault, and Lulli in the "tragedy-ballet" of *Psyche*, and then wrote and produced two light comedies of his own particular style—*Les Fourberies de Scapin* and *La Comtesse d'Escarbagnas*. 1672 had one (but as Herrick says of his Sappho, "a principal") in *Les Femmes Savantes*, where the satire of the *Précieuses Ridicules* was repeated more seriously and with a rather regrettable touch of personality, but no doubt with heavier metal brought to bear and in the spirit of a deeper criticism of life. And then February 1673 saw, in *Le Malade Imaginaire*, the last and not the least of the triumphs of his peculiar manner. Although desperately ill, he played the title-part several times to the life, playing it on the 17th to the death. Either on the stage or immediately after coming home, he broke a blood-vessel, died, and was buried four days later, at night and with maimed rites, permission for which his widow had, with much effort, obtained from the ecclesiastical authorities.[12] . . .

As to the charges, direct and indirect, of plagiarism, it cannot, at this time of day, be necessary to say much. It is practically acknowledged by all critics whose opinion is of the slightest value that such charges are only valid against

[12] Who were still smarting over *Tartuffe* and *Don Juan*. Ed.

bad writers—that the good writer may "take his property"
(in Molière's own attributed and very likely genuine words)
where he finds it. But another charge or class of charges, less
fully outlined in the above dialogue, requires ampler dealing.
From the very first the keen eye of professional jealousy saw
that the word to use against Molière was *farce*. "Farce" is
the critical *tarte à la créme*. And, as sometimes happens in
such cases, the defenders have played into the hands of the
attack by exhibiting a sort of nervous "confession and avoid-
ance" of it. . . . Then, exaggerating this nervousness still
farther, they try to make of these two masterpieces (*Tartuffe*
and *Le Misanthrope*), if not also of *Don Juan*, something
like tragedies, to throw a tragic air over Molière's whole
career, to lament his necessity of writing roaring farces for
the city and wishy-washy entertainments for the Court. . . .

Why should it be so difficult to take Molière for what he
is—the Master of the Laugh? and so tempting to make him
something else—a great poet, a great moralist, a fashioner
of terrible tragedies under comic veils? I believe (If I could
only put it in his own words!) I could hit pretty well on
what his own thoughts in the matter would be, and a famous
passage it would make! In the English sense Molière is hardly a "poet" at all—he had no occasion to be so, though he is
an admirable versifier in his own easy way (*not* easy to do),
and the mingled awe and admiration with which the French
regard the tricks he plays with the stiff language and prosody
of their classic tongue make a very funny mixture. As for
his morality, it is practically never bad and seldom if ever
careless; but he does not make it his first or his direct object
in all cases. . . .

But the part to be allotted to seriousness in his theatre generally is, I admit, a much more difficult question and not to
be settled offhand. You must read Molière long, and you
must read him not in scraps or separate plays, but continuously, before you really apprehend his essence.

For it is not an essence of style and form, as Milton's is
almost wholly and Dante's to a great extent. It is not an essence of craftsmanship like Dryden's, or Racine's, or, in a
lesser way still, Pope's. It is not the power of creating a special less or more limited world of his own, like (in very different ways) the essence of Spenser, or Ariosto, or Balzac, or
Dickens. It is not quite—though it comes nearer to these—
the power of investing everything with actual life, which belongs to Shakespeare supremely, and to Scott, Thackeray,
Fielding, in different ways and degrees. It does not exactly
transform everything by passing it through a bath of bur-

lesque irony like Rabelais, or romantic irony like Cervantes, or indignant irony like Swift. It only asks everything which suggests itself "Can you help me to make men laugh?" and if so, it takes the thing and makes it do this. With the rest it *n'a que faire*, as the French phrase goes. It has no business for them; they may be excellent things for other artists and other methods, but not for it and for *him*. . . .

Molière was not old; he was almost exactly the age of Shakespeare when he too died—less "tragically," as they say, but also with a parcel of work done, such as makes it, though natural, almost absurd to wish for more. . . . If God has given you brains, and courage, and the upward countenance; if you have loved; if you have had your day and lived your life, what more do you want? Molière had had and done all this. . . .

A LIST OF MOLIÈRE'S PLAYS:

The Bungler's Jealousy (1645?), *The Flying Doctor* (1648?), *The Blunderer* (1655), *The Spiteful Love* (1658), *The Precious Young Women* (1659), *Sganarelle* (1660), *Dom Garcia of Navarre* (1661), *The School for Husbands* (1661), *The Nuisances* (1661), *The School for Wives* (1662), *The Criticism of "The School for Wives"* (1663), *The Improvisation at Versailles* (1663), *The Forced Marriage* (1664), *The Princess of Élide* (1664), *Tartuffe* (1664), *Dom Juan* (1665), *Love, the Doctor* (1665), *The Misanthrope* (1666), *The Doctor in Spite of Himself* (1666), *Mélicerte* (1667), *A Comic Pastoral* (1667), *The Sicilian* (1667), *Amphitryon* (1667-8), *George Dandin* (1668), *The Miser* (1668), *Monsieur de Porceaugnac* (1669), *The Magnificent Lovers* (1670), *The Bourgeois Gentleman* (1670), *Psyche* (1671), *The Pranks of Scapin* (1671), *The Countess of Escarbagnas* (1671), *The Scholarly Ladies* (1671), *The Imaginary Invalid* (1673).

SUGGESTIONS FOR FURTHER READING ON MOLIÈRE:

Bishop, Morris (tr. and ed.). *Eight Plays by Molière*. New York: Random House, Inc. (Modern Library, Inc.), 1957.

Lancaster, H. Carrington. *A History of French Dramatic Literature in the Seventeenth Century.* 9 vols. Baltimore: The Johns Hopkins Press, 1929-42.

Moore, W. G. *Molière, a New Criticism.* New York: Oxford University Press, Inc., 1950.

Palmer, John. *Molière.* New York: Harcourt, Brace & Company, Inc., 1930.

Schwartz, I. A. *The Commedia dell'Arte and Its Influence on French Comedy in the Seventeenth Century.* (Comparative Literature Series.) New York: Institute of French Studies, Inc., 1933.

Turnell, Martin. *The Classical Moment.* New York: New Directions, 1948.

IN FRENCH ONLY:

Audiberti, Jacques. *Molière Dramaturge.* L'Arche, 1954.
Jouvet, Louis. *Molière. Conferencia,* 1937.
Lanson, Gustave. *Molière et la Farce. Revue de Paris,* 1901.
Simon, Alfred. *Molière par lui-même.* Editions du Seuil, 1957.

NOTE: A critical note on Molière, "From *An Essay on Comedy,*" by George Meredith, will be found on p. 522.

THE IMAGINARY INVALID

A Comedy in three acts, two musical interludes
and a grand finale

By Jean-Baptiste Poquelin, called Molière

FIRST PERFORMED AT THE
THÉÂTRE-FRANÇAIS ON FEBRUARY 10, 1673

Translated by Mildred Marmur

CHARACTERS

ARGAN, *an imaginary self-imagined invalid*
BELINE, *second wife of Argan*
ANGELIQUE, *Argan's daughter, beloved of Cleante*
LOUISON, *younger daughter of Argan, and Angelique's sister*
BERALDE, *Argan's brother*
CLEANTE, *Angelique's suitor*
Monsieur DIAFOIRUS, *a doctor*
THOMAS DIAFOIRUS, *his son, and Angelique's suitor*
Monsieur PURGON, *Argan's doctor*
Monsieur FLEURANT, *Argan's apothecary*
Monsieur BONNEFOY, *a notary*
TOINETTE, *Argan's servant*

*The scene takes place in Paris, in Argan's sitting room.
Act I is preceded by a pastoral ballet.*

ACT I

ARGAN (*sitting at a table in his room, adding up his bills with small round counters*): Three and two make five and five make ten, and ten make twenty. Three and two make five. "Plus, on the twenty-fourth day of the month, one small enema, soothing and softening, to moisten, liquefy, and refresh the gentleman's intestines." What I like about Monsieur Fleurant, my apothecary, is that his bills are always so politely phrased. "The gentleman's intestines, thirty pieces." All very good, Monsieur Fleurant, but it is not enough to be polite. You should also be reasonable and not try to swindle a poor invalid. Thirty pieces for one enema! You only charged me twenty last time. And twenty in apothecary language means ten. So there we are, ten. "Plus, on the aforementioned day, one cleansing enema consisting of a double dose of rhubarb, rose-honey, and other ingredients according to prescription, to sweep, cleanse, and polish the gentleman's lower stomach. Thirty pieces." Allow me to adjust, ten. "Plus, on the evening of the aforementioned day, one hepatic, soporific, and somniferous tonic to encourage Monsieur's sleep. Thirty-five." I will not argue that one. It did help me to sleep. Ten, fifteen, sixteen, and seventeen pieces, six farthings. "Plus, on the twenty-fifth day of the month, one fine purgative and fortifying medicine consisting of fresh cassia, Levantine senna, and other ingredients prescribed by Monsieur Purgon, to expel and evacuate the gentleman's bile. Four pounds." Ah, Monsieur Fleurant, you're not serious. You must learn to live with sick people. Monsieur Purgon did not instruct you to ask four pounds. There, let us say three, if you please. Twenty and thirty pieces. "Plus, on the aforementioned day, one astringent potion to relax Monsieur. Thirty pieces." Let us add ten and fifteen. "Plus, on the twenty-sixth day of the month, one enema to chase the gas from Monsieur's intestines, thirty pieces." Ten, Monsieur Fleurant. "Plus, one enema as above, the evening of the same day, thirty pieces." Ten, Monsieur Fleurant. "Plus,

43

on the twenty-seventh day of the month, one excellent medicine designed to aid in speeding away the ill humors of
Monsieur, three pounds." Good, twenty and thirty pieces.
I'm pleased to see that you can be reasonable. "Plus, on the
twenty-eighth day of the month, one dose of clarified and
sweetened buttermilk, to soften, temper, and refresh Monsieur's blood. Twenty pieces." Why don't we say ten? "Plus,
one soothing and fortifying potion consisting of twelve grains
of bezoar, syrup of lemon, syrup of pomegranate, and other
ingredients, according to prescription. Five pounds." Easy,
easy, Monsieur Fleurant. If you go on like this, I shall refuse
to be sick any more. Be satisfied with four. Twenty and forty
pieces. Three and two make five, and five make ten, and ten
make twenty. Sixty-three pounds, four pieces, six farthings.
So, during this month I have taken one, two, three, four,
five, six, seven, eight medicines; and one, two, three, four,
five, six, seven, eight, nine, ten, eleven, twelve enemas. But
last month I had twelve medicines and twenty enemas. No
wonder I feel worse this month. I shall tell Monsieur Purgon
to look into the matter. Now let me get rid of all this. Where
is everyone? They take no notice of me. They're never here
when I want them! (*Rings bell to summon the servants.*) They
never listen. And my bell isn't loud enough. (*Rings again.*)
It's no use! (*Rings more.*) They're all deaf. Toinette! (*Rings
bell with all his might.*) Toinette! I am growing angry. (*Stops
ringing and shouts at top of his lungs.*) You hussy, come
here immediately! How can they leave a poor invalid all
alone like this! (*Rings.*) What shall I do? (*Rings again.*) Oh,
God! They will leave me here to die. (*Keeps ringing.*)

   TOINETTE (*running into bedroom*):   Coming!
   ARGAN: Oh, you witch! You vixen!
   TOINETTE (*pretends she banged her head*):   The devil take
your impatience! You rush me around so much that I banged
my head against the shutter.
   ARGAN (*furious*):   Quiet, you . . . you creature!
   TOINETTE (*in order to interrupt him and keep him from
shouting, keeps clutching her head and saying*):   Oh!
   ARGAN: About . . .
   TOINETTE: Oh!
   ARGAN: About an hour ago . . .
   TOINETTE: Oh!
   ARGAN: You left me . . .
   TOINETTE: Oh!
   ARGAN: Shut up and let me shout at you.
   TOINETTE: Shut up? I can't speak a word the way my
head is hurting.

ARGAN: You've made me scream myself hoarse.

TOINETTE: And you made me crack my skull, which is just as bad. So we're even, thank you.

ARGAN: How dare you!

TOINETTE: If you shout at me, I will cry.

ARGAN: To leave me . . .

TOINETTE (*still interrupting*): Oh!

ARGAN: You want to . . .

TOINETTE: Oh!

ARGAN: Quiet! At least let me have the pleasure of shouting at you.

TOINETTE: Shout all you want, I'm perfectly willing.

ARGAN: But you keep interrupting me.

TOINETTE: If you enjoy shouting, I have the right to enjoy complaining. It's only fair. Oh!

ARGAN: All right, all right. Here, take this away. (*Rises and gives her the counters and the bills.*) How did my enema come out this morning?

TOINETTE: Your enema?

ARGAN: Yes. Did I pass enough bile?

TOINETTE: I beg your pardon! Do you expect me to mess about with those things? Monsieur Fleurant can stick his nose into them. He's the one who makes the profit.

ARGAN: See that my next one is prepared. I'm supposed to have it in a little while.

TOINETTE: Those two gentlemen—Monsieur Fleurant and Monsieur Purgon—are having a fine time with your body. They know they've latched on to a good thing in you. I'd love to ask them just what's wrong with you to make them keep prescribing so many different medicines.

ARGAN: Quiet, ignoramus! You have no right to interfere with my medical advisers. Call my daughter, Angelique. I have something to tell her.

TOINETTE: Here she comes. She must be reading your mind.

(*Enter* ANGELIQUE.)

ARGAN: Ah, Angelique. You've come at the right time. I wanted to talk to you.

ANGELIQUE: Yes, Father?

ARGAN (*running to his bedpan*): Wait. (*To* TOINETTE.) Give me my walking stick. I'll be back in a minute.

TOINETTE (*in mock encouragement*): Hurry, Monsieur, hurry.

(*Exit* ARGAN, *running.*)

ANGELIQUE (*looking wistfully at her*): Toinette . . .

TOINETTE: What?

ANGELIQUE: Look at me.

TOINETTE: I'm looking.

ANGELIQUE: Toinette!

TOINETTE: "Toinette" what?

ANGELIQUE: Can't you guess what I want to talk to you about?

TOINETTE: I have a good enough idea. About our young lover. For six days now he's been the sole topic of our conversation and you're miserable the moment we stop talking about him.

ANGELIQUE: If you know it, why don't you mention him first and spare me the embarrassment?

TOINETTE: You don't give me enough time. Besides, it's impossible to talk about him enough to suit you.

ANGELIQUE: Oh, I know! And it makes me so happy that I can discuss him with you, Toinette. Tell me, do you think I'm wrong to feel this way about him?

TOINETTE: I really don't know.

ANGELIQUE: Am I a fool to give in to my feelings?

TOINETTE: I wouldn't say that.

ANGELIQUE: And do you think I should be cold when he's so tender about his love for me?

TOINETTE: Heaven forbid!

ANGELIQUE: Don't you agree that Fate arranged our meeting?

TOINETTE: Yes.

ANGELIQUE: And don't you think that the way he defended me without knowing who I was shows what a good person he is?

TOINETTE: Yes.

ANGELIQUE: That no one could have acted more generously?

TOINETTE: I agree.

ANGELIQUE: And that he did it with the greatest charm in the whole world?

TOINETTE: Oh yes.

ANGELIQUE: And Toinette, don't you think he's very handsome?

TOINETTE: Definitely.

ANGELIQUE: That he's the handsomest young man who ever lived?

TOINETTE: No question about it.

ANGELIQUE: That there's something noble about him even

when he speaks—let alone when he acts!

TOINETTE: Absolutely.

ANGELIQUE: That no girl could wish to hear anything more romantic than what he says to me?

TOINETTE: Without a doubt.

ANGELIQUE: And that there's nothing worse than the way they keep me locked up and prevent me from seeing him?

TOINETTE: Oh yes.

ANGELIQUE: But Toinette dear, do you think he loves me as much as he says he does?

TOINETTE: It's always hard to distinguish between sincerity and good acting. And I've seen some very convincing actors in my day.

ANGELIQUE: Toinette, what do you mean? Oh dear, the way he speaks, could it be possible that he's lying to me?

TOINETTE: You'll know soon enough. He wrote you yesterday that he was going to ask your father for your hand in marriage. If he does, you can be sure of him.

ANGELIQUE: Toinette, if he deceives me, I'll never believe another man in my life.

TOINETTE: Hush, your father's coming back.

(*Re-enter* ARGAN, *who sits down in his chair.*)

ARGAN: Ah yes, my dear. I have some news for you that you probably don't expect. I've been asked for your hand in marriage. What's that? You're laughing. Well, marriage is a pleasant word. There's nothing more amusing for a girl. Ah, nature, nature! To look at you, I don't think I have to ask if you're willing.

ANGELIQUE: I'm bound to do whatever you command, Father.

ARGAN: I am delighted to have such an obedient daughter. The matter is settled then. I have consented.

ANGELIQUE: It's my duty to obey you blindly, Father.

ARGAN: Your stepmother wanted me to send you to a convent, and your little sister Louison with you. She's been talking about it for a long time now.

TOINETTE (*aside*):   The dear lady knows what she's doing.

ARGAN: She was very reluctant to consent to this marriage, but I convinced her and gave my word.

ANGELIQUE: Oh, Father, I'm so grateful to you for your kindness.

TOINETTE (*to* ARGAN):   I must say, Monsieur, that I am also grateful to you. This is the most sensible thing you've done in your life.

ARGAN: I haven't seen the young man yet, but I'm told that we'll both be pleased.

ANGELIQUE: Oh yes, Father.

ARGAN: Do you know him?

ANGELIQUE: Since you have consented I can speak freely. We happened to meet six days ago. Since then we've become steadily fonder of each other and that is why he's asked you for my hand.

ARGAN: They didn't tell me that, but I'm pleased just the same. So much the better if it happened that way. They say he's a handsome young man.

ANGELIQUE: Oh yes, Father.

ARGAN: And tall. Charming.

ANGELIQUE: Very.

ARGAN: With a kind face.

ANGELIQUE: Very kind.

ARGAN: Intelligent and well born.

ANGELIQUE: Yes. Very much so.

ARGAN: Trustworthy.

ANGELIQUE: The most trustworthy person in the world!

ARGAN: Speaks Latin and Greek very well.

ANGELIQUE: I didn't know that.

ARGAN: And he'll be a doctor of medicine in three days.

ANGELIQUE: He will?

ARGAN: Yes. Hasn't he told you?

ANGELIQUE: No, not a word. Who told you?

ARGAN: Monsieur Purgon.

ANGELIQUE: Does Monsieur Purgon know him?

ARGAN: What a question! Of course he knows him. He's his nephew.

ANGELIQUE: Cleante is Monsieur Purgon's nephew?

ARGAN: Cleante? We are talking about the young man you're going to marry.

ANGELIQUE: Of course.

ARGAN: Of course. He is Monsieur Purgon's nephew and the son of his brother-in-law, Doctor Diafoirus. And his name is Thomas Diafoirus and not Cleante, and this morning we contracted for the marriage, Monsieur Purgon, Monsieur Fleurant, and I. And tomorrow your fiancé is coming here with his father. What's the matter? Why have you turned so pale?

ANGELIQUE: I'm afraid, Father, that you were talking about one person and I thought you meant someone else.

TOINETTE: What's all this about? A joke? A farce? A wealthy man like you marrying his girl off to a doctor?

ARGAN: Yes, I am, insolent wench. What's it to you?

TOINETTE: Please, Monsieur, not so loud and not so insulting. Can't we discuss something without being carried away? Let's speak calmly. Let's hear your reason for such a marriage.

ARGAN: My reason is simple. I am feeble and ailing and I would like to have a doctor as my son-in-law so that I can have all the treatments and prescriptions and free consultations I need without going outside the family.

TOINETTE: That's better. Now you're talking sense and you do have a reason. But, sir, put your hand on your heart—are you really sick?

ARGAN: The impudence of you! Am I really sick, really sick!

TOINETTE: Very well, sir, very well. You're sick, let's not fight about it. Very sick, I agree. Even sicker than you think. But your daughter should marry a husband for *her* reasons, and since she's not sick there's no reason for her to marry a doctor.

ARGAN: I am giving her this doctor for my benefit. A dutiful daughter should be delighted to marry someone who will be useful for her father's health.

TOINETTE: May I make a suggestion, Monsieur?

ARGAN: What?

TOINETTE: Stop thinking about this marriage.

ARGAN: Why?

TOINETTE: Why? Because your daughter will never agree to it.

ARGAN: She won't agree?

TOINETTE: No.

ARGAN: My daughter won't agree?

TOINETTE: Your daughter won't agree. She'll tell you that she doesn't want anything to do with Monsieur Diafoirus, nor with his son Thomas Diafoirus, nor with any member of the Diafoirus family anywhere in the world.

ARGAN: But I want something to do with them. Besides, the match is even better than it seems. This son is the sole heir of Monsieur Diafoirus, and that's not all; Monsieur Purgon, who has no wife or child, is bequeathing everything he owns to him because of this marriage and Monsieur Purgon is a man with an income of eight thousand pounds a year.

TOINETTE: He must have killed a lot of people to get that rich.

ARGAN: Eight thousand pounds a year is good in itself, but besides that there's also the father's wealth.

TOINETTE: That's all very well, sir, but let's come back to the point. I advise you, between you and me, to find her another husband. She wasn't destined to be Madame Diafoirus.

ARGAN: But I want her to be.

TOINETTE: Don't say that.

ARGAN: Why not?

TOINETTE: Just don't.

ARGAN: Why shouldn't I say it?

TOINETTE: People will say you don't think before you speak.

ARGAN: People can say anything they want. I tell you she's going to honor the agreement I've made.

TOINETTE: I'm sure she won't do it.

ARGAN: I will force her to.

TOINETTE: I tell you she won't.

ARGAN: She does, or I put her into a convent.

TOINETTE: You will?

ARGAN: Yes, I will.

TOINETTE: Ha!

ARGAN: What do you mean, "Ha!"?

TOINETTE: You won't put her into a convent.

ARGAN: I won't put her into a convent?

TOINETTE: No.

ARGAN: No?

TOINETTE: No.

ARGAN: Just listen to her! I won't put my daughter into a convent if I want to?

TOINETTE: No, I tell you.

ARGAN: Who will stop me?

TOINETTE: You yourself.

ARGAN: Me?

TOINETTE: Yes. You won't have the heart.

ARGAN: Oh yes I will.

TOINETTE: You're fooling yourself.

ARGAN: No, I'm not.

TOINETTE: Your fatherly affection won't let you.

ARGAN: Affection won't sway me.

TOINETTE: A little tear or two, her arms around your neck, a "papa darling" said with the right note of sadness, will be enough.

ARGAN: It won't do a thing.

TOINETTE: Oh yes it will.

ARGAN: I tell you I won't give in.

TOINETTE: Nonsense.

ARGAN: There's no use saying "nonsense."

TOINETTE: I know you very well. You're naturally kind-hearted.

ARGAN (*angry*):   I'm not kindhearted; I can be mean when I want to be.

TOINETTE: Careful, sir, you forget how sick you are.

ARGAN: I insist that she get ready for the husband I've chosen for her.

TOINETTE: And I insist that she do no such thing.

ARGAN: What has this world come to when a servant can speak to her master like this!

TOINETTE: When a master doesn't consider what he's doing, a sensible servant has the right to correct him.

ARGAN (*running after her*):   You insolent slut! Just let me get my hands on you.

TOINETTE (*running away*):   It's my duty to stop you from doing anything dishonorable.

ARGAN (*furious, chasing her around his chair, cane in hand*):   Just you come here, I'll teach you how to talk to me.

TOINETTE (*running to the other side of the chair*):   I have to keep you from behaving like a fool!

ARGAN: Witch!

TOINETTE: I'll never consent to this marriage.

ARGAN: Hussy!

TOINETTE: I refuse to let her marry Thomas Diafoirus.

ARGAN: Quiet!

TOINETTE: And she'll obey me quicker than you.

ARGAN (*stops chasing her*):   Angelique, stop her!

ANGELIQUE: Oh, Father, don't upset yourself so.

ARGAN (*to* ANGELIQUE):   If you don't stop her, I'll disinherit you.

TOINETTE: And if she obeys you, I'll disinherit her.

ARGAN (*drops into chair, exhausted*):   Oh! I can't run any more. She will send me to my grave.

(*Enter* BELINE.)

ARGAN: Come here, my love.

BELINE: What's the matter, darling?

ARGAN: Help me.

BELINE: What's wrong, my little angel?

ARGAN: My love!

BELINE: My darling.

ARGAN: They're making me very angry.

BELINE: Who, dearest?

ARGAN: That awful Toinette is more impertinent than ever. She made me furious, dearest.

BELINE: Don't excite yourself, sweetheart.

ARGAN: She argued with me for an hour about everything I want to do.

BELINE: There, there, my poppet.

ARGAN: And she had the gall to tell me that I'm not sick.

BELINE: That is impertinent!

ARGAN: Darling, you know how sick I am.

BELINE: Yes, my turtledove. She's wrong.

ARGAN: That girl will put me into an early grave!

BELINE: I'm here to protect you, my sweet.

ARGAN: She's the cause of all my bile.

BELINE: Don't listen to her, my angel.

ARGAN: How long now have I been asking you to get her out of the house?

BELINE: Dearest, there are no servants without faults, and we must put up with their bad qualities because of the good ones. Toinette is careful and clever and above all faithful, and you know how difficult it is to find servants we can trust these days. Toinette!

TOINETTE: Yes, Madame?

BELINE: Why do you make my husband angry?

TOINETTE (*sweetly*):   Me, Madame? I don't know what you mean. I try to please Monsieur in every way.

ARGAN: The liar!

TOINETTE: He told us that he wanted to marry his daughter off to the son of Monsieur Diafoirus and I said I thought it was a good marriage for her, but that it seemed more sensible to put her into a convent.

BELINE: There's nothing wrong with that. I agree with her.

ARGAN: Don't believe her, my pigeon. She tried to provoke me in hundreds of ways.

BELINE: I believe *you*, dear. There now, sit back. Listen, Toinette. If you make my husband angry again, I will dismiss you. Now, give me his fur wrap and some pillows so that I can settle him into his chair. Poor dear, you're all out of sorts. Pull your nightcap down to your ears. The fastest way to catch cold is to let the air touch your ears.

ARGAN: My dove, how good you are to me.

BELINE (*tucking the pillows in around him*):   Lift yourself so that I can put this one under you. Let's put this one here and this one on the other side. And this one behind your back and this one under your head.

TOINETTE (*drops a pillow over his head and runs away*):   And this one to protect you from the night air!

ARGAN (*furious, throws all the pillows at her*):   Devil! You want to smother me?

(*Exit* TOINETTE, *running, followed by* ANGELIQUE.)

BELINE: What happened?

ARGAN (*breathless*):   I can't bear any more.

BELINE: What's wrong? She only wanted to help.

ARGAN: You don't know how vicious she can be, my treasure. She's upset me completely and I'll need more than eight medicines and twelve enemas to recover.

BELINE: My little angel, calm yourself.

ARGAN: My precious, you're my only consolation.

BELINE: Poor little one!

ARGAN: Sweetheart, as I told you, I'm going to make my will so that I can show you how I appreciate your love.

BELINE: Darling, please don't talk about it. The very mention of the word "will" makes me shiver.

ARGAN: I asked you to talk to your notary about it.

BELINE: He's in the parlor. I brought him with me.

ARGAN: Call him in, dearest. (*Exit* BELINE *and re-enter immediately, followed by* NOTARY.) Come in, Monsieur de Bonnefoy, come in. Please sit down. My wife tells me that you're a very honest man, sir, and a good friend of hers. I've asked her to speak to you about a will I want to draw up.

BELINE: No. I can't bring myself to talk about such things.

NOTARY: She has told me of your intentions, and of the plans you've made for her. I must tell you that you won't be able to give her anything in your will.

ARGAN: Why?

NOTARY: Common Law is against it. It might be possible if you were in a land where written law prevailed. But it can't be done in Paris or in most of the other common law domains. The only settlement which may be made by a husband and wife is a gift between them during the lifetime of both, and even this requires that there be no surviving children, either of both parents or of one, on the expiration of the first partner.

ARGAN: What an outrageous state of affairs when a husband can leave nothing to a wife who loves him dearly and takes such good care of him! I'd like to ask my lawyer what I can do about this.

NOTARY: It's a waste of time to go to the lawyers. They're usually very strict about these matters. They think it's a crime to arrange one's affairs outside the law. They're difficult people and they refuse to acknowledge the necessity

for subterfuge. But there are people you can consult who
are much more accommodating; who can adjust certain pro-
hibited matters; who know how to eliminate legal difficulties
and circumvent common law by various subtle methods.
We're forced to be adaptable in our work, sir, or we could
do nothing and my whole profession would not be worth one
farthing.

ARGAN: My wife was right when she told me that you
were an honest and a clever man. How can I arrange to
leave my fortune to her and disinherit my children?

NOTARY: How? You quietly select a close friend of your
wife and leave everything in your will to him; and he can
pass it over to her later on. You can also pretend to contract a great number of debts with various creditors, who
will lend their names to your wife and provide her with
documents attesting the validity of her claims. And during
your lifetime you're free to give her money or any notes
payable to the bearer which you may have.

BELINE: My dearest, don't torment yourself with all this.
If anything happens to you, I don't want to live.

ARGAN: My turtledove!

BELINE: Yes, my love. If I am unfortunate enough to
lose you . . .

ARGAN: My devoted wife!

BELINE: Life would mean nothing to me.

ARGAN: My treasure!

BELINE: And I'd follow you to the grave to show you
how much I love you.

ARGAN: My dearest, you're breaking my heart. Please
stop crying, I beg of you.

NOTARY (to BELINE): Your tears are premature. We'll
come to that style later.

BELINE: Oh, Monsieur, you don't know what it is to
have a husband you love dearly.

ARGAN: If I die, my love, my one regret would be that
we haven't had a child. But Monsieur Purgon has promised
to let me have one.

NOTARY: It's still possible.

ARGAN: I must make my will out, dearest, the way Monsieur recommends. But to be safe I'm going to give you
20,000 gold pieces which I've been keeping behind a panel
in my bedroom, and two notes which are owed to me by
Monsieur Damon and Monsieur Gerante. They're both payable to the bearer.

BELINE: No! no! I don't want any part of them. How
much did you say there was behind the panel?

ARGAN: Twenty thousand, my love.

BELINE: Please don't mention money to me. I can't bear it. How much are the notes worth?

ARGAN: One is for four thousand, dearest, and the other for six.

BELINE: All the wealth in the world, my beloved, is worth nothing to me without you.

NOTARY (*to* ARGAN):   Would you like me to draw up the will?

ARGAN: Yes, sir, but we'll be more comfortable in my other room. Help me there, my sweet, if you please.

BELINE: Come, my poor darling.

(*Exit* BELINE, ARGAN, NOTARY. *Enter* TOINETTE *and* ANGELIQUE.)

TOINETTE: There they go with a notary, and talking about a will. Your stepmother doesn't waste a second. I'm sure that she's plotting with your father to deprive you of your inheritance.

ANGELIQUE: I don't care if he gives away his fortune—I just don't want him to give away my heart. Don't you see, Toinette, how my love is being threatened? Promise you won't abandon me now when I need you most.

TOINETTE: Me, abandon you? I'd rather die. Your stepmother's wasting her time making friends with me. I've never liked her and I've always been on your side. I'll manage to help you somehow, but I must change my tactics. I'll have to hide my affection for you and pretend to agree with your father and stepmother.

ANGELIQUE: Please try to get word to Cleante about this marriage they've decided on.

TOINETTE: I have no one to send except that old money-lender, Polichinelle. He's in love with me and he'll make me pay him quite a few kisses. But I'm happy to do this for you. It's too late tonight. I'll send him off tomorrow as early as possible. He'll be delighted to . . .

BELINE (*from next room*):   Toinette!

TOINETTE: I must go. Good night and don't worry. I'll take care of everything.

FIRST INTERMISSION

(*The scene shifts to the street outside* ARGAN's *house. It is nighttime and* POLICHINELLE *has come to serenade his lady.*)

POLICHINELLE: Oh love, love, love, love! Poor Polichinelle, what lunatic notions have you taken into your head? What are you up to, you poor mad creature? You neglect your business and watch it dwindle down to rack and ruin; you've stopped eating; you hardly even drink; and you can't sleep at night. And all of this for whom? For a dragon, an absolute dragon, a devil of a wench who snubs you and laughs at everything you say. But what's the use of trying to be logical? It's love. I've got to be as crazy as the next one. Not the best thing in the world for a man of my age, but what can I do? I can't force myself to be reasonable. Old hearts are overwhelmed as easily as young.

I've come to try and soften my tigress with a serenade. Sometimes there's nothing so touching as a lover singing his grievances at his mistress' door. (*Picks up his lute.*) I can accompany myself with this. Oh night, lovely night! Carry my laments to the bed of my inflexible love.

(*Sings.*) [1]

> Night and day I love you true
> And beg for your reply
> If you say yes, you'll comfort me
> If you say no, I'll die.
>
> I long for you when we're apart
> And pray that soon we'll meet
> But time runs out and I'm alone
> Aggrieved and in defeat.

[1] Molière has the song in Italian.

56

> Night and day I love you true
> And beg for your reply
> If you say yes, you'll comfort me
> If you say no, I'll die.
>
> If I should perish from my love
> Remember me at night
> Pretend at least to pity me
> And soothe my sorry plight.
>
> Night and day I love you true
> And beg for your reply
> If you say yes, you'll comfort me
> If you say no, I'll die.

(*An* OLD WOMAN *appears at the window, and answers* POLICHINELLE *in a mocking manner.*)

OLD WOMAN (*sings*):
> You can't fool me
> I know your type
> You lie to win a maiden ripe
> But when you've won
> You blithely leave
> And let the girl in silence grieve.
>
> You can't fool me
> I've seen your kind
> It makes me laugh at girls so blind
> Who heed your words
> And then are left
> In misery at pride bereft!

POLICHINELLE (*hears Violins*): What's this impertinent sound? Who dares to interrupt my song? (*Violins.*) Quiet! Stop, you violins. I wish to bemoan my cruel love in peace. (*Violins.*) I said stop! It's my turn to sing. (*Violins.*) Quiet! (*Violins.*) Can't you hear me? (*Violins.*) Are you making fun of me? (*Violins.*) I can't stand this noise! (*Violins.*) Devil take you! (*Violins.*) I'm getting very angry! (*Violins.*) Won't you ever stop? (*Violins stop.*) Ah, thank God! (*Violins.*) Still? (*Violins.*) A pox on violins! (*Violins.*) What awful music! (*Violins.*) (*Violins keep playing, but* POLICHINELLE *starts making fun of their melody.*) La, la, la, la, la, la, la. (*Violins.*) La, la, la, la, la, la la. (*Violins.*) La, la, la, la la. (*Violins.*) All right then, it's beginning to amuse me! Play on, you violinists, I like that tune. (*No more music.*) Come now, keep playing. Please? That's the way to shut them up. Musicians do just the opposite of what you ask them. Before I sing again, I must play a little tune to get in the right key. (*Picks lute up, pretends to play it, mouthing the sound it should make.*) Plan, plan, plan. Plin plin plin. Plin tan plan. Plin plin. This awful weather makes the strings too loose. Plin, plan. I hear a noise. Let's hide the lute near this door.

NIGHT PATROL (*composed of several men, some of whom now come running on stage and sing*):

> Who goes there?
> Who goes there?

POLICHINELLE: What new nonsense is this? People talking in music?

NIGHT PATROL (*sing*):

> Who goes there?
> Who goes there?
> Who goes there?

POLICHINELLE (*frightened*):   Me, me, me.

NIGHT PATROL (*sing*):

> Who goes there?
> Who goes there?
> We're asking who goes there?

POLICHINELLE: Me, me, I tell you.

NIGHT PATROL (*sing*):

> And who are you?
> And who are you?

POLICHINELLE: Me, me, me, me, me, me.

NIGHT PATROL (*sing*):

> Tell us your name.
> Tell us your name.
> Don't make us wait longer.

POLICHINELLE (*with a display of bravado*):   My name is "Go hang yourself."

NIGHT PATROL: Come, lads, let's grab this impertinent pup!

(*More men, VIOLINISTS and DANCERS, enter on stage, looking for POLICHINELLE in the dark.*)

POLICHINELLE: Who goes there? (*VIOLINISTS play and DANCERS dance.*) Who are those villains I hear? (*VIOLINISTS and DANCERS again.*) Well? (*They continue playing and dancing throughout this speech.*) Hey there! Where are my footmen? 'Pon my word, I'll see you hanged yet! Champagne, Poitevin, Picard, Basque, Breton! Give me my musket. (*Pretends to shoot.*) Bang! (*All fall and then stand up and run away, as* POLICHINELLE *laughs.*) Hah, hah, hah! Look at the way I scared 'em! What silly folk to be afraid of me, when I'm afraid of everyone. The trick is to play the brave gentleman. If I hadn't lorded it up a bit they'd have nabbed me. Hah, hah, hah! (*Part of* NIGHT PATROL *steal back on stage at his words and grab him by the neck.*)

NIGHT PATROL: We've got him! He's ours, boys, ours! Quick, some light! (*Rest of* NIGHT PATROL *comes back on stage with lanterns.*) You traitor! So it's you! Scoundrel! Knave! Rogue! Idler! Thief! Pickpocket! How dare you frighten us?

POLICHINELLE (*sings*):
>   Gentlemen, I was tipsy
NIGHT PATROL (*sing*):
>   No excuse, you thieving gypsy
>   We'll take you to jail
>   Where you'll stay without bail!
POLICHINELLE: But I'm no thief.
NIGHT PATROL (*sing*):
>   We'll take you to jail
>   Where you'll stay without bail!
POLICHINELLE: I'm a citizen of this city.
NIGHT PATROL (*sing*):
>   To jail
>   Without bail!
POLICHINELLE: What did I do?
NIGHT PATROL (*sing*):
>   To jail . . .
POLICHINELLE: Gentlemen, please let me go.
NIGHT PATROL (*sing*):
>   The answer is no.
POLICHINELLE: Please?
NIGHT PATROL (*sing*):
>   No.
POLICHINELLE: I beg of you.
NIGHT PATROL (*sing*):
>   No.
POLICHINELLE: Show me some charity?
NIGHT PATROL (*sing*):
>   No.
POLICHINELLE: In the name of Heaven!
NIGHT PATROL: No, no!
POLICHINELLE: Have mercy?
NIGHT PATROL (*sing*):
>   You're cowardly and tipsy
>   An idle thieving gypsy

We'll take you to jail
Where you'll stay without bail!

POLICHINELLE: Is there nothing that can soften your hearts, my lords?

NIGHT PATROL (*sing*):

You could easily describe us
As softhearted and sincere
So why not try to bribe us
With six pistolets for beer?

POLICHINELLE: Alas, kind sirs, I swear I haven't even one farthing on me.

NIGHT PATROL (*sing*):

If you won't give us the money
There's another choice to make
Thirty cracks to start you stinging
Or twelve smacks to make you ache.

POLICHINELLE: If I must choose one of the two, I'll take the cracks.

NIGHT PATROL (*sing*):

Get ready, you scoundrel
And don't dare oppose
Get ready, you scoundrel
And count all the blows!

(*They dance around him and lash his hand in rhythm.*)

POLICHINELLE: One and two, three and four, five and six, seven and eight, nine and ten, eleven and twelve, and thirteen and fourteen and fifteen.

NIGHT PATROL (*sing*):

Don't think you can fool us
We're intelligent men
If you're skipping the numbers
We'll start over again!

POLICHINELLE: Gentlemen! My poor head can't count any more. You've made it feel like a mashed potato. Can't I be whipped instead?

NIGHT PATROL (*sing*):

If you'd rather be whipped
On the back of your hide
We'll be happy to please you—
You can feel how we've tried!

(NIGHT PATROL *whip him on back in rhythm.*)

POLICHINELLE: One, two, three, four, five, six, oh oh oh! I can't take any more. Here's the money.

NIGHT PATROL: Ah, what a good man! What a beautiful and noble soul! Good-by Lord Polichinelle, good-by.

POLICHINELLE: Good night, gentlemen.

NIGHT PATROL: Good-by, Baron Polichinelle.

POLICHINELLE: At your service.

NIGHT PATROL: Good-by, Prince Polichinelle, good-by.

POLICHINELLE: Your servant, gentlemen. Farewell.

(Exeunt all, dancing with glee at the money they have received. The scene shifts back to ARGAN'S *sitting room.)*

ACT II

(TOINETTE *and* CLEANTE *are discovered.*)

TOINETTE (*opening door*): May I help you, sir? Oh, it's you. What a surprise! Why did you come?

CLEANTE: To find out what my future holds, to talk to Angelique and see how she feels about me and to ask what she plans to do about this disastrous marriage.

TOINETTE: I see. But you can't be that blunt with Angelique. You have to create an air of mystery. Besides, you know how carefully she's guarded. They never let her out of the house, or allow her to talk to anyone. The only reason we met you that first day at the theater was that an old aunt of hers had invited us out. And we've been careful not to tell anyone about you.

CLEANTE: It doesn't matter, I've come not as Cleante, but as a friend of her music teacher. He's allowed me to say that he sent me in his place.

TOINETTE: Here comes her father. Stand back a little and let me tell him you're here.

(*Enter* ARGAN.)

ARGAN (*not seeing anyone*): Monsieur Purgon told me to walk back and forth in my room twelve times each morning but I forgot to ask if he meant the length or the width.

TOINETTE: Sir, there is a—

ARGAN: Quiet! You've shattered my nerves. Don't you know better than to shout at sick people that way?

TOINETTE: I wanted to tell you . . .

ARGAN: Quiet, I said!

TOINETTE: Sir . . . (*She pretends to speak.*)

ARGAN: What?

TOINETTE: I said that . . . (*Still pretending.*)

ARGAN: What the devil are you saying?

TOINETTE (*shouting*): I said that there's a gentleman here who wants to talk to you.

ARGAN: Show him in. (TOINETTE *beckons to* CLEANTE.)

CLEANTE: Sir . . .

TOINETTE (*poking fun*):   Don't speak so loud. You may shatter his nerves.

CLEANTE: Sir, I'm delighted to see that you're out of bed and looking so much better.

TOINETTE (*pretends to be angry*):   Looking better? Oh, no! He's getting worse and worse.

CLEANTE: I heard that the gentleman was better and it seems to me that he looks very well.

TOINETTE: Looks well? He looks terrible. Only his enemies would insult him by saying he looks better. He's never been this sick before.

ARGAN: She's right.

TOINETTE: He walks, sleeps, eats, and drinks like the rest of us, but that doesn't stop him from being deathly ill.

ARGAN: She's right.

CLEANTE: I'm very sorry to hear this, sir. I've come on behalf of your daughter's singing teacher, who is a good friend of mine. He had to go to the country for a few days and he asked me to continue her lessons so that she won't forget what she has already learned.

ARGAN: I understand. (*To* TOINETTE.) Tell Angelique to come here.

TOINETTE: I think it would be better to show the gentleman to her room, sir.

ARGAN: No. Have her come here.

TOINETTE: He won't be able to teach her properly in front of other people.

ARGAN: Of course he will.

TOINETTE: But it will only make you dizzy. And in the state you're in right now, you mustn't be upset, or have your nerves shattered.

ARGAN: It's perfectly all right. I love music and I'll be very happy to . . . Ah! There she is. (*To* TOINETTE.) Go see if my wife is dressed. (*Enter* ANGELIQUE. *Exit* TOINETTE.) Come here, girl. Your music teacher has gone to the country and has sent this gentleman to teach you in his place.

ANGELIQUE (*seeing* CLEANTE):   Oh!

ARGAN: What's the matter? Why are you so surprised?

ANGELIQUE: Because . . .

ARGAN: What is it? What's bothering you?

ANGELIQUE: Oh, Father, something very strange is happening to me.

ARGAN: What?

ANGELIQUE: I dreamed last night that I was in the most

terrible trouble and that someone, just like this gentleman, passed by. I asked him to help me and he came to my rescue. So you can imagine how surprised I was to find someone with the same face as in my dream.

CLÉANTE: It would be no hardship to occupy either your thoughts or your dreams, Mademoiselle, and I'd be the happiest of men if you considered me worthy enough to come to your aid in a moment of need. There's nothing I would not do for . . .

(*Enter* TOINETTE, *laughing.*)

TOINETTE: Sir, I'm all on your side now and I take back everything I said yesterday. Monsieur Diafoirus and his son have come to pay you a visit. How fortunate you are! [2] You're about to see the most handsome and witty young man in the world. He said only two words but they were delightful. Your daughter will be enchanted by him.

ARGAN (*to* CLÉANTE, *who pretends he is about to go*):   Don't go away. My daughter is getting married shortly and her fiancé is here. She hasn't met him yet.

CLÉANTE: It's very kind of you to invite me to witness this happy occasion, sir.

ARGAN: He's the son of an eminent doctor. The wedding is going to take place four days from today.

CLÉANTE: Excellent.

ARGAN: Try to get word to her music teacher to come.

CLÉANTE: I'll be sure to do it.

ARGAN: We would be honored by your company as well.

CLÉANTE: You honor me too much, sir.

TOINETTE: We'd better get ready; here they are.

(*Enter Messrs.* DIAFOIRUS *and* FOOTMEN.)

ARGAN (*putting his hand to his nightcap but not removing it*):   Monsieur Purgon has ordered me to keep my head covered, sir. You, being a member of the profession, will understand.

M. DIAFOIRUS: We wish to help the ailing in our visits, not to make them uncomfortable.

ARGAN: Sir, I accept . . . (*They speak alternately, interrupting and confusing each other.*)

M. DIAFOIRUS: Sir, my son Thomas and I . . .

---

[2] The pun in the original, *Que vous serez bien engendré!*, defies the translator. It is a play on the verb *engendrer*, meaning "to engender," and *gendre* meaning "son-in-law."

ARGAN: With great pleasure . . .

M. DIAFOIRUS: Have come . . .

ARGAN: The honor of receiving you, and . . .

M. DIAFOIRUS: In order to express . . .

ARGAN: I wish I were able . . .

M. DIAFOIRUS: Our delight . . .

ARGAN: To pay you a visit . . .

M. DIAFOIRUS: At the honor you do us . . .

ARGAN: And assure you of it.

M. DIAFOIRUS: In receiving us . . .

ARGAN: But you, sir, know . . .

M. DIAFOIRUS: Into the heart . . .

ARGAN: How a poor invalid . . .

M. DIAFOIRUS: Of your family.

ARGAN: Can do no more . . .

M. DIAFOIRUS: And to assure you . . .

ARGAN: Than affirm to you . . .

M. DIAFOIRUS: That in any medical matters . . .

ARGAN: That he will seek every opportunity . . .

M. DIAFOIRUS: As well as in anything else . . .

ARGAN: To demonstrate . . .

M. DIAFOIRUS: We are always ready . . .

ARGAN: That he is at your service.

M. DIAFOIRUS: To demonstrate our loyalty. (*Turns to his son.*) Come here, Thomas, and present yourself.

THOMAS DIAFOIRUS (*a tall, simple-minded young man, fresh out of the University, awkward in everything he does*): Should I start with the father?

M. DIAFOIRUS: Yes.

THOMAS DIAFOIRUS (*to* ARGAN, *in a mechanical tone*):   Sir, I come to greet you, to find, cherish, and respect in you a second father, and a second father, if I may say so, to whom I owe more than to the first. He created me, but you chose me. He received me out of necessity but you preferred me over all others. What he gave me came from his body, but what you offered me came from your soul and, since the spiritual faculties are superior to the physical, I shall owe you that much more and I shall hold doubly precious our future affiliation, for which I come today to offer you—in advance—my very humble and very sincere respects.

TOINETTE: Three cheers for advanced education which produces such clever men!

THOMAS DIAFOIRUS: Did I say it right, Father?

M. DIAFOIRUS: *Optime.*

ARGAN (*to* ANGELIQUE):   Why don't you welcome the young man?

THOMAS DIAFOIRUS (*to his father*): Shall I kiss her hand?

M. DIAFOIRUS: Of course.

THOMAS DIAFOIRUS (*to* ANGELIQUE): Madame, Heaven was just to endow you with the name of Mother, because one can . . .

ARGAN: You're talking to my daughter, not my wife.

THOMAS DIAFOIRUS: Where is your wife?

ARGAN: She's coming.

THOMAS DIAFOIRUS: Shall I wait for her, Father?

M. DIAFOIRUS: You may greet Mademoiselle first.

THOMAS DIAFOIRUS: Mademoiselle, just as the statue of Memnon [3] emitted its harmonious sounds when the rays of the sun fell upon it, so do I now feel myself suffused with euphony at the sunshine of your beauty. The naturalists tell us that the flower known as heliotrope turns unceasingly toward the diurnal orb; in that same manner shall my heart from this day forward yearn toward your resplendent eyes, which shall henceforth be my lodestars. Please permit me, Mademoiselle, to place today at the altar of your charms, the offering of this heart whose lifelong ambition and hope shall be to remain your humble, faithful, and obedient servant and spouse.

TOINETTE (*laughing*): That's what learning does for you! Shows you how to drop real compliments.

ARGAN: And what do you think about that?

CLEANTE: The gentleman speaks brilliantly, and if he is as good a doctor as he is an orator, it will be a pleasure to be one of his patients.

TOINETTE: Absolutely. It'll be wonderful if his leeches are as good as his speeches.

ARGAN: Bring my sofa over here. And bring chairs for everyone. (FOOTMEN *bring chairs*.) Sit down over there, daughter. (*To* M. DIAFOIRUS.) You see, sir, how everyone admires your son. You must be a happy man to have a boy like him.

M. DIAFOIRUS: I have reason to be pleased with him, sir, and not merely because he's my son. Everyone who sees him says that he's a lad without one mean bone in his body. He's never had the lively imagination or the enthusiastic spirit which you find in some people, but precisely because of that I always knew that he would have a dependable mind, which is very necessary for the exercise of our art. As a child he was never naughty or lively; he was always gentle, quiet, and

---

[3] A statue which reputedly gave out musical sounds when hit by the sun's rays.

well behaved, never saying a word and never playing at little games like other children. I had a laborious time teaching him to read. He didn't know one letter of the alphabet until he was nine years old. "Good," I told myself, "the late-blooming trees bear the best fruit; it's much more arduous to carve on marble than on sand, but the writing endures longer, and this slow comprehension, this leaden imagination is the foretaste of a sound judgment." When he went off to school it was not easy for him. But he braced himself against all difficulties and his teachers would continually praise his diligence and his effort. Finally, by hammering away at it, he managed to obtain his degrees gloriously and I can say in all modesty that in the two years he has been at his advanced studies, no other student has made more noise in the discussions. He has proved himself a formidable adversary, and whenever a new theory is proposed he will argue to the death against it. He is firm in dispute and sticks like a Turk to his principles; he never changes his mind, and he pursues an argument into the very last stronghold of logic. But what pleases me above all else and where he most follows my example is the way he clings to the opinions of the old school of medicine. He has never tried to understand or even listen to the reasoning or the evidence of those so-called discoveries of our century—the circulation of the blood and similar nonsense.[4]

THOMAS DIAFOIRUS (*pulls long scroll from his pocket and offers it to* ANGELIQUE):   I have composed a document supporting my position against the circulationists and if your father permits (*bows toward* ARGAN) I shall take the liberty of presenting it to you as my spiritual offering.

ANGELIQUE: It is meaningless to me, sir. I don't know a thing about such matters.

TOINETTE (*takes the scroll*):   Take it, take it! It's worth having for the drawings. It'll look pretty in the bedroom.

THOMAS DIAFOIRUS (*bows once more toward* ARGAN):   If Monsieur permits further, I would like to invite you out one day to hear my dissertation while a woman is being dissected.

TOINETTE: A cozy afternoon's entertainment! Some young men have plays put on for their ladies, but a dissection is much more gallant.

M. DIAFOIRUS: As for marriage and propagation, I assure you that our doctors have pronounced him highly suitable. He is prolific to the point of praise and he has the tem-

---

[4] There were still some doctors as late as 1673 who refused to acknowledge Harvey's theory, proposed in 1619, that blood circulated through the body. Molière is making fun of them.

perament necessary to beget and procreate well-formed children.

ARGAN: Aren't you going to present him at court, sir, to try to secure him an appointment as royal doctor?

M. DIAFOIRUS: To be frank with you, the thought of practicing on nobility has never seemed pleasant to me. I have always found that it is better for us to be public practitioners. It is more comfortable. We need answer to no one for our actions and as long as we practice according to the professional rules no one pays heed to the results. The nobility are difficult. They always insist on being cured.

TOINETTE: That's funny. Who do they think they are, expecting you poor gentlemen to cure them? That's not why you go to them. You're there to tell them what medicine to take and what fees to pay. If they want to get better, that's up to them—if they can.

M. DIAFOIRUS: Exactly. We are only obliged to treat them.

ARGAN (*to* CLEANTE): I'd like my daughter to sing for the guests.

CLEANTE: I was waiting for the word from you, sir; it just occurred to me that your guests might like to hear her sing a scene from a new short opera. (*Gives* ANGELIQUE *a paper.*) Here's your part.

ANGELIQUE: My part?

CLEANTE: Don't worry. I'll explain what the scene is. (*Aloud.*) I'm not a very good singer but it will do if I make myself heard. I trust you will forgive me in view of Mademoiselle's need for a partner.

ARGAN: Are the lyrics beautiful?

CLEANTE: It's more of an impromptu opera, and you will be hearing only a rhythmic prose—a sort of free verse—such as passion and necessity would dictate to two people reciting their own words as they come from within.

ARGAN: Good, good. Let's hear it.

CLEANTE: This is the subject of the scene. A shepherd is watching an outdoor entertainment which has just begun, when his attention is drawn by a noise nearby. He turns around and sees a ruffian speaking arrogantly to a shepherdess. At first he is merely protecting a lady, as any man should, but after he has beaten the ruffian for his insolent ways, he goes nearer to the shepherdess and sees a young girl from whose eyes, the most beautiful eyes he has ever seen, flow tears which to him are the most beautiful tears in the world. "Alas!" he says to himself, "how could anyone be cruel to this lovely creature? Is there even one inhuman, barbaric individual who would not be touched by these tears?"

He takes the trouble to coax away those tears that he finds beautiful, and the lovely shepherdess thanks him for his help in such a charming, tender, and heartfelt manner that the shepherd cannot resist. Each word, each look, is a fiery shaft into his heart. "Does my deed merit these words? What would I not do, to what lengths would I not go, what dangers would I not risk to enjoy for one moment the sweetness of such gratitude?" The entertainment continues but he sees nothing of it, although he laments at its end that it was too short, since now that it is over he must be parted from his shepherdess. And from this first glimpse, this first moment, he is plunged into all the emotions of a violent love that has lasted several years. Soon he is miserable at her absence and tormented at no longer seeing this girl whom he has seen only once. He does all he can do to see once more that beloved face which haunts him continually, but the shepherdess is kept away from him in seclusion. His great love makes him resolve to ask for her hand. Without her he no longer wishes to live. He obtains permission from her when she answers a letter he was bold enough to send. But at the same time, he is informed that her father has arranged for her to marry another man and that the celebrations for the wedding are about to take place. Imagine the poor shepherd's heartbreak. He is overwhelmed by a mortal sadness. The monstrous thought of seeing his beloved in the arms of another is unbearable and his desperation helps him find a way to enter her home, and find out from her what fate has decreed for him. In her home he sees the preparations for what he fears most. His unworthy rival, sponsored by a whim of her father, arrives. He sees this ridiculous figure winning the shepherdess and the sight fills him with an anger that is difficult to master. He gazes sadly at his beloved. Her respect for her father's presence prevents her from speaking out, but her eyes are eloquent. Finally he can no longer control himself and he speaks in this fashion: (*Sings.*)

> Beautiful Philis, I cannot bear it
> Break this cruel silence and reveal
>   your heart to me
> Tell me my destiny
> Shall I live or shall I die?

ANGELIQUE (*sings*):

> You see me, Tircis, sad and melancholy
> Forced into this marriage which
>   frightens you.
> I lift my eyes to the Heavens, but

I see your face instead and I sigh.
I have said enough.

ARGAN: I never knew my daughter could sing a new song
without stumbling over the words.

CLEANTE (*sings*):

Beautiful Philis
Can it be that Tircis who loves you
Should be blessed enough
To find a place in your heart?

ANGELIQUE (*sings*):

I cannot hide it
In the extremity in which I find myself
Yes, Tircis, I love you.

CLEANTE (*sings*):

O heavenly words!
Have I heard clearly?
Say it again, Philis
Let me not doubt it.

ANGELIQUE (*sings*):

Yes, Tircis, I love you.

CLEANTE (*sings*):

Please, Philis, once more.

ANGELIQUE (*sings*):

I love you.

CLEANTE (*sings*):

Say it one hundred times.
Never tire of saying it.

ANGELIQUE (*sings*):

I love you, I love you
Yes Tircis, I love you.

CLEANTE (*sings*):

O Gods, O kings! You have mankind
at your feet
Is your happiness equal to mine?
But one thought, Philis
Troubles my bliss.
A rival, a rival.

ANGELIQUE (*sings*):

Ah! I loathe him more than death
And his presence, as it is to you
Is a cruel torture to me.

CLEANTE (*sings*):

But your father commands the wedding.

ANGELIQUE (*sings*):

I shall die
Rather than ever consent to it.
I would rather die, I would rather die.

ARGAN: And what does her father say to all that?

CLEANTE: Nothing.

ARGAN: What a stupid father to allow such nonsense without a word.

CLEANTE (*sings*):

Oh my love . . .

ARGAN: No, enough of that! Your little drama is in very bad taste. This shepherd Tircis is an impudent rascal and this shepherdess Philis an insolent girl to talk like that in front of her father. (*To* ANGELIQUE.) Show me that paper. Aha! And where are the words you sang? All I see here is music.

CLEANTE: Haven't you heard, sir? Just recently a new way was invented to write lyrics with notes.

ARGAN: I see. I am at your service, young man. Good-by. We could have done without your impertinent little opera.

CLEANTE: I wanted to please you.

ARGAN: Foolishness does not please me. (*Exit* CLEANTE. *Enter* BELINE.) Ah, here is my wife. Dearest, this is the son of Monsieur Diafoirus.

THOMAS DIAFOIRUS (*begins a speech which he has memorized, but his memory fails and he cannot continue*):   Madame, Heaven was just to endow you with the name of Mother, because one can see on your face . . .

BELINE: Monsieur, I am delighted to have the honor of your acquaintance.

THOMAS DIAFOIRUS: Because one can see on your face . . . Because one can see on your face . . . Madame, you interrupted me in the middle of my sentence and you've made me forget my speech.

M. DIAFOIRUS: Thomas, you will recite it another time.

ARGAN: I wish you had been here earlier, my love.

TOINETTE: Ah, Madame! You missed hearing about the second father and the statue of Memnon and the flower known as heliotrope.

ARGAN: Come, daughter, take the gentleman's hand and pledge yourself to him.

ANGELIQUE: Father . . .

ARGAN: "Father?" What does "Father?" mean?

ANGELIQUE: Please don't rush this matter. At least give us the time to know each other and to learn to love each other. A marriage can't be happy without love.

THOMAS DIAFOIRUS: I have already learned to love you, mademoiselle, and I don't need to wait any longer.

ANGELIQUE: You are more prompt than I, sir, and I must tell you that you haven't yet made enough of an impression on me.

ARGAN: Nonsense! You'll have all the time you need
after you're married.

ANGELIQUE: Father, please give us some time. Marriage
is a bond to which no one should be submitted by force,
and if the gentleman is sincere he won't even want to accept someone who is given to him against her will.

THOMAS DIAFOIRUS: *Nego consequentiam,* mademoiselle.
I can be sincere and still be willing to accept you from your
father.

ANGELIQUE: The wrong way to make yourself beloved of
a woman is to go against her will.

THOMAS DIAFOIRUS: We read of the ancients, mademoiselle, that they used to take the girls they were going to
marry from their father's houses by force so that it wouldn't
look as if the girls were going willingly into the arms of
men.

ANGELIQUE: The ancients were the ancients, sir, and we
are alive today. Pretense is not necessary in our century,
and when a marriage pleases us, we are quite capable of
accepting it without being forced. Be patient; if you love
me you ought to want all that I want.

THOMAS DIAFOIRUS: I do, mademoiselle, but not where
my love is concerned.

ANGELIQUE: But the great sign of love is to submit yourself to the will of the beloved.

THOMAS DIAFOIRUS: *Distinguo,* mademoiselle. In that
which does not concern possession, *concedo;* but in that
which concerns it, *nego.*

TOINETTE (*to* ANGELIQUE): You're wasting your time.
The gentleman is fresh out of college and he'll have an answer to any argument. Why keep resisting and refuse the
glory of being attached to the faculty body?

BELINE: She may have some other match in mind.

ANGELIQUE: If I did, madame, I wouldn't be ashamed
to admit it.

ARGAN: Well! I see how much I count here.

BELINE: If I were you, my love, I would not force her
to marry. I know very well what I would do.

ANGELIQUE: I know what you mean, madame, and I
know your kind intentions toward me. But perhaps your
advice will not be good enough to be heeded.

BELINE: So, virtuous and honest daughters like you
laugh instead of obeying their fathers and carrying out their
orders. It used to be different.

ANGELIQUE: A daughter's duty has its limits, madame,
limits that are protected by both common sense and our laws.

BELINE: In other words, you aren't considering this marriage and you wish to have a husband of your own choosing.

ANGELIQUE: If my father doesn't wish to give me a husband who pleases me, then I beg of him at least not to force me to marry one I cannot love.

ARGAN: Gentlemen, I beg your pardon for all this.

ANGELIQUE: Everyone has a purpose in marrying. For myself, I want a husband I can love dearly and I hope to make him the one love of my life. I admit that I will choose him carefully. Some women marry solely to escape from the constraint of their parents and to place themselves in a position where they can do as they please. There are others, madame, who marry out of sheer interest, for a settlement, and to be able to enrich themselves by the death of their husbands. These women move unscrupulously from one husband to the next in order to inherit their possessions. It's true that this type isn't too particular about husbandly qualities.

BELINE: You're arguing very eloquently today. I'd like to know what you mean by this.

ANGELIQUE: Mean, madame? What could I mean except what I say?

BELINE: You are an insufferably stupid girl!

ANGELIQUE: You would love to provoke me to some impertinent remark. But you won't succeed.

BELINE: You are impossibly insolent!

ANGELIQUE: You speak in vain, madame.

BELINE: And you have a ridiculous pride, and a presumption which makes everyone laugh.

ANGELIQUE: It will do you no good, madame. I shall remain unprovoked in spite of you, and I am going to remove myself from your sight so you will no longer have even a hope of succeeding.

ARGAN (*to* ANGELIQUE, *who is on her way out*): Listen. Four days from now, you will either marry Monsieur or go into a convent. (*Exit* ANGELIQUE.) Don't worry. I will make her listen to me.

BELINE: I hate to leave you, my dove, but I must go into town. I shall return soon.

ARGAN: Go, my sweet, and stop by at your notary's to see if he's taken care of our little matter.

BELINE: Good-by, my little boy.

ARGAN: Good-by, my angel. (*Exit* BELINE.) How that woman loves me. It is unbelievable.

M. DIAFOIRUS: We are going to take leave of you, monsieur.

ARGAN: Would you tell me how I look to you?

M. DIAFOIRUS (*checks his pulse*): Here, Thomas, take the patient's other arm and see if you can find his pulse properly. *Quid dicis?*

THOMAS DIAFOIRUS: *Dico,* that his pulse is the pulse of an ailing man.

M. DIAFOIRUS: Good.

THOMAS DIAFOIRUS: That it is hardening, if not hard.

M. DIAFOIRUS: Very good.

THOMAS DIAFOIRUS: It fights the fingers.

M. DIAFOIRUS: *Bene.*

THOMAS DIAFOIRUS: It leaps and bounds.

M. DIAFOIRUS: *Optime.*

THOMAS DIAFOIRUS: Which points to some disorder in the splenic parenchyma, that is to say, the spleen.

M. DIAFOIRUS: Excellent.

ARGAN: But Monsieur Purgon says that it's my liver.

M. DIAFOIRUS: Ah, yes. Hmm. You see, when you say "parenchyma" it means either one or the other because of the close link of the two by the *vas brevis* of the pyloris and the bile ducts. I imagine he allows you to have roast meat only?

ARGAN: No, only boiled.

M. DIAFOIRUS: Ah, yes. Hmm. Roast, boiled, exactly the same. He counsels you prudently and you could not be in better hands.

ARGAN: How many grains of salt should I put into my eggs, sir?

M. DIAFOIRUS: Six, eight, or ten, in even numbers. For medicines, always uneven numbers.

ARGAN: Farewell, gentlemen.

(*Exeunt* DIAFOIRUS, *father and son. Enter* BELINE.)

BELINE: I am on my way out, darling, but I thought I should stop and tell you about something you must look into. There was a young man in Angelique's room just now. He ran off as soon as he saw me.

ARGAN: A young man with my daughter?

BELINE: Yes. Louison was with them. She'll be able to tell you about it.

ARGAN: Send her here, my love, send her here. (*Alone.*) Oh, the brazen hussy! Now I understand her resistance!

(*Enter* LOUISON.)

LOUISON: What do you want, Papa? Stepmama said you wanted to see me.

ARGAN: Yes. Come here. Over here. Turn around. Look up. Head high. Look me in the face. Well?

LOUISON: What, Papa?

ARGAN: So!

LOUISON: What?

ARGAN: Don't you have something to tell me?

LOUISON: If you would like to hear a story, I will tell you the fable of the Donkey's Skin or the one about the Crow and the Fox which I just learned.

ARGAN: That is not what I want to hear.

LOUISON: What then, Papa?

ARGAN: Little devil. You know very well what I mean.

LOUISON: No I don't, Papa.

ARGAN: Is that how you obey me?

LOUISON: What?

ARGAN: Haven't I told you to come and tell me everything you see?

LOUISON: Yes, Papa.

ARGAN: And have you done so?

LOUISON: Yes, Papa. I told you everything I saw.

ARGAN: And have you seen anything today?

LOUISON: No, Papa.

ARGAN: No?

LOUISON: No, Papa.

ARGAN: Are you sure?

LOUISON: I'm sure, Papa.

ARGAN: In that case I will give you something to see. (*He reaches out for a birch rod.*)

LOUISON: Papa!

ARGAN: Aha! Little minx. You didn't tell me you saw a man in your sister's room?

LOUISON (*crying*): Papa!

ARGAN (*grabs her by the arm*): This will teach you not to lie.

LOUISON (*falls to her knees*): Please forgive me, Papa. Sister made me promise not to tell, but I will.

ARGAN: First, I'm going to hit you for lying. Then we'll see about the rest.

LOUISON: Forgive me, Papa.

ARGAN: No.

LOUISON: Please, Papa, don't hit me.

ARGAN: You deserve it.

LOUISON: Please!

ARGAN (*pulls her closer*): Come here.

LOUISON: Papa, you've hurt me. I'm dying! (*She plays dead.*)

ARGAN: Oh, my God! Louison, Louison, what have I done? Oh Lord! Louison! My daughter! What sort of monster am I? This accursed rod, if only I had never seen it! My poor baby, my poor little Louison!

LOUISON: Don't cry, I'm not dead all over.

ARGAN: You little devil! I forgive you this time, but only if you tell me everything.

LOUISON: Yes, I will. I promise.

ARGAN: Be careful. This little finger knows everything and it will tell me if you lie.

LOUISON: Only don't tell Sister that I told you, please.

ARGAN: I won't.

LOUISON (*first looks around to see if anyone is listening*): It's like this. A man came into Sister's room when I was there.

ARGAN: And?

LOUISON: I asked him what he wanted and he said he was her singing teacher.

ARGAN (*aside*): So that's what it was about! (*To* LOUISON.) And then?

LOUISON: Sister came back.

ARGAN: And then?

LOUISON: She told him, "Go away, go away. Please go away. You're making me miserable."

ARGAN: And then?

LOUISON: He didn't want to go away.

ARGAN: What did he tell her?

LOUISON: All kinds of things.

ARGAN: Like what?

LOUISON: He said lots of things: that he loved her, that she was the most beautiful girl in the world.

ARGAN: And then?

LOUISON: Then he kissed her hand.

ARGAN: And then?

LOUISON: Then Stepmama walked past and he ran away.

ARGAN: Nothing else?

LOUISON: No, Papa.

ARGAN: My little finger says there's more. (*Puts finger to ear.*) Wait a minute. Aha! My little finger tells me you left something out.

LOUISON: Your finger is lying, Papa.

ARGAN: Be careful.

LOUISON: Don't believe it, Papa. It's lying. Cross my heart!

ARGAN: Perhaps. We shall see. Go back and be sure to keep your eyes open. Away with you! (*Exit* LOUISON.) Ah! There are no children left. What a kettle of fish. I don't even have the time to think about my illness. I just can't take any more!

(*Enter* BERALDE.)

BERALDE: Good day, Brother. How are you?

ARGAN: Bad, very bad.

BERALDE: What's the matter?

ARGAN: You wouldn't believe how weak I am.

BERALDE: I'm sorry to hear that.

ARGAN: I don't even have the strength to speak.

BERALDE: I came to suggest a husband for Angelique.

ARGAN (*stands up*):   Don't talk to me about that hussy! She's a brazen wench and I'm going to put her into a convent before the next two days are up.

BERALDE: I'm happy to see that my visit has helped you regain some of your strength. We'll talk about Angelique later. I met some entertainers on the way over; I brought them with me to cheer you up and put you in a more receptive frame of mind for the things I want to talk to you about. They are gypsies dressed like Moors, and I'm sure you'll enjoy their songs and dances. They're worth more than one of Monsieur Purgon's prescriptions. Come.

SECOND INTERMISSION

(*Several* GYPSIES, *dressed like Moors, file into* ARGAN'S
room and sing and dance.)

FIRST FEMALE MOOR (*sings*):
> Let's bask in the sunshine
> Of youthful bliss
> When girls are twenty
> What joy to kiss!

> But the lovely pleasure
> Of which I sing
> Without true love
> Has no meaning.

> So seize your moments
> While you may
> Care's for tomorrow
> And love's for today.

SECOND FEMALE MOOR (*sings*):
> When a girl is wooed
> She can never resist
> To the man who is wooing
> She runs and gets kissed

> But the warnings that she gets
> About the tears she'll spill
> Make her hesitate
> To give in to his will.

THIRD FEMALE MOOR (*sings*):
> It's heaven to love at twenty
> And heaven to be loved in return
> But if the young man should leave you
> You're left to despair and to yearn.

FOURTH FEMALE MOOR (*sings*):
> It's not that the boy may leave me

78

Nor that I'll be alone
But the rascal may well bereave me
By taking my heart with his own!

SECOND FEMALE MOOR (*sings*):
      Whom should we love
      And cherish for life?

FOURTH FEMALE MOOR (*sings*):
      Must we submit
      To love's fearful strife?

ENSEMBLE (*sings*):
We must submit
We must give in
We must take the good with the bad;
For the good when it's good, is so very good
That the bad when it's bad can't be bad!

(MOORS *all dance and play with the monkeys they have brought with them.*)

ACT III

BERALDE: Well, Brother, what do you say? Didn't that do you as much good as a dose of rhubarb?

TOINETTE: Nothing is as good as a good dose of rhubarb.

BERALDE: Hush! (*To* ARGAN.) Can we talk for a few minutes?

ARGAN: Wait, I'll be right back.

TOINETTE: Here, sir, you're forgetting that you can't walk without your cane.

ARGAN: You're right.

(*Exit* ARGAN.)

TOINETTE: Please keep trying to help your niece.

BERALDE: I'll do everything I can to get her what she wants.

TOINETTE: We must stop this ridiculous marriage he's set his mind on. I think it might be a good idea to bring our own type of doctor into the house, someone who would put him straight about Monsieur Purgon and make him look ridiculous. But there's no one around to do it. Maybe I should play a trick I've been thinking of instead.

BERALDE: What kind of trick?

TOINETTE: A comic imitation. If he won't learn by being taught, perhaps he'll learn if we make fun of him. Let me take care of that part and you do what you can. Here's our man!

(*Exit* TOINETTE. *Enter* ARGAN.)

BERALDE: Before we start, Brother, may I ask you to control your temper while we talk?

ARGAN: Of course.

BERALDE: To answer my questions without any bitterness?

ARGAN: Agreed.

BERALDE: And to discuss the matters we have to consider with detachment?

ARGAN: Agreed, agreed! What an introduction!

BERALDE: How does it happen, Brother, that with all your wealth, and with just one daughter—because I'm not counting the little one—how does it happen that you talk about sending her to a convent?

ARGAN: How does it happen, Brother, that I am master of my household and free to do as I please?

BERALDE: Your wife hasn't lost any time in advising you to get rid of your daughters like this. I'm quite sure she would be delighted to see them both become nuns, out of religious fervor, of course.

ARGAN: Aha! Now we have it. The poor woman is the first to be criticized. She's the one who's always in the wrong, and everyone's against her.

BERALDE: No, Brother, not at all. She has the best intentions in the world toward your family and is without any kind of self-interest. She's wonderfully tender to you and incredibly kind and affectionate to your children. There's no doubt about it. Let's not talk about her any more. Let's return to your daughter. For what reasons, Brother, do you wish to marry her off to a doctor's son?

ARGAN: For this reason, Brother: to obtain the sort of son-in-law I need.

BERALDE: That's not your daughter's responsibility. Besides, there's someone more suitable for her.

ARGAN: That may be, but the other one suits me.

BERALDE: Is she to marry a man for you or for herself?

ARGAN: He should suit both of us. I want to bring the people I need into the family.

BERALDE: With that kind of reasoning, if the little one were old enough, you'd marry her off to an apothecary?

ARGAN: Why not?

BERALDE: Are you always going to be infatuated with your apothecaries and your doctors; will you always insist on being sick in spite of nature and other people?

ARGAN: What do you mean?

BERALDE: I mean that I see no man less sick than you, and that I wouldn't ask for a better constitution than yours. The proof that you're healthy and that your body is in extremely good condition is that with all the trouble you've taken, you haven't been able to ruin your health and you haven't died of all those medicines they've made you swallow.

ARGAN: But don't you realize that those medicines are

what save me? Monsieur Purgon says I would die within three days if I stopped taking care of myself.

BERALDE: If you aren't careful, he'll take good care of you right into the next world.

ARGAN: Let's be reasonable, Beralde. Don't you believe in the power of medicine?

BERALDE: No. And I don't see that it's necessary to believe in it for its own sake.

ARGAN: Really? You don't accept something everyone else does, something which has been revered in every century?

BERALDE: Far from accepting it, I find it, between you and me, one of the greatest follies of mankind. To be philosophic about the matter, I see no funnier pretense, nor anything more ridiculous, than a man who wants to interfere in the recovery of another.

ARGAN: Why don't you believe that one man can cure another?

BERALDE: Because the workings of our body have been mysteries up to now and men do not understand them. Nature has placed veils before our eyes which are too thick for us to see through.

ARGAN: So doctors know nothing according to you?

BERALDE: Nothing at all. The majority of them know the humanities very well, can speak a fluent Latin, can give the Greek name for any illness, and diagnose and categorize it, but when it comes to curing, they don't know a thing.

ARGAN: At least we can agree that doctors know more than other people.

BERALDE: They know what I just told you, which doesn't cure anyone, and their entire art consists in a meaningless pomposity, in a hypocritical double-talk which gives you words for reasons and promises for results.

ARGAN: But there are other people as wise and clever as you, and you know that they consult doctors when they are sick.

BERALDE: It's a mark of human weakness and not proof of medical skill.

ARGAN: Yet the doctors themselves must believe what they practice since they use it on themselves.

BERALDE: There are some among them who make money although they know as little as their patients and others who know more than their patients and still make money. Your Monsieur Purgon, for example, is not a shrewd man; he is all doctor, from head to toes; a man who believes in his rules more than in all the mathematical proofs, and who would consider it a crime if someone wanted to examine them. He sees nothing doubtful, difficult, or obscure in medicine. With his zeal for preventive tactics, his unquestioning confidence, and his lack of common sense, he prescribes enemas and bloodletting without rhyme or reason: he never even thinks about it. It isn't necessary for him to have evil intentions; he'll dispatch you with the best will in the world, and in killing you, he'll be doing what he did to his own wife and children and what he would do to himself if the necessity arose.[5]

ARGAN: You have an old grudge against him, Brother. But let's get to the point. What should a man do when he is sick?

BERALDE: Nothing.

ARGAN: Nothing?

BERALDE: Nothing. All he need do is rest. Nature herself, when we rely on her alone, pulls us gently out of the disorder into which we've fallen. Our anxiety and our impatience are what spoil everything. Nearly everyone dies of medicine and not of illness.

ARGAN: But don't you agree, Beralde, that we can help nature along by certain measures?

BERALDE: My God! Those are just notions that we like to play with, Argan. Mankind is prone to optimistic daydreams because they flatter us or because they promise us certain benefits. When a doctor talks to you about helping or easing Mother Nature, about removing harmful influences from her, about giving her what she needs, about restoring her to full control of her functions; when he talks to you about restoring the blood, adjusting the intestines and the brain, soothing the chest, repairing the liver, strengthening the heart, re-establishing and maintaining normal body temperature, and knowing the secrets of longer life—when he talks to you about all this he's merely telling you the story of medicine. And when you find the truth out by experience you'll see that none of it is true; you'll be as disillusioned as if you had awakened from a beautiful dream only to find it wasn't real.

ARGAN: In other words, all the knowledge in the world is concentrated in your head and you know more than all the great doctors of our century.

BERALDE: When it comes to great doctors, talk is one

---

[5] Probable allusion to one of the royal doctors, Guénaut, who was reputed to have prescribed his favorite remedy, antimony, for his wife, daughter, two sons-in-law, and one nephew, all of whom died of it.

thing and action another; to hear them speak they're the most able men in the world. To see them in action, they're the most ignorant.

ARGAN: And you are a great doctor, I suppose. I'd love to have one of those gentlemen here to show up your arguments and make you change your tune a bit.

BERALDE: I'm not making it my business to fight the entire medical profession; everyone can think as he pleases, to his advantage or his peril. What I am saying about it is just between you and me, and I had hoped to sway you a little away from your misconceptions. I was going to amuse you and take you to see a comedy by Molière on the subject.

ARGAN: That Molière of yours is a scoundrel with those comedies he writes. I find his habit of poking fun at honest men like doctors very impertinent.

BERALDE: He's not poking fun at doctors; he's poking fun at the practice of medicine.

ARGAN: It's all right for him to stick his nose into medical matters; the insolent rogue laughing at examinations and prescriptions, attacking the medical profession and putting those respectable gentlemen into his plays!

BERALDE: Whom should he put into his plays if not people from all walks of life? Kings and princes are portrayed every day and they're certainly equal to the doctors.

ARGAN: What a rascally whelp! If I were one of his doctors, I'd revenge myself for his impudence and let him die without treatment if he became ill. Whatever he said, whatever he did, I wouldn't prescribe the slightest bloodletting, or the smallest enema, and I'd say to him, "Die, die! That will teach you to make fun of the Faculty."

BERALDE: You're certainly angry at him.

ARGAN: He's a blundering fool and if the doctors are smart they'll do as I say.

BERALDE: He'll be still smarter than the doctors. He won't ask for any help.

ARGAN: So much the worse for him if he doesn't get any treatment.

BERALDE: He has reason not to want any. He maintains that it's only useful for those who are vigorous and hearty enough to withstand treatment when they're already sick. He himself has just enough strength to bear his sickness.

ARGAN: What idiotic reasoning! Listen, Beralde, let's not talk about that creature any more because it heats up my bile and you'll only make me sick.

BERALDE: Very well. And to change the subject let me

tell you that you shouldn't take such violent action and put your daughter into a convent just because you're growing angry at her. You really shouldn't become so blind with rage over the choice of a son-in-law. On a matter like this you should take a girl's feelings into consideration. After all, it's for her entire life and the happiness of a marriage depends on it.

(*Enter* MONSIEUR FLEURANT, *syringe in hand.*)

ARGAN: Ah! With your permission, Brother.

BERALDE: What in the world are you going to do?

ARGAN: Take a little enema. I'll be through soon.

BERALDE: You're joking! Can't you go for one moment without enema or medicine? Put it off until later and rest a while.

ARGAN: Come back tonight, Monsieur Fleurant, or perhaps tomorrow.

M. FLEURANT (*to* BERALDE): What right have you to meddle with a prescription and prevent Monsieur from taking my enema? You certainly have your nerve!

BERALDE: Away with you, sir. It's easy to see that you aren't accustomed to speaking to people's faces.

M. FLEURANT: You have no right to make fun of my medicines and make me waste my time. I came here with a good prescription and I'm going to tell Monsieur Purgon how I was stopped from carrying out his orders and doing my duty. You'll see, you'll see . . .

ARGAN: Beralde, you're going to cause me trouble.

BERALDE: The trouble of not taking an enema that Monsieur Purgon prescribed! Once more, Argan, is there no way to cure you of doctoritis? Do you really want to spend the rest of your life drowning in their remedies?

ARGAN: You speak as if I were a healthy man! You'd change your tune fast enough if you were in my shoes. It's easy to talk against medicine when you're in good health.

BERALDE: And what's wrong with you?

ARGAN: You're going to make me very angry! I only wish that you felt as sick as I do and then we'd see how you'd talk. Ah! Here is Monsieur Purgon.

(*Enter* MONSIEUR PURGON *and* TOINETTE.)

M. PURGON: I have just heard some very interesting news; that my prescriptions are sneezed at and that you refuse to follow my orders.

ARGAN: It's not that . . .

M. PURGON: Daring, isn't it, for a sick man to rebel against his doctor?

TOINETTE: How frightful!

M. PURGON: An enema which I had the pleasure of preparing with my own two hands!

ARGAN: But I didn't . . .

M. PURGON: Invented and composed according to all the rules of medicine!

TOINETTE: He is wrong.

M. PURGON: And it would have produced magnificent results in the intestines.

ARGAN: My brother . . .

M. PURGON: To send it back so scornfully!

ARGAN (*pointing to* BERALDE): It's his . . .

M. PURGON: Outrageous!

TOINETTE: Absolutely.

M. PURGON: An enormous outrage against medicine.

ARGAN (*still pointing to* BERALDE): He's the cause of . . .

M. PURGON: A crime of lese-majesty which can't be sufficiently punished!

TOINETTE: You're right!

M. PURGON: I would like you to know that from this day forward I shall no longer treat you.

ARGAN: But my brother . . .

M. PURGON: I wish no further connection with you.

TOINETTE: You're doing the right thing.

M. PURGON: And, in order to break off all connections with you, here is my will which I altered in favor of my nephew for his wedding! (*He tears it up.*)

ARGAN: My brother did all those terrible things.

M. PURGON: To make fun of my enema!

ARGAN: Bring it back, I'll take it.

M. PURGON: I would have cured you in just a little while.

TOINETTE: He doesn't deserve it.

M. PURGON: I was going to irrigate your body and evacuate all the evil humors.

ARGAN: Oh, Beralde!

M. PURGON: And I needed no more than a dozen medicines to empty out your bowels.

TOINETTE: He doesn't deserve your care.

M. PURGON: But since you did not want to be cured by me . . .

ARGAN: It's not my fault!

M. PURGON: Since you have denied the obedience owed to one's doctor . . .

TOINETTE: That calls for vengeance.

M. PURGON: Since you have rebelled against the remedies prescribed for you . . .

ARGAN: No, I haven't!

M. PURGON: I am abandoning you to your unhealthy constitution, to your disordered intestines, to the corruption in your blood, to the bitterness of your bile and to the turbidity of your humors.

TOINETTE: Well done!

ARGAN: My God!

M. PURGON: And I predict that in less than four days you will be incurable!

ARGAN: Have mercy on me!

M. PURGON: That you will develop bradypepsia.

ARGAN: Monsieur Purgon!

M. PURGON: Bradypepsia will lead to dyspepsia.

ARGAN: Monsieur Purgon!

M. PURGON: Dyspepsia will lead to apepsy.

ARGAN: Monsieur Purgon!

M. PURGON: Apepsy will lead to lientery.

ARGAN: Monsieur Purgon!

M. PURGON: Lientery will lead to dysentery.

ARGAN: Monsieur Purgon!

M. PURGON: Dysentery will lead to dropsy.

ARGAN: Monsieur Purgon!

M. PURGON: And dropsy will lead to the loss of life, and that is how far you will have brought yourself by your folly.

(*Exit* MONSIEUR PURGON.)

ARGAN: Oh, I am as good as dead. Brother, you have murdered me.

BERALDE: Why? What's wrong with you?

ARGAN: I can't take any more. I can already feel the doctors revenging themselves.

BERALDE: Argan, you are mad. I wouldn't like anyone to see how you're carrying on. Think for a minute, please, take hold of yourself and stop wallowing in your imagination.

ARGAN: Did you hear what strange sicknesses he threatened me with?

BERALDE: What a simple soul you are!

ARGAN: He says I'll be incurable before the next four days are up.

BERALDE: And what does it matter what he says? To
listen to you it would seem that Monsieur Purgon controls
your lifeline and that he can lengthen and shorten it as he
wishes, by some kind of supreme authority. Remember, you
control your destiny. Monsieur Purgon's anger is as likely to
make you die as his medicines are likely to keep you alive.
Here's a chance, if you want, to learn to do without a doctor; or, if you are the sort of man who can't do without
one, it's easy enough to find another one who will run you
a little less risk.

ARGAN: But he's familiar with all my troubles and he
knows how to treat them.

BERALDE: You're a very prejudiced man. You look at
matters in an extremely strange fashion.

(*Enter* TOINETTE.)

TOINETTE: Sir, there's a doctor who wants to see you.

ARGAN: Which doctor?

TOINETTE: A doctor of medicine.

ARGAN: I asked you who he is.

TOINETTE: I don't know him but he looks exactly like
me. If I weren't sure that my mother was a virtuous woman,
I'd say that he was a younger brother she'd provided me with
since my father's death.

ARGAN: Send him in.

(*Exit* TOINETTE.)

BERALDE: Your wishes are anticipated. One doctor leaves
you, another appears.

ARGAN: I'm dreadfully worried that you're going to cause
me more trouble.

BERALDE: Again! Are you still harping on that?

ARGAN: Listen, I'm worried about all those sicknesses
I don't know, those . . .

TOINETTE (*enters, disguised as a doctor*):   Kind sir, I
have come to pay you a visit and offer you my humble serv-
ices for all the bloodlettings and enemas you may need.

ARGAN: Most obliged to you, sir. (*To* BERALDE.) The very
image of Toinette!

TOINETTE: Would you excuse me for a moment, sir? I
forgot to give my valet some instructions; I'll be right back.

ARGAN: Wouldn't you say that he's the spitting image of
Toinette?

BERALDE: There's a strong resemblance. But it's not the

first time I've seen something like that. History is full of such little tricks of nature.

ARGAN: I am very surprised and . . .

TOINETTE (*enters, dressed as herself, having returned so rapidly that it is difficult to believe she just appeared as the doctor*): Did you call, sir?

ARGAN: What?

TOINETTE: Didn't you call me?

ARGAN: I? No.

TOINETTE: My ears must have deceived me.

ARGAN: Wait a minute. You'll be able to see how that doctor resembles you.

TOINETTE: I don't have all day, you know. I've got things to do downstairs and I already saw him.

ARGAN: If I didn't see the two of them, I'd think it was just one person.

BERALDE: I've read some fascinating stories about this type of resemblance. And we've seen people being deceived about such matters in our own day.

ARGAN: This time, I would have been fooled. I would have sworn it was the same person.

(*Enter* TOINETTE, *dressed as the doctor.*)

TOINETTE: I humbly beg your pardon, sir.

ARGAN (*to* BERALDE): Amazing!

TOINETTE: You won't take offense, sir, at my curiosity to see such a famous invalid as yourself. Your reputation which extends far and wide will excuse the liberty I have taken.

ARGAN: I am at your service, sir.

TOINETTE: I notice that you keep staring at me. How old would you say I am?

ARGAN: I imagine that you're no older than twenty-six or twenty-seven.

TOINETTE: Aha! I am ninety.

ARGAN: Ninety?

TOINETTE: Yes. You see the effect of the secrets of my art, which enable me to remain young and vigorous like this.

ARGAN: Well! Here's a handsome young man for ninety.

TOINETTE: I am a traveling doctor and I go from town to town, from province to province, and from kingdom to kingdom to seek out worthy subjects for my art, to find invalids who deserve my treatment, and who are capable of profiting by the great and beautiful secrets that I have found in medicine. I consider it beneath me to play with that hodgepodge of minor ailments, those trifles of rheumatism or pneumonia, those passing fevers and dizzy spells and headaches. I want important ailments; persistent fevers with delirium, scarlet fever, plagues, advanced cases of dropsy, flourishing pleurisies with chest complications—those are what please me; with those ailments I can prove myself. And I would be happy, sir, if you had all the illnesses I just named, if all the doctors had abandoned you to your agony in desperation, so that I could show you how excellent my treatment is and how much I desire to assist you.

ARGAN: I am very grateful for your kind intentions, sir.

TOINETTE: Let me check your pulse. Come now, beat the way you should. I'll make you run the way you're supposed to. You impertinent pulse, I can see that you don't know me yet. Who is your doctor?

ARGAN: Monsieur Purgon.

TOINETTE: That name is not written on my list of great doctors. What does he say is the matter with you?

ARGAN: He says it's my liver; other doctors say it's my spleen.

TOINETTE: They are all ignoramuses. It's your lungs.

ARGAN: My lungs?

TOINETTE: Yes. What are your symptoms?

ARGAN: I have head pains occasionally.

TOINETTE: Exactly. Lungs.

ARGAN: And sometimes I feel that there's a fog in front of my eyes.

TOINETTE: Lungs.

ARGAN: Sometimes I get heart pains.

TOINETTE: Lungs.

ARGAN: Sometimes I feel weak all over.

TOINETTE: Lungs.

ARGAN: And sometimes I have terrible pains in the stomach, colic pains.

TOINETTE: Lungs. Do you have a powerful appetite?

ARGAN: Yes, sir.

TOINETTE: Lungs. Do you like to drink a drop of wine?

ARGAN: Yes, sir.

TOINETTE: Lungs. You take a little nap after meals and you fall asleep easily?

ARGAN: Yes.

TOINETTE: Lungs, lungs, lungs! What does your doctor allow you to eat?

ARGAN: He prescribes soup.

TOINETTE: Ignorant fool.

ARGAN: And some chicken.

TOINETTE: Ignorant fool.

ARGAN: Veal.

TOINETTE: Ignorant fool.

ARGAN: Beef stock.

TOINETTE: Ignorant fool.

ARGAN: Fresh eggs.

TOINETTE: Ignorant fool.

ARGAN: And tiny prunes at night to relax the stomach.

TOINETTE: Ignorant fool.

ARGAN: And especially to drink my wine diluted.

TOINETTE: *Ignorantus, ignoranta, ignorantum.* You must drink your wine strong, and to thicken your blood, which is too thin, you must eat substantial pieces of beef and pork, good Dutch cheeses, rice and oatmeal, and chestnuts and scones to bind and conglutinate. Your doctor is a sham. I am going to send you one of my representatives and I shall come to see you from time to time when I am in this city.

ARGAN: You are very kind to me.

TOINETTE: What the devil are you doing with that arm?

ARGAN: What?

TOINETTE: If I were you, I'd have that arm cut off right away.

ARGAN: Why?

TOINETTE: Don't you see that it's drawing all the nourishment away from the other side?

ARGAN: Yes, but I need my arm.

TOINETTE: You have a right eye there that I would also have removed if I were in your shoes.

ARGAN: Remove an eye?

TOINETTE: Don't you realize that it is intruding on the other one and stealing all its esculence? Believe me, have that eye removed as fast as possible. You'll see better from the left eye.

ARGAN: There's no hurry for that.

TOINETTE: Good-by. I'm sorry to have to leave you so soon but I must be present at a post-mortem on a man who died yesterday.

ARGAN: A man who died yesterday?

TOINETTE: Yes, to see what should have been done to cure him. Good-by.

ARGAN: You know that an invalid can't show you out.

(*Exit* TOINETTE.)

BERALDE: There's a doctor who really speaks intelligently.

ARGAN: Yes, but he goes a bit too fast.

BERALDE: All great doctors are like that.

ARGAN: Cut off one arm and remove one eye so that the other works better! I'd rather it didn't work that well. A nice operation, to leave me half blind and amputated!

TOINETTE (*returns, pretending to talk to someone*):   Go along with you! I don't think that's very funny.

ARGAN: What's the matter?

TOINETTE: That doctor of yours. He wanted to check my pulse.

ARGAN: Imagine that, at the age of ninety!

BERALDE: Listen, Argan, since Monsieur Purgon has broken with you, won't you let me talk to you about this match you are proposing for your daughter?

ARGAN: No, Brother, I want to send her into a convent because she has opposed my wishes. I know quite well that there's some little romance brewing. I've found out about a secret meeting that no one knows I've discovered.

BERALDE: But Brother, when there is a preference is it criminal and offensive when it's going to lead to an honorable conclusion like marriage?

ARGAN: I don't care what it is, she's going to be a nun. I have decided.

BERALDE: You're looking to please someone.

ARGAN: I understand. You always come back to the same thing. The thought of my wife sticks in your throat.

BERALDE: Since we must speak frankly, yes, I do mean your wife; and I can't stand your stubborn convictions about her any more than I can your medical nonsense. I can't stand to see you walk blindly into the traps she sets for you.

TOINETTE: Oh, sir, don't talk that way about Madame. She's a woman you can't criticize, a woman without affectation and she loves Monsieur and he loves her. . . . You can't say such things.

ARGAN: Ask her about the affection she lavishes on me.

TOINETTE: It's true.

ARGAN: Her worry about my illness.

TOINETTE: Absolutely.

ARGAN: And all the care and trouble she takes for me.

TOINETTE: No question about it. (*To* BERALDE.) Would you like me to prove to you how Madame loves Monsieur? (*To* ARGAN.) Monsieur, please let me show him how wrong he is and set him straight.

ARGAN: How?

TOINETTE: Madame is going to come back. Stretch out

on the lounge and pretend to be dead. You'll see how miserable she'll be when I tell her the news.

ARGAN: I'm willing.

TOINETTE: But don't let her be miserable too long; she might die of despair.

ARGAN: Let me take care of it.

TOINETTE (*to* BERALDE):   Hide in that corner.

ARGAN: Isn't there some danger in pretending to be dead?

TOINETTE: No, of course not. What danger would there be? Just lie down. (*Softly.*) It will be fun to show your brother up. Here's Madame. Keep still.

(*Enter* BELINE.)

TOINETTE (*pretending not to see* BELINE):   Oh heavens! Oh miserable me! What a terrible accident!

BELINE: What's the matter, Toinette?

TOINETTE: Oh, madame!

BELINE: What is it?

TOINETTE: Your husband is dead.

BELINE: My husband is dead?

TOINETTE: Yes. The poor man is gone.

BELINE: Are you sure?

TOINETTE: Yes. No one knows about the tragedy yet. I was here all alone. He expired in my arms. Look at him all stretched out.

BELINE: Thank God! I'm relieved of a great burden. What a fool you are, Toinette, to let yourself feel so miserable.

TOINETTE: I thought I was supposed to cry, madame.

BELINE: Don't be silly, it's not worth it. What sort of loss is his death? What use was he on earth? A nuisance to everyone, filthy, disgusting, always with a medicine or an enema in his stomach, wiping his nose, coughing, spitting, dullwitted, boring, ill-tempered, tiring everyone out and scolding his servants day and night.

TOINETTE: Quite a funeral oration.

BELINE: You'll have to help me carry out my plan, Toinette, and I assure you that you'll be rewarded. It's lucky no one knows about this yet. Let's carry him into his bed and keep his death quiet until I've done what I have to. There are some papers and money I want to take. It's not fair. I've spent the best years of my life with him without any profit. Come here, Toinette, let's take his keys first.

ARGAN (*sits up suddenly*):   Not so fast!

BELINE: Agh!

ARGAN: So, my good wife, this is how you love me?

TOINETTE: Agh, agh! The corpse isn't dead.

ARGAN (*to* BELINE, *who leaves*):   I am very glad to see your real feelings for me, and to have heard your touching little eulogy. That was a warning to keep me wiser in the future and to prevent me from doing many things.

BERALDE (*steps out of his hiding place*):   Well, Brother, now you see.

TOINETTE: My goodness. I wouldn't have believed it. I hear your daughter; get back into position and let's see how she takes your death. It's not a bad thing to know; and since you've started, you'll soon learn how your whole family feels about you. (BERALDE *hides himself again*.)

TOINETTE (*pretending not to see* ANGELIQUE):   Oh heavens! What a terrible catastrophe! Oh unhappy day!

ANGELIQUE: What's the matter, Toinette? Why are you crying?

TOINETTE: I have sad news for you.

ANGELIQUE: What?

TOINETTE: Your father is dead.

ANGELIQUE: My father is dead, Toinette?

TOINETTE: Yes, there he is. He had an attack a little while ago and died of it.

ANGELIQUE: Oh God! What a tragedy! What a cruel blow! Must I lose my father, the one person left to me on this earth? And, worse misery, at a moment when he was angry with me? What shall I do in my misfortune and what consolation shall I find after this great loss?

(*Enter* CLEANTE.)

CLEANTE: What's the matter, my love? Why are you crying?

ANGELIQUE: I'm crying for the dearest and most precious thing I could lose in life. I'm crying because my father is dead.

CLEANTE: Oh no! How terrible! An unexpected blow! I had asked your uncle to plead my case with him and I was coming here to pay my respects and to try to win his consent for our marriage.

ANGELIQUE: Ah, Cleante, let's not talk about it any more. Let's forget all thought of marriage. After losing my father I am going to enter the convent and give up the world forever. Yes, Father, I resisted your desires before, but now I want to carry out at least one of your intentions, to make up for the unhappiness I fear I caused you. (*Falls to her knees.*) Allow me, Father, to give you my word here and now and to kiss you to show my sincerity.

ARGAN (*kissing* ANGELIQUE):   My daughter!

ANGELIQUE: Agh!

ARGAN: Come here. Don't be afraid, I'm not dead. Ah, you are my flesh and blood, my very own child; and I am delighted to have seen your true good nature.

ANGELIQUE: Oh, Father, what a wonderful surprise! Since the Heavens were kind enough to return you to me, please allow me to kneel at your feet and beg something from you. If you don't approve of my heart's yearning, if you refuse to let me marry Cleante, I beg of you, at least don't force me to marry someone else. It's the only thing I ask of you.

CLEANTE (*falls to knees*):   Monsieur, please listen to her prayers and mine and don't oppose our love for each other.

BERALDE: Brother, can you persist in refusing?

TOINETTE: Sir, can you resist so much affection?

ARGAN: Let him become a doctor, and I'll consent to the marriage. (*To* CLEANTE.) Yes, become a doctor, and I'll give you my daughter.

CLEANTE: Gladly, sir; if that's all that's necessary to become your son-in-law, I'll become a doctor, even an apothecary if you like. It's a trifling matter and I would do many more things to win Angelique.

BERALDE: But, Brother, I have an idea. Why don't you become a doctor yourself? Think how convenient it will be if you learn how to cure yourself.

TOINETTE: That's true. It's the best way for you to recover fast; there's no illness daring enough to approach a doctor.

ARGAN: I think you're making fun of me, Brother. I'm not the right age to be a student.

BERALDE: To be a student! You know enough already; there are many doctors who are no more clever than you.

ARGAN: But you have to speak Latin well and know all kinds of sicknesses and remedies.

BERALDE: You'll learn all that when you put on the medical robe and hat. You'll become even more clever afterwards than you want.

ARGAN: You mean I'll learn to discuss ailments as soon as I wear the robe?

BERALDE: Yes. As soon as you talk in cap and gown any nonsense becomes science and any foolishness becomes wisdom.

TOINETTE: You know, sir, your beard alone counts for a

lot; the beard makes up more than half the doctor.

CLEANTE: Whatever you decide, I'm ready.

BERALDE: Would you like the ceremony to take place soon?

ARGAN: What do you mean, soon?

BERALDE: I mean soon. And in your house.

ARGAN: In my house?

BERALDE: Yes. I have some friends among the Faculty. They can come by in a little while and perform the ceremony in your parlor. It won't cost you a farthing.

ARGAN: But what shall I say? How shall I answer?

BERALD: They'll instruct you in short order, and they'll write down what you have to say. Go get dressed. I'll send for them.

ARGAN: Well, we'll see.

(*Exit* ARGAN.)

CLEANTE: What are you planning, sir, and what do you mean by those friends of yours among the Faculty?

TOINETTE: What are you planning?

BERALDE: To have a little fun this evening. My actor friends have worked out a little musical interlude based on a doctor's graduation; I'd like all of us to take part in the entertainment, with my brother leading the performance.

ANGELIQUE: But, Uncle, I think you're making a little too much fun of my father.

BERALDE: It's not so much making fun as adjusting to his fantasies. All of this is strictly between us. We'll all take parts and amuse each other. It's Mardi Gras time and we're allowed to play. Come, let's get ready.

CLEANTE (*to* ANGELIQUE):   Is it all right with you?

ANGELIQUE: Yes, since my uncle is leading us.

FINALE

A comic interpretation of the swearing in of a doctor. Several FOOTMEN *come into the room and arrange benches. Their movements are in rhythm. Then the entire troupe files in: eight men carrying syringes, six* APOTHECARIES. *twenty-two* DOCTORS, ARGAN, *eight dancing* SURGEONS, *and two singing* SURGEONS.)

PRESIDENT (*in a pompous manner*): Most sapient doctors, professors of medicine, gathered here; and you gentlemen, Surgeons and Apothecaries, faithful executors of the pronouncements of the Faculty; and the residuum of the company: Greetings! I bid you honor, wealth, and hearty appetites. It is impossible for me to admire the medical profession enough. What a beautiful and distinguished thing it is! By its name alone this surprising miracle has kept people of all walks of life fit and flourishing for centuries. We are aware of our great reputation throughout the earth, and we know also how the great and small alike are infatuated with us. They view us as gods as they hasten to take the cures we have prescribed. Princes and kings submit to our commands. Therefore it behooves us to maintain our position, our reputation, and our honor and to take heed that we receive into our learned Faculty only those persons capable and worthy of fulfilling our honorable functions. For this reason you are now convoked. And I believe that you will find a worthy candidate for a medical degree in the learned man who stands before you and whom I deliver unto you, for interrogation and profound examination on every topic.

FIRST DOCTOR: If our worthy President so authorizes me, and also the learned doctors and illustrious witnesses, I shall ask the most learned Candidate, whom I respect and honor, the cause and reason for which opium induces sleep.

ARGAN: I am asked by the learned doctor the cause and the reason for which opium induces sleep. To which I answer that it is because it is a soporific!

97

CHORUS: He answers with skill, with skill, with skill.

SECOND DOCTOR: With the permission of our worthy President, of the learned Faculty, and of the company assembled for our discussions, I shall ask thee, learned Candidate, what are the remedies which one should prescribe for the ailment known as dropsy.

ARGAN:

> Give an enema first
> Then a blood vessel burst
> Then purge till they thirst.

CHORUS: He answers with skill, with skill, with skill.

THIRD DOCTOR: If it suit our worthy President and the learned Faculty, I shall ask you, esteemed Candidate, what remedies you judge appropriate for consumptives, tuberculotics, and asthmatics.

ARGAN:

> Give an enema first
> Then a blood vessel burst
> Then purge till they thirst.

CHORUS: He answers with skill, with skill, with skill.

FOURTH DOCTOR: The esteemed Candidate has spoken brilliantly on these maladies. But, if I do not bore our worthy President, or the learned Faculty, or any of the honorable company, I shall put a question to him. Yesterday a sick man came under my care. He has a high fever with convulsions, excruciating headaches, a terrible pain in the side, and great difficulty in breathing. Kindly tell me what to do, esteemed Candidate.

ARGAN:

> Give an enema first
> Then his blood vessel burst
> Then purge till he thirst.

FIFTH DOCTOR: But if the ailment persists and cannot be cured, what should be done then?

ARGAN:

> Once the enema's fed
> Keep the bleeder in bed
> And purge till he's dead!

CHORUS: He answers with skill, with skill, with skill.

PRESIDENT: Do you swear to observe the statutes prescribed by the Faculty with good sense and discernment?

ARGAN: I swear.[6]

PRESIDENT: To follow the established opinion whether right or wrong in every consultation?

---

[6] At this first "I swear" Molière had the initial coughing up of blood which led to his death a few hours after the fourth performance. He managed to finish out the scene.

ARGAN: I swear.

PRESIDENT: With this venerable and esteemed head-cov-
ering, I give and concede unto you the virtue and power of
practicing medicine, of purging, bleeding, lancing, carving,
cutting, and killing with impunity in every part of the
world.

(SURGEONS *and* APOTHECARIES *bow to* ARGAN *in rhythm.*)

ARGAN: Great masters of the science of rhubarb and
liver pills, it would doubtless appear as inept and ridiculous
were I to praise you as it would if I undertook to put light
on the sun, stars into the heavens, waves into the ocean,
and roses into springtime. Please accept my one word of
thanks to your learned body. To you I owe much more than
to nature or my father. Nature and my father made a man
out of me but you made me a doctor, which is far more
important. This honor, favor, and grace has engraved itself
for eternity in the heart you behold before you.

CHORUS: Long live, long live, long live the new doctor
who speaks so well! May he eat, drink, bleed, and kill for
thousands and thousands of years!

(SURGEONS *and* APOTHECARIES *dance, accompanied by
music, voices, hand clapping, and the tapping of apothecaries' mortars.*)

FIRST SURGEON: May he see his learned prescriptions
fill the shops of every surgeon and apothecary.

CHORUS: Long live, long live, long live the new doctor
who speaks so well! May he eat, drink, bleed, and kill for
thousands and thousands of years!

SECOND SURGEON: May every year be a good and favor-
able one for him: may he have only plagues, smallpox, fevers,
pleurisies, hemorrhages, and dysenteries!

CHORUS: Long live, long live, long live the new doctor
who speaks so well! May he eat, drink, bleed, and kill for
thousands and thousands of years!

(DOCTORS, SURGEONS, *and* APOTHECARIES *leave ceremoni-
ously, in the order of their rank.*)

RACINE: Andromache

JEAN RACINE (1639–1699)

Racine spent his formative years at the Jansenist seminary
of Port-Royal near Chevreuse, a tiny town about twenty
miles out of Paris, beyond Versailles. His mother had died
when the boy was fourteen months old, after the birth of his
sister, Marie, and his father died two years later in February
1643. Young Racine's aunt had already retired to Port-Royal
—later his grandmother would follow her example—and
one of the three founders of the institution, Antoine Le
Maître, took charge of the boy, treated him as his son
(for the purposes of discipline, at any rate), and referred to
himself as the orphan's "papa." Le Maître was a former lawyer who had "withdrawn from the world" a year before
Racine's birth. He continually reminded his protégé that
"the world is an enemy of piety," and in one letter he wrote:
"Youth must always allow itself to be led, and not try to
emancipate itself."

Between his fourteenth and sixteenth years Racine was
sent from Port-Royal to the Collège de Beauvais, which was
also, in Le Maître's words, "sympathetic to Jansenism." Then
he went back to Port-Royal, where he stayed until he was
almost nineteen (1658), to round off his Jansenist indoctrina-
tion and to complete his classical studies: he was an unusu-
ally good Greek scholar. His first exposure to "the impious
world" was in Paris, where he studied philosophy for two
years at the Collège d'Harcourt.

Away from the Port-Royal atmosphere, he acquired a
taste for the theater and wrote three plays, which he offered
to leading theater companies in Paris who declined to produce them. His aunt, grandmother, and "papa" were upset to
learn that he was applying himself to as disreputable a profession as the theater, and urged him to go to his uncle's
parish in the south of France, so that he could prepare himself for a ministry. Racine stayed with his uncle at Uzès in
Languedoc Province for two years (1661–1663), and then,
when no clerical appointment seemed to be opening up for

him, he went back to Paris and took up his writing again. His first literary effort was a crafty piece of work called *An Ode on the King's Convalescence*, which brought him into immediate favor with Louis XIV, and won him an award of six hundred livres.

His fourth play, *The Thebaide*, was accepted by Molière, who presented it at the Palais-Royal. *The Thebaide* has a powerful theme, taken from Sophocles' Oedipus triology— the dispute between Oedipus' sons for the throne of Thebes. But the explosion of death and suicide at the end of *The Thebaide* is almost comic, and the structure of the play is weak. Still, it contains some finely controlled dramatic verse and one episode, Act IV, Scene 3, promises the greatness of the later *Andromache* and *Phaedra*.

The production by Molière's troupe in 1664 was heavily criticized and so was the Molière production of Racine's next play, *Alexander the Great*. Racine therefore "paid Molière back," as one French critic puts it, by furtively setting up another production of *Alexander* with Molière's competitors, the Hôtel de Bourgogne company (who are slyly mocked in several of Molière's plays). Actually, *Alexander* is not much of a play. It has less urgency than *The Thebaide* and its resolution, when Alexander forgives one of the kings of India who has dared to stand up to him, is reminiscent of Augustus' act of mercy at the end of Corneille's *Cinna*, written twenty-five years earlier. More interesting than the play itself is the fact that it was the occasion for Racine's breaking off relations with the other two great French dramatists of the seventeenth century. Corneille praised the style but had reservations about the tragic conception. Racine, who had asked for Corneille's opinion, was furious when he got it. Molière, on the other hand, was angry at Racine partly because Racine had sneaked his play away to an enemy troupe and partly because he had taken Molière's leading tragedienne, the beautiful Marquise du Parc (and her husband), with him. The husband later returned to Molière.

Racine now proceeded to escape more vigorously from his Port-Royal background. In the twelve years that followed he cavorted about Paris, enjoying its high and low life, making friends (with the critic and satirist, Boileau, among others) and enemies, living with actresses who performed in his plays, and finding time to write eight fine dramas, beginning with his greatest success, *Andromache*, and ending with a "failure," *Phaedra*, the play for which he is today most esteemed.

The next twelve years of Racine's life were a contrast to the previous twelve. After *Phaedra* was hissed by a houseful of enemies and their employees—it is, perhaps, some indication of Racine's success, as well as his prickly temperament, that so many people disliked him so actively—on New Year's Day, 1677, he broke with the theater and three months later became, with Boileau, joint royal historiographer, a sinecure carrying light duties and comfortable compensation. That was in March; in June he married Catherine de Romanet who, according to one historian, was plain, dull, and semiliterate but, according to the journal *Mercure Galant,* was a lady of "wealth, wit, and good birth."

Racine now settled down to a quiet life at court; he renounced the theater and re-established contact with Port-Royal and the Jansenists. Become pious and reserved, he now gave up much of his writing time to theological and historical disputes. The poetry he wrote during this period delineates the conflict in him between his affection for the world as it was and his religious idealism, based on his Port-Royal training. Particularly revealing are the lines:

> *Je ne fais pas le bien que j'aime*
> *Et je fais le mal que je hais.*

("I do not practice the good I love; I practice the evil I hate.")

He could not give up the theater altogether. He wrote two more plays based on stories from the Bible, *Esther* (1689) and *Athaliah* (1691). He remained on close terms with the king until the publication of his *Address on the Sufferings of the People* in 1697. The last two years of his life were unhappy and painful. He contracted a liver disease toward the end of 1698 and never recovered. He died on April 21, 1699, in his sixtieth year and was buried, at his own wish, at Port-Royal.

A LIST OF RACINE'S PLAYS:

Theagene and Chariclea (1659); *Amasia* (1660); *The Loves of Ovid* (1660–61); *The Thebaide* (1664); *Alexander the Great* (1665); *Andromache* (1667); *The Pleaders,* Racine's only comedy (1668); *Britannicus* (1669); *Berenice* (1670); *Bajazeth* (1672); *Mithridatus* (1673); *Iphigenia* (1674); *Phaedra* (1677); *Esther* (1689); *Athaliah* (1691).

SUGGESTIONS FOR FURTHER READING ON RACINE:

Bentley, Eric. (ed.). *The Classic Theatre,* Vol. 4, *Six French*

Plays. Phaedra, trans. by Robert Lowell. New York: Doubleday & Company, Inc. (Anchor Books), 1961.

Muir, Kenneth. *Racine: Five Plays.* New York: Hill & Wang, Inc. (Dramabooks), 1960.

Sainte-Beuve, Charles-Augustin. *Portraits of the Seventeenth Century, Historic and Literary.* Trans. by Katharine P. Wormeley. New York: G. P. Putnam's Sons, 1925.

Turnell, Martin. *The Classical Moment.* New York: New Directions, 1948.

Vinaver, Eugène. *Racine and Poetic Tragedy.* Trans. from the French by P. Mansell Jones. New York: Hill & Wang, Inc., 1959.

IN FRENCH ONLY:

Brisson, Pierre. *Les Duex Visages de Racine.* Gallimard.

Goldmann, Lucien. *Jean Racine, Dramaturge.* In the series *Les Grands Dramaturges.* Paris: L'Arche.

———. *Le Dieu Caché.*

NOTE: A critical essay on Racine, "The Return of *Andromache,*" by Robert Kemp, will be found on p. 528.

THE CHARACTERS IN *ANDROMACHE*

Racine's *Andromache* is set shortly after the end of the Trojan War. The events of the war and the people who took part in it diverge in details from Homer, the primary source of information, through the Greek and Roman historians and dramatists including Virgil. According to the fairly recent archaeological discoveries of Schliemann and Sir Arthur Evans and others, there is good reason to believe that some of the battles and other happenings in the *Iliad* and the *Odyssey,* if not the *Aeneid,* are based on historical fact. The personalities involved in the war, however, gods included, seem to be partly legend, partly the invention of Homer, and partly the embroidery of Aeschylus, Sophocles, Euripides, Virgil, and other authors, all of whom quite rightly took dramatic license in their retellings of the war's aftermaths.

The brief recapitulation that follows is necessarily generalized, but it may serve as a reference for the reader of *Andromache.*

The Trojan War was provoked when PARIS, prince of Troy and son of PRIAM, the king of Troy, stole HELEN, the Spartan queen, and took her back to Troy with him.

MENELAUS, Helen's husband, the king of Sparta, and AGAMEMNON, his brother, the king of Mycenae, summoned up a massive army, consisting of soldiers from many Greek

čity-states—Argos, Corinth, Troezen, and others less famous—and led this army against Troy in order to recover
Helen. After ten years of fighting, the Greeks (also known
as Achaeans or Danaans) gained secret entry into Troy by
hiding in the wooden horse and then vanquishing the Trojans inside their own walls.

But this defeat could not take place until ACHILLES, the
mightiest of the Greek warriors, had joined in the battle and
slain HECTOR, the brother of Paris, the son of Priam, and
the hero of Troy.

After Troy had been sacked ASTYANAX, Hector's baby son,
was thrown from the castle battlements by the conquering
Greeks, and ANDROMACHE, his mother, Hector's widow, was
given as a prize of war to PYRRHUS (also known as Neopto-
lemus), the son of Achilles, to be his slave and concubine.
Pyrrhus, however, was already contracted by marriage to
HERMIONE, the daughter of Menelaus and Helen. Hermione
was naturally jealous of Andromache, particularly as Andromache had borne MOLOSSUS, a son to Pyrrhus, whereas
she, Hermione, had remained childless. She therefore called
upon ORESTES, her first cousin, the son of Agamemnon, to
help her take revenge on Pyrrhus. Orestes was in love with
Hermione and, to execute her revenge and to win her for
himself, he killed Pyrrhus.

This is a crude outline of the story used by Euripides
in his short drama *Andromache*. In the course of his play,
Orestes kills Pyrrhus, Andromache and Molossus are
spared, Hermione goes off with Orestes, and the goddess
Thetis swoops down from Olympus at the end and predicts
that a whole line of "Molossian kings" will descend from
the child Molossus.

Racine moved his play forward to an earlier time than
Euripides' (to shortly after the destruction of Troy) and to
a different place, Epirus (Euripides' play took place in Thes-
saly, on the other side of the Greek peninsula). Readers will
notice a number of other modifications in the story. But
Racine kept the same four protagonists, Andromache, Pyrrhus, Hermione, and Orestes, and kept them in roughly the
same relationship. By making the modifications, Racine was
able to construct his play so that each of the four main
characters was subjected to a personal conflict between
honor (or duty) and love (or passion). The child in Racine's
play was Andromache's first baby, Astyanax, not her second
one, Molossus. In the third paragraph of his preface to the
published edition of *Andromache*, Racine explains and de-
fends this switch. (See pages 105-106.)

RACINE'S SECOND PREFACE TO *ANDROMACHE*

Virgil in the third book of the *Aeneid*—it is Aeneas who speaks:

> The sigh of high Phaeacia soon we lost,
> And skimm'd along Epirus' rocky coast.
> Then to Chaonia's port our course we bend,
> And, landed, to Buthrotus' heights ascend.

> . . . .
> By chance, the mournful queen, before the gate,
> Then solemniz'd her former husband's fate.
> Green altars, rais'd of turf, with gifts she crown'd:
> And sacred priests in order stand around,
> And thrice the name of hapless Hector sound.

> . . . .
> With eyes dejected, in a lowly tone,
> After a modest pause, she thus begun:
> "Oh, only happy maid of Priam's race,
> Whom death deliver'd from the foe's embrace!
> Commanded on Achilles' tomb to die,
> Not forc'd, like us, to hard captivity,
> Or in a haughty master's arms to lie.
> In Grecian ships, unhappy we were borne,
> Endur'd the victor's lust, sustain'd the scorn!
> Thus I submitted to the lawless pride
> Of Pyrrhus, more a handmaid than a bride.
> Cloy'd with possession, he forsook my bed,
> And Helen's lovely daughter sought to wed;

> . . . .
> Till young Orestes, pierc'd with deep despair,
> And longing to redeem the promis'd fair,
> Before Apollo's altar slew the ravisher." [1]

Here, in very few lines, is the entire theme of this tragedy. Here are the locale, the action, the four principal actors and even their personalities, except for Hermione, whose jealousy and fits of anger are quite pronounced in the *Andromache* of Euripides.

This is almost the only thing I am borrowing from the latter. Because, even though my tragedy bears the same name as his, the treatment is very different. Andromache, in the Euripides version, fears for the life of Molossus, the son

---

[1] In the translation of John Dryden from the original Latin. *Ed.*

105

she has borne to Pyrrhus, whom Hermione wishes to have slain along with his mother. But here there is no mention of Molossus: Andromache knows no husband other than Hector, no son other than Astyanax. In this way, I felt I was conforming to the view that we now have of this princess. Almost everyone who has heard Andromache mentioned knows her only as Hector's widow and Astyanax's mother. No one feels that she should love another husband or another son; and I don't believe that her tears would have made the impression they did make on my audience, had they been shed for a son other than the one she bore to Hector. True, I was forced to have Astyanax live longer than he actually did; but I am writing in a country where this liberty will not be ill received. Even omitting Ronsard, who chose this same Astyanax for the hero of his *Franciade,* who among us does not know that our original kings are reputed to be descendants of this son of Hector's, and that our ancient chronicles spare the young prince's life, after the destruction of his country, in order to make him the founder of our monarchy?

Euripides was much more daring in his tragedy *Helen:* he openly shocks the accepted beliefs about Greece; he assumes that Helen has never set foot in Troy, and that after the burning of the city, Menelaus finds his wife in Egypt, whence she has never departed; all this based on a supposition which only the Egyptians accepted, as we can see in Herodotus.

I don't believe that I need Euripides' example to justify the small liberty I have taken. There is a world of difference between destroying the very heart of a myth and merely altering those few incidents which change almost completely from one version to the next. Thus Achilles, according to most of the poets, can only be wounded in the heel, although Homer, who doesn't believe him invulnerable in any part of his body, has him wounded in the arm. Or Sophocles, who has Jocasta die right after the recognition of Oedipus, in contrast with Euripides, who has her live until the battle and death of her two sons. And it is in view of several contradictions of this sort that a former critic of Sophocles points out very wisely "that we should not waste time quibbling about the changes the poets may have made in a myth; but that we should rather devote ourselves to considering the excellent use they made of these changes and the ingenious manner in which they were able to accommodate the myth to their theme."

Translated by Mildred Marmur

ANDROMACHE

By Jean Racine

FIRST PERFORMED AT THE HÔTEL DE BOURGOGNE
ON NOVEMBER 17, 1667

Translated by Lionel Abel

CHARACTERS

ANDROMACHE, *widow of Hector and now captive of Pyrrhus*
PYRRHUS, *son of Achilles and now king of Epirus*
ORESTES, *son of Agamemnon, in love with Hermione*
HERMIONE, *daughter of Helen, promised to Pyrrhus*
PYLADES, *friend of Orestes*
CLEONE, *confidant of Hermione*
CEPHISE, *confidant of Andromache*
PHOENIX, *commander under Achilles and later under Pyrrhus*
FOLLOWERS *of Orestes*

*A city in Epirus. The play takes place in one of the rooms
in Pyrrhus' palace.*

ACT I

(ORESTES *and* PYLADES.)

ORESTES: My faithful friend, seeing you again, I know my fortune must change; my fortune—it is already less at odds with me; it is almost mine. Just think, on this shore, which I was afraid my ship would bring me to, whom did I first see but you, my Pylades! I never imagined six months ago that I would meet you again at the court of Pyrrhus.

PYLADES: I thank the Gods for preventing me from returning to Greece, our home! Now, I thank them! And even for the storms which sank my ships, just off this shore! In this place of exile, Orestes, I have had much to fear; but mainly my fears were for you. I was always afraid some new danger might beset you which I, your friend, would not be able to share. Most of all, I feared your melancholy . . . and I was afraid that Heaven, so often cruel in helping, might help you to your death. Death, I thought, was what you wanted. But now I see you magnificently accompanied, richly attended; you don't look, Orestes, like a man who came here to die.

ORESTES: Alas! Do I know why I came? Love brought me in search of a lady who is so unloving; at this moment, I cannot say for myself what fate will have to say later on. I don't know whether I came looking for life or death.

PYLADES: So you are still a slave to love, still asking love to tell you what to do! And after all you have suffered from love! Pain, I see, has taught you nothing. Do you suppose that Hermione, who was so pitiless in Sparta, is going to be at your beck and call here in Epirus? Remember, once you were ashamed of the vows you made her. Reflect, once you were able to hate her. You no longer spoke of her to me. In not speaking of her, my lord, you took me in.

ORESTES: If that was deceit, then I was the one deceived. My friend, don't be so hard with me. After all, you know my love for you, and besides, I am so unhappy. Did I ever

hide my heart from you? You knew my desires, my one desire, you watched while it grew strong. You heard my first
sighs and when at last Menelaus bestowed his daughter on
Pyrrhus, the avenger of his honor, it was to you I revealed
my whole despair. Since then, you have seen me drag my
tedium from sea to sea. I knew that you were ready to follow me anywhere, if only to soothe my rage from time to
time, and save me, regularly, from myself. . . . But to my
story. . . . Pylades, I became aware that Hermione despite
my love for her had fixed her heart on Pyrrhus and wanted
his love. It was then that my own heart, wounded, formed a
new resolve: to forget Hermione, to punish her. Why had
she scorned me? I pretended to believe that I could do this;
in some way I did believe it; I actually thought that my
desire to harm her sprang from hatred; I forgot that she was
beautiful; I thought myself safe. I believed that I could see
her once more and not be moved. Calm and self-deceived, I
returned to Greece. The princes of the land were at that
moment meeting to find means of countering a new peril. I
joined with the others. I was hoping for war, the chance of
glory. I hoped that in battle I might find new objects for
concern, that my feelings might again be stirred, and that
love would leave my heart. Will you not wonder, Pylades?
I do! What is that fatal bent in me which makes me turn my
steps toward the very trap from which I ought to run, and
at top speed? On every side I heard Pyrrhus denounced,
threatened; all Greece was against him; everyone said he
had forgotten his own father, his own kin, and was even
nurturing at his court the future enemy of Greece, Astyanax, Hector's son—so young, so to be pitied—but still the
one link remaining between any still living Trojan and all
the kings dead and buried under the ruins of Troy. I heard
how Andromache to save her child had tricked Ulysses: she
substituted someone else's son for Hector's; this was the boy
the Greeks executed. I learned that Pyrrhus, forgetful of
Hermione's beauty, was on the point of offering his heart
and his crown to Andromache. Menelaus would not credit
the rumor, but at the same time, took note of it. Why had
the marriage of Pyrrhus to his daughter Hermione been for
so long postponed? In the flood of anxiety where the heart
of Menelaus was sinking, my heart was borne upwards. A
new opportunity for me: I might still conquer her. At first I
flattered myself that my victory would take the form of revenge; and then Hermione took up her old place in my heart.
Pylades, I knew that the fire in me was not dead; rather
my hatred was dead; I could love Hermione forever. I asked

the Greeks to send me as their emissary to Pyrrhus. Thus it is I am here. Apparently I came to make Pyrrhus yield up this boy whose life is a threat to all the cities of Greece. But what do I really want? Not to rob Pyrrhus of Astyanax, but to snatch Hermione from his arms. My love is stronger than ever it was. What is there to fear now? Since all my efforts to resist have proved futile, I have no choice but to give myself blindly to a hope of joy which has shown itself stronger than I. Pylades, I love Hermione; I came here to find her, to make her yield to me, to bring her back with me; if I cannot do that, at least I can force her to watch me die. You know something of Pyrrhus, Pylades. What will be his next move? What is his secret thought? Or don't you know what's happening at his court, what's happening in his heart? Does he plan to keep his word to Hermione? Or will he yield her up? Do you know, Pylades?

PYLADES: I cannot promise you, Orestes, what Pyrrhus himself may be unwilling to give. It's true that he does not seem the happier because of Hermione's love. He himself loves Hector's widow. She, for her part, has treated his passion with indifference and even contempt. Every day he tries to weaken her or to frighten her. He threatens her son's life, causes her to weep and then tenderly wipes away her tears. Many a time he has turned toward Hermione, repeated his first vows to her, and sighing, cast himself at her feet, but less with love than with rage. How can one predict the action of a man who is not his own master? Pyrrhus is no longer himself; he is perfectly capable, I should say, of punishing the woman he loves and marrying the woman he hates.

ORESTES: But you have said nothing about Hermione. Her marriage has been postponed; her beauty is without power; what can her feelings be?

PYLADES: Her hope is to make others believe that Pyrrhus is inconstant because she has been cruel to him. She seems to think against all evidence that he will again beg her to accept his love; but I have seen her weep; she weeps a great deal, I think, when she is alone. Yet she pretends to be ready to leave Epirus at any time, always stays, and sometimes cries out your name, Orestes, calling on you to come to her aid.

ORESTES: No! She couldn't have called on me! But if she did, I must go to her. I'll go at once. . . .

PYLADES: First you must accomplish your mission. You await the king; talk with him, tell him that all the Greeks have joined against Hector's son. When told of their hate for the child, he will not yield him up; he loves the mother; his passion for the mother will become still more fierce. The more the Greeks try to part him from her, the more will they unite the two. Be firm: ask for everything so as to be sure you get nothing. He's coming.

ORESTES: And you go and tell Hermione that I am here, and that I came only for her.

(*Exit* PYLADES *and enter* PYRRHUS *and* PHOENIX.)

ORESTES: Before I speak to you, my lord, on behalf of all the Greeks, allow me to say first of all that I am proud to be their spokesman; I am about to confer with the son of Achilles, with you who conquered Troy. Yes, my lord, we admire your deeds, even as we extol your father's: Hector fell before him, Troy died under your feet; you have shown the world that the son of Achilles is able to take his father's place; all Greece has been made happy by such audacity. Nevertheless, this must be said too: You have done something Achilles would never have dared do, and Greece grieves because of it: You have given comfort and refuge to a survivor of the war with Troy, permitting yourself to be touched with pity for Hector's son and heir. Have you forgotten, my lord, what Hector was like in battle? The people of Greece remember him well. Just to mention his name is enough to make our daughters, our widows tremble: Think of all the Greeks Hector slew; today there is not a family among us which does not demand a reckoning with his unfortunate son. And what might not this son attempt some day? Perhaps he'll turn up in our ports suddenly, and like his father, torch in hand, set fire to our ships. Dare I say openly what I think? You yourself are not without fear of the reward you may get for all your concern; you, too, suspect that the dead hero's son may punish you one day for having protected his life. My lord, give us of Greece what we ask. Avenge us, save yourself, and destroy an enemy who is all the more to be feared since he counts on using you in order to fight us.

PYRRHUS: Why is all Greece so interested in me? I thought the people there had many other problems, much graver cares. And when I heard you were their emissary I assumed at once that you had come on a mission of great scope, of real grandeur. I find it hard to believe that you, the son of Agamemnon, were chosen for nothing better than this mission. And I find it hard to believe, too, that a people so accustomed to victory should now be involved in a conspiracy to take the life of a child. In whose name is the boy to be sacrificed? Has Greece any right now to take his life? And why should I be the only Greek not allowed to dispose of a captive? You know perfectly well that when the conquerors of Troy, black and bloodied by its smoking walls, were wondering how to divide their loot, we all agreed that chance, which thrust Andromache and her son into my hands, would be the arbiter. Hecuba wept her last tears in the tent of Ulysses! Cassandra went to Argos with your father! Did I make objection? Did I say then how Ulysses and Agamemnon should be judged? You are afraid that Troy will be born again and that the son of Hector will plot to take my life in revenge for my having spared his? I say you are requiring of me a prudence not befitting a king. For my part, I have never learned to fear dangers so far off. I think of what Troy was once—rich in heroes, circled with proud walls, mistress of Asia—and then I think of all that happened to it. What remains of Troy now? Its towers are dust and cinders. It is a river of blood washing a barren plain. What else is Troy? A boy in irons. Am I supposed to fear that this stricken Troy still hopes for revenge on us? If the death of Hector's son was really decreed, then why was it postponed for a whole year? Could he not have been slain with Priam himself? With so many dead on every side the boy could have been put to death without any of us suffering a pang. At that moment whatever we did seemed just. Old age and childhood could not depend on their weakness then to weaken our will. Victory and the dark, both more cruel than we, made it easier for us to kill, and our blows fell upon no matter whom. I think now that my own spite against our victims was much too bitter, too harsh. Should cruelty outlast anger? Should I go against my own present pity and at my pleasure, unpressed by danger, soil my hands with a boy's blood? No, no; let the Greeks seek some other victim. Let them hunt down some other Trojan survivor. My wrath is spent. Here in Epirus I will spare the child the Greeks spared at Troy.

ORESTES: By cunning and trickery, another boy was substituted for Hector's son and executed. Moreover, it is not the people of Troy but Hector that we fear. Yes, the Greeks want to strike the father again, by striking his son. Hector let our blood; only in his blood can our anger end. They will come here to Epirus for Astyanax. Forestall them.

PYRRHUS: No, let them come! It would delight my old resentment to see them try to make a second Troy of this my city, confusing in their hatred friend and foe, no longer able to distinguish the one who gave Greece victory from

those he conquered for Greece. This will not be the first
injustice done by the Greeks. I remember their treatment of
Achilles. Who gained by it? Hector. Some day Hector's son
in his turn may profit from their injustice, too.

ORESTES: Then you are ready to rebel against Greece?

PYRRHUS: I did not conquer for Greece in order to become her slave.

ORESTES: I think Hermione will have something to say
about this. Think of her beauty; you will think more kindly of
her father.

PYRRHUS: Hermione, sir, may be mine and forever. I
can still love her without submitting to Menelaus; perhaps
some day I will be able to reconcile the need to act greatly
with true love. I suggest that you yourself see the daughter
of Helen. I know that you are closely allied in blood. Once
you have spoken to her I shall not keep you here. You may
tell the Greeks that I shall not do what they wish.

(*Exit* ORESTES.)

PHOENIX: But you are sending him to a woman he
loves!

PYRRHUS: It is said that he always loved her.

PHOENIX: Perhaps he still does. He may offer her his
love again; she may accept. . . .

PYRRHUS: May love take both of them. Yes, let it take
both of them, each the other's prisoner, off to Sparta! They
can sail at any time. Those are my orders. Yes, Hermione
can go, and take my boredom with her.

PHOENIX: Sir . . .

PYRRHUS: I cannot tell you everything now. Andromache
approaches. Leave us.

(*Enter* ANDROMACHE *and* CEPHISE.)

PYRRHUS: Madam, were you looking for me? I hope so:
The hope is sweet; don't deny it me.

ANDROMACHE: I was on my way to where my son is
kept under guard. You have allowed me to see once a day
all that I still possess of Hector, of Troy. I was going, my
lord, to cry, since you permit it, with my son. I have not
kissed him today.

PYRRHUS: The Greeks, madam, may soon give you further
reason to weep.

ANDROMACHE: But why? What do they want now? Has
any Trojan escaped you?

PYRRHUS: Their hatred for Hector is not yet dead: they fear his son.

ANDROMACHE: How could my child frighten them? This unhappy boy, who does not even know that he is the captive of Pyrrhus, or the son of Hector.

PYRRHUS: The Greeks still demand his life. The son of Agamemnon himself has come with an order that the boy be executed—and at once.

ANDROMACHE: Will you give the boy up? Are you that cruel? Does my love for the child make him a criminal? Alas! Are the Greeks afraid that he will avenge his father, or only that he will dry his mother's tears? To me he would have been both father and husband. But I am about to lose him; again you are going to strike me; this time fatally.

PYRRHUS: On the contrary, madam, I have decided to be merciful. I acted. You have no cause now to weep. The Greeks have threatened me with war. But even if they come here with a thousand ships to demand your son, even if the blood of the same people who fought for Helen must be spilled over this land, even if ten years from now I shall have to see my palace burning, I will not yield. I will defend your son, and at the risk of my own life. You see the dangers I invite to please you. But won't you look at me with even a little kindness? I am hated by the Greeks, importuned on all sides, am I to expect cruelty from you, too? These arms will fight for you, but will you not accept with them the heart that loves you? Or must I, about to do battle in your cause, think of you as one more enemy?

ANDROMACHE: Think what will be said of you in Greece, my lord, if you take my part not for love of justice but for love for me. . . . Must a heart as great as yours be so weak? Your resolve is so generous; shall it be said that you were moved by passion? I am your captive, ever sad, and without any love for life; do you expect me to love you? And how can you love a woman whom you yourself condemned to be always in tears? Should you not, sir, respect the unhappiness you have brought on an enemy? Save the boy; restore a son to his mother; deny the request of those who want his life, but do not ask me to pay you back for this by yielding up my heart. Can you not protect my son without thinking of me? That would be hard for most men, but you are the son of Achilles.

PYRRHUS: Will nothing change your feelings? Will you never stop hating me? Must I still be punished? I know what I did at Troy; I killed many who loved you, and whom you loved. But think how many times your eyes have punished me for those deeds! Andromache, you must know by now that you are able to make me pay for all the tears I caused you. I am full of remorse; you know it; you have only to look at me, and I am bowed down with guilt. I taste all the sadness I brought on Troy: your captive, now in bonds, I have more fires in me than ever I lit; I myself know more cares, tears, anxieties than I have caused you. Alas! Was I ever as cruel to you as you now are to me? Let us stop punishing each other. We have the same enemies; let us unite; speak the words I want to hear you say and you shall have your son again; I will be his father; I myself will teach him to avenge Troy; I shall punish the Greeks for your sufferings and for my own. One glance from you and I can undertake anything. Ilium can be reborn. In less time than it took the Greeks to destroy it, I will rebuild Troy; there I shall crown your son.

ANDROMACHE: But what can such glory mean to me now? I promised all that to my son when his father was alive! No, sacred walls of Troy, I do not want to see you restored—you did not save Hector from death. An unhappy woman, sir, asks for less than you offer; my tears ask you for no more than exile in safety with my son. Let us go where the Greeks cannot find us, where even you cannot. Let me hide my boy and mourn my husband. Your love has made others hate me. Return, I beg of you, to the daughter of Helen.

PYRRHUS: How can I, madam? Oh, you torment me! How can I give Hermione the heart you have taken from me? I promised her marriage, she came to Epirus, thinking to reign here with me. Fate willed that both of you should come to Epirus, you as a captive, she to marry your conqueror. But tell me one thing I have done to please Hermione? One would think—your charm being all-powerful, hers neglected—that she came here the captive and you to rule! Hermione would be happy if a single one of my countless sighs by chance escaped my feeling and went not toward you but toward her.

ANDROMACHE: But she has no reason not to love you, sir. What have you ever done that she cannot accept? That she must forget? She will not reject you for what you did at Troy. Was her love given once and for all to a husband now dead? And what a man that husband was! His death made your father's fame. Achilles is known now throughout the world for having spilled Hector's blood; and you, like him, shall always be remembered for having made me weep.

PYRRHUS: Perhaps I must do as you wish: forget you, or

rather, hate you, but my desire has grown too violent to halt at indifference. Know this: my heart from now on shall feel love without limit or nothing but hate. And if you make me hate you, expect no mercy. Your son will have to pay. Greece asks it of me, and I am not going to risk my honor for the sake of a thankless woman.

ANDROMACHE: Then the boy dies! He has only his mother's tears and his own innocence to defend him. . . . And perhaps his death will put an end to me and to my sorrow. For his sake I prolonged my life and its griefs; following my son I may perhaps see my husband again. Thus, sir, you can reunite the three of us. . . .

PYRRHUS: Go and see your son, madam. Perhaps the sight of him will caution your love and free it from anger. I shall look for you later to learn what all of our fates are to be. . . . One last word: When you embrace the boy, madam, think this: you, and only you can save him.

ACT II

(HERMIONE *and* CLEONE.)

HERMIONE: Perhaps you are right. I will see him. Or rather, I'll let him see me. I think he deserves that much. But, Cleone, if I had any self-respect, I would refuse to see him. . . .

CLEONE: Why, madam? Isn't he the very Orestes you told me you wanted to see again? The Orestes whose love and constancy you have praised so often?

HERMIONE: His love, which I never wanted, will not be fooled now, but will see at once just how things stand. And he will be the one to feel pride. That's why I am afraid to see him! He'll note at once that my humiliation is equal to his own hurt. And he'll say to himself, "Is this the proud Hermione? She scorned me; look at her; she was rejected . . . whom can she scorn now? Her heart, which was so haughty, has now learned pain." Think of it!

CLEONE: What have you to fear, madam, from a man who has been for so long under your spell? Do you expect insults from a lover? He brings you the heart he has not been able to offer anyone else. . . . But you still haven't told me what your father advised. . . .

HERMIONE: Unless Pyrrhus disposes of the boy and stops postponing our marriage, my father's orders are to leave with Orestes.

CLEONE: In that case, you must see Orestes and hear him out. This is an intrigue; Pyrrhus started it. You must make the next move. You have to act. And I think you told me you have come to hate Pyrrhus. . . .

HERMIONE: I do hate him! I will hate him! He has forgotten my love for him. He was near to me—he has gone to another. I loved him too much not to hate him now.

CLEONE: Then leave, madam. And since Orestes loves you . . .

HERMIONE: I want to give my anger time to grow strong.

I need time to plan. . . . I may leave. Yes. But Pyrrhus must be in despair when I go. . . . That much I owe him.

CLEONE: Are you going to expose yourself to more punishment? He loves his captive and flaunts that love. He has done enough to make you hate him. Can he still hurt you? If you haven't broken with him already, how will you ever be able to?

HERMIONE: You want to hurt me, too, Cleone! Well, you can! I don't know myself now. I am afraid to know my own thoughts. I beg this of you: Try not to understand me. Try not to believe all that you know to be true. Think this instead: think there is no love in me, praise my force, my will, believe that in his scorn my heart grew hard . . . believe all this, and make me believe it, too. You want me to leave Epirus? He won't stop me; let's be off then, and stop envying the prisoner who made him her captive. . . . Yes, let's be gone. . . . But what if he should remember his vows to me, what if true feeling again fills his heart, what if he were to throw himself at my feet and beg for mercy? What if, God of love, you were to deliver him to me bound hand and foot, what if he himself wanted that? But all he wants, I think, is to insult me, injure me. So we shall remain here, if only to be in their way, to be their bad luck. He is about to break a solemn vow and the Greeks think him a criminal. I wish they would demand the boy's mother, too. I wish her all the hurt she made me feel. She must lose. Lose him, or become his victim. May he be the one to order her death!

CLEONE: How can you think of this unhappy woman as your rival? Do you suppose that her heart, so burdened with sorrow, is interested in making her tormentor sigh with love? Look at her, and you see at once that Pyrrhus is no solace to her. For why is she so unhappy? And why doesn't she yield to the man who loves her?

HERMIONE: Would I had been as hard! I should not even have answered his words. I did answer, and what I said, unhappily, I meant. I thought it was possible to be sincere without risk to oneself. And he got not one cold glance from me. I asked of none but my heart what I should say to him. But who would have acted differently once he had sworn such solemn vows? I wonder if I seem to him now as I did then. You will recall how everything favored him: He had avenged my family, the Greeks were exultant, our ships were freighted with the loot of Troy, his father's exploits had been dimmed by his own deeds, and I thought,

Cleone, that his love for me was even stronger than mine for him. My heart . . . you were the traitor, you were dazzled by his fame, you let Pyrrhus betray me. But however I feel about Pyrrhus, I recognize a certain virtue in Orestes. At least he can love me without my loving him. He may even know how to make himself loved. Admit him.

CLEONE: Madam, he is here.

HERMIONE: Already?

(*Enter* ORESTES.)

HERMIONE: May I believe, sir, that some remaining tenderness for me brings you here; knowing as you do that I am sad? Or am I to think that duty alone brought you?

ORESTES: You know, madam, that my love is both fatal and blind; Orestes is doomed always to return to you, swearing each time that he will never come again. I know that each glance from you is another wound, and that each step I take toward you is another hope broken. I know all that. I blush for it. But I call the Gods to witness: they heard my last good-bys. I went wherever I could expect death; thus I might be free of my vows, and end my pain. I even went begging my death of strange and cruel tribes who sacrifice men to their gods; they closed their temples to me and would not spill my blood. Finally I sought you out and what I ask now is the desired death your glance is able to inflict. Despairing, all I expect of you is coldness and indifference. I want you to forbid me to feel the slightest hope. All you have to do is to say again what you have always said. For a whole year, madam, my one aim has been to come to you as a victim, a victim the Scythians would have cut to pieces, had they been as cruel as you are.

HERMIONE: I think, sir, that you came here on a mission which concerns all of Greece, and not just your own ills, whether caused by me or by the Scythians—think of all the kings you represent. They sent you here to avenge them and not to satisfy your own passion—or to die, for that matter. Think, sir, of the duty you took upon yourself when you came here.

ORESTES: I have already discharged my mission. Pyrrhus has refused to comply with the will of Greece. He has dismissed me, madam, and is prepared to defend Hector's son for reasons known only to him.

HERMIONE: The traitor!

ORESTES: So I am about to leave Epirus. But first I want to know from your lips what my fate is to be. I think I know it already. I can almost hear your hatred for me, pronouncing my doom, even without words.

HERMIONE: You who say you are sad, will you always be unjust to me? Why do you say I hate you? When was I cruel to you? I came to Epirus at my father's command. How do you know that I have not secretly felt some of the sorrow you feel? Are you the only one who can suffer? Do you suppose I never wept? Haven't you enough imagination to conceive that at moments I may have defied my clear duty and wished to see you again?

ORESTES: You wanted to see me! My gracious princess, is it really to me you have said those words? I beg you, open your eyes. Do you see who is standing in front of you? It is Orestes, madam, Orestes, whom you have always scorned.

HERMIONE: I see you. Yes, you, whose love for me first told me that my beauty has a certain power. You, indeed, whose many virtues I cannot but praise, you whom I have pitied, and whom I may even learn to love.

ORESTES: I understand my fate. Your heart is for Pyrrhus. Your good wishes are for me.

HERMIONE: Orestes, don't wish for Pyrrhus' luck. Do you want me to hate you?

ORESTES: If you could hate me, why then I could still hope to be loved. How your glance stabs me! You would like to love me, I think, but I know I can never please you. And since it is love that we finally obey, even in turning toward me you have my rival mainly in mind. My feeling for you is so tender, my respect for you so real. Everything would speak in my behalf if only you were able to listen. . . . But I know it is Pyrrhus you want, no matter what you say, no matter what you think, and no matter what he—Pyrrhus—wants. For the truth is that he scorns you; his heart belongs elsewhere.

HERMIONE: Who told you Pyrrhus scorns me? Did he say it? In so many words? Did you see this in his glance? Could the sight of me fill a man with scorn? Am I incapable of binding another's heart to mine? I am sure I can find favor in some men's eyes.

ORESTES: Continue your attack, madam. It would appear now that it is I who scorn you. But haven't I given proof of my constancy? Your beauty has overwhelmed me, and you say that I am the witness to its weakness. I show scorn for you? I think you would like my rival to show a like scorn!

HERMIONE: His hatred, his love do not matter to me. Arm all Greece against the rebel. Warn him what his rebellion will cost; make Epirus a second Ilium. Go! Act! Then come to me and accuse me of loving him.

ORESTES: I say it now. For if you loved me, I think you
would return with me to Greece and not remain here as
Pyrrhus' hostage. Come with me and join all hearts against
him.

HERMIONE: Once I'm gone he'll marry Andromache.

ORESTES: What if he does?

HERMIONE: Think of the disgrace to Greece if he marries
Hector's widow.

ORESTES: And you still say you hate him! Madam, love is
a flame one cannot smother. The flame reveals you. It burns
in your words, in your eyes, even when you say nothing.
You cannot hide that blaze.

HERMIONE: I see now, sir, that you have come here
armed against anything I can say, ready to interpret any
hatred in me for Pyrrhus as the effect of love. Let me make
myself clear. Then you may be able to act. I came here out
of duty, and duty keeps me. I may leave only when either my
father or Pyrrhus orders me to. Go to him, then, and speaking for my father, tell him that an enemy of Greece can
never be my husband. Let him decide whether he wants me
or Andromache. He must either give you her son or break
with me. If he decides for her, I shall return to Greece
with you.

(*Exit* HERMIONE.)

ORESTES: Yes, you shall go with me. The matter is settled. I know whom Pyrrhus wants. He wants the Trojan.
The sight of any other woman offends him. He wants nothing better than an excuse to break with you. If I say to him
what you want me to say, the thing is done. You will be mine,
in all your beauty. Let Hector's son and widow remain in
Epirus; Hermione goes with me to forget this land and its
king. . . . He approaches. What luck! May love make him
forget how lovely Hermione is.

(*Enter* PYRRHUS *and* PHOENIX.)

PYRRHUS: I was looking for you, sir, to tell you that I
overspoke myself against your argument. Afterwards I felt
the force and justice of your appeal. I realized that I had
been on the point of disavowing my father, Greece, and
myself, too. No, Orestes, I shall not restore Troy, ren-
dering vain all that my father and I did. You were angry;
but you had a right to be. My soldiers are ready to surrender Astyanax.

ORESTES: A stern decision. And certainly a most prudent one. Yes, now you can have peace—and at no greater cost than the poor child's blood.

PYRRHUS: Peace. And I intend that this peace we both wish for shall be an enduring one. To that end, I shall marry Hermione. This greatly desired event lacked only you for its witness. And here you are, representing Greece, Menelaus, and in addition, your dead father, the great Agamemnon. Communicate my decision to Hermione. Tell her that tomorrow we shall marry. You yourself shall join our hands.

(*Exit* ORESTES.)

PYRRHUS: Well, Phoenix, is love my master still? You look at me as if you didn't know me.

PHOENIX: My lord, I know you again. You are restored to Greece and to yourself, and no longer the puppet of a trivial passion. Once again you are Pyrrhus, the son of Achilles, and even his rival for glory. You have triumphed again over Troy.

PYRRHUS: My real triumph begins today. For only today can I enjoy it; in conquering love, my heart is at last proud, no longer enslaved. Consider all the troubles I shall avoid, the whole long train of ills that follow love, unfailingly. I was ready to sacrifice my obligations, even my friends. . . . A single glance could have made me do all that. The Greeks were on the point of uniting against me, and I even took pleasure in the thought that I was about to destroy myself.

PHOENIX: My lord, your present sternness makes me happy, and . . .

PYRRHUS: You saw how she treated me. . . . I thought fear for her son would make her yield to me. It only made her weep the more; a hundred times she called on Hector. I offered to defend her son, and do you know how she answered me? "Then you will be defending Hector," she said. "Take note of his eyes, his posture. The boy already has Hector's daring." And embracing Astyanax, she said, "It is you, my dear dead husband, whom I kiss." What does she expect of me? Does she think I won't touch the boy when I see that loving him satisfies her?

PHOENIX: That's gratitude! Forget her, my lord.

PYRRHUS: She counts on her beauty, I suppose, and expects me to overlook her anger and cast myself at her feet. But I shall see her at my feet, Phoenix, and I shall be unmoved. She is the widow of Hector, and I am the son of Achilles: too much hate separates Andromache and Pyrrhus.

PHOENIX: Suppose you start afresh by not talking about her. See Hermione. You will forget your vexation in trying to please her. Ask for her hand yourself, and don't send a rival who loves her to do this for you.

PYRRHUS: Do you suppose that if I marry Hermione, Andromache will feel any pain?

PHOENIX: Does she still occupy your thoughts? What are her joy or spite to you? What still draws you toward her?

PYRRHUS: The truth is, Phoenix, that I haven't told her everything I had in mind to. I've only expressed part of what I feel. She still doesn't realize the kind of enemy I can be. I shall see her again. I want her to face me once more and make me hate her once and for all. Then, Phoenix, I shall really be able to humiliate her. Come along.

PHOENIX: Do you want me to urge you to go to her? Go then. Swear to her that you love her, give her cause to scorn you again.

PYRRHUS: You think that I am still trying to find excuses for her and can find satisfaction only in her?

PHOENIX: You're in love with her. That's all there is to it.

PYRRHUS: I—love her? Her? I love a woman who dares to hate me for my very kindness to her? She is without friends, without kin, without hope from anyone. I can take her son's life; perhaps I ought to. She comes from a foreign land. She is no better than a slave in Epirus. I was ready to give her, and her son, everything. I offer her my whole service and she thinks of me as her persecutor! No, I must be revenged. I've sworn it. I shall give her good cause to hate me this time by sacrificing her son. Let her tears never stop now! What name will she find to call me, I wonder, in her grief? What a scene awaits her today, Phoenix! She'll die of it. And I'll help her die. I shall stab her to the heart.

PHOENIX: Why announce your plan? Why test your weakness at this point?

PYRRHUS: I know what you mean. Overlook a lingering tenderness for her. You have seen the last burst of a dying passion. Come, I shall follow your counsel, Phoenix, from now on. What shall I do? Shall I yield up the boy? Must I see Hermione?

PHOENIX: See her, my lord, and repeat your vows of love. . . .

PYRRHUS: I will, Phoenix, I will. . . .

ACT III

(Orestes *and* Pylades.)

PYLADES: I hear angry words, my lord . . . but I don't hear your true voice. . . . My advice is—

ORESTES: I don't want advice. I will not be reasonable: to live means only to prolong my sufferings. I will take her with me or die. My decision is fixed; now I shall act.

PYLADES: Then I suppose you'll take her with you. Take her and my blessing. But just reflect one moment. You don't want Pyrrhus to know your plans. Be wary, be calm. Don't give your scheme away. You are at the court of Pyrrhus; Hermione is betrothed to him. She is the last person you should see in the state you are in now. And you are waiting for her!

ORESTES: No doubt you're right. I suppose, in my rage I hoped to find her with him. . . .

PYLADES: And then?

ORESTES: You think I'm mad. But do you think you could keep your calm if wounded as I have been? He says he will marry Hermione tomorrow, and will do me the honor of letting me give her to him! I'll kill him first. . . .

PYLADES: Are you accusing him of calculation? How do you know that the man, tormented by his own desires, is not as much to be pitied as you are?

ORESTES: I know him. He is flattered by my despair. Without me, without my love for her, he would have turned her down; until I came she did not interest him. He wants her in order to take her from me. And it was all settled. I had won Hermione. She would have left him forever. Her heart, advised both by love and by spite, asked only to be rejected by him once and for all to give itself to me. Pylades, she listened to me, spoke to me, pitied me. One word would have been enough.

PYLADES: You believe that?

ORESTES: I do believe it. Her anger had gone too far against him.

125

PYLADES: And I tell you, sir, Pyrrhus was never loved by her as much as he is right now. Do you think when he seemed ready to let you take her, he had no plan to detain her at the last moment? Take my advice: Instead of taking her with you, quit her forever. What joy can you have of a woman who will always hate you, and always regret a marriage nearly consummated?

ORESTES: Joy? I don't expect joy. And still I want to take her with me. Is Pyrrhus to have her? And am I to leave this land with nothing but unspent rage? You want me to quit her and to try to forget her? No, I can think of something better than that. I'll take her; keep her close to my own torment. I don't propose to be unhappy and alone. I don't want her to pity me. I want to make her fear me. May she be condemned to tears, and curse me as I have wanted to curse her.

PYLADES: Well, you will have been a most extraordinary envoy. Abduction and then rape. . . .

ORESTES: So be it. Suppose our cities applaud my deeds, do you think Hermione will be less indifferent to my tears? If I am scorned in Epirus, what is the admiration of all Greece worth? To be altogether frank, I must tell you this, too: I am sick to death of my unavailing innocence. I think there must be an unjust power and purpose which ignores the criminal and dogs the innocent. I am what the gods have made of me. And now I ought at least to merit their hatred, justify it, and enjoy the rewards of crime—I who have been punished, though innocent. But why should you thrust yourself in front of blows aimed only at me? You have been my friend and I think I have been an affliction to you. Go. Shun a man who is unhappy, abandoned, a man on the point of sinning. Pylades, pity has made you weak. Be strong. Go. Pyrrhus is surrendering the boy. Take him to the Greeks.

PYLADES: I'll go with you, my lord, and we'll seize Hermione. Should I become disloyal to you, fearing for myself? You can depend on me, Orestes. I am your friend and you are in love. Advise your men. Our ships are ready to sail. I know every crooked turn in the palace; it's right by the sea; tonight it will be easy to bring Hermione secretly to your ship.

ORESTES: My friend, I shall once again make use of you and of your friendship. I know you will forgive me as you have in the past, in thinking of all my misfortunes, which you alone pitied. Forgive me, a madman, who has lost everything he loves, who is hated by the world, and who hates himself. Who knows? It may be my turn some day. . . .

PYLADES: Hide your purpose, sir, that's what I want you to do. Don't reveal your plan before you act. Forget your griefs, forget even your love for Hermione until you have her secure. She's coming.

ORESTES: Go. Later, bring her to me. I'll be ready.

(*Exit* PYLADES, *enter* HERMIONE *and* CLEONE.)

ORESTES: Through my efforts, madam, you have conquered. I've talked with Pyrrhus, and he is going to marry you. The feast is being prepared.

HERMIONE: That's how the talk runs. And I've also been told you were looking for me, that you wanted to be the first to tell me this.

ORESTES: You feel no anger for him now?

HERMIONE: Who would have thought that finally Pyrrhus would show constancy of heart, that his passion would now be so strong, that he would turn to me when I was on the point of breaking with him? But perhaps he's only afraid of the Greeks. And is thinking, above all, of his own interests. Maybe even now he is less in my power than you are.

ORESTES: Let me reassure you, madam. Pyrrhus loves you. He is in your power now, which means you will do nothing to displease him.

HERMIONE: Sir, I can do nothing against fate. I was promised to Pyrrhus and can hardly take from him what I did not choose to give. You know very well that no princess is ever free to love. For a princess, the glory of obeying is all. I was about to go with you; you must realize that for your sake I almost strayed from my duty.

ORESTES: We all have the right to love. Your heart was yours to give. It's true I had hopes. Well, you have given your heart to Pyrrhus, but your aim was not to wound me. I accuse not you but fate. But why should I weary you with my complaint? You know your duty, and mine is to spare you the sad sight of me.

(*Exit* ORESTES.)

HERMIONE: Isn't it strange, Cleone, that he did not show anger?

CLEONE: Don't think he's not hurt. I pity him the more since he himself brought about his own undoing. Your marriage was again and again postponed. He spoke to Pyrrhus and the marriage is to take place.

HERMIONE: Do you think Pyrrhus made his decision out of fear? Of what would he have been afraid? What does he have to fear from a people who for ten long years fled from Hector, and who, so many times, were dismayed by Achilles' refusal to fight, and looked for refuge even in burning ships? Without the son of Achilles the Greeks would still be begging Helen of the still unpunished Trojans. No, Cleone, Pyrrhus is not at war with himself; this is no stratagem; what he does he wills. If he is to marry me, it can only be because he loves me. Let Orestes, if he likes, blame me for all his griefs. There is no entertainment in the fellow. He has nothing to offer me but tears. Pyrrhus again is mine! Cleone, you cannot know the extent of my happiness. For to know that you would have to know Pyrrhus better. You have heard of his deeds. But who can sum up all that he is? Intrepid, chivalrous, always victorious, charming, and in the end, even constant. What does he lack? Nothing.

CLEONE: Hide your joy, madam. Here comes your rival in tears.

HERMIONE: Am I not to be allowed one moment of happiness?

(*Enter* ANDROMACHE *and* CEPHISE.)

ANDROMACHE: You turn to go, at the sight of me! Madam, there must be some pleasure to you in seeing Hector's widow in tears? It is not jealousy which brings me here. I do not envy your conquest of the heart of Pyrrhus, your possession of his love. The only man I loved and must still love I saw struck down by a cruel hand. My passion for Hector still lives. It is with him still. What remains to me is his son. Some day perhaps you'll know what it is to love a son. I hope you shall never come to know how much pain that love can give, when all the good things of life have been taken from you, excepting only your son, and he is threatened. I remember how the Trojans after ten years of fighting threatened your mother, Helen; did you know that I persuaded Hector to protect her against his own people? You have some power over Pyrrhus, as I had over my husband. And there is no reason to fear his son, who in losing Hector lost everything. Let me hide the boy on some deserted island. What can I, his mother, teach him that you have to fear? All I can teach him is how to endure his lot.

HERMIONE: I truly sympathize. . . . But duty forbids me to interfere when the order comes from my father. It was my father who put Pyrrhus in his present mind. And who could speak more persuasively to Pyrrhus than you, madam? You have the power to move him, or had such power. Perhaps you can still get him to defend your son. I will support you if he does.

(*Exeunt* HERMIONE *and* CLEONE.)

ANDROMACHE: I expected to be refused, but not with such scorn, such cruelty, Cephise. I'll go to Pyrrhus myself.

CEPHISE: One glance from your eyes can still confound Hermione and Greece. And here is Pyrrhus himself, looking for you.

(*Enter* PYRRHUS *and* PHOENIX.)

PYRRHUS (*to* PHOENIX):   Where is the princess? Didn't you tell me I would find her here?

PHOENIX: I thought she was here.

ANDROMACHE (*to* CEPHISE):   You see how much power I have over him!

PYRRHUS: What's that she said? Did you hear, Phoenix?

ANDROMACHE: There is no one to whom I can turn.

PHOENIX: Come, my lord. You were looking for Hermione.

CEPHISE (*to* ANDROMACHE):   You must speak now, madam.

ANDROMACHE: He has promised the Greeks my son.

CEPHISE: But he hasn't surrendered the boy yet.

ANDROMACHE: He will, he will!

PYRRHUS (*to* PHOENIX):   Won't she even notice that we're here? The pride of that woman!

ANDROMACHE: I don't know what to say to him now.

PYRRHUS (*to* PHOENIX):   I shall now turn Hector's son over to our friends from Greece.

ANDROMACHE (*throwing herself at his feet*):   No, merciful, my lord! . . . But if I am mistaken about you, if you are not merciful, then at least surrender the boy's mother with him. You said you were my friend! Can you be entirely without pity? Am I never to be forgiven?

PYRRHUS: Phoenix will tell you I have given the Greeks my word.

ANDROMACHE: But you said you would face any peril to help me.

PYRRHUS: When I said that, I was blind. Now my eyes are open. And when I was blind, you could have had anything you asked. But you didn't know the right way to ask. Now it's too late.

ANDROMACHE: My lord, I was never sure that you were really attentive when I sighed, when I wept. Forgive the pride remaining to me, the last remnant of a great heritage; but I think you know that Andromache would never have cast herself at the feet of anyone but you.

PYRRHUS: I think you hate me and want to owe me nothing. And as for the boy, your son, I think you would love him less once you owed his safety to me. You have more hatred for me than for all of the Greeks put together. So content yourself with your hatred of me. Come, Phoenix.

ANDROMACHE: Then I must rejoin my husband.

CEPHISE: Madam!

ANDROMACHE: What can I say to him now? He knows my sufferings, for he it was who caused them. My lord, you see to what I am reduced; I saw my father dead, our palace ablaze, all my kin slaughtered, the body of my husband dragged in the dust around Troy; his only son and I were taken prisoner, meant for chains. But a son is everything! I breathe, I am alive, and sometimes I even find solace in the thought that fate exiled me here and not elsewhere; and I think, too, that my son is not so unlucky for all his bad luck, since if he must be a captive, he is your captive. I thought you would make of his prison a place of refuge. Priam when he kneeled was respected by Achilles; from the son of Achilles I expected more kindness! Oh, Hector, forgive my credulity! I was foolish enough to think your foe incapable of crime. Despite all he did, I believed he would be magnanimous. All I ask of Pyrrhus now is that he take me and your son to you, put an end to his hatred and our sufferings by mingling our ashes in the same dust.

PYRRHUS: Leave us, Phoenix. (*Exit* PHOENIX.) Madam, I can still save your son. And haven't you realized that the tears I cause you to shed are the very weapons you use against me? I should have come here more strongly armed. But, madam, look at me for one moment. See if I seem so severe a judge, or an enemy who wants to hurt you. Are you going to force me to betray you? For the sake of your son, let us not hate each other. Save your son. Now it is I who am begging you. And is it right that I should be the one to ask you to let him live? Must I cast myself at your feet for his sake? For the last time I implore you, save him. I am breaking my pledged word for you, conjuring up enemies against me. I will send Hermione back to Greece, placing on her brow instead of my crown an affront not to be endured. I will take you to the very temple where the wedding ceremony for her is being prepared and I myself will place upon your head the crown that was to be hers. I advise you not to scorn the offer I am making now. Your only choice is to die or to rule with me. My heart is tired of your ingratitude and wants to be sure of something. Uncertain expectation means threats, tears, still more sighs. I shall die if I lose you, but I shall die if I keep waiting for you to yield. Think of what I have said, while I am gone. I shall return to take you to the temple where your son will await you. And there I shall act, either as your lover or as your enemy. You shall be my wife, or the boy dies.

(*Exit* PYRRHUS.)

CEPHISE: As I predicted, despite all the Greeks do, you in the end will be the mistress of your fate.

ANDROMACHE: Alas! What can you be thinking? I have no other course now than to condemn my son to death.

CEPHISE: There is such a thing as being too faithful, too constant. There is such a thing as being virtuous to the point of crime. I think Hector himself would entreat you to be less firm.

ANDROMACHE: You want me to marry Pyrrhus?

CEPHISE: Yes, marry Pyrrhus for the sake of your son; otherwise Pyrrhus will surrender the boy to the Greeks. Do you think the ghosts of your family will blush for you? Do you think Hector himself would scorn a king who is ready to place you on the throne of your ancestors, and is prepared to fight against the very men he led against Troy? I ask you to think of this: Pyrrhus has forgotten that his father was Achilles.

ANDROMACHE: Because he does not remember, does that mean I must forget? Must I forget great Hector, gasping out his life, dragged, bloodying the dust, around the walls of Troy? Must I forget my father, face downward, skull split, his blood bubbling against the altar which his hands still clasped? Cephise, should not you, too, remember; Cephise, should you forget—that night when a whole people were thrust pell-mell into the lasting dark? See Pyrrhus, wide-eyed, finding his way to me by the light of our burning palace, hacking a path toward me over the bodies of my dead brothers, Pyrrhus smeared with blood and avid for still more slaughter. Hear again the shouts of the victors, hear the screams of the dying, choked by the fires or ripped by steel! And see Andromache lost in all that horror! This was how Pyrrhus first appeared to me; such are the deeds for which he won fame. Can you still ask me to be his bride? No, for

I shall never be his accomplice. My son and I will be his last victims. Hatred like mine can never be enslaved!

CEPHISE: Then your son must die. His life depends on you.

ANDROMACHE: And now I remember also, Cephise, how his life was entrusted to me. My son, my only joy, who so resembles Hector, the son Hector left me, the pledge of both our loves! Alas! I remember that day when Hector's courage made him seek out Achilles only to find death; he asked for his son and taking him in his arms said to me, "I do not know what fate awaits me, I leave you my son as a pledge of my love to you. If he loses me, I know that he will still have me, having you. If the memory of a happy marriage is dear to you, then show this boy how much you loved his father." And can I see the boy's blood spilled? Must all his ancestors perish with him? Barbarous king! Must Astyanax die because of me? If I hate you, he is innocent of hate. It was I who reproached you for your deeds; my boy doesn't even know what those deeds were. And yet it is he who must die. My son, the sword is at your throat. I can prevent its thrust. But can I? No, you shall not die. I'll find Pyrrhus. Cephise, you must find him for me.

CEPHISE: What am I to say to him?

ANDROMACHE: Tell him I love my son enough to . . . Do you think he has sworn to kill the boy? Could love make him so savage?

CEPHISE: Madam, you must conciliate him.

ANDROMACHE: Go, tell him . . .

CEPHISE: What shall I tell him?

ANDROMACHE: But do I have the right to promise Pyrrhus anything? Speak to me, husband, Trojans, father! My son, you have slain your mother.

CEPHISE: But what have you decided to do?

ANDROMACHE: To pray to Hector.

ACT IV

(ANDROMACHE, CEPHISE.)

CEPHISE: There can be no doubt of it, madam: it was your husband, it was Hector, who by a miracle caused you to yield. He wants Troy to rise again and his son to be its king. Pyrrhus gave his word that he would restore Troy. All he wanted from you was your trust. He will give you all you desire: allies, soldiers, a throne. Happy to have your heart, he is ready to give anything you ask. You shall rule over him and his people. Is this tyranny, and is such a tyrant to be hated? He is as nobly concerned to support your son against the Greeks as you are. Do you know what he has done? Anticipating reprisals from the angry Greeks, he has placed your son under the care of his best men, while he himself goes unguarded. The ceremony is now being prepared, and you have given your word.

ANDROMACHE: I shall be there, but first let us see my son.

CEPHISE: Why now? Henceforth you will be able to see him any time you like, heap gifts on him, and no one will count the number of times you kiss him. You will see your son grow up not as a slave but as the founder of a new line of kings!

ANDROMACHE: Cephise, I am going to see him for the last time.

CEPHISE: I don't understand. . . .

ANDROMACHE: Cephise, you are one person from whom I cannot hide my real feelings. You have always been loyal, but I did hope that you knew me better. Did you think that Andromache could be faithless, that she could betray a husband whose only remaining life is in her? Is that the love I promised him? But Hector's son must not die; I had to make sure of that. In marrying me Pyrrhus makes himself the boy's defender, and I shall trust him in the role he asked to have. I know that Pyrrhus is violent, but I think he is sincere, too, and I believe he will do even more than he promises. I rely now on the anger of the Greeks; their hatred will give Hector's son a father. Therefore I shall pledge my life to Pyrrhus, we shall exchange vows at the altar, and I shall tie him to my son by eternal bonds; then I shall take my own life, saving my virtue, and paying what I owe to Pyrrhus, to my son, to my husband, and to myself. This is the innocent stratagem my love has hit on. This is what my husband would have asked me to do. I will rejoin Hector and my ancestors.

CEPHISE: Alas!

ANDROMACHE: But you must live, Cephise, live for Hector's son. I entrust my boy to you. Keep alive the hope of a new Troy. Astyanax may still give our city many kings. Stay close to Pyrrhus and make him keep his vow to me. You may even speak of me to him and tell him that when I accepted his offer of marriage, it was not coldly. I did commit myself and my son to him, and he ought not, when I am gone, to resent me. In leaving him my son, at least I show him respect. Instruct the boy about his race, its heroes, teach him to model himself on their deeds. Tell him what they did, rather than what they were. Tell him of his father's courage, and sometimes speak to him of me, too. And may he never take it into his mind to avenge either me or Troy; I am leaving him to a master he must not fight against; let pride in his ancestors not stir him against Pyrrhus. . . . He is Hector's son, all that remains of Hector, and for this boy I shall have betrayed Hector and Pyrrhus, too, and sacrificed my life.

CEPHISE: Must you, madam?

ANDROMACHE: I do not want to see your tears. Remember, Cephise, my fate is in your keeping. Hermione is coming. Let us withdraw.

(*Exeunt* CEPHISE *and* ANDROMACHE. *Enter* HERMIONE *and* CLEONE.)

CLEONE: I marvel at your reserve. I don't understand it. You haven't said one word, madam. This latest cruelty of Pyrrhus seems hardly to interest you—and I have seen you tremble merely hearing Andromache's name spoken. If Pyrrhus simply honored her with a glance you were unable to endure it. Madam, he is on the point of marrying her! He is going to make her the vows and give her the crown pledged to you. And so far I have not heard you complain! You are far too calm, madam! Wouldn't it be better . . .

HERMIONE: Have you sent for Orestes?

CLEONE: He is on his way, madam; and he is coming to throw himself at your feet, ready to serve you without hope of reward. You do not have to fear that you will displease this man. Here he is.

(*Enter* ORESTES.)

ORESTES: Can it really be that for once you want to see Orestes as much as he wants to see you? Or am I flattering myself? Do your eyes look at me with pleasure at last? Now what is it you want?

HERMIONE: Sir, I want to know if you love me.

ORESTES: I think you are perfectly well informed of that. My oaths, my perjuries, my flight from you and return to you, my pleas, my wounds, and finally my despair are surely witnesses to my sincerity.

HERMIONE: If you avenge me, I shall believe you.

ORESTES: Madam, I shall. Let there be a new war like the war against Troy. You shall be Helen, I, Agamemnon. We shall bring on this land all the horrors of Troy.

HERMIONE: Not so fast, my lord. I don't want to avenge an insult to that point. My aim is not to exalt the insolence of an enemy. I would rather be less extreme, more prudent, and get the kind of revenge I want. Why risk everything in a battle which I am not certain to win? But if you are going to avenge me, you must do so within the hour and in your own person. If you delay I shall think that you are refusing my request. You must hurry to the temple, you must kill him. . . .

ORESTES: I must kill whom?

HERMIONE: Pyrrhus.

ORESTES: Pyrrhus!

HERMIONE: Can it be that you hesitate? Aren't you afraid that I'll tell you not to kill him? And do not tell me that he has rights of any kind. Whatever they are, I want to forget about them.

ORESTES: Never fear that, madam. Your appeal to me makes him a criminal. We shall be avenged, I agree. But not as you suggest. Let us be his enemies, not his murderers. Let's bring about his ruin honestly. Do you want me to bring the Greeks his head instead of his answer to them? I am the envoy of Greece. Do you want me to behave like an assassin? Let Greece decide his fate. Let him die publicly, hated by all. Remember, though, here he reigns, here he is master.

HERMIONE: Isn't it enough for you that I have sentenced him? Isn't it enough for you that I, offended, ask you that a victim be sacrificed to me? Is Hermione not worth the corpse of a tyrant? And isn't it enough for you, sir, that I hate this man, and that I once loved him? I will be frank. This traitor knew how to please me. Whether because of my feelings or because of my father matters not at all now. I want you to know this: Despite my pledges which he shamefully spurned, despite the horror of his treachery to me, as long as he lives you must fear that I may forgive him. As long as he lives you cannot be sure that I will continue to hate him. I am capable of loving him tomorrow, Orestes. I am asking you to kill him—today.

ORESTES: You want me to kill him? Otherwise you'll forgive him? So be it. If I must, I can. But it will take some planning. I must find a way to him. Remember I have only just come to Epirus. You expect me with one blow to overthrow an empire; and you give me a day, an hour, a single moment in which to achieve all that? I am to kill Pyrrhus in front of all his subjects? Very well, but I must consider how. Tonight. Yes. . . . Tonight I'll avenge you.

HERMIONE: Tonight? But by then he'll have married Andromache! The wedding takes place today. The temple is now being prepared, my shame is about to be made public, and his crime against me consummated. Nor is there reason for you to delay. Pyrrhus goes to the ceremony unguarded; he has ordered his men to watch over Hector's son. Pyrrhus is at your mercy, Orestes. He is careless of his life. Are you going to be more careful than he is? Arm my followers and your men. Pyrrhus has betrayed me, deceived you, and scorned us all. I am not now the only one who hates him. . . . Well, speak up. He can't escape you. Lead your men to the temple. The thing done by your men or by you—it does not matter. Return to me with his blood upon you and then tell me you love me.

ORESTES: But wait, madam, think. . . .

HERMIONE: I have thought, sir. I choose not to argue. I wanted to give you a chance to please me, but I see that you, as always, prefer losing to doing. Leave me. Boast of your constancy to others, and let me prepare my vengeance. I have offered my heart twice today; it has been refused twice. I shall go myself to the temple where you are afraid to go to win my favor. I'll be able to come close to my enemy and pierce that heart I could not move. Then, I'll pierce my own heart, and despite him, unite us in death. He deceived me, betrayed me. . . . All the same, Orestes, I think

I would rather die with him than live to love you.

ORESTES: He shall die by my hand. You shall owe his death to me.

HERMIONE: And I will be your reward. But go at once. See that our ships are ready to sail.

(*Exit* ORESTES.)

CLEONE: No good will come of this, madam. No good to you.

HERMIONE: The only thing I want now is revenge. But should I have left my revenge to someone else? Pyrrhus is not as guilty to Orestes as he is to me. I would hold the dagger more firmly, strike with it more surely—his blood would stain my hands and Pyrrhus would know that he had fallen victim to me. Will Orestes tell Pyrrhus that he was slain for my sake? Go, find Orestes, tell him to let the traitor know that my hatred, not the state's enmity, is the cause of his death. Hurry, Cleone. If he dies not knowing that I killed him, I shall have lost him and my vengeance, too.

CLEONE: But here is Pyrrhus himself.

HERMIONE: Find Orestes. Tell him not to act, Cleone, until he sees me again.

(*Enter* PYRRHUS *and* PHOENIX.)

PYRRHUS: I know you were not expecting me, but I had to see you, and I assure you my aim is not to justify what I am doing with false arguments. I don't argue well for what I don't believe, and I know my guilt toward you. Yes, I am about to marry Hector's widow, and I plan for her what I promised you. Do you know what I would say to you if I were not the kind of man I am? I would tell you that your father and mine on the battlefield of Troy promised each other that you and I would marry without asking you or me what we ourselves wished. But I won't insist on this point; I did agree to the marriage when it was proposed. My ambassadors came to your court and promised my heart to you; in so doing they spoke for me, or at least not against my wishes. You came to Epirus, but when I saw you at last it was with the eyes of a man who had already seen another beauty he could not resist. I tried to free myself from the spell cast on me by Andromache; I really wanted to be constant and keep the vows I had made you. I received you as if you were already my bride and believed until today that my word had more power over me than the violence in my heart. How wrong I was! Andromache has taken from me this heart she herself hates. She will break her sacred vows to Hector; I, my vows to you. So, madam, vent your rage against me. I have betrayed you, I have sacrificed you, not for happiness, no—only for sorrow, and yet I could not do otherwise. I think the rage you feel against me is just; express it and you will help me, too. Heap insults on me; madam, whatever you omit to say against me my own heart will supply.

HERMIONE: Perhaps you mean what you say, my lord, but for my part, I think you do not rate yourself highly enough; cannot you commit crimes without thinking yourself culpable? After all, is it right that a conqueror should be obliged to keep his promise to a woman? Inconstancy has its delights. Should you be denied them? I think you come here with no other aim than to show me the pleasure you feel in breaking your vows to me. Why should your pledged word or any duty tie you to me? Woo a princess of Greece, fall in love with a Trojan woman, break off with me, beg me for my hand again, and then turn once more from the daughter of Helen toward Hector's widow. Why not? Crown in turn the princess and the slave; sacrifice Troy to the Greeks and after that all Greece to Hector's son! Will not these actions show the world that you are master of your destiny, a hero not enslaved by his own words? Let people call you perjurer or traitor, why should that matter to you? In any case you will have pleased your wife. I think you came to inspect my pallor so as to be able to describe it to her when you hold her in your arms. I am sure you would like to see me following her chariot in tears, but, my lord, I think you have enjoyed yourself enough today. Why look for more conquests, you who already have so many hollow victories to your credit? Didn't you beat down Hector's old father and, watching him die in front of his grandchildren, stab him yet again with your sword to draw out every last drop of his old man's blood? Didn't you butcher all the Trojans? Didn't you kill Polyxena with your own hands in front of all the Greeks who begged you to spare her life? Why shouldn't I expose my breast to those blows which only you know how to give?

PYRRHUS: Madam, I well remember and regret what I did in avenging your mother. I could charge her with the blood I've spilled, but I've decided to forget what's past, and I thank heaven that you have no admiration for me; now I can be innocent and hope for happiness. My heart is too prone to blame itself; it should have known you better. I see that my guilt toward you was really insulting. I condemned myself for being inconstant, assuming that I was loved. You don't want me, I know that. Our hearts were never involved. You were going to yield to duty in marrying me, and I the same. Nothing forced you to love me.

HERMIONE: You think I never loved you. You can say that to me when for your sake I scorned all the princes of Greece! I came seeking you here in your land and I am still here despite your infidelity. I have told my Grecian warriors to keep your cruelty to me secret, and I waited for your heart to show itself again faithful to me. I believed that sooner or later you would yield me what you promised and what you owed. You were faithless, still I loved you. Think what I would have felt for you if you had been constant. At this very moment when your cruel lips calmly tell me my fate, I am forced to wonder, traitor, if I am not still in love with you. But, my lord, if the happiness of pleasing you has been granted her by heaven, then marry her. I consent, but do not force me to witness the ceremony. Perhaps these are the last words I shall ever say to you. Postpone the marriage for just one day. Tomorrow you can do what you will. But you do not answer me. I know what is in your mind. You are counting the minutes spent with me as minutes lost to you. You want to be with Andromache and can barely even speak to me. You are talking to her right now in your heart. Your eyes are looking for her. I shall not detain you. Go. Swear to her the vows you made me. Go, and profane the gods who have not forgotten the oaths that bound you to me. Take your heart which has forgotten me to the holy altar. Go, and go quickly; Hermione may be there before you.

(*Exit* HERMIONE.)

PHOENIX: My lord, I beg you not to overlook what an enraged woman who wants vengeance can do. She is strongly supported in Epirus. The Greeks sustain her. Orestes still loves her, and for her love might . . .

PYRRHUS: Andromache awaits me. Guard her son.

ACT V

HERMIONE: Lost! What have I done? What should I do now? I don't know whether what I feel is pleasure or pain. Aimless in this palace, I cannot now tell love from hate. . . . That cruel traitor! How coldly he dismissed me, not even feigning the slightest pity. Did he show any sign of grief or regret, for even one moment? Was I able to extract from him a single sigh? Deaf to my sighs, calm when I showed fear, did he even notice that I was on the point of weeping? And still I pity him. My weak heart pleads for him! The thought of the blow now threatening him makes me tremble. Ready to avenge myself, I am also ready to forgive! But no, I must be angry! Let the blow fall. Let Pyrrhus fall! I lose him; he, life. At this very moment my rage causes him to smile, and he calculates that the storm within me will end when I cry. He thinks me weak; he thinks, too, that with one hand I'll thrust aside the dagger my other hand holds. He thinks of me as I was; I was loving. He counts on that. Right now at the temple he thinks he will get what he desires. He has not tried to find out whether I desire his life or his death. And I have to decide which I prefer and without any help from him. Kill him, Orestes! Strike him again! I shall let Orestes act. Pyrrhus must die if for no other reason than that he could not foresee his death. . . . And because he forced me to want his death. Is it that I want? Did I really order it? Is the death of the man I love to be my act of love? My heart was so delighted in the past to talk about this prince's deeds, this prince to whom I was destined, before he planned the marriage which today he will not live to enjoy. . . . But did I come from so far, cross so many seas, only to bring about his ruin, only to assassinate him? May he, before he dies . . . (*Enter* CLEONE.) What have I done, Cleone? What have you come to tell me? . . . Tell me of Pyrrhus.

CLEONE: He is the proudest and most loving of men, at the height of his desires. I saw him go toward the temple, triumphantly leading his new conquest, his eyes lit with joy

140

and hope, drunk with the pleasure of seeing Andromache, who, for her part, did not seem to hear the joyous shouts of the crowd, but always remembering Troy, incapable of either loving or hating, seemed to obey the wishes of Pyrrhus without pleasure but without protest.

HERMIONE: But what of Pyrrhus? Has he consummated his crime? And, Cleone, did you see his face? Did you observe his expression? Did he seem to you calm in his great joy? Did he once look toward the palace? Tell me, did he notice you were there? And did he blush at seeing you? Did he admit his guilt, showing uneasiness, or was he proud to the end?

CLEONE: Madam, he sees no one, nothing. His fame and safety seem not to be in his mind any more than you are. He does not seem to know who is following him, so intent is he on his new adventure. He has placed his picked men around Hector's son, apparently thinking the boy the only one in danger. Phoenix himself is in charge of the boy and has taken him to a refuge far from the temple and the palace. The boy's safety seems to be the only thing that worries Pyrrhus.

HERMIONE: He must die. What did you learn from Orestes?

CLEONE: Orestes entered the temple with his Greek followers.

HERMIONE: So be it. Is he prepared to avenge me?

CLEONE: I cannot tell you that.

HERMIONE: You don't know? Why don't you know? Am I betrayed by Orestes, too?

CLEONE: Orestes worships you, but I think his mind, attacked by many scruples, counsels him to love, but also to think of honor. He respects Pyrrhus for his crown, because he is the son of Achilles, and I think he respects Pyrrhus for what he is. Orestes fears the Greeks; he fears the anger of the world. He would like to bring you the head of his rival, after having beaten him in battle, but he does not want to be called an assassin. . . . He entered the temple still undecided whether he had come there to be a spectator or a murderer.

HERMIONE: No, he'll do nothing, he'll watch the spectacle and not interfere with it. I know his lack of courage. He is afraid of death. Yes, death is what he fears. My mother armed all of Greece to fight for her. For ten long years she watched twenty kings die whom she had never before seen. All I am asking for is the death of a traitor, and I have entrusted a lover to avenge me. . . . He can do it without risk.

Am I to be guilty and not avenged? Come, I must myself act in my own cause. May cries of grief fill the temple, preventing the consummation of the ceremony. Perhaps the couple has already been joined; they shall not be united long! In the confusion I shall not pick or choose a victim. Everyone there, even Orestes, will seem to me like Pyrrhus. I will die but, at least, in dying, I will be avenged. And I shall not die alone.

(*Enter* ORESTES.)

ORESTES: Madam, the deed is done. You have been obeyed. Pyrrhus is dying now at the altar where he was to be married.

HERMIONE: He is dead!

ORESTES: He is dying, and my Greek followers have washed away the stain to your honor with his blood. I promised you the deed, and against my inclination, raced to the temple where my Greek followers were placed in the crowd around the altar. Pyrrhus recognized me at once, but never lost heart. His audacity seemed to be excited by my presence. Perhaps he thought that all of Greece, defied in her ambassador, would add a new luster to his marriage. Joyfully placing his crown on the brow of Andromache, he said: "I give you my crown and my vows of faith. I promise your son a father's friendship; I call the Gods to witness: this is my oath to the boy's mother. All his enemies are mine; I recognize him as the king of Troy." These words, applauded by the people of Epirus, caused our Greeks to answer with cries of rage. The faithless king was hemmed in on all sides. I could not get close enough to strike him. Everyone fought for the glory of being his killer. I saw him struggle for a while, all bloody, trying to escape their blows: finally, he fell by the altar. I pushed my way through the terrified crowd to reach you, my princess, and bring you to the port where soon we shall meet our friends smoking with the blood of him you wanted dead.

HERMIONE: What have they done?

ORESTES: You must forgive their impatience. I know you think they betrayed your vengeance. I know you wanted my own hand to strike the first blows, so that Pyrrhus, in dying, would know you ordered his death. But it was my fever which inspired them to act; I was the one who brought them to the temple, and you can take credit for the death their arms simply executed. You really were the one who struck Pyrrhus.

HERMIONE: Traitor, your crime belongs to you, only to you. Go, get your Greeks to admire your fury. Go! I disavow your deed. You fill me with horror. Savage, what have you done! You have cut off a glorious life. How could you, cruel Orestes, strike him today? And tell me this. Who made you the arbiter of his fate? Why did you assassinate him? What had he done? By what right did you act? Who told you to do this?

ORESTES: Didn't you yourself, madam, order his death?

HERMIONE: Did you have to believe the words of a woman mad with love? Couldn't you read my real thoughts behind my words? Didn't you notice that in my rage my heart always gave the lie to what I said? When I wished his death, did you have to agree? Shouldn't you have asked me to repeat my words at least a hundred times in order to be sure of their real meaning? Shouldn't you have come to consult me before the deed, come back to consult me again, or perhaps even have avoided me entirely? Why not leave my revenge to me? What brought you to this place, which I came to in order not to see you? Here is the result of your detested love: you brought me the unhappiness which pursues you. Your mission here made Pyrrhus incline to my rival, to his misfortune. At least I could have gone to him when he was in trouble. Perhaps he would have loved me. At least he pretended to love me once. Good-by. You can go. I shall stay in Epirus. I renounce Greece, Sparta, my whole family. I think of Greece now as the land which produced the monster you are.

(Exit HERMIONE.)

ORESTES: Is this Hermione I heard? For whom, then, did I make myself guilty of murder? She has called me a traitor and an assassin. Is it Pyrrhus who is dying? Am I still Orestes? Gods! I stifled my own reason. I murdered a king I honored. In one day I violated the rights of a sovereign, the duty of an envoy, and my duty to men. I also violated the sanctity of an altar. I have become a traitor and an assassin. And for whom did I make myself sin? For a thankless woman, who even if Pyrrhus had not died would have refused to see me again, a woman to whose hatred I am wedded! And when I did what she bid, she asked me to give her back his blood and his life. She loves him! And I am the monster! She will not let me see her again. And in fleeing me she leaves in payment all the ill I did to please her.

(*Enter* PYLADES.)

PYLADES: We must go quickly, my lord. Either we leave this palace now or we may never leave it. For the moment our Greek soldiers are holding the gateway, but they are being attacked on all sides by the people of Epirus, who support Andromache, treating her as their queen and us as their enemies. Andromache herself, who was so unyielding to Pyrrhus, now shows him all the devotion of a faithful widow, orders that he be avenged, and perhaps sees a chance now to get revenge for Troy and for Hector. Let us go before we are entirely surrounded. Our friends will join us; and while Hermione occupies the populace, we can slip out and save our skins.

ORESTES: Hermione? I'll go with her. I do not want to survive her sentence of me. Go! I committed the crime; I am ready to expiate it.

PYLADES: Hermione, my lord? I think you should forget her. You were always the instrument and the object of her anger. Are you going to attempt some new outrage in the land of the dead? Because she is dying, must you perish, too?

ORESTES: Did I hear that Hermione is dying?

PYLADES: You didn't know? Returning here, we met her racing madly toward the temple. She found Pyrrhus borne by his soldiers, anxious to avenge him. Doubtless she was overwhelmed by the sight of the dead hero. . . . From the gateway we saw her lean over the body of Pyrrhus, dagger in hand, raise her eyes to heaven, stab herself, and fall.

ORESTES: Praised be the Gods! My bad luck is even worse than I could have hoped for! Yes, I praise you, heavens above, for your perseverance, devoted without respite to my punishment. You have led me to the very height of sorrow. Your hatred is pleased by my grief. After all, what was I born for, except to be an instance of your anger, the paradigm of all those who are unhappy? Well, I can die content that my fate is perfect. Where are the two lovers? To consummate my joy, I must drown myself in their blood and in mine; I would like to see the two of them even as I die; let the three hearts which could not beat to the same rhythm be reunited. The thickness of night surrounds me suddenly. From whence did all this blackness come? Why do I shudder? What horror seizes me? May heaven be praised. I see around me such pools of blood. . . .

PYLADES: My lord!

ORESTES: Pyrrhus, must I meet you again? Must I find,

no matter where, a rival whom I hate? Pierced by so many dagger blows, how can you still be alive? Wait, wait! Here is the blow I kept for you. But what do I see now? Hermione embraces him. She arrives just in time to ward off the blow that would really kill him. What hatred for me there is in her glance! What are those demons and serpents that follow in her train? Daughters of Hell, are your hands ready to seize me? Is it because of me that those serpents in your hair hiss with hate? Have you come to take me off to eternal night? Come then, Orestes yields to you, Furies. Only one thing I ask: do not substitute yourselves for Hermione. She knows how to torture me better than you can. I bring her my heart. Let her devour it!

PYLADES: He has lost his senses. Time presses. Let us use to best advantage this moment of his transport. Now that his rage, like his reason, is subdued, let us try to save him.

BEAUMARCHAIS: *The Barber of Seville*

PIERRE-AUGUSTIN CARON DE BEAUMARCHAIS
(1732–1799)

Like Molière and Voltaire before him and Courteline after him, Beaumarchais chose his own surname; he also gave it aristocratic coinage by prefacing it with a "de," which he dropped after the French Revolution. His father was André Caron, a watchmaker to the king, with a modest establishment in the Rue St. Denis, slightly north of the Île de la Cité in Paris. (Today, just under a mile to the east, and running parallel, is the Boulevard Beaumarchais.) Pierre Caron attended boarding school each morning, without distinguishing himself, and took religious instruction each afternoon, without becoming particularly pious. At thirteen, he was confirmed and left school to work for his father. Occasionally, he sold watches without telling his father; he also ran about with a fast crowd of youngsters during working hours and in the evening, and while at his watchmaker's bench taught himself music: the harp, the violin, and the flute. His father, after three years, was goaded into banishing him from the house and business, and let him return only after Pierre signed a six-point treaty of good behavior.

From then on, he rallied himself and settled down to study (in his own time) the great French writers, mathematics, and mechanics. When he was twenty-one, he developed a new, simplified watch escapement; he showed it to a rival watchmaker named Lepaute who admired it so much that he appropriated the idea. Pierre submitted this case of infraction to the Royal Academy of Sciences, and won. Following the public interest that the case aroused, he sought and gained the title Watchmaker to the King, and confirmed his reputation for ingenuity by constructing "the smallest watch ever made," which he set in a ring and sold to Mme. de Pompadour.

Not long after this he met the young wife of an old man, Francquet, a Controller of the Royal Kitchen, or rather, she introduced herself to him by dropping her watch and taking it to him for repair. She was rapidly smitten by Caron's good looks and confident presence and not only took him to her husband, but persuaded that gentleman to pass on his duties and title to the young watchmaker. In January 1756 old Francquet died and ten months later, when the Francquet estate had been settled on the widow, with the assistance of Beaumarchais and his lawyer, he married her and moved into her luxurious, well-servanted quarters in Versailles, near the palace. From now on, he added "de Beaumarchais" to his name and proceeded to step lightly in court circles.

The following year his wife contracted typhus and died suddenly. Beaumarchais had to return his wife's property to her first husband's relatives, but managed to retain his court appointment by teaching music to the two daughters of Louis XV. He combined this work with a high-sounding position, the duties of which were to prosecute rabbit poachers on the king's preserves. In the few cases of prosecution that he undertook, Beaumarchais showed formidable skill in law and oratory, which in France are perhaps the same thing. His official functions, however, did not prevent him from enjoying liaisons with several ladies, from indulging in duels (in one he killed a knight, in another he wounded a marquis), and from provoking envy at court.

In 1764 he went to Spain to shame a grandee who had "compromised" one of his two sisters living in Madrid. The shaming over, he stayed in Spain for a further eleven months, making the cultural rounds and meeting Iberian ladies, one of whom he presented to the Spanish king, Charles III, with beneficial results all around.

Back in Paris, he wrote his first play, *Eugenia,* a melodramatic comedy of court intrigue, which took him seven versions to get right. It was performed in 1767 at the Théâtre-Français and caused some bad feeling which, together with sharply worded whispers that were circulated by other members of court society, alienated him from Louis XV.

In April 1768 he married a young widow, who eight months later gave birth to a son. Beaumarchais then went to work on his second play, *The Two Friends,* or *The Merchant of Lyon,* which was produced and generally disapproved of in 1770. On the poster outside the theater, a disappointed spectator wrote under the title *The Two Friends:* "by a man who has none."

In November of that same year his second wife died, and his son survived her by only two years. During this wrecking of his personal life, Beaumarchais had been polishing the draft of a comic opera, *The Barber of Seville.* By 1774 the play was ready for staging, but during that year Beaumarchais engaged in a drawn-out and complicated litigation, which began when he attempted to recover some money owed to him and ended in name-slinging and a public scandal with many prominent people maligned. Beaumarchais lost, was deprived of his civil rights, and, in spite of the sympathy of such men as Voltaire and Rousseau, decided to go to England and let a few tempers cool off.

By carrying out certain duties for Louis XV and his grandson and successor, Louis XVI—principally by suppressing certain libels being written about the French royal family in England—Beaumarchais vindicated himself and returned to France. In 1775 *The Barber*, which in its musical form had been rejected by the Italian Players, was mounted as a five-act play. But the audience grew restless during the fifth act; Beaumarchais thereupon cut, scraped, sharpened, and generally improved the text, reducing it to four acts. "I removed," he said, "the fifth wheel from the chariot." Three days later, the second performance was a triumph. There were fewer digs, but the ones left penetrated deeper.

Beaumarchais then took off again for England, to pay off the ambisexual Chevalier d'Eon, who was threatening to publish libels against the king, and sullying the fair name of France by appearing alternately in men's and women's clothes. While in England, Beaumarchais conspired with various American representatives and, for the sake of France's sugar islands, extracted one million francs from Louis XVI to assist the revolutionaries in the then British colony. In the year that followed, he set up a trading company of his own and sent munitions and materials to the value of six million francs to America, most of which was never repaid. A warship that he had outfitted especially to convoy the goods across the Atlantic was captured by the British. Altogether he lost about four million francs on his American dealings. At the same time—his credit was still good—he was making regular loans to a number of friends, including an impoverished prince and princess who understandably addressed him as BONmarchais.

His next enterprise was to set up a printing firm to publish the complete works of Voltaire in a luxury edition of seventy-two volumes. This took him a number of years, but the complete works eventually appeared, at a further, enormous loss to Beaumarchais.

In 1781 *The Marriage of Figaro*, Beaumarchais's successor to *The Barber*, was accepted by the Théâtre-Français, but Louis XVI, who had heard a reading of the play and hated it, canceled the performance thirty minutes before the curtain was due to rise. The play was not performed for another three years; then it was a rousing success. Mozart started to write his opera based on it that same year.

Beaumarchais's third marriage, to a Mlle. Villermawlaz (they already had a daughter aged eight), came in the middle of more court cases, this time against him, for slander, but the prosecution's arguments were obviously based on malice, and Beaumarchais won. Somehow surviving more unprofitable business deals, he came intact through the French Revolution, which began in 1789; he was sympathetic to its aims and took part in it eagerly as an adviser to the Commune, but as a professed former nobleman he was suspect: his house was raided several times; he was imprisoned and freed and finally fled to England, where a businessman to whom he owed money had him sent to debtors' prison.

In his cell he wrote *Six Epochs, the Most Painful Nine Months of My Life,* which he smuggled out; it was published in France and helped to raise enough money to get him out of jail. He returned home and almost immediately was sent abroad again as a Commissioner of the Republic; while he was out of the country, his enemies managed to get him branded as an *émigré,* an enemy of the regime, who had fled out of the country. Seals were placed on his property six times and six times they were removed. He was "investigated" five times and five times he was cleared, largely owing to the efforts of his wife, who had remained in France with their daughter. During this time, Beaumarchais traveled penuriously through England, Holland, and northern Germany. In 1796 the "erasure" of his name as an *émigré,* once and for all, meant that he could come back to Paris and join his wife and daughter and his daughter's fiancé.

At sixty-four, although he was slower on his feet and with his tongue, and although he was now deaf enough to need an ear trumpet, Beaumarchais settled into something like his old, hectic life, helping to produce his plays, writing letters on dozens of topics to dozens of people, including members of the American Congress which had failed to recognize its old debts to him. His last play had been *The Guilty Mother,* which featured the same characters as *The Marriage,* but now older, wiser, more serious and more dull. It had flopped in 1792 on its first production, but was revived several times with varying receptions.

In the midst of this new whirl of activities, on the night of 17-18 May 1799, Beaumarchais died in his bed of an apoplectic stroke, at the age of sixty-seven. According to his friend Gudin, his face was set in a peaceful half-smile.

A LIST OF BEAUMARCHAIS'S PLAYS:

Eugenia (1766); *The Two Friends* (1770); *The Barber of Seville* (1775); *The Marriage of Figaro* (1781); *Tarare,* an opera (1785); *The Guilty Mother* (1786).

SUGGESTIONS FOR FURTHER READING ON BEAUMARCHAIS:

Dalsemé, René. *Beaumarchais.* Trans. by Hannaford Bennett. New York: G. P. Putnam's Sons, 1929.

Hall, Evelyn Beatrice. *The Friends of Voltaire.* New York: G. P. Putnam's Sons, 1907.

Kite, Elizabeth. *Beaumarchais and the War of American Independence.* Boston: Richard G. Badger (The Gorham Press), 1918.

de Loménie, Louis Leonard. *Beaumarchais and His Times.* Trans. by Henry S. Edwards. New York: Harper's, 1857.

Newman, Ernest. *Great Operas,* Vol. I, pp. 34-74, *The Barber of Seville.* New York: Random House, Inc. (Vintage Books, Inc.), 1958.

Rivers, John. *Figaro, The Life of Beaumarchais.* London: Hutchinson, 1922.

IN FRENCH ONLY:

Bailly, Auguste. *Beaumarchais.* Paris: Fayard, 1945.

Latzarus, Louis. *Beaumarchais.* Paris: Plon, 1930.

Le Barbier de Sèville and *Le Mariage de Figaro,* texts with notes, published in the Classiques Larousse edition.

A LETTER FROM
BEAUMARCHAIS TO THE READER [1]

The author, modestly dressed, bows, and presents his play to the reader.

Sir:

I have the honor to offer you a new little work of my own creation. I would like to catch you in one of those happy moments when you are free from cares, content with your health, your business, your mistress, your dinner, your stomach, and you can delight for a moment in reading my *Barber of Seville;* for only under these conditions will you be an amusable man and an indulgent reader.

But if some accident has impaired your health; if your business is not going well; if your beauty has been false to her promises; if your dinner was bad, or your digestion difficult, pray put my *Barber* to one side; the moment is not right for it: examine your accounts, study your adversary's brief, reread that treacherous, secret note addressed to your Rose, or peruse Tissot's masterpieces [2] on temperance and reflect on their political, economic, dietetic, philosophic, or moral values. . . .

Beaumarchais' Dramatic Theories

. . . I have been heartily assured that when an author emerged broken-backed but triumphant in the theater, all that he needed, sir, was to be approved by you and torn to pieces by a few newspapers in order to have won every literary laurel. Thus my glory is assured if you are good enough to grant me the laurels of your approval, for I am given to understand that a few reviewers will not refuse me their abuse.

[1] From "A Temperate Letter on the Failure and the Criticism of *The Barber of Seville,*" written as a prefatory note to the play in its first published edition, 1775. *Ed.*

[2] Tissot was a contemporary of Beaumarchais and wrote popularized books on medicine. *Ed.*

Already one of them, employed by *Bouillon*,[3] has honored me by assuring his subscribers that my play was without plan, without unity, without characters, void of intrigue, and bereft of comedy.

Another reviewer, who is even more naïve, gave a frank account of my play, then added to his critical laurel this flattering praise of my person: "The reputation of M. Beaumarchais has indeed sunk, and honest people are convinced at last that once the peacock's feathers are plucked from him, only a nasty, black, brazen, voracious crow will remain. . . ."

Vicissitudes of "The Barber" and of Theater in General

. . . That is how men are: if you are successful, they welcome you, support you, pet you, they are honored to know you; but beware of stumbling in your career: at the slightest setback, my dear friends, remember that there *are* no more friends.

And that is exactly what happened to us the day after that saddest of opening nights. You would have seen the *Barber's* faint friends scatter, hide their faces, or flee; the women, who are normally so brave and protective, sink into their hoods up to their feathered hairdos and lower their eyes in confusion; the men run around to each other, publicly apologizing for the good things they had said about my play, and blaming my accursed first reading for all the false pleasures they had tasted. It was a case of total desertion, absolute abandonment.

Some men turned their eyes to the left as I passed on the right, affecting not to see me. Others with more courage—first making very sure that no one was watching—dragged me into a corner and said: "How did you manage to put that illusion over on us? For you must agree, my friend, that your play is the flattest platitude in the world."

"Alas, gentlemen, I read my platitude quite as flatly as I wrote it, but in the name of your goodness in speaking to me again after my disgrace, and to uphold your second judgment, do not allow the play to be repeated on the stage; for if, by mischance, it were played as I read it, you would perhaps be deluded anew, and you would be angry at me in no longer knowing when you were right and when wrong. God forbid that."

Not one of them believed me. They let the play be performed again, and for once I was a prophet in my own coun-

---

[3] A contemporary journal. *Ed.*

try. Poor Figaro, beaten down by the muttering of the league of critics and almost buried on Friday,[4] did not behave like Candide: my hero took heart and on Sunday he rose again. And his vitality could not be weakened by fasting through an entire Lent or by the hardships of seventeen public performances. But who knows how long this will last? Our nation is so fickle and giddy that I would not want to swear that people will even be aware of Figaro in five or six centuries.

Plays, gentlemen, are to their authors what children are to women: they cost more pain than they give pleasure. Follow their careers: no sooner do they see the light of day than a swollen style is detected and hot censorship has to be applied; some of them have never recovered from it. Instead of treating them gently, the cruel pit bullies them and knocks them down. And often, while the actor is supposed to be cradling them, he injures them. Lose sight of them for an instant and you find them—alas!—lying about all over the place, tattered and disfigured, with sections nibbled out of them, and covered with criticisms. If they escape all these ills and illuminate the world for one moment, they are overtaken by the most deadly fate of all —oblivion. They sink into the abyss and are lost forever in the vast tomb of dead books. . . .

What Criticism Should Be—What It Is

Let us see, if you will, whether the reporter from *Bouillon* observed in his review the friendly nature and especially the candor which are the marks of good criticism.

"The play is a farce," he said.

So let us ignore all its qualities. The bad name a foreign cook gives to French stews does not change their flavor; it is only when they fall into his hands that the stews lose their taste. Let us analyze what *Bouillon* calls farce.

"The play," he said, "has no plan."

Is it because the plan is too simple that it escapes the wisdom of this adolescent reviewer?

An amorous old man intends to marry his ward on the following day; a young man who is more clever forestalls him, and on that very day captures the girl in the guardian's house, right under his nose, and makes her his wife. There you have the foundation on which a comedy, a tragedy, a drama, or an opera could be built with equal success. Is Molière's *Miser* anything else? Or [Racine's] *Mithridates*?

[4] Opening night, February 23, 1775. *Ed.*

The classification of a play, like that of any other work, depends less on its plot than on the characters who put that plot into action.

As for me, all I wanted to build on this foundation was a lighthearted, amusing play, an intrigue. I had no need of a black villain; it was enough for my schemer to be a comic, happy-go-lucky fellow who laughs equally at the success and failure of his enterprises. Thus the work, instead of developing as a serious drama, turned into a very gay comedy. And because the guardian is a little less stupid than those who are usually deceived in the theater, the play has more action and, more important, the schemers need to be more resourceful.

Reply to Some Objections

"The play is a series of improbabilities," continues this journalist, who is an accredited and privileged writer for *Bouillon.*

"Improbabilities!" . . . Let us look into them, just for enjoyment.

His Excellency Count Almaviva, whose intimate friend I am honored to have been for a long time, is a young lord, or rather, was, for age and responsible duties have since transformed him into a very grave man, such as I have become myself. His Excellency was, then, a young Spanish lord, as vital and passionate as all the lovers of his nation, which is thought to be cold but is merely lazy.

He had been secretly pursuing a beautiful lady whom he had caught a glimpse of in Madrid and whose guardian had swiftly brought her home. One morning, as he was walking beneath her windows, in Seville, where he had been trying for a week to attract her attention, chance brought Figaro the barber to the same spot.

"Ah, chance," my critic will say, "and if chance had not brought the barber to that spot on that day, what would become of the play?"

"It would have begun, my friend, at some other time."

"Impossible. According to you, the guardian was getting married the next day."

"Then there wouldn't be any play; or if there had, it would have been different. Is a thing improbable because it could have happened otherwise? . . ."

. . . Chance, then, brings Figaro the barber to this same spot; he is a good talker, a bad poet, a daring musician, a guitar-slapper, and the count's former valet. He is established now in Seville, is equally successful with beards, romances, and marriages, and wields the barber's lancet as adroitly as the druggist's pump. He is the terror of husbands, the darling of wives, and exactly the man we were looking for. Investigation shows that what we call passion is nothing but desire inflamed by obstacles; thus our young lover might have been content merely to dream about a beautiful woman if he had met her in society, but because she was imprisoned and it was impossible for him to marry her— he fell in love.

But to recite the entire play to you here, sir, would be to question your wisdom. . . . You will certainly see that "all the troubles the count has to go to" are *not* "simply to allow him to put back a letter," which is only a property in the plot. He is trying to break into a stronghold defended by a vigilant, suspicious old guardian; to fool a man who catches on to every maneuver right away, and obliges his enemy to operate rather slowly so as not to be defeated on the first try.

And when you realize that the whole idea of the denouement is that the guardian has locked his door and given his passkey to Bazile, so that only the two of them can enter for the marriage later, you can only be astonished that such an honest critic toys with his reader's trust, or is mistaken, when he writes: "The count takes the trouble to reach the balcony with Figaro by climbing a ladder, although the door is not locked."

And when, finally, you see the unfortunate guardian who was betrayed by his very precautions, compelled to sign the count's marriage contract and to sanction what he was not able to prevent—you will leave it to the critic to decide this question: Was that guardian an "imbecile" for not understanding an intrigue that was completely hidden from him, when the critic himself, from whom nothing was hidden, was not able to understand any better?

If the critic *had* followed the plot would he still have neglected all the good things in the work?

I can forgive him for not noticing how the first act brightly introduces and displays the characters.

I am sympathetic that he found no trace of comedy in the big second-act scene where the girl manages to mislead her mistrustful, angry guardian about a letter delivered in his presence, and to make him ask pardon on his knees for his suspicions.

I am not at all surprised that he did not say a single word about the third-act scene of Bazile's stupefaction, which

seemed to be such a novelty in the theater and entertained
so many spectators.

I will even overlook his failure to suspect that the author
had deliberately plunged into a last-act predicament, by
having the ward confess to her guardian that the count had
stolen the key, a predicament that the author unscrambles
in two words, and for a playful moment gives his audience
something new to worry about.

I accept his failure to see that although this is one of
the liveliest plays in the theater, it was written without the
least equivocation, without one thought, one single word
which would alarm even the modesty of the nobility in their
enclosed boxes.[5] Nevertheless, all this is something of a
feat, sir, in a century when respectability has become almost
as hypocritical as morals have become relaxed. I grant your
point. Naturally, none of this is worth the attention of such an
important critic.

But how is it that he could not admire something that
made every virtuous man in the audience spill tears of
tenderness and pleasure? I mean the filial piety of Figaro,
who could not forget his mother: "You know this guardian
then?" the count says to him in the first act. "Like my own
mother," Figaro replies. A miser would have said: "Like my
pockets." A dandy would have answered: "Like myself." An
ambitious man: "Like the road to Versailles." And the journalist from *Bouillon:* "Like my bookseller"—Each man's comparisons centering on the object that interests him most.

"Like my own mother," said the tender and respectful son.

Let us pass silently over his sharp reproach to the young
lady, for having "all the faults of a badly bred girl." True,
he does try to avoid stating the consequences of the imputa-
tion by blaming it on others: he employs that banal, impersonal phrase—as if somebody else had written it—"One
finds in the young lady," etc. One finds!

What did he want her to do? Instead of yielding to a very
likable young lover who proves to be a titled man of quality,
should our charming young lady marry the gouty old doctor?
A fine future he has planned for her! And because she is
not of Monsieur's opinion, she has "all the faults of a
badly bred girl!"

Some knowing people noticed that I had fallen into the
mistake of criticizing and poking fun at French customs in
a play set in Seville, when, for the sake of consistency, I

[5] *Petites loges,* boxes behind the orchestra from which one could
observe without being observed. *Ed.*

should have concentrated on Spanish customs. They are right: I had thought about that and to bring the believability nearer perfection, I had at first resolved to write the play and have it performed in the Spanish language; but a man of taste pointed out to me that it would perhaps lose a little of its gaiety for the Parisian public, which made me decide to write it in French. You can see that I made a multitude of sacrifices for the sake of gaiety, but did not succeed in loosening the frown on the face of *Bouillon*'s reviewer.

Another amateur [playwright] seized on a moment when many people were in the lobby to reproach me in the gravest tone because my play resembled *You Can't Think of Everything*.[6]

"Resemble, sir! I maintain that my play IS *You Can't Think of Everything*."

"How is that?"

"Well, sir, you haven't yet thought of everything in my play."

The amateur stopped short and everyone laughed much more to think that the man who reproached me about *You Can't Think of Everything* is a man who has never thought of a single thing.

A few days after (this is more serious), at the house of a lady who was indisposed, a solemn gentleman—black suit, hair on end, the head of his cane forming a crow's beak which brushed the lady's hand—courteously offered several misgivings concerning the accuracy of the arrows which I let fly at doctors.

"Sir," I said to him, "are you a friend of one of them? I should be deeply sorry if a mere flippant remark . . ."

"Not at all: I see that you don't know me; I never take anyone's side; I am speaking now on behalf of medical practitioners in general."

I tried hard to imagine who this man might be. "In the case of humor," I added, "you know, sir, that people never ask if the story is true, only if it is good."

"Do you think you will fare any better in this discussion than you did in the earlier ones?"

"Admirably put, Doctor," said the lady. "What a monster he is! Daring to speak so badly of us. Let us join forces."

At the word "doctor," I knew that she was speaking to her private physician.

"It is true, dear lady and sir," I replied modestly, "that I have permitted myself a few trifling errors, for the lighter

6 Comic opera by Sedaine and Monsigny. *Ed.*

they are, the less grave their consequences. After all, there are two powerful groups whose influence is felt throughout the universe and who share the world—and nobody can dethrone them, not even the envious among us: beautiful women will always reign through pleasure and doctors through pain; and radiant health will let us conquer love, just as sickness will make us surrender to medicine. . . ."

Conclusion

But I am drifting too far from my subject. Let us return to *The Barber of Seville*. Or on second thoughts, sir, let us not return. Enough has been said about a romp. Without realizing it, I could fall into the error for which we Frenchmen are rightly reproached: of always writing frivolous verses about major concerns and huge dissertations on minor ones.

I am, sir, Your most respectful, humble and obedient servant,

The Author.

Translated by Joyce Bermel

THE BARBER OF SEVILLE

OR THE USELESS PRECAUTION

by Pierre-Augustin Caron de Beaumarchais

FIRST PERFORMED AT THE COMÉDIE-FRANÇAISE
ON FEBRUARY 23, 1775

Translated by Albert Bermel

CHARACTERS

COUNT ALMAVIVA, a Spanish grandee
DR. BARTHOLO, guardian of Rosine
ROSINE, young lady of noble birth, ward of Bartholo
FIGARO, a barber, former valet of Almaviva
DON BAZILE, an organist, Rosine's singing teacher
PUBERTY (LA JEUNESSE), an old servant of Bartholo
LIVELY (L'ÉVEILLÉ), a young servant of Bartholo
A NOTARY
AN ALCALDE or Spanish magistrate
POLICEMEN and other SERVANTS

ACT I

(The stage represents a street in Seville, with grilled windows; THE COUNT is alone, pacing to and fro, dressed in a flowing brown cloak and low-brimmed hat. He takes out his watch.)

COUNT: The day is advancing more slowly than I thought. She usually appears at the window much later than this. Never mind; it is better to be too early than to miss that moment of seeing her. If one of my friends at the court guessed that I was a hundred leagues away from Madrid and spending my mornings under the windows of a woman I have never spoken to, he would take me for a romantic of Queen Isabella's time.[1] Well, why not? Every man pursues his own happiness. Mine is in the heart of Rosine. But why follow a woman as far as Seville, when Madrid and the court offer such a selection of easy pleasures? Ah, that is exactly why I ran away. I am bored with these unending conquests of women whose motives are self-interest, social climbing, or vanity. It is sweet to be loved for oneself. And if I could be sure that this disguise—damn, an intruder.

(FIGARO comes in, wearing a guitar, attached bandolier-fashion by a wide ribbon. He has a pencil and paper in his hand.)

FIGARO *(singing)*:

> Let us not pine.
> It eats us alive.
> But the fire of a good wine
> Helps us revive.
> Without wine, a man
> Is a meaningless loon.

[1] Late fifteenth century. Isabella the Catholic lived from 1451 to 1504. She sponsored Columbus' voyage in 1492.

> He lives out a gray span
> And dies off too soon.

That's not bad. Up to now. What next?

> And dies off too soon . . .
> Yes, good wine and idleness
> Fight for my heart . . .

No, they don't fight, they rule there together, peacefully:

> *Reign* in my heart.

Can you say "reign"? I don't see why not. When you're writing a comic opera, you can't stop to look at every word. Nowadays, if a thing isn't worth saying, you sing it.

> Yes, good wine and idleness
> Reign in my heart. . . .

I'd like to end with something beautiful, brilliant, glittering, something with a kick in it. (*He goes down on one knee and writes as he sings.*)

> Reign in my heart.
> If one takes my tenderness,
> The other gives me happiness.

No, no. That's flat. That's not it. I need a clash, an antithesis:

> If one is my mistress
> The other . . .

Yes, perfect:

> The other's my tart.

Well done, Figaro. (*He writes as he sings.*)

> Yes, good wine and idleness
> Reign in my heart.
> If one is my mistress,
> The other's my tart.
> The other's my tart.
> The other's my tart.

Just wait until there's an orchestra behind it, and I'll show you critics if I don't know what I'm talking about. (*He sees the* COUNT.) I've seen that reverend somewhere before. (*He stands up.*)

COUNT (*aside*):   I'm sure I know that man.

FIGARO: No, he isn't a reverend. That haughtiness, that nobility . . .

COUNT: That grotesque shape . . .

FIGARO: I wasn't wrong: it's Count Almaviva.

COUNT: I believe it's that rogue Figaro.

FIGARO: It certainly is, my lord.

COUNT: Fool, if you say one word . . .

FIGARO: It's you all right, my lord. I recognized you. You always honored me with that kind of friendly greeting.

COUNT: I can't say I recognized you. Look how fat and flabby you are. . . .

FIGARO: What do you expect, sir? That's poverty for you.

COUNT: Poor creature. What are you doing in Seville? I gave you references for a job with the government.

FIGARO: I took that job, and don't think I'm not grateful, my lord.

COUNT: Call me Lindor. Can't you see by my disguise that I don't want to be known?

FIGARO: I'll go away.

COUNT: No, stay here. I am waiting for something, and two men standing and talking look less suspicious than one walking about on his own. So pretend we're talking. Now, about the job . . .

FIGARO: The minister took Your Excellency's recommendation into account and, without hesitation, made me assistant medicine-mixer.

COUNT: For all army hospitals?

FIGARO: No, for all the royal stud farms in Andalusia.

COUNT (*laughing*):   A fine beginning.

FIGARO: It wasn't bad. I was in charge of bandages and drugs, and I often sold good horse medicine to men. . . .

COUNT: Which killed the king's subjects.

FIGARO: Ah, there's no universal remedy. But sometimes they got over it. They're tough people in Galicia, Catalonia, and Auvergnat.

COUNT: Why did you give it up?

FIGARO: It gave me up. Someone told the government what I was up to:

"Crooked-fingered Envy, with pale and livid hue . . ."

COUNT: Spare me that. Do you write poetry too? I saw

you kneeling and scribbling and singing over there before.

FIGARO: That was exactly my trouble. When someone reported to the minister that I was composing bouquets of verse—and rather well, if I say so myself—dedicated to Chloris,[2] and that I was sending puzzles and madrigals to the newspapers, and then when he learned that I was suddenly in print, he took a dim view of it and made me give up my job, on the pretext that literature and business don't go together.

COUNT: Good reasoning. But couldn't you make him understand?

FIGARO: I thought it was better for him to forget about me. A great man is doing you enough good when he isn't doing you harm.

COUNT: You're not telling me everything. When you were in my employ, you were a pretty slovenly character.

FIGARO: Well, my lord, you can't expect a poor man to be perfect.

COUNT: Lazy, disorganized . . .

FIGARO: A servant is expected to be as virtuous as his master, my lord, but do you know many masters who are fit to be good servants?

COUNT (laughing):   A sharp point. And so you retired to this city?

FIGARO: No, not straight away.

COUNT (stopping him):   One moment. I thought she was . . . Keep talking. I am still listening.

FIGARO: Back in Madrid, I thought I'd try my literary talents out again, and the theater seemed to be the most likely field of honor. . . .

COUNT: God save us!

FIGARO (during this speech, the COUNT watches the blind of ROSINE's window):   I can't think why I wasn't the greatest success; I filled the orchestra with solid supporters; they had hands like washboards. I insisted: no gloves or canes—nothing that might deaden the applause—and, on my honor, before the opening, everyone in the café across the street [3] seemed to be on my side. But the critics turned up in force. . . .

COUNT: Ah, the critics. And the author's preparations were undermined?

----

[2] Generic name for short poems addressed to a lady on her birthday, wedding, etc.

[3] A dig at the café opposite the Comédie-Française.

FIGARO: It can happen to anybody. They booed me. But if ever I get that audience together again . . .

COUNT: You'll have your revenge by boring them to death?

FIGARO: I'll have my revenge. I'm saving it for them, by Christ.

COUNT: Are you still angry enough to swear about it? In the Palace of Justice, you know, you have only twenty-four hours to curse your judges.

FIGARO: In the theater you have twenty-four years; a lifetime is too short to get over my kind of resentment.

COUNT: It's good to see how you enjoy your anger. But you haven't told me what made you leave Madrid.

FIGARO: Must have been my good angel, sir, since I've been lucky enough to find my old master again. I saw that the men of letters in Madrid were a pack of wolves, always attacking each other. Authors were beset by their cousins, their critics, their booksellers, their censors, the people who envied them and the people who imitated them—all these insects, these mosquitoes, fastened themselves to the skin of the unfortunate authors and sucked them dry. And so I left Madrid, tired of writing, bored with myself, disgusted with other people; my debts heavy and my pockets light; convinced once and for all that the useful income from a razor is better than the doubtful honors of a pen. I took my baggage on my back and traveled philosophically through the two Castiles, La Mancha, Estremadura, Sierra Morena, and Andalusia, being acclaimed in one town, jailed in another, but always on top of events; praised by these people, denounced by those people; helping out in good times, making do in bad times, taunting all the fools and daunting all the knaves; laughing at my misfortune and clipping every beard I came across. And here I am at last in Seville, where you see me ready to serve Your Excellency in whatever capacity you desire.

COUNT: Who gave you such a joyful philosophy?

FIGARO: Lady Misfortune. I force myself to laugh at everything for fear of being forced to weep at it. What do you keep looking at over there?

COUNT: Let's get away.

FIGARO: Why?

COUNT: Come on, dolt. You'll ruin my plans.

(They go out. The blind on the first floor of the house is pulled back and BARTHOLO *and* ROSINE *appear at the window.)*

ROSINE: How delightful to breathe this fresh air! The window is so rarely open.

BARTHOLO: What is that paper you are holding?

ROSINE: Some verses from *The Useless Precaution*, which my singing teacher gave me yesterday.

BARTHOLO: What is *The Useless Precaution*?

ROSINE: It's a new comedy.

BARTHOLO: Another play, eh? More of this modern rubbish? [4]

ROSINE: I don't know.

BARTHOLO: The newspapers and the government are to blame. This is a barbarous century!

ROSINE: You're always abusing our poor century.

BARTHOLO: Pardon the liberty. What has it produced that it should be praised? Every kind of stupidity: freedom of thought, the law of gravity, electricity, religious tolerance, inoculation, quinine, the encyclopedia—and plays that anybody can understand. . . .

(*The paper falls out of* ROSINE's *hands, into the street.*)

ROSINE: Oh, dear. My song! My song fell while I was listening to you. Hurry down after it, sir, hurry; it will blow away.

BARTHOLO: When you're holding something, hold on to it. (*He leaves the balcony.*)

ROSINE (*looks back inside and hisses into the street*): Psst, psst. (*The* COUNT *appears.*) Pick up the paper, quickly, and hide. (*The* COUNT *bounds forward, picks up the paper, and goes off.*)

BARTHOLO (*coming out of the house and looking about*): Where is it? I can't see anything.

ROSINE: Under the balcony, at the foot of the wall.

BARTHOLO: I can't see a thing. Did anybody else pass by?

ROSINE: Not that I saw.

BARTHOLO (*to himself*): And I'm soft enough to look for it. Bartholo, you're an indulgent old fool. This will teach you never to open street windows. (*He goes in again.*)

ROSINE (*still on the balcony*): My plight has driven me to do this: I am alone, trapped, and persecuted by an objectionable man. Is it a crime to escape from slavery?

BARTHOLO (*coming on to the balcony*): Come inside, young lady. I am to blame if your song is lost; it was bad

4 Bartholo did not like plays. Perhaps in his youth he had written some tragedy. . . . [Note by Beaumarchais.]

luck but it won't happen again, I promise you. (*He locks the window with a key.*)

(*The* COUNT *and* FIGARO *re-enter cautiously.*)

COUNT: Now that they've gone inside, let's look at this song, which must contain some hidden message. It is a letter.

FIGARO: He asked what *The Useless Precaution* was!

COUNT (*reading eagerly*): "I am curious to know why you are interested in me. As soon as my guardian goes out, sing the tune to these verses, casually, and let me know the name, the rank, and the intentions of the man who seems to be so obstinately concerned with the unfortunate Rosine."

FIGARO (*imitating* ROSINE'S *voice*): Oh, dear. My song! My song fell. Hurry down after it, sir, hurry! (*He laughs.*) These women! Do you want to make the most innocent one deceitful? Then lock her up.

COUNT: My dear Rosine!

FIGARO: Now I understand why you are wearing that disguise, my lord; you're planning to court her.

COUNT: Correct. But if you tattle . . .

FIGARO: Figaro tattle? My lord, I'm not going to pour out those highfalutin phrases about honor and devotion to reassure you; people break them every day. All I want to say is: my self-interest is in your hands; weigh it, balance it, and . . .

COUNT: Good enough. You may as well know that six months ago, on the Prado,[5] I happened to meet a young woman of such beauty—well, you have just seen her. I sent throughout Madrid to find her. No luck. A few days ago I discovered that she is called Rosine, that she is an orphan of noble blood, and that she is married to an old doctor of this city named Bartholo.

FIGARO: A pretty little bird. Not easy to dislodge from the nest. But who told you she was the doctor's wife?

COUNT: Everybody.

FIGARO: That's a story he invented when he got back from Madrid to mislead the young men of Seville and keep them away. She is still only his ward. But before long . . .

COUNT (*spiritedly*): Never! Not after that piece of news! I'd made up my mind to risk everything just to apologize to her—and I find she's free. There isn't a moment to lose. I must get her to love me, and then I must snatch her away from him. How well do you know this guardian?

5 **One** of the principal streets of Madrid.

FIGARO: Like my own mother.

COUNT: What kind of a man is he?

FIGARO: A fine, fat, short, young old man, going gray, sly, spry, and secretive, who pries and spies and grumbles and groans, all at the same time.

COUNT (*impatiently*):   Yes, I have seen him. But his character?

FIGARO: Brutal, miserly, loving, and excessively jealous of his ward, who hates him like death.

COUNT: Then how can he please her?

FIGARO: He can't.

COUNT: Even better. Is he honest?

FIGARO: Just enough to keep him this side of the gallows.

COUNT: Better still. I'll punish a rascal while I'm rewarding myself.

FIGARO: Then you'll serve the public and private welfare at the same time. Truly, sir, a masterpiece of morality.

COUNT: You say he locks his door because he's afraid of young men?

FIGARO: Of everybody. If he could, he'd make the place airtight.

COUNT: That's not so good. Do you have any way of getting in?

FIGARO: Haven't I just: First, the house I live in belongs to the doctor, who lets me stay there gratis.

COUNT: Aha!

FIGARO: Yes. And I agree, in return, to pay him a rent of six gold coins a year, also gratis.

COUNT (*impatiently*):   But you're his tenant?

FIGARO: That's not all: I'm his barber, his surgeon, and his apothecary. Every razor, lancet, and syringe in his house is wielded by the hand of yours truly.

COUNT (*embracing him*):   Figaro, you are my friend, my guardian angel, my liberator, my savior.

FIGARO: I see. Now I'm useful to you we're close friends. Talk about passion . . .

COUNT: Lucky Figaro. You are going into that house to see my Rosine, to *see* her. Do you realize how lucky you are?

FIGARO: A typical lover's remark. Am *I* in love with her? I only wish you could take my place.

COUNT: If we could get past the servants who are watching . . .

FIGARO: That's what I was thinking.

COUNT: Just for twelve hours.

FIGARO: Keep servants busy with their own affairs and they don't interfere with other people's.

COUNT: I agree. What about it?

FIGARO: The pharmacy . . . I've just thought of a harmless way to keep them quiet. . . .

COUNT: Villain!

FIGARO: I'm not going to hurt them, am I? They all need my drugs. It's only a question of treating them all at the same time.

COUNT: But the doctor may become suspicious.

FIGARO: We must work so fast that the suspicion will never be born. I have an idea: the regiment of the Royal Infanta is coming into town.

COUNT: The colonel is a friend of mine.

FIGARO: Good. Get hold of a cavalryman's uniform and present yourself at the doctor's house with a billeting order. He'll have to put you up. Leave everything else to me.

COUNT: Excellent.

FIGARO: It might be good if you looked a bit sozzled.

COUNT: Why?

FIGARO: And be impudent with him.

COUNT: Why?

FIGARO: So that he doesn't get wind of anything. He'll think you're more anxious to sleep than to plot in his house.

COUNT: Good idea. What will you be doing?

FIGARO: Never mind me. We'll be lucky if he doesn't recognize you; still, he's never seen you. How are you going to introduce yourself?

COUNT: That will be tricky.

FIGARO: It may be too hard a part for you to play. A cavalryman, and drunk . . .

COUNT: Are you serious? Listen to this. (*In a drunken tone.*) Is this the residence of Doctor Bartholo?

FIGARO: Not bad at all. But a little more intoxication around the knees. (*In a drunker tone.*) Is this the residence of Doctor Bartholo?

COUNT: No, that's how commoners get drunk.

FIGARO: The best way. And the most enjoyable.

COUNT: The door is opening.

FIGARO: That's our man. Let's keep out of the way till he's gone.

(*They hide.* BARTHOLO *comes out of the house.*)

BARTHOLO (*looking inside*):   I'll be right back. Don't let anybody in. (*To himself.*) I was stupid to have come down.

The moment she asked me I should have stopped and thought. . . . And Bazile still hasn't come. He is supposed to make all arrangements for the secret marriage tomorrow; and not a word from him. I'll go and see what's holding him up. (*Exit.*)

COUNT: What was that? He's marrying Rosine in secret, tomorrow?

FIGARO: The harder it is to succeed, sir, the more necessary it is to try.

COUNT: Who is this Bazile who is involved in the marriage?

FIGARO: A poor devil who teaches the young lady music; in love with his art, a petty swindler, so out of money that he'll go down on his knees for the smallest coin, and no trouble at all for us to deal with, my lord. (*Looking up at the window.*) There she is, there she is.

COUNT: There who is?

FIGARO: Behind her blind, up there, up there! Don't look, though, don't look.

COUNT: Why not?

FIGARO: Remember what she wrote: "Sing the verses casually." In other words, sing as if you were singing to yourself, just for the sake of singing. Ah, there she is again.

COUNT: Since she's already interested in me without knowing who I am, I'll keep this name Lindor; it'll be better to hide my title until I've won her. (*He unfolds the paper that* ROSINE *dropped.*) But what can I sing to this music? I can't just make up lines.

FIGARO: Yes you can. Sing whatever comes to you. In love the heart assists the mind. Take my guitar.

COUNT: What do I do? I hardly know how to hold it.

FIGARO: Is there actually something a man like you doesn't know? With the back of your fingers: strum, strum, strum. . . . You can't sing without a guitar in Seville. You'll be recognized and rooted out in no time. I'll be here, if you need any help.

(*He goes close to the wall, below the balcony. The* COUNT *sings and walks about, accompanying himself on the guitar.*)

COUNT:

> You ask me to give you my name,
> But, unknown, I dared to adore you.
> After naming myself I implore you
> To allow me to love you the same.

FIGARO (*low*):   It's going well. Keep it up.
COUNT:

> I am Lindor, a man of low birth,
> My pledge is a simple, sincere one:
> I wish I could offer my dear one
> High rank and estates of great worth.

FIGARO: I'll be damned. I couldn't do better myself, and this is my vocation.
COUNT:

> I'll tenderly sing of my love,
> My love that is not yet requited,
> I'll think of you and be excited
> To know you are listening above.

FIGARO: For that verse you deserve—(*Kisses the hem of the* COUNT's *cloak.*)
COUNT: Figaro.
FIGARO: Your Excellency?
COUNT: Do you think she heard me?
ROSINE (*singing inside*):

> Everything tells me that Lindor is charming
> And that I must love him constantly . . .

(*A window slams. The singing stops.*)

FIGARO: Now do you think she heard you?
COUNT: She closed her window. Evidently someone came into her room.
FIGARO: Poor child! Her voice was shaking. She is yours, my lord.
COUNT: She was singing to a melody from *The Useless Precaution*, too. "Everything tells me that Lindor is charming." What style! What perception!
FIGARO: What dishonesty! What love!
COUNT: Figaro, do you think she'll give in to me?
FIGARO: She won't give you up. She'd rather leap out of that window.
COUNT: It's settled. I belong to Rosine . . . for life.
FIGARO: You forget, my lord, that she can't hear you now.
COUNT: One more thing, Figaro: she is going to be my wife; and if you serve me well and don't tell her my

name . . . well, you understand me, you know me. . . .

FIGARO: I'm on your side, all of me. Come, Figaro, fly toward fortune, my boy.

COUNT: We'd better move away, before anyone becomes inquisitive.

FIGARO: My lord, I shall enter this house and, with the aid of my black arts, I shall wave my wand once and put vigilance to sleep and bring love awake, battle jealousy, baffle intrigue, and overturn all obstacles. You, sir, must go to my house and wait there in soldier's uniform, with a billeting order and gold in your pockets.

COUNT: Gold? For whom?

FIGARO: Gold. Just gold, that's all; gold is the sinews of intrigue.

COUNT: Say no more, Figaro. I'll bring a pile of it.

FIGARO (*moving away*): I'll join you shortly.

COUNT: Figaro!

FIGARO: What?

COUNT: Your guitar.

FIGARO (*coming back*): Forgetting my precious guitar, me! I'm losing my mind. (*Takes it and goes.*)

COUNT (*calling after him*): Where's your house, numskull?

FIGARO (*coming back*): Amnesia, it's caught up with me at last. My shop is a few steps away from here, my lord; it's painted blue with lead window frames, three basins in the air,[6] the eye in the hand, and a big sign over the door: "Figaro." (*Rushes off.*)

---

[6] The insignia of the barber surgeon in France; the three bowls were to catch the blood of patients during "bleedings." The other sign, the "eye in the hand," was to indicate the barber's dexterity, as though his hands could see where they were going.

ACT II

(ROSINE's *quarters in* BARTHOLO's *house. The window at the rear is closed by a grilled ironwork shutter.* ROSINE *is alone at a table with a lighted candle in a candlestick. She takes some paper and writes on it.*)

ROSINE: Marceline is sick; all the men are busy; and nobody will see me writing. I don't know if these walls have ears and eyes or if my Argus has an evil spirit that reports back to him, but I cannot say a word or take a step that he doesn't know about immediately. Ah, Lindor. (*She closes the letter.*) I'll seal this letter, although I don't know when or how I'll be able to give it to him. I saw him through my window, talking to the barber Figaro for a long time. I like Figaro; he has often shown pity for me; if only I had a chance to speak to him. (FIGARO *comes in.*) Mr. Figaro, I am glad to see you.

FIGARO: Aren't you well, madam?

ROSINE: Not too well, Mr. Figaro. I'm dying of boredom.

FIGARO: I believe you. Only fools thrive on it.

ROSINE: You were chatting away to somebody outside. I couldn't hear what you were saying, but . . .

FIGARO: A relative of mine, a very promising young fellow, full of wit, imagination, and talent, and very good-looking.

ROSINE: Yes, I can imagine that. What is his name?

FIGARO: Lindor. He has no money, but if he hadn't left Madrid suddenly he could have found a good job there.

ROSINE: He will find one somewhere else, Mr. Figaro. A young man of that description will make his mark.

FIGARO (*aside*): Good, good. (*Aloud.*) But he has one great weakness, which may work against him.

ROSINE: A weakness, Mr. Figaro? A weakness, are you sure?

FIGARO: He is in love.

ROSINE: In love—and you call that a weakness?

173

FIGARO: Well, only in relation to his lack of money.

ROSINE: Fate is unkind. And has he told you whom he loves? I'm just curious. . . .

FIGARO: Madam, you are the last person I can talk to about this.

ROSINE (*quickly*):   Why, Mr. Figaro? I am discreet. This young man is your relative and I am very interested in him. Do tell me who she is.

FIGARO (*watching her cunningly*):   Imagine the prettiest little darling, sweet, tender, fresh, delightful and appetizing, light-footed and slender-figured with plump arms and rosebud lips—and hands!—and cheeks!—and teeth!—and eyes!

ROSINE: Does she live in this city?

FIGARO: In this part of it.

ROSINE: In this street, by chance?

FIGARO: Two paces away from me.

ROSINE: How convenient . . . for your relative. And this person is . . . ?

FIGARO: Haven't I as good as told you her name?

ROSINE: That is the one thing you forgot, Mr. Figaro. So tell me, tell me quickly; if someone comes in I won't know.

FIGARO: Do you insist, madam? Well then, she is . . . the ward of your guardian.

ROSINE: The ward . . . ?

FIGARO: Of Doctor Bartholo, yes, madam.

ROSINE (*with emotion*):   Ah, Mr. Figaro, I don't believe you.

FIGARO: And he is burning to come here and talk to you himself.

ROSINE: You make me nervous, Mr. Figaro.

FIGARO: It's no good being nervous. Once you give in to the fear of evil, you begin to feel the evil of fear. Besides, I have just got rid of all your guards until tomorrow.

ROSINE: If he loves me, he should prove it by remaining absolutely quiet about it.

FIGARO: Now, now, madam. Can love and peace live in the same heart? Youth is unhappy because it is faced with this terrible choice: love without peace, or peace without love.

ROSINE (*lowering her eyes*):   Peace without love . . . seems . . .

FIGARO: Very dull. Love without peace is a lot more exciting; and frankly, if I were a woman . . .

ROSINE (*embarrassed*):   Certainly, a young lady cannot prevent a young man from admiring her.

FIGARO: And my relative admires you enormously.

ROSINE: But if he did something rash, Mr. Figaro, we'd be lost.

FIGARO (*aside*):   We would, too. (*Aloud.*) Why don't you forbid him to? Send him a note. A note is powerful.

ROSINE (*giving him the letter she has just written*):   I haven't time to rewrite this, but tell him about it . . . be sure to tell him . . . (*She listens.*)

FIGARO: Nobody there.

ROSINE: . . . that I am doing it out of pure friendship.

FIGARO: Why not say "love"? Love is much more open.

ROSINE: No, out of pure friendship, understand that. I'm afraid of all the complications. . . .

FIGARO: You think he may turn out to be a will o' the wisp. But remember, madam: the wind that carries a will o' the wisp can make a bonfire blaze and that bonfire is the human heart. When he talks about you he breathes out so much heat that he almost scorches me. And I'm an outsider.

ROSINE: Hush, I hear my guardian. If he finds you here . . . Hide in that closet with the harp, and make your way downstairs, quietly, as soon as you can.

FIGARO: Keep calm. (*Aside, holding up the letter.*) This is worth all my talk put together. (*Goes into the closet.*)

ROSINE: I'll die of worry until I know he's safely outside. I like Figaro. He's a fine, honest man, a good relative. Ah, here comes the tyrant. Back to my embroidery. (*She snuffs out the candle, sits down, and takes a piece of embroidery on a frame.*)

(BARTHOLO *storms in.*)

BARTHOLO: Curse him, that mad, vile shark of a Figaro. A man can't step out of his house for an instant and find it the same when he gets back. . . .

ROSINE: Who has made you so angry, sir?

BARTHOLO: That damn barber, who has just wrecked my entire household in one swoop: he gave Lively a sleeping powder, and Puberty a sneezing powder; he took blood from Marceline's foot; he even interfered with my mule: he put a poultice over the eyes of the poor, blind beast. He owes me a hundred crowns and he'll do anything to cancel out the debt. But wait till he brings me his bills. And look—nobody in the antechamber. The house is as empty as a barrack square and completely unprotected.

ROSINE: Nobody can come in except you, sir.

BARTHOLO: I would rather worry without need than live

without heed. The world is full of swindlers and pirates. Didn't one of them snatch your song this morning, while I was going down to get it?

ROSINE: You're making a fuss about nothing. The paper may have been picked up by the wind or by a passer-by. How do I know?

BARTHOLO: It was nothing whatever to do with the wind or with a passer-by. It's strange but whenever a woman seems to drop papers by accident someone is always waiting to pick them up.

ROSINE: *Seems*, sir?

BARTHOLO: Yes, *seems*, madam.

ROSINE (*aside*):   What a nasty old man.

BARTHOLO: But that's the last time it will happen. I am going to lock the grille.

ROSINE: Don't stop at that: wall up the windows. There's not much difference between a prison and a dungeon.

BARTHOLO: Yes, the windows that open onto the street—not a bad idea. That barber didn't come in to see you, did he?

ROSINE: Are you worried about him too?

BARTHOLO: I worry about everybody.

ROSINE: You answer so politely.

BARTHOLO: Trust the whole world and you'll soon find yourself with a good wife who deceives you, good friends who seduce her, and good servants who assist them.

ROSINE: Don't you even admit that a person could have scruples about letting herself be seduced by a man like Figaro?

BARTHOLO: Who the devil understands women and their scruples?

ROSINE: If it takes a man to please a woman, sir, how is it that you displease me?

BARTHOLO: How—? What do you mean? . . . You still haven't answered my question about the barber.

ROSINE (*furiously*):   Then I will. Yes, he did come in here. I did see him. I did speak to him. And I found him very pleasant. And may you die of rage from knowing it. (*Exit.*)

BARTHOLO: Where are you, you dogs, you servants, you bribe-takers? Puberty! Lively, Lively, curses on you both!

(LIVELY *comes in yawning, almost asleep.*)

LIVELY: I—ah, aah, er, ah.

BARTHOLO: Where were you when the barber came in, you plaguey nincompoop?

LIVELY: Sir, I was ah . . . aah, ah . . .

BARTHOLO: Up to some trickery, I bet. Didn't you see him?

LIVELY: I certainly did; from what he said I was quite ill, and he must have been right because I began to ache all over as soon as he told me. Ah, aah, ah . . .

BARTHOLO (*imitating him*): Aah, ah! As soon as he told me . . . Where is that no-good Puberty? How dare he drug a youngster like you without consulting me about the prescription! There's some knavery going on behind my back.

(*Enter* PUBERTY, *an old man on a crutch. He sneezes several times.*)

LIVELY (*still yawning*): Puberty? Is that you?

BARTHOLO: Stop that sneezing on my time. Save it till your day off.

PUBERTY: That makes fifty . . . fifty times in the last minute. (*He sneezes.*) I'm a wreck.

BARTHOLO: Now, listen: I asked you both if anyone came into Rosine's room, and you didn't tell me that this barber . . .

LIVELY: Is Figaro "anyone"? Eh? I . . . ah . . .

BARTHOLO: I bet this scoundrel is in cahoots with him.

LIVELY (*crying like a drunk*): Me, sir, in cahoots . . . ?

PUBERTY (*sneezing*): But, sir, is there no . . . is there no justice?

BARTHOLO: Justice is for dregs, like you, to argue about. I'm the master here and what I say goes.

PUBERTY (*sneezing*): But cripes, right is right. . . .

BARTHOLO: Only when I say so. If idiots like you were ever allowed to be right, what would become of discipline?

PUBERTY (*sneezing*): I'm giving notice. This is a terrible job; it's like being in hell.

LIVELY (*sobbing*): A poor, honest man is called a dreg.

BARTHOLO: Get out, then, you poor, honest man. (*He imitates their sneezes and yawns.*) With your aah's and your tchoo's, yawning and sneezing in my face. (LIVELY *goes out, weeping still.*)

PUBERTY: I swear to you, sir, that it would be impossible to stay in this house if it weren't for Miss Rosine. (*Exit, sneezing.*)

BARTHOLO: What a state that Figaro has got them into! I can see what the thief is up to: he thinks that by administering expensive drugs he's found a way to pay back my hundred crowns without opening his wallet.

(*Enter* DON BAZILE. FIGARO, *who is still hidden in the closet, looks out and listens from time to time.*)

BARTHOLO: Ah, Don Bazile, you've come to give Rosine her music lesson.

BAZILE: That's not important at the moment.

BARTHOLO: I stopped at your house, but you were not in.

BAZILE: I'd gone out to check something for you. And I heard some rather upsetting news.

BARTHOLO: For you?

BAZILE: No, for you. Count Almaviva is here in Seville.

BARTHOLO: Talk quietly. The man who was looking all over Madrid for Rosine?

BAZILE: Yes. He's staying in the Square, and he goes out every day in disguise.

BARTHOLO: This may be serious. What can I do?

BAZILE: We could soon frighten him away if he were an ordinary citizen.

BARTHOLO: Yes. Ambush him one evening; we'd be armed and protected. . . .

BAZILE: *Bone deus!* I know! Why not start a scandal about him? Get a few rumors going and once they're started, add to them. Watch them grow.

BARTHOLO: A curious way to get rid of a man.

BAZILE: Slander, sir, defamation! Don't belittle it. I've seen it destroy the most honest men. Believe me, there's no flat lie, no horror, no absurdity that the scandalmongers in a big city won't gulp down if you tell it right. And the people here gulp like nobody's business. You start with a faint rumor, skimming the earth like a swallow before a storm, *pianissimo*, a murmur, a melody, gently spreading its poison. Somebody passes it on and *piano, piano,* it slips cunningly in and out of ears. The harm is done, but it mounts, it blossoms, and passes in ringing chords *rinforzando* from mouth to mouth at Satan's own speed. Then suddenly—who knows how?—you see Slander rear up, hiss, swell, and grow into a monstrous hurricane before your eyes. And it flings itself about, whirls and reaches out and crushes, plucks up and pulls down, flashes lightning and booms thunder, and becomes, heaven be praised, a general shout, a public *crescendo,* a universal *chorus* of hate and condemnation. Who could stand up to that?

BARTHOLO: What's all this nonsense, Bazile? And how is this *piano-crescendo* business supposed to help me?

BAZILE: That is how people defeat their enemies. This

is how you can defeat *your* enemy before he has a chance to get near you.

BARTHOLO: But I intend to marry Rosine before she even learns that this count exists.

BAZILE: In that case, let's not waste any more time.

BARTHOLO: What's delaying us? I made you responsible for all the details.

BAZILE: Yes, but you've been tight on expenses; when you have dissonances, such as an unequal marriage, an unfair relationship, a gross injustice, you must bring them into harmony by means of gold.

BARTHOLO (*giving him money*):   Take as much as you need. Now let's get on with it.

BAZILE: That's what I like to hear. Tomorrow, everything will be arranged. It's up to you to see that nobody tells Rosine anything today.

BARTHOLO: Trust me. Will you come back this evening, Bazile?

BAZILE: Don't bank on it. Organizing your marriage will keep me busy all day; don't bank on it.

BARTHOLO (*going with him*):   Allow me.

BAZILE: Don't bother, Doctor, don't bother. I can find my way out.

BARTHOLO: It's not that. I want to make sure the front door is closed behind you. (*They go out.*)

(FIGARO *reappears.*)

FIGARO: Oh, these precautions! Yes, close the front door, close it, and when I go out I'll open it again for the count. This Bazile is a crafty scoundrel. Luckily, he's even more of a fool. You need an estate, a family, a name, a rank, in other words, quality, if you want to become a professional scandalmonger. But a Bazile! Oh, no. He'll start inventing stories and nobody will believe him.

(ROSINE *comes running in.*)

ROSINE: What—are you still here, Mr. Figaro?

FIGARO: Luckily for you, madam. Your guardian and your singing teacher thought they were alone, and talked openly. . . .

ROSINE: And you listened to them? You know, that was very naughty.

FIGARO: To listen? But that is the only way to hear properly. And here's what I heard: your guardian is making arrangements to marry you tomorrow.

ROSINE: How frightening!

FIGARO: Don't be frightened. We'll keep him so busy that he won't have time to think about it.

ROSINE: He's coming back. Go out down the little staircase. You're making me die of fright.

(FIGARO *hastens out. Re-enter* BARTHOLO.)

ROSINE: Was somebody here with you, sir?

BARTHOLO: Don Bazile; I've just seen him out. You can't be too careful. You'd have been happier if it was Figaro, eh?

ROSINE: It makes no difference to me.

BARTHOLO: I'd like to know what the barber had to say to you that was so important.

ROSINE: Shall I tell you the truth? He gave me a report on Marceline's health, and from what he says she isn't too well.

BARTHOLO: He gave you a report! I'll bet he came to deliver a letter.

ROSINE: From whom? Please tell me.

BARTHOLO: Oh, from . . . from someone that women never admit they know. How do I know? It may have been a reply to the paper that fell from the window.

ROSINE (*aside*): He hasn't missed a thing. (*Aloud.*) If so, it would serve you right.

BARTHOLO: If so? It *is* so. After all, you have been writing.

ROSINE (*embarrassed*): It will be interesting if you can prove that.

BARTHOLO (*taking her right hand*): I don't need to. See, your finger still has an ink stain on it. Aha, you cunning girl.

ROSINE (*aside*): You repulsive old creature.

BARTHOLO (*still holding her hand*): A woman thinks she's safe just because she's alone.

ROSINE: That may be, but you haven't proved anything. Let go, sir, you're twisting my arm. It so happens that I burnt myself when I was sewing next to this candle, and I've always heard that it's best to dip a burn in ink. So that's what I did.

BARTHOLO: So that's what you did? Let's see if we can find a second piece of evidence to confirm the first. Here's the notebook; there were six sheets in it; I count them every morning, and I didn't forget this morning.

ROSINE (*aside*): I'm a fool—

BARTHOLO (*counting*): Three, four, five . . . (*He looks up.*)

ROSINE: The sixth one . . .

BARTHOLO: Yes, I notice that the sixth one is missing.

ROSINE: I used it to make a cone for some candies I gave Figaro for his little girl.[7]

BARTHOLO: Indeed? And this pen nib, which was new—how did it become dirty? When you were addressing the candy cone to Figaro's little girl?

ROSINE (*aside*): Jealousy is this man's first instinct. (*Aloud.*) I used it for redrawing a faded flower on the jacket I'm embroidering for you.

BARTHOLO: How nice! If you want to be believed, my girl, you mustn't blush as you tell one lie after another. You haven't learned that yet.

ROSINE: Who wouldn't blush, sir, to see you drawing such false conclusions from such innocent behavior?

BARTHOLO: Yes, I must be wrong. You burnt your finger, you dipped it in the ink; you made a candy cone for Figaro's daughter, and you embroidered my jacket. What could be more innocent? But what could be more guilty than piling up all those lies to conceal one single fact: *I am alone,* you thought; *nobody can see me. I can lie to my heart's content.* But your fingertip is still black, the nib is dirty, the paper is missing. Well, one can't think of everything. But from now on, young lady, whenever I go into town, every door in this house will be double-locked. (*The* COUNT *enters, in cavalry uniform, swaying drunkenly and singing: "Reveille, reveille, time to get up in the morning . . ."*) A soldier? What does he want? Go into your bedroom, girl.

COUNT (*advancing and still humming*): Which one of you ladies is Doctor Barcarolle? (*Aside, to* ROSINE.) I am Lindor.

BARTHOLO: The name is Bartholo.

ROSINE (*aside*): He said he was Lindor.

COUNT: Barkalo, Barmy-o, who cares? What I want to know is, which one of you is it? (*To* ROSINE, *handing her a paper.*) Take this letter.

BARTHOLO: Which one? You can see very well that I'm Bartholo. Rosine, go inside. This man has been drinking.

ROSINE: That's why I'd better stay, sir. You'll be alone with him. Soldiers sometimes behave with more courtesy in front of a woman.

BARTHOLO: Go in, go in. I'm not afraid.

---

[7] Figaro's daughter is not explained by Beaumarchais. In a succeeding play, *The Marriage of Figaro,* he weds Suzanne, a chambermaid.

COUNT: It's all right. I recognized you right away by your description.

BARTHOLO: What's that you're hiding in your pocket?

COUNT: Something I'm hiding in my pocket, so that you can't tell what it is.

BARTHOLO: My description! These people always think they're talking to other soldiers.

COUNT: Do you think it would be so hard to describe you? (*Sings.*)

Shiny head with a big, bald top.
Different-colored eyes that glare and pop.
Creeping walk, like a beaten-up hound.
Sluggish gray body that slops around.
Shoulder on the right too high by a foot.
Wooden complexion, with ingrained soot.
Nose the shape of an unmade bed.
Balloonlike legs with lead-heavy tread.
Squalling tone from a grumbling throat.
Greedy and destructive and as vicious as a stoat.
A scraggy old, baggy old, cheap-minded churl. . . .
In short, sir, of doctors you are the pearl.

BARTHOLO: Do you realize that you've insulted me? Is that what you came for? Get out this instant.

COUNT: Get out? Now is that a nice thing to say? Do you now how to read, Doctor Buffalo?

BARTHOLO: That is an insolent question.

COUNT: Don't let it annoy you. I'm at least as much of a doctor as you are. And between doctors . . .

BARTHOLO: You're what?

COUNT: Yes, didn't I tell you? I'm the regimental horse doctor. That's why they sent me here—to lodge with a colleague.

BARTHOLO: How dare you compare me with a blacksmith!

COUNT (*singing*):

A simple horse doctor like me can't pretend
That my art is as highly selective
As yours is, my dear Hippocratical friend,
For you can be much more effective:
With the aid of odd drugs and extortionate fees
And pills and diverse medications,
You eliminate not merely pain and disease
But also your patients.

Is that polite enough for you?

BARTHOLO: It's typical of an ignorant shyster like you to decry the first, the greatest and the most useful of the arts. . . .

COUNT: Certainly the most useful to those who practice it.

BARTHOLO: An art whose successes the sun shines upon.

COUNT: An art whose failures the earth tries to conceal.

BARTHOLO: It's obvious that you are not used to talking to anything but horses.

COUNT: But isn't it well known that a horse doctor always cures his patients without talking to them, whereas a doctor always talks to his patients . . .

BARTHOLO: Without curing them? Is that what you were going to say?

COUNT: You've already said it.

BARTHOLO: Who the devil sent this drunken idiot here?

COUNT: Careful; next you'll be spilling epigrams, you lovable old man.

BARTHOLO: What do you want? What have you come for?

COUNT (*pretending to be angry*):   He's trying to make me lose control. What do I want? Can't you see?

(ROSINE *comes running in.*)

ROSINE (*to* COUNT):   Please don't lose your temper, Mr. Soldier. (*To* BARTHOLO.)   Speak to him nicely. He doesn't know what he's doing or saying.

COUNT: You are right. But he's the one who doesn't know what he's doing or saying. We do, don't we? I'm polite and you're pretty . . . that's enough. I've just decided: from now on I'm not going to deal with anyone in this house but you.

ROSINE: And what can I do for you, Mr. Soldier?

COUNT: A small favor, my dear. I hope I am making myself clear?

ROSINE: I'm following the message. . . .

COUNT (*showing her the letter*):   No, take the letter, the letter. (*To* BARTHOLO.)   All you have to do, and I say this with the greatest respect, is to give me a bed for the night.

BARTHOLO: Is that all?

COUNT: That is all. Read this love letter that our quartermaster has sent you.

BARTHOLO: Let me see. (*The* COUNT *hides the letter and gives him another paper.*) "Doctor Bartholo will receive, feed, accommodate, and sleep . . ."

COUNT (*leaning over his shoulder*):   Sleep is the word . . .

BARTHOLO: "For one night only, the undernamed scholar and member of the horse regiment: Lindor . . ."

ROSINE: It is Lindor; that proves it.

BARTHOLO (*swiftly, to* ROSINE): What was that?

COUNT: Well, was I wrong, Doctor Go-below?

BARTHOLO: This man seems to be out to wound me in every way possible. Go to hell with your Go-belows and Buffaloes and tell your impertinent quartermaster that, since I went to Madrid, I've been exempted from accommodating soldiers.

COUNT (*aside*): That's a blow.

BARTHOLO: Ah, my friend, that sobers you up a little. And now you can clear out without wasting any more time.

COUNT (*aside*): I was afraid of this. (*Aloud.*) If you're exempted from lodging soldiers, you're not exempted from being polite. Before I clear out I want to see your certificate of exemption, even if I can't read it.

BARTHOLO: That's no problem. It's in this desk.

COUNT (*softly, without moving*): My lovely Rosine!

ROSINE: Lindor, I'm so happy to see you.

COUNT: Take this letter.

ROSINE: Not now. He's watching.

COUNT: Take out your handkerchief. I'll drop this. (*Approaches.*)

BARTHOLO: Careful, careful, soldier. I don't like strange men to go near my wife.

COUNT: Oh, she's your wife?

BARTHOLO: What else?

COUNT: I took you for her great-grandfather, paternal, maternal, or eternal. There are at least three generations separating you.

BARTHOLO (*reading a document*): "Upon the good and faithful evidence that has been given us . . ."

COUNT (*knocking the papers to the floor*): I don't have to listen to all that garbage. . . .

BARTHOLO: Do you realize, soldier, that if I call my men I can have you thrown out? And that's what you deserve.

COUNT: Ah, a battle? With pleasure. That's my trade, fighting. (*Takes a pistol from his belt.*) And here's what I use to throw dust in their eyes. Have you ever seen a battle, my dear?

ROSINE: No, and I never want to.

COUNT: Nothing is as much fun as a battle. There (*he pushes* BARTHOLO *back*) is the enemy on one side of the ravine, and here we are on the other. (*Aside.*) Take out your handkerchief. (*He spits on the floor.*) And there is the ravine.

(ROSINE *takes out her handkerchief. He drops the letter between her and him.*)

BARTHOLO (*bending forward*): Ah!

COUNT (*picking up the letter*): Stand back. I'm about to teach you the secrets of my trade. Now, there's a cautious woman for you. Isn't that a love letter that fell out of her pocket?

BARTHOLO: Give it to me.

COUNT: Easy, Grandpa. It's not your business. How would you like strange people to pick up your quack prescriptions?

ROSINE (*holding out her hand*): It's mine. I know what it is. (*She takes the letter and puts it in her pocket.*)

BARTHOLO: Will you get out?

COUNT: Yes, I'll get out. Good-by, Doctor. No hard feelings? I have a small request, my dear man: pray that Death may spare me for a few more campaigns. Life has never been so precious before.

BARTHOLO: Go on, get out. Do you think I have a credit account with Death?

COUNT: Why not? You're a doctor. After all you've done for Death, she shouldn't be able to refuse you anything.

(*He goes out.* BARTHOLO *watches him leave.*)

BARTHOLO: At last. (*Aside.*) Now to get around her.

ROSINE: You must admit, sir, that he's a merry young man. Drunk or not drunk, he's obviously neither foolish nor illiterate.

BARTHOLO: We're lucky to be rid of him, my love. And now, aren't we both curious to read that paper he gave you?

ROSINE: Which paper?

BARTHOLO: The one he pretended to pick up for you.

ROSINE: Oh, the one that fell from my pocket. It's from my cousin, the officer.

BARTHOLO: I have an idea that it fell from his pocket.

ROSINE: No, from mine.

BARTHOLO: Well, it won't hurt to look at it.

ROSINE: I don't remember what I did with it.

BARTHOLO (*pointing to her pocket*): In there.

ROSINE: I wasn't thinking.

BARTHOLO: Of course, of course. It's something idiotic, you'll see.

ROSINE (*aside*): I'll have to make him angry. There's no other way to refuse.

BARTHOLO: Give it to me, then, my heart.

ROSINE: Why are you insisting, sir? More suspicions?

BARTHOLO: Why don't you want to show it to me?

ROSINE: I've already told you, sir, that this paper is a letter from my cousin, which you opened yesterday before you gave it to me. And while we're on that subject, I'd like to say that you have no right to take such a liberty.

BARTHOLO: I don't understand.

ROSINE: Do I open your mail? Why should you interfere with mine? If you are jealous, it's insulting; if you are trying to show your authority, it's revolting.

BARTHOLO: What? Revolting? You've never spoken to me like that before.

ROSINE: Just because I haven't protested before, it doesn't mean that you have the right to go on insulting me.

BARTHOLO: What insults are you talking about?

ROSINE: It's unheard of for a person to open another person's mail.

BARTHOLO: Even his wife's?

ROSINE: I'm not your wife yet. And if I were, why should you humiliate your wife? You wouldn't do it to a stranger.

BARTHOLO: You're trying to switch the conversation away from that note which is undoubtedly a letter from some lover. But I am determined to see it.

ROSINE: You will not see it. If you come any nearer, I'll run out of the house and ask the first passer-by to protect me.

BARTHOLO: He'll refuse.

ROSINE: We'll see about that.

BARTHOLO: You think we are in France, where women always get their own way. To close that fantasy out, I'll shut the door.

ROSINE (*as he is going*):   Now what can I do? I know— change the two letters around and let him find my cousin's. (*She lets her cousin's letter show out of her pocket.*)

BARTHOLO (*coming back*):   Now for the letter.

ROSINE: What right have you to look at it?

BARTHOLO: The unanswerable right—of the stronger.

ROSINE: You'll have to kill me before I give it up.

BARTHOLO (*stamping his foot*):   Don't waste time . . . I want it now.

ROSINE (*falling into a chair and pretending to be ill*):   This is a disgrace.

BARTHOLO: Give me that letter or face my anger.

ROSINE: I am so unhappy. . . .

BARTHOLO: What's wrong with you?

ROSINE (*muttering*):   An unbearable future.

BARTHOLO: Rosine!

ROSINE: I am suffocating.

BARTHOLO: She does look ill.

ROSINE: I'm getting weaker. I am dying.

BARTHOLO (*feels her pulse and says, aside*):   There's the letter. I'll read it, while she doesn't realize what's happening.

ROSINE: Nothing but misery left for me.

BARTHOLO (*aside, still holding her wrist*):   How eager we are to learn what we fear to know.

ROSINE: I am for the grave.

BARTHOLO: It must be her perfume that causes those spasms. (*He reads the letter behind the chair, still feeling her pulse.* ROSINE *raises herself a little, looks at him slyly, nods to herself, and pretends to move restlessly again.*) Oh, God. It *is* her cousin's letter. And I was so worried. How can I calm her down? She mustn't know I've read this. (*Pretends to sit her up, and slips the letter back in her pocket.*)

ROSINE (*sighing*):   Ah . . .

BARTHOLO: Now then, my child, it's nothing at all: the vapors rising inside you to your brain, that's all. Your pulse is normal. (*He takes a medicine bottle from a cabinet.*)

ROSINE (*aside*):   He has put the letter back. Good.

BARTHOLO: Here you are, Rosine dear. A little spirit water.

ROSINE: I don't want anything from you. Leave me.

BARTHOLO: Perhaps I was too forceful about that letter.

ROSINE: It's nothing to do with the letter. It's your way of asking for things that makes me furious.

BARTHOLO (*on his knees*):   Forgive me. I admit I was wrong. Here I am at your feet, ready to make amends.

ROSINE: Forgive you? When you believe this letter is not from my cousin?

BARTHOLO: It makes no difference whether it's from him or somebody else. Don't tell me.

ROSINE (*handing him the letter*):   You see, when you ask me properly you can have anything. Read it.

BARTHOLO: Your honesty has convinced me. I was unkind to suspect you.

ROSINE: Read it anyway.

BARTHOLO (*moving away*):   God forbid that I do you such an injury.

ROSINE: You will annoy me if you refuse.

BARTHOLO: No, let it be my sign of confidence in you. I think I'll go and see how poor Marceline is getting on. Would you like to come?

ROSINE: I'll come up in a moment.

BARTHOLO: Now that we have made up, my dear, give me your hand. Ah, if you could only love me you would be so happy.

ROSINE: If you could only please me, perhaps I could love you.

BARTHOLO: I shall please you, I shall. When I say that, I mean it. (*Goes out.*)

ROSINE: Lindor, he says that he will please me. Now I can read this letter which almost got me into so much trouble. (*She reads and cries out.*) Too late. He advises me to remain on bad terms with my guardian. I had that beautiful quarrel going and now I've patched it up. When he gave me this letter I felt myself blushing to the eyes. My guardian is right: I do give myself away; I haven't the sophistication of a woman of the world. But an unjust man can soon turn an innocent girl into a schemer.

ACT III

(BARTHOLO's *study*.)

BARTHOLO (*alone and sad*): What a temper that girl has! She seems to have calmed down now, but who gave her the idea of not having her piano lesson with Don Bazile? She must have guessed that he is mixed up in this marriage arrangement. (*A knock on the door.*) You do everything you can to please women, but if you forget one tiny thing, just one . . . (*Another knock.*) I'll see who this is.

(*The* COUNT *comes in, dressed as a young scholar, in a jacket, breeches, high socks, priest's cloak, neck ruff.*)

COUNT: Peace and joy on this house forevermore.

BARTHOLO (*shortly*): Nobody ever made a more appropriate wish. What do you want?

COUNT: Sir, I am Alonzo, a licensed instructor . . .

BARTHOLO: I don't need an instructor.

COUNT: . . . of music, the pupil of Don Bazile, organist of the Grand Convent, who has the honor of teaching music to your ward. . . .

BARTHOLO: Yes, I know all that—he's an organist and he has the honor and so on. What about it?

COUNT (*aside*): What a man. (*Aloud.*) A sudden sickness has forced him to take to his bed. . . .

BARTHOLO: To his bed, Bazile! Just as well that he informed me. I'll go and see him at once.

COUNT (*aside*): Damn! (*Aloud.*) When I say he's in bed, sir, I mean that he is staying in his room.

BARTHOLO: Only indisposed? Well, we'll go, anyway. Lead the way; I'll follow you.

COUNT (*embarrassed*): Sir, he asked me to . . . Can anybody hear us?

BARTHOLO (*aside*): Some rascal or other. (*Aloud.*) No, sir. Speak up, don't be mysterious. Talk freely, if you can.

189

COUNT (*aside*): The old scourge. (*Aloud.*) Don Bazile asked me to tell you . . .

BARTHOLO: Louder. I am deaf in one ear.

COUNT (*raising his voice*): Certainly. Count Almaviva, who is staying at the Square . . .

BARTHOLO (*nervously*): Not so loud.

COUNT (*louder*): . . . left his house this morning. It was through me that Don Bazile discovered that Count Almaviva . . .

BARTHOLO: Quietly, please. *Please!*

COUNT (*just as loudly*): . . . was in this city, and I have discovered that Miss Rosine has written to him. . . .

BARTHOLO: She has? My dear friend, please don't shout, I beg of you. Why don't we sit down and chat quietly? Now, you say you've discovered that Rosine . . .

COUNT (*noisily*): That's right. Bazile thought you ought to know about this correspondence and asked me to show you her letter; except that you take things too badly. . . .

BARTHOLO: I do? Don't you worry about the way I take things. But please, please, keep your voice down.

COUNT: You said you're deaf in one ear.

BARTHOLO: I am sorry, Señor Alonzo, if I seemed suspicious and blunt; but I am surrounded by schemers and traps . . . and then your bearing, your age, your manner . . . I'm sorry. So, you have the letter?

COUNT: All in good time, sir, now that you are talking politely. But I am afraid someone may be listening.

BARTHOLO: Who? My servants are all helpless; Rosine has shut herself in her room to sulk. The devil has taken over this house. But I'd better make sure. . . . (*Goes to* ROSINE's *room and opens the door gently.*)

COUNT (*aside*): I'm hemmed in by spite. Must hold on to the letter for the time being. I shall have to run. Better never to have come than to show it to him. If I can only warn Rosine, though, it will be a master stroke to show it to him. . . .

BARTHOLO (*coming back*): She's sitting next to the window, with her back to the door, reading that letter from her cousin, which I looked at. Now let's see your letter.

COUNT: Here it is. (*Aside.*) She is reading my letter.

BARTHOLO (*from the letter the* COUNT *has given him*): "Since you have told me your name and rank . . ." Ah, treachery! It is certainly her handwriting.

COUNT (*nervously*): Now it's your turn to keep your voice down.

BARTHOLO: What are you planning, my friend?

COUNT: When this is all over, you will be her husband, I assure you. Bazile is making arrangements at this moment with a lawyer. . . .

BARTHOLO: For my marriage?

COUNT: Of course. Why else would I warn you against telling her? He told me to say that everything would be ready tomorrow. Then, if she objects . . .

BARTHOLO: She will.

COUNT (*trying to reclaim the letter;* BARTHOLO *holds on to it*):   . . . that's when I can be of service to you. We will show her the letter and, if necessary (*mysteriously*), I'll even tell her that I got it from a woman who had wheedled it away from the count. Do you understand? The shame, the anguish, will make her . . .

BARTHOLO: Ah, slander! Now, my dear boy, I am convinced that you are working for Bazile. But to prevent her from thinking this is a conspiracy, shouldn't she meet you first?

COUNT (*trying not to appear anxious*):   That is what Don Bazile thought. But how can we do it? Time is running out. . . .

BARTHOLO: I'll tell her that you are taking his place. You could give her a music lesson, couldn't you?

COUNT: Anything to please you. But take care not to make her think there's a plot against her. Don't be melodramatic. What if she suspects something?

BARTHOLO: She won't. I'll introduce you myself. You look more like a disguised lover than an official friend.

COUNT: Do you think that will help the deception?

BARTHOLO: I'm sure of it. She is in a terrible mood this evening. But as soon as she sees you . . . Her harpsichord is in that closet. You can play it while you're waiting for her. I'll persuade her to come in somehow.

COUNT: Be sure not to mention the letter to her.

BARTHOLO: I won't. Not before the crucial moment. It would lose its effect. You never have to repeat anything to me. No, you never have to repeat anything to me. (*Exit.*)

COUNT: I've done it. What a hard man to handle! Figaro was right about him. I could tell I was lying badly; that made me even more hesitant. And he has eyes like knives. If I hadn't thought of the letter, I swear I'd have been dismissed like an idiot. They're arguing in there. Suppose she won't come out? (*He goes to the door and listens.*) She refuses to meet me. All my efforts have been wasted. No, here she comes. I'd better not show myself at first. (*Hides in the closet.*)

ROSINE (*pretending to be angry*): It's useless to talk to me, sir. I have made up my mind. I don't want to hear another word about music.

BARTHOLO: But listen, my dear, it's Señor Alonzo, the pupil and friend of Don Bazile, and chosen by him to be one of our witnesses. A little music will soothe you.

ROSINE: Spare yourself the trouble. If I sing this evening, it will only be because . . . But where is this music teacher that you are afraid of sending away? (*The* COUNT *comes out of the closet quietly.*) I'll tell him what I think of him and of Don Bazile. (*She sees the* COUNT.) Oh!

BARTHOLO: What's wrong?

ROSINE: Nothing, nothing.

BARTHOLO: She is ill again, Señor Alonzo.

ROSINE: No, I am not ill. But as I was turning—oh! . . .

COUNT: You twisted your foot, madam?

ROSINE: What? Yes, I twisted my foot. The pain is awful.

COUNT: I saw you do it.

ROSINE (*looking at the* COUNT): The pain went straight to my heart.

BARTHOLO: A seat, a seat! There isn't an armchair here. (*Goes for one.*)

COUNT: Ah, Rosine.

ROSINE: You are too rash.

COUNT: I have a thousand things to tell you.

ROSINE: He won't leave us alone.

COUNT: Figaro will help us.

BARTHOLO (*bringing in an armchair*): Here you are, my darling, sit down. It doesn't look as if she'll be able to take her music lesson this evening, Señor Alonzo; it'll have to wait. Good night.

ROSINE (*to* COUNT): No, stay. The pain is not so severe now. (*To* BARTHOLO.) I have been unfair to you, sir. I'd like to make it up to you, by following your good example. . . .

BARTHOLO: Oh, you sweet, dear little thing. But you have been so upset that I don't want you to strain yourself in the least. Good-by, señor.

ROSINE (*to* COUNT): One moment, please. (*To* BARTHOLO.) If you stop me from taking my lesson, sir, I shall think that you don't want me to prove how sorry I am.

COUNT (*quietly, to* BARTHOLO): Take my advice: don't cross her.

BARTHOLO: Anything you wish, my love, I am so eager not to displease you, I'll stay here during the whole lesson.

ROSINE: No need to, sir. I know that you don't like music.

BARTHOLO: This evening I shall love it.

ROSINE (*aside, to* COUNT): I can't get rid of him.

COUNT (*taking a piece of paper from the desk*): Would you like to sing this, my lady?

ROSINE: Yes, it's a very nice song from *The Useless Precaution.*

BARTHOLO: *The Useless Precaution* again.

COUNT: It's all the rage today. It's a song about spring, a very sweet melody. And, now, if you'd like to try it . . .

ROSINE: With pleasure. I love the idea of spring; the young days of Nature. Winter has disappeared and the heart becomes sensitive, like a slave who has been locked up for a long time and then appreciates his liberty more than ever.

BARTHOLO (*to* COUNT, *quietly*): Her head's still full of romantic ideas.

COUNT (*quietly*): You realize where they can lead?

BARTHOLO: Yes, yes. (*He sits in the armchair he brought in for* ROSINE.)

ROSINE (*sings*):

> When love doth bring
> The first of spring
> To fire the flowers
> And warm the hours
> And overjoy young hearts—
> A bird sings praises
> To the sun
> A new lamb grazes,
> Everyone
> Is glad when springtime starts.

COUNT (*sings*):

> And Lindor dreams in happiness
> Of being loved by his shepherdess.

ROSINE (*sings*):

> For though they may be
> Watched and spied on
> Not knowing who can
> Be relied on—
> This is the test
> That makes love surer,
> Stronger and purer. . . .
> Yes, lovers are deeply impressed:
> The spring of the year is best.

(BARTHOLO *has fallen asleep, and the* COUNT *has been kissing* ROSINE's *hands while she was singing. Now that she has stopped,* BARTHOLO *wakes up. The* COUNT *stands up.* ROSINE *begins to sing the second verse again.* BARTHOLO *is again lulled to sleep. Finally:*)

COUNT: Madam, you sang that with great feeling.

ROSINE: You flatter me, sir. It was your encouragement. . . .

BARTHOLO (*yawning*):   I must have dozed off during that charming interlude. What with patients all the time, I have to run here and there, and as soon as I sit down and take the weight off my legs, it's good night again. (*Gets up and pushes the armchair back.*)

ROSINE (*softly, to the* COUNT):   Figaro isn't coming.

COUNT: We'll have to spin out the talk.

BARTHOLO: You know, I keep telling old Bazile, there must be something for Rosine to study that's a bit livelier than all these grand arias which go up and down with the trills and the frills and the doh-soh-me-doh-me-soh's. They're like burial marches. Give me those catchy little melodies we used to sing when I was a lad; they were so easy to remember. I used to know them all. For instance . . . (*He scratches his head to help his memory, then sings, snapping his fingers and thumbs and kicking up his knees.*)

> Oh, my pretty Rosinette,
> Will you marry me and get
> The monarch of the merry swains . . .

(*To the* COUNT, *laughing.*) In the original song it was Fanchonette, but I substituted Rosinette to bring it up to date. Ha, ha, ha, ha. Pretty smart, eh?

COUNT (*laughing*):   Yes, devastating.

BARTHOLO (*singing*):

> Oh, my pretty Rosinette,
> Will you marry me and get
> The monarch of the merry swains,
> Youth and tenderness and brains?
>
> I may not be handsome, yet
> I know how to play.
> When the night gets dark as jet
> Every cat looks gray.

(*He sings the last verse again, dancing to the rhythm.* FIGARO *comes in behind him and mimics his movements from behind. Noticing* FIGARO:) Hello, Mr. Barber. Step forward. You are a charming fellow.

FIGARO (*bowing*):   Sir, it's true that my mother said so once, but since then I've become somewhat less sightly. (*Aside, to the* COUNT.) Everything is under control, my lord.

(*During this scene, the* COUNT *tries his hardest to talk to* ROSINE, *but after* FIGARO's *entrance,* BARTHOLO *becomes watchful, and the* COUNT *and* ROSINE *have to play a sort of dumb game during the following exchange of dialogue.*)

BARTHOLO: Have you come back to purge and bleed and drug my household again?

FIGARO: Unfortunately, sir, not every day is a holiday, but when it comes to doing those routine little things that have to be done, I'm always at your command. . . .

BARTHOLO: Oh, yes? Then what do you say, Mr. Activity, to that poor creature who is yawning and falling asleep on his feet? Or to the other poor fellow who has been sneezing his nose off for the last three hours?

FIGARO: What would I say to them? Well, to the one who is sneezing, I would say: "God bless you." And to the one who is falling asleep, I would say: "Go to bed." And I wouldn't charge either of them for the advice.

BARTHOLO: No, but you'll charge them for the bleeding and the drugs, won't you? And what about my poor, blind mule, with his eyes blocked up by a poultice?

FIGARO: That won't stop him from seeing anything that he missed before.

BARTHOLO: Just let me find it on the bill, that's all. I don't believe in these expensive jokes.

FIGARO: Men have hardly any choice between stupidity and folly; so where I can't make a profit, I try to make some pleasure. Long live joy. Who knows if the world will last for another three weeks?

BARTHOLO: It would be better for both of us, Mr. Reason-Twister, if you paid me my hundred crowns without any more evasion.

FIGARO: Do you doubt my honesty, sir? I would never deny that I owe you one hundred crowns. I would rather owe you them for the rest of my life.

BARTHOLO: And by the way, how did your daughter like the candies?

FIGARO: What candies are you talking about?

BARTHOLO: The ones you took in the paper cone this morning.

FIGARO: Damned if I remember . . .

ROSINE (*interrupting*): I hope you remembered to give them to her, Mr. Figaro. I asked you to tell her they were from me.

FIGARO: Oh, the candies. The candies from this morning. Of course. I'm so stupid. I'd forgotten all about them. They were excellent, madam, delicious.

BARTHOLO: Yes, excellent, delicious! As delicious as the taste of your own words, when you have to eat them. Words seem to be your stock-in-trade.

FIGARO: What's wrong now, sir?

BARTHOLO: A fine reputation you're giving yourself.

FIGARO: A high reputation, I hope, sir.

BARTHOLO: Make sure you're not underneath when it starts to fall, sir.

FIGARO: I'll take your advice, sir.

BARTHOLO: Don't turn away from me, sir. When I argue with a fool, I never give in.

FIGARO: We differ there, sir. I always give in. (*Turns his back on* BARTHOLO.)

BARTHOLO: What was that he said, Señor Alonzo?

FIGARO: You think you're talking to some village barber, who can handle nothing but a razor. But I, sir, wield a pen too. When I was in Madrid, if it hadn't been for those envious . . .

BARTHOLO: You should have stayed in Madrid. Why did you change your profession?

FIGARO: I had no choice. Put yourself in my place.

BARTHOLO: Not likely. I'd be saying such idiotic things.

FIGARO: You haven't started too badly. I appeal to your colleague who is daydreaming over there to bear me out.

COUNT: I am not his colleague.

FIGARO: Oh? I saw you here and assumed that you were working together.

BARTHOLO (*angrily*): What have you come for? Have you brought the young lady another letter? Perhaps I should step outside.

FIGARO: You are so rude to the lower classes. No, sir, I came in order to shave you, that's all. Isn't today your day?

BARTHOLO: Come back some other time.

FIGARO: What other time? Tomorrow morning, I have to give all the men in the barracks their laxatives. I have an exclusive contract; I had to bribe heavily to get it. So I have no time to waste. Would you like to go into your room?

BARTHOLO: No, I would not. Why can't you shave me in here?

ROSINE (*scornfully*): How gentlemanly! Why not in my room?

BARTHOLO: Don't be annoyed, my dear. You still have to finish your lesson. I didn't want to miss the pleasure of hearing you.

FIGARO (*aside, to the* COUNT): We'll never get him out of here. (*Aloud.*) Lively! Puberty! Come on! Water, a basin and everything else I need to shave the doctor.

BARTHOLO: It won't do you any good to call them. I had to send them to bed, exhausted, harassed, and helpless after your treatment.

FIGARO: All right, I'll get the things myself. They are in your room, aren't they? (*Aside to the* COUNT.) I'll soon get him outside.

BARTHOLO (*takes out his bunch of keys, then reflects*): No, I'll go. (*Aside to the* COUNT, *as he goes out.*) Keep an eye on them. (*Exit.*)

FIGARO: We missed a great opportunity there. He was going to give me his key ring. I think the window key is on it.

ROSINE: Yes, it's the brand-new one.

(BARTHOLO *comes back.*)

BARTHOLO (*aside*): I don't know what I was thinking of, to let that crafty barber stay in here. (*Aloud.*) Here. (*Gives him the bunch of keys.*) In my room, under the desk. Don't touch anything else.

FIGARO: It would serve you right if I did, you're so suspicious. (*Aside, as he goes out fingering the key.*) See how Heaven helps the righteous. (*Exit.*)

BARTHOLO (*aside, to the* COUNT): He's the wretch who took the letter to the count.

COUNT: He looks irresponsible to me.

BARTHOLO: He won't catch me again.

COUNT: I'm sure the worst is over.

BARTHOLO: Everything considered, I thought it was safer to send him to my room than to leave him here with her.

COUNT: They couldn't have said anything. I would have overheard.

ROSINE: Gentlemen, it isn't very polite to keep whispering. What about my lesson?

(*A noise, off, as of breaking china.*)

BARTHOLO: What was that crash? That clumsy barber must have dropped everything on the stairs. . . . My finest china! (*He runs out.*)

COUNT: Figaro has found a way to give us a moment together. I think I know how to rescue you, if you will listen to these instructions.

ROSINE: Of course, Lindor.

COUNT: I'll climb up to your window. I received your letter this morning, but I was forced to say that . . .

(BARTHOLO *and* FIGARO *come back.*)

BARTHOLO: I was right. Everything is broken, shattered.

FIGARO: It was hard luck. I couldn't see a thing on the stairs. (*He shows the key to the* COUNT.) As I was coming up, the key got caught in the banister rail . . .

BARTHOLO: Why didn't you take more care? The key got caught! Clever man!

FIGARO: Find somebody cleverer, then.

(DON BAZILE *comes in.*)

ROSINE: Don Bazile!

COUNT (*aside*): That's a nuisance.

FIGARO (*aside*): That's a disaster.

BARTHOLO: Ah, Bazile, my friend, I'm glad you're fit again. No after-effects from your illness, eh? I was very worried by what Señor Alonzo told me. Ask him if I wasn't ready to rush off to see you. If he hadn't kept me from going . . .

BAZILE: Señor Alonzo?

FIGARO (*stamping on the floor*): Why do I have to put up with all these hindrances? Two hours for one rotten beard. What kind of a customer are you?

BAZILE (*looking around in bewilderment*): Gentlemen, will you please explain to me—

FIGARO: No. You can talk to him after I go.

BAZILE: But I must . . .

COUNT: You must not say one word, Bazile. Do you think you're telling the doctor anything he doesn't already know? I told him that you asked me to give the music lesson for you.

BAZILE: The music lesson? Alonzo? What is this . . . ?

ROSINE: Hush. Quiet.

BAZILE: Are you in this too?

COUNT (*aside, to* BARTHOLO): Tell him about our arrangement.

BARTHOLO (*aside, to* DON BAZILE): Don't give us away, Bazile, by saying that he isn't your pupil. You'll spoil everything.

BAZILE: My pupil . . . ? (*Quietly.*) I came to tell you that the count has moved to . . .

BARTHOLO: Yes, I know. Keep quiet.

BAZILE: Who told you?

BARTHOLO: He did, of course.

COUNT (*joining in quietly*): Of course I did. Just listen.

ROSINE (*quietly to* BAZILE): Is it so hard for you to keep quiet?

FIGARO (*quietly to* BAZILE): Great oaf. He's deaf.

BAZILE: Who the devil's deceiving whom? Everybody's in on the secret.

BARTHOLO (*aloud*): What happened with the lawyer?

FIGARO: He has the whole evening to tell you about the lawyer.

BARTHOLO: Just one thing: are you satisfied with him?

BAZILE (*bewildered*): With the lawyer?

COUNT (*smiling*): Haven't you seen him?

BAZILE (*irritated now*): No, I haven't seen him.

COUNT (*quietly to* BARTHOLO): Do you want him to explain everything in front of her? Send him away.

BARTHOLO (*quietly, to the* COUNT): You're right. (*To* BAZILE.) But what was that illness that took you suddenly?

BAZILE (*furiously*): I don't know what you're talking about.

COUNT (*slipping him a purse*): The doctor means, why did you come here when you weren't well?

FIGARO: He's as white as a corpse.

BAZILE (*looking at the purse*): I'm beginning to understand.

COUNT: Put yourself to bed, my dear Bazile. You don't look fit and we're worried about you. Go to bed.

FIGARO: His face is all drawn. Go to bed.

BARTHOLO: On my word, you could see the fever from a mile away. Go to bed.

ROSINE: Why did you come out? It may be catching. Go to bed.

BAZILE: I think I'd better go to bed.

EVERYBODY: Yes. Go to bed.

BAZILE (*staring at them in turn*): As a matter of fact, I do think it might be wise for me to go home. I don't feel quite up to my ordinary standards.

BARTHOLO: Till tomorrow, then—if you are better.

COUNT: Bazile, I shall be round to see you early.

FIGARO: Take it from me: Your bed should be good and warm.

ROSINE: Good night, Don Bazile.

BAZILE (*aside*):   God help me, I don't understand a thing. If it weren't for this purse . . .

EVERYBODY: Good night, Bazile, good night.

BAZILE: If you all say so. Good night. (*They all see him to the door.*)

BARTHOLO (*professionally*):   That man is definitely not well.

ROSINE: His eyes were rolling.

COUNT: It's a chill of some kind.

FIGARO: Did you see how he was muttering to himself? As if we weren't here? (*to* BARTHOLO.) Well, are you ready now? (*Sits him in a chair and puts a sheet around him; they are at the other end of the room from the* COUNT *and* ROSINE.)

COUNT: Before we conclude the lesson, madam, I must mention one thing that will be essential to the progress of your technique in this art that I am trying to teach you. (*He whispers to her.*)

BARTHOLO (*to* FIGARO):   You seem to be standing in my way deliberately, to stop me from seeing . . .

COUNT (*to* ROSINE):   We have the key to the window. We'll be here at midnight.

FIGARO (*tucking the sheet around* BARTHOLO's *neck*):   From seeing what? If it were a dancing lesson, I'd let you see. But a singing lesson? Oh, oh!

BARTHOLO: What's wrong?

FIGARO: Something went in my eye. (*Puts his head near.*)

BARTHOLO: Don't rub it.

FIGARO: The left eye. Do you think you could get it out?

(BARTHOLO *takes* FIGARO's *head, looks over it and sees the* COUNT *and* ROSINE *whispering. He pushes* FIGARO *violently away and goes behind the others to listen to their conversation.*)

COUNT: About your letter: I needed an excuse to stay here . . .

FIGARO: Ahem, ahem.

COUNT: My disguise didn't seem to be working again . . .

BARTHOLO (*coming between them*):   So your disguise didn't seem to be working . . .

ROSINE: Oh!

BARTHOLO: Very good. In front of me, under my very eyes, you dare to commit such an outrage!

COUNT: What is the matter, sir?

BARTHOLO: Alonzo, eh? It looks like treachery to me.

COUNT: Senor Bartholo, if you often behave in this ridiculous way, I am not surprised that the young lady is reluctant to be your wife.

ROSINE: His wife? What? To spend my days with a jealous old man who offers me slavery for happiness?

BARTHOLO: How dare you say that!

ROSINE: Say it? I'll shout it! I will give my heart and my hand to anybody who can rescue me from this loathsome prison. (*She goes out.*)

BARTHOLO: I'm choking with anger.

COUNT: It is difficult, sir, for a young woman—

FIGARO: Yes, a young woman and an old man, that's what's troubling his senile head.

BARTHOLO: I caught them in the act. You damn barber, I'd like to . . .

FIGARO: I'm getting out. He's mad.

COUNT: So am I. He is mad. (*They go out.*)

BARTHOLO: Mad, am I? Crooks, rogues, slaves of Satan, trying to turn my house into hell. I hope he carries you all off. Mad, am I? I saw them as clearly as I can see this desk . . . and then they face me brazenly. The only man who can tell me what has really happened is Bazile. Come here, somebody. . . . Oh, I forgot; there's nobody. A neighbor, a passer-by, it doesn't matter. It's enough to make me mind my lose—lose my mind!

ACT IV

(*During the entr'acte music, the sounds of a storm are heard. When the curtain rises the stage is dark.* BARTHOLO *enters, followed by* DON BAZILE, *with a lantern in his hand.*)

BARTHOLO: What's this, Bazile? You don't know him? How is that possible?

BAZILE: If you asked me a hundred times, I'd give you the same answer. If he handed you Rosine's letter, he must be one of the count's messengers. But to judge by the magnificent sum of money he gave me, he could even be the count himself.

BARTHOLO: How can we know? By the way, that money he gave you—why did you take it?

BAZILE: He seemed to be in league with you. I didn't know what was going on. And whenever it's difficult for me to make up my mind about anything, a purse always convinces me. Besides, as the proverb goes: whatever is worth taking . . .

BARTHOLO: I know: is worth . . .

BAZILE: Keeping.

BARTHOLO (*surprised*): You mean: is worth earning.

BAZILE: I arrange my proverbs to suit circumstances. Variations on a theme. But to get back to the point: how far are you prepared to go?

BARTHOLO: In my place, Bazile, wouldn't you go all out to get her?

BAZILE: No, I would not, Doctor. When it comes to property, ownership is not important; it's enjoyment that makes a man happy. I suggest that if you marry a woman who doesn't love you, you leave yourself open—

BARTHOLO: To deception?

BAZILE (*laughing*): Well, sir, there have been a good number of deceptions this year. I wouldn't put myself out to win a heart that doesn't want me.

BARTHOLO: You are you. It is better for her to weep with me than for me to die without her.

BAZILE: If it's life or death to you, Doctor, then marry her.

BARTHOLO: I intend to. Tonight.

BAZILE: Good-by, then. But remember, when you are talking to her about Figaro and the count, make them seem blacker than hell.

BARTHOLO: Leave it to me.

BAZILE: It's slander, Doctor. Slander. You can't beat it.

BARTHOLO: Here is Rosine's letter; that fellow Alonzo gave it to me. He showed me it without realizing that I could make good use of it.

BAZILE: Good-by; we'll all be here at four o'clock.

BARTHOLO: Why not earlier?

BAZILE: Impossible; the notary is booked.

BARTHOLO: For a marriage?

BAZILE: Yes, at the barber Figaro's house. His niece is getting married.

BARTHOLO: He hasn't got a niece.

BAZILE: He told the notary that he has.

BARTHOLO: I'll swear he's involved in this plot. What is he up to now?

BAZILE: Do you think that . . . ?

BARTHOLO: Those people are clever. I'm not comfortable about this. Go back to the notary and bring him here with you at once.

BAZILE: It's raining; the weather is fierce; but nothing can hold Don Bazile back when he is under contract. Where are you going?

BARTHOLO: To see you out. Figaro has disabled all my servants. I am alone here.

BAZILE: I have my lantern.

BARTHOLO: Here is my master key. I'll wait for you. Whatever happens, nobody but the notary and yourself will be able to come in.

BAZILE: With those precautions, you can't go wrong.

(*They go out. Enter* ROSINE.)

ROSINE: I thought I heard somebody talking. Midnight has struck and Lindor has not come. This bad weather should have helped him. . . . He was sure of not meeting anybody. Ah, Lindor, if you have let me down . . . What is that noise? Oh, it's my guardian. I'll go back inside.

BARTHOLO (*holding up a lamp*): Rosine, since you aren't in your room . . .

ROSINE: I am just going to bed.

BARTHOLO: You won't sleep in this weather, and I have some urgent matters to discuss.

ROSINE: What do you want with me, sir? Isn't it enough to be tormented by you in daylight?

BARTHOLO: Listen to me, Rosine.

ROSINE: I will—tomorrow.

BARTHOLO: One moment, that's all. Please.

ROSINE (*aside*): If he has found out . . .

BARTHOLO (*showing her the letter*): Do you recognize this letter?

ROSINE (*startled*): Where did you get it?

BARTHOLO: I am not going to reproach you, Rosine; at your age a person makes mistakes. But I am your friend, believe me.

ROSINE: I don't want to talk to you any more.

BARTHOLO: This letter, which you wrote to Count Almaviva . . .

ROSINE: To Count Almaviva?

BARTHOLO: You can see what kind of a man he is. As soon as he received it, he gave it to another woman as a keepsake.

ROSINE: Count Almaviva!

BARTHOLO: You can hardly believe this, can you? You are young and inexperienced and gullible. But you were being drawn into a trap. This woman has told me everything; apparently she regards you as a rival. It makes me shudder. This was a plot by Almaviva, Figaro, and this Alonzo, who claimed to be a pupil of Bazile; that is not his real name; he is only an agent for the count. They were planning to mislead you and ruin your name.

ROSINE: Horrible. What, Lindor, that pleasant young man . . . ?

BARTHOLO: Ah, (*aside*) his name is Lindor. . . .

ROSINE: And doing it for Count Almaviva . . . for another man . . .

BARTHOLO: That's what I was told when I was given this letter.

ROSINE: What an indignity! A man has deceived me. He will be punished for it. Sir, you wanted to marry me?

BARTHOLO: You know how deep my feelings are.

ROSINE: If they have not changed, I am yours.

BARTHOLO: Wonderful. The notary will be here tonight.

ROSINE: There is something else. Oh, God, I have been

so humiliated! He is going to come in through that window. He and Figaro stole the key from you.

BARTHOLO (*looking at the key ring*): So they did, the scoundrels. Don't worry, my child, I won't leave you.

ROSINE: What if they are armed?

BARTHOLO: You may be right. I would lose my revenge. Go up to Marceline's room and double-lock yourself in. I'll go out and get help, and wait for them outside the house. I'll have them arrested as thieves. We'll be revenged and rescued at the same time: a double pleasure. Trust my affection; I shall make you happy again.

ROSINE: Please forgive my mistakes. I have been punished enough.

BARTHOLO: Now to lay the ambush. I know how to deal with them. (*Exit.*)

ROSINE: He thinks he can make me happy again when I am so unhappy. (*She cries into her handkerchief.*) What can I do? Lindor will be here any moment. I'd like to stay and argue with him, to see how he tries to trick me. That is what I need to save myself from him. I must. A noble face, a gentle manner, a tender voice . . . and he is nothing but a mercenary. I am so unhappy. . . . What's that? Somebody is opening the window. (*She runs out.*)

(*The* COUNT *appears at the window, with* FIGARO; *they are wearing cloaks.*)

FIGARO (*outside*):   Somebody ran away. Shall I go in?

COUNT (*outside*):   A man?

FIGARO: No.

COUNT: It was Rosine. Your face frightened her away.

FIGARO: I believe it. (*Jumps into the room.*) Well, here we are, in spite of the rain, thunder, and lightning.

COUNT: Help me in. (*He jumps inside.*) Victory at last.

FIGARO (*throwing off his cloak*):   We're soaked through. Charming weather for fortune hunting. What do you think of this night, my lord?

COUNT: For a lover, superb.

FIGARO: Yes, but for an accomplice . . . ? And suppose we're caught here?

COUNT: You're with me, aren't you? I'm worried about something else: how to persuade her to leave this house with us immediately.

FIGARO: As far as the fair sex is concerned, you have the three big passions on your side: love, hatred, and fear.

COUNT (*looking into the darkness*):   How can I tell her

right out that the notary is waiting at your house to marry us? She'll think I'm too bold; she'll say it's a risk.

FIGARO: If she says you're too bold, you can say she's cruel. Women love to be called cruel. And if she loves you as much as you hope, tell her who you are. Then she won't doubt your feelings.

(FIGARO *lights the candles on the table.*)

COUNT: Here she is. My lovely Rosine.

ROSINE (*in a cool voice*): I was beginning to fear that you were not coming, sir.

COUNT: A charming fear. I don't wish to take advantage of the circumstances; I am offering you a share in my poverty; but wherever you choose to live, I swear on my honor . . .

ROSINE: Sir, you would not be here if you were not taking my heart with my hand. It is not your fault if the circumstances are . . . irregular.

COUNT: Rosine, can you accept the companionship of a man without fortune or birth?

ROSINE: Fortune, birth! These are things that come by chance. Simply assure me that your intentions are pure. . . .

COUNT (*kneeling*): Rosine, I adore you.

ROSINE: Stop! You dare to say that, to lie? You adore me! I'm not in danger any longer. I was waiting for that word. I detest you. But before I leave you to your remorse (*crying*) I want you to know that I did love you; I thought I would be happy sharing your poverty. I was ready to leave everything and follow you. But you took advantage of my trust. I know now that you were working for this despicable Count Almaviva, that you were going to sell me to him. Do you recognize this letter?

COUNT: Did your guardian give it back to you?

ROSINE: Yes, and I am grateful to him.

COUNT: I am so glad of the chance to explain it to you. I gave it to him to win his confidence, and I have been trying to tell you about it. It is true then, Rosine, that you love me?

FIGARO: My lord, you wanted a woman who would love you for yourself. . . .

ROSINE: What did he say? "My lord"?

COUNT (*throwing off his cloak, and appearing in magnificent costume*): My darling, now I can tell you the truth; I am not Lindor; I am Count Almaviva. I am dying of love; I have spent six months trying to find you.

ROSINE (*slumping into his arms*):   Ah!

COUNT: Figaro!

FIGARO: Nothing to get upset about, my lord. She's overcome with joy, and that's the best way to be overcome. There
you are, she's coming to already. God, she's beautiful.

ROSINE: Ah, Lindor—I mean, my lord—I have been
wicked. I promised to marry my guardian tonight.

COUNT: Rosine . . .

ROSINE: I was nearly punished: I would have spent my
life hating you. The worst fate of all, Lindor, is to hate when
one was made to love.

FIGARO (*at the window*):   My lord, they've cut off our
escape. The ladder is gone.

COUNT: Gone?

ROSINE: It's the doctor. I believed him. I told him everything; I gave away the whole story. He knows that you are
here, and he is coming up with the police.

FIGARO: They're opening the street door.

ROSINE: Lindor . . . (*She runs into his arms.*)

COUNT: Rosine, you love me, and I am not afraid of
anybody. You will be my wife. And that will be our first
punishment on the old man. . . .

ROSINE: No, Lindor. Have pity on him. My heart is
too full of love to leave any room for vengeance.

(*Enter* DON BAZILE *and* NOTARY.)

FIGARO: It's our notary, my lord.

COUNT: And Bartholo's friend Bazile with him.

BAZILE: What's happening?

FIGARO: This is lucky. How did you . . . ?

BAZILE: This is a mistake. How did you . . . ?

NOTARY: Are these the happy people who are to be con-
joined?

COUNT: Yes, sir. You were supposed to marry this
young lady and me tonight at Figaro's house; but we have
chosen this house instead, for reasons that we will explain.
Have you got the contract?

NOTARY: Have I the honor of addressing His Excellency
Count Almaviva?

FIGARO: You have.

BAZILE (*aside*):   If that's why he gave me the master
key . . .

NOTARY: I have two marriage contracts, my lord. We
must not confuse them. This one is yours; and here is
Señor Bartholo's. He is also going to marry a young lady

named Rosine. Apparently, the two ladies are sisters who have the same name.

COUNT: Let's sign the contract, anyway. Perhaps Don Bazile will sign as the second witness? (*The* COUNT *and* ROSINE *sign.*)

BAZILE: But Your Excellency, I don't understand. . . .

COUNT: My dear Bazile, you are upset by a nothing, and astonished by everything.

BAZILE: But my lord, if the doctor . . .

COUNT (*throwing him a purse*): Don't be awkward. Sign quickly.

BAZILE: Ah, but . . .

FIGARO: What's the difficulty now?

BAZILE (*hefting the purse*): There isn't any. But when I give my word, I have to have a heavy reason for breaking it. (*He signs.*)

(*Enter* BARTHOLO, *with an* ALCALDE [*Spanish magistrate*], POLICEMEN, *and* SERVANTS *with torches.*)

BARTHOLO (*seeing the* COUNT *kissing* ROSINE'S *hand and* FIGARO *embracing* DON BAZILE): Rosine, with these scoundrels! (*Grabs the* NOTARY *by the throat.*) Arrest the lot of them. I've got this one.

NOTARY: I am your notary.

BAZILE: He's your notary. Are you joking?

BARTHOLO: How did you come to be in here?

BAZILE: How did you come to be out of here?

ALCALDE (*pointing to* FIGARO): One moment. I know this man. What are you doing in this house at this late hour?

FIGARO: This early hour, you mean. It's nearer morning than night. I came with His Excellency my lord the Count Almaviva.

BARTHOLO: Almaviva!

ALCALDE: Then these people are not thieves?

BARTHOLO: Forget about that now. (*To the* COUNT.) Anywhere else, my lord, I am your humble servant, but in my house, rank does not mean anything, and I ask you to leave.

COUNT: No, rank doesn't mean anything here; I have nothing over you except Rosine's preference. She has just given me her hand.

BARTHOLO: Is that true, Rosine?

ROSINE: Quite true. Why are you surprised? Didn't I say that I would punish the man who deceived me?

BAZILE: You see, Doctor. I told you it was the count himself.

BARTHOLO: I don't care about that. This marriage is ridiculous. Where are the witnesses?

NOTARY: Everything was in order. I called on these two gentlemen to assist me.

BARTHOLO: What! Bazile, you signed?

BAZILE: What else could I do? This man (*indicating the* COUNT) always has his pockets full of irresistible arguments.

BARTHOLO: I don't give a damn for his arguments. I will use my authority.

COUNT: You have lost it by abusing it.

BARTHOLO: The young lady is a minor.

FIGARO: She has just come of age.

BARTHOLO: Who is talking to you, crook?

COUNT: The young lady is noble and beautiful. I am a man of rank, and I am young and rich. She is now my wife. Is anybody prepared to dispute this marriage which honors us both?

BARTHOLO: I will not give her up.

COUNT: She does not belong to you any more. I shall ask the law, which you were kind enough to bring, to decide whether or not she should be protected against your violence. Our magistrates are the true guardians of the oppressed.

ALCALDE: That is correct. This man's resistance to an honorable marriage indicates that there may have been some misappropriation of his ward's property. He will have to give a full account of her possessions.

COUNT: As long as he agrees to the marriage, I won't pursue this any further. He can keep all property.

FIGARO: Except my bill for one hundred crowns. Let's not lose our heads about this.

BARTHOLO: They were all against me. I stuck my head into a wasp's nest.

BAZILE: You've got it out of a wasp's nest. The girl is gone—but the money remains. The money, old man.

BARTHOLO: Leave me alone, Bazile. All you think of is money. What do I care about money? Do you think money is my only motive? (*He signs.*)

FIGARO: You see, my lord, these two belong to the same family.

NOTARY: But, gentlemen, I am a little bewildered. Are there not two young ladies with the same name?

FIGARO: No, sir. They are only one.

BARTHOLO: And after I took away the ladder to make sure of my marriage! I lost because I was not cautious enough.

FIGARO: Not clever enough. Let's admit it, Doctor: when love and youth unite to deceive an old man, anything he does to try to stop them can only be called a useless precaution. . . .

HUGO: *Hernani*

VICTOR HUGO (1802–1885)

Hugo, the most prolific and versatile French poet of the nineteenth century, was also the most determined and impressive philanderer in history; his "affairs" extended—if we can believe his diary—into his eighty-fourth and final year. The example may have been set for him by his parents, both of whom had other partners throughout the childhood of Victor-Marie and his two older brothers. His parents were divorced when he was sixteen, after many quarrels and reconciliations, and during his young years Hugo traveled to and from Elba, Corsica, Italy, and Spain and across France, as his mother repeatedly joined and ran away from his father. The older Hugo was a soldier-poet, who rose to the rank of general and, under Napoleon, governor of Avellino province in Italy and later Guadalajara in Spain.

The two younger sons went to school in Spain and in Paris, where they learned to translate Virgil and Lucretius and Horace before they were twelve, wrote poetry and studied mathematics, science, and drawing. By the time he left boarding school in Paris, in 1819, Hugo had written *The Devil's Castle*, a melodrama in three acts (when he was ten); *Irtamena*, a tragedy in five acts, dedicated to his mother and appealing to the spirits of Racine and Voltaire for protection; *Athelia*, or *The Scandinavians*, two acts of an unfinished tragedy; *Inez de Castro*, a melodrama in two acts (Inez was a character in Montherlant's play *Queen After Death*, 1942); and an epic poem, *The Flood*. As he passed out of the world of children, Hugo wrote in a poem: "Fame, to you I aspire."

His father gave him and his brother an allowance to pay for courses and books at law school. The boys used the money to found a magazine, *Le Conservateur Littéraire* (*The Literary Conservative*), named after Chateaubriand's

Le Conservateur; the magazine had a short, vigorous life of sixteen months until, in March of 1821, it was swallowed up by another magazine. Hugo himself wrote most of the articles, on a broad range of subjects, including theater. After the magazine's demise, he, Alfred de Vigny, and other poet-critics directed their romantic outpourings into another magazine, *La Muse Française* (*The French Muse*), which was also short-lived.

In 1822 Hugo married Adèle Foucher; the Hugos and the Fouchers had been friendly since Victor and Adèle were children. Within eight years the young couple had three daughters and two sons. Besides his prose and poetry, Hugo had written during those same years three full-length plays. The first of these to be given any kind of a public showing was *Cromwell,* "a drama, rather than a tragedy," to a reading of which Hugo invited Sainte-Beuve, a young but influential critic, who was to become Hugo's close and lifelong friend and—despite this friendship—Mme. Hugo's lover. Hugo explained that the play *Cromwell* had "a great deal of Shakespeare" in it. Sainte-Beuve was thrilled by the drama, but took exception to certain "excesses" in the writing. Hugo put *Cromwell* to one side, came back to it fourteen years later, and rewrote three acts, but never finished it.

The second of the three plays was *Amy Robsart,* which Hugo adapted from *Kenilworth;* Scott was all the rage with the Romantic young French writers of the time. Hugo cannily had this play performed in the name of Paul Foucher, his seventeen-year-old brother-in-law; it was a hopeless failure with the public. The third play, *Marion de Lorme,* a tragedy that heaped fictional extravagance on seventeenth-century fact, portraying Louis XIII with disrespect and Cardinal Richelieu with hatred, was read aloud to a group of Hugo's friends, including Vigny, Balzac, Mérimée, Musset, Lamartine, and Dumas. The writers praised it wildly, and *Marion* was accepted for production four days later by the Théâtre-Français, but was not allowed to be played after the first few performances. As compensation, the king offered Hugo a pension, which he refused. He then sat down and toiled over a new play, *Hernani,* which he finished in twenty-eight days. This play proved acceptable, and the opening night was set for February 25, 1830. Like *The Barber of Seville* and many other great French plays, it was set in Spain, and the hero was named after the Spanish village of Ernani, where Hugo had once stayed as a child.

In the five months before the production, Hugo and his friends organized a claque of supporters from among the bearded, shaggy-haired, demonstrative art students of Paris, to fill the pit and "crush" hecklers and protests. The students were led by Théophile Gautier, who wore for the occasion a deservedly remembered "rose-colored—not red—doublet."

While Hugo ran to and from rehearsals, talked severely to the actors and the leading actress, Mlle. Mars, about how their lines should be enunciated and gave instructions to his hairy storm troops, he was writing poetry steadily and trying to settle the estate of his recently deceased father— whose mistress was contesting the claims of Hugo and his family.

With so much and such violent support from the pit, *Hernani* could not help being a success. Between the fourth and fifth acts, a publisher made a swift deal with Hugo: five thousand francs for the first printing. One of the actors later wrote that the uproar during the fifth act "did nobody any good except the box office." The reviews next day were either vigorously in favor (as in *Le Globe*) or viciously against (as in *Le National*), but business at the theater boomed, cheered on by Hugo's supporters rather than by the general public. The night of February 25, 1830, is still commemorated in France as a major theatrical occasion, in every sense.

If *Hernani* was written in a twenty-eight-day rush, Hugo now showed that he could break his own record. He finished *Le roi s'amuse*, another verse play, in twenty-one days and the following month (July 1832) completed a play in prose, *Lucrezia Borgia*, in twelve days. *Le roi s'amuse* was banned after the first night—as was the original libretto for Verdi's *Rigoletto*,[1] which lifted the basic plot of this play—but *Lucrezia Borgia* was a hit, with Mlle. Georges and the great actor Frédérick Lemaître starring. Between 1833 and 1838 Hugo went on to write *Mary Tudor* (in twenty-four days), *Angelo*, the opera *La Esmeralda* (to Louise Bertin's music), and *Ruy Blas*.

It was during the rehearsals that Hugo met a twenty-six-year-old actress named Juliette Druot, "the most beautiful woman in Paris," and became the latest and last in a succession of her lovers: Juliette remained faithful to Hugo, in spite of great provocation, to the end of her long life. But by 1840 she had been supplanted by a younger actress, Léonie d'Aunet. The affair with Léonie led to a national scandal, instigated by Léonie's husband. The couple were indict-

---

[1] The name "Rigoletto" is an Italianized twisting of the French "Triboulet," the name of the jester in *Le roi s'amuse*. *Ed.*

ed and tried. Hugo (who had been made a viscount) was let off, but Léonie was sent to prison and later to a convent.

Undaunted by the scandal, Hugo became involved with a number of other women—and with national politics. He had changed from a monarchist to an antimonarchist and wrote pamphlets against the election laws and attacking the ambitions of Louis-Napoléon. He was one of the initiators of the uprising of the people in December 1851; four hundred people were killed in the riots, which failed, and Hugo had to flee out of the country, first to Brussels and later to the Channel Islands of Jersey and Guernsey.

He lived in exile for almost twenty years, writing at top speed, striding the acreage of Guernsey, taking cold showers and rubbing himself down with horsehair brushes, attending to the wants of his family and of Juliette Druot, who had come to join him. The family eventually grew bored and returned to Paris, except for one of his sons, François-Victor, who was busily translating all 120,000 lines of Shakespeare's plays into French.

During these exiled years Hugo wrote almost no drama, but produced several of his most important novels, books of literary criticism, and political tracts. Two of the novels, *Les Misérables* and *The Toilers of the Sea*, were immediate best sellers in France, although they had to be published in Belgium.

Hugo did not return to Paris until September 3, 1870, when France was attacked by Bismarck and the Second Empire dissolved. He was a national hero, and received a tremendous welcome from a waiting crowd as his train pulled in.

During the last fifteen years of his life, he remained a leading figure in the literary and political worlds. His plays were repeated; his affairs with actresses (including Sarah Bernhardt), and other women inspired a continuous flow of what might be called "gratitude poetry"; he finished another important novel, on the post-revolutionary years, *Quatre-Vingt-Treize* (*Ninety-Three*) in 1872, *The Art of Being a Grandfather* in 1879 (by which time he had outlived both his sons and two of his daughters), and a play, *Torquemada*, in its final, revised version.

He was elected to the French Assembly in 1871, from which he quickly resigned when he saw little chance of achieving his progressive plans to abolish the death penalty, to establish women's rights, and to promote the United States of Europe; but five years later he became a member of the Senate. He was also, by this time, the senior member of the French Academy.

He was seized by lung congestion on May 21, 1885 and died the following day. His body lay in state below the Arc de Triomphe, during a nationwide day of mourning, and was buried in the Panthéon.

A LIST OF HUGO'S PLAYS:

The Devil's Castle and *Hell on Earth* (both 1812); *Irtamena* (1816); *Athelia,* or *The Scandinavians* (1817); *Inez de Castro* (1817 or 1818); *Cromwell,* later called *The Twins* (1826); *Amy Robsart* (1825); *Marion de Lorme* (1829); *Hernani* (1829); *Le Roi s'amuse* (1832); *Lucrezia Borgia* (1832); *Mary Tudor* (1833); *Angelo* (1835); *Ruy Blas* (1838); *The Burgraves* (1842); *The Wet Forest* (1854); *The Grandmother* (1865); *One Thousand Francs Reward* (1866); *The Intervention* (1866); *On the Edge of a Wood* (1873); *Torquemada* (completed in 1882). Other plays of uncertain dates: *Possibly Gavroche's Brother; Madame Louis XIV; The Devil in Five Acts; End of Satan; Welf, castellan d'Osbor.*

SUGGESTIONS FOR FURTHER READING ON HUGO:

Maurois, André. *Olympio, The Life of Victor Hugo*. Trans. from the French by Gerard Hopkins. New York: Harper & Brothers, 1956.

Pendell, W. D. *Victor Hugo's Acted Dramas and the Contemporary Press*. Baltimore: The Johns Hopkins Press, 1947.

Stevenson, Robert Louis. "Victor Hugo's Romances," in *Familiar Studies of Men and Books*. New York: E. P. Dutton and Company, Inc. (Everyman 765)

(Stevenson is concerned here with Hugo's novels, not with his plays.)

Swinburne, Algernon Charles. *A Study of Victor Hugo*. London: Chatto & Windus, 1886.

IN FRENCH ONLY:

Gaudon, Jean. *Victor Hugo, Dramaturge*. L'Arche, 1955.
Le Breton, A. *Le Théâtre Romantique*. Boivin.
Lote, G. *En Preface à Hernani, Cent ans après*. Librairie Universitaire, 1930.
Zola, Emile. *Nos Auteurs Dramatiques*. Charpentier, 1881.

NOTE: A critical essay on Hugo, "The Work of Victor Hugo," by Algernon Charles Swinburne, will be found on p. 534.

HERNANI

by Victor Hugo

English version by Linda Asher

FIRST PERFORMED AT THE COMÉDIE-FRANÇAISE ON
FEBRUARY 25, 1830

CHARACTERS

Hernani
Don Carlos
Don Ruy Gomez de Silva
Doña Sol de Silva
Duke of Bavaria
Duke of Gotha
Duke of Lutzelburg
Don Sancho
Don Matias
Don Ricardo
Don Garci Suarez
Don Francisco
Don Juan de Haro
Don Gil Tellez Giron
First Conspirator
A Mountaineer
Iaquez
Doña Josefa Duarte
A Lady
Other Conspirators, Mountaineers, Lord, Soldiers, Pages, etc.

The action of the play takes place in Spain, in 1519.

ACT I

THE KING

(*Saragossa: a bedchamber. It is night. A lamp on the table.*)

(*Scene 1.* DOÑA JOSEFA DUARTE, *an old woman in black, with the bodice of her gown ornamented in jet, in the style of Isabella the Catholic; she draws the crimson window drapes and arranges a few chairs. There is a knock at a small hidden door on the right. She listens; there is a second knock.*)

DOÑA JOSEFA: Has he arrived already? (*Another knock.*) It *is* from the secret stairway, no doubt of that. (*A fourth knock.*) Quick, then—I must open it. (*She opens the covered door.* DON CARLOS *enters, his cloak across his lower face, and his hat low over his eyes.*) Good evening to you, sir. (*She leads him in. He opens his cloak and reveals a rich outfit of velvet and silk, in the fashion of Castile in 1519. She looks at him more closely, and draws back, astonished.*) What? Señor Hernani—but it is not you! Help! Guards!

DON CARLOS (*gripping her arm*): Two more words out of you, old woman, and you die! (*He stares hard at her; she subsides into terrified silence.*) Is this the apartment that belongs to Doña Sol? They tell me she is promised to her uncle, the old duke—a gracious lord, proud, venerable, and decrepit. They say this beauty spurns all other men, but that she loves a smooth-faced youth, and every night she meets this young lover—without whiskers or mustache—beneath the very nose of the old man. Is this all true? (*She is silent; he shakes her arm.*) Well? Will you answer me?

DOÑA JOSEFA: You forbade me to speak even two words, my lord.

DON CARLOS: I asked for only one—a yes or no. Doña Sol de Silva *is* your mistress? Speak.

DOÑA JOSEFA: Yes. Why?

DON CARLOS: No matter. And her old fiancé, the duke —he is out at present?

DOÑA JOSEFA: Yes.

DON CARLOS: She must be awaiting her young man, then?

DOÑA JOSEFA: Yes.

DON CARLOS: Oh, I could die!

DOÑA JOSEFA: Yes.

DON CARLOS: Duenna—is this where they meet?

DOÑA JOSEFA: Yes.

DON CARLOS: Hide me here somehow!

DOÑA JOSEFA: Hide you!

DON CARLOS: Yes.

DOÑA JOSEFA: But why?

DON CARLOS: No matter why.

DOÑA JOSEFA: You're asking me to hide you?

DON CARLOS: Yes—somewhere here.

DOÑA JOSEFA: Never!

DON CARLOS (*drawing a knife and a purse at once from his sash*):   Madame, do me the honor of choosing—this purse or else this blade.

DOÑA JOSEFA (*taking the purse*):   You must be the devil.

DON CARLOS: Yes, I am.

DOÑA JOSEFA (*opening a narrow closet in the wall*): Come in here.

DON CARLOS (*looking in*):   This box?

DOÑA JOSEFA (*closing it*):   If it does not suit you, leave.

DON CARLOS (*opening it again and examining it*):   It will do perfectly. (*With another glance inside.*) Is this the stable where you keep your broomstick between rides? (*He cramps himself into it with difficulty.*) Ouff!

DOÑA JOSEFA (*clasping her hands in horror*):   A man— here in this room!

DON CARLOS (*from the still-open closet*):   Oh, then your lady was expecting a woman?

DOÑA JOSEFA: Good heavens—I hear her coming now— please, my lord, close the door, quickly! (*She pushes the door shut.*)

DON CARLOS (*from inside*):   Remember, duenna—say one word, and you shall die.

DOÑA JOSEFA (*alone*):   Who is this man, Good Jesus! Shall I call for help? But whom can I call? Except my lady and myself, all the palace is asleep. Well, the other one will be arriving soon, and this is his affair—he has a good sword. May the Lord save us from perdition! (*Weighs the purse in her hand.*) After all, it's not as though he were a common thief.

(DOÑA SOL *enters, in white;* DOÑA JOSEFA *hides the purse.*)

(*Scene 2*)

DOÑA SOL: Josefa!

DOÑA JOSEFA: My lady?

DOÑA SOL: I am afraid—Hernani should be here by now. (*Sound of steps at the small door.*) Listen—I hear him now on the stair. Open before he knocks—and be quick—hurry!

(JOSEFA *opens the tiny door.* HERNANI *enters, in a great cloak and broad hat. Underneath he is dressed as an Aragonese mountaineer, in gray, with a leather jerkin; a sword, a dagger, and a horn are at his waist.*)

DOÑA SOL (*running to him*): Hernani!

HERNANI: Doña Sol! At last you stand before me, and the voice I hear is yours! Ah, why must fate set my path so far from yours? I need you to help me forget the rest of this unhappy life.

DOÑA SOL: Your cloak is drenched! Is it raining so hard?

HERNANI: I do not know.

DOÑA SOL: You must be chilled.

HERNANI: It is nothing.

DOÑA SOL: Take off that cloak.

HERNANI: Doña Sol, my beloved, tell me this—when you fall to rest at night, all calm, and innocent and pure—when a happy sleep half opens your fresh lips, and when its finger closes your dark eyes—does some angel come and tell you how dear a thing you are to me, a man deserted and rebuffed by all the world?

DOÑA SOL: You are so late, my lord! But tell me, are you cold?

HERNANI: Beside you I only burn! When a fierce love rages in my head, when my heart swells with its own swirling tempests—then how can I feel nature's cloud outside, with all its flash and storming?

DOÑA SOL (*unfastening his cloak*): Come—give me your cape. And your sword too.

HERNANI: No—this is another friend, as innocent and loyal as you. Doña Sol, the old duke, your uncle, your promised husband—is he away?

DOÑA SOL: Yes, this hour belongs to us.

HERNANI: This hour, and nothing more! No more than just an hour for our love! And afterwards, I must forget, or die. My angel, one hour with you when I would ask for all of life and all eternity!

DOÑA SOL: My Hernani!

HERNANI (*bitterly*):   How fortunate I am, that the duke has left the palace! Like a miserable thief I force the door —I creep within and see you, and steal an hour of your sweet song and gaze from the old man. And I am lucky, and others envy me for stealing an hour from him, while he steals my whole life.

DOÑA SOL: Please, Hernani. (*Handing the cloak to the old woman.*) Josefa, dry his cloak. (JOSEFA *goes out.* DOÑA SOL *sits down, and gestures to* HERNANI *to come closer.*) Come here by me.

HERNANI (*not hearing her*):   So the duke is away from the castle. . . .

DOÑA SOL (*smilingly*):   How tall you are!

HERNANI: He is gone awhile—

DOÑA SOL: Dear Hernani, let us not think about the duke.

HERNANI: But we must think about him! That old man loves you, and will marry you. . . . He took a kiss from you the other day—not think about him!

DOÑA SOL (*laughing*):   Is that what's thrown you into such despair? An uncle's kiss—and on the brow besides! Almost a fatherly caress. . . .

HERNANI: No; a lover's kiss, a husband's—the kiss of a jealous man. Oh, my lady, you will soon belong to him! Do you realize that? The foolish, stooped old man, he needs a wife to end his journey and complete his day—and so the chilly specter takes himself a young girl! The mad old man! Does he not see that while he marries you with one hand, death weds him by the other? He comes so heedlessly to thrust himself into our love—when he should instead be measuring himself for the gravedigger! Doña Sol, who made this match? You were forced to it, I hope?

DOÑA SOL: The king desires it, they say.

HERNANI: The king! the king! My father died upon the gallows, condemned by his! And though we have grown older since that day, my hatred is still fresh toward the old king's ghost, his widow, and his son—toward all his flesh. He is dead, he counts no more; but when I was a child I made a vow to avenge my father on his son. Carlos, king of the Castiles—I have sought you everywhere, for the loathing between our houses does not die! Our fathers struggled without pity or remorse for thirty years; now, with our fathers dead, nothing has changed. They died in vain, for their enmity lives on; peace has not yet come to them, for their sons still stand, and still pursue the duel. So it is you, Carlos, who made this shameful match! So much the better. I sought for you, and here you are astride my path.

DOÑA SOL: You frighten me.

HERNANI: I have sworn to carry out a curse, and I must frighten even myself. Listen. The man they have betrothed you to, Don Ruy de Silva, is duke of Pastraña; he is a nobleman of Aragon, a count and grandee of Castile. He cannot give you youth, my sweet young girl; but in its place he offers you such gold, such jewels and gems that your brow will shine among the glittering crowns of royalty. His duchess will hold such power and pride, splendor and wealth, that many a queen could envy her. Such is the duke. While I—I am poor; as a child I had nothing but the forests where I roamed barefoot. I too may own some glowing coat of arms, hid now by clotted blood; I too may have rights that now are cloaked in the folds and shadows of a black gallows-cloth; unless my waiting be in vain, perhaps one day those rights will flash out from this sheath again as I draw my sword. Meanwhile, a jealous heaven has granted me nothing but air, and light, and water—no more than the dowry it offers every man. Let me free you now from one of us, the duke or me. You must choose between us: marry him, or come with me.

DOÑA SOL: I shall go with you.

HERNANI: To live among my rough companions? They are outlaws, whose names the hangman already knows, men whose blades never grow blunt, nor their hearts tender—each of them with some blood vengeance that whips him on. Would you come and be the queen of such a band? For I never told you this—I am an outlaw! When I was hunted through the land of Spain, only old Catalonia welcomed me like a mother into her forests, her harsh mountains, her rough rocks where only the soaring eagle peers. Among her highlanders, her solemn, poor, free men, I grew to manhood; and tomorrow if I sound this horn, three thousand of them will come. . . . You shiver—think again. Would you follow me into the trees, over the hills, along the river's edge? To the land of men who look like the devils in your dreams? And live in doubt, suspecting everything—eyes, voices, footfalls, rustlings—and sleep on the bare grass, and drink from the stream; and as you nurse some waking child at night, to hear musket balls go hissing by your ear?

Would you be an outlawed wanderer with me, and if need

be, follow me to where I shall follow my father—onto the scaffold?

DoÑa Sol: I will follow you.

Hernani: The duke is prosperous and powerful—his life is good. There is no stain on his old family name. The duke can do what he will. He offers you not just his hand, but treasure, titles, and contentment.

DoÑa Sol: We will leave tomorrow. Hernani, do not condemn me for my new boldness. Are you my demon or my angel? I cannot tell—but I am your slave. Wherever you go I will go. Stay, or depart—I belong to you. Why? I cannot say. I need to see you, and must have you near, and have you all the time. When the sound of your step fades, then I think that my heart has stopped its beat; you are gone, and I am gone from myself. But no sooner does that beloved footfall sound in my ear again, than I remember life and feel my soul come back to me!

Hernani (*taking her in his arms*): My love!

DoÑa Sol: At midnight, then, tomorrow. Bring your men to my window, and clap your hands three times. You will see —I will be strong and brave.

Hernani: Do you realize now what I am?

DoÑa Sol: My lord, what does it matter? I am going with you.

Hernani: No—since you want to follow me, impulsive woman, you must learn what name, what rank, what soul, what destiny is hidden in this rough Hernani. You would take a brigand; but would you have a banished man?

Don Carlos (*clattering the cupboard door open*): Will you never finish telling her your tale? Do you suppose it's pleasant, cramped into this closet?

(Hernani *starts back, astonished.* DoÑa Sol *cries out and flies into his arms, staring fearfully at* Don Carlos.)

Hernani (*his hand on his sword hilt*): Who is this man?

DoÑa Sol: Great heavens! Help! Help, guards!

Hernani: Quiet, Doña Sol! You'll waken angry eyes! When I am with you, please, whatever comes, never call for any hand but mine to aid you. (*To* Don Carlos.) What were you doing there?

Don Carlos: I can hardly claim I was out for a gallop through the woods.

Hernani: When a man banters after he offends, only his heir is likely to enjoy the joke.

Don Carlos: One good line deserves another. Sir, let us

speak frankly. You love this lady; you come to watch your eyes in hers each night: very good. I love her too, and want to know who it is I have seen so often entering by the window while I stay at the door.

HERNANI: I swear you shall leave the way I enter, sir.

DON CARLOS: We shall see. So then, I offer my lady my love too. Let us share her, shall we? I've seen such goodness in her soul, so much tender feeling, that I should think she had enough for two lovers. And so, tonight, I thought to bring my plans to fruit. I was mistaken for you, and slipped in by surprise; I hid, I listened—you see how frank I am—but in this slot I hardly heard a word, and nearly suffocated. Besides, my French vest was crumpling badly. I am coming out.

HERNANI: My dagger is uneasy in its hiding place too, and eager to come out.

DON CARLOS (*acknowledging the challenge*): As you like, sir.

HERNANI (*drawing his sword*): En garde!

(DON CARLOS *draws his own.*)

DOÑA SOL (*throwing herself between them*): Hernani! No!

DON CARLOS: Peace, señora.

HERNANI: Tell me your name.

DON CARLOS: Tell me your own!

HERNANI: I am keeping it a deadly secret for another man—one day he will lie beneath my conquering knee and feel my name in his ear, and my knife at his heart.

DON CARLOS: Then what is that man's name?

HERNANI: What can it mean to you? On guard! Defend yourself!

(*They cross swords.* DOÑA SOL *falls trembling onto a chair. Knocking at the main door.*)

DOÑA SOL (*rising in alarm*): Someone is at the door! (*The duel stops.* JOSEFA *enters through the small door, highly agitated.*)

HERNANI (*to* JOSEFA): Who is knocking there?

DOÑA JOSEFA (*to* DOÑA SOL): My lady, a terrible thing! The duke has just returned!

DOÑA SOL (*wringing her hands*): The duke! Then there is no hope. . . .

DOÑA JOSEFA (*glancing about her*): Gracious Lord—the stranger, and these swords—they're battling! This is a fine affair!

(*The two adversaries slip their swords back into the sheaths.* DON CARLOS *wraps himself in his cloak and pulls his hat down over his eyes. The knock is heard again.*)

HERNANI: What shall we do?

(*Another knock.*)

A VOICE OUTSIDE: Doña Sol, open the door. It is I.

(DOÑA JOSEFA *takes a step toward the door, but* HERNANI *stops her.*)

HERNANI: No.
DOÑA JOSEFA (*fingering her rosary*):   Good Saint James, help us through this trial!

(*More knocking.*)

HERNANI: We must hide. (*He points to the closet.*)
DON CARLOS: In that closet again?
HERNANI (*opening its door*):   Go on in, yes; it will hold the two of us.
DON CARLOS: Lord no, it's far too small.
HERNANI: Let us leave then, through the secret door.
DON CARLOS: Good night. I shall stay here.
HERNANI: You will pay for this! (*To* DOÑA SOL.) Can I barricade the door?
DON CARLOS (*to* JOSEFA):   Open it.
HERNANI: What is he saying?
DON CARLOS: Open it, I say! (*She is standing bewildered. The knocking is repeated.* DOÑA JOSEFA *goes trembling to answer it.*)
DOÑA SOL: Lord in heaven, help me!

(*Scene 3*)

DON RUY GOMEZ DE SILVA (*white-haired, white-bearded, dressed in black*):   Men at this hour in my niece's room! Guards, come closer—this calls for brighter light! (*To* DOÑA SOL.) By Saint John of Avila, there are three of us here— two more than should be, madam! (*To the young men.*) You young cavaliers, what business have you here? When the Cid lived, and in Bernardo's day, those two giants of Spain and of the world moved through the Castiles doing honor to the aged and granting women the safeguard of their shields. Those were powerful men—their iron and their steel rode lighter on their shoulders than your velvet does on you. Those men respected a gray beard; they brought their love to consecration in the church and betrayed no man, and their reason was that they must keep the honor of their line. When they desired a woman, they wed her unsullied and in full daylight before the eyes of all, and with their sword, or halberd, or lance firmly in hand. But these criminals who skulk by dark, trusting only the night with their shameful deeds—who steal a woman's honor behind her husband's back—I tell you that the Cid, the ancestor of us all, would have named them vile and forced them to their knees. He would degrade their rank, for they are mere usurpers of nobility; he would deface their coat of arms with a slap of his sword.

Ah, what regret I feel as I think of it—how those men of other times would deal with men today!

Why are you here? To tell me I am an old man, at whom the young shall sneer? Will they laugh at me, who fought at Zamora? When I pass by, white-headed, will they laugh? Not you—no, you at least will not be there to laugh!

HERNANI: Duke—

DON RUY: Silence! . . . You have your swords, your daggers, your lances; you have hunting, and banquets, festivals, and falcons; songs to sing at evening under a balcony, plumes in your hats, and cloaks of silk, and balls and tournaments, and youth, and joy—and yet you children weary of all that! You must have a new plaything; you cast about and pick an old man for it—and now, you have smashed the toy! But God willing, the pieces will spring up whole again and burst in your very teeth! Come out with me!

HERNANI: My lord duke—

DON RUY: Come out with me! Draw your swords! Gentlemen, was this only a whim? Was it? There is a treasure in my house—a young girl's honor, the honor of a woman and of a whole family. I love this girl; she is my niece, and soon she will exchange her ring for the one I wear. I believe her to be chaste and pure, and sacred to all men. It happens that I leave the house an hour, and a thief slips in through the door to steal my honor. Wash off your hands, you soulless men—by no more than a touch you taint our women. Or better—have I still something more for you? (*He pulls off his gold collar of knighthood.*) Here, take and trample this, my Golden Fleece! (*Throws off his hat.*) Wrench out my hair, make it a lowly thing, and tomorrow go and boast throughout the town that never in their shameless games have scoundrels defiled a nobler head, nor whiter hairs.

DOÑA SOL: My lord—

DON RUY (*to his servants*):   Guards—my hatchet, and my knife, and my Toledo blade. And you two, come out with me now!

DON CARLOS (*stepping forward*):   Duke, there is more pressing business first. I came to tell you of Maximilian, emperor of Germany: he is dead. (*He throws off his cloak, and uncovers his face.*)

DON RUY: Are you joking? . . . God, it is the king!

DOÑA SOL: The king!

HERNANI (*his eyes flaring*):   The king of Spain!

DON CARLOS: Yes, Carlos of Spain. My lord duke, then, do you understand? My grandsire the emperor has died; I heard this only now, and hastened here in person to tell you of the news, as a loyal and beloved subject. I came by dark, and incognito, to ask your guidance—all quite simple, and yet see what confusion you arouse!

(DON RUY *sends his servants away with a sign. He draws closer to* DON CARLOS, *whom* DOÑA SOL *watches in fear and surprise.* HERNANI *gazes attentively on, from his corner.*)

DON RUY GOMEZ: But why that long delay before the door was opened?

DON CARLOS: With good reason—you come with a whole escort. When a state secret brings me to your house, am I expected to confide in all your men?

DON RUY: Highness, forgive me! Appearances—

DON CARLOS: Good father, I named you governor of the Figueras castle. Now who will govern you?

DON RUY: Forgive me—

DON CARLOS: Enough. We'll talk no more of it, my lord. Well. The emperor is dead.

DON RUY: Your highness' grandfather—he is dead?

DON CARLOS: I stand before you now heavy with grief.

DON RUY: Who will succeed him?

DON CARLOS: A Saxon duke, perhaps; or Francis the First of France, who is one of the contenders.

DON RUY: Where will the electors meet?

DON CARLOS: At Aix-la-Chapelle, I think, or Spires or Frankfurt.

DON RUY: And our own Spanish king, whose days God guard, has he never considered the throne of empire for himself?

DON CARLOS: Incessantly.

DON RUY: It goes to you by right.

DON CARLOS: I know it.

DON RUY: Your father was archduke of Austria; and I hope the electors will recall that the man who has just fallen from the imperial purple to the shroud was your ancestor.

DON CARLOS: Besides, I am a citizen of Ghent.

DON RUY: I saw your grandfather once when I was young —alas, I am the last survivor of a whole century; everyone else has died now. He was a superb, a mighty emperor.

DON CARLOS: Rome is on my side.

DON RUY: Valiant, firm—and yet no tyrant—that head well suited the old Germanic body! (*He bends to kiss the king's hands.*) I pity you—so young and made to know so terrible a grief.

DON CARLOS: Sicily belongs to me; the pope wants it back again. An emperor cannot own Sicily; thus he makes me emperor; and I, the docile son, give Naples over. Let us first win the eagle and then we'll see whether I let his wings be clipped!

DON RUY: What joy that old ruler would feel to see your already broad brow assume his crown. My lord, we weep with you for that very great and good and Christian emperor!

DON CARLOS: The holy father is nimble. What is Sicily, after all: an island dangling from my realm; a ragged tag, a remnant that hangs off Spain and trails along beside her. He will say this: "What use have you, my son, for that misshapen shred of land that clings by a mere thread to the imperial world? Your empire is badly shaped. Quick now, the shears, and let us cut it off."

Most holy Father, thanks! For if fortune is good to me, I shall expect to stitch a couple of those pieces back again onto the holy empire; and if some few strips are missing here and there, I'll patch my estates together again with duchies and with islands!

DON RUY: May you find consolation. There is an empire of just men where the dead are found again, still holier and grander than they were in life.

DON CARLOS: This King Francis the First is an ambitious man. No sooner does the emperor die than he ogles the throne! He already has his France—a fine piece of Christian land, and well worth holding to. My grandfather the emperor used to say to King Louis, "If I were God the Father, and I had two sons, I should make the elder God, and the other king of France." (*To the duke.*) Do you suppose that Francis has a chance?

Don Ruy: He has a habit of success.

Don Carlos: Everything would have to be amended. The Golden Bull forbids a foreigner to reign.

Don Ruy: But in that respect, Your Highness, you are king of Spain.

Don Carlos: But I am a citizen of Ghent.

Don Ruy: His latest campaign has made King Francis very strong.

Don Carlos: The eagle who may hatch upon my crest can spread his wings wide too.

Don Ruy: Does Your Highness know Latin?

Don Carlos: Only poorly.

Don Ruy: That is a pity. The German nobles like to be addressed in Latin.

Don Carlos: They will be satisfied with a noble Spanish. For mark my words, it makes small difference what tongue a voice may speak, if it speaks strongly enough.

I am setting out for Flanders. Your king, dear Silva, must return to you as emperor. The king of France will do all that he can to win his way; I must overtake him. I shall go shortly.

Don Ruy: Will you leave us, sire, with Aragon still unpurged of these new bandits who raise their brazen heads throughout our mountainland?

Don Carlos: I shall leave orders with the Duke of Arcos to wipe them out.

Don Ruy: And will you also command their leader to let himself be taken?

Don Carlos: Who is their leader—his name?

Don Ruy: I do not know it. But he is said to be a formidable man.

Don Carlos: Nonsense. I know that just now he is hidden in Galicia, and can be taken with a few militia troops.

Don Ruy: Then the rumors are false that say he is nearby?

Don Carlos: Completely false. . . . You will give me a bed for the night.

Don Ruy (*bowing to the floor*):   Thank you, sire. (*Calling his servants.*) All of you, do honor to the king, my guest.

(*The servants bring torches, and the duke orders them into two rows to the door in rear. Meanwhile* Doña Sol *draws imperceptibly closer to* Hernani; *the king watches the pair of them.*)

Doña Sol (*low to Hernani*):   Tomorrow at midnight, beneath my window—do not fail. And clap three times.

Hernani (*softly*):   Tomorrow night . . .

DON CARLOS (*to himself*): Tomorrow! (*And aloud to* DOÑA SOL, *toward whom he moves with courtly gesture.*) Allow me to escort you. (*He leads her to the door; she exits.*)

HERNANI (*his hand inside his breast, on the pommel of his dagger*): My faithful blade! ...

DON CARLOS (*returning, aside*): Our friend has the expression of a man who is trapped. (*He draws Hernani aside.*) I did you the honor, sir, of touching your sword. I could mistrust you for a hundred different reasons—but King Carlos has no taste for betrayals. Go. I am willing to protect you in your flight.

DON RUY (*coming closer and indicating* HERNANI): Who is this gentleman?

DON CARLOS: One of my followers. He is leaving now.

(*They go out with the servants and the torches, the duke ahead of the king, with a candle in his hand.*)

(*Scene 4*)

HERNANI (*alone*): One of your followers—yes, King! Your follower, true! Night and day, and step by step, I follow you. A knife in my fist I go, my eye fixed on your trail—my race in me pursues your race in you. And now besides, you are become my rival. For a moment I hung hesitant between love and hatred; my heart was not large enough to hold both you and her. In loving her I forgot the hatred for you that weighs on me; but since you wish it, since you yourself come to remind me, good! I remember! My love bends the uncertain scales, and falls now wholly to the side of hatred. Yes, I am one of your followers. No courtier dancing in your accursed halls, no noble lord kissing your shadow, no steward denying his own man's heart for your heart's whim, no palace dog trained to slink at the king's heel, will dog your step more diligently than I! All that those Castilian grandees want of you is some pointless title, some shiny trinket, some golden sheep to hang about their throats; I'm not so foolish as to yearn so small! What I want from you is no vain favor—it is your body's soul, your vein's blood; I want what a fuming, conquering knife can dredge out from a heart's dark root. Lead on before me! I shall follow you. My vengeance is alert, it moves with me and speaks into my ear. Lead!

I am here, I watch and I listen; my step seeks yours sound-
lessly, pursues it, and draws close. By day, my king, you'll
never turn your head but you shall find me motionless and
dark amid your celebration. By night you shall not turn your
eyes, my king, but you shall see my burning eyes glow
hot behind you! (*He goes out the small door.*)

ACT II

THE BANDIT

(*Saragossa. A patio in the Silva palace. At left, the palace's high walls, with a balconied window. Beneath the window is a small door. At right and rear are houses and streets. It is night. Here and there in the buildings a few windows are still showing light.*)

(*Scene 1.* DON CARLOS, DON SANCHO SANCHEZ DE ZUÑIGA, DON MATIAS CENTURION, DON RICARDO DE ROXAS, *all four arrive onstage, with* DON CARLOS *at their head. Their hats are pulled low and they are enveloped in long cloaks whose lower edges are lifted by their spears.*)

DON CARLOS (*surveying the balcony*): There is the balcony, and the door, just as she said. . . . My blood is boiling hot. (*Pointing to the unlit window.*) No light there yet! (*His eyes rove over the other lighted casements.*) Lights everywhere that are no use to me, and none where I would see one!

DON SANCHO: That traitor; my lord—you simply let him leave?

DON CARLOS: Yes.

DON MATIAS: And he may have been the bandit general!

DON CARLOS: He might have been their general or their drummer boy, but no sceptered king ever bore himself more nobly.

DON SANCHO: What was his name, my lord?

DON CARLOS (*his eyes on the casement window*): Muñoz— . . . Fernan— . . . (*He suddenly remembers something.*) A name that ends in *i*.

DON SANCHO: Hernani, possibly?

DON CARLOS: Yes.

DON MATIAS: Hernani? Then it *was* the chief!

233

Don Sancho (*to the king*): Do you remember anything of what he said?

Don Carlos (*who has not taken his eyes from the window*): I could not hear a thing in their damned closet.

Don Sancho: But why let him go when he was in your hands?

Don Carlos (*turning slowly and staring at him*): Count of Monterey, do you question me? (*The two lords draw back and are silent.*) Besides, that is not what concerns me now. I want his mistress, not his head. I want her black eyes, friends! The loveliest in the world! Two mirrors! Two black beams of light, two dark torches! I heard nothing of their babble but these few words: "Tomorrow, come at midnight" —but they are the important ones. A perfect arrangement, gentlemen, I think you will agree: while this winsome bandit dallies at some murder or other, or digging someone's grave, I come at my ease and make off with his dove.

Don Ricardo: Your Highness, it were more decisive to take the dove by killing off the vulture.

Don Carlos (*to Don Ricardo*): A valuable suggestion, Count! Your hand is quick!

Don Ricardo (*bowing deeply*): By what title does the king please to name me count?

Don Sancho (*angrily*): That was an error!

Don Ricardo (*to Don Sancho*): The king called me count.

Don Carlos: That's enough. (*To Don Ricardo.*) I dropped that title. Pick it up.

Don Ricardo (*bowing again*): Thank you, Highness.

Don Sancho (*to Don Matias*): A fine count—a count by accident!

(*The king walks about stage rear, looking at the lighted windows impatiently. The two noblemen converse in the foreground.*)

Don Matias (*to Don Sancho*): But what will the king do, once he has the woman?

Don Sancho (*watching Ricardo out of the corner of his eye*): Make her a countess, and then a lady in waiting; then, if he has a son by her, it will be king.

Don Matias: Oh, come now. A bastard? Count, even a king can never draw a king out of a countess.

Don Sancho: He'll make her a marquise then, my dear marquis.

Don Matias: Bastards are brought up to be the viceroys

of conquered countries—that is how they are used.

(DON CARLOS *comes back.*)

DON CARLOS (*looking about at all the lighted windows*): They are watching us like dozens of jealous eyes. . . . Well, finally—two have just gone out. Now for the rest of them! Gentlemen, how long these waiting minutes! Who can make the time move faster?

DON SANCHO: We often wonder in Your Highness' court.

DON CARLOS: And meanwhile my people are saying it of you. (*The last bright window dims.*) The last of them is out! (*He turns toward the balcony of* DOÑA SOL's *room; it is still dark.*) You damned glass, when will you turn light? This night is very dark. Doña Sol, come shine like a star in all this blackness! (*To* DON RICARDO.) What time is it?

DON RICARDO: Nearly midnight.

DON CARLOS: This business must be done with soon—the other one may come at any moment!

(DOÑA SOL's *window brightens. Her shadow is visible on the lighted panes.*) Friends—a torch—her shadow at the window! No dawn was ever more beautiful to me than this one. I must be quick: give the signal she is waiting for, and clap my hands three times. In an instant, friends, you'll see her! . . . But our number will frighten her, perhaps—go, the three of you, into the shadow there, and watch for him. We'll share the loving pair among us—I take the lady, and you three the brigand.

DON RICARDO: A thousand thanks.

DON CARLOS: If he comes, get to him quickly and stun him with your swords. Then, while he is still unconscious, I'll go off with the girl; we shall meet later. But be sure not to kill him. He is a valiant man, and a man's death is a serious thing.

(*The two noblemen bow and leave.* DON CARLOS *waits till they disappear, then claps twice. At the second, the window opens, and* DOÑA SOL *appears on the balcony.*)

(Scene 2)

DOÑA SOL (*from the balcony*): Is it you, Hernani?

DON CARLOS (*to himself*): I must not speak! (*He claps his hands once more.*)

Doña Sol: I shall come down.

(*She closes the window, and the light goes out. A moment later, the small door opens and she emerges, a lantern in her hand and a cloak over her shoulders.*)

Doña Sol: Hernani! (Don Carlos *pulls his hat low over his face, and hurries to her.*) That is not his step! (*She turns to go back.* Don Carlos *runs to her and holds her by the arm.*)

Don Carlos: Doña Sol!

Doña Sol: And not his voice!

Don Carlos: What more adoring voice could you desire? It is still a lover's voice, and a royal lover's besides.

Doña Sol: The king!

Don Carlos: Wish or command—a kingdom is yours to have! For the man whose gentle grasp you would break is the king your lord, and Carlos is your slave!

Doña Sol (*struggling to free herself*):   Hernani, help me!

Don Carlos: You fear the wrong man—this is not your bandit holding you; it is the king!

Doña Sol: No. *You* are the bandit! Do you feel no shame? I blush with it for you. Are these the exploits for a king to boast? To come by night and take a woman by force? My bandit is worth a thousand of you! If a man's birth matched his nobility—if God gave rank according to men's hearts, then he would be the king, and you the criminal!

Don Carlos (*trying to draw her with him*):   Madame—

Doña Sol: Have you forgotten that my father was a count?

Don Carlos: I shall make you a duchess.

Doña Sol (*pushing him away*):   Shame! (*She draws back a few steps.*) There can be nothing of the sort between us, Don Carlos. My aged father poured out his blood for you. I am a noblewoman, I come from that proud blood—too haughty for a concubine, and too lowly for a bride.

Don Carlos: Princess!

Doña Sol: Go offer your love games to common girls, King Carlos; else, if you dare to treat me in such disgraceful manner, I can show you quite clearly that I am a lady and a woman both.

Don Carlos: Well then, come share my throne and my name too. Come—you shall be queen, and empress besides—

Doña Sol: No. That is a ruse. Besides, Your Highness, I must speak honestly—no matter if you were another man,

I would rather wander with Hernani, my own king; rather live outside the world, and the law, in hunger, and thirst, forever hunted and in flight, rather share his sorry destiny from day to day, share his solitude, his battles and his exile, his grief, his poverty, his fear—I would rather all that than be empress to any emperor.

DON CARLOS: How fortunate he is!

DOÑA SOL: He is a pitiful exile!

DON CARLOS: But fortunate even so, for he is loved. I am alone, and an angel walks with him. Do you loathe me?

DOÑA SOL: I do not love you.

DON CARLOS (*seizing her violently*): Whether you love me or not can make no difference—you will come! My hand is stronger than yours—you will come. I want you! We shall soon see if I am king of Spain and of the Indies for nothing.

DOÑA SOL (*struggling*): Have pity on me, my lord! You are king! You are royal! You have but to select a duchess, a marquise, or a countess. The loyal ladies of the court can always find a love that's ready made to answer yours. But my exiled beloved, what did the miserly heavens ever grant to him? You have Castile, Aragon, and Navarre; and Murcia and León; ten other realms, and Flanders; you have India with all its golden mines! You own an empire vast beyond any other king's, a domain so wide it never sees a setting sun! And with all of this, could you, the king, take a poor girl from him who has nothing else? (*She throws herself to her knees. He tries to draw her away.*)

DON CARLOS: Come! I do not hear your words. Come, and if you will, I give you any four of my Spains. Which will you have? Come, choose them! (*She struggles in his arms.*)

DOÑA SOL: For my honor's sake, I want nothing of you but this dagger, sir! (*She wrenches the knife from his belt. He releases her and falls back.*) Come forward now! Take a single step!

DON CARLOS: So that is how she plays! I do not wonder now that she should love a rebel! (*He moves to take a step; she raises the dagger.*)

DOÑA SOL: One step and I kill you and myself. (*He draws back again. She turns away and cries loudly.*) Hernani! Hernani!

DON CARLOS: Quiet!

DOÑA SOL (*the knife ready*): One step, and all is over!

DON CARLOS: Madam! Now you have gone too far; I can be gentle no longer. I have three men here to force you . . .

HERNANI (*springing from behind him*): There is one you did not count!

(*The king turns and sees* HERNANI *poised behind him in the shadows, his arms crossed under his long cloak, and the broad border of his hat raised.* DOÑA SOL *cries out, runs to* HERNANI, *and throws her arms around him.*)

(*Scene 3*)

HERNANI (*motionless, his arms still crossed and his glittering eyes set on the king*): As God is my witness, I did not want to confront you now, nor here.

DOÑA SOL: Hernani, save me from him!

HERNANI: Be calm, my love.

DON CARLOS: What are my men doing in the town to have let this gypsy chieftain pass? Monterey! (*He calls.*)

HERNANI: Your men are in the hands of mine—no use to cry out for their powerless swords. For any three that came to your call, sixty would run to mine. Sixty, and every one of them worth four of yours. So . . . we shall settle our quarrel between the two of us. You raised your hand against this girl! It was an unwise move, my lord king of Castile; a coward's act.

DON CARLOS (*smiling disdainfully*): My lord bandit, let there be no reproach from you to me.

HERNANI: He laughs! I am no king; but when a king insults me, and then scoffs, my rage springs up and lifts me to his height. Beware, for when I am offended, men fear my angry brow more than any kingly crest! You are mad if you have some illusion of hope. (*He seizes the king.*) Do you know whose hand grips you now? Listen. Your father sentenced mine to death. For that I hate you. You took my title and my estate. For that I hate you. We love the same woman, both of us. For that I hate you, I hate you for everything—I hate you from my soul!

DON CARLOS: Very well.

HERNANI: And yet this evening my hatred seemed far away. I felt only one desire, one heat, one need—Doña Sol! I hastened here, full of love—and I find you in this vile attempt on her! I had forgotten you, but you are set across my path! You are mad, Don Carlos! You are caught in your own snare without help, or hope of escape. I have you in my hand! You are alone, surrounded by furious enemies. What will you do?

DON CARLOS (*proudly*): You dare to question me!

HERNANI: I will not have you struck down by some strange hand—my vengeance must not elude me now. No one but I shall touch you; defend yourself. (*He draws his sword.*)

DON CARLOS: I am the king, your master. Strike; but I will not duel with you.

HERNANI: If you recall, only yesterday you crossed your blade with mine.

DON CARLOS: Yesterday it still could be. I did not know your name, nor you my rank. Today you know who I am and I know you.

HERNANI: Perhaps.

DON CARLOS: No duel, then. Assassinate me.

HERNANI: Do you suppose that kings are sacred to me? Draw your sword!

DON CARLOS: You must murder me. (HERNANI *draws back.* DON CARLOS *sets his eagle eyes on him.*) Do you believe your bandit gangs can roam through our towns at will? Striped with gore and stained with murder as you are, do you believe that you can still strut and pose as noble men, and expect that we should dignify your knives by striking ours against them? Are we such gullible victims? No, crime holds you in its grip; it trails you where you go. And we—are we to duel with you? Never. Murder me.

HERNANI (*brooding and thoughtful, stands for a few seconds gripping and releasing the hilt of his sword; then he turns abruptly back to the king, and snaps the sword-blade against the flagstones*): Then leave here. (*The king half turns back toward him, and stares haughtily at him.*) Go.

DON CARLOS: Very well, sir. In a few hours I shall return. My first concern will be to call for the prosecutor. Is there a price already set upon your head?

HERNANI: Yes.

DON CARLOS: From this day forward you shall be considered a traitor and a rebel. I warn you of this; I shall pursue you everywhere. I hereby place you under the ban of the kingdom.

HERNANI: I am already banished.

DON CARLOS: Good.

HERNANI: But France is close by Spain; it will be a haven.

DON CARLOS: I shall be emperor. I set you under the ban of all the empire.

HERNANI: As you will. I have the rest of the world to

defy you from. There are many other lands where your power
cannot reach me.

DON CARLOS: And when I have the world?

HERNANI: Then I shall have my grave.

DON CARLOS: I will put an end to your insolent activities.

HERNANI: Revenge is lame; it comes with halting steps
—but it does come.

DON CARLOS (*half laughing, disdainful*):   That I should
touch the woman this outlaw loves!

HERNANI (*his eyes blazing again*):   Have you forgotten
you are still within my grasp? You would-be Roman Caesar,
do not remind me that you lie frail and small in my hand's
cup; that if I were to clench this too-honorable fist, I should
crush the imperial eagle in the egg!

DON CARLOS: Then do so.

HERNANI: Go! Leave this place! (*He takes off his mantle
and throws it over the king's shoulders.*) Take my cloak,
and go; without it you could not pass alive among my men.
(*The king wraps himself in the cloak.*) You may leave in
safety now. My thirsting rage will let no hand but mine cut
off your life.

DON CARLOS: Remember how you spoke to me tonight,
and ask no mercy of me when we meet again. (*He goes out.*)

(*Scene 4*)

DOÑA SOL (*seizing HERNANI's hand*):   Let us go now
quickly!

HERNANI (*holding her away, with gentle gravity*):   My
love, you have determined to join more firmly in my misery each day; to hold to it always, and to share my days
without reserve until they end. Your scheme is a noble one,
and one that is worthy of so steadfast a heart. But Lord God,
you can see it is too late now to accept so much of her, and
heedlessly to carry off to my lair this beauteous gem a king
wants for his own; to have my Doña Sol follow me and to
own her, to take her life and wed it to my own, to lead her off
with no shame or remorse—there is no time! The scaffold
looms too near!

DOÑA SOL: What are you saying?

HERNANI: I defied the king to his face, and he will
punish me for having dared to free him. He is gone; perhaps

already in his palace, gathering his men, his soldiers, and his noblemen; calling his executioners ...

DOÑA SOL: Hernani! I am frightened! Then hurry—we must leave now together!

HERNANI: Together ... no. No. The time for that is past. Doña Sol, when first you revealed yourself to me, so good, and kind enough to love me with a willing love, I dared to offer you everything I have: my mountain, my woods, my stream. Your sympathy emboldened me; I offered you my outlaw's bread, and half the green and tufted bed the forest gives me. But to offer you half my gallows—oh no, my Doña Sol—the gallows is mine alone.

DOÑA SOL: Yet you promised to share everything.

HERNANI (*falling to his knees*): My saint! At this moment when death perhaps is near, when my dark destiny draws to a dark close, I must tell you this: banished, and burdened by a solemn mission born in a bloody cradle; and as black as is the grief that shades my life—I am a happy man, and call upon all men to envy me! For you have loved me, for you have told me so, for you have leaned and blessed my cursed brow!

DOÑA SOL (*bending over him*): Hernani!

HERNANI: How kind is the fate that set this flower at the chasm's edge for me! (*He rises.*) And I speak not for your sake; I speak for the listening heavens, and for God.

DOÑA SOL: Let me go with you.

HERNANI: It would be a crime to wrench out the flower as I fall into the abyss! No, I have breathed its perfume, and that is enough. Go link the life I've troubled to another man's. Marry the old duke. I myself unbind you. I return into my night. And you—be happy, and forget!

DOÑA SOL: No, I shall come with you. I want my share of your shroud! I shall go where you go!

HERNANI (*grasping her in his arms*): Ah, let me go alone! (*He turns from her with a convulsive movement.*)

DOÑA SOL (*mournfully, and clasping her hands*): Hernani, you would go from me! So, foolish woman, you give your life and see it turned away; and after so much love, and so much pain, you do not earn even the joy of dying by his side.

HERNANI: I am a banished man! I am outlawed! I bring misfortune!

DOÑA SOL: You are a thankless man.

HERNANI (*turning back to her*): Then no! no, I shall stay. You desire it—then I am here. Come ... oh come into my arms! I shall stay, and for as long as you shall want me. Let us forget the others. We shall stay here. (*He seats her on a bench.*) Sit here on this stone. (*He settles at her feet.*) Flames from your eyes wash over my lids; sing me some song as you used to sing at evening, with tears in your dark eyes. Let us be happy! And drink, for the cup is filled, for this hour is ours, and all the rest is madness. Speak to me, sing, and say: Is it not sweet to love and to know you are adored? To be true? To be alone? And is it not sweet to speak our love at night, when all's at rest? . . . Oh let me sleep and dream upon your breast. Doña Sol! My love, my beauty!

(*Sound of alarm bells in the distance.*)

DOÑA SOL (*rising, frightened*): The alarm! Do you hear it? The alarm!

HERNANI (*still on his knees*): No . . . they are tolling our marriage. (*The sound of bells grows louder. There are cries, torches, and lights at all the windows, on all the roofs, in every street.*)

DOÑA SOL: Hernani, flee! Almighty God! All Saragossa is alight!

HERNANI (*half rising*): Our wedding shall be lit by torches!

DOÑA SOL: A deathly wedding! A marriage of the tomb!

(*Sound of swords and cries.*)

HERNANI (*reclining again on the stone bench*): Come lie here in my arms!

(*A mountaineer runs in, his sword in hand.*)

MOUNTAINEER: Sir, long columns of militia and police are entering the square! Be quick, my lord! (HERNANI *rises.*)

DOÑA SOL (*pale*): You were right; he did prepare this.

MOUNTAINEER: Men—to the rescue!

HERNANI (*to the* MOUNTAINEER): I am ready. All is well. (*Cries offstage:* "Death to the bandit!") Your sword. (*To* DOÑA SOL.) Then farewell!

DOÑA SOL: You are lost through my doing! Where will you go? (*Pointing to the small door.*) Come this way! We can leave by that open door.

HERNANI: Abandon my comrades? What are you saying?

DOÑA SOL: This clamor stabs my heart. (*She holds* HER-NANI.) Remember that if you die, I die!

HERNANI (*holding her close*):   One kiss!
DOÑA SOL: My husband! My Hernani! Oh, my master!
HERNANI (*kissing her brow*):   Alas—it is our first.
DOÑA SOL: It is perhaps our last.

(*He leaves. She falls to the bench.*)

ACT III

THE OLD MAN

(The Silva Castle, in the mountains of Aragon. The portrait gallery of the Silva family: a large hall in which the portraits form the decor, in rich frames with ducal coronets and golden blazons. In rear, a tall gothic door. Between every two portraits stands a full panoply of armor, a suit representing each of the different centuries.)

(Scene 1. DOÑA SOL, pale, standing by a table; DON RUY GOMEZ DE SILVA, seated in his great ducal chair of oak.)

DON RUY GOMEZ: At last! Today, within an hour, you shall be my duchess, and I no longer an uncle. And you will embrace me—but have you forgiven me? I was wrong, I know; I caused you shame, and made your cheek turn pale. My doubts surged up too soon; I should not have condemned you thus before I heard you. How false appearances can be—how unjust we are! Two fine young men were there indeed with you; still, I should not have believed my eyes. But what can you expect, my poor child, from an old man like me?

DOÑA SOL *(motionless and grave)*: You still return to that. Who has blamed you for it?

DON RUY GOMEZ: I myself! I was wrong. I should have known a Doña Sol would allow no lovers courting—not such a woman as you, nor one whose heart is flushed with good Spanish blood.

DOÑA SOL: It is good and pure blood indeed, my lord; perhaps it will soon be seen.

DON RUY GOMEZ *(rising and going toward her)*: Understand, a man is not master over himself, when he loves as I love you, and when he is old. Why might a man be jealous, and even cruel? Because he is old. Because grace and fairness, youth in another man all make for fear, all threaten him. Because he is envious of others, and ashamed of himself. What a mockery is this limping love—it brings a drunken fire back to the heart, it makes the soul young again,

244

but it forgets the body! Often when some young shepherd goes by—ah yes, it's come to that—as we pass, he singing and I musing, he to his green pasture, I to my dark halls, often I murmur low beneath my breath "How gladly I would give my battlements, my ancient ducal keep; and I would give my fields and forestlands, and the vast herds that browse upon my hills, my ancient name, my title, and all my ruins, and all my old forbears who soon will welcome me among them —I would give it all for his new-thatched cottage and for his youthful brow!" His hair is black, his eye gleams like your own; you might see him and say "A young man!" And then think of me who am old. I know this. I bear the Silva name, but it is no longer enough. And my mind is ever running on this theme. You see how great a love I bear you. I would give all I have to be young and fair as you. But what am I dreaming of, I young and fair? I who must go so long before you to the grave!

DOÑA SOL: Who can tell?

DON RUY GOMEZ: But believe me, Doña Sol; such gay gallants as those can give no love more lasting than fine phrases. Let a girl love and give her faith to such a man, she may die of it and he will laugh. All those young cockerels, with their bright wings and with their languid song—their love molts like their plumage. The aged ones, whose tone and tints are muted by the years, have a more trusty wing and they are better, though less fair to see. We love well. Our steps may be heavy, our eyes dull, perhaps, and our brows deep-lined—but the heart does not show the crease of age. Alas! When an old man loves, one must go gently; the heart is always young, and it still can bleed. My love is no crystal toy that gleams and trembles; it is a stern and solid love— deep, sure, paternal, friendly, carved of the same oak as my ducal throne. See then how I love you—and I love you too a hundred other ways, as one loves the dawn, as one loves flowers, and as one loves the skies. To know that I shall see you every day—you with your graceful step and your pure brow, the rich fire in your proud eye—I laugh, and in my soul I feel an endless joy.

DOÑA SOL: Alas!

DON RUY GOMEZ: And then, you know, when a man is waning limb by limb, when he stumbles against the marble of the tomb—the world thinks well of the woman watching over him; an innocent dove, an angel sheltering him and suffering a useless antique good only for death. It is a sacred work, and they are right to praise it, when a devoted heart performs this crowning good—to console a dying man until he ends his day—and even perhaps without love, has all the look of love.

Ah, you shall be my woman-hearted angel, who still sweetens the soul of a pitiful old man, and helps to bear the weight of his last years—a daughter in respect, a sister in compassion.

DOÑA SOL: Far from preceding me, you may well follow, my lord. Youth is not reason enough for living. Often the old ones linger, the younger go before; suddenly their eyelids drop like an open tomb whose stone falls back to place.

DON RUY GOMEZ: What mournful talk! I must scold you, my child—a day like this is holy and joyful. But the hour is late; how is it you are not ready for the chapel? Hurry then, and dress yourself. I shall count every second. Put on your wedding gown!

DOÑA SOL: There still is time.

DON RUY GOMEZ: Not much of it. (*A page enters.*) What does Iaquez want of us?

PAGE: My lord, a man—a pilgrim or a beggar—is at the door and asks you for asylum.

DON RUY GOMEZ: Whatever he may be, good fortune enters with the stranger. Let him come. Has there been a report from the outside? What do they say of the treacherous bandit who fills our forests with his rebel acts?

PAGE: Hernani is done for; the mountain lion is finished.

DOÑA SOL (*aside*): Oh God!

DON RUY GOMEZ: What?

PAGE: The band has been destroyed. They say the king himself set after them. Hernani's head is worth a thousand crowns; but I have heard he is dead.

DONA SOL (*aside*): Without me, Hernani!

DON RUY GOMEZ: Thanks be to heaven! the rebel's dead! Now, my dear, we can truly rejoice. Go and prepare yourself, my love, my pride! Today's a double holiday!

DOÑA SOL (*aside*): . . . A wedding dress for widow's weeds! . . . (*She goes out.*)

DON RUY GOMEZ (*to the page*): Send her the jewel case I prepared for her. (*He sits down again in his armchair.*) I want to see her adorned like a madonna; I want her gentle eyes and all my jewels to make her so beautiful a pilgrim would fall upon his knees at sight of her. Oh—and the one who has begged shelter of us, tell him to enter, and ask his pardon. Quickly. (*The page salutes and goes out.*) Leaving a guest to linger at the door! A shameful thing.

(*The rear door opens.* HERNANI *appears, disguised as a pilgrim. The duke rises and goes toward him.*)

(*Scene 2*)

HERNANI (*stopping on the threshold*): My lord, peace and happiness!

DON RUY GOMEZ (*saluting him with a gesture of his hand*): Peace and happiness to you, my guest! (HERNANI *enters. The duke sits again.*) You are a pilgrim?

HERNANI: Yes. (*He bows.*)

DON RUY GOMEZ: You come from Armillas?

HERNANI: No. I took another road. There was fighting there.

DON RUY GOMEZ: The outlaw's men?

HERNANI: I do not know.

DON RUY GOMEZ: And Hernani, their leader—what of him? Do you know?

HERNANI: Who is this man, my lord?

DON RUY GOMEZ: You do not know him? A pity, then you shall not win the bounty for him. Hernani is a rebel who has gone too long unpunished. If you go to Madrid, you still may see him hang.

HERNANI: I am not going there.

DON RUY GOMEZ: The reward goes to whatever man can take him.

HERNANI (*aside*): Let them come!

DON RUY GOMEZ: Where are you bound for, good pilgrim?

HERNANI: My lord, I go to Saragossa.

DON RUY GOMEZ: For a vow made to some saint? to Our Lady?

HERNANI: Yes, Duke—to Our Lady.

DON RUY GOMEZ: Of Pilar?

HERNANI: Of Pilar.

DON RUY GOMEZ: It would be an empty soul that did not fulfill the vows made to the saints. But when you have accomplished yours, have you no further plans? To see the Lady of the Pillar is all you want?

HERNANI: Yes, I want to see the torches and the candles burn; to see Our Lady glowing in her brilliant shrine, with all her golden vestments, and then turn home again.

Don Ruy Gomez: Very good. Your name, my brother?
I am Ruy de Silva.

Hernani (*hesitating*): My name . . . ?

Don Ruy Gomez: You need not pronounce it, if you so
choose. None has the right to demand it here. Have you not
come to ask asylum?

Hernani: Yes, Duke.

Don Ruy Gomez: Thank you. Be welcome; stay here, my
friend, and want for nothing. As for your name, you are
called my guest. Whoever you be, it is well. I'd welcome
Satan himself with peace of mind, if God sent him to me.

(*The double door at rear opens. Doña Sol enters, dressed
in Castilian wedding costume of the period. Behind her are
pages and attendants; two women carry upon a velvet cushion
a chiseled silver box which they place upon a table. It holds
a rich array of jewels, a duchess' coronet, bracelets, collars,
necklaces, pearls, and diamonds in a tumbled heap. Hernani, breathless and startled, his eyes burning, stares at
Doña Sol without listening to the duke.*)

(Scene 3)

Don Ruy Gomez (*continuing*): Here is my own holy
lady. A prayer to her will bring you good fortune. (*He goes
to offer his hand to Doña Sol, who is still pale and grave.*)
My lovely bride, come forward. What? You wear no ring, and
still no coronet?

Hernani (*in a thunderous voice*): Who here would earn
a thousand crowns? (*All turn toward him, astonished. He
rips off his pilgrim's robe, throws it to the door, and appears
in his mountaineer's outfit.*) I am Hernani.

Doña Sol (*aside, joyfully*): He is alive!

Hernani (*to the valets*): I am the man they seek. (*To the
duke.*) You asked if I were called—what, Perez, or Diego?
No, I am named Hernani. It is a name much greater, an exile's
name, an outlaw's name! You see this head? It is worth
enough to pay for your whole feast! (*To the attendants.*) I offer it to all of you. You will be well rewarded! Take it! Tie my
hands, and bind my feet—bind them! No, that is needless;
there is a chain that holds me and that I shall never break!

(*Horror on Doña Sol's part.*)

DON RUY GOMEZ: Madness—my guest is a madman!

HERNANI: Your guest is a bandit.

DOÑA SOL: Do not listen to him!

HERNANI: I have said what I have said.

DON RUY GOMEZ: A thousand golden crowns! Sir, the sum is a high one, and I cannot be sure of all my men.

HERNANI: What does it matter? So much the better if there is one among them who will do it. (*To the attendants.*) Give me up! Sell me!

DON RUY GOMEZ (*trying to quiet him*): Be still! Someone may take you at your word.

HERNANI: My friends, it is a matchless opportunity! I tell you I am the criminal, the rebel—I am Hernani!

DON RUY GOMEZ: Quiet!

HERNANI: Hernani!

DOÑA SOL (*her voice faint, in his ear*): Oh be still, my love!

HERNANI (*half turning toward her*): There is a wedding here! and I shall share in it! My bride awaits me too. (*To the duke.*) She is less lovely than your own, my lord, but no less faithful. Her name is Death. (*To the servants.*) Not one of you steps forward?

DOÑA SOL (*low*): Have pity on me!

HERNANI (*to the servants*): Hernani! A thousand crowns in gold!

DON RUY GOMEZ: It is the devil himself!

HERNANI (*to the young servant*): Come, you there; you can win the bounty; you shall be rich, and from a servant become a man again. (*To the other unmoving men.*) And you, you tremble too! Oh, have I not misery enough!

DON RUY GOMEZ: Brother, in touching your head they risk their own. Were you Hernani, were you a thousand times worse; if the reward for your head were more than gold, were it a whole empire, I still must protect you in this house against the king himself, for as my guest you are here by will of God. May I die if a single hair falls from your brow. (*To DOÑA SOL.*) My niece, within the hour you shall be my wife. Go to your rooms. I must order the castle armed, and bar the door. (*He goes out, and the servants follow him.*)

HERNANI (*glancing despairingly at his weaponless sash*): Not even a knife!

(*When the duke has gone, DOÑA SOL starts to follow her ladies off, then stops. When they have disappeared, she comes anxiously back to HERNANI.*)

(*Scene 4.* HERNANI *gazes coldly at the nuptial jewel casket on the table, and seems almost unaware of her. Then he raises his head abruptly, and his eyes flare.*)

HERNANI: I compliment you! You cannot imagine how thoroughly charming I find your ornaments . . . Enchanting; really, quite admirable. (*He moves to the casket.*) The ring is most tasteful; I like the coronet; the necklace is lovely work, the bracelet quite rare—but a hundred, a hundred times less so than the woman who can hide such perfidy behind so pure a brow! (*He examines the box again.*) And what have you paid for all of this? A little of your love? Why, excellent! That is nothing at all. Good God! To so betray, to feel no shame, and still live on! (*Looking through the jewel box.*) But perhaps though, after all, these are no more than painted pearls, and copper that seems gold, and glass and lead; unreal diamonds, false sapphires, false gems and glittering stones! If that is so, then your heart is false as well, Duchess—false as these ornaments, and you are only gilt! (*He goes back to the case.*) But no. No. It is all real, all good, and every piece is fine. He would not dare to cheat, so near the grave. There is nothing lacking. (*He takes one piece after another from the case.*) Necklets, brilliants, ear pendants . . . a ducal coronet, a ring of gold—marvelous! A fitting thanks to steadfast, true, and deepest love—the precious jewel case!

DOÑA SOL (*going to the casket; she reaches beneath the jewels, and draws out a dagger*):   You have not reached deep enough. Here is the knife I took from King Carlos with my holy Lady's help, when he was offering me a throne; and I refused, for you who vilify me.

HERNANI (*dropping to her feet*):   Oh—I beg from my knees—let me wipe those bitter beloved tears out from your sorrowing eyes. Take my blood for your tears!

DOÑA SOL (*softened*):   Hernani! I love you and forgive you. I feel only love for you.

HERNANI: She has forgiven me, and loves me! But how can I forgive and love myself again, after what I have said? My heavenly angel, show me where you have walked, and let me kiss the pavement where it was.

DOÑA SOL: My love!

HERNANI: No, I cannot be but hateful to my eyes! Listen, say to me: "I love you!" Assure a doubtful heart, and tell me. Often a woman's lips have healed many pains with those few words.

DOÑA SOL (*absorbed, unhearing*): How could he think my love so short of memory? That lusterless men could shrink a heart wherein his name has entered down to the size of other loves, however noble the world might think them!

HERNANI: I have blasphemed! Doña Sol, if I were in your stead, I should have had enough; I should be weary of this wild fool, of this brooding, senseless man who knows not how to kiss till he has wounded. I should tell him "Go." Turn me away, you must! And I shall only bless you, for you were good, and kind; for you have borne me far too long already, for I am evil—I would darken your days with my black nights.

It is too much—your spirit is high and good and pure; if I am bad, why should you suffer for it? Wed the old duke, he is a good man, and noble; he owns Olmedo from his mother, Alcala from his father. Once more I bid you, be rich with him; be happy! Do you know what splendid gifts my own generous hand can offer you? A dowry of sorrow. A choice between blood and tears. Exile, chains, death, the constant fear around me—there is your golden necklace, and your handsome crown, and never has proud husband offered his bride a richer treasure chest of pain and mourning! Marry the old man, I tell you. He deserves you. Who would ever match my doomed head with your clear brow? Who ever, seeing the two of us—you calm and fair, me violent and perilous, you tranquil and blossoming like a shaded flower, me storm-tossed against a thousand different reefs—who would think to say our fates are joined by a single law? No. God, who determines good things, did not make you for me. I have no heaven-sent right to you. I am resigned. I have your heart, but I have it by theft. I hand it to another, worthier man. Heaven has never consented to our love. When I told you it was your destiny, I lied. And in any case, farewell to all revenge and love! My day is done. I'll go then, futile, with my double dream, unable either to win love or to punish. I should have been built to hate, but I can only love! Forgive me, and flee! These prayers are all I ask; do not refuse them, for they are my last. You live, and I am dead. You must not wall yourself into my tomb with me.

DOÑA SOL: Ungrateful love!

HERNANI: Mountains of Aragon! Galicia, Estremadura! I bring misfortune to all who join with me. I have taken your best sons to serve my claims; relentless, I have sent them into battle, and they are dead of it. They were the most val-

iant in all of valiant Spain. And they are dead. They have
fallen in the mountains, all of them upon their backs as
brave men do, before God; if they were to open their eyes
again, they would see the blue heavens. And this is what I
do to all who join me. Is this a destiny that you should want
to share? Doña Sol, take the duke—take hell itself, take the
king! Anyone is better! There is not one friend left who
thinks of me; everything else has gone, and now your turn
has come to leave me too, for I must live alone. Flee my con-
tamination; do not make a religion of love. Oh, have mercy
on yourself, and flee! . . . Perhaps you think me a man like
all the rest, a rational thing who first perceives his goal and
then will move straight toward it. Do not be fooled—I am
not such a man. I am a resistless energy—the blind and deafened agent of doleful mysteries, a soul of sorrows bound
together with darkness. Where am I bound? I cannot say.
But yet I feel myself hurled on by some impulsive gale, some
wild determination. I fall, and fall, and never do I rest. . . .
If once, gasping for breath, I dare to turn my head, a voice
commands "Go on!"; and the chasm is a deep one, and the
depth of it is red with blood or flame! And meanwhile,
along my headlong course, all things are crushed, or die.
Woe to him who comes close to me! Oh, flee! Turn from my
fated path. Against my will I'll do you injury!

DOÑA SOL: Oh God!

HERNANI: My devil is a fearsome one—the single miracle
he cannot work is my happiness. And you are happiness!
So you are not meant for me; seek out another man. Heaven
has rejected me; if ever it should smile upon my fate, do
not believe in it! It would only be in irony. Marry the
duke.

DOÑA SOL: It still was not enough—you tore my heart
and now you crush it. You do not love me now.

HERNANI: You are my heart, my soul! The glowing
hearth that warms me by its flames is you! Do not hate me
that I flee, my love.

DOÑA SOL: I do not hate you. But I shall die of it.

HERNANI: Die? For whom? For me? Could you die for so
little?

DOÑA SOL (letting her tears come):   It is all!

HERNANI (sitting beside her):   You weep, and once more
through my doing. And who will punish me? For you, I know,
will pardon me again. Can you ever know what pain I feel
when even a single tear drowns the radiance in your eyes?
For their brightness is my joy. Oh, my friends are dead! I
am a fool. Forgive me. I want to love, but I do not know the

way—and yet I love so deeply! Weep no more—let's rather die. If I owned a world I would give it to you. What misery this is!

DOÑA SOL (*throwing herself at his neck*):   Oh my proud, my noble lion! I love you.

HERNANI: How supreme a blessing love would be, if one could die of loving too well!

DOÑA SOL: I love you, my lord! I love you and I am wholly yours!

HERNANI (*dropping his head onto her shoulder*):   How sweet a dagger blow would be from you. . . .

DOÑA SOL (*imploring*):   Have you no fear that God will punish you for words like those?

HERNANI (*still leaning on her breast*):   Let him unite us then! . . . You wish it—let it be! I have fought against it!

(*They gaze ecstatically at one another in an embrace, hearing nothing, seeing nothing else, and totally absorbed in their own gaze.* DON RUY GOMEZ *enters by the door at rear. He sees them and stops frozen on the doorsill.*)

(*Scene 5*)

DON RUY GOMEZ (*motionless, his arms crossed, on the threshold*):   Then this is hospitality's reward!

DOÑA SOL: It is the duke! (*The two turn as if shocked awake.*)

DON RUY GOMEZ (*still unmoving*):   Are these my wages, guest? Run, my lord host, and see if the wall is high enough, if the gate is strongly barred and the archer in his tower; go look once, and once again, about your castle for our sake. Look through your arsenal for armor that will fit—try on your battle trappings again at sixty years! And here's our kind of loyalty in payment for your good faith. You do that for us; we shall do this for you. Saints in heaven! I have lived more than sixty years, and seen a hundred bandits, with lawless and untrammeled soul; often, as I drew my dagger from its sheath, I have flushed the hangman's game where I walked. I have seen murderers, forgers, traitors; and faithless grooms serve poison to their masters. I have seen men die without the cross, and without prayer. I saw Sforza, and Borgia; I see Luther now—but never have I seen evil so great as to betray one's host in the face of heaven's thunder!

I come from other times. So black a treason petrifies an old man on the threshold of his home; the aging master, as he waits to fall, takes on the aura of a statue carved for his own tomb. Moors and Castilians! Tell me, what is this man? (*He raises his eyes and runs them over the portraits that circle the hall.*) Oh all ye Silvas who hear me now, forgive me if I say this to you—forgive me if my wrath pronounces hospitality a poor adviser!

HERNANI (*rising*):   Duke—

DON RUY: Silence! (*He takes three or four slow steps into the hall, and again looks about him at the Silva portraits on the walls.*) Sacred departed ones! My ancestors! Men of iron! You who see all that comes from heaven and hell—tell me, my lords, tell me—what is this man? He is not Hernani, no; his name is Judas! Oh strain to speak, and tell me who he is! (*Crossing his arms.*) Have you ever in your times seen such a thing? No!

HERNANI: My lord duke—

DON RUY GOMEZ (*still to the portraits*):   Do you see this? The villain wants to speak! But you can read better in his soul than I. Oh do not hear him, he is a knave! He will tell you he sees that my own hand longs to drench my house with blood; that perhaps my heart is brewing some revenge amid its storm, some vengeance like the feast of the Seven Heads.[1] He will declare he is an exile, and that the name of Silva will ring with all the horror of the Lara name. He will say he is my guest, and yours as well. . . . My fathers, oh my sires, say, am I to blame? Judge now between us!

HERNANI: Ruy Gomez de Silva, if ever a noble brow was raised to heaven, if ever there was fine heart, or lofty soul, they are yours, my lord! I who speak to you am guilty; I have nothing more to say than that I am most surely damned. Yes, I desired to take your bride from you; I did wish to soil your marriage bed, and that is infamous. I have life and blood in me—you have the right to spill it, then wipe your sword, and think no more of it.

DOÑA SOL: My lord, the fault is mine, not his! Strike me instead!

HERNANI: Be silent, Doña Sol. This moment is supreme; this time belongs to me, and it is all I own. Then let me talk to the duke. Sir, believe these last words from my lips: I swear that I am guilty, but be at peace, for she is innocent. That is the whole tale—I guilty and she pure. Your

---

[1] The heads of his seven children were served up to their father at table by their uncle, Ruy Velasquez de Lara.

good faith must go to her, and the thrust of a sword or knife to me. Then toss the body away and wash the floor if you wish; it matters not.

DOÑA SOL: *No!* I alone have done it all! Because I love him. (DON RUY *starts at this word, and turns a terrible gaze on* DOÑA SOL. *She throws herself to her knees.*) Yes, forgive me. I love him, my lord.

DON RUY GOMEZ: You love him! (*To* HERNANI.) Then tremble! (*A blare of trumpets outside. The page enters. To the page*:) What is that sound?

PAGE: It is the king himself, my lord, with a troop of archers, and his herald.

DOÑA SOL: The king! A final stab of fate!

PAGE (*to the duke*): He demands to know the reason why the gate is closed, and wants it opened.

DON RUY GOMEZ: Open to the king. (*The page bows and leaves.*)

DOÑA SOL: He is lost!

(DON RUY *goes to one of the paintings, which is his own portrait, the last on the left; he touches a spring, the portrait turns out like a door, and shows a hiding place in the wall. He turns to* HERNANI.)

DON RUY GOMEZ: Step in here, sir.

HERNANI: My life belongs to you. Surrender it, my lord; I hold it ready. I am your prisoner.

(*He steps into the hiding place.* DON RUY *touches the spring again, and the painting moves back into place.*)

PAGE (*returning*): His Highness the King. (DOÑA SOL *quickly lowers her veil. The double door opens.* DON CARLOS *enters outfitted for war, followed by a crowd of gentlemen armed as he is, and halberdiers, arquebusiers, and crossbowmen.*)

(*Scene 6.* DON CARLOS *advances slowly, his left hand on the hilt of his sword, his right inside his bosom, and stares at the duke in anger. The duke steps before the king and bows deeply. Silence. Suspense and fear in the atmosphere. Finally the king, reaching the duke, lifts his own head abruptly.*)

DON CARLOS: How is it that today, my cousin, your gate

is so firmly locked? By the very saints, I had thought your
blade more rusty by now! I should not have imagined it
would be so quick to flash in your fist again when we should
come to see you. (DON RUY GOMEZ *attempts to speak, but
the king continues, with an imperious gesture.*) It is a little
late to play the young man! Do we wear a turban? Are we
named Boabdil, or Mohammed, and not Carlos—answer!—
that you should lower the portcullis or raise the bridge before us?

DON RUY GOMEZ (*bowing*):   Highness—

DON CARLOS (*to his men*):   Take the keys and seize the
gates. (*Two officers go out. Several others arrange the soldiers into triple file in the hall, from the king to the main
door.* DON CARLOS *turns again toward the duke.*) So, you
yearn to awaken dead mutinies: God in heaven—if you
dukes assume such airs with me, the king will act the king!
I shall go about among the lofty mountain peaks and crush
their lordships in their battlemented nests with my own war-
ring hands!

DON RUY GOMEZ (*straightening*):   Highness, the Silvas
are loyal—

DON CARLOS (*interrupting him*):   Answer me without
guile, Duke, or I shall have your eleven towers razed to earth.
A spark still glows from the extinguished blaze; from all the
slaughtered bandits, their chief survives. Who is concealing
him? It is you! This Hernani, this vicious rebel—you are
hiding him here within your castle now!

DON RUY GOMEZ: My lord, it is true.

DON CARLOS: Very well. I want his head—or else your
own, you understand, my cousin?

DON RUY GOMEZ (*bowing*):   You shall be satisfied.

(DOÑA SOL *hides her face in her hands and falls into a
chair.*)

DON CARLOS (*softening*):   Ah, you improve. Now give me
my prisoner.

(*The duke crosses his arms, lowers his head, and remains
thoughtful for a few moments. The king and* DOÑA SOL
*watch him in silence, and with contrary emotions. Finally
the duke raises his head, goes to the king, takes his hand, and
leads hims slowly up to the oldest of the portraits, the one
starting the row at the spectator's right.*)

DON RUY GOMEZ (*showing the portrait to the king*):

This is the oldest of the Silvas, the forefather, the ancestor, the great man! Don Silvius, who three times was Roman consul. (*Moving to the next portrait.*) Here is Don Galceran de Silva, the other Cid. At Toro, near Valladolid, there is a golden case that holds his remains, and a thousand candles burn around the shrine. He liberated León from the tribute of the hundred virgins.[2] (*He passes to another.*) Don Blas, who by his own decision and his conscience placed himself in exile, for having given the king poor counsel. (*At another.*) Christoval. At the battle of Escalona, the king Don Sancho was forced to flee on foot, and the furious blows fell harshest around his royal white plume. He cried out "Christoval!" Christoval took on the plume and gave his horse. (*At the next.*) Don Jorge, who paid the ransom for Ramirez, king of Aragon.

DON CARLOS (*crossing his arms and looking at* DON RUY *from head to toe*): Don Ruy, by God, I wonder at you! I want my prisoner now!

DON RUY (*moving to another portrait*): This is Ruy Gomez de Silva; he was named Grand Master of Saint James and of Calatrava.[3] His giant armor would far surpass our size. He took three hundred flags, won thirty battles; he conquered Motril for the king, and Antequera, Suez, and Nijar, and died a pauper. Highness, salute them. (*He himself bows and uncovers his head, then goes on to another. The king listens to him with growing impatience and anger.*) Beside him, Gil his son, beloved by noble hearts. His hand upon an oath was worth a king's. (*At another.*) Don Gaspard, the glory of Mendoza and of Silva! Every noble house has some alliance with the Silvas, Highness. The house of Sandoval dreads and weds us in alternation; Manrico's line is envious, the Laras jealous, and Alencastro hates us. Our feet touch all the dukes at once, and our foreheads all the kings.

DON CARLOS (*annoyed*): Do you make sport of us?

DON RUY (*going to other portraits*): Here is Don Vasquez, called the Wise; and Don Jaime, called the Strong. One day as he went by he stopped Zamet and a hundred Moors alone. I shall pass over others, some better still! (*As the king makes an angry gesture, he moves past a great many of the paintings, and stops at the last three portraits at the spectator's left.*) My noble grandfather. He lived for sixty years, keeping his promised word even to Jews. (*At the*

---

[2] A yearly levy extorted by the victorious Moors there.

[3] Orders of chivalry.

next-to-last.) This old man, this holy face—this is my father. He was a great man, although he came the last. The
Moors at Granada had taken prisoner Count Alvar Giron,
his friend. But my father gathered six hundred soldiers to
find and free him. He had a Count Alvar Giron carved out in
stone, and carried the statue with him, swearing by his patron
saint that never would he turn back until the stony count
itself should turn about and seek retreat. He battled, reached
the count, and saved him.

DON CARLOS: My prisoner, Duke!

DON RUY GOMEZ: He was a Gomez de Silva. When in
this house one sees the portraits of these heroes, this is what
one says—

DON CARLOS: My prisoner, and instantly!

(DON RUY GOMEZ *bows deeply before the king, takes his
hand and leads him to the last portrait, the one behind which
he has hidden* HERNANI. DOÑA SOL *watches him anxiously,
and the others are silent and attentive.*)

DON RUY GOMEZ: This portrait is my own. And I thank
you, King Carlos; for what you ask is that on seeing it, all
men should say "This last one, the son of such heroic race—
he was a traitor that sold his guest away."

(*Joy on* DOÑA SOL's *face; a murmur of astonishment among
the others present. The king, disconcerted, moves off in fury,
and keeps silence for several moments, his lips trembling and
eyes blazing.*)

DON CARLOS: Duke, your castle is in my way, and I shall
throw it down!

DON RUY GOMEZ: For you would indeed pay me for his
head, Your Highness, would you not?

DON CARLOS: For such defiance as this, I shall level all
its towers, and order nettles sown where once it stood.

DON RUY GOMEZ: Better that nettles grow where my
towers rose, than that a stain should mark the Silva name.
(*To the portraits.*) Is that not so, my fathers?

DON CARLOS: Duke, his head is ours, and you had promised me—

DON RUY GOMEZ: I promised one or the other. (*To the
portraits.*) Is that not so, my sires? (*Touching his own head;
to the king.*) I give you this one. Take it.

DON CARLOS: I thank you, Duke—but I lose by this arrangement. The head I need is young; once severed, it must
be lifted by the hair before the people. But yours! What use
have I for it? The headsman would seek in vain to grasp its
hair. You have not even enough to fill the hand!

Don Ruy Gomez: Highness, do not insult me! My head is still a good one, and easily worth a rebel's thatch, I think. You disdain a Silva head?

Don Carlos: Give us Hernani!

Don Ruy Gomez: My lord, I have spoken.

Don Carlos (*to his men*): Search everywhere! In every wing, in every cellar and tower—

Don Ruy Gomez: My dungeon is as faithful as myself. Alone it knows the secret that I know, and both of us will guard it well.

Don Carlos: I am the king.

Don Ruy Gomez: Unless they build my tomb up, stone by stone, from my demolished castle, they will find nothing.

Don Carlos: Pleas and threats are all in vain! Give me the bandit, Duke, or I will demolish head and castle both!

Don Ruy Gomez: I have spoken.

Don Carlos: Well then, instead of one, I shall take two heads. (*To the* Duke of Alcala.) Jorge, arrest the duke.

Doña Sol (*tearing off her veil and throwing herself between the duke and the guards*): Carlos, you are an evil king!

Don Carlos: Good Lord, what is this? Doña Sol!

Doña Sol: Highness, you have not a Spaniard's heart!

Don Carlos (*disturbed and hesitant*): Madam, you are too harsh toward the king. (*He approaches* Doña Sol, *and speaks low to her.*) You yourself have put this fury in my heart. A man turns saint or monster by your touch. How quickly one grows evil when one is loathed! I was already great; if you had wished it, perhaps I might have been the lion of Castile! You have made me its tiger with your rage. And now that tiger roars. Be silent, then. (Doña Sol *looks at him. He bows.*) However, I'll obey. (*He turns back to the duke.*) My cousin, I respect you. Your scruples after all have something worthy in them. Be loyal to your guest, and disloyal to your king. Very well, I pardon you and am the better man. I shall only take your niece with me as hostage.

Don Ruy Gomez: Only!

Doña Sol (*shocked and frightened*): Take me, my lord?

Don Carlos: Yes, you!

Don Ruy Gomez: So you exact no more than that of me? Oh, what splendid clemency! Oh, generous victor, to spare the head and torture the heart instead! Fine mercy, this!

Don Carlos: Make your choice—Doña Sol or the traitor. I must have one of them.

DON RUY GOMEZ: Ah, you are the master!

(DON CARLOS *approaches* DOÑA SOL *to take her away. She retreats toward* DON RUY GOMEZ.)

DOÑA SOL: Save me, my lord! (*She stops; then, to herself.*) But I must! My uncle's head or his—no, sooner myself. (*To the king.*) I go with you.

DON CARLOS (*aside*): By all the saints! What an excellent idea this was! You shall have to soften finally, my girl! (DOÑA SOL *moves with deliberate step toward the box that holds the jewels; she opens it and takes the dagger out, hiding it in her bosom.* DON CARLOS *comes up beside her and offers her his hand.*) What have you there?

DOÑA SOL: Nothing.

DON CARLOS: Some precious jewel?

DOÑA SOL: Yes.

DON CARLOS (*smiling*): Let us see it.

DOÑA SOL: Later you shall. (*She gives him her hand and prepares to go with him.* DON RUY GOMEZ, *who has remained motionless and deeply absorbed in thought, turns and takes a few steps, shouting.*)

DON RUY GOMEZ: Doña Sol! Heaven and earth, my Doña Sol! . . . Since this man has no heart in him—castle, come to my aid! Crumble, you weapons and fortress walls, fall in upon us all! (*He runs to the king.*) Leave me my child! I have nothing but her, my king!

DON CARLOS (*dropping* DOÑA SOL'S *hand*): My prisoner, then!

(*The duke drops his head, and seems caught by a tortured hesitation; then he raises his eyes and gazes at the portraits, clasping and stretching his hands toward them imploringly.*)

DON RUY GOMEZ: Have pity on me, my fathers! (*He takes a step toward the hiding place;* DOÑA SOL'S *eyes follow him in anguish. He turns back toward the portraits; to them:*) Oh, hide your eyes—your gaze will hold me back! (*He advances falteringly as far as his portrait, then turns back to the king again.*) It is your will?

DON CARLOS: Yes.

(*The duke raises his trembling hand toward the spring.*)

DOÑA SOL: God in heaven!

DON RUY GOMEZ: No! (*He throws himself at the king's feet.*) Have pity, take my head!

DON CARLOS: Your niece!

DON RUY GOMEZ (*rising*):   Then take her! And leave me my honor.

DON CARLOS (*gripping* DONA SOL's *trembling hand*): Farewell, Duke.

DON RUY GOMEZ: Until we meet again. (*His eyes follow the king, who moves slowly off with* DOÑA SOL; *then he puts his hand to his dagger.*) God protect you, Highness! (*He comes forward again, and stands motionless, hearing and seeing nothing; his gaze is fixed, his arms crossed on his chest, which rises and falls in a convulsive rhythm. Meanwhile, the king goes out with* DOÑA SOL, *and all the courtiers go gravely after him, two by two, each in order of his rank. They speak low among themselves.*)

DON RUY (*to himself*):   King, as you leave my home rejoicing, my ancient loyalty leaves my weeping heart. (*He raises his eyes, looks about him, and sees that he is alone. He dashes to the wall, takes down two swords from a display there, compares and examines them, and sets them on a table. This done, he goes to the portrait, pushes the spring, and opens the secret door.*)

(Scene 7)

DON RUY: Come out. (HERNANI *appears at the doorway of the hiding place.* DON RUY *points to the two swords on the table.*) Choose one of them. Don Carlos has left my house; now you must settle with me. Choose, and do it swiftly. . . . Come now! Your hand is trembling!

HERNANI: A duel! Old man, we cannot fight one another.

DON RUY GOMEZ: And why not? Are you afraid? Or is it that you are not noble? Damnation! Noble or not, any man who injures me is gentleman enough to cross his sword with mine!

HERNANI: Old man—

DON RUY GOMEZ: Kill me, or die yourself.

HERNANI: Die—yes. You have saved me despite my will, and so my life is yours to take.

DON RUY GOMEZ: That is your wish? (*To the portraits.*) You see that he asks it. (*To* HERNANI.) Very well; then say your prayer.

HERNANI: I make my last to you, my lord.

DON RUY GOMEZ: Address the other Lord.

HERNANI: No—no, to you! Old man, strike me, with anything, knife, dagger, sword! But grant me this last joy, in pity's name—Duke, before I die, let me see her!

DON RUY GOMEZ: See her!

HERNANI: Or at least let me hear her voice once more —only one last time!

DON RUY GOMEZ: Hear her voice!

HERNANI: My lord, I understand your jealousy; but death already clutches at my young life—forgive me. Tell me that I may hear her voice again, even if it must be without the sight of her. And I shall die tonight. Only to hear her! Fill my last longing—how contented I should breathe out my life, if you would let my soul look into hers again, into her eyes, before I fly to heaven! I shall not speak to her—you will be there, my father. And take me afterwards!

DON RUY GOMEZ (*looking amazed at the open door of the cupboard*): Can that closet be so deep, so tightly sealed, that he heard nothing?

HERNANI: I heard nothing at all.

DON RUY GOMEZ: I was forced to yield him Doña Sol, or you.

HERNANI: Yield her to whom?

DON RUY GOMEZ: The king.

HERNANI: You fool! He loves her!

DON RUY GOMEZ: Loves her!

HERNANI: He has stolen her from us! He is our rival!

DON RUY GOMEZ: My God! . . . Men! To your horses, your horses! We must go after the abductor!

HERNANI: Listen. Vengeance that is well planned makes far less noise as it comes. I belong to you; you have the right to kill me. But do you wish to use me first, to avenge your niece and her honor? Let me share in your revenge! Ah, grant me that share—if I must fall and kiss your feet, I do it, but let us both pursue the king! Come, I shall be your striking arm—I shall avenge you, Duke. And afterwards you can slay me.

DON RUY GOMEZ: And then, just as today, you will give yourself up to death?

HERNANI: Yes, Duke.

DON RUY GOMEZ: How do you swear it?

HERNANI: Upon my father's head.

DON RUY GOMEZ: And will you swear to recall the vow yourself?

HERNANI (*handing him the horn he takes from his belt*): Take this horn. Whatever may happen, when you wish it, lord, and in whatever place, when you feel that it is time for me to die, then sound this trumpet, nothing more. It shall be done.

DON RUY GOMEZ (*offering him his hand*):   Your hand. (*They clasp hands. Then, to the portraits*:) And you, my fathers—you all are witness to it!

ACT IV

THE TOMB

(*Aix-la-Chapelle: the underground crypt that holds the tomb of Charlemagne. The great vaults of Lombard architecture, arches, massive low pillars, their capitals carved with birds and flowers. To the right, Charlemagne's tomb with a small bronze door, low and arched. A single lamp hung from the height of an arch picks out its inscription: Carolus Magnus. It is dark. The far end of the cavern cannot be seen; it is lost among the arcades, the stairs and pillars that merge and disappear into the dimness.*)

(*Scene 1.* DON CARLOS *and* DON RICARDO DE ROXAS, *with a lantern in his hand. Full cloaks, hatbrims pulled low.*)

DON RICARDO (*his hat in his hand*):   This is the place.
DON CARLOS: It is here that the conspiracy will meet—and I shall have them all in the hollow of my hand! My Lord Elector of Treves, this is the place and you have lent it to them. . . . It is an admirable choice—a black plot flourishes in the air of catacombs, and tombstones are good for sharpening stilettos. And yet the game is crucial—a life is at stake, my lords assassins. We shall see. Well, they are wise indeed to choose a sepulcher for such a conference; they will have less distance to go. (*To* DON RICARDO.) Do these caverns stretch far beneath the ground?
DON RICARDO: Down to the castle-fort.
DON CARLOS: More space than I shall need.
DON RICARDO: Others on this side go as far as the monastery of Altenheim. . . .
DON CARLOS: Where Rudolph killed Lothair. Good—now once again, Count, recite me all the names and grievances: where, why, and how.
DON RICARDO: Gotha—
DON CARLOS: I know why that good duke would plot with them: he wants a German emperor for Germany.

264

Don Ricardo: Hohenburg—

Don Carlos: Hohenburg, I think, would rather choose hell with Francis at its head, than heaven itself with me.

Don Ricardo: Don Gil Tellez Giron—

Don Carlos: Saint Mary and Castile! So he is in revolt against his king, the traitor!

Don Ricardo: They say he found you with Lady Giron, the evening of the day you made him baron. He would avenge the honor of his sweet wife.

Don Carlos: And thus turns rebel against Spain? . . . Who else is there?

Don Ricardo: The Reverend Vasquez, the bishop of Avila, is said to be among them.

Don Carlos: Is that to avenge his wife's dishonor too?

Don Ricardo: Then Guzman de Lara is discontent; he wants the collar of your knighthood.

Don Carlos: Ah! Guzman de Lara—if he wants only a collar, he will have it.

Don Ricardo: The duke of Lutzelburg. As for his intentions—

Don Carlos: The duke of Lutzelburg stands just a head too tall.

Don Ricardo: And Juan de Haro, who wants Astorga.

Don Carlos: Those Haros have always earned the headsman twice his wages.

Don Ricardo: That is the list.

Don Carlos: You have named only seven, Count, and I had been warned of more.

Don Ricardo: There are some bandits besides, engaged by Treves, or France. . . .

Don Carlos: Men without a true allegiance, whose everready knives turn toward the fattest purse like compass needles toward the pole.

Don Ricardo: I did make out two more conspirators, both of them newly arrived. One young, one old.

Don Carlos: Their names? (Don Ricardo *shrugs his shoulders; he does not know.*) Their ages then?

Don Ricardo: The younger one seems twenty.

Don Carlos: What a pity!

Don Ricardo: The elder, sixty at least.

Don Carlos: The one is too young, the other too old. Too bad; I shall take care of them. The headsman can count upon my help when it is needed. My sword will not be kind to treachery, and I shall lend it when his ax grows dull; and if the scaffold cloth should prove too small, I shall stitch my imperial purple onto it. But shall I indeed be emperor?

DON RICARDO: The college of electors is gathered now to vote.

DON CARLOS: I cannot tell—they will name Francis the First, or else their Saxon, their Frederick the Wise—ah, Luther is right, Europe is in bad times! Fine men to choose a sacred majesty, reasons of gold alone can sway their mood. A Saxon heretic! An imbecilic count palatine, and a primate of Treves who is a libertine! The Bohemian king will vote for me. But Hessian princes even smaller than their fiefs— young idiots and debauched old men. Oh, crowns—there are many crowns, but heads? only try to find one! Dwarfs all of them, that laughable council, whom I could carry off like Hercules draped in my lionskin. Without their purple mantles, they would none of them have a skull as large as Triboulet's![4] . . .

I lack three voices, Ricardo! And lacking them, I shall lack everything! Oh, I would give Toledo, Ghent, and Salamanca or any three cities they could wish, for three more votes! For those three voices—mark thee, Count, I would give up three cities in Castile or in Flanders! For I could take them back another time. (DON RICARDO *bows deeply to the king, and puts his hat on his head.*) You cover your head before me?

DON RICARDO: My lord, you called me "thou"; (*He bows again.*) thus I am made a grandee.

DON CARLOS (*aside*):   Ah, you pitiful things, so ambitious for a pittance! A self-seeking breed of animals, who follow their single strand of purpose through our own concerns! This is a shabby barnyard where they beg shamelessly of the king, and he dispenses scraps of greatness to all these famished beasts. (*Reflectively.*) Only God and the emperor are great—and the holy father. The rest, the kings and dukes— what are they?

DON RICARDO: Indeed, I hope they will select Your Highness for the throne.

DON CARLOS (*aside*):   Highness! Am I still only highness? Must misfortune follow me? If I should remain only king . . .

DON RICARDO (*aside*):   Enough—emperor or not, I am now a grandee of Spain.

DON CARLOS: How will they announce his name when they elect the German emperor?

DON RICARDO: If it is the duke of Saxony, a single cannon shot. Two for the king of France, and three if it is Your Highness.

---

[4] Fool at the courts of Louis XII and Francis I; main character in *Le roi s'amuse* (1832), which play Verdi later adopted for *Rigoletto*.

Don Carlos: And then Doña Sol! Everything has joined
to irritate and wound me! Count, if fortune falls my way
and makes me emperor, quickly bring her here. Perhaps she
will find a Caesar more to her taste.

Don Ricardo (*smiling*):   Your Highness is most generous.

Don Carlos (*interrupting him haughtily*):   Silence, upon
that subject! I have not yet said what I wish opinion to be.
When will we know the council's choice?

Don Ricardo: Within the hour at latest, I think.

Don Carlos: Three voices more! Only three. . . . But
first we must crush this plotting rabble here, and afterwards
see who will have the empire. (*He counts on his fingers and
stamps his foot.*) Still three votes too few! The others have
it! Yet that Cornelius Agrippa predicted them—he saw thirteen stars in the celestial sea come sailing swiftly toward
my northern one. I'll have the empire then! . . . But on the
other hand, they say that Abbé Jean Trithème prophesied
for Francis. I should have helped the auguries along by military means, for then fate would be clear! Predictions by the
best of sorcerers come best to birth when a good army serves
as midwife; an army with its cannon and its pikes, with soldiers, horsemen and with marching tunes will lead a waver-
ing fate in the right direction. Which of the two is better,
Cornelius Agrippa or Jean Trithème? The one with regi-
ments behind his words; the one who makes his points with
iron lance, who underlines them with troops and mercenaries; their swords can set imperfect fortune straight, and
mold the event according to the prophet.

They are poor fools who aim to have the empire of the
world, who with proud eye and brow declare "It is my
right!" They have a thousand cannon stretched in rows,
whose hot breath could melt cities; they've vassals, soldiers,
horses, and one assumes that they will march to their goal
over the conquered peoples. . . . But no! When they have
reached the great crossroads of human destiny, where
many paths lead to the pit and one leads to the throne, they
hardly take three steps but stop in indecision; wondering,
they try in vain to read the book of fate; they hesitate, uncertain of themselves; and, caught by doubt, go running to
the neighboring necromancer, to ask their way!

(*To* Don Ricardo.) Leave me now; the traitors' league will
soon be here. Oh—and the key to the tomb?

Don Ricardo (*handing it to him*):   My lord, you will remember the Count of Limburg, the guardian here? He gave
me the key, and he does all that's in his power for your
sake.

DON CARLOS (*dismissing him*):   Do everything as I have ordered you. Everything!

DON RICARDO (*bowing*): I go at once, Your Highness.

DON CARLOS: I need three cannon shots, you said?

(DON RICARDO *bows and leaves.* DON CARLOS, *left alone, falls into a deep reverie. His arms cross, his head falls to his chest; then he lifts it and turns toward the tomb.*)

(*Scene 2*)

DON CARLOS: Charlemagne, forgive me! These silent vaults should not reverberate with any but solemn words. You must be indignant at hearing our ambition hum about your monument. . . . Charlemagne is here! You somber sepulcher, how can you hold so great a spirit and yet not burst? Are you truly there, giant creator of a world? And can you stretch your length within those walls? . . . It is a spectacle to astound the mind, as it was before he came, and as he later made it! A vast structure with two men at its top, elected lords to whom each king is subject. Each state and duchy, military fief, kingdom, and march—almost all are hereditary reigns; yet the people sometimes have their pope or Caesar. The mechanism works, and one chance corrects another; so equilibrium comes, and order triumphs. Electors in cloth of gold, and scarlet cardinals—the sacred double senate that stirs the earth—are but display, and God will have His will. An idea may rise one day born of the times; it grows, and burns, and spreads, and mingles with all things; takes human form, grips hearts, and carves a furrow; many a king will trample it underfoot, or gag its voice. But if one day it penetrates the diet, or the papal conclave, then suddenly the kings will see the once-enslaved idea loom up, with globe in hand or the tiara on its brow, and bow their royal heads beneath its feet.

The pope and emperor are everything. Nothing is on earth but for or by them. A sublime mystery dwells in them, and heaven, from which they hold their privilege, endows them with a feast of peoples and of kings; heaven keeps them underneath its thunderous canopy of cloud, seated alone at table where God serves them up the world. Side by side, they sit to rule and sentence, arranging the universe as a reaper does his field. All that is occurs between those two. The kings stand at the door, breathing the savory steam of dishes carried past, staring through the window, watchful, agitated, and rising on their toes to see. Beneath them the world falls into ranks and groups. They do and they undo. One absolves, the other cuts. The one is truth, the other might. Their purpose is contained within them; they are because they are. When they emerge from the sanctuary, both equal, the one in purple, the other in his white soutane, the dazzled universe in terror regards these two halves of God, the pope and the emperor.

Emperor! To be emperor—oh fury, not to be, and to feel one's heart filled with courage! How fortunate was he who sleeps within this tomb; how great was he! And it was still finer in his time. The pope and the emperor: they were more than two men. Peter and Caesar—in themselves the two Romes were joined, each fertilized the other by mystic marriage, giving new form and soul to human kind; melding peoples and kingdoms as they wished to form a new Europe, and both of them by their hands refashioning the bronze that still remained of the old Roman world. A lofty fate—and yet, this tomb is his. Is all so trivial then, that this is where it ends? To have been prince, and king, and emperor—to have been the sword and been the law . . . a giant, with Germany for his pedestal, with Caesar for his title, and Charlemagne for name! To have been greater than Hannibal, or than Attila, as great as all the world—and this is where it ends!

Then scheme for empire, and see the dust an emperor leaves! Cover the earth entire with fanfare and with tumult; raise and build your endless empire; slash and carve out an enormous edifice—do you know what will remain one day? Ah, lunacy—this stone! And of the title and the triumphal name? A few letters, that serve to teach a child his spelling! However high the goal your pride envisions, here is the last limit! Oh empire! I do not care—I touch at it, and find it to my liking. Something tells me: "You shall have it." It shall be mine . . . if it only were! Oh heaven, to be what is beginning! Alone, upright, atop the enormous spiral; to be the keystone in the arch of all the states arranged one on the other, to see beneath one all the many kings, and wipe one's sandals on them.

To see beneath the kings the feudal houses, margraves and cardinals, doges, and dukes with floral seals; then bishops, abbots, heads of clans, great barons! Then priests and soldiers next; then in the shadow, far below the peak whereon we stand—deep within the chasm—are men!

Men—a mass, a sea, great rumbling, tears and cries, some-

times a bitter laugh—a whole lament that wakes the startled
earth, and through a hundred thousand echoes reaches us
as a skirl of trumpets! Men! . . . Cities, towers, a vast swarm
of high church belfries to ring their gongs! (*Musingly*.) A
base of human nations, bearing on their shoulders the enormous pyramid that leans on the two poles; living waves that
grasp it always in their hollows, and float it pitching on their
vast swells; waves that shift everything about, and at its
upper reaches topple thrones like footstools, so that all kings
cease their vain disputes and raise their eyes to heaven.

Kings! Look down beneath you! Ah, the people—that
ocean—that never-resting wave, where nought can be cast
in but stirs the whole! A swell that may crush a throne or
rock a tomb! Mirror wherein a king will rarely find a handsome image of himself. If he should sometimes gaze into
that dark swell, he'd see at bottom numberless empires, great
shipwrecked vessels swaying in its ebb and flow—empires
that had disturbed the ocean's stream and now exist no
more!

To think of ruling over all of that! To mount up to that
pinnacle if the electors call—to climb there, conscious that
one is but a man! To see the chasm below! If only I do not
at that same moment grow dazed with vertigo—oh, shifting
pyramid of kings and countries, your summit is so narrow!
Woe to the fearful foot! By whom should I hold steady?
Suppose I stumble at feeling the world shudder beneath my
feet! At feeling the earth live, and surge, and pulse! Or when
I have that globe between my hands, what then? Shall I be
capable of carrying it? What is there in me? Emperor, my
God! to fill the role of king was hard for me! Surely the
man is rare whose soul can stretch with fortune. But I—
who shall make me great? Who will be my guide and give
me counsel?

(*He falls to his knees before the tomb*.) Charlemagne—
you shall! Since God, before whom all obstacles fall back,
has taken our two majesties and set them face to face, then
from the depths of this your grave imbue my heart with
something sublime! Ah, show me all things from their every
aspect, show me that the world is small, for I dare not lay
my hand on it. Show me that within this tower of Babel, rising from shepherd to Caesar to the skies, each man at his
own rank delights himself, admires what he is, observes the
man beneath him and cannot help but mock. Teach me
your secrets of conquest and of rule, and tell me that it is
better to punish than forgive—is this not so? If it is true
that sometimes the world's clatter wakes a great shadow in

his lonely resting place; if it is true his wide bright tomb can open suddenly, and throw the world a flare in its dark night—if these things are true, emperor of Germany, then tell me, what can a man do when he comes after Charlemagne?

Speak! Though it mean your sovereign breath in speaking must crack this bronze door across my brow! Or rather let me enter alone within your sanctuary, and see your face in death—do not repulse me by an icy breath, but raise yourself upon your bed of stone, and let us talk. Yes, even though you should tell me, in your fateful voice, of matters that darken the eye and pale the brow! Speak, and do not blind your fearful son, for your tomb must be so full with light! Or else, if you will say nothing, let me study that deeply peaceful head, as if it were a world; let me measure you carefully, oh giant, for nothing here below is great as is thy dust! Let the ashes guide me if the spirit would not.

(*He puts the key to the lock.*) We shall go in. (*He draws back.*) But what if he should speak to me indeed? if he is there, awake and upright, walking with slow steps! And I should reappear with my hair white! Still—I shall enter. (*Sound of footsteps.*) Someone is approaching. Who but I could dare to come here at this hour, and rouse the home of such a corpse? Who is it? (*The noise is closer.*) Ah, I had forgotten—it is my murderers. Let us go in then.

(*He opens the door to the tomb and closes it behind him. Several men come on, with muffled steps, hidden in their cloaks and hats.*)

(*Scene 3. The conspirators; they move about among themselves, clasping hands and exchanging a few words in low voices.*)

FIRST CONSPIRATOR (*who alone carries a lighted torch*): *Ad augusta.*

SECOND CONSPIRATOR: *Per angusta.*

FIRST: May the saints protect us.

THIRD: May the dead serve us.

FIRST: God keep us.

(*Sounds of steps in the darkness.*)

SECOND: Who goes there?

VOICE: *Ad augusta.*

SECOND: *Per angusta.*

(*Other conspirators appear. Sound of footsteps again.*)

FIRST CONSPIRATOR (*to the* THIRD): Look there, another's coming.
THIRD: Who goes there?
VOICE IN SHADOWS: *Ad augusta.*
THIRD: *Per angusta.*
(*Still others appear, with signs of greeting.*)

FIRST: Good, we are all here. Gotha, give us your report. My friends, the dark awaits the light.

(*All the conspirators seat themselves on tombs in a half circle. The first conspirator passes among them, and from his torch each lights a candle and holds it in his hand. Then the first conspirator takes a seat silently upon a tomb at the center of the circle and higher than the others.*)

DUKE OF GOTHA (*rising*): Friends, this Charles of Spain, a foreigner through his mother, lays claim to the Holy Empire.
FIRST CONSPIRATOR: He shall have the grave instead.
GOTHA (*throwing his torch to the ground and grinding it out with his foot*): May his skull be as this flame!
ALL: May it be!
FIRST: Death to him!
GOTHA: May he die!
ALL: May he be slain!
DON JUAN DE HARO: His father was a German.
DUKE OF LUTZELBURG: His mother was Spanish.
GOTHA: He is Spanish no longer, and not a German. Death!
ONE OF THE CONSPIRATORS: What if the electors were to name him emperor at this moment?
FIRST: They name him? Never!
DON GIL TELLEZ GIRON: What does that matter, friends! If we strike the head, the crown will die with it.
FIRST: Whatever he may be, if he wins the Holy Empire, he becomes mighty and august, and only God can touch him.
GOTHA: The surest way is to act before he gains that state.
FIRST: He shall not be elected.
ALL: He shall not have the Empire!
FIRST: How many hands are needed to wind him in his shroud?

ALL: Only one.

FIRST: How many strokes to the heart?

ALL: Only one!

FIRST: Who will do it?

ALL: All of us!

FIRST: Our victim is a traitor. They are choosing an emperor; let us make a high priest. We shall draw lots.

(*All the conspirators write their names on their tablets, tear off the sheet, roll it up, and go one after the other to drop it into the urn on one of the tombs.*)

FIRST CONSPIRATOR: Let us pray. (*They all kneel. The* FIRST *rises.*) May the chosen one put his faith in God, strike like a Roman, and die like a Hebrew! He must brave the wheel and pincers, sing at the rack, and laugh at the fiery brand; he must do all to kill and die in resignation! (*He draws one of the parchment sheets from the urn.*)

ALL: What name is it?

FIRST (*loudly*): Hernani.

HERNANI (*emerging from the group*): I've won! Ah revenge, I have you now, you whom I have pursued so long!

DON RUY GOMEZ (*moving through the crowd and taking* HERNANI *aside*): Let me take your place!

HERNANI: No, upon my life! My lord, do not grudge me my fortune! It is the first time that luck has come to me!

DON RUY: You have nothing. Then listen—I give you my fiefs, my castles, and my vassalages—a hundred thousand peasants in my three hundred villages—I give them all to you, my friend, for the right to strike that blow!

HERNANI: No!

GOTHA: Your weaker arm would strike with less effect, old man.

DON RUY GOMEZ: Silence! If not the arm, I have the spirit for it! Do not judge the blade by the rust that coats its scabbard. (*To* HERNANI.) You belong to me.

HERNANI: My life is yours, yes. But his belongs to me!

DON RUY GOMEZ (*drawing the horn from his waist*): Listen, my friend: I give you back this horn.

HERNANI (*shaken*): What? My life? Ah, what does it mean to me? My vengeance is at hand! God is with me in this. I have my father to avenge, and more perhaps! Would you give her to me?

DON RUY GOMEZ: Never! But I yield up this horn!

HERNANI: No.

DON RUY GOMEZ: Reflect upon it, boy!

HERNANI: Duke, leave me my prey.

DON RUY: Then be accursed for denying me that joy.
(*He replaces the horn in his belt.*)

FIRST CONSPIRATOR (*to* HERNANI):   Brother, before they
can elect him, it would be well to watch for Carlos on this
very night—

HERNANI: Fear not! I know how to put a man into his
grave.

FIRST: May any treason fall back upon the traitor, and
God be with us! And if he should fall without having slain,
then, counts and barons, we shall continue it! Let us swear
to strike, each of us in turn, without evasion—for Carlos
must die.

ALL: We swear it!

GOTHA (*to the* FIRST CONSPIRATOR):   Upon what, my
brother?

DON RUY GOMEZ (*upending his sword, taking it by the
tip and raising it over his head*):   Let us swear upon this
cross!

ALL (*raising their swords*):   May he die unrepentant.

(*A far-off cannon shot is heard. They all stop, silent. The
door to the tomb opens slightly;* DON CARLOS *appears on
the threshold. Pale, he listens. A second shot. A third. He
opens the door wide, but without stepping forward; he stands
motionless on the doorsill.*)

(*Scene 4*)

DON CARLOS: Go on, my lords! The emperor is listening.
(*All the torches go out at once. Deep silence. He moves
a step in the shadows, so dark that the mute and motionless conspirators are scarcely visible.*) Silence and darkness!
the swarm emerges from the black, and now returns there.
Do you believe somehow that all of this will seem a dream,
and that because you have put out your flares, I shall take
you all for stone figures seated on their tombs? But a moment since, my statues, your voices were still loud! Come
now! raise up your lowered heads, for Charles the Fifth is
here! Strike me now—take even a step. Let us see it, do you

dare? No, you dare not. Your torches flamed like blood beneath these vaults; and my breath alone sufficed to put them out. But look, turn your quavering eyes—I did extinguish many, but I light many more. (*He strikes the iron key on the bronze door of the tomb; at the sound, the depths of the cavern fill with soldiers bearing torches and halberds. At their head are the* DUKE OF ALCALA *and the* MARQUIS OF ALMUÑAN.) Come here, my falcons! I have the nest, and I have the prey! (*To the* CONSPIRATORS.) Now I bring light in my turn. Look, the sepulcher's aflame. (*To the soldiers.*) Come forward, all of you; this is a flagrant crime.

HERNANI (*looking at the soldiers*): That is better now. Alone, he seemed too large. At first I thought that it was Charlemagne; it is only Charles the Fifth.

DON CARLOS (*to the* DUKE OF ALCALA): Constable of Spain! (*To the* MARQUIS OF ALMUÑAN.) Admiral of Castile, come forward! Disarm them all. (*The plotters are surrounded and disarmed.*)

DON RICARDO (*running up and bowing to the ground*): Majesty!

DON CARLOS: I name thee alcalde of the palace.

DON RICARDO (*bowing again*): Two electors are come to congratulate Your Sacred Majesty, in the name of the Golden Chamber.

DON CARLOS: Let them come in. (*Low, to* RICARDO.) Doña Sol.

(RICARDO *salutes and leaves. The* KING OF BOHEMIA *and the* DUKE OF BAVARIA *enter with torches and trumpet flourishes; both are clothed in their gold-embroidered mantles, with crowns on their heads. A large cortege follows them, made up of German lords carrying the imperial banner— the two-headed eagle with the Spanish shield at its center. The soldiers form an aisle to the emperor for the two electors. They salute him deeply and he returns it by raising his hat.*)

DUKE OF BAVARIA: Charles, King of the Romans, Most Sacred Majesty, Emperor! The world is now within your hands, for the Empire is yours. Yours, the throne that every monarch covets! Frederick, Duke of Saxony, was first elected; but he judged you more worthy of it, and declined. Come then, receive this crown and take the globe. The Holy Empire, King, invests you with its purple robe; it arms you with its sword, and you are great.

DON CARLOS: I shall thank the council on my return. Go

now, my lords. Thank you, my brother Bohemia, and my cousin Bavaria. Go now—and I myself must leave.

KING OF BOHEMIA: Charles, our ancestors were friends; my father loved your father, and their sires too loved each other. Charles, you are so young a man to face disturbing fortunes—tell me, would you wish that I should be your brother among brothers? I knew you as a child, and I cannot forget—

DON CARLOS (*interrupting him*): King of Bohemia, you are most familiar! (*He presents his hand for the* KING *to kiss, and to the* DUKE OF BAVARIA, *then dismisses the two electors, who bow deeply.*) Go now. (*They leave with their suites.*)

CROWD: Long live the emperor!

DON CARLOS (*aside*): I am emperor! And everything has made way for me. Emperor! through the refusal, though, of Frederick the Wise!

(DOÑA SOL *enters, led by* RICARDO.)

DOÑA SOL: Soldiers! and the emperor—oh God, I did not expect this! Hernani!

HERNANI: Doña Sol!

DON RUY (*beside* HERNANI, *to himself*): She does not even see me!

(DOÑA SOL *runs to* HERNANI; *his defiant stare stops her.*)

HERNANI: My lady!

DOÑA SOL (*drawing the knife from her bodice*): I have his dagger still.

HERNANI: My beloved!

DON CARLOS: Silence, all of you. (*To the plotters.*) Have you recovered your determination? It is fitting that I show the world a lesson here. Lara the Castilian, and Saxon Gotha —all of you—what did you come here to do? Speak!

HERNANI (*stepping forward*): Sire, it is a simple thing, and we can tell you of it: we were writing the sentence upon Balthazar's wall. (*He draws his knife and brandishes it.*) We render unto Caesar what is Caesar's.

DON CARLOS: I see. (*To* DON RUY GOMEZ.) And you, Silva—a traitor!

DON RUY GOMEZ: Which of us two is traitor, sire?

HERNANI (*turning to the other* CONSPIRATORS): He has what he desires—our heads and empire both! (*To the* EM-

PEROR.) A king's blue robe could hinder your steps. This purple suits you better; it does not show blood.

DON CARLOS (to DON RUY GOMEZ): My cousin Silva—this is crime enough to strike your barony from your coat of arms. It is high treason, Don Ruy; consider that well.

DON RUY GOMEZ: Count Julians are made by King Rodrigos.[5]

DON CARLOS (to the DUKE OF ALCALA): Take only the dukes or counts. The rest—

(DON RUY GOMEZ, the DUKE OF LUTZELBURG, the DUKE OF GOTHA, DON JUAN DE HARO, DON GUZMAN DE LARA, DON GIL TELLEZ GIRON, and the BARON OF HOHENBURG step out of the group; HERNANI remains with it. The DUKE OF ALCALA surrounds the lords with guards.)

DOÑA SOL (aside): He is safe!

HERNANI (stepping forward): I claim my place among these others! (To DON CARLOS.) Since this is a matter of the ax; since Hernani the humble peasant would slip beneath your feet unpunished; since his brow is no longer worthy of your sword; since one must be a nobleman to die, I rise. God who awards the scepter and who gave it you, God made me Duke of Segorbia and Cardona, the Marquis of Monroy, Count Albatera and Viscount of Gor—and lord of lands whose number or whose names I cannot count. I am Juan of Aragon, grand master of Avis, born in exile—the banished son of a father slaughtered by your father's word, King Carlos of Castile! Murder is a family affair between us. You have the scaffold; we have the knife. Thus, heaven made me a duke, and exile a mountaineer. I have whetted my sword against the hills and tempered it in rushing streams; but since all my preparation must come to nothing—(he puts on his hat, and says to the other conspirators)—cover your heads, all you grandees of Spain! (All the nobles do so. To DON CARLOS.) Yes, King—our heads have the right to fall before you covered! (To the prisoners.) Silva, Haro, Lara—men of title and of race—open your ranks to Juan of Aragon! Dukes and counts, give me my place! (To the courtiers and guards.) I am Juan of Aragon, king, headsmen and grooms. And if your scaffolds are too small, change them for others! (He joins the group of captured lords.)

DOÑA SOL: Why did he speak?

DON CARLOS: True, I had forgotten that whole story.

[5] This Visigoth king defiled the count's daughter, and was killed by him.

HERNANI: The man whose flesh has bled remembers better. And the wrong forgotten by the offender lives on still active in the injured heart.

DON CARLOS: Then I am the son of men who felled your fathers' heads—that is title enough for me.

DOÑA SOL (*throwing herself to her knees before the emperor*): Sire, pardon! Pity, sire—be merciful! Or else then kill us both by the same stroke, for he is my beloved, my husband! I live in him alone. Oh, I tremble, sire; find the compassion to kill the two of us together! Majesty, I lie at your sainted feet! I love him! He is mine, as the empire is yours! Oh mercy! (DON CARLOS *watches her, impassive.*) What dark idea absorbs you now?

DON CARLOS: Rise, Duchess of Segorbia, Countess Albatera, Marchioness of Monroy. . . . (*To* HERNANI.) What are your other names, Don Juan?

HERNANI: Who is it says these things? The king?

DON CARLOS: No, the emperor.

DOÑA SOL (*rising*): Great heavens!

DON CARLOS (*indicating her to* HERNANI): Duke, here is your wife.

HERNANI (*his eyes raised to heaven, and* DOÑA SOL *in his arms*): God of justice!

DON CARLOS (*to* DON RUY GOMEZ): Cousin, you are jealous and proud in your nobility, I know. But an Aragon may wed a Silva.

DON RUY GOMEZ (*darkly*): It is not for my nobility.

HERNANI (*gazing lovingly at* DOÑA SOL, *and holding her close*): Ah, I feel my hatred vanishing. . . . (*He throws down his dagger.*)

DON RUY GOMEZ (*watching the pair*): Shall my rage burst from me? Ah no—senseless love, and senseless grief. . . . They would pity your old Spanish head. Burn flameless, old man—love and suffer secretly. Let your heart be consumed, but not a cry, for they would laugh.

DOÑA SOL (*still in* HERNANI'S *arms*): My duke!

HERNANI: I have nothing left in my heart but love.

DOÑA SOL: What happiness . . .

DON CARLOS (*aside, his hand upon his breast*): Quiet, my heart that still is young and full of love! Let intellect rule now, for too long you have had your way. Henceforward all your loves, and alas, your only mistresses are Germany and Flanders and old Spain. (*He eyes his banner.*) The emperor is like the eagle, his companion: in the heart's stead there hangs only an escutcheon.

HERNANI: You are Caesar indeed!

DON CARLOS (*to* HERNANI): Your heart is worthy of your noble line, Don Juan. (*Indicating* DOÑA SOL.) And worthy too of her. On your knees, Duke! (HERNANI *kneels.* DON CARLOS *takes off the collar of the Golden Fleece, and sets it around* HERNANI's *neck.*) Receive this collar. (DON CARLOS *draws his sword and taps him three times upon the shoulder.*) Be faithful. In the name of Saint Stephen, Duke, I name thee knight. (*He raises and embraces him.*) But you have the best and sweetest collar yet, one I have not, and one that even the highest rank can lack: the arms of a beloved woman loving you. Ah, you shall be happy; and I, I am emperor. . . . (*To the conspirators.*) I know your names no more, sirs. Hatred and anger—I would forget them all. Go then; I pardon you. This is the lesson I must give the world. It shall not be in vain that the emperor Charles the Fifth succeeds to Charles the First, the king; nor that, before a mourning, orphaned Europe, a law should change a Catholic highness into a sacred majesty.

(*The plotters fall to their knees.*)

CONSPIRATORS: Glory to Carlos! Hail!
DON RUY GOMEZ (*to* DON CARLOS): And so I alone remain condemned to suffering.
DON CARLOS: And I.
DON RUY (*aside*): But unlike him, I have not forgiven!
HERNANI: Who is it has changed us all?
ALL (SOLDIERS, CONSPIRATORS, NOBLES): Long live Germany and Charles the Fifth!
DON CARLOS (*turning toward the tomb*): Honor to Charlemagne! Leave the two of us together now. (ALL *exeunt.*)

(*Scene 5*)

DON CARLOS (*alone; he bows before the tomb*): Are you content with me? Have I stripped away the pettiness of kings, Charlemagne, and am I indeed become another man? May I join my helmet to the Roman miter? Have I the right to bend the fortunes of the world? Have I a firm and steady foot, one that may walk upon this path, all strewn with vandal's ruins, that you have beaten out for us with your broad sandals? Have I caught your flame to kindle my own torch?

And understood the voice that sounds within your tomb? Ah,
I was alone and lost before an empire, a whole howling
world that plots and threatens me—there is the Dane to
punish, the Holy Father to pay; Venice and Suleiman;
Luther, Francis the First—a thousand jealous blades already
gleaming in the dark, snares and hidden reefs, and enemies
unnumbered; twenty peoples, and each of them enough to
frighten twenty kings—all hurrying and urgent, all to do at
once. And I cried out to you: "How shall I start?" And you
replied: "My son, by clemency!"

ACT V

THE WEDDING

(*Saragossa. A terrace of the palace of Aragon. At stage rear, a flight of stairs down into the garden. At right and left, two doors opening onto the terrace, which is enclosed by a balustrade topped by two rows of Moorish arcades; above and through them are visible the palace gardens, fountains in the shade, clumps of trees with lights moving among them, and beyond it all the Gothic and Arab lines of the brightly lit palace. It is night. We hear faraway trumpet flourishes. Persons in masks and dominoes, single or in groups, cross over the terrace here and there. In the foreground, a group of young lords, their masks in hand, are laughing and chattering noisily.*)

(*Scene 1.* DON SANCHO SANCHEZ DE ZUÑIGA, DON MATIAS CENTURION, DON RICARDO DE ROXAS, DON FRANCISCO DE SOTOMAYOR, DON GARCI SUAREZ DE CARBAJAL.

DON GARCI: Well, here's to joy, and long live the lovely bride!

DON MATIAS (*watching the balcony*): All Saragossa is hanging out of its windows tonight.

DON GARCI: And so it should! There has never been a wedding with gayer lights, nor a gentler night, nor for a handsomer pair!

DON MATIAS: The emperor is good!

DON SANCHO: Marquis, I remember a dusky night when we went out with him to try our chance. Who could have told that it would end this way?

DON RICARDO (*interrupting him*): I was there too. (*To the others.*) Listen to this tale. Three lovers—one a bandit destined for the block, and a duke, and then a king—all three lay siege to a single woman's heart. When the battle clears, who holds it? It is the bandit.

DON FRANCISCO: But nothing is astonishing in that. In

281

Spain as everywhere, love and luck turn on a play of loaded dice. The thief will always win!

DON RICARDO: And I, I've made my fortune by watching the course of love. First count, then grandee, then alcalde of the court; I have spent my time quite well, and none observed me.

DON SANCHO: Your secret is to hang about the king's path . . .

DON RICARDO: And turn my rights and actions to advantage.

DON GARCI: You profited by his preoccupation.

DON MATIAS: What is the old duke doing now? Having his coffin built?

DON SANCHO: Marquis, do not scoff. He is a valiant man. And he loved Doña Sol. Sixty years had turned his hair to gray, and one day made it white.

DON GARCI: He has not appeared again in Saragossa, they say.

DON SANCHO: Would you have this festival send him sooner to the grave?

DON FRANCISCO: And the emperor? how is he?

DON SANCHO: The emperor is sad today; Luther distresses him.

DON RICARDO: That Luther is fine cause for worry and alarm! With three or four armed men I'd take him easily.

DON MATIAS: He is disturbed by Suleiman as well.

DON GARCI: Oh, Luther, Suleiman, Neptune, the devil, Jupiter—what are they all to me? The women are pretty, the masquerade's a good one, and I've laughed all evening long!

DON SANCHO: Those are the things that count.

DON RICARDO: Garci is right—on holidays I am no longer myself; when I pull on a mask I fully believe I have a different head entirely!

DON SANCHO (low to MATIAS): If only each day were a holiday!

DON FRANCISCO (pointing to the door at right): My lords, is that not the bridal apartment?

DON GARCI (nodding): They will appear in just a moment.

DON FRANCISCO: Do you think so?

DON GARCI: I am sure of it!

DON FRANCISCO: Good! The bride is so very beautiful.

DON RICARDO: How generous the emperor is—to think this rebel Hernani should have the Golden Fleece—and be wed—and pardoned too! If he had taken my advice, the emperor would have given the outlaw a bed of stone, and the lady one of down.

DON SANCHO (*low to* DON MATIAS):   Ah, how my blade would love to slit his throat—that false, tinsel lord, all patched together with string! A count's doublet stuffed with a steward's soul!

DON RICARDO (*drawing near*): What are you saying?

DON MATIAS (*low to* DON SANCHO):   Count, let's have no quarrels here! (*Aloud to* DON RICARDO.) He was singing me one of Petrarch's sonnets to his love.

DON GARCI: Gentlemen, among the flowers and the women, and all these brightly colored costumes, have you noticed that specter leaning at the parapet and dimming the feast with his black domino?

DON RICARDO: I have indeed!

DON GARCI: Who is it?

DON RICARDO: Well, from his height, his manner, it must be Don Prancasio, the admiral.

DON FRANCISCO: No.

DON GARCI: He has not taken off his mask.

DON FRANCISCO: He has been cautious not to. It is the duke of Soma, who wants to draw attention—nothing more.

DON RICARDO: No, the duke spoke to me.

DON GARCI: Who is he then? Look now, there he goes.

(*A black domino slowly crosses the terrace at the rear. All turn to watch him, without his seeming to notice.*)

DON SANCHO: If the dead walk, that is their step.

DON GARCI (*approaching the dark figure*): Good sir! . . . (*The figure turns and stops;* GARCI *draws back.*) Gentlemen, I swear, a flame gleams in his eyes!

DON SANCHO: If he is the devil, he has found the man to talk to. (*He goes to the black domino, who stands motionless.*) Evil one! Have you come to us from hell?

MASKED FIGURE: I do not come; I go there. (*He continues his progress and disappears by the flight of stairs. All watch him go with a kind of horror.*)

DON MATIAS: His voice comes from the grave!

DON GARCI: Enough now! what's frightening otherwise is only amusing at a ball!

DON SANCHO: It is some sorry joke!

DON GARCI: Or if it's Lucifer who's stopped to watch us dance while on his way to hell, then let us dance!

DON SANCHO: It is certainly some game.

DON MATIAS: We shall find out tomorrow.

Don Sancho (*to* Don Matias): Look below, I beg you. Where is he now?

Don Matias (*leaning over the balustrade*): He has gone down the staircase. I see no more of him.

Don Sancho: A droll trick . . . (*musingly*) it is strange. . . .

Don Garci (*to a lady passing by*): Marquise, shall we dance this one together? (*He bows and presents his hand.*)

Lady: My dear sir, you know my husband counts the ones we dance together.

Don Garci: Only the more reason. If he finds pleasure in that, he shall count, and we shall dance, you and I. (*The lady gives him her hand, and they go out.*)

Don Sancho (*thoughtfully*): It is curious, indeed.

Don Matias: Here is the bridal pair! Silence!

(*Enter* Hernani *and* Doña Sol *hand in hand.* Doña Sol *wears a magnificent bridal costume;* Hernani *is all in black velvet, the Golden Fleece about his neck. Behind them, a crowd of masked figures, ladies and lords forming a retinue. Two halberdiers in rich livery follow them, and four pages precede them. All present separate and bow as they pass. Fanfare.*)

(*Scene 2*)

Hernani (*saluting*): My dear friends!

Don Ricardo (*going up to him and bowing*): Your happiness is ours, Excellency!

Don Francisco (*gazing at* Doña Sol): Holy Saint James! . . .

Don Sancho (*to* Don Matias): It is late. Shall we go now?

(*All of them move forward to greet the pair and then leave, some through the door, others by the stairway in rear.*)

Hernani (*moving with them*): God keep you all!

Don Sancho (*the last to go, grips his hand*): I wish you joy. (*He leaves.*)

(Hernani *and* Doña Sol *remain alone. The sound of*

footsteps and voices fades and disappears completely.
Throughout the beginning of the following scene, the far-
away trumpets and the lights diminish gradually, and dark-
ness and silence return.)

(*Scene 3*)

DOÑA SOL: They all have gone, at last.

HERNANI (*attempting to draw her into his arms*): My
dearest love!

DOÑA SOL (*blushing and drawing back*): It—it is late,
I think.

HERNANI: My angel, it is always late for us to come together!

DOÑA SOL: All the activity was tiring me. Do you not
find, my dear lord, that so much gaiety turns happiness
numb?

HERNANI: It is true. Happiness is a thing of gravity. It
seeks for hearts of bronze, and carves itself there slowly;
pleasure startles it away by tossing flowers to it. Joy's smile
is much more close to tears than it is to laughter.

DOÑA SOL: In your eyes, that smile is daybreak. (HER-
NANI *tries to lead her toward the door. She flushes.*) Soon.

HERNANI: I am your slave—yes, linger, linger! Do what
you will, I ask you nothing. You know what you would
have; you can do only good. I shall laugh if you desire it,
or sing. My soul burns. Ah, tell the volcano to smother its
flame—the volcano shall close its gaping chasms, and rim
its sides with flowers and green grass. For the giant is held
captive, Vesuvius is enslaved; its lava-boiling heart must not
affect you. It is flowers you would have? Very well! Then
the spitting volcano must do its best to burst with blossom!

DOÑA SOL: How kind you are to a poor woman, Hernani my heart!

HERNANI: What name is that, my lady? Ah, never call
me by that name again, I beg of you! You remind me then
of all I have forgotten. I know that once upon a time, in
some dream, there lived a Hernani, whose eye glinted like a
sword—a man of night and of the mountains, an outlaw who
wore the word "revenge" scrawled everywhere upon him, a
miserable man who trailed a curse behind him! But I do not
know this Hernani. I am a man who loves the meadows,
and flowers, and woods, and the nightingale's soft song; I

am Juan of Aragon, and wed to Doña Sol! I am a happy man!

DOÑA SOL: I too am happy!

HERNANI: What do I care for the rags I left behind me at the door? Here I am returned to my saddened palace; an angel of the Lord awaits me on the stair. I enter, and set upright the shattered columns; I light the fire, I open wide the casements, and tear the growth from between the flag-stones in the court—I am nothing now but joy, enchantment, love.

Let them return my towers, my cellars and bastilles, my crest and seat within the council of the Castiles; give me my Doña Sol, all flushed, and her brow bent low—let the two of us be left alone, and the rest is past, forgotten. I have seen nothing, said and done nothing. I begin anew, wipe everything away, forget! Be it wisdom or madness, I have you, I love you, and you are all my joy!

DOÑA SOL (*examining his collar*):   How handsome this collar is against the velvet black!

HERNANI: You saw the king dressed thus before myself.

DOÑA SOL: I did not notice it. What is another man to me? And then besides, is it the velvet, or the satin? No, my duke, it is your throat that suits the gold so well. You are noble and proud, my lord. (*He urges her off again.*) Soon! A moment yet! Look at me, do you see? This is joy, and I am weeping with it! Come look upon the lovely night! (*She goes to the balustrade.*) Only a moment, my duke! Only for long enough to breathe and gaze. All is dimmed now, the flares and festive tunes. Only the night and us. Perfect delight. . . . Say then, do you not feel that dreaming nature still half watches over us with love? There is not a cloud. All is at rest, as we are. Come, breathe the rose-perfumed air with me. No torches, not a sound. All is still. A while ago the moon climbed up from the horizon, and as you spoke your voice and its trembling light both pierced my heart together. I felt myself joyful and calm, oh my beloved; I should have liked to die then.

HERNANI: Who'd not forget all things at that celestial voice? Your tones are a song that has nothing human left in it. And like a traveler carried on a stream, who slips upon the waters through a summer night, and sees a thousand flowery fields slide past him, my bewitched spirit goes wandering in your reveries. . . .

DOÑA SOL: This silence is too dark, this peace is too profound. Would you not set a star there in the sky? Or hear a night voice sing out suddenly, all tender and sweet? . . .

HERNANI (*smiling*):   Capricious girl—only a moment since, you yearned for the light and singing to be done!

DOÑA SOL: The celebration, yes! But a bird who would sing above the meadow, a single nightingale amid the moss and shadow, or else a distant flute. . . . Such music is sweet; it brings its harmony into the soul, and sets a thousand voices singing in the heart like heavenly choirs! Oh, how lovely it would be! (*The distant sound of a horn is heard.*) God! My prayer is answered!

HERNANI (*starting; aside*):   Ah no, it cannot be!

DOÑA SOL: An angel heard my thought—your guardian angel!

HERNANI (*bitterly*):   Yes, my guardian angel! (*The horn is heard again. Aside.*) Again!

DOÑA SOL (*smilingly*):   Don Juan, I recognize the sound of your own horn!

HERNANI: Yes.

DOÑA SOL: Have you then some part in this serenade?

HERNANI: Some part—yes.

DOÑA SOL: Unpleasant wedding feast—how much more I love the horn deep in the wood. And then besides, it is your horn, and so like your own voice.

(*Sound of the horn again.*)

HERNANI (*aside*):   The tiger is there, and howling for his prey!

DOÑA SOL: Its music fills my heart with delight, Don Juan.

HERNANI (*rising, in terrible fury*):   Call me Hernani! Hernani! For I have not yet done with that terrible name!

DOÑA SOL (*trembling*):   What is wrong?

HERNANI: The old man!

DOÑA SOL: My God! What horror in your eyes! What is it?

HERNANI: The old man, laughing in the dark! Can you not see him?

DOÑA SOL: What wildness is this? What old man?

HERNANI: The old man!

DOÑA SOL (*falling to her knees*):   I beg you from my knees, tell me, what secret tears at you? What is it?

HERNANI: I gave my oath!

DOÑA SOL: Your oath? (*She watches all his movements anxiously. He stops suddenly and wipes his hand over his brow.*)

HERNANI (*aside*):   What did I nearly tell? I must spare

her. (*Aloud.*) Nothing, nothing. What did I say to you?

DOÑA SOL: You said—

HERNANI: No—no. I was distressed. I am a little ill, it is nothing. . . . I did not mean to frighten you.

DOÑA SOL: Is there something you need? Tell me, I am your servant!

(*The horn begins again.*)

HERNANI (*aside*):   He demands it, and he has my pledge! (*He feels at his waist, but finds no sword, no dagger.*) Nothing there! It should be done by now!

DOÑA SOL: Do you suffer such pain?

HERNANI: An old wound, one I thought had healed. It has reopened. (*Aside.*) She must be sent away. (*Aloud.*) Doña Sol, beloved, listen. The box I carried with me always in less happy days—

DOÑA SOL: I know the one you mean—what do you want of it?

HERNANI: There is a vial inside; it holds a remedy to end the pain I feel. Go!

DOÑA SOL: I go, my lord. (*She leaves by the door of the marriage chamber.*)

(*Scene 4*)

HERNANI (*alone*):   So this is what he would make of my good fortune! This is the fateful finger that gleams upon the wall! Oh, how sardonically fate laughs at me! (*He falls into a deep, convulsive reverie; then turns abruptly.*) Well? . . . But all is still. . . . I hear nothing approach. . . . Could I have been mistaken?

(*The masked figure in its black domino appears at the head of the stairs.* HERNANI *stops, frozen.*)

(*Scene 5*)

MASK: "Whatever may happen, when you wish it, and in whatever place—when you feel that it is time for me to

die, then sound this trumpet, nothing more. It shall be done."
The dead were witness to that pact. Well now, and is it done?

HERNANI (*his voice low*): It is he!

MASK: I come now to your home, and tell you it is time.
Now is the hour I choose. I find you late.

HERNANI: Very well. What is your will? What would
you do with me? Speak.

MASK: You may choose—the knife or poison. I have
brought both with me. We shall go together.

HERNANI: So be it.

MASK: Shall we pray?

HERNANI: What does it matter?

MASK: Which will you take?

HERNANI: The poison.

MASK: Very well. Give me your hand. (*He gives a small
flask to* HERNANI, *who takes it, paling.*) Now drink—and
let me finish it.

HERNANI: Oh, Duke, have pity! Tomorrow! Ah, if you
have still a heart, or even a soul—if you are more than a
specter from the flames, one of the damned dead, a phan-
tom or a demon till eternity—if God has not yet set the
hideous mark of "Never" on your brow—if you have
known this highest joy, to love at twenty years of age, and
to marry your beloved—if ever a cherished woman has trem-
bled in your arms, then wait until tomorrow! Tomorrow
come for me!

MASK: What a fool you are to say this! Tomorrow! Tomorrow! You must be mocking me! The bells you rang this
morning tolled your end! What would become of me, this
night? I should die of it, and who would come and take you
afterwards? Shall I go alone to death? Young man, you must
come with me!

HERNANI: No! No, you devil, I free myself from you—I
shall not obey!

MASK: I suspected you would not. Very well. For after
all, how did you swear this vow? On nothing so important,
after all—only your father's head. That can be overlooked.
Youth's vows are frivolous.

HERNANI: My father! Father! Oh, I shall go mad!

MASK: No, it is only perjury and treason.

HERNANI: Duke!

MASK: Since the sons of Spanish houses play so lightly
now with pledges and denials, farewell! (*He makes as if to
go.*)

HERNANI: Stay!

MASK: Well then—

HERNANI: Cruel old man! (*He raises the vial.*) I turn about and trace my steps back to the door of heaven!

(DOÑA SOL *returns, but does not see the masked figure, who stands at the rear.*)

(*Scene 6*)

DOÑA SOL: I could not find your box—

HERNANI (*aside*): She has returned! And at so terrible a moment!

DOÑA SOL: I startle him, he shudders at my voice! . . . What have you in your hand? No—what have you in your hand? Answer me! (*The domino approaches and unmasks. She cries out as she recognizes* DON RUY.) It is poison!

HERNANI: Great heaven!

DOÑA SOL (*to* HERNANI): What have I done to you? What hellish mystery! You meant to betray me, Don Juan!

HERNANI: I should have hid it from you. When the duke saved me I promised him that I would die at his command. Aragon must pay its debt to Silva.

DOÑA SOL: You belong to me, and not to him. What do I care for any other of your vows? (*To* DON RUY GOMEZ.) Duke, love makes me strong. I shall defend him, against you and all the world.

DON RUY GOMEZ (*immobile*): Defend him if you can against a sworn pledge.

DOÑA SOL: What pledge?

HERNANI: I did swear it.

DOÑA SOL: No, no—nothing shall bind you! It cannot be! It is a crime! Murder! Madness!

DON RUY GOMEZ: Duke, let us proceed.

(HERNANI *makes as if to obey*. DOÑA SOL *tries to draw him away*.)

HERNANI: No, Doña Sol; I must. The Duke has my word, and my father is watching from above.

DOÑA SOL (*to* DON RUY GOMEZ): You would do better to tear their young from the tigers than the one I love from me! Do you know this Doña Sol? For a long while, compassion for your age and for your sixty years made me the docile daughter, all innocent and mild. But now you see my eyes are wet with tears of rage. (*She draws a dagger from her bodice.*) And do you see this dagger? Ah, you mad old man, do you not fear the knife, when the eye has already sent its threat? Take care, Don Ruy, my uncle; I am of your line! Listen to me. Were I your very daughter, woe to you if you should lift your hand against my husband! (*She throws down the knife, and falls to her knees before the duke.*) Mercy! Alas, my lord, I am only a woman! I am weak, my strength stops short within my soul. I break too easily. I fall to your feet! Ah, I implore you, have pity on us!

DON RUY GOMEZ: Doña Sol!

DOÑA SOL: Forgive! We Spaniards speak our pain in hasty words, you know that. You were not cruel before! Have pity! Uncle, you kill me in wounding him! Pity—I love him so!

DON RUY GOMEZ (*darkly*):   You love him too well!

HERNANI (*to* DOÑA SOL):   Do you weep?

DOÑA SOL: No, no, my love—you must not die! No, I will not let you! (*To* DON RUY.) Be merciful today! I shall be fond of you as well!

DON RUY GOMEZ: After him! Do you think to appease the thirst that harrows me with such remnants of love—of friendship—no, even less than that! (*Pointing to* HERNANI.) He is the only one. He is everything. But I, what need have I for pity? What can I do with your affection? Oh, fury! He, he would have your heart, your love, the throne, and he would offer me the alms of a kind glance from you! And if a word were needed to calm my wild desires, he would tell you "Say this, and nothing more," cursing below his breath the avid beggar who gets the leavings in the empty cup. Shame! and mockery! No. It must be ended. Drink!

HERNANI: He has my word, and I must keep it.

DON RUY GOMEZ: Drink!

(HERNANI *brings the vial to his lips.* DOÑA SOL *throws herself upon his arm.*)

DOÑA SOL: Not yet! Both of you, ah hear me!

DON RUY GOMEZ: The grave is open, and I cannot wait.

DOÑA SOL: A moment! My lord, and my Don Juan! Ah, both of you, you are so harsh! What do I ask of them? An instant only, I ask no more! A moment to let this sorry woman speak what is in her heart! Oh let me speak!

DON RUY GOMEZ (*to* HERNANI):   I cannot wait.

DOÑA SOL: My lords, you make me tremble! What have I done to you?

HERNANI: Her cry undoes me!

DOÑA SOL (*still clutching his arm*): You see I have a thousand things to say!

DON RUY GOMEZ (*to* HERNANI): Death is waiting.

DOÑA SOL (*still hanging from* HERNANI's *arm*): Don Juan, when I have spoken, you shall do what you will. (*She snatches the vial from him.*) I have it now! (*She raises the vial to the gaze of* HERNANI *and the astonished old man.*)

DON RUY GOMEZ: Since I must deal here with two women, Don Juan, I shall go elsewhere to seek souls. You make fine vows upon the blood you spring from; I shall go now among the dead and speak of it to your father. Farewell. (*He takes a few steps away.* HERNANI *holds him back.*)

HERNANI: Duke, stop! (*To* DOÑA SOL.) Alas, I implore you, would you see me a man of false word, a felon, a perjurer? Would you have me go about the world with treason written on my brow? For pity's sake, give me back that poison! by our love, by our immortal souls . . . !

DONA SOL (*somberly*): You wish it? (*She drinks.*) Here, take it now.

DON RUY GOMEZ (*aside*): Then it was meant for her!

DOÑA SOL (*handing* HERNANI *the half-empty vial*): Take it, I tell you!

HERNANI (*to* DON RUY): You see this, vile old man!

DOÑA SOL: Do not be angry with me; I saved your share for you.

HERNANI (*taking the vial*): Lord God!

DOÑA SOL: You would not have left mine for me. You! You have not the heart a Christian wife has. You cannot love as a Silva loves. But I have drunk first and am at peace. Go on! Drink if you wish!

HERNANI: Alas, what have you done, my wretched love!

DOÑA SOL: It is you who forced me to it.

HERNANI: It is a hideous death!

DOÑA SOL: No, why should it be?

HERNANI: This potion takes us to the grave!

DOÑA SOL: Were we not to sleep together through this night? What difference in what bed?

HERNANI: My father, you have your revenge on me, for I forgot you! (*He puts the vial to his lips.*)

DOÑA SOL (*throwing herself upon him*): Ah heaven! What unearthly agony! Ah, throw that flask far from you! My reason's wandering. Stop! Alas, my Don Juan, this poison is a living thing! It opens out a hundred-toothed hydra in the heart that gnaws and clutches and devours! Ah, I did not know one

ould feel such hideous pain! What is that thing? Pure
ire! Do not drink it! You would suffer too horribly!

HERNANI (*to* DON RUY): Ah, your soul is wicked!
Could you not choose a different way for her? (*He drinks,
and throws down the vial.*)

DOÑA SOL: What are you doing?

HERNANI: What have you done?

DOÑA SOL: Come, oh my young love, come to my arms.
(*They sit by one another.*) Is it not a terrible pain?

HERNANI: No.

DOÑA SOL: So now begins our wedding night! Am I not
strangely pale for a young bride?

HERNANI: Ah!

DON RUY GOMEZ: Now destiny is done.

HERNANI: What torment! That Doña Sol should suffer,
and I watch!

DOÑA SOL: Be calm. It is better now. Soon we shall
open our wings together, and move toward some new brightness. Let us fly side by side toward a better world. . . . A
kiss, though; only a kiss! (*They embrace.*)

DON RUY GOMEZ: Oh, what pain to see them. . . .

HERNANI (*his voice weakening*): Oh, blessed be heaven;
it gave me a life hemmed in by chasms and haunted by
shades; but when I wearied of so hard a road, it let me
drop to sleep, with my lips pressed to your hand!

DON RUY GOMEZ: They are happy!

HERNANI (*his voice weaker and weaker*): Come, come
. . . Doña Sol . . . it is dark. Are you in pain?

DOÑA SOL (*her voice as faint*): Nothing, nothing now. . . .

HERNANI: Do you see flames within the shade?

DOÑA SOL: Not yet.

HERNANI (*with a sigh*): Here . . . (*He falls.*)

DON RUY GOMEZ (*raising his head, then dropping it*):
Dead!

DOÑA SOL (*disheveled, half rising from her bench*): Dead!
No, not dead! we are asleep. He sleeps. You see, he is
my husband. We love one another. This is where we shall
lie. It is our bridal night. (*Her voice failing.*) Do not awaken
him. He is weary. (*She turns* HERNANI'S *head to her.*) Turn
your face to me, my love. Nearer . . . nearer still. . . . (*She
falls back.*)

DON RUY GOMEZ: Dead! Oh, I am damned! (*He kills
himself.*)

LABICHE AND DELACOUR:
Pots of Money

EUGÈNE LABICHE (1815–1888)

Labiche, born and raised in Paris, came from what a social psychologist might call the lower-middle-to-lower-middle-middle class. Not much is known—or if known, recorded —of his personal life. He was evidently the kind of child every parent secretly wishes for. He had a placid temper and a gay but obedient disposition. He was in the habit of making quietly self-deprecating remarks about himself and humorous comments about others without, on the one hand, talking about himself unduly or, on the other hand, giving offense. He was not studious and never particularly devoted to Latin or Greek or "cultural" matters in general, but he had a sharp enough mind and retentive enough memory to pass examinations and to bring home good reports from his school, the Collège Bourbon. When his father suggested that he should study law, Eugène went unprotestingly to the law courses and came through with above-average grades. When his father thought that Eugène should take the standard, mind-broadening tour through Switzerland, Italy, and Sicily before settling down to a career, Eugène obediently left home, took the prescribed route and returned with a presumably broader mind.

At twenty, he had several friends who were journalists and were able to help him to find work with a number of small papers, including *Chérubin* and *La Gazette des Théâtres*. His parents did not mind that he had not gone into a legal practice. After all, he was not a bohemian: he dressed, talked, thought, and behaved like a satisfactory bourgeois; he did not associate with any red-vested romantics; he brought home a respectable wage; he had no grudges against anybody, no enemies; he ate whatever his mother cooked and relished it.

When he was twenty-four, Labiche published a humorous novel, *La Clef des Champs* (*The Key of the Fields*): nobody was surprised, nobody was annoyed. Two years later, he wrote his first play, *Monsieur de Coyllon,* or *The Infinitely*

Polite Man, in collaboration with two established playwrights whom he had met on the outskirts of Parisian theater life. The play did not generate any ripples of talk or influence, but it did give a break to Grassot, a comedian who later became very famous. Labiche was not discouraged. He enjoyed his "scribbling," as he called it, and went on to scribble some more little plays which were concerned with lower-middle-middle-class merchants, their foibles and their problems in getting their daughters married and dowered. The plays were designed for laughs and were written on a personal or local level, ignoring the cultural, political, and economic revolutions going on around them at the instigation of such men as Hugo, Balzac, Delacroix, Courbet, Baudelaire, Louis Blanc, and Saint-Simon. They were rather like today's domestic comedies on television, storms in suburban teacups, sometimes flat enough to be in saucers.

Labiche hit his stride in 1848 (the year in which the French monarchy collapsed—February—and recovered—December) with a one-act called *Young Man in a Hurry,* but another play performed the same year, *The Champenois Club,* was more satirical and biting—Labiche was discernibly laughing *at* the middle classes, and not with them—and it flopped. Labiche was by now popular with theater managers, however. He could turn out a slick little laughing-piece at a few days' notice, and was always willing to rewrite to order.

In 1851 he wrote his first full-length play, a five-act, in collaboration with one of his early partners. *The Italian Straw Hat* was an immediate hit. Francisque Sarcey, the most influential reviewer of the mid-nineteenth century, called it a "revolution in vaudeville," and it has gone on to become the most popular comedy of this type in French literature, as well as a remarkable silent motion picture (1927) under the direction of René Clair. The original production of *Le Chapeau de Paille d'Italie* enjoyed three hundred performances. The following year Labiche wrote and had staged six plays and sketches (*pochades*), all to order; he followed them with *The Vultures in Pursuit,* another five-act, written with Marc-Michel, in which the satirical spirit returned and the men of the money market were seen as flesh-eating ravens or vultures. But the message was a little too personal for most of the audience and the play failed badly.

Nevertheless, Labiche was now pulling in a good income from his writing, enough, at any rate, to buy him a substantial acreage of farming-and-hunting property in La Sologne, about eighty miles south of Paris and twenty-five miles east-southeast of Orléans in the great bend of the Loire River. By this time (1853), he was married and had a family as well as a desire to promote himself to the rank of gentleman-farmer.

Having conquered the "vaudeville" formula, Labiche again tried to break away from it, but met with only lukewarm receptions for *Les Marquises de la Fourchette* and *The Miser in Yellow Gloves.* But his next play, a four-act, *Monsieur Perrichon's Journey* (1860), was so enthusiastically received by public and reviewers alike that Labiche had indisputably become the first comic dramatist of his day. In the next four years he wrote twenty-odd plays, culminating in *Myself,* which was commissioned by the Comédie-Française, and earlier that same year (1864) *Pots of Money* (*La Cagnotte,* which means literally, "the kitty"), the last of his three five-act plays, and subsequently one of the most popular of Labiche's works in France.

From 1865 on, Labiche spent most of his time on his estate in La Sologne, coming back to Paris only for the rehearsals of his plays. He was elected mayor of the commune and seemed to enjoy his local duties. In 1870, when the Prussians invaded France, Labiche managed to secure from them a promise not to shoot hostages by claiming that he would rather face shooting himself than deliver up guerrillas. The Prussians did not press him.

In 1875 Philippe Gille, a journalist, collaborated with him on *Gladiator's Thirty Millions,* which did not do very well, although a young actress named Sarah Bernhardt was warmly applauded in the role of Suzanne, the *cocotte.* The following year he collaborated with Émile Augier, his friend, counselor and co-playwright, on *The Martin Prize,* a three-act comedy, and with Legouvé on a one-act, *Grasshopper Among the Ants.* And this was his last play. At the age of sixty-one Labiche resolutely gave up writing, saying that it was "better to retire from the theater too soon than too late." He passed the remaining thirteen years of his life on his farms where, according to Augier, he grew wheat and pine-trees, cattle and sheep, ate and drank as heavily and zestfully as ever—he was a big, stout man—and took part in local activities with great fervor.

Augier persuaded him to reprint his complete works in one series; his plays had been published by twenty-six different houses. Labiche agreed reluctantly, and only on condition that Augier would write the preface, which he did, claiming that the plays gain 100 per cent in reading over performance, since they are then divorced from stage trickery and business. This is rather like saying that a conjuror can perform better without an audience because then nobody can see what he is up to.

Actually, only 57 of Labiche's total of 160 or so plays were included in the *Complete Works;* they had been written with twenty different collaborators, with all of whom Labiche was still on good terms. (Of the plays included in the *Complete Works,* only six were written by Labiche alone, and they are all one-acts.)

After the publication of the *Complete Works,* there was a revival of interest in Labiche's plays, particularly the earlier successes like *The Italian Straw Hat, Monsieur Perrichon's Journey,* and *Pots of Money.* As a result, Labiche was proposed for the French Academy and took his seat in November 1880. It is not known if he made any contributions to the Academy; he remained a modest, pleasantly mannered man, who never traded on his reputation. In 1888 he died at home on his estate, and was nationally mourned.

A LIST OF LABICHE'S PRINCIPAL PLAYS:

(Those included here represent a tiny fraction of Labiche's output. He did not himself consider most of the others worth reprinting in his *Complete Works.*)

The Italian Straw Hat (1851), *The Vultures in Pursuit* (1853), *The Affair in the Rue de Lourcine* (1857), *The Miser in Yellow Gloves* (1858), *A Gentleman Has Burned a Lady* (1858), *M. Perrichon's Journey* (also translated under a multitude of other titles, 1860), *Dust in Your Eyes* (1861), *M. Montaudouin's 37 Sous* (1862), *Célimare the Beloved* (1863), *Myself* (1864), *Pots of Money* (1864), *Grammar* (1867), *The Happiest of the Three* (1870), *Must It Be Said?* (1872), *Twenty-Nine Degrees in the Shade* (1873), *Gladiator's Thirty Millions* (1875), *The Martin Prize* (1876), *Grasshopper Among the Ants* (1876).

SUGGESTIONS FOR FURTHER READING ON LABICHE:

Very little has been written about Labiche in English. Émile Augier's preface to Labiche's *Complete Works,* translated by Mary Douglas Dirks, appears in *The Tulane Drama Review*, Winter 1959. The only biography is in French, *Eugène Labiche, Sa Vie, Son Oeuvre*, by Philippe Soupault (Editions du Sagittaire, 1945). Reviews of many Labiche plays can be found in Francisque Sarcey: *Forty Years of Theatre*.

See also Henri Bergson's famous essay *Le Rire, essai sur la signification du comique* (translated by Wylie Sypher in an Anchor Book under the title *Laughter*), in which a number of important references are made to, and examples drawn from, Labiche's scenes and situations.

NOTE: A critical essay in which reference is made to Labiche, "The Psychology of Farce," by Eric Bentley, will be found on p. 540.

POTS OF MONEY
(LA CAGNOTTE)

A Comedy in Five Acts

by Eugène Labiche and A. Delacour

FIRST PERFORMED IN PARIS IN 1864

Translated by Albert Bermel

CHARACTERS [1]

BOURSEY, *a man of independent means*
DANNE, *a rich farmer*
CORDEN, *a pharmacist*
SYLVAIN, *son of Danne*
FELIX, *a young lawyer*
PENURI, *a tax collector*
POCHE, *a marriage broker*
CHUTE, *an assistant police commissioner*
LEONIDA, *sister of Boursey*
BLANCHE, *daughter of Boursey*
BENJAMIN, *a waiter*
JOSEPH, *servant of Poche*
TRICOT, *a fruit merchant*
MADAME CARAMEL, *a grocer*
SECOND WAITER
THIRD WAITER
POLICEMAN

France in the 1860's. The first act takes place in the village of Endives-Under-Glass; the other four acts, in Paris.

[1] Some of the characters' names have been slightly modified from the French.

ACT I

(*A provincial living room in the village of Endives-Under-Glass.* BLANCHE *and* LEONIDA *are seated round a small table, knitting or crocheting.* PENURI *is reading a newspaper.* BOURSEY, DANNE, CORDEN, *and* FELIX *are playing cards.*)

BLANCHE: Aren't you joining the card game this evening, Aunt Leonida?

LEONIDA: Yes, very shortly.

FELIX: It's my turn to drop out. You can take my place in five minutes.

LEONIDA: It's not your turn. It's somebody else's. But he doesn't seem to be moving.

CORDEN: Don't think I didn't hear that.

PENURI: Well, well! (*Lowering the newspaper.*) Here's a curious advertisement.

EVERYBODY: What's that?

PENURI: Listen. "Young, attractive, majestic lady, with annual income of five thousand francs, bracket, from well-selected shares, close the bracket, would like to meet honest man, widower or bachelor, with romantic disposition. Must be in good health, reasonably provided, and not too old. No fortune necessary. Objective: marriage and a modest home in a small, well-situated town. For information, write to Box 44, care of this newspaper, and enclose stamped, addressed envelope. No frivolous replies, please."

BOURSEY: That's an old one. It's been appearing in the paper, on and off, for three years now. I pass. My tooth is killing me.

PENURI: Imagine anybody replying to that kind of an advertisement. It's indecent. The woman is shameless.

LEONIDA: I don't see anything wrong with it. A poor, forgotten person, sitting out her life in some corner of the provinces, waiting for happiness. And somewhere else a man, alone, who could be that happiness. And suddenly, perhaps, the personal column brings them together.

CORDEN: They say there have been some nice matches through the personal column. As a bachelor, I must say I read it from time to time and dream all sorts of dreams. . . .

DANNE: Bunkum! If you want to marry somebody you hang about together and it happens naturally. Take me: when I came across my late wife and took a fancy to her we started going together right away. I went to her house, she came to my house, and before we knew it—bang! That's how people get married.

BOURSEY: Come on, come on. Let's get back to the game.

LEONIDA (*standing up*): Nine-fifteen. My turn.

CORDEN: Wait till we finish one more hand.

FELIX: No, I'll drop out. You can take over my hand. (*He changes seats with* LEONIDA.)

CORDEN: You want to keep playing all the time. I never met such a greedy cardplayer.

LEONIDA: What are you complaining about? You're still in the game, aren't you? Show some manners for a change. If you can.

CORDEN: Listen to who's talking. The most bloodthirsty cardplayer in—

BOURSEY: Stop it! You're always squabbling, you two. Remember you're the godmother and godfather of the bell-ringer's son. Try to behave like a godmother and godfather.

DANNE (*to* LEONIDA): He did give you that diamond pendant, after the christening.

CORDEN: Yes. Sometimes I forget how generous I am. (*He deals the cards.*)

BLANCHE (*to* FELIX): Now you have a quarter of an hour of boredom ahead.

FELIX: These are the most beautiful quarter-of-an-hours of my life, Mademoiselle Blanche, the ones I spend beside you.

CORDEN: What have you got there?

BOURSEY: An ace.

CORDEN: Good. I pass.

BOURSEY: What?

CORDEN: You don't want me to trump you, do you?

BOURSEY: Don't you know what I mean when I say an ace? I mean a two. (*Everybody laughs.*) I don't see what's funny about that.

DANNE: You two haven't got your sign system worked out properly. When I have an ace, I press my lips together like this, and I open my nostrils like this. It always works.

LEONIDA: So that's what you're getting at when you make faces. Oh, we forgot the kitty. Blanche, bring the kitty over.

BLANCHE (*holding out an earthenware pot to each of the players in turn*): One franc, please.

DANNE (*putting in his franc*): It's ruinous, this game.

BLANCHE (*testing the weight of the pot*): The pot is getting nice and heavy.

FELIX: And what about the other three, all full up?

DANNE: So they should be full up, after a whole year.

BOURSEY: I don't want to boast, but I think that was a pretty good idea of mine.

CORDEN: What do you mean? It was my idea.

BOURSEY: Excuse me. You may have suggested that we start a kitty. . . .

CORDEN: I may have? I did.

BOURSEY: But you wanted to open it every Saturday and spend the proceeds on wine.

DANNE: That would have been good.

BOURSEY: Do you think my house is a bar?

CORDEN: I didn't say anything about bars. What I said was—

LEONIDA: That wouldn't have been fair to the ladies. We don't drink, except occasionally. We would have been the ones to suffer, as usual.

BOURSEY: That's why I decided to enlarge your idea, by letting the funds add up for an entire year. And now we have a real sum of money to spend; it may be as much as two hundred francs.

EVERYBODY: Oh!

BOURSEY: Two hundred francs, I say. Perhaps more: we shall soon know. At nine-thirty the year is up and the kitty is to be counted. Now, suppose we do have two hundred francs . . .

DANNE: What a celebration!

BOURSEY: We can do something really worth while. We'll hold a dinner that will make the last Firemen's Banquet look like a snack.

LEONIDA: Let's get on with the game. I have three—

BOURSEY: I am sorry that Penuri, our wise and worthy tax collector—

PENURI (*looking up from his paper*): Me?

BOURSEY: —did not see fit to join us and pay his contributions.

PENURI: Gambling is an immoral practice for a man who holds public office.

FELIX: I'm the public notary, and I don't see anything immoral in a friendly game.

BLANCHE: And how about Father? He's commander of the fire brigade.

PENURI: That's different. Your father is not, properly speaking, a public official.

BOURSEY (*standing up*): What am I then? I think I've done enough for my country not to be insulted by a mere tax collector.

PENURI: I'm not insulting—

BOURSEY: I should think not. People forget too easily that I am the one who presented the community with its only fire pump.

DANNE: Yes, but it's never been used. It's going rusty.

BOURSEY: It's not my fault if there are no fires. What am I supposed to do—go around the village setting fires right and left, just so that my pump can be used?

LEONIDA (*banging the table*): Are we playing or are we not? I have three—

BOURSEY (*sitting down*): I was waiting for you to call.

DANNE: Well, she's obviously got something good there, so I pass.

CORDEN: So do I.

BOURSEY: So do I.

LEONIDA: How's that? (*She lays her cards on the table.*)

BOURSEY: Good enough.

LEONIDA: Another four francs. Thank you, gentlemen. (*She scoops up the money.*)

BLANCHE (*getting up and going to the door*): Look what's arrived. Two special deliveries from Paris. One for you, Auntie. And one for Monsieur Danne.

LEONIDA: For me? Thank you. (*She looks at the writing on the envelope, turns red, and puts it away hastily.*)

BOURSEY: Who's it from?

LEONIDA: Oh, nobody special. My dressmaker in Paris. I'll read it later. Er—whose turn?

BOURSEY: A special delivery from your dressmaker?

LEONIDA: She's always anxious to let me know about her new styles.

DANNE (*having put on his glasses*): Ah, it's from my boy. He's written to tell me how he's doing at that school of agriculture. He told me he wanted to be a photographer. But I gave him a clout that knocked all those ideas out of his head. "You're going to be a farmer," I said, "like your father, and his father. Because a farmer is—"

BOURSEY: Yes we know all that. Let's get on with the game.

DANNE: Wait till I read this letter from my boy.

BOURSEY: Oh, no.

CORDEN: Not again.

DANNE (*reading*): "My dear Dad, I am writing to tell you that they are very satisfied with me here. I've been promoted to the cowshed. . . ."

BOURSEY: The rest of us don't want to hear these intimate details about cowsheds. Read to yourself.

DANNE: If I read aloud, it's not for your benefit. It's for mine. You're not supposed to be listening. If I don't read aloud, how can I understand what I'm reading? (*Continues to read noisily.*) ". . . to the cowshed. They gave me my own sick cow to look after. . . ."

BOURSEY: Looks as if we have to wait until he's finished.

DANNE: "She is very sick. She doesn't drink. She doesn't eat. She coughs and sneezes all the time." Poor beast. She's caught a cold. "They say here that she may not last. . . ." (*Deeply moved, he passes the letter to* BOURSEY.) Read it for me. I can't see the words. My eyes are too wet. Poor creature.

BOURSEY: Courage. Don't get upset. She isn't dead yet. (*Reading.*) "As for me, I'm all right." There, you see, he's all right. He says so.

DANNE: Yes, but the cow . . .

BOURSEY: "We have been ploughing every morning. They are ploughing me to death. They want to get the seeds planted, but it won't stop raining. Still, as the proverb says:

>   When February's wetter
>   The dunghill is better . . . ."

DANNE: He's got it the wrong way round:

>   The dunghill is better
>   When February's wetter.

It's true, though. And I'll tell you why—

CORDEN: Finish it off quickly, Boursey, or we'll never get through this hand.

BOURSEY: Here comes the end. "Love and affection and best wishes from your respectful son, and will you please send my monthly allowance as soon as possible. Sylvain."

EVERYBODY: At last.

LEONIDA: Where did we get to?

BLANCHE: Father, it's nine-thirty.

CORDEN: Time to count the kitty.

DANNE: Pass.

CORDEN: Pass.

BOURSEY: Pass.

LEONIDA: Pass.

BOURSEY: That tooth is murdering me. Blanche, collect the last contributions.

BLANCHE (*going around with the earthenware pot*):   One franc each, please.

DANNE: Ruinous, this game.

BLANCHE: What's this you've given me, a foreign coin? Oh, no, it's a button.

DANNE: Excuse me, a mistake. Here you are. One franc.

BOURSEY: Now let's burn the cards.

DANNE: Don't get reckless. Some of them still have corners.

LEONIDA: Excuse me. I'm just going out to read this letter from my dressmaker. (*Exit.*)

BOURSEY: Now, gentlemen. We will proceed to the counting of the kitty.

CORDEN: The sooner the better.

BOURSEY: Blanche, bring me your workbasket. (*She empties out her workbasket on a table, and brings it to him, with a small hammer.*) And Blanche, bring in the other three pots of money.

FELIX: I'll help you. They may be heavy. (*He and BLANCHE go out together.*)

BOURSEY (*taking the hammer*):   There is only one way I know to open these pots and that is to break them.

DANNE: Don't break them. You might be able to use them. Let me have them. I'll find a way to get the money out without breaking them.

BOURSEY: I wish I knew what to do about this tooth.

CORDEN: Break the pots.

BOURSEY: In a moment. (*Puts the pot and the basket down and holds his jaw.*)

DANNE: I'll tell you what to do about that tooth. First you take a live mole, no more than three to three-and-a-half months old—

BOURSEY: How do you recognize a mole that's three-and-a-half months old?

DANNE: It takes practice.

PENURI: I'll tell you what's better. You take a mouthful of milk. And you keep it in your mouth all night. You don't swallow it.

BOURSEY: What if I fall asleep?

PENURI: That's all right. Fall asleep if you like. But don't swallow the milk.

CORDEN: As a professional, licensed pharmacist, may I offer a suggestion?

PENURI: A pharmacist is not a dentist.

CORDEN: Why waste money on a dentist? Do you remember how I operated on the colonel two years ago? That was a beautiful extraction.

BOURSEY: Was it easy?

CORDEN: Easy.

BOURSEY: Did it hurt?

CORDEN: How could it hurt? It was scientific. I tied a string around his tooth and attached it to the tail of a donkey. I fired one round of my service revolver, which I keep loaded for these occasions. The animal leaped forward and the tooth came from its socket like the bullet from my revolver. The colonel has never stopped thanking me since. I can do the same for you.

BOURSEY: I'll think about it. The tooth has stopped aching now. Let's get back to the kitty. (*Picking up the hammer.*) One, two, three. (*He smashes the pot.*)

DANNE: Look at all those francs.

BOURSEY: Let's get down to it. Stack them in twenties. (*They begin to count.*)

CORDEN: Three, four, five . . .

DANNE: Six, seven, eight . . .

BOURSEY: Nine, ten . . . No, what am I talking about? You're putting me off.

DANNE: I didn't say a word.

BOURSEY: You said, "Seven, eight," and that made me say, "nine, ten." Can't you count to yourself?

DANNE: No.

BOURSEY: Now I don't know where I am.

PENURI: Nor do I.

CORDEN: Let's start again. Four, five . . .

DANNE: Six, seven, eight . . .

BOURSEY: Nine, ten. No, we're doing it again. I know what. We'll all go to different corners of the room, and— (*seeing* BLANCHE *and* FELIX *coming back with the pots*) I have a better idea. You take a pot for yourself, Danne old man, and go into my bedroom with it. Corden and Penuri, you can take a pot each into my study; one of you use the desk, the other one the table. And I'll stay here.

PENURI: And we'll all come back in here afterwards for the grand total.

EVERYBODY: Yes.

CHORUS (*they sing*):

> Since it's growing rather late,
> And the pots are here to smash,
> Let us end this one-year wait
> And proceed to count the cash.

(DANNE *goes out on the left,* CORDEN *and* PENURI *on the right, each carrying his pot of money.* BOURSEY *sits down again.*)

BOURSEY: Two, four, six . . .

BLANCHE (*to* FELIX):   Ask him now, while he's alone.

FELIX: Perhaps I should wait until he's not so busy.

BLANCHE: You've already put it off for three days.

FELIX: He's had that toothache for three days.

BLANCHE: He feels better today.

BOURSEY: Money, money, money. (*Gurgling with delight.*) That makes the first hundred.

BLANCHE: Now. While he's laughing. Quick.

FELIX: I haven't thought out what to say. . . .

BLANCHE: Be brave. Just ask him. Don't waste time thinking.

FELIX: I wanted to lead up to it slowly.

BLANCHE: No, be direct. Take him by surprise. "Please, may I marry your daughter?" Isn't that simple?

FELIX: Yes. (*She pats his hand and goes out.*) No. I wish I could stop shaking. It's ridiculous. A proposal. What could be easier? (*Bracing himself.*) Sir. He didn't hear me. Sir. Monsieur Boursey.

BOURSEY: Twelve, thirteen. What is it?

FELIX: You will be able to tell, by the emotion in my voice—

BOURSEY: Every time you speak to me I lose count.

FELIX: You'd just reached thirteen.

BOURSEY: That's it. Thirteen, fourteen, fifteen.

FELIX: —by the emotion in my voice, as I say. . . . What *was* I going to say? Try again. In the three months during which I have known your daughter . . .

BOURSEY: Why don't you give me a hand? It'll go quicker.

FELIX: With pleasure.

BOURSEY: In stacks of twenty.

FELIX: In those three wonderful months, I have come to experience . . .

BOURSEY: Start counting.

FELIX (*taking a load of coins*):   Two, three . . . to experience a feeling that can only be called . . .

BOURSEY: One, two . . .

FELIX: Six, seven . . . that can only be called love. And I would therefore like . . .

BOURSEY: Three, four . . .

FELIX: Eight, nine . . . to ask for her hand . . . Ten, eleven . . .

BOURSEY: Seven, eight . . .

FELIX: —for her hand, twelve, thirteen, fourteen . . . in marriage . . .

BOURSEY: Look at that. A button. That's the second one I've found.

FELIX (*louder*): I humbly ask for your daughter's hand.

BOURSEY: Just a minute. Eighteen, nineteen, twenty. Another pile. They're really adding up. (*Starting to count again.*) One, two, three . . . My dear Felix . . . four, five, six . . . I understand the honor you do me in making this proposal.

FELIX: Thank you, sir, thank you.

BOURSEY: Where was I?

FELIX: Six.

BOURSEY: Oh, yes. Six, seven, eight . . . And I promise to consider it carefully. . . . Another button. Somebody's been filling up the kitty with them. Do we know any tailors?

FELIX: It wasn't me, sir.

BOURSEY: Nine, ten . . . Marriage, my boy, has its joy and its sweetness. It also has its responsibilities. . . .

FELIX: I know. All my live I have believed in . . .

BOURSEY: Now, what have we got? (*He points to the piles of coins.*)

FELIX: I have my practice. Nothing extraordinary at present, but in the future . . .

BOURSEY: Five here and three there. Eight. Eight twenties: one hundred and sixty.

FELIX: It might go as high as forty-five thousand.

BOURSEY: Forty-five thousand. What? Where? (*Irritably.*) This is no good, Felix. I'm talking kitties and you're talking dowries. (*Piling the money into the basket.*) I'm going into the kitchen to count in peace.

FELIX: At least, may I hope that—

BOURSEY (*going out right*): You can hope for whatever you like—as long as my daughter loves you. If I catch the man who put all those buttons in the kitty . . . (*Exit.*)

FELIX: She does love me. She told me so. Before I even asked her. I'll tell her the old boy said yes. (*He runs out. LEONIDA comes in, carrying the letter.*)

LEONIDA: When I read the first line I almost passed out. It's happened. He's found somebody for me. I have to be in Paris tomorrow evening at eight o'clock. Do I dare to?

Yes, I must. It may be a question of my future happiness. If only I knew what to do and how to go. If only my mother were still alive. She would have known how to advise me. She would have said—she would have said: Go. So I shall go. But suppose they get suspicious? And that's not all. How can I travel all that way by myself? I wonder if my brother would come with me. I'll have to tell him. No, I daren't. What shall I do? I must confide in somebody. (*Enter* BLANCHE.)

BLANCHE: Oh, Aunt Leonida, you don't know how happy I am.

LEONIDA: What right have you to be happy at a serious time like this?

BLANCHE: Felix has just asked Father if I can marry him, and Father said that he can hope.

LEONIDA: What? Are you in love with Felix?

BLANCHE: I suppose I must be, otherwise I wouldn't want to marry him.

LEONIDA: That's interesting.

BLANCHE: Why?

LEONIDA: He has fair hair.

BLANCHE: What's wrong with that?

LEONIDA: And so have you. That means that you will lead a peaceful life, with no problems and no upsets, a calm life, like two sheep grazing in the same field.

BLANCHE: Sheep! Let me tell you that Felix is a charming and intelligent boy. He just had a marvelous idea.

LEONIDA: To marry you?

BLANCHE: To spend the kitty on a ball. We could invite the whole village.

LEONIDA: That would be delightful. But when, did you say?

BLANCHE: Tomorrow. Do you know what tomorrow is? Mardi Gras.

LEONIDA: Tomorrow, oh. Of course, a ball would be quite pleasant. But I have another suggestion for spending the kitty. Not quite as exciting as a ball, but more useful perhaps.

BLANCHE: What could be more useful than a ball?

LEONIDA: Suppose we all went to Paris for the day?

BLANCHE: But what good would that do?

LEONIDA: We could look in the shops. You're getting married, and you'll want to start thinking about china and curtain fabrics and nightgowns and so on. You could look for your trousseau, without *saying* so, of course.

BLANCHE: So I could. How clever you are, Aunt Leonida.

LEONIDA: Yes. You'll have to speak to your father about it. Don't tell him exactly why you want to go.

BLANCHE: Mardi Gras in Paris. Perfect. Here he is. Let me speak to him. (BOURSEY *comes in.*)

BOURSEY: All counted up. What a total! It makes the blood rush to my head.

BLANCHE: Father, you don't look very well.

LEONIDA: He looks fine.

BOURSEY: Of course I do. Wait till I tell you how much we have here.

BLANCHE: That toothache must be painful.

BOURSEY: I'd forgotten all about it.

BLANCHE: Your cheek is all swollen.

LEONIDA: I can't see it.

BOURSEY: Now you mention it, it is beginning to throb again.

BLANCHE: Poor Father. Does it hurt very much?

BOURSEY: It does now.

BLANCHE: If I were you . . .

BOURSEY: You'd put a live mole aged three to three-and-a-half months in your mouth. The trouble is, how do you tell the age of a mole?

BLANCHE: No. If I were you I'd go to a dentist.

BOURSEY: There isn't one in the village.

BLANCHE: There are plenty in Paris. The best dentists in the world.

LEONIDA (*aside*): She's not as sheepish as she looks.

BOURSEY: Don't joke with me. Go all the way to Paris for the sake of a tooth?

BLANCHE: Two little tiny hours by train.

BOURSEY: But the expense.

BLANCHE: You could do it for nothing.

BOURSEY: How?

BLANCHE: You could pay all the expenses from the kitty. We could all go.

BOURSEY: So we could. We could all go, and we could spend the kitty in Paris.

BLANCHE: You could have your tooth pulled out, we could look around the shops . . .

LEONIDA: I could keep my appoint—

BOURSEY: Your what?

LEONIDA: We could visit the monuments.

BOURSEY: Yes. The Panthéon, the Tower of Saint Jacques, the Champs Élysées . . .

BLANCHE: The Louvre, the Eiffel Tower, the Concorde . . .

LEONIDA: The Tuileries, the Luxembourg Gardens . . .

BOURSEY: The Follies . . .

BLANCHE: But wait. Suppose the others don't want to go?

BOURSEY: They will have to be convinced. Leave that to me.

(CORDEN, DANNE, PENURI *and* FELIX *return.*)

PENURI: Gentlemen, here is the total of the portion of the kitty that was placed in my jurisdiction. Upon counting and rechecking the result I find that my portion comes to one hundred and thirty-one francs. I must add, however, since we are interested in complete totals, that I have found a number of buttons, namely five, among the coins.

CORDEN: So have I.

BOURSEY: And I.

BLANCHE (*looking at* DANNE):   Buttons, eh?

DANNE: Somebody must have made a mistake.

CORDEN: I have one hundred and twenty-eight francs and four buttons.

BOURSEY: I have one hundred and five francs. And nine buttons.

DANNE: I have one hundred and twenty-seven francs.

BOURSEY: And no buttons?

DANNE: No buttons.

BOURSEY: That's strange.

PENURI (*who has written down the totals*):   That, gentlemen, gives us an over-all total of four hundred and ninety-one francs.

EVERYBODY: Ah!

PENURI: Plus eighteen buttons.

BOURSEY: A very nice kitty.

CORDEN: Magnificent.

DANNE: I thought it would be bigger.

CORDEN: So it would have been—without the buttons.

BOURSEY: And now, gentlemen, the great moment has come when we must deliberate and vote on how the kitty shall be spent.

EVERYBODY: Yes, yes! (*They sit around the table in the center.*)

FELIX (*appearing at the back*):   Have you counted it up?

BOURSEY: Yes, we have. Come in. We need your vote. We are all good friends, gentlemen, and even if our votes diverge, we still respect each other's opinions. Who wants to speak first?

CORDEN }
DANNE } (*standing up together*):   I do!

BOURSEY: I can see that we are full of suggestions this evening. Which one of you asked first?

CORDEN }
DANNE } I did!

BOURSEY: This is becoming difficult.

PENURI: The custom in deliberative assemblies is for the younger man to give way in favor of the older.

BOURSEY: That solves it. Corden, you have the floor. . . .

CORDEN: Thank you. But I believe that Danne is older than I am.

DANNE: I am not. I've always been younger than you, much younger, as long as I remember.

CORDEN: It's not true. I refuse to speak first.

BOURSEY: Gentlemen, gentlemen, I was counting on a brilliant discussion, with flashing remarks from man to man, from friend to friend. And all I hear is petty squabbling.

CORDEN (*standing up*):   Very well. I'll speak first. Not because I'm the oldest, but because I am the most reasonable.

PENURI: Good for you.

CORDEN: I shall be brief. . . .

BOURSEY (*graciously*):   That's a pity.

CORDEN: Thank you. Here we are with this considerable and unexpected sum of money. We must spend it in a manner worthy of our positions; we are, after all, not unimportant men in this village. I therefore propose that we write to my friend Chevet and order a large turkey, stuffed with truffles. (*Murmurs of disagreement.*)

BOURSEY (*shaking a little bell*):   Ladies, gentlemen. Please. We shall listen to everybody's suggestion in turn . . . even the most stupid ones.

CORDEN: Eh?

LEONIDA: I'm against truffles. I don't like them.

BLANCHE: Nor do I.

BOURSEY: They also happen to upset my stomach.

DANNE: I prefer mushrooms. Fried.

CORDEN: I'm sticking to truffles.

BOURSEY: Right. Next opinion. Danne?

DANNE: The weather is fine and my old buggy is big enough for all of us. Let's go to Cressy and spend the day at the fair.

EVERYBODY: No, no. Terrible idea. Waste of time. Ridiculous . . . etc.

BOURSEY (*ringing his bell*):   Order, order. One at a time.

CORDEN: I still think that a fat turkey, overflowing with truffles . . .

DANNE: You didn't let me tell you about the fair. You see the sideshows, the snakes, the magicians, the donkeys with two heads, and the fat woman. She's really something to see. And sometimes they let you touch her. It's fun, that is.

FELIX: Excuse me, I have a much better suggestion. . . .

BLANCHE (*in a hiss*): Don't talk about the ball. It's all been changed. We have something else.

FELIX: Oh, it's changed?

BOURSEY: All right, Felix. Go ahead.

FELIX: I—um—er—I need a few more minutes to think.

PENURI: Although I have not contributed to the kitty, perhaps you will allow me to give you an outside, objective view. I have a proposal which, I am sure, will please everybody. If you don't wish to hear it, just say so, but you'll be sorry if you neglect this valuable and unifying motion.

BOURSEY: Go ahead, Monsieur Penuri, for God's sake.

PENURI: The most desirable attribute in woman is maidenly virtue. Ladies and gentlemen, virtue is on the decline. We must revive it, encourage it.

DANNE: What's that got to do with us?

PENURI: Why not hold a carnival, and select the most virtuous girl in the village of Endives-Under-Glass to be the queen of the carnival?

CORDEN: How can you tell who is the most virtuous girl?

PENURI: That would be up to the judges.

CORDEN: Who are the judges?

PENURI: We are.

CORDEN: Much easier to buy a turkey, a thumping great turkey swamped with truffles, and have done with it.

DANNE: Or drive to the fair in my buggy and spend a whole day with the fat lady and the snakes and—

BOURSEY: Order. Silence. This is my house, so I shall speak last. I claim all your attention.

BLANCHE: Good old Daddy.

BOURSEY: Ladies and gentlemen, Paris is the capital of the world. It has the finest dentists in the world. . . .

PENURI
DANNE } What?
CORDEN

BOURSEY: I mean it is the center of the arts, industry, and entertainment. Paris has everything. I therefore propose that we take the excursion train tomorrow to Paris.

BLANCHE } Bravo!
LEONIDA }

DANNE: No good. I've been to Paris before. I passed through it forty-one years ago on the way to Lille.

CORDEN: An excursion? But we'll have no money left for eating. I would have thought that a giant turkey, brimming with truffles . . .

BOURSEY: But truffles don't agree with the rest of us. They make us ill.

CORDEN: Paris will make me ill.

BOURSEY: But if the majority decides on Paris . . .

CORDEN: The majority would never—

BOURSEY: We'll see. Let's proceed to the vote.

EVERYBODY: The vote. The vote.

PENURI: Shall I, as the only impartial member of this assembly, take charge of the ballot box?

BOURSEY: Yes. Good idea. (*He hands out a sheet of paper to each person.*) The ballot box. (*He gives* PENURI *a hat.*)

PENURI: One, two, three, write. (*Everybody except* BLANCHE *and* PENURI *writes.*) No crossings-out or you spoil your ballot paper. Has everybody decided? The ballot is closed. (*He takes the papers and puts them in the hat. To* LEONIDA.) Now we will count the votes. (*He takes out the papers one at a time.*) One turkey with truffles . . .

CORDEN: Hooray.

PENURI: Silence, please. Paris. (*Cheers from* FELIX, BOURSEY, LEONIDA *and* BLANCHE.) Paris. (*More cheers.*) The fair at Cressy.

DANNE: Hooray, very good, terrific, that's for me.

PENURI: And the final vote is for Paris. (*More cheers.*) Total number of votes: five. Votes for Paris: three. An absolute majority for Paris.

CORDEN: I suppose we'll be able to get a decent meal there.

DANNE: We can go to the cattle market and the slaughter-houses. I have a cousin who works in one of the slaughter-houses. He'll show us round.

BOURSEY: There's one other thing: we certainly won't spend the whole of our four hundred and ninety-one francs on the fare. We'll have something left over for our personal needs, such as visiting dentists and so on.

DANNE: That reminds me: I could do with a new pickax.

CORDEN: I've just thought of something too, foolish perhaps, but—

BOURSEY: What is it?

CORDEN: Nothing, nothing. (*Aside.*) It may be a question of my future happiness.

LEONIDA (*aside*): I'll be able to keep my appointment.

BOURSEY: Let's all have an early night. We'll have to catch the five twenty-five tomorrow morning.

BLANCHE (*to* FELIX): How are you going to get up?

FELIX: I won't sleep. I'll be too excited thinking about you.

CHORUS (*they sing*):
> What a lucky group are we—
> Off to Paris in the train.
> One whole day to stay and see
> All the sights upon the Seine.

ACT II

(Paris. A large, elegant restaurant.)

BENJAMIN *(arranging a table)*: Is that a customer? At this time of the morning?

SYLVAIN *(entering hesitantly)*: No, it frightens me. It's too luxurious.

BENJAMIN: May I help you, monsieur? What are you looking for?

SYLVAIN: Some information. Last night I was at the Casino and I met a young lady who calls herself Miranda the Sensitive.

BENJAMIN: I know her.

SYLVAIN: Good. Then she really exists. I was beginning to wonder after those drinks last night. She told me to meet her here for lunch.

BENJAMIN: At this time of the morning?

SYLVAIN: No, a bit later. But I wanted to know beforehand if it's possible for the two of us to eat lunch in a private booth for seventeen francs. That's all I have.

BENJAMIN: Seventeen francs—well, we could certainly give you something.

SYLVAIN: I don't just mean rolls and coffee. I'm entertaining a young lady, don't forget.

BENJAMIN: I could do you a nice sheep's cheek in vinegar.

SYLVAIN: Sounds appetizing.

BENJAMIN: Or a steak—rather thin, rather narrow, but a steak. Or an omelette made with one egg.

SYLVAIN: Perfect. We shall also want dessert. Something unpretentious. At an unpretentious price.

BENJAMIN: How about stewed prunes?

SYLVAIN: You're joking.

BENJAMIN: Or a strawberry tart?

SYLVAIN: Fresh?

BENJAMIN: This week's.

SYLVAIN: Plenty of crust?

BENJAMIN: Acres.

SYLVAIN: Plenty of strawberries?

BENJAMIN: Dozens.

SYLVAIN: Put two strawberry tarts aside. (*Takes out a cigar case.*) Have a cigar.

BENJAMIN: Thank you, monsieur. Oh no, this is the cabbage-leaf type. I only smoke Havanas.

SYLVAIN: So do I, when I can afford them. But my father doesn't allow me enough to buy more than one Havana a month.

BENJAMIN: A tightwad, eh?

SYLVAIN: He's the finest of men, my father. But a peasant, after all. He has a farm at Endives-Under-Glass, and he thinks he can turn me into a farmer too.

BENJAMIN: It's a noble profession.

SYLVAIN: Yes, but too earthy for my taste. I wanted to be a photographer, and specialize in girls . . . you know: models, standing under waterfalls or kissing trees. But Dad wouldn't hear of it. He sent me to this school at Grignon.

BENJAMIN: To learn farming?

SYLVAIN: Yes, but I don't know a cauliflower from a carrot. As soon as I got there they stuck me in the cowshed, and in twenty-four hours they had me carting manure all over the place. Two days later I left . . . without telling Dad, of course.

BENJAMIN: Suppose he finds out?

SYLVAIN: That's where I've been smart. I write to him every month. I go back to Grignon to post the letter and pick up my monthly allowance: one hundred francs.

BENJAMIN: A hundred francs—that's rough.

SYLVAIN: It is after the first few days. From the fifth of the month on I'm always in debt. I wish I knew some way to earn a little on the side. Something not too strenuous. Tell me, what do you make a month at this job?

BENJAMIN: Depends on the tips. About three hundred on the average.

SYLVAIN: That would do me nicely. I wouldn't be ashamed to wait in a café.

BENJAMIN (*coldly*):   There's nothing to be ashamed of.

SYLVAIN: It would suit me. Always in the money. Tips. Plenty of women around.

BENJAMIN (*persuading himself*):   And it's very satisfying work. Creative.

SYLVAIN: I bet. What's your name?

BENJAMIN: Benjamin.

SYLVAIN: Good for you. Listen, Ben, if you hear of an opening for a bright young man, keep me in mind, will you?

BENJAMIN: Certainly.

SYLVAIN: And you'll save me a booth for lunch?

BENJAMIN: Number four, monsieur. By the window, facing onto the boulevard.

SYLVAIN: Perfect. If I'm not here when Miranda arrives, tell her to wait on one of those chairs. I don't want her to start spending before I get here.

BENJAMIN: Very good, monsieur. Don't worry about it.

SYLVAIN: Thanks, Ben. You're a pal. Come and have a coffee with us at lunch time.

BENJAMIN: Thank you, monsieur. (SYLVAIN *goes out.*) He called me Ben! That's the kind of person I like: no swank, even though he comes from a good family.

(*Noises from outside. Sounds of running feet. Shouts of "Stop thief, stop thief." Another waiter comes in.*)

SECOND WAITER: Did you see that? A pickpocket. He got away.

BENJAMIN: Where?

SECOND WAITER: Right outside the restaurant. He tore off around the corner.

BENJAMIN: Did you see him?

SECOND WAITER: No. He snatched somebody's watch and disappeared.

BENJAMIN: It doesn't pay to carry a watch these days.

(SECOND WAITER *goes out. Enter* BOURSEY, DANNE, CORDEN, LEONIDA, *and* BLANCHE.)

DANNE: First time I ever saw a thief close up. He looked just like anybody else. Talk about exciting. I'm glad we came to Paris, after all. It's a good beginning to the day.

LEONIDA: I've never seen anybody run at that speed before.

BOURSEY: He went right by me. If I'd reached out I could have touched him.

CORDEN: It was your duty to stop him.

BOURSEY: I'm safer minding my own business. We didn't come to Paris to catch crooks. Interfere with a man like that and he might give you a nasty knock. (*Noticing* BENJAMIN.) Waiter!

BENJAMIN: Monsieur?

BOURSEY: How's your food?

BENJAMIN: Very good, monsieur.

DANNE: Bring some in. I'm starving.

BENJAMIN: Now?

DANNE: Yes. Immediately now.

BENJAMIN: Would you like a booth, gentlemen?

LEONIDA (*going to the nearest table*): We would not. Booths are for loose women.

BOURSEY: That told him.

BENJAMIN: Don't get annoyed, ladies. Sit where you like. I'll bring you a menu. (*Aside.*) People who are hungry before lunch. . . . Must come from the backwoods.

(*He goes off.* BOURSEY *lays his umbrella on another table.* CORDEN *and* LEONIDA *put their overnight bags, and packets wrapped in brown paper, on other tables.* DANNE *has a bundle tied up in a red, spotted handkerchief, which he puts in the middle of the table at which they are sitting.*)

BOURSEY: That's the way. Unload your stuff.

DANNE: Don't worry, I will. I brought my old shoes to change into. (*He puts them on.*)

BOURSEY: We'll make this restaurant our headquarters. If the lunch is good and cheap, we'll come back for dinner.

BLANCHE: Can you imagine Felix missing the train like that after he promised me he wouldn't oversleep?

BOURSEY: Lawyers. They're not used to getting up before the afternoon.

LEONIDA: I'm tired. Let's sit down. (*She and* BLANCHE *do so.*)

BOURSEY: Don't get too comfortable. We're only staying for a bite. We want to see all the sights and there isn't too much time.

CORDEN: Whose fault is that? The first sight we saw this morning was the dentist's waiting room.

BOURSEY: Corden, I don't wish you any harm. But if you ever break a leg, I shall consider it my duty to go to the doctor with you, and to see that your pain is relieved as soon as possible.

DANNE: How does your tooth feel now?

BOURSEY: Fine. First he started to play about with my gum. That didn't help. Then he tugged the tooth out in one clean movement. I forgot to tell you: it was only ten francs. . . .

CORDEN: Very cheap.

BOURSEY: . . . So I took the money from the kitty.

CORDEN: Ten francs. I could have done it for three, with a donkey.

BENJAMIN (*re-entering*):   The menu.

BOURSEY (*taking it*):   That's my decision.

CORDEN: It's everybody's decision.

BOURSEY: If you're going to keep questioning my authority, I'm going home.

BLANCHE: Father . . .

LEONIDA: Gentlemen . . .

CORDEN: I didn't say a thing.

DANNE: Don't start fighting in public. We ought to explain to this man (*he indicates* BENJAMIN) that we're in Paris to enjoy ourselves. We want to eat like kings.

BOURSEY: Nothing but the best.

DANNE: We have a lump sum to get rid of—found money, you might say.

BENJAMIN (*aside*):   I don't like it. Who are these people?

BOURSEY: Advise us.

BENJAMIN: I have some juicy mutton chops with—

BOURSEY: No, no mutton.

CORDEN: We eat it every day.

DANNE: I sell it.

BENJAMIN: Or some Chateaubriand steaks . . .

CORDEN: No, no steak.

BOURSEY: Let me explain the situation. We don't want beef, mutton, veal, chicken, duck, or goose.

DANNE: Nor do we want potatoes, cabbages, beans, or peas.

BENJAMIN: Let me think. How about a slice of canteloupe melon for the ladies?

BLANCHE: Yes. I love melon.

LEONIDA: So do I. I adore it.

BENJAMIN: Two slices?

BOURSEY: Just a minute. Let's check the price. (*To* DANNE *and* CORDEN.) You can't trust these city waiters. "Melon, per slice, one franc."

CORDEN: In February, off season? That's dirt cheap.

DANNE: They're giving it away.

BOURSEY (*to* BENJAMIN):   Melon for everybody.

BENJAMIN: Five slices of canteloupe. (*Writes it down.*)

BOURSEY: Make it ten slices.

BENJAMIN: And what to follow?

CORDEN (*taking the menu*):   "Pâté de Nerac."

DANNE: I don't know what it is, but I like the sound of that.

CORDEN: So do I.

BOURSEY: How much is it?

CORDEN: Two francs.

BOURSEY: That's not dear.

DANNE: They're giving it away.

BOURSEY (*confidentially, to the others*): I always seem to land up in the right places. I have a nose for them. (*To* BENJAMIN.) That Nerac business—bring a large helping for everybody.

BENJAMIN: Five pâtés. And what could you like for entrée?

BOURSEY: An entrée too? Well, why not? The prices are so reasonable. Have you got something delicate and unusual?

DANNE: This is a special occasion.

CORDEN: It says here that they have tournedos à la plenipotentiary.

(*They all crowd round the menu.*)

LEONIDA: What is it made of?

BENJAMIN: It's a new dish. A chef's special. Hunks of stag meat with minced quail, strained anchovies, olives, marinated oysters, lettuce, and truffles.

CORDEN: Truffles. That's for me.

DANNE: And me.

EVERYBODY: And me.

BOURSEY: Tournedos à la plenipotentiary for everybody. Well done.

LEONIDA: And something sweet for the ladies.

BLANCHE: Oh yes.

DANNE: And some Roquefort cheese. Strong enough to make me sit up.

BOURSEY: What have you got in the way of dessert?

BENJAMIN: I can offer you a floating palace à la Radetzki or a froufrou à la Pompadour.

BOURSEY (*to* BLANCHE): Which do you prefer?

BLANCHE: You choose for me.

CORDEN: The floating palace must be light—if it floats. (*They laugh.*)

BOURSEY (*to* BENJAMIN): We'll take the lightest floating palace you have. (*More laughs.*)

CORDEN: The balloon variety. (*Hysterical laughter.*)

(DANNE *slaps* BENJAMIN *on the back.*)

BENJAMIN (*aside*): Comedians, comedians. (*Aloud.*) It's rather early. The chef will need about half an hour to prepare the dishes.

BOURSEY: That's all right. We'll leave our things and stroll around the Concorde and up the Champs Élysées.

BLANCHE: Or along the Rue de Rivoli to look at the shops.

LEONIDA (*to* BOURSEY):   Stay here with me, Theodore. I have something to tell you. It's important.

BOURSEY: But I want to see the Concorde and the—

LEONIDA: Please. It's a matter of life and—

BOURSEY: All right, all right. (*To* BLANCHE.) Your aunt is a little tired. I'll stay here with her. You others go off by yourselves.

CORDEN: I have an errand. There's something I want to buy near here.

DANNE: Don't you worry, Blanche. We'll go off together and have a good time on our own, eh? (*He digs her in the ribs.*)

CHORUS (*they sing*):

> First $\left\{ \begin{array}{l} \text{we'll} \\ \text{you'll} \end{array} \right\}$ look in all the stores
>
> All along the street.
>
> Then $\left\{ \begin{array}{l} \text{we'll} \\ \text{you'll} \end{array} \right\}$ hurry back in force,
>
> Just in time to eat.

(DANNE *gives his arm to* BLANCHE. CORDEN *goes out by himself.*)

BOURSEY: Now then. About this matter of life and—

LEONIDA: Yes. I don't know how to tell you.

BOURSEY: You left your handbag in the train? I'm not buying you another one.

LEONIDA: No, it's not that. Theodore, you are my brother, my only friend, the only person I can trust. Promise you won't be angry with me.

BOURSEY: For what?

LEONIDA: Promise first.

BOURSEY: Not till I know what I'm promising.

LEONIDA: Theodore, I have been wicked.

BOURSEY: You? You've never been wicked in your life. You wouldn't know how to be.

LEONIDA: I should have asked your permission.

BOURSEY: I wouldn't have given it.

LEONIDA: That young lady you've been reading about for four years in the paper, in the advertisement . . .

BOURSEY: The one who wants a modest home in a small, well-situated town?

LEONIDA: Yes.

BOURSEY: What about her?

LEONIDA: Theodore, I—

BOURSEY: So that's it. So that's how you've been spending your money. Well, it wasn't a bad idea. Except that it didn't work.

LEONIDA: But it has worked. Read this letter. I received it yesterday at home.

BOURSEY: From your dressmaker.

LEONIDA: I'm sorry I lied to you. I was embarrassed. (*Gives him the letter.*)

BOURSEY: It's signed X. Who is X?

LEONIDA: It's Monsieur Poche, a marriage broker.

BOURSEY: The cattle-monger!

LEONIDA: Not cattle, Theodore, please.

BOURSEY: "Mademoiselle, come to Paris as soon as you can. I have just the man for you. A gentleman in a high position, dark, gay, good-looking. I have arranged to introduce you to him at my salon tomorrow night at eight o'clock. . . ."

LEONIDA: That's tonight.

BOURSEY: "Be on time, and bring some of the family with you for him to meet. The address is 55 Rue Joubert. . . ." We'll have to let him know we're in Paris.

LEONIDA: I've already done it. I couldn't sleep last night, so I sent him a telegram.

BOURSEY: There was no need for that. Minimum price for a telegram is three francs. A letter would have been enough.

LEONIDA: Theodore, can I count on you to come with me?

BOURSEY: Of course you can. Don't I want your happiness as much as I want my own?

LEONIDA: What shall we do about Corden and Danne?

BOURSEY: We'll take them with us. We won't tell them why. They can be the rest of the family.

LEONIDA: I'm so glad you're not angry. (*Kisses him.*) I've been a burden to you for too long.

BOURSEY: A burden? Not at all. But naturally I'm glad you'll be going off on your own. It'll be good for you. You've been turning a bit sour in the last few years.

LEONIDA: I like that. You should talk. I've never met such an impossible person to live with. I can tell you frankly that if this hadn't happened now—

BOURSEY: Shush. Here comes somebody.

(*Enter* SYLVAIN.)

SYLVAIN: Miranda must be here by now.

BOURSEY }
LEONIDA }   Sylvain!

SYLVAIN: Oh. (*Forcing a smile.*) Monsieur Boursey, Mademoiselle Leonida, what a treat to meet you in Paris.

BOURSEY: Yes. Your father is with us.

SYLVAIN: Really? It must be my lucky day.

BOURSEY: Yes, he's out looking at the shops with Blanche. But he'll be back shortly.

SYLVAIN: Here?

BOURSEY: Yes, for lunch.

SYLVAIN: Well, if he's visiting the shops, why don't I go out and look for him? (*He starts to go out and sees* BLANCHE *and* DANNE *coming in.*) Trapped.

DANNE: Here we are again. I bought a brand new pickax. You don't know how I've dreamed about having a new pickax.

BLANCHE: I can think of nothing more charming than walking along the Champs Élysées with a man who is swinging a pickax.

SYLVAIN (*aside*): Better make the best of this. (*Coming forward.*) Hello, Dad.

DANNE: My boy. (*Embraces him with a kiss on both cheeks.*) Well, son, how is she?

SYLVAIN: Who's that?

DANNE: Your poor old cow.

SYLVAIN: It's kind of you to remember. She's still bad.

LEONIDA (*to* BOURSEY): Have you made a note of all the gifts we have to deliver in Paris?

BOURSEY: Yes. I'll never do any favors again. Somebody gave me an old boot here to take somewhere. I think I'll dump it under the table and forget about it.

DANNE: How is it you're not at the school?

SYLVAIN: I decided to . . . that is, I was sent . . . You see, the cow is sick, so they asked me to take it to the doctor at Alfort.

DANNE: They put you in charge of it?

SYLVAIN: Yes.

DANNE: My boy! I always knew you had a great future. So they have cow-doctors nowadays. Well, well.

SYLVAIN: I stopped off in Paris on the way back. Lucky I met you. While we're here you might as well give me next month's allowance. You'll save the postage.

DANNE: Good idea. (*Takes out his wallet.*) Wait a minute, though. You're on your own here. You might lose it.

SYLVAIN: Of course I won't.

DANNE: You stay with us for the day, son, and I'll give it to you this evening, before you leave for Grignon.

BOURSEY: That reminds me. We all have an invitation for this evening.

DANNE: Where?

BOURSEY: A delightful evening, music, pastries, punch . . . with a friend of mine. (*To* LEONIDA.) What's his name again?

LEONIDA: Poche.

BOURSEY: Poche. Dear old Poche, one of my oldest and dearest friends. He's in the match business.

BLANCHE: Will there be any dancing?

BOURSEY: Certainly. All the time. This is a big evening.

BLANCHE: I have no evening dress.

BOURSEY: It's informal.

DANNE: I can leave my pickax in the cloakroom. Is it all right if my boy comes along?

BOURSEY: With pleasure. It'll add to the family—to the company.

SYLVAIN: I'd be glad to come, Dad, but—

DANNE: You're coming. No arguments. I want you to learn how to behave with high-class people. (*Puts his pickax on a nearby table.*) I'll give you your money when we leave there.

SYLVAIN: What's the address?

LEONIDA: 55 Rue Joubert. Ask for Monsieur Poche.

SYLVAIN: I'll be there. Dad, I'll see you—

LEONIDA: Don't keep talking, Sylvain. We have to sort out the gifts. Get the bags onto the tables.

(*They empty their overnight bags and parcels on the tables.*)

BOURSEY: Well, this is a nice load to get rid of. Rings, bracelets, fans, letters . . . we must have brought the whole countryside with us. How can we deliver all these gifts in one day?

BENJAMIN: I wonder what they're up to with those parcels. (*Goes closer.*)

BOURSEY: The first thing to do is to share it out equally.

BENJAMIN: Sharing it out, eh? I'll have to watch this. (*Goes even closer. Voice from a distant table: "Waiter, waiter."*) Oh, damn! Coming!

(*Enter* CORDEN, *puffing and red in the face, looking as if he has a pillow under his shirt.*)

CORDEN: Whew. Hope I didn't keep you waiting. Hello, Sylvain. (SYLVAIN *nods to him gloomily*.)

LEONIDA: You look as if you haven't stopped running since you left.

CORDEN: I was in a hurry.

BOURSEY: What's wrong with your chest?

CORDEN: Does it show?

BOURSEY: You're all puffed up like a pigeon. It looks as if your stomach has moved up to your neck.

CORDEN: I was going to tell you: I've been embarrassed by my stomach for some time; it has a tendency to sag. So I thought: while we're in Paris I might as well get a good thick belt to hold it up.

BLANCHE: A corset.

CORDEN: A health belt. So I bought one. Out of the kitty.

EVERYBODY: Shame. A disgrace. Out of our money, etc.

BOURSEY: It hasn't done you any good. You had a fat belly; now you've got a fat chest. Squeeze the belt a bit tighter and you'll have a fat head.

CORDEN: The salesman told me it looked fine, but it's doing wicked things to my ribs.

BENJAMIN: Luncheon is served.

EVERYBODY: Good. At last. I'm famished, etc.

DANNE (*to* SYLVAIN): Sit down and have a bite with us, son.

SYLVAIN: I've eaten, thank you. (*Aside.*) Miranda isn't here yet. (*Aloud.*) I'll see you later.

DANNE: Stay here. Look at all this food. (*Holding* SYLVAIN's *arm.*) Have a chair.

BENJAMIN: Here's a chair. (*To* SYLVAIN.) I've found a job at The Smiling Bull.

SYLVAIN: Tell me afterwards. Thank you, waiter.

BOURSEY: What a fragrant melon!

LEONIDA: Delicious.

DANNE: Only one franc a slice.

CORDEN: I'll never live to enjoy it. My belt is crushing me.

DANNE: What do you think of my new pickax, son?

SYLVAIN: Very beautiful.

DANNE: Look at it. I bet they haven't got any pickaxes like that at your school, eh?

SYLVAIN: Nothing quite that ferocious. They have a few small ones.

DANNE: Are you growing many beetroots down there?

SYLVAIN: Not too many—a beetroot here, a beetroot there.

DANNE: You can't beat beetroots. But you have to give them plenty of dung, tons of it.

CORDEN: I can see some truffles. Pass me a few.

DANNE: And how about turnips? Are you growing turnips?

SYLVAIN: Oh yes. We're very big on turnips. Turnips wherever you look.

BOURSEY: Is he ever going to stop with his vegetables?

DANNE: Can't beat turnips. They're like parsnips. You have to give them plenty of dung. Pile it on.

CORDEN: Hurry up with those truffles. I wish I could take this belt off.

DANNE: And carrots. Are you growing many carrots?

SYLVAIN: The place is alive with them. I've grown thousands myself. They're my specialty.

DANNE: Good for you. You can't beat carrots. But you have to smother 'em in dung.

BOURSEY: You and your dung. Do you have to keep talking about it while we're eating?

DANNE: If it wasn't for dung you wouldn't be eating at all. Right, Son?

SYLVAIN: Yes, Dad.

DANNE: You see? My boy says so, and he's a farmer, like me.

LEONIDA: But at table . . .

DANNE: No good being soft-mouthed about it. Everything you eat—bread, meat, red radishes, white turnips, green cucumbers—where does it all come from, hey?

EVERYBODY: From dung.

BOURSEY: Now shut up about it. You've wrecked my appetite.

BLANCHE }
LEONIDA } And mine.

CORDEN: Not mine. I'm still waiting for the truffles.

DANNE: Tell me, Son. Do you kill many pigs down there?

BOURSEY: Here we go again.

DANNE: Show me how you go about killing a pig, a real fat porker.

SYLVAIN (looking round uneasily): I just—kill it.

DANNE: There's a right way and a wrong way. You roll your sleeves up like this. You take the animal's head in this hand . . .

EVERYBODY: Go home! Dry up! Give us a break! It's disgusting, etc.

SYLVAIN (standing up): Well, I'll push off.

DANNE: Where are you going?

SYLVAIN: Back to Alfort to see how the cow is. I'll see you later.

DANNE (*holding him back*): Have a glass of wine first.

SYLVAIN: Thanks, I don't want one now.

DANNE: Drink up, Son. It's good for the shoulders. (*Gives* SYLVAIN *a glass of wine.* SYLVAIN *drinks it.*) That's better, isn't it? Straightened you out, didn't it?

SYLVAIN: Yes, thanks. Good-by for now, everybody. See you later. (*Aside.*) I'll come back when they've finished.

DANNE: You can get your money this evening, Son.

SYLVAIN: I'll be there. Fifty-five Rue Joubert. Ask for Poche. (*Exit.*)

DANNE: He's a good boy. Do anything for me. Loves the soil.

BOURSEY: Has everybody finished? We don't want to spend all day in here. Waiter, the bill.

BENJAMIN: Right away, monsieur.

LEONIDA: First we'll get rid of the gifts.

CORDEN: Then we'll take a look at the Arch of Triumph.

BENJAMIN: Your bill, monsieur.

BOURSEY: Now then . . . here, what's this? Four hundred and fifty-two francs? Where did that come from?

EVERYBODY: What? Four hundred and fifty-two francs? Impossible, etc.

BOURSEY (*to* BENJAMIN, *who is bringing in glasses of liqueurs*): What are those?

BENJAMIN: Liqueurs.

BOURSEY: Take them away.

CORDEN: We didn't order any liqueurs.

BENJAMIN: They're on the house. You don't pay for them.

BOURSEY: Take them away. Four hundred and fifty-two francs. Where does that come from? You thought to yourself, "Out-of-towners," didn't you? "I'll take them for everything they've got."

BENJAMIN: But monsieur . . .

BOURSEY: We can be as smart as you, you know.

BENJAMIN: The prices are all written on the menu.

BOURSEY: Give me a menu.

BENJAMIN: With pleasure, monsieur. (*Brings one over.*)

BOURSEY (*snatching it*): You see: melon—one franc per slice.

DANNE: It says ten francs on the bill. Swindle!

BENJAMIN: It is ten francs, monsieur. You can't see the zero because of the frame on the menu.

EVERYBODY: Oh!

CORDEN: But look at this pâté de Nerac. Two francs a portion.

BENJAMIN (*taking the menu back*):   Twenty francs, monsieur. The frame is hiding the zero again.

EVERYBODY (*peering over*):   Oh!

LEONIDA: We've been robbed.

DANNE: All the zeroes are hidden.

BOURSEY: I refuse to pay. Where is the manager?

BENJAMIN: In the other dining room over there. If you'd like to discuss it with him . . .

BOURSEY: I certainly would. Let's go.

EVERYBODY (*they sing*):   Let's go.

> Someone's trying to cheat us
> When we're in the right.
> We won't let them beat us.
> We'll go out and fight.

(BOURSEY, DANNE, LEONIDA *and* BLANCHE *troop out.* CORDEN *is still sitting.*)

CORDEN: I don't like to argue about meals, especially when my stomach feels as if it's two-thirds of the way up my body. I ought to go out and get some fresh air; it might make a difference. I keep thinking about that advertisement. I wrote to the newspaper. They told me to apply to a fellow named Poche, at 55 Rue Joubert. I could nip over and see him, and meet the others later. Who knows?—it may be a question of my future happiness. Waiter!

BENJAMIN: Monsieur?

CORDEN: Is Rue Joubert far from here?

BENJAMIN: No, monsieur. You go out of the door, turn right, and it's the second on the right.

CORDEN: Thank you. When my companions return, will you tell them I'll meet them on top of the Arch of Triumph in one hour?

BENJAMIN: Yes sir.

CORDEN: Happiness, here I come. (*He goes out. Noise of a violent argument from the next room.*)

BENJAMIN: They're battling away like wild animals. Anybody'd think they hadn't ordered the most expensive dishes on the menu.

(BOURSEY *comes in, followed by the others.*)

BOURSEY (*shouting back*):   Call anybody you like. I'm not paying.

DANNE: I'd rather go to court.

SECOND WAITER (*going out left*):   A policeman? Yes, boss, there's one outside.

BOURSEY: Bring the entire police force, for all I care.

BLANCHE: Father, they may . . .

BOURSEY: They can't do a thing. I laugh in their faces. Ha, ha, ha.

LEONIDA: I thought they'd at least reduce the bill. And all they tell us is that the liqueurs were free.

DANNE: It's a mockery. We didn't even drink them.

BENJAMIN: Monsieur, the other gentleman told me to tell you that . . .

BOURSEY: You again? Get out of my sight. (BENJAMIN *leaves*.) Collect your things, everybody, as if we're going to walk out. Then they'll have to give way.

(*They pick up their parcels.* DANNE *takes his pickax and* BOURSEY *his umbrella. The* SECOND WAITER *comes back with a* POLICEMAN.)

SECOND WAITER: There they are. They wouldn't pay.

BOURSEY: You mean we wouldn't let ourselves be swindled.

LEONIDA: Melon at ten francs a slice!

DANNE: Ten slices. That's a hundred francs. Did you ever hear of anything like it?

POLICEMAN: Let me see the menu.

(BENJAMIN *gives it to him.*)

BOURSEY: Some menu. It's full of hiding places and secret zeroes. Can you see what they've done with that frame around the edges? (*He gesticulates with his umbrella. A watch falls out of it.*)

POLICEMAN: What's that?

EVERYBODY: A watch.

POLICEMAN: Who owns it?

BOURSEY: It's not mine.

EVERYBODY: Nor mine.

POLICEMAN: The chain is broken or cut. This watch has been stolen. How did it get inside your umbrella?

BOURSEY: I didn't put it there. You can't tell the time from a watch that's inside an umbrella.

BENJAMIN (*to* POLICEMAN):   Search them. They've got all kinds of loot in their parcels and pockets.

POLICEMAN: So you don't know where the watch came from and you refuse to pay your bill. You'd better come along with me, all four of you, to the station.

DANNE: What station?

POLICEMAN: The police station. (*To* BENJAMIN.) And bring your menu. They'll pay you there.

BLANCHE: What are they going to do to us?

BOURSEY: Don't be afraid, my child. An honest man is never afraid to be judged by the law of his country. Follow me.

(*Chorus*):

LEONIDA
BLANCHE
DANNE
BOURSEY
} Take us to the station.
Let the law decide
If their accusation
Has been justified.

BENJAMIN
SECOND WAITER
} Drag them to the station.
Tie them up inside,
Under observation
Till they can be tried.

POLICEMAN: Come down to the station.
Do not try to hide
From investigation
If you haven't lied.

(*They all go out, except the* SECOND WAITER.)

SECOND WAITER: Jailbirds, the lot of them. I bet they're a gang.

(FELIX *enters hastily and sits at a table.*)

FELIX: Waiter, bring me a steak. Rare. I'm in a hurry.

SECOND WAITER: Right away, monsieur.

FELIX: I had to take a later train. Where can they have got to? I've already been to the Panthéon and the Tower of Saint-Jacques. After I've eaten I'll try the Concorde and the Champs Élysées.

SYLVAIN (*entering*): They've gone at last. I wonder if Miranda—

FELIX: Sylvain!

SYLVAIN: Hello, Felix. You weren't with the others, then?

FELIX: Have you seen them?

SYLVAIN: They were here a few minutes ago.

FELIX: Blanche too? (SYLVAIN *nods*.) Where are they now? Which way did they go?

SYLVAIN: I have no idea.

FELIX: Damn!

SECOND WAITER: Your steak, sir. It's very rare.

FELIX: Rare? It's raw.

SYLVAIN: Waiter—oh, you're not the same one. Have you seen a young lady here? She's expecting me.

SECOND WAITER: A very highly dressed lady, monsieur? Yes, she's in booth four. She's already had thirty francs worth of drinks.

SYLVAIN: Thirty francs? Is she having an alcohol rub?

WAITER (*as a woman's voice calls: "Waiter"*): There she is again. She's waiting for her melon.

SYLVAIN: Melon! Thirty francs worth of drinks! I'd better get away. Tell her I've been ordered to sit on a jury . . . for two weeks. (*He rushes out. The woman's voice is heard again, calling the* WAITER.)

FELIX: Waiter, bring me some bread.

SECOND WAITER: Bread for number five. Melon for number four. Coming, coming! (*He hurries off.*)

ACT III

(Waiting room in a police station. A table, a chair, a bench, and a police-station quartet: BOURSEY, BLANCHE, LEONIDA, *and* DANNE, *who are shown in by the* POLICEMAN. *They line up and sing, to a Mozartean melody.)*

CHORUS:

>Gloom without measure.
>Happiness foiled.
>This day of pleasure
>Has now been spoiled . . .
>This day of pleasure
>Has now been spoiled.

POLICEMAN: Wait here, please. I'll call Monsieur Chute.
BOURSEY: Chute, who's he?
POLICEMAN: The assistant police commissioner. He'll want to question you. *(Exit.)*

(They put their parcels on the table.)

DANNE: What are we going to say when they question us?
BOURSEY: Stop waving your pickax. You'll stick somebody with it.

(DANNE puts his pickax in a corner.)

LEONIDA: Do you think they'll torture us?
BOURSEY: Keep calm. It's all a misunderstanding.
LEONIDA: Perhaps so, but here we are in prison.
BOURSEY: We are not in prison. We are in the police station. People walk into the police station every day. And walk out again.
DANNE: If you'd listened to me we'd be in Cressy now, at the fair, with the snakes and Siamese twins and fat women. It's your fault.

BOURSEY: That's it—blame me. How could I know that they stuff watches in your umbrella in Paris?

DANNE: Who told you to bring your umbrella?

BOURSEY: Corden told me, that's who. (*Turning.*) Corden, it's your— Where is he?

DANNE: I haven't seen him since we left the restaurant.

BLANCHE }
LEONIDA } Neither have I.

BOURSEY: Trust him to scuttle away at the first sign of danger.

DANNE: He probably hid under a table.

BLANCHE: At least, he is free.

BOURSEY: I would not exchange my chains for his liberty.

BLANCHE: Chains? I hope they don't lock us up.

BOURSEY: Leave it to me. I'll handle this man myself. He's only an assistant, isn't he? I'll talk to him confidentially. I'll make myself known.

DANNE: I'll tell him all about the kitty.

LEONIDA: I'll explain that we came to Paris to see the sights.

BLANCHE: And the shops.

BOURSEY: Now listen to me, all of you. If the four of us talk at once, we're lost. One firm, clear voice must speak for us all.

DANNE: We need a lawyer.

BLANCHE: I wish Felix were here.

BOURSEY: What we need is a calm, eloquent, quietly persuasive man. Luckily, we have such a man at our disposal— with us. . . .

DANNE: Thank you.

BOURSEY: I venture to say that you will find all these qualities in me.

BLANCHE: Yes, let Father speak for us.

DANNE: Good enough. Don't be nervous. I'll be right behind you.

BOURSEY: Quiet, here he comes.

(*Enter* CHUTE.)

CHUTE: Ah, there are four of you.

DANNE: For the time being.

CHUTE: Sit down, won't you? (*Goes to the desk and consults some papers.*)

BOURSEY: You are too kind, Commissioner. We thank you from the bottom of our innocent hearts. (*They sit on the bench.* BOURSEY *speaks to the others in an undertone.*) Keep calm. Smile freely, like people who have nothing to fear. (*They all smile.*) Very good. Stay like that.

CHUTE (*looking up*):   It appears that a watch was discovered in an umbrella belonging to one of you. Why are you all grinning at me like that?

BOURSEY: To show that our consciences are easy.

CHUTE: Tell me about the watch.

BOURSEY (*standing up*):   In the life of every man, Commissioner, as in the life of every country, there are moments of crisis, when—

CHUTE: Very likely. Now explain about the watch.

BOURSEY: Before going into the murky details of this affair, which could sully the lives of an entire family, I think it is my duty as a man, as a father, as a citizen, to proclaim my respect for the law of this country. I am proud to be—

CHUTE: Will you please answer my question?

DANNE: Your Worship, he's telling the truth.

CHUTE: All right, let's hear your version. Take off your hat.

DANNE: Thank you, Your Worship; it doesn't trouble me.

CHUTE (*to* BOURSEY):   You sit down.

DANNE: You see, we wouldn't be here, except for the kitty. We caught the five twenty-five this morning . . .

BLANCHE: And Felix must have overslept . . .

CHUTE: About the watch . . .

BOURSEY (*standing up*):   Commissioner, if you will allow me . . .

CHUTE: Sit down. (DANNE *and* BOURSEY *sit down.*) No, not you (*to* DANNE). Carry on with what you were saying. Stand up, man.

DANNE: I said we should have gone to the fair at Cressy. With the fat woman, and so on. But the others voted against it.

CHUTE: Let's get this straight. You came to Paris this morning.

BOURSEY (*standing up*):   From Endives-Under-Glass.

CHUTE: Sit down. (BOURSEY *and* DANNE *sit.*) You came to see the sights . . .

DANNE (*standing up*):   It was the kitty.

BOURSEY (*standing up*):   We came here, Commissioner, to admire the great city of Paris.

CHUTE (*to* BOURSEY):   All right, if you insist on talking. (*To* DANNE.) Sit down. (*They both sit down.*) Not you (*to* BOURSEY). Stand up again. (*To* DANNE.) And take off your hat. Now, you were saying?

BOURSEY: I wasn't saying a thing. He (*pointing to* DANNE) was talking.

CHUTE: Let's start again. How did this stolen watch get into your umbrella?

BOURSEY: As commander of the Endives-Under-Glass fire brigade, invested with the full responsibility of that onerous position . . .

DANNE: He gave the community a fire pump.

BOURSEY: I think I have always done my duty for my country. . . .

DANNE: As a farmer and the son of a farmer—

LEONIDA: I'm afraid we don't know anything about the watch.

CHUTE: Now we're getting to it.

BLANCHE (*standing up*): We haven't done anything wrong.

LEONIDA (*standing up*): Our lives have been pure and stainless.

CHUTE: That's enough. Sit down.

BOURSEY (*standing up*): Look into my past. It will answer for my future.

CHUTE: Silence. Sit down, all of you. Listen to me. I'm sure that you're harmless, the lot of you. There is no charge against you. You can go.

EVERYBODY: Hooray. We're free. No charge, etc.

(LEONIDA, BLANCHE, *and* BOURSEY *stand up joyfully.* DANNE, *who is on the end of the bench, goes down with it.*)

CHUTE: But be careful. The authorities are watching you. (*He rings a bell and sits down again.*)

BOURSEY: I told you we'd be safe if you trusted in me. (*To* DANNE.) Why did you talk so much? You nearly got us into trouble.

CHUTE: Oh, I forgot. There is a witness. (POLICEMAN *enters.*) Bring in the waiter. (*Enter* BENJAMIN.) What have you got to say?

BENJAMIN: Nothing. All I want is for them to settle the bill.

CHUTE: What bill?

BENJAMIN: Their lunch bill. They wouldn't pay it. (*He hands the bill to* CHUTE.)

BOURSEY: Four hundred and fifty-two francs—never!

DANNE: We're not paying for all those zeroes around the edges.

CHUTE: Let me see: melon, pâté, tournedos a là plenipotentiary; this is an expensive meal. Why did you refuse to pay?

BOURSEY: Because we were not aware . . .

DANNE: They tried to swindle us. They're thieves.

BENJAMIN: There may be thieves in this room, but I'm not one of them.

EVERYBODY: What?

CHUTE: What do you mean by that? You'd better explain yourself.

BOURSEY: Yes, you'd better.

BENJAMIN: It's true. If the police ever look in your bags and parcels, they'll see what you are.

BOURSEY: Our parcels?

DANNE: What's he getting at?

CHUTE (opening the bags and parcels): Rings, bracelets, fans . . . Where did all this come from?

LEONIDA: They are gifts for us to deliver.

DANNE: Which proves that we're honest folk who can be trusted with other people's belongings.

BENJAMIN: Some honest folk.

DANNE: Why, you table-clearing, plate-washing, young— (he starts toward BENJAMIN. A chisel falls out of his overcoat pocket.)

POLICEMAN (picking it up and handing it to CHUTE): A chisel.

DANNE: It's mine.

CHUTE: A burglar's tool.

BOURSEY: I bet you bought that out of the kitty too.

DANNE: Of course I did. That's what the kitty was for.

CHUTE (he speaks to the POLICEMAN. Then): In your own interests, I think we'd better get you to give a sworn testimony.

BOURSEY: I think I've done enough for my country. It's not my fault if we never had a fire.

DANNE: We're honest folk.

BLANCHE: We haven't done anything wrong.

CHUTE: That's enough. Follow the policeman outside, the ladies too. I'll call you back when I want you.

POLICEMAN: Outside, all of you. Hurry up. (They go out slowly, protesting.)

DANNE: Stop pushing. (Exit.)

CHUTE: Now then, tell me everything you know. At what time did they go into your restaurant?

BENJAMIN: It was barely nine o'clock. I was sweeping out when I heard somebody on the boulevard shouting: "Stop, thief."

CHUTE (*taking notes*):   Go on.

BENJAMIN: These people came rushing in. They looked frightened to me. They ordered lunch, all the best dishes on the menu, and they said they had plenty of money. "Found money," they said.

CHUTE: That's serious. Go on.

BENJAMIN: Some of them went out while the dishes were being prepared. That stout woman stayed behind with the leader of the gang. She told him she had committed a fault. I was listening. When the others came back they emptied the loot out on the table . . . jewelry, fans, rings. They shared it out, and the leader of the gang said: "This is a nice load to get rid of."

CHUTE: Yes, it all ties up. Go on.

BENJAMIN: One of them came in later than the others, a fat one. The policeman didn't get a chance to pinch him. He got away. He had something under his jacket. I couldn't see what it was. It made him all bloated. It must have been a sack, at least.

CHUTE: More plunder. Yes. Go on.

BENJAMIN: Well, after they'd eaten their fill, they refused to pay. That's it.

CHUTE: I see. Well, you can go now. You'll be called as a witness.

BENJAMIN: What about my bill?

CHUTE: You'll be paid at the registrar's office. Go out that way. (BENJAMIN *goes out of another door.* CHUTE *rings.* POLICEMAN *reappears.*) Bring those people in again.

POLICEMAN (*at the threshold*):   Back in here. Get a move on.

(BOURSEY, LEONIDA, BLANCHE, *and* DANNE *re-enter.*)

EVERYBODY: It's a disgrace. Honest folk like us. Shame, horror, etc.

BOURSEY: I protest, in the name of civilization.

CHUTE: About what?

BOURSEY: They emptied our pockets.

LEONIDA: They confiscated all our property.

BOURSEY: Our money, our watches, our parcels. All they left us was our handkerchiefs.

DANNE: And who needs them?

BOURSEY: It's an affront to our rights.

CHUTE (*standing up*):   Enough of these fine words. I know you now. You're one of those gangs who descend on Paris during festivals. You wait till the evening comes, then you roll drunks and snatch purses.

EVERYBODY: Roll what? Do what? Snatch what? etc.

DANNE: Your Worship. As a farmer and the son of a farmer . . .

CHUTE: You can stop playing yokels now. I know what you are. I've just sent for a cart to take you all to prison.

EVERYBODY: To prison!

CHUTE: You're a gang of pickpockets. (*He goes out.*)

LEONIDA: What is a pickpocket?

BOURSEY: It's a kind of tailor. Um—after a suit is finished . . .

BLANCHE: It means a thief.

BOURSEY: Impossible! We're not thieves.

DANNE: They're going to put us in prison.

BOURSEY: That's what he said. We're in trouble now. Oh, injustice!

(*They hear the double door being closed on them outside.*)

BLANCHE: We're locked in.

LEONIDA: And Monsieur Poche will be waiting for us this evening. My happiness is destroyed. My future is ruined.

BLANCHE: Felix won't want to marry me now.

DANNE: Sylvain won't find us this evening. I'll have to send his money by mail. More expense.

BOURSEY: My friends, are you ready to risk everything in one great enterprise?

EVERYBODY: Well? What is it? What do you mean? etc.

BOURSEY: Speak low. I am going to propose a course of action that may live in the annals of historic endeavor. . . . Don't be afraid. You all remember the fate of the Count of Monte Cristo. He was imprisoned in the Bastille because the king's mistress hated him. He stayed there for thirty-five years.

BLANCHE: Thirty-five years!

DANNE: I thought that was Robinson Crusoe.

LEONIDA: No, it was Latude.

BOURSEY: Latude, what are you talking about? Now, I think of it, though, it was Latude. Forget about Monte Cristo. Now, what I propose is that we escape. What do you say to that?

DANNE: Just let me out. But how?

BLANCHE: The door is locked from the outside.

BOURSEY (*tiptoeing across the room*): But there is still a window. (*They rush across after him.*) Hush! Not a murmur. Don't let them hear.

LEONIDA: But the ladies . . . how about us?

BOURSEY: We are only one flight up. Below is a courtyard, and I can see a pile of . . .

DANNE: Manure! There it is. Nice and soft to land on. Like a featherbed.

LEONIDA: But how about this evening? We won't be able to go out like that, smelling . . .

BOURSEY: Ah, look what I've discovered. A rope.

EVERYBODY: A rope! How lucky! Just what we need! Etc.

BOURSEY: I'll go out first. You wait here. I'll bring a ladder, and it'll be easy for the rest of you. (*He seizes the rope. There is a clanging outside.*) Oh God, it's on the end of a bell. (*Sound of bolts being drawn outside.*) Keep calm. Keep smiling.

(*They sit down on the bench. DANNE looks at it fearfully, then sits at CHUTE's desk. POLICEMAN enters. They all smile at him.*)

POLICEMAN: Who rang that?

DANNE: That what?

POLICEMAN: That bell.

BOURSEY: Somebody in the courtyard outside.

POLICEMAN: Don't be impatient. The van will be here soon. (*He goes to the window, pulls a bar across it, and padlocks the bar in place.*)

DANNE: Look at the size of that padlock.

BOURSEY (*rummaging in his pockets*): And not a thing left to bribe him with. Excuse me, Inspector. They've taken away all my money, but if you ever happen to be passing through or near Endives-Under-Glass, my house and table are at your disposal.

POLICEMAN: What do you mean?

BOURSEY: Come and have dinner with us. And I'll make you a handsome present.

POLICEMAN: Oho! Attempted bribery, eh? *That'll* be something to add to the evidence. (*Exit.*)

LEONIDA: You made it worse.

BOURSEY: I was trying to—

DANNE: Wait. They've forgotten something. My pickax.

BOURSEY: Why couldn't they have forgotten something that would be useful to us?

DANNE: But it is. My lovely new pickax. It's all sharp and pointed. I'll dig a hole in the wall and we can walk out through the next house.

EVERYBODY: Wonderful. Better than the window. Easy, etc.

BOURSEY: Get down to it. (DANNE *lifts his pickax.*) No, stop. They'll hear you. It's no use.

LEONIDA: What can we do?

DANNE: Why don't you all sing? Sing as loud as you can. Drown me and the pickax.

BLANCHE: What songs do we know?

LEONIDA: There's my aria from *The Barber of Seville.* (*Singing.*) "*Una voce poco fa . . .*"

BOURSEY: No, it's loud, but not noisy enough. Do you remember that song I wrote for the firemen's banquet? "A tired old man"? (LEONIDA *and* BLANCHE *nod.*) Good. Off you go. (*To* DANNE.) Wait till the first line, then start banging. Now, put plenty of expression into it. (DANNE *swings his pickax.*)

CHORUS:

> A tired old man
> Once knocked on my door.
> His clothes were so dirty
> He must have been poor.
>
> So dirty, so dirty,
> His clothes were so dirty,
> His trousers and shirt, he
> Just must have been poor.

(*At the end of the chorus some lumps of plaster fall away.*)

DANNE: I forgot about that. What are we going to do with the plaster?

BOURSEY: In our pockets, quick. (*They pick up the debris and put it in their pockets.*) Right, second verse.

CHORUS:

> But where could we put him
> To lie down and rest?
> Except in the cellar—
> Yes, that would be best.
> The cellar, the cellar,
> Away in the cellar . . .

(*The door bolts grind open.*)

BOURSEY: They're coming. What can we do about the hole? How can we hide it?

DANNE: We can't. We're finished.

BOURSEY: Leonida! You stand in front of it. There.

DANNE: Good. She's just wide enough.

BOURSEY: Don't move an inch. Smile!

(CHUTE *comes in. They all smile at him.*)

CHUTE: I forgot to take your names for the testimony. You first.

BOURSEY: Theodore Athanasia Boursey, of Endives-Under-Glass, commander of the—

CHUTE: Don't start that again. The young lady?

BLANCHE: Blanche Rosalie Boursey.

CHUTE: And you?

DANNE (*standing with his pickax behind his back*): Leonard Robert Danne.

CHUTE (*to* BOURSEY):   Is this lady (*pointing to* LEONIDA) your wife?

LEONIDA (*coming forward*):   No, I am his sister. I am unmarried.

BOURSEY: Don't move!

CHUTE: Come here. I'm not going to bite you.

LEONIDA: I'm comfortable here.

CHUTE: Come forward. (LEONIDA *approaches him slowly.* DANNE *swiftly takes her place in front of the hole.*) Now, what is your name?

LEONIDA: Zelmira Leonida Boursey.

CHUTE: That's all. We're having some trouble finding a cart. It's Mardi Gras, all the vehicles are out. But we'll have one here soon. (*He goes out with the* POLICEMAN.)

DANNE: Back to work. Keep singing.

BOURSEY: Second verse again.

CHORUS: But where could we put him
               To lie down and rest?
               Except in the cellar.
               Yes, that would be best.

               The cellar, the cellar,
               Away in the cellar . . .

DANNE: That's enough. The hole's gone through.

LEONIDA: Saved!

BOURSEY: Quiet now.

DANNE: I'll see where we've got to. Pooh! Stinks of tobacco. (*Reappearing hurriedly.*) We're finished. It's the policemen's lounge. There are three of them in there.

BOURSEY: Quick. Try and fill up the hole again before they come back.

POLICEMAN (*entering*):   Transport's ready. We commandeered a taxi. Hurry, before you get up to more mischief. What's this? A hole in the wall? Who did that?

DANNE: The mice.

POLICEMAN: A pickax, eh? Attempted escape, eh? Now you're really in the juice. (*Blows a whistle. Two other* POLICEMEN *enter.*)

POLICEMEN:

> Drop them in the clink
> Get them under locks
> Before they have a chance to think
> We'll have them breaking rocks.

PRISONERS:

> Save us from the clink
> Spare us all the locks
> Before we have a chance to blink
> They'll have us breaking rocks.

ACT IV

(In Paris. The marriage salon owned and run by POCHE. *We are in the "meeting room," just off the main hall, spacious, brilliantly lit by a candelabra—altogether an atmosphere of vulgar splendor.* JOSEPH, *the servant, is skimming the woodwork with a dustcloth or encouraging the fire. Enter* POCHE.)

POCHE: Haven't you finished yet, Joseph?

JOSEPH: Almost, monsieur. Shall I see to the lights in the other room?

POCHE: The main salon. Yes, by all means. Do it now. This is a big evening. Money will flow. A young lady is coming from Endives-Under-Glass with a dowry of one hundred thousand francs. Did you order the ice cream and the pastry? Did you get the dancing partners?

JOSEPH: Yes, monsieur. They're all there, except for Anatole.

POCHE: What's happened to him?

JOSEPH: He wanted an increase. He said he won't work for less than ten francs on Mardi Gras.

POCHE: Ten francs—the robber! I offer him five francs for an easy evening's work, and I'm paying for the white gloves. It's adequate, isn't it?

JOSEPH: That's what I told him.

POCHE: I admit that he's my best man. He has an insolent manner that the ladies seem to love. He's only a hairdresser's assistant, after all, but the other night somebody took him for the English ambassador.

JOSEPH: And he smells so good.

POCHE: That's true. You always think he's just been fished out of a bottle of lavender water. That goes down well in the salon.

JOSEPH: He said he'd send one of his friends along to replace him.

POCHE: I'm sorry about this. He was my star attraction.

Well, never mind. For ten francs we can do without him. Put the lights on in the main salon, but nowhere else. (JOSEPH *goes out*.) Seven forty-five. If I'm not mistaken, my beautiful Leonida will be here on the dot of eight. (*Takes a note from his pocket and reads it*.) I'll just refresh myself on the list of personal particulars. "Dark, flowing hair," that's good. "Warm, golden complexion," even better. "Sad and tender temperament"—that could be a problem—"mellowed by a natural sweetness"—excellent—"docility"—I'm not sure about that—"and spontaneous good humor"—ah, she came through. "Which shines in my eyes and lights up my personality." She's a poet. "In other words, I am gay, unaffected, gentle, overwhelmingly charming and modest." She certainly knows how to make out a prospectus. "Since I was a child, my life has been devoted to my brother, a widower, who is many years my senior. He is an irritable, uncouth, surly loudmouth, and yet I have never complained of my fate, either to him or to anybody else. My soft pink lips have remained sealed, and I have cared for him with the undemanding affection of a saint." I wonder if she's religious. "If the gentleman you have found for me is suitable, I would consent to share a home with him in a small, well-situated town. . . ."

(SYLVAIN *enters*.)

SYLVAIN: Are you Poche?

POCHE: Yes. What do you want?

SYLVAIN: I've come for the evening. . . .

POCHE (*aside*):   Anatole's replacement! (*Aloud*.) Wait there. I'll look you over. (*He puts his papers down*.)

SYLVAIN: What a way to treat guests.

POCHE: Now. Turn round, slowly. Not bad. I like your jacket, but your trousers could have done with another pressing. The creases should be like knives.

SYLVAIN: You know how it is. You wear what you have.

POCHE: There's a button missing from your sleeve. I don't like that.

SYLVAIN (*aside*):   Next he'll want to wash behind my ears.

POCHE: Go into the dressing room. One of the girls will replace that button.

SYLVAIN (*aside*):   They really take care of you here.

POCHE: I don't have to remind you that I expect impeccable behavior, chaste language—no doubtful words or smutty allusions—and a firm, upright stance. There. (*Straightens* SYLVAIN's *shoulders*.)

SYLVAIN: I know that. You have to be careful what you say to ladies.

POCHE: One other thing: you're not to touch the ice cream or the bonbons.

SYLVAIN: But I thought—

POCHE: It doesn't matter what you thought. The agreement is that you are entitled to one cake and a cup of tea during the course of the evening.

SYLVAIN: I can't stand tea. It makes me vomit.

POCHE: Vomit—that's a word I don't like. When the tray of tea is brought round, say something like: "My doctor forbids me to indulge in it." Be a man of the world. It's not so hard.

SYLVAIN: I'll try.

POCHE: Wait here. I'll get your gloves. (*He takes a pair of gloves from a table.*)

SYLVAIN: What are these for?

POCHE: Only one of them is to be worn, on your left hand. You hold the other one, and keep your right hand bare, for greeting guests. There are your five francs.

SYLVAIN: Five francs?

POCHE: No discussions, please. I've had enough trouble this evening with Anatole. Five francs for gentlemen and three for ladies; it's the standard rate.

SYLVAIN: Well, if it's the standard rate . . . (*puts the money in his pocket*). Seventeen and five—twenty-two. Good.

POCHE: What's that about twenty-two?

SYLVAIN: Just a little private arithmetic. I can afford a meal tonight.

POCHE: Tell Anatole from me that if he drops out again at such short notice, he's finished.

SYLVAIN: You keep talking about Anatole. Anatole who?

POCHE: Anatole your friend.

SYLVAIN: I don't know any Anatoles.

POCHE: Who sent you then?

SYLVAIN: My dad. He said go to 55 Rue Joubert and ask for Monsieur Poche. So here I am.

POCHE: Ah, now I understand. Your father wants me to find you a wife.

SYLVAIN: Does he?

POCHE: Obviously. I beg your pardon, monsieur. I took you for one of my . . . But now I see that you are a client.

SYLVAIN: About this wife business . . .

POCHE: So I'll trouble you for the gloves and the five francs.

SYLVAIN: You want them back? I was just getting used to

them. (POCHE *is already taking the gloves out of his hands.* SYLVAIN *returns the money.*)

POCHE: Please have a chair. I'll sign you in the clients' register. You'll be in company with some of the finest names in France. (*He opens a creaking great book, after undoing the padlock.*)

SYLVAIN: You could use a little grease on those hinges.

POCHE: May I please have your name?

SYLVAIN: You can borrow it. Sylvain Jerome Danne.

POCHE: Oh, what a name!

SYLVAIN: What's wrong with it?

POCHE: It's magnificent.

SYLVAIN: Thank you.

POCHE: Don't mention it. That will be one hundred francs security, please.

SYLVAIN: Oh no. No security. Tell you what: with a magnificent name like mine, couldn't you give way on the hundred francs?

POCHE: Impossible. It's for the preliminary paper work.

SYLVAIN: Dad didn't say anything to me about a hundred francs. You'd better talk to him when he comes.

POCHE: Is he coming this evening? Splendid. Then we'll settle later.

(JOSEPH *comes in.*)

JOSEPH: Monsieur, your guests are arriving. . . .

POCHE (*closing his book and looking through a door*): Good. The girls are here. I'll start grouping them.

SYLVAIN (*looking over his shoulder*):   You can group me with that plump one over there.

POCHE: Come with me . . .

(*He goes out, followed by* SYLVAIN.)

JOSEPH: The boss is going to be tied up this evening. Gives me a chance to make hay with the ice cream and the cups of tea.

CORDEN (*entering*):   Very nice. Very nice. They've really dressed it up. (*He is clad in high style.*)

JOSEPH: It's the gentleman who was here this morning. I'll tell the boss. (*Exit.*)

CORDEN (*admiring himself in a glass*):   Very impressive. Suits me beautifully. And a perfect fit, considering it was all hired at short notice. How are those two grease stains? Gone, that's good. I can still smell the stain remover, though. Benzine. It stinks. I drenched myself in cologne, but the benzine is winning. I should have left the stains. She might not have noticed them. Now she won't be able to get near me. Well, it's too late to retreat now. There's too much at stake. I'm dying to see her. Either she's beautiful, as she says in the advertisement, or she's ugly. If she's beautiful—happy days; I'm only a man, after all; I'm not made of marble. If she's ugly; well, I'm not so young myself, and with a dowry that large she'll be well worth my fifty francs deposit. I estimate our value this way: she has five thousand a year; add that to my four thousand from the pharmacy; that makes nine. I'll be able to set her up in a little business on the side; perfumes or ladies' underwear or tobacco, snuff and stationery—to keep her occupied. Let's be conservative and say that brings in another thousand a year: that makes ten. I'll be on a level with Boursey. I'll present the community with another pump. He'll be furious. There's only one obstacle. Poche tells me that I have a rival. The meeting was arranged for him. Still, as Poche says, may the better man win. (*Admiring himself again.*) My rival is going to have a hard time beating that. (*Sniffing.*) I only wish I could do something about that benzine. I wonder what happened to Boursey and the others. I waited for two hours on top of the Arch of Triumph; I didn't come down till the man drove me away, ten minutes after closing time. It's not very nice of them to let me down like that. I'll have a word with Boursey about it when I see him. I'll probably meet them on the last train going back tonight. (*Enter* POCHE.) Good evening. Am I late?

POCHE: Not at all. It's the young lady. I'm still waiting for her. (*Inspecting* CORDEN.) Very good. The vest is stylish.

CORDEN: Isn't it?

POCHE: But you shouldn't throw out your chest like that. You bulge.

CORDEN: It's the belt. I mean, it's natural.

POCHE: What's that curious odor?

CORDEN: I can't smell anything. Tell me, is my rival here yet?

POCHE: Yes, he's strolling about in one of the other rooms.

CORDEN: Let me see him.

POCHE: I'm afraid I can't.

CORDEN: Is he good-looking?

POCHE: Not bad.

CORDEN: Better than me?

POCHE: Well . . .

CORDEN: Confidentially.

POCHE: He is a little less—broad.

CORDEN: What does he do for a living?

POCHE: He works.

CORDEN: Has he got any medals, titles, or decorations?

POCHE: Not that I know of.

CORDEN: Then we're on a par. Don't forget that you promised to let me have first crack at the lady.

POCHE: Rest assured. (*Looking at his watch.*) I hope she doesn't let me down.

(JOSEPH *comes in with a tray of ice cream and pastry.*)

JOSEPH: Monsieur.

POCHE (*eagerly*): Has she arrived?

JOSEPH: No sir. It's Amanda. I saw her eating an ice cream and a pastry.

POCHE: The hussy. I'll give her pastry. (*To* CORDEN.) Excuse me, an important visitor has just arrived. (*He goes out.*)

CORDEN: He has a very fine clientele.

JOSEPH (*offering the tray*): Ice cream or pastry, monsieur?

CORDEN: I'll have one of each—to start with. Oh, you have three kinds of ice cream. Which smells the strongest?

JOSEPH: I beg your pardon, sir?

CORDEN (*He sniffs the flavors*): I'll take the chocolate. (*Aside.*) Now I'll look in the other rooms. I may see my rival. (*Exit.*)

JOSEPH: Just time for a quick pastry. (*He stuffs one into his mouth.*) Somebody's coming. (*He hurries out with his mouth full of pastry.*)

BOURSEY (*entering*): In here. Quick! Close the door behind you. (LEONIDA, BLANCHE, *and* DANNE *come in behind him.*) Are you sure nobody followed us?

BLANCHE: Certain. We didn't stop running.

LEONIDA: A fine way to go to a ball.

BLANCHE: Ah, a fire. (*She goes and warms herself near it.* LEONIDA *joins her.*)

BOURSEY: Free at last!

DANNE: I could do with something to eat.

BOURSEY: So could we all.

JOSEPH (*entering*): Ice cream or pastries, ladies and gentlemen?

BOURSEY: Pastries! Look at them!

DANNE: Just leave the tray here.

JOSEPH: I'm sorry, monsieur, I am not permitted to.

BOURSEY: I'll pass them around. (*He passes them, one at a time, to* DANNE, *who passes them on to* BLANCHE *and* LEONIDA, *putting a few in his pocket on the side.*) Young man (*To* JOSEPH), will you tell Monsieur Poche that the Bourseys are here from Endives-Under-Glass?

LEONIDA: Including Mademoiselle Leonida.

DANNE: And Danne the farmer, son of a farmer.

JOSEPH: With pleasure, monsieur. (*He goes to the door.*)

DANNE (*stopping him*): You don't want to carry that heavy tray with you. Put it down here till you come back.

JOSEPH: I have to take it round the salon, monsieur. (*He goes out.*)

DANNE: Come back soon.

(CORDEN *enters.*)

CORDEN: I can't get rid of this benzine smell. It's worse than a gas leak.

BOURSEY: Corden. What are you doing here? Do you know Poche?

CORDEN: Why, I—of course I do. Known him for twenty years. An old friend.

BOURSEY: You never mentioned him to me before.

CORDEN: Don't talk to me in that tone, Boursey, after what you have on your conscience.

BOURSEY: You're hardly the one to talk about conscience.

CORDEN: Walking out on me like that, leaving me on top of the Arch of Triumph till after closing time. It was windy as hell.

DANNE: So were you as windy as hell.

BOURSEY: Skulking away at the first sign of danger.

DANNE: Hiding under tables.

CORDEN: I didn't skulk anywhere. I was waiting on top of the Arch of Triumph. . . .

BOURSEY: I'm surprised that you didn't feel ashamed at the sight of that monument dedicated to courage and honor.

CORDEN: Are you questioning my courage and honor, monsieur?

BOURSEY: I am not questioning them. I am denying them, monsieur.

CORDEN: I refuse to stomach that kind of an insult, monsieur.

BOURSEY: Take your corset off, then you'll be able to stomach anything, monsieur.

LEONIDA: Don't start quarreling now.

BLANCHE: Father, please.

DANNE: Come on, boys, shake hands. We're all children of Endives-Under-Glass, aren't we? We're friends.

BOURSEY: We were. I was not the one who broke up the friendship. I will not shake hands with a coward.

BLANCHE: Father, stop that kind of talk.

LEONIDA: Haven't we had enough trouble for one day?

BOURSEY: Very well. I yield to the persuasions of my family. (*He shakes hands with* CORDEN.)

CORDEN: Now tell me what happened to you.

BOURSEY: We were battered by the tempest of destiny. Our lives were in the balance. . . .

DANNE: It was all because of the watch and the chisel.

CORDEN: What was?

DANNE: The reason why they took us to the prison.

CORDEN: What prison? Who?

BOURSEY: All four of us, in a taxi.

DANNE: The policeman was sitting in front with the driver.

CORDEN: You were in a taxi with a policeman. . . .

BOURSEY: We had to find a way to escape.

CORDEN: From a taxi?

DANNE (*to* BOURSEY):   You're muddling him up. Let me explain. (*To* CORDEN.) You see, the pickax didn't work. We went through to the policemen's lounge. And the rope didn't work either. It was on the end of a bell.

CORDEN: Yes . . .

DANNE (*to* BOURSEY):   Now he understands. You can fill in the details.

BOURSEY: We drove down the boulevard in a taxi; the police cart hadn't arrived. The taxi had to go slowly because of the crowds. There was a Mardi Gras procession, with trumpets blowing as the main float went by, and the crowd shouted, "There it is, there it is." The policeman, who was sitting in front, looked out of the window to the right to see what was going on. At the same moment, on the left, four clowns who had finished in the procession made a sign to the cab driver to stop, because they thought he was free. So we got out and they got in. And the policeman was still looking out of the other window.

BLANCHE: And the traffic moved on. . . .

BOURSEY: And the four clowns went to prison with the policeman. (*They all laugh helplessly, except* CORDEN.) And we got away in the crowd.

DANNE: I'd like to have seen that policeman's face when he found the four clowns in the back. (*They laugh again.*) Now do you understand?

CORDEN: Not a word.

DANNE: It must be that belt. (*Punches him playfully in the tummy.*) Ooh, you smell terrible!

CORDEN: Just a little benzine. I'll find something to neutralize it. (*He goes out.*)

DANNE: So that's it. He drinks benzine. I always wondered. . . .

BLANCHE: That reminds me. I'm thirsty.

DANNE: So am I. Must be the pastry. Let's find that tray.

LEONIDA: You two go. Theodore and I will stay here.

(DANNE *gives* BLANCHE *his arm. They go out.*)

LEONIDA: I wonder where Monsieur Poche is.

BOURSEY: I'm very curious to meet that man.

LEONIDA: Is my hair terrible?

BOURSEY: No, but your shoes are covered with dust. It's lucky that I still have my handkerchief. (*Takes it out. A lump of plaster falls from his pocket.*) There goes a piece of the police station. (*He rubs his handkerchief over her shoes.*)

LEONIDA: Hurry, hurry. He may come in.

BOURSEY: I know that this is going to be a waste of time. I'd never have the luck to marry you off at your age.

(LEONIDA *is about to retort when* POCHE *appears.*)

POCHE: Good evening, good evening. I'm so glad to see you.

BOURSEY: Oh. (*He lifts his handkerchief from* LEONIDA'S *shoes and pretends to be blowing his nose. Large smudges appear on his face.*) I am Theodore Boursey.

POCHE: Delighted to meet you. And where is the lovely Leonida?

LEONIDA (*lowering her eyes*):   Here I am.

POCHE: Good heavens!

LEONIDA: What did you say?

POCHE: I am surprised, mademoiselle. When you filled out the prospectus, you did not do yourself justice.

BOURSEY: Be honest. There isn't a dog's chance, is there?

LEONIDA: Theodore, how dare you!

POCHE: I think there is every chance. The young lady would make a handsome wife. I think she is capable of inspiring a great passion. . . .

BOURSEY: You can say that, after seeing her?

LEONIDA: Theodore, you're a beast.

BOURSEY (*to* POCHE): Have you really got somebody who might be interested in her?

POCHE: Certainly, if all goes well.

BOURSEY: But will it? Look at her again.

LEONIDA (*to* POCHE): This is the man on whom I have thrown away my young years.

BOURSEY: I'll be only too happy if he can fix you up. But you'll have a hard time. She's a sour old bird.

POCHE: Please. Not at all.

LEONIDA: He's a wicked, spiteful man, Monsieur Poche.

BOURSEY: And a terrible problem to feed. She won't eat beef or mutton. We have all that beef and mutton left over. We have to throw it out.

POCHE: Not so loudly, please. Someone may hear you. A suitor.

BOURSEY: You've actually got a suitor out there? The poor fool.

POCHE: I have two of them.

LEONIDA (*overjoyed*): Shall I go out and see them or will they come in and see me?

POCHE: Don't be in too much of a hurry, mademoiselle. You're not exactly dressed for the part.

LEONIDA: Why not?

POCHE: You should have an evening dress, something alluring, something low-cut.

LEONIDA: I haven't got one.

BOURSEY: If we have to go out looking for an evening dress at this hour. . . .

POCHE: That won't be necessary. We have everything you need here. I'll take you to my costume mistress. By the time she's finished with you, no man will be able to resist you.

BOURSEY: Look here, if you can really take her off my hands, I'll add twenty thousand to the dowry.

LEONIDA: Theodore, darling, that makes up for all your insults. (*Kisses him.*)

BOURSEY: But only if you get married.

POCHE: With one hundred and twenty thousand francs? Inevitable. Last week I married off an eighty-year-old lady for half that amount. Everything will be fine. Now, you hurry along, mademoiselle, and get dressed.

BOURSEY: I could use a wash myself.

(*He goes out with* LEONIDA.)

POCHE: Five feet eight inches, and solid up and down. But still, 120,000 francs . . . (*Noticing the plaster on the floor.*) A lump of plaster. (*Picks it up and puts it in his pocket.*) I hope the building is safe. (*Looks worriedly at the ceiling.*) It must have broken off the cornice.

(SYLVAIN *comes in, dragging* DANNE *by the arm.*)

SYLVAIN: He's in here, Dad, and he wants to talk to you.

POCHE: Another prospect for Leonida.

SYLVAIN: This is my dad.

POCHE: Good evening, monsieur. Allow me to thank you for the confidence you have shown in me by visiting my establishment.

DANNE: They told me I could just walk in.

POCHE: Indeed you may. Some of the finest families in France are among my clientele. I spoke to your son earlier this evening. A fine, upstanding young gentleman. I can see that he takes after you.

DANNE: Yes, he's a good boy.

POCHE: Don't worry about him any more. I am going to find him a lovely wife.

DANNE: Very kind of you to put yourself out.

POCHE: Not at all. It is my work and my pleasure.

DANNE (*to* SYLVAIN): Say thank you to the man.

SYLVAIN: Thank you. Talking about wives, there's a plump little girl in the other room. If you could dig up something along those lines . . .

POCHE: We will try. Please have a seat.

DANNE: Don't mind if I do. (DANNE *and* SYLVAIN *sit down.*)

POCHE: You've come at the right time. My register is full of bargains, some new, some not so new, some—shall we say?—used. (*Opens the creaking book.*)

DANNE (*to* SYLVAIN): What's he opening that thing for?

SYLVAIN: To take out a few of the finest names in France.

DANNE: Have a cake. (*He takes two out of his pocket, gives one to* SYLVAIN *and eats the other himself.*) I've got cream all over my pockets.

POCHE: Now, what have we here? I never divulge names, you understand. Discretion is my hallmark. Number 2403, that's a possible match. She brings a dowry of fifty thousand francs.

DANNE: I want something better than that.

SYLVAIN: So do I.

POCHE: I'll look farther. (*He turns the pages.*)

(DANNE *reaches into his pocket for a pastry, pulls out a lump of brick, and bites into it.*)

DANNE: Ow, a brick! I've broken my jaw. (*Drops the brick.*)

POCHE: Here's number 9827. Dowry: eighty thousand francs.

DANNE: That's better.

POCHE: "Perfect health. Blameless character. Will play the piano, if desired. . . ."

DANNE: We don't go in for that kind of thing.

POCHE: There is only one drawback. She has one eye. . . .

SYLVAIN: A squint?

POCHE: No, it's a perfectly good eye. But she hasn't got another to go with it. I might as well tell you now; you'd be sure to notice it.

DANNE: We've got nothing against one eye, have we, Son?

SYLVAIN: But Dad—one eye . . .

DANNE: You see the same things with one eye as you see with two. She's not blind.

POCHE: No, wait. I've just thought of something even better to offer you. A superb woman . . .

SYLVAIN: Anything like the plump little girl in the other room?

POCHE: Very similar. And this, let me tell you, is a woman with a heart. She has given some of her early years to caring for a crotchety, arthritic old man.

DANNE: We don't mind that, do we, Son?

SYLVAIN: I haven't got arthritis.

POCHE: Dowry: 120,000 francs.

DANNE: That's for us!

SYLVAIN: Bring her in!

DANNE: Listen, what about this? My boy can have the eighty thousand francs. . . .

SYLVAIN: The one-eye?

DANNE: Yes, the one-eye. And I'll take the 120,000.

POCHE: You? By all means.

SYLVAIN: That's no good. I want a wife, not a stepmother. Besides, you're senile.

DANNE: I don't know. Sometimes, on a Sunday evening, after a day's rest, there's a lot of life in me. (*He pirouettes clumsily.*)

POCHE (*lathering his hands in air*):   So now we have two young men to marry. First, I will register you, one at a time.

DANNE: That's right, register us.

POCHE: Two hundred francs please.

DANNE: What for?

POCHE: One hundred for you and one hundred for your son. For security.

DANNE: Let me see the girls first.

POCHE: I'm sorry. Money first.

DANNE: Girls first.

POCHE: It isn't our practice.

DANNE: Then I won't get married. Nor will my boy.

POCHE: As you wish. (*Closes his register.*)

SYLVAIN: Dad, don't stop now. Offer him half.

DANNE: Can't. Haven't got a single franc on me. It was the police. They even took away our kitty.

SYLVAIN: But I was depending on you for my allowance. (*He stamps out.*)

POCHE: One hundred and twenty thousand francs. Isn't it worth two hundred?

DANNE: Not till I see the girls. Which way did my boy go? (*Exit.*)

POCHE: A pity. Well, there are two of them left. (*Goes to the door and beckons* CORDEN *in.*) This way, please.

CORDEN: Is she here yet?

POCHE: Yes.

CORDEN: Have you seen her? Is she a blonde? I'm partial to blondes.

POCHE: No, she's a brunette. And the dowry has changed. It has gone up from one hundred to one hundred and twenty thousand francs. But, as I say, she's a brunette.

CORDEN: That's good. I'm partial to brunettes.

POCHE: What's this? (*He picks up the piece of brick dropped by* DANNE.) The place is falling apart. (*He looks up fearfully.*)

CORDEN: Anything wrong?

POCHE: That's the second one. (*Puts the brick in his pocket.*)

CORDEN: I'm getting anxious. Present me.

POCHE: Wait here. I'll send her in.

CORDEN: How soon?

POCHE: Now. I'll see that you are not interrupted. Remember . . . That's strange. This whole place smells of cologne.

CORDEN: Don't worry about that. You were saying: "Remember . . ."

POCHE: Yes. Remember not to throw your chest out so far. You're bulging again. In a different place. (*Exit.*)

CORDEN: My belt is slipping. I ought to take it off. But someone might see. She might see. I hope she likes me. (*He goes to the mirror.*) I wish I had time to comb my hair again.

No, it's too late. (*Enter* LEONIDA *in evening dress.*) What does she want? Hello.

LEONIDA: Hello. (*She looks about the room.*)

CORDEN: I am—expecting someone in here.

LEONIDA: So am I.

CORDEN: Your brother was looking for you before, in another room.

LEONIDA: I'll speak to him later. I haven't had a dance yet. Would you escort me into the ballroom? I don't want to go in alone.

CORDEN: With pleasure. You don't mind if I leave you afterwards? I'm going outside.

LEONIDA: Not at all.

(*They go out, arm-in-arm, just as* POCHE *comes in.*)

POCHE: Where did they get to? They couldn't have run away. They hardly met. Unless they're trying to get out of paying my commission . . .

(LEONIDA *and* CORDEN *reappear at opposite ends of the room.*)

LEONIDA: I thought you were going outside. . . .

CORDEN: I thought you wanted to dance. . . .

POCHE (*coming between them*):   Well, what have you two lovebirds been saying to each other? Is everything all right? (*They gape at him.*) Well, is it a match? (*To* CORDEN.) She's the one. (*To* LEONIDA.) He's the one.

CORDEN: What? Old Leonida?

LEONIDA: What? Fatty Corden! I don't want him.

CORDEN: I don't want her.

LEONIDA: We know each other.

CORDEN: We've been playing cards together for twenty years.

LEONIDA: Is this why you brought me all the way to Paris?

CORDEN: Is this why I hired an expensive evening jacket and outfit? I want my security back.

POCHE: Now, keep calm. This is only your first encounter. I have many others. Some of the finest names in France.

CORDEN: I'm going for my coat. I'll be back in five minutes for my money. (*Exit.*)

LEONIDA: I'm heartbroken. Let me have my dress back.

POCHE: Now wait, Mademoiselle Leonida. He doesn't

count. I have another man waiting to see you, the one I wrote to you about. A man in a very high position. Wait there.

(*He goes out.* LEONIDA *walks to the mirror, pats her hair, powders her nose, adjusts the shoulders on her dress.* POCHE *comes in with* CHUTE. LEONIDA *has her back to them.*)

POCHE: There she is, by the mirror. Good luck.

CHUTE: Good evening, mademoiselle.

LEONIDA: Good evening. (*She turns and recognizes him.*)

CHUTE: I have heard so much about you. . . . (*She turns away hastily.*) Is anything wrong?

LEONIDA: No, it's the excitement.

CHUTE: I understand. (*Aside.*) She's a big girl, but attractive. And shy. I'm sure I know her face. (*Aloud.*) Didn't I see you at the theater last Tuesday?

LEONIDA: I don't think so. I don't go to the theater. (*Aside.*) He doesn't remember me.

CHUTE: Or at the Museum of Oriental Art, perhaps?

LEONIDA: No, I don't like museums.

CHUTE: I may be wrong, but I have a good memory for faces. Especially such a pretty face as yours. I know that you have given some of your early years to caring for an old man, but I am sure that you could never have been more desirable than you are now.

LEONIDA: Thank you.

CHUTE: Were you in the Mardi Gras procession today?

LEONIDA: The Mardi Gras? What is that?

CHUTE: I've seen you very recently. I should remember where.

LEONIDA (*still turned away*): Does it matter?

CHUTE: No, I suppose not. Would you like to dance?

LEONIDA: I don't care for dancing. Couldn't we stay here, like this, and talk?

(BOURSEY *bursts in.*)

BOURSEY: Well, how's it going? What do you think of her?

CHUTE (*recognizing him*): Now I know you, both of you.

BOURSEY: It's the commissioner. (*He goes out again at high speed, followed by* LEONIDA.)

CHUTE: Stop! Stop those people!

(DANNE *wanders in, from the other end of the room.*)

DANNE: I'm dying of thirst. It's those pastries.

CHUTE: The other one!

DANNE: His worship! (*He rushes out again.*)

CHUTE: They're all here. The whole gang. After them! Police, police! (*He pulls a whistle out of his pocket and blows it while he is running after* DANNE.)

ACT V

(*A street in Paris. At the rear, a building under construction, with planking in front. On the left a grocery store with a sign in front: "Laiterie," and in smaller letters: "Lait— Beurre—Fromage—Oeufs Frais." To one side of the store is a fruit shop, with a sign: "Aux Halles de Paris, Fruits et Légumes." As the curtain goes up,* TRICOT, *the owner of the fruit store, is just opening up.*)

TRICOT: What with the trumpets and fireworks and the shouting, I didn't close my eyes all night. Thank the Lord that's over for another year.

(MADAME CARAMEL *comes out of the grocery store and arranges some eggs on the stand in front.*)

MME. CARAMEL: Lovely morning, Monsieur Tricot.
TRICOT: Yes, but what a night it was! Bedlam, Babylon, Jericho. I see you're getting the fresh eggs out for the beginning of Lent.
MME. CARAMEL: Same as always. I picked out the biggest and freshest ones and put them aside, two weeks ago.
TRICOT: There's nothing like a fresh egg for Lent. Personally, I stick to fish.
MME. CARAMEL: You don't know what's good for you.

(*Sound of a trumpet.*)

TRICOT: Don't tell me they're starting up again. I'm going in. *Salut*, Madame Caramel.
MME. CARAMEL: *Salut*, Monsieur Tricot.

(*She puts out a few more eggs, leaves the basket with the remaining eggs in front, and goes into her shop. One of the planks at the back is pushed aside and* BOURSEY's *head appears cautiously and looks to either side.*)

361

BOURSEY: Nobody about. I'll risk it. (*Pushes his way out, past the plank.*) We spent the night in there. We had just rushed out of Poche's place when we ran into Chute, the assistant commissioner, and four of his men. Leonida almost fainted. We couldn't run carrying her, so we took shelter in this building, which is still under construction. It was my idea. All the best ideas come from me. The others are helpless. I'm the only man of action. Corden keeps groaning, and Danne keeps losing his temper. Anyway, Blanche and Leonida bedded down on some sawdust and workmen's overalls, and the rest of us slept in wheelbarrows. I'm so stiff from lying in one position all night that you could put wheels under me and trundle me away.

(CORDEN *pokes his head through the planks.*)

CORDEN: Psst, psst!
BOURSEY: What's that? Oh, it's you. You scared the wits out of me.
CORDEN: Is it clear?
BOURSEY: Yes.

(CORDEN *comes out laboriously, still wearing his evening clothes.*)

CORDEN: What a trip! My God, what a trip!
BOURSEY: You haven't stopped saying that all night. I could hear you from my wheelbarrow.
DANNE: Hisst!

(CORDEN *and* BOURSEY *spin in fright.*)

BOURSEY: Now *he's* starting.
DANNE: Is it all right to come out?
BOURSEY: Yes.

(DANNE *squeezes out. Like the other two, he is covered with plaster and dust.*)

DANNE: I've had enough of this. It can't go on any longer.
BOURSEY: What do you want to do about it?
DANNE: I protest, that's what. Sleeping in wheelbarrows, nothing to eat for dinner but pastries, cream all over my pockets, and no breakfast.
CORDEN: What a trip! My God, what a trip!

BOURSEY: Stop complaining. As soon as my sister wakes up we'll catch the first train home.

DANNE: How? They took everything away from us except our handkerchiefs, and we can't buy tickets with them. I've had enough of this. It can't go on any longer. I protest.

BOURSEY: *We* have no money, that's true, but Corden has.

CORDEN: Who says so?

BOURSEY: You weren't with us at the police station, were you?

DANNE: Of course he wasn't.

CORDEN: Excuse me, I had only 114 francs in my pocket, for personal expenses, when we left.

BOURSEY: That's enough to get us home.

DANNE: Stop arguing and hand it over.

CORDEN: It's all gone.

DANNE }
BOURSEY } Where?

CORDEN: That rogue Poche took a hundred francs from me so that I could see your sister. And I'd been seeing her at the card table for nothing for the last twenty years.

BOURSEY: But you should have fourteen francs left.

CORDEN: I spent them on the belt.

BOURSEY: At least you still have your watch.

CORDEN: No, I had to leave it with the tailor who lent me this outfit. I was counting on the kitty for the money to pay him. He still has my clothes and my watch.

BOURSEY: Let's go and return the suit.

CORDEN: In this condition? And without any money to pay for the hiring?

BOURSEY: Then we're stuck.

CORDEN: What a trip! My God, what a trip!

DANNE: I've had enough of this. It can't go on any longer. I protest.

BOURSEY: We'll never get anywhere if you two keep on like that. Let's put our trust in Providence and think hard.

(*They think.* CORDEN *suddenly lets out a cry that makes the other two start.*)

CORDEN: Ah, look what I've found in my vest pocket: fifty centimes.

BOURSEY: What did I tell you? It's Providence.

DANNE: Some Providence. What can you do with fifty centimes for the five of us? Let me take care of them.

BOURSEY: No, they belong to the community. We'll take a vote on what to do. Who's going to speak first?

CORDEN }
DANNE } I am.

BOURSEY: Don't let's start that again. Corden, you're the oldest. Let's have your contribution.

CORDEN: Gentlemen . . . what a trip, my God, what a trip!

BOURSEY: Yes. Go on.

CORDEN: That's all I have to say.

BOURSEY: That's all I expected from you. Danne?

DANNE: I suggest we buy as much bread and sausage as we can afford with the fifty centimes.

BOURSEY: And after you've eaten—what then?

DANNE: I don't know. We'll think about it later.

BOURSEY: Neither of those suggestions gets us very far.

CORDEN: What do you expect? I'm overwhelmed by our bad luck.

BOURSEY: With me, it's the opposite. I find my true stature under conditions of adversity. I grow. I thrive on danger and difficulties. I was born for great achievements.

CORDEN: What are you going to do?

BOURSEY: First, I am going to buy a stamp for twenty centimes.

DANNE: You can't eat a stamp.

BOURSEY: That leaves thirty centimes. Then I shall write to our friend Penuri, the tax collector, and ask him to send us five hundred francs.

CORDEN: Five hundred francs!

DANNE: We're saved!

BOURSEY: Put it down to my unfailing ingenuity.

CORDEN: But wait a minute. How can he send us the money? We have no return address.

DANNE: And how can we live till the money arrives?

BOURSEY: Fellow citizens of Endives-Under-Glass, believe in me, trust me. In the old days, when I used to stay in Paris, I always put up at the Hotel Driftwood. I used to tip the people there heavily. They're sure to remember me.

CORDEN: Well?

DANNE: What about it?

BOURSEY: I'll tell Penuri to send the money to us, care of the Hotel Driftwood. In the meantime, we'll take rooms there and live comfortably until the money reaches us.

CORDEN: I'll be able to get my clothes back.

BOURSEY: What do you say to that?

CORDEN: You're a genius.

DANNE: A superman.

BOURSEY: No, I am not a superman. I merely happen to be gifted. Now I am going to buy a stamp, then I shall borrow a pen and ink, and the letter will go out by the next post. In the meantime, you two can try to wake Leonida. (*He goes out.*)

CORDEN: Yes, wake Leonida. But how? She's snoring like a trumpet.

DANNE: Wish I had a jug of cold water to tip down her back.

(BLANCHE *pushes aside the plank, and helps* LEONIDA *through.*)

BLANCHE: Careful with your dress, Aunt Leonida.

CORDEN }
DANNE }　Here she is.

LEONIDA (*yawning, and still in her evening gown*): Where are we? Why am I wearing this dress?

DANNE: Give her another ten minutes to come alive.

TRICOT (*coming out in front of his shop and looking at them*): What, more processions? (*He goes in again.*)

BLANCHE: I think it's raining.

CORDEN: I'm frozen. While we're waiting, why don't we find a warm store and go inside? We can look at the merchandise. It's better than standing here.

BLANCHE: Good idea. Let's find a dress shop or a china store.

DANNE: Don't buy anything.

BLANCHE: Aren't you coming with us?

DANNE: No, somebody has to wait here for your father.

CHORUS:　　Let us fly
　　　　　　Before the storm
　　　　　　To a store where it's dry
　　　　　　And clean and warm.

(CORDEN, BLANCHE, *and* LEONIDA *go off, leaving* DANNE *alone.*)

DANNE: I didn't tell the others. I have one pastry left. A bit squashed, but it's food.

(*Takes it out and eats it.* BOURSEY *appears, pursued by a waiter.*)

BOURSEY: It's only twenty-five centimes in Endives-Under-Glass.

WAITER: It's forty centimes in Paris.

DANNE: What's wrong?

BOURSEY: The post office wasn't open, so I went into a cafe to borrow a pen and ink. They said I had to buy something; I ordered a glass of sugared water, which is only twenty-five centimes . . .

WAITER: Forty centimes . . .

DANNE: Did you drink it?

BOURSEY: Yes.

DANNE: You'll have to pay him.

BOURSEY: I can't. I spent twenty of our fifty centimes on a stamp from the machine. (*To* WAITER.) Take thirty. That's all I have left.

WAITER: If you haven't got the money you shouldn't order.

BOURSEY: I'll have a little more respect from you, please. You don't even know who I am. (*To* DANNE.) Call me Commandant.

WAITER: You can call yourself major-general if you like, but you'll still pay up.

BOURSEY: Very well. You'll have to come back with me to my hotel.

DANNE (*admiringly*): He never runs out of ideas.

WAITER: Is it far away?

BOURSEY: No, it's the Hotel Driftwood.

WAITER: So you're staying at the Hotel Driftwood?

BOURSEY: I am indeed.

WAITER: That's interesting. It was pulled down twelve years ago.

BOURSEY: Oh. (*To* DANNE.) I've sent the letter off.

DANNE: Five hundred francs gone.

WAITER: You're nothing but a couple of cheap crooks.

BOURSEY: Why, you insolent young . . .

DANNE: Don't fight, don't fight!

(*He grabs* BOURSEY, *who is about to throw himself at the* WAITER, *and swings him back by the arm. Caught off balance,* BOURSEY *staggers into the front window of the fruit store. There is a tinkle of glass.*)

TRICOT (*coming outside and standing with his hands on his hips*): One broken shop window. That will be three hundred francs.

BOURSEY (*sitting on the ground*): Now we have two creditors.

(SYLVAIN *comes on the scene. His clothes are awry, his jacket is back to front. He is very drunk.*)

SYLVAIN (*singing*):

> Here is my heart, take it.
> Here is my heart, break it.
> Here is my heart, make it
> Yours . . .

DANNE: My boy. We're saved!

BOURSEY (*to* TRICOT *and the* WAITER): Now you will be paid.

SYLVAIN: Hello, Dad.

DANNE: Where's your wallet? (*Reaches into* SYLVAIN'S *pocket.*) What's this? A false nose.

BOURSEY (*reaching into the other pocket*): Here's his wallet. (*Opening it.*) Ten centimes.

DANNE: Is that all?

BOURSEY: Ten and thirty makes forty. (*To the* WAITER.) Here are your miserable forty centimes. (*The* WAITER *takes the money and goes.*) That's one debt out of the way.

TRICOT: What about my three hundred francs?

BOURSEY (*fumbling in his own pockets*): Just a moment. Let me have another look through my clothes.

DANNE: How is it you're not at the school?

SYLVAIN: I said good-by to the school. Good-by, school, I said. And now I'm going to be a waiter. I have a job at The Smiling Bull.

DANNE: You're drunk, you good-for-nothing. I'll give you Smiling Bull.

SYLVAIN: I'm still thirsty. Waiter, another glass of Beaujolais. (DANNE *gives him a furious push.* SYLVAIN *crashes into the basket of eggs.*)

EVERYBODY: Ah!

MME. CARAMEL (*coming out swiftly*): All my eggs broken, my fresh-laid eggs.

DANNE: I'll send you some more.

MME. CARAMEL: You will not. You'll pay me twenty-five francs.

BOURSEY: Now we have two creditors again, and it's worse than before.

SYLVAIN: Don't cry, old girl. You can come to my place. I haven't got any eggs, but I will give you a chair.

DANNE: His place!

BOURSEY: He has a house.

DANNE: We're saved. We'll sell his furniture. (*To* SYLVAIN.) Where do you live?

SYLVAIN: In a tall building. Ah, um, wait a minute. You go past this bridge—

BOURSEY: Which bridge?

SYLVAIN: I don't remember. Yes, I do remember. I live at number 118.

DANNE: What street?

SYLVAIN: That's hard. I don't know that.

DANNE: Idiot!

BOURSEY: Animal!

SYLVAIN: I'm not comfortable here. (*He staggers over to a bench, sits down, and falls asleep. Some cries are heard from nearby.* CORDEN, LEONIDA, *and* BLANCHE *pant in.*)

DANNE: What's happening?

CORDEN: A crowd of children were chasing me and shouting: "Scarecrow, scarecrow, feed him to the birds."

LEONIDA: And when we went into a dress shop, the woman thought I was a tourist and said: "Madame, you're a day late for the carnival."

CORDEN: What a trip, my God, what a trip!

TRICOT: How much longer are we supposed to wait?

BLANCHE: What do these people want?

TRICOT: My window.

MME. CARAMEL: My eggs.

BOURSEY: I'd forgotten about them. (*He starts to fumble in his pockets again.* DANNE *does the same.*) How are we ever going to get out of this? (*Suddenly, looking at* LEONIDA.) I know a way.

DANNE: We're saved.

CORDEN: What is it?

BOURSEY: Leonida . . . her diamond pendant . . . they forgot to take it.

DANNE: Of course. We can sell it.

CORDEN: No.

LEONIDA: No.

BOURSEY: I know how you feel. It was a present from Corden when you were a godmother and he was a godfather. But we can't think about that now. Give it to me. I'll run to the nearest jeweler and get what I can for it.

CORDEN: Stop! It's useless.

EVERYBODY: Why?

CORDEN: I don't know how to tell you. It's not a diamond. It's an imitation. . . .

EVERYBODY: Paste! False! A hoax, etc.

CORDEN: It's not my fault. I was in a hurry. I didn't have time to look for a diamond.

LEONIDA: You cad!

DANNE: You rat!

BOURSEY: You blackguard! No man of honor would give a lady an imitation diamond.

CORDEN: Anyway, I couldn't afford a real one.

TRICOT: I'm not going to waste all day waiting for you.

MME. CARAMEL: Pay us now or . . .

BOURSEY: Give us another minute. (*He and* DANNE *make a pretense of going through their pockets again.*)

TRICOT: Not another second. I'm going to call my friend, the assistant police commissioner.

EVERYBODY: The commissioner!

DANNE: His worship!

BOURSEY: No, please, I beg of you—

(FELIX *enters.*)

FELIX: At last! Here you are.

EVERYBODY: Felix!

DANNE: *We're saved!*

BOURSEY (*to* FELIX): My boy, we're delighted to see you. My daughter is yours. Now.

BLANCHE: Thank you, Father.

FELIX: Thank you, Father.

BOURSEY: And now—have you any money?

FELIX: Why, yes.

EVERYBODY: He has money!

BOURSEY: Pay these people for me. Twenty-five francs to this woman; three hundred francs to this man.

FELIX: Blanche . . .

BOURSEY: Pay them now.

FELIX: Certainly. I don't know what this is all about, but still . . . (*He gives* TRICOT *and* MME. CARAMEL *the money, and they go back into their shops.*)

CORDEN: It's lucky that you turned up.

FELIX: I've been looking for you since yesterday morning. I've been to every monument and park in Paris. Last night I was watching the procession, hoping to see you when I spotted the thief.

EVERYBODY: What thief?

FELIX: The thief who took my watch on the boulevard yesterday. I recognized him immediately, and grabbed him just as he was putting his hand into somebody else's pocket.

BOURSEY: Did you get your watch back?

FELIX: No. He said he'd thrown it into somebody's umbrella.

BOURSEY: Mine. My umbrella.

DANNE: So that's how it got there. This time we really are saved.

BOURSEY: They'll have to admit we were innocent.

CORDEN: They'll have to give us back the kitty.

BOURSEY: Felix, my daughter is yours.

FELIX: Thank you, thank you. (*He goes to take* BLANCHE's *hand.*)

BOURSEY (*pulling* BLANCHE *away*): But first, have you any money?

FELIX: More money?

BOURSEY: To pay for lunch. We haven't eaten yet.

SYLVAIN (*waking up*): Lunch? Very good, monsieur. I'm going to be a waiter.

DANNE: You'll wait in the cowshed. I'm taking you back to Endives-Under-Glass. I'll make a farmer of you yet.

BOURSEY: After lunch we'll pay a visit to our friend the commissioner.

DANNE: I'll ask him for my pickax.

BOURSEY: He will give us our kitty back and this time we'll celebrate at home.

CORDEN: Yes, with a bouncing great turkey buried under truffles.

FELIX }
BLANCHE } No, a ball. . . .

DANNE: No, the fair at Cressy. . . .

BOURSEY: Order, order! We'll put it to the vote. Who wants to speak first?

EVERYBODY: I do!

BOURSEY: We'll decide when we get back. Now, gentlemen, give your arms to the ladies and we will all go to lunch.

EVERYBODY: To lunch!

CHORUS (*they sing*):
<blockquote>
So it's good-by to Paris,
The big, bad city,
Which tried to embarrass
Us out of our kitty.
Before another day can pass
We'll be back in
  back in
  back in
Dear old Endives-Under-Glass.
</blockquote>

ROSTAND: *The Romantics*

EDMOND ROSTAND (1868–1918)

Rostand is the only major French playwright from the south of France, although his plays are, in many respects, more "Parisian" than any other playwright's, because of their attempts to be continuously witty, charming, rhetorical, and sophisticated. He was born in the Rue Montaux in Marseille to Eugène Rostand, a former journalist who had translated Catullus into French verse and was now a comfortable publicist and scholar, and whose brother, Alexis, Rostand's uncle, was a financier and amateur composer who had written a locally popular song cycle.

Rostand studied at the Lycée de Marseille, where he was apparently a bright and chirpy scholar. At the age of thirteen he founded a school newspaper which was written by several other boys and himself and lasted for five issues. He went on to complete his general studies at Stanislas College in Paris, then attended a law school. At the age of nineteen he won first prize in a competition, for an essay on "The Sentimental Novel and the Naturalistic Novel" in which his preference was for the former, and this at a time when the naturalistic style of writing was in heavy vogue. In 1890 he published a collection of poems, *Musardises,* of which he presented one copy to the granddaughter of Marshal Gérard, Rosemonde, who was also a poet. He married her that same year.

The young couple settled in Paris, and in 1894 Rostand submitted a one-act, *The Two Pierrots,* to the management of the Comédie-Française. It was turned down. According to Mme. Rostand, her husband—who had had one small play, *The Red Glove,* performed in Marseille—decided that if he was going to be rejected it might as well be for a three-act as for a one-act. He therefore went home and wrote *The Romantics,* which the Comédie-Française board unanimously accepted.

The play was agreeably enough received to ease the way for Rostand's next two plays, *The Faraway Princess,* based on the exploits of a Provençal poet, and *The Woman of Samaria,* a drama with a biblical setting, in both of which the feminine lead was played by Sarah Bernhardt.

By this time Rostand was respected enough in public and in private theatrical circles to be approached by the great actor Coquelin, who wanted a part specially written for him. As a young student, Rostand had inscribed in one of his notebooks, "A fine play in verse . . . will I ever find it in my heart?" His output up to that time had not satisfied this yearning to write a poetic drama on an heroic scale. For his subject he chose an earlier southern poet, Cyrano, who came from a small town on the Dordogne River, Bergerac, and was a friend and rival of Molière. The "heroic comedy" was written and staged in 1897, the year in which *The Woman of Samaria* was also produced, with Coquelin in the title role of the poet-swordsman with the unwieldy nose and incomparable gift of oratory. The part was a magnification of Straforel, the professional "bravo" of *The Romantics*. Press and public and literary critics went wild over *Cyrano de Bergerac*. The thirty-year-old Rostand was hailed as the legitimate successor to Hugo, to Molière, to Shakespeare; he was poetry incarnate; he had breathed new being into the great tradition of French drama; the heroic alexandrine had again come alive. He had remade the most popular French hero of all, the man who, in the words of one French critic, Jean-Aubry, "by dint of talking, creates the belief that he has acted."

Rostand, having triumphantly created the tragicomic hero, now turned his attention to the fully tragic hero, and built his next drama around the Duke of Reichstadt, the exiled son of Napoleon who dreamed of recapturing his father's glory but was too young, sickly, and tender to inspire leadership, and who died at the age of twenty-one. The role of The Young Eagle (*l'Aiglon*) was played by Bernhardt in 1900 and although the play was not greeted as rapturously as *Cyrano* had been, was far superior to any other plays being written in France, and the following year the author, at thirty-three, was made a member of the French Academy.

During the winter rehearsals of *L'Aiglon*, Rostand, who was physically frail, contracted a mild case of bronchial pneumonia, possibly from his continual coming-and-going between the warm theater and the cold streets of Paris. His doctor advised him to move to a milder climate; he went with his wife and two young sons to the Basque country and stayed first in a "health hotel" and later in a magnificent house on an estate called Arnaga, near the village of Cambo on the lower slopes of the Pyrenees.

Here Rostand lived out his life, reading and writing steadily, taking long, slow walks through his gardens and park, and fending off curious locals and visitors from Paris. Rostand's arrival in the quiet Pays Basque apparently turned the postal system there upside down. Among the swarm of letters and telegrams that came to him was a congratulatory message from the Italian poet D'Annunzio. The local telegrapher, unused to any telegrams other than

the usual birth, death, and marriage greetings, passed on
the message as "How are the wings of your mule?"—the
word "mule" being a sub-Freudian slip for "muse."

All kinds of rumors crept out of Cambo and into the
French newspapers. Rostand's next play would be about
Joan of Arc, about Don Quixote, about Faust, about
Polichinelle, about Don Juan, about Penelope and Ulysses.
Most of these subjects were, in fact, considered by Rostand
during his later years; he did translate *Faust*, and he did
begin a play on Don Juan, which was published incomplete
in 1921, three years after his death. Yet he could not seem
to satisfy his own exacting standards. He was a neat, elegant
man who kept writing beautifully groomed verse in faultless
handwriting, but most of it he tore up. He could not come
to grips with a subject that would top, or even equal, his
former successes.

As early as 1902 it became known that he was working on
a drama of Chantecler, the cockerel, the symbol of the
French spirit, as a new vehicle for Coquelin. But in spite of
pressure from Paris, Rostand would not release a script. He
had finished one draft in 1903, but he continued to trim, re-
touch, and polish the enormously long, enormously ambitious
drama, tucking two or more witticisms, references, and verbal
jugglings into almost every line of the four overloaded acts.
So much publicity and hullabaloo preceded the eventual opening of the play in 1910 that, in one critic's words, "even a
Macbeth or an *Oedipus* would have disappointed the public."
Coquelin had died without seeing even a draft version of the
play, and the leading role was taken by Lucien Guitry.

Chantecler, in which all the characters are birds (with the
exception of one dog), was intended to be an elaborate satire
and comment on French life and is comparable to Aristo-
phanes' *The Birds* and Orwell's *Animal Farm*. But it proved
too self-indulgent for the audience. The nonstop jests and
word plays mouthed by every character flew across the footlights and died in open space; the audience could not take more
than a fraction of them in, and was bewildered by the others.

For the last eight years of his life Rostand wrote no more
plays for production, although two fragments, *The Sacred
Wood* and *The Last Night of Don Juan*, were published after
his death. Neither of these has the power of Rostand's
earlier work, which had reached its summit with Cyrano,
although *Don Juan* has an unorthodox theme: it is an anti-
heroic treatment of the celebrated seducer, who has now
become impotent and disillusioned—an idea that was recently revived in a play by Henry de Montherlant.

Rostand was afflicted until the end of his life with acute bronchitis and a steadily worsening neurasthenia. He husbanded his energies by remaining in bed until late each morning, and there read, according to his sons' tutor, every new novel, play, and book of poetry that was written. Sometimes, after meals he would read aloud from other people's works—the passages that pleased him—to his family. He read with great concentration and care, in the studied voice of an actor, his eyes only a few inches from the words and his mustache brushing the paper. In the late afternoon he would stroll to the end of his garden to admire a trio of stone statues that formed a sort of shrine—busts of Shakespeare, Hugo, and Cervantes, who had been his models.

He died on December 2, 1918, shortly after the end of World War I.

A LIST OF ROSTAND'S PLAYS:

The Red Glove (1889), *The Two Pierrots* (1894), *The Woman of Samaria* (1897), *Cyrano de Bergerac* (1897), *The Eaglet* (*L'Aiglon*) (1900), *Chantecler* (1910), *The Sacred Wood* (1916?), *The Last Night of Don Juan* (1917–18).

SUGGESTIONS FOR FURTHER READING ON ROSTAND:

There is no full-length book on Rostand in English and very little biographical material. The best article is G. Jean-Aubry's "Edmond Rostand" in *The Fortnightly Review*, 1919. Chesterton has a section on Rostand in his book *Five Types*, as do Ludwig Lewisohn in *The Modern Drama* and T. S. Eliot in *Selected Essays*.

There are three books worth consulting in French: *Edmond Rostand*, by his wife, Rosemonde Gérard Rostand; *Edmond Rostand: Biographie-Critique*, by Louis Haugmard; and *Edmond Rostand: Son Oeuvre*, by Lautier and Keller. Readers will also find interesting biographical sidelights in "Rostand à Arnaga," by Raymond Lerouge in the *Revue des Deux Mondes*, April 1930; and in "Rostand: Mémoires d'Enfance," by Paul Brulat in *La Revue Mondiale*.

NOTE: Critical essays on Rostand, "The Essence of Rostand's Greatness," by Cleveland Moffett, and *"Les Romanesques* in Philadelphia," by Edward Childs Carpenter, will be found on pp. 554 and 556.

THE ROMANTICS

A Comedy in Three Acts

by Edmond Rostand

FIRST PERFORMED AT THE COMÉDIE-FRANÇAISE,
ON MAY 21, 1894

Translated by Barrett H. Clark

CHARACTERS

SYLVETTE
PERCINET
STRAFOREL
BERGAMIN, Percinet's *father*
PASQUINOT, Sylvette's *father*
BLAISE, *a gardener*
A WALL (*not a speaking part*)

Swordsmen, musicians, Negroes, torch-bearers, a notary, four witnesses, and other supernumeraries.

The action takes place anywhere, provided the costumes are pretty.

ACT I

(*The stage is divided by an old wall, covered with vines and flowers. At the right, a corner of* BERGAMIN's *private park; at the left, a corner of* PASQUINOT's. *On each side of the wall, and against it, is a rustic bench.*

As the curtain rises, PERCINET *is seated on the top of the wall. On his knee is a book, out of which he is reading to* SYLVETTE, *who stands attentively listening on the bench which is on the other side of the wall.*)

SYLVETTE: Monsieur Percinet, how divinely beautiful!
PERCINET: Is it not? Listen to what Romeo answers: (*Reading.*)

"It was the lark, the herald of the morn,
  No nightingale: look, love, what envious streaks
  Do lace the severing clouds in yonder east.
  Night's candles are burnt out, and jocund day
  Stands tiptoe on the misty mountain tops:
  I must begone"—

SYLVETTE (*interrupts him, as she listens*): Sh!
PERCINET (*listens a moment, then*): No one! And, mademoiselle, you must not take fright like a startled bird. Hear the immortal lovers:

"*Juliet*: Yon light is not the daylight, I know it, I,
It is some meteor that the sun exhales,
To be to thee this night a torch-bearer,
And light thee on thy way to Mantua:
Therefore stay yet, thou need'st not to be gone.

Romeo: Let me be ta'en, let me be put to death;
I am content, so thou wilt have it so.
I'll say, yon gray is not the morning's eye,
'Tis but the pale reflex of Cynthia's brow;
Nor that is not the lark, whose notes do beat
The vaulty heaven so high above our heads:
I have more care to stay than will to go:
Come, death and welcome"—

377

SYLVETTE: No, he must not say such things, or I shall cry.

PERCINET: Then let us stop and read no further until tomorrow. We shall let Romeo live! (*He closes the book and looks about him.*) This charming spot was expressly made, it seems, as a cradle for the beautiful lines of Will Shakespeare.

SYLVETTE: The lines *are* beautiful, and the soft air here is a divine accompaniment. And see, these green shadows! But, Monsieur Percinet, what makes them beautiful to me is the way you read!

PERCINET: Flatterer!

SYLVETTE (*sighing*): Poor lovers! Their fate was cruel. (*Another sigh.*) I think—

PERCINET: What?

SYLVETTE: Nothing!

PERCINET: Something that made you blush suddenly.

SYLVETTE: Nothing, I say.

PERCINET: Ah, that's too transparent. I see it all: you are thinking of our fathers.

SYLVETTE: Perhaps—

PERCINET: Of their terrible hatred for each other.

SYLVETTE: The thought often pains me and makes me cry when I am alone. Last month, when I came home from the convent, my father pointed out your father's park, and said to me: "My dear child, you see there the domain of my mortal enemy, Bergamin. Never cross the path of those two rascals, Bergamin and his son Percinet. Do you promise? If not, I shall cast you off as an enemy. Their family has always hated ours." And I promised. But you see how I keep my word.

PERCINET: Did I not promise my father to do the same, Sylvette? Yet I love you.

SYLVETTE: Holy saints!

PERCINET: I love you, my dearest!

SYLVETTE: It's sinful.

PERCINET: Very—but what can we do? The greater the obstacles to be overcome, the stronger the desire. Sylvette, kiss me!

SYLVETTE: Never! (*She jumps down from the bench and runs off a few steps.*)

PERCINET: But you love me?

SYLVETTE: What?

PERCINET: My dear girl: I, too, sometimes think of us and compare us with those other lovers—of Verona.

SYLVETTE: But I didn't compare—!

PERCINET: You and I are Juliet and Romeo; I love you

to despair, and I shall brave the wrath of Pasquinot-Capulet and Bergamin-Montague!

SYLVETTE (*coming a little nearer to the wall*): Then we love each other. But how has it happened so soon, Monsieur Percinet?

PERCINET: Love is born, we do not know how or why, because it must be born. I often saw you pass my window—

SYLVETTE: I saw you, too!

PERCINET: And our eyes spoke in silence.

SYLVETTE: One day I was gathering nuts in the garden by the wall—

PERCINET: One day I happened to be reading Shakespeare. See how everything conspired to unite two hearts!

SYLVETTE: And a little gust of wind blew my scarf in your direction.

PERCINET: I climbed to the wall to return it—

SYLVETTE (*climbing the wall again*): I climbed too!

PERCINET: And since that day, my dear, I have waited at the same hour, here by this wall; and each time my heart beat louder and faster, until I knew by your soft laugh that you were near!

SYLVETTE: Now since we love, we must be married.

PERCINET: I was just thinking about that.

SYLVETTE (*solemnly*): I, the last of the Pasquinots, hereby pledge myself to you, the last of the Bergamins.

PERCINET: What noble recklessness!

SYLVETTE: We shall be sung in future ages!

PERCINET: Two tender children of two hard-hearted fathers!

SYLVETTE: But perhaps the hour is at hand when our fathers' hatred may end?

PERCINET: I doubt it.

SYLVETTE: I have heard of stranger things. I can think of half a dozen—

PERCINET: What, for instance?

SYLVETTE: The crown prince comes riding past some day—I run to him and kneel and tell him the story of our love and of our fathers' hatred. The prince asks to see my father and Bergamin, and they are reconciled.

PERCINET: And your father gives me your hand!

SYLVETTE: Yes. Or else, you languish, the doctor declares you cannot live—

PERCINET: And asks: "What ails you?"

SYLVETTE: And you answer: "I must have Sylvette!"

PERCINET: And his pride is then forced to bend.

SYLVETTE: Yes. Or else: an aged duke, having seen my

portrait, falls in love with me, sends a squire to sue for my hand, and offers to make me a duchess.

PERCINET: And you say, "No!"

SYLVETTE: He is offended, and some dark night when I am in the garden, thinking of you, he seizes me. I scream!

PERCINET: And I instantly spring over the wall, dagger in hand. I fight like a tiger. I—

SYLVETTE: You lay low three or four men. Then my father rushes in and takes me in his arms. You tell him who you are. His heart softens, he gives me to my rescuer. Your father consents, for he is proud of your bravery.

PERCINET: Then we live happily together for years and years.

SYLVETTE: This is not at all impossible, is it?

PERCINET: Someone's coming!

SYLVETTE (*forgetting herself*):   Kiss me!

PERCINET (*kissing her*):   This evening, at eight, then? As usual? You will come?

SYLVETTE: No.

PERCINET: Yes!

SYLVETTE (*disappearing behind the wall*):   Your father! (PERCINET *jumps quickly from the wall.*)

(*Enter* BERGAMIN.)

BERGAMIN: Ah, I find you here again, dreaming in this corner of the park!

PERCINET: Father, I love this old corner! I adore this bench over which the vines of the wall have so gracefully draped themselves. See, what graceful arabesques these festoons make! The air is purer there.

BERGAMIN: By the side of this wall?

PERCINET: I love it!

BERGAMIN: I see nothing lovable about it!

SYLVETTE (*aside*):   He can't see why!

PERCINET: But it is charming, all covered with ivy and creeper. See here, what honeysuckle! This hundred-year-old wall, with its clinging vines, its constellations of flowers, looking through the crannies, kissed by the summer sun, makes the bench a throne fit for kings!

BERGAMIN: Nonsense, you harebrained youth! Do you mean to tell me that this wall has eyes?

PERCINET: Ah, what eyes! (*Turns toward the wall.*) Of soft azure, yet dazzlingly blue; let but a tear come to dim your brightness, or a single kiss—

BERGAMIN: But the wall hasn't eyes, you idiot!

PERCINET: See this vine, though! (*He plucks part of the vine from the wall and graciously presents it to his father.*)

SYLVETTE (*aside*):   How clever!

BERGAMIN: How stupid! But I know now what has turned your silly head: you come here to read! (SYLVETTE *starts as she hears this.* PERCINET *also shows signs of fear as his father pulls the book from the youth's pocket.*) Plays! (*He drops the book in horror.*) And verse! Verse! That's what has turned your head. Now I see why you talk about eyes and honeysuckle. I tell you, to be useful, a wall doesn't have to be beautiful. I am going to have all this green stuff taken away, and the bricks relaid and the holes stopped up. I want a white wall and a high one to keep the neighbors from looking into our park. I want no vines and honeysuckles. Along the top I'll sprinkle broken glass—

PERCINET: Have pity!

BERGAMIN: No pity! I insist on it! Glass—all along the top of the wall! (SYLVETTE *and* PERCINET *are in despair.* BERGAMIN *sits down on the bench.*) And now, I have something to say to you. (*He rises and examines the wall.*) If the wall hasn't eyes, it may possibly have ears. (*He is about to stand on the bench, when* PERCINET *takes fright and* SYLVETTE *clings close to her side of the wall, making herself as small as she can.* BERGAMIN *decides not to scale the wall, but motions to his son to do so.*) See whether some curious listener—?

PERCINET (*climbing to the top and leaning over so that* SYLVETTE *can hear him*):   Till tonight!

SYLVETTE (*giving him her hand, which he kisses*):   I'll come as the clock is striking! I adore you!

BERGAMIN (*to* PERCINET):   Well?

PERCINET (*jumping down—to his father*):   No one!

BERGAMIN (*reseating himself*):   Well, then, my boy, I should like to see you married.

SYLVETTE (*aside*):   Oh!

BERGAMIN: What's that?

PERCINET: Nothing.

BERGAMIN: I thought I heard a cry?

PERCINET (*looking into the air*):   Some wounded bird, perhaps.

BERGAMIN: I have given the matter my undivided attention, and have chosen a wife for you. (PERCINET *whistles and walks away.*) I am serious; I intend to force you, if necessary. (PERCINET *continues whistling.*) *Will* you stop that confounded whistling! The young woman is rich—she's a jewel!

PERCINET: I want none of your jewels!

BERGAMIN: I'll show you, you insolent young—

PERCINET (*grasping his father's cane, which is raised as if to strike him*): Spring has filled the bushes with the songs of birds; the streams accompany the love-notes of wild birds.

BERGAMIN: Rascal!

PERCINET (*still holding the cane*): The whole world laughs and sings farewell to April. The butterflies—

BERGAMIN: Ruffian!

PERCINET (*as before*): Wing their way across the meadows, to make love to their adored flowers! Love—

BERGAMIN: Villain!

PERCINET: Love opens the heart of all nature. And you ask me to consent to a marriage of reason!

BERGAMIN: Of course I do!

PERCINET (*passionately*): No, no, no, Father. I swear by this wall—which hears me, I hope—that my marriage will be more romantic than any of the world's love stories! (*He runs out.*)

BERGAMIN (*pursuing him*): Wait until I catch you—!

SYLVETTE: Now I understand why Papa hates that odious old man!

(*Enter* PASQUINOT, *left.*)

PASQUINOT: Well, mademoiselle, what are you doing here?

SYLVETTE: Nothing. Taking the air.

PASQUINOT: Alone? But, you silly girl, are you not afraid?

SYLVETTE: Not in the least.

PASQUINOT: Near this wall? I forbade you to come near it! You see that park over there? That belongs to my greatest enemy!

SYLVETTE: I know it, Father dear.

PASQUINOT: Why, here you are exposed to any insult, any —if those rascals knew that my daughter were walking alone in this park—it makes me shiver to think of it. I'm going to have the wall repaired, and erect a huge iron grill on top.

SYLVETTE (*aside*): He'll never do it—it would cost too much!

PASQUINOT: Now go into the house—quick! (*She goes out,* PASQUINOT *glowering at her.*)

BERGAMIN (*heard from the other side of the wall, as he enters*): Take this note at once to Monsieur Straforel.

PASQUINOT (*running to the wall and climbing to the top of it*): Bergamin!

BERGAMIN (*doing likewise*): Pasquinot! (*They embrace.*)

PASQUINOT: How are you?

BERGAMIN: Pretty well.

PASQUINOT: How's your gout?

BERGAMIN: Better. And how is your cold?

PASQUINOT: The horrible thing still troubles me.

BERGAMIN: Well, the marriage is arranged!

PASQUINOT: What?

BERGAMIN: I heard everything—I was hidden in the bushes. They adore each other!

PASQUINOT: Bravo!

BERGAMIN: We must bring matters to a head. (*He rubs his hands.*) Ha, ha! Now we can do as we had planned—

PASQUINOT: Yes, and tear down the wall.

BERGAMIN: And live together.

PASQUINOT: Joining our properties.

BERGAMIN: By marrying our children. But I wonder whether they would be so anxious if they knew we wished it? A marriage arranged beforehand is not so tempting to two young children so romantic as ours. That is why we had to keep our own wishes a secret. I felt sure that after they had been separated—Sylvette in the convent, Percinet at school —they would thrive on their secret love. That is how I came to invent this hatred of ours. And you even doubted its success! Now all we have to do is to say yes.

PASQUINOT: But how can it be done? Remember, I've called you a scoundrel, fool, idiot—

BERGAMIN: Idiot? Scoundrel was sufficient.

PASQUINOT: Now, what pretext—?

BERGAMIN: Your daughter herself has given me an inspiration. This evening they are to meet here at eight. Percinet comes first. At the moment Sylvette appears, mysterious men in black will emerge from the shadows and start to carry her off. An abduction! She screams, then our young hero gives chase, draws his sword—the ravishers pretend to flee—I arrive on the scene, then you—your daughter is safe and sound. You bless the couple and drop a few appropriate tears; my heart is softened. End of scene.

PASQUINOT: A stroke of genius.

BERGAMIN (*modestly*):   Yes—I think it is. Look—see that man coming? It's Straforel, the professional kidnaper I wrote to a few minutes ago. He is to superintend the abduction.

(STRAFOREL, *in an elaborate swordsman's costume, appears at the back of* BERGAMIN's *park, and swaggers downstage.*)

BERGAMIN (*descending from the wall and bowing low to*

STRAFOREL):   Allow me to introduce you to my friend Pasquinot.

STRAFOREL (*bowing*):   Messieurs! (*He raises his head and sees no* PASQUINOT.)

BERGAMIN (*pointing to* PASQUINOT *on the crest of the wall*):   There, on the wall! Now, my dear master, does my plan meet with your approval?

STRAFOREL: It does. It is most simple.

BERGAMIN: You must act quickly, you understand?

STRAFOREL: And say nothing.

BERGAMIN: A make-believe abduction and stage fight with swords.

STRAFOREL: I understand perfectly.

BERGAMIN: You must have skillful swordsmen—I can't have my boy hurt. He is my only child.

STRAFOREL: I will see to that myself.

BERGAMIN: Good. In that case, I shall fear nothing.

PASQUINOT (*aside to* BERGAMIN):   Ask him the price?

BERGAMIN: For an abduction, maestro, how much do you charge?

STRAFOREL: That depends, monsieur, on the kind you wish; we have them at all prices. In an affair of this kind, however, nothing should be spared. If I were in your place, I should have a first-class abduction.

BERGAMIN (*surprised*):   Then you have many classes?

STRAFOREL: Indeed I have. I have the ordinary vulgar abduction in a cab, with two men dressed in black—that's rarely used; the daylight abduction; the midnight abduction; the pompous abduction in a court carriage, with powdered servants—wigs are extra—with mutes, Nubians, brigands, musketeers, anything you like! The abduction in a post chaise, with two, three, four, five horses, or more if you wish; the discreet and quiet abduction, in a small carriage— that one's rather disappointing; the rollicking abduction, in which the victim is carried away in a sack; the romantic abduction in a boat—but a lake is necessary!—the Venetian abduction, in a gondola—ah, you have no lagoon! Moonlight abduction, or the abduction on a dark and starless night —those moonlight abductions are quite the style, though they are a little expensive! Besides these, there is the abduction by torchlight, with cries and screams, and clash and shock of arms; the brutal abduction, the polite abduction; the classical one with masks; the gallant abduction to the accompaniment of music; but the latest, most stylish, gayest of all, is the sedan-chair abduction!

BERGAMIN (*scratching his head—aside to* PASQUINOT): Well, what do you think?

PASQUINOT: Hm, what do you?

BERGAMIN: I think that we should do everything in the best possible way, no expense spared. Let us give our young fantasy-lovers something they'll not soon forget. Let's have it with masks, dark mantles, torches, music, and a sedan-chair!

STRAFOREL (*taking notes*):   A first-class, then, with all extras.

BERGAMIN: That's it.

STRAFOREL: I shall return soon. (*To* PASQUINOT.) Remember, monsieur, to leave the door of your park open tonight.

BERGAMIN: Very well, it shall be done.

STRAFOREL (*bowing*):   My compliments. (*Turning to go.*) One first-class—with extras. (*He goes out.*)

PASQUINOT: The honest man, he went without telling us the price!

BERGAMIN: Everything is arranged. Now we'll demolish the wall, and live together. A single home!

PASQUINOT: And a single rent!

BERGAMIN: We'll make wonderful improvements to the park.

PASQUINOT: We'll trim the yew trees. . . .

BERGAMIN: And sand the paths. . . .

PASQUINOT: We'll have statues of ourselves, interwined with flowers. . . .

BERGAMIN: And the lawns are too dull. . . .

PASQUINOT: We'll brighten them with crystal bowls. . . .

BERGAMIN: We'll build a new fish pond. . . .

PASQUINOT: And a fountain, with an egg dancing on it. And a rock. . . .

BERGAMIN: Our dearest wishes are realized!

PASQUINOT: And we'll grow old together!

BERGAMIN: Dear old Pasquinot!

PASQUINOT: Dear old Bergamin! (*They embrace.* SYLVETTE *and* PERCINET *enter, from each side of the stage, and see their fathers embrace.*)

SYLVETTE: Oh!

BERGAMIN (*aside to* PASQUINOT):   Your daughter!

PERCINET: Oh!

PASQUINOT (*aside to* BERGAMIN):   Your son!

BERGAMIN (*aside to* PASQUINOT):   Pretend to fight! (*Their embrace is transformed into a struggle.*) Rascal!

PASQUINOT: Fool!

SYLVETTE (*pulling her father's coattails*):   Papa!

PERCINET (*doing the same with his father*):   Papa!

BERGAMIN: Let us be!

PASQUINOT: He insulted me!

BERGAMIN: He struck me!

PASQUINOT: Coward!

SYLVETTE: Papa!

BERGAMIN: Thief!

PERCINET: Papa!

PASQUINOT: Bandit!

SYLVETTE: Papa!! (SYLVETTE and PERCINET finally succeed in separating the fathers.)

PERCINET (dragging his father away):   Go in now, it's late.

BERGAMIN (trying to go to the wall again):   I can't control myself. Just let me—! (PERCINET takes him out.)

PASQUINOT (also trying to return to the wall):   I'll kill him!

SYLVETTE (dragging PASQUINOT out):   The air is so damp! Think of your rheumatism! (They go out.)

(Little by little it grows dark. For a moment the stage is empty. Then, in PASQUINOT's park, enter STRAFOREL and swordsmen, musicians, and torchbearers.)

STRAFOREL: I see one star already. The day is dying. (He places his men about the stage.) Stay there—you there—and you there. The hour is near. You will see, as the clock strikes eight, a figure in white enter on this side. Then I whistle— (He looks at the sky again.) The moon? Splendid! Every effect is perfect tonight! (Examining the costumes of his band.) The capes and mantles are excellent. Look a little more dangerous, over there! Now, ready? (A sedan chair is brought in.) The chair over there in the shade. (Seeing the Nubians who carry the chair.) The Nubians are good! (Speaking at a distance.) Torches, there, you understand you are not to come until you receive the signal? (The faint reflection of the torches is seen at the back of the stage, through the underbrush. Enter the musicians.) Musicians? There—at the back. Now, a little distinction and life! Vary your poses from time to time. Stand straight, mandolin! Sit down, alto! There. (Severely to a swordsman.) You, first mask, don't look so harmless—I want a villainous slouch! Good! Now, instruments, play softly—tune up! Good—tra la la! (He puts on his mask.)

(PERCINET enters slowly from the other side of the stage. As he speaks the following lines, the stage becomes darker, until at the end, it is night.)

PERCINET: My father is calmer now. The day is dying, and the intoxicating odor of the elder blossoms is wafted to me; the flowers close their petals in the gray of the evening—

STRAFOREL (*aside to the violins*): Music! (*The musicians play softly until the end of the act.*)

PERCINET: I tremble like a reed. She is coming!

STRAFOREL (*to the musicians*): Amoroso!

PERCINET: My first evening meeting—I can scarcely stand! The evening breeze sounds like the fluttering of her dress. Now I can't see the flowers, but I can smell them. Ah, this great tree, with a star above it—Music? Who—? (*A pause.*) Night has come. (*After another pause, a clock strikes eight in the distance.* SYLVETTE *appears at the back of her park.*)

SYLVETTE: The hour has struck. He must be waiting.

(*A whistle is heard.* STRAFOREL *rises in front of* SYLVETTE, *and torchbearers appear in the background.* SYLVETTE *screams. The swordsmen seize and put her into the sedan chair.*)

SYLVETTE: Help! Help!

PERCINET: Great Heavens!

SYLVETTE: Percinet, they are carrying me off!

PERCINET (*leaping to the wall*): I am coming! (*When he reaches the top of the wall, he draws his sword, jumps down on the other side, and engages four or five swordsmen in combat. They flee before him.*) There, and there, and there!

STRAFOREL (*to the musicians*): Tremolo. (*The violins now play a dramatic tremolo.*)

STRAFOREL: Per Bacco, he's the devil, that boy. (PERCINET *now engages* STRAFOREL *in a duel.* STRAFOREL, *after a few thrusts, puts his hand to his breast.*) I—I'm mortally wounded! (*He falls.*)

PERCINET (*running to* SYLVETTE, *who sits in the sedan chair*): Sylvette! (*He kneels to her.*)

SYLVETTE: My hero.

PASQUINOT (*entering*): Bergamin's son! Your hero? Your hero? Why, then I give you to him!

SYLVETTE *and* PERCINET: Heavens!

(BERGAMIN *now appears on his side of the wall.*)

PASQUINOT (*to* BERGAMIN, *who is seen on top of the wall*): Bergamin, your son is a hero! Let us forget our quarrels, and make these children happy!

BERGAMIN (*solemnly*):   I no longer hate you.

PERCINET: Sylvette, don't speak loud: I know I ar
dreaming. But don't wake me!

BERGAMIN: Our hatred is ended in the marriage of ou
dear children. (*Indicating the wall.*) Henceforth let there b
no Pyrenees!

PERCINET: Who would have believed that my fathe
could change so!

SYLVETTE: I told you everything would turn out happily

(*While the lovers go upstage with* PASQUINOT, STRAFOREL *rise*
and hands a folded paper to BERGAMIN.)

BERGAMIN (*aside*):   What is it? This paper—your signature? What is it, if you please?

STRAFOREL (*bowing*):   Monsieur, it's my bill! (*He lies*
down again.)

ACT II

(*Scene: The same, except that the wall has disappeared. The benches which were formerly against it are removed to the extreme right and left. There are a few extra pots of flowers and two or three plaster statues. To the right is a small garden table, with chairs about it.*

As the curtain rises, PASQUINOT *is sitting on the bench to the left, reading a paper.* BLAISE *is at the back, busy with his rake.*)

BLAISE: So the notary comes tonight, Monsieur Pasquinot? It is pleasant, now that the wall is down, and you living together this past month. It was high time, I'm thinking. The little lovers must be happy!

PASQUINOT (*raising his head and looking about*): So you like it without the wall, Blaise?

BLAISE: The garden is superb!

PASQUINOT: Yes, my property has increased a hundred per cent! (*Poking a tuft of grass with his foot.*) Have you watered the grass? (*Furiously.*) You have no business doing that during the day!

BLAISE: But Monsieur Bergamin told me to!

PASQUINOT: What a waste! He seems to think that the more grass is watered the better it becomes. Well, take those plants out of the greenhouse. (*As* BLAISE *begins arranging plants which he gets from the greenhouse—just offstage— enter* BERGAMIN *at the back.*)

BERGAMIN (*watering some flowers from a large watering can*): Dear me, these plants never get enough water! (*To a tree.*) Hey there, old man, you never get enough to drink, do you? There's for you! (*Laying down the watering can, he looks about him with satisfaction.*) Yes, it is better now. Very pretty—those statues there are a decided improvement. (*Catching sight of* PASQUINOT.) How are you? (*No answer.*) How are you? How are you? (PASQUINOT *raises his head.*) Well?

PASQUINOT: My friend, why ask that? We see each other all the time!

BERGAMIN: Oh, very well. (*Seeing* BLAISE *arranging the*
389

plants.) Take those plants back! (BLAISE, *not knowing what to do, takes them back immediately.* PASQUINOT *raises his eyes, shrugs his shoulders, and then resumes his reading.* BERGAMIN *walks back and forth, and finally sits down near* PASQUINOT. *There is a pause.*) I used to come here every day in silence—

PASQUINOT (*laying aside his paper*): I, too—it was most enjoyable.

BERGAMIN: The secret!

PASQUINOT: The danger!

BERGAMIN: Enjoyable. . . .

PASQUINOT: Most enjoyable. . . .

BERGAMIN: Climbing upon the wall to talk. . . .

PASQUINOT: Risking our ribs and our limbs. . . .

BERGAMIN: Crawling under bushes. . . .

PASQUINOT: Getting our clothes green. . . .

BERGAMIN: It was enjoyable.

PASQUINOT: Most enjoyable.

BERGAMIN: And the things we had to say about each other—!

PASQUINOT: Very enjoyable—Bergamin?

BERGAMIN: Pasquinot?

PASQUINOT: Something's lacking now.

BERGAMIN: I don't think so. (*After a moment's reflection.*) Yes, I do. Funny—are you losing your sense of the romantic? (*He looks at* PASQUINOT *and says, aside:*) His vest is always one button short. It's disgusting! (*He rises and walks back and forth.*)

PASQUINOT (*looking over his paper—aside*): He looks like some immense beetle. (*He pretends to be reading as* BERGAMIN *passes him.*)

BERGAMIN (*aside*): See the ridiculous way he reads! (*He whistles as he walks away upstage.*)

PASQUINOT (*aside*): Whistling! Oh, Heavens! Don't do that, whistling makes me nervous.

BERGAMIN (*with a smile*): Remember the mote in your neighbor's eye. You get on *my* nerves sometimes.

PASQUINOT: I do?

BERGAMIN: You tell the same story twenty times a day.

PASQUINOT: Why I—

BERGAMIN: And when you sit down you swing your foot like a pendulum. At meals you roll your bread in a most disgusting manner.

PASQUINOT: Ha, you take me to task for my irritating mannerisms! But let me tell you, you are no less unpleasant. You are ridiculous and thoroughly selfish. I know now what the trouble is: the wall—with it, we were happy, now we don't live at all.

BERGAMIN: We didn't do this for ourselves, did we?

PASQUINOT: No, we did not!

BERGAMIN: It was for our children.

PASQUINOT: For our children, yes. Let us therefore suffer in silence, and regret our former liberty.

BERGAMIN: Parents have to make sacrifices.

(SYLVETTE and PERCINET appear at the left, upstage, arm in arm.)

PASQUINOT: —Sh—the lovers!

BERGAMIN (looking at them): See them! How they love each other! Like the old pilgrims of love, they return each day to the sacred spot.

(The lovers, who have meantime disappeared, reappear on the opposite side of the stage, and come down toward the old men.)

PASQUINOT: If they are talking as they usually do, their conversation will be well worth listening to!

(BERGAMIN and PASQUINOT retire behind a tree.)

PERCINET: I love you.

SYLVETTE: I love you. (They stop.) Here is the famous spot.

PERCINET: Yes. He fell here, that big fellow, pierced to the heart.

SYLVETTE: There was I, like Andromeda.

PERCINET: And I was Perseus!

SYLVETTE: How many were there against you?

PERCINET: Ten!

SYLVETTE: Oh, there were twenty at least, not counting the big leader.

PERCINET: Or thirty—there must have been!

SYLVETTE: Tell me once more how you managed it?

PERCINET: They fell—like cards in a row!

SYLVETTE: Our story should be put into a poem!

PERCINET: It shall be.

SYLVETTE: How I love you!

PERCINET: I adore you!

SYLVETTE: A dream come to life! I would never think of marrying a commonplace little husband picked out by my father!

PERCINET: Indeed?

SYLVETTE: No, no, not the way husbands are usual
given to young girls.

PERCINET: No, *you* would never have thought of ma
rying the son of your father's best friend.

SYLVETTE (*laughing*):   Indeed not. Have you noticed ho
bad-tempered our fathers have been lately—?

PERCINET: Yes, like dogs.

BERGAMIN (*aside*):   Hm!

PERCINET: And I know the reason why. This new a
rangement is not the best thing for their property. Our fa
thers are very good people, you know, but they haven'
much soul, and our brilliant adventure puts them in th
shade—

PASQUINOT (*aside*):   How's that?

SYLVETTE: You see, they are fathers of celebrated lovers
Poor fathers, how they have been deceived!

PASQUINOT (*aside*):   Ha, ha!

PERCINET: Yes, Fate has been with us!

BERGAMIN (*aside*):   Ha, ha!

SYLVETTE: And tonight the marriage contract is to be
signed!

PERCINET: I must have musicians.

SYLVETTE: Then go quick.

PERCINET: I'll run.

SYLVETTE (*calling him back*):   I'll take you as far as the
gate. (*They go upstage, arm in arm.*) We are at least as great
as the most celebrated lovers.

PERCINET: We shall take our place with Romeo and
Juliet!

SYLVETTE: Aminta and her shepherd.

PERCINET: Pyramus and Thisbe.

SYLVETTE: And so many others! (*They disappear, but
their voices are heard outside.*)

VOICE OF PERCINET: Francesca and Paolo.

VOICE OF SYLVETTE: Petrarch and Laura.

(BERGAMIN and PASQUINOT emerge.)

PASQUINOT: See how well your plan has succeeded! Our
children are quite mad, thanks to you!

BERGAMIN: Your daughter, with her famous abduction,
is most aggravating.

PASQUINOT: Your son thinks he is a hero. He gets on my
nerves.

BERGAMIN: But the worst of it all is that they think we

are two idiotic old fools whom they have deceived. I don't like it at all.

PASQUINOT: Why didn't you think of it before, wise man? I'm going to tell them everything.

BERGAMIN: No, please don't do that—at least not until after the signing of the contract. Let us not say a word until then.

PASQUINOT: Very well. But meantime, here we are caught in the net of your own making.

BERGAMIN: But my dear friend, you admired the plan!

PASQUINOT: A fine plan it turned out to be.

BERGAMIN (*aside*): He irritates me.

(SYLVETTE *enters gaily, with flowers in her hand. She waves to* PERCINET *in the distance, then comes downstage.*)

SYLVETTE: Good day, Papa. Good-day, Father-in-law-to-be!

BERGAMIN: Good day, daughter-in-law-to-be!

SYLVETTE: My, my, what a bad humor you are in!

BERGAMIN: It's Pasquinot's fault—he—he—

SYLVETTE (*waving her flowers in* BERGAMIN's *face*): Sh! Please don't quarrel. Of course, I understand, you can't behave quite as old friends and you like to quarrel a little, in a friendly way—

BERGAMIN: Of course, our hatred was so great.

SYLVETTE: A mortal hatred, too! When I think what you've said about Papa—oh, dear! I used to sit by the wall and hear every word! And to think you never once suspected that I came there to meet Percinet—

PASQUINOT (*ironically*): Ah, I—

SYLVETTE: We came every day at the same hour. (*To* BERGAMIN.) Ha, ha, I can still hear Percinet telling you that he was going to marry—"most romantically"! And he kept his word!

BERGAMIN (*put out*): Really? And do you think that if I had wished—?

SYLVETTE: Now, now, now! I know lovers' dreams are always realized, and that fathers who are mortal enemies always end by falling into each other's arms.

PASQUINOT: Oh, let me laugh!

SYLVETTE: But we proved it!

BERGAMIN: I could say something—

SYLVETTE: What?

BERGAMIN: Nothing!

SYLVETTE (*to* BERGAMIN): You seem changed. What do you mean?

BERGAMIN: I mean—

PASQUINOT: Why, with one word, we could—(*Aside.*) I can't tell her! (*He walks upstage two or three steps.*)

SYLVETTE: Well, if you have nothing to say, why not keep quiet?

PASQUINOT (*angrily*): Keep quiet? Nothing to say? Do you imagine that everything just happened? How do you think people could come into my park through the iron gates?

BERGAMIN: Do you imagine for one instant that young ladies are carried off like that nowadays?

SYLVETTE: Do I—? What are you saying?

BERGAMIN: That will do! It is high time you knew the truth. I tell you, the victory was on the side of the old men!

SYLVETTE: But—

PASQUINOT: In old plays the father was always the dupe. Nowadays, we do the duping! Would either of you have loved the other if you had been told to do so? No.

SYLVETTE: Then perhaps you suspected—?

PASQUINOT: Of course we did.

SYLVETTE: Our meetings?

BERGAMIN: I heard you every time!

SYLVETTE: But the benches?

PASQUINOT: We put them there on purpose.

SYLVETTE: The duel?

BERGAMIN: A trick—prepared beforehand.

SYLVETTE: The kidnapers?

PASQUINOT: Actors!

SYLVETTE: Then my abduction—? It was all a joke!

BERGAMIN (*searching in his pocket*): Joke? Here's the bill!

SYLVETTE (*snatching the bill from him*): Give it to me! (*She reads.*) "Straforel, Confidential affairs: One abduction, setting and scenery—for purposes of bringing about a marriage—" Oh! "Eight assistants at five francs a head; eight masks—"

BERGAMIN (*to* PASQUINOT): I think we told her too soon!

SYLVETTE (*continuing*): "One sedan chair, with porters; latest style, with red trimmings—" (*Laughing, she throws the bill on the table.*)

PASQUINOT: Then she isn't angry?

SYLVETTE (*graciously*): A charming idea! But, truly, Monsieur Bergamin, do you think I love Percinet merely because of your trick?

PASQUINOT: She takes it very well.

BERGAMIN (*to* SYLVETTE): You're not offended?

PASQUINOT: Are you going to tell Percinet?

SYLVETTE: Oh, no. Men are so stupid!

BERGAMIN: Very sensible. But I had an idea—(*Taking out his watch.*) Now we must see about the contract. (*Offering his hand to* SYLVETTE.) We are still good friends?

SYLVETTE: Of course!

BERGAMIN (*turning about once more before he goes out*): You don't blame me, do you?

SYLVETTE (*sweetly*):   Not in the least! (BERGAMIN *and* PASQUINOT *go out. As they leave,* SYLVETTE *bursts into a rage.*) How I hate that Bergamin!

(*Enter* PERCINET.)

PERCINET: Still here? Ah, I see; you did not want to leave this sacred spot—

SYLVETTE (*sitting on the bench to the left*):   Outrageous!

PERCINET: There is where you saw me, like Amadis, put thirty of the ruffians to flight!

SYLVETTE: No: ten!

PERCINET (*going to her*):   Dearest, what is the matter? Are you troubled? Your eyes are not so bright as they were. I know! This marvelous place makes you sad sometimes. Are you sad because our balcony—our Verona balcony—is destroyed?

SYLVETTE (*impatiently*):   Oh, dear!

PERCINET: But the wall still exists in our memories. That wall which cradled our love—

SYLVETTE (*aside*):   Will he never end!

PERCINET: You remember not long ago, you said our story should be put into a poem?

SYLVETTE: Yes?

PERCINET: Well, I have occasionally written verses.

SYLVETTE: Are you going to write our story?

PERCINET: Listen to this; I thought it out when I was walking. "The Fathers Who Are Mortal Enemies." First canto—

SYLVETTE: Oh!

PERCINET (*ready to declaim*):   Er—

SYLVETTE: Oh!

PERCINET: What is the matter?

SYLVETTE: I imagine I am too happy—I'm nervous—I don't feel well. (*She bursts into tears.*) I'll be fine in a moment. Let me be! (*She turns her back and hides her face in a handkerchief.*)

PERCINET (*surprised*):   I'll leave you for a moment.

(*Aside.*) On a day like this, it's only natural—(*He goes to the right, sees the bill on the table, takes a pencil from his pocket, and sits down.*) I'll just jot down those lines. (*He picks up the bill, and starts to write; notices the writing and reads aloud.*) "I, Straforel, having pretended to be killed by a sword thrust from a foolish young blade, hereby render account for torn clothes and wounded pride: forty francs." (*Smiling.*) What is it? (*He continues reading to himself, and his smile dies away.*)

SYLVETTE (*wiping her eyes*): He *would* fall from the clouds if he knew! I must be careful!

PERCINET (*rising*): Well, well, well!

SYLVETTE (*going toward him*): What is it?

PERCINET (*hiding the bill*): Nothing. (*Aside.*) Now I see why the body was never found!

SYLVETTE (*turning around to show* PERCINET *her dress*): You've said nothing about my dress today?

PERCINET (*preoccupied*): Blue is not becoming. I always prefer you in pink.

SYLVETTE (*aside*): What is the matter? Can he have found out? (*She looks toward the table.*) The bill? (*She runs to the table.*)

PERCINET: What are you looking for?

SYLVETTE: Nothing. Now let me hear your poem.

PERCINET: No.

SYLVETTE: Please!

PERCINET: No.

SYLVETTE: But I want to hear it.

PERCINET: The verses are not good.

SYLVETTE: Oh! (*Aside.*) I think he knows!

PERCINET (*aside*): I think she knows!

BOTH (*each to the other*): You know! (*After a pause, they laugh.*) Ha, ha, ha!

PERCINET: Isn't it funny?

SYLVETTE: Very.

PERCINET: We were made to play a farce—our fathers were the best of friends all the time!

SYLVETTE: Good neighbors.

PERCINET: I'll wager they are cousins, too!

SYLVETTE (*bowing*): I am about to marry my cousin!

PERCINET: My cousin!

SYLVETTE: How nice and respectable!

PERCINET: Classic!

SYLVETTE: Of course, I had dreamed of a more romantic marriage—but it is comforting to know that our love coincides with our—duty!

PERCINET: And the material interests of our fathers.

SYLVETTE: An excellent marriage, in short: a marriage of convenience! And our poor idyll!

PERCINET: Gone!

SYLVETTE: Gone! So I'm the good little girl of the family!

PERCINET: And I the obedient little son! But it was only as Romeo that I appealed to you!

SYLVETTE: Well, you are no longer that!

PERCINET: And do you think you are Juliet?

SYLVETTE: Now you're bitter.

PERCINET: And you cynical.

SYLVETTE: If you were ridiculous, it is my fault?

PERCINET: I at least had a partner!

SYLVETTE: I, too! Poor Blue Bird, you are beautifully plucked!

PERCINET (*bitterly*):   A prearranged abduction!

SYLVETTE: Farce, all of it!

PERCINET: And I your hero! All our poetry was bought and paid for. Our beautiful bubble is now a tiny fleck of soap. Farewell, Shakespearean lovers—we have nothing in common with you!

SYLVETTE: Nothing!

PERCINET: In place of a divine drama, we played an infamous parody.

SYLVETTE: Our nightingale was a sparrow!

PERCINET: And the immortal wall a Punch-and-Judy theater. We were the puppets, worked by our fathers.

SYLVETTE: But how much more ridiculous we should be if we loved each other less than we do!

PERCINET: We must now love more than ever.

SYLVETTE: But we do—we adore—

PERCINET: The word is not a bit too strong.

SYLVETTE: Love can console us. Can it not, my treasure?

PERCINET: Certainly, my jewel.

SYLVETTE: Good-by then, my dearest.

PERCINET: Good-by, my darling.

SYLVETTE: I shall dream of you, my heart.

PERCINET: And I of you.

SYLVETTE: Good night. (*She goes out.*)

PERCINET: So this is how I have been treated!—But who is this? See the long mustaches—I don't know him—

(STRAFOREL *enters and walks majestically toward* PERCINET.)

STRAFOREL (*with a profound bow*): I have come to collect a small bill.

PERCINET: Are you an upholsterer?

STRAFOREL: Run along, young man, and tell your papa I am waiting for him.

PERCINET: What is your name?

STRAFOREL: My name is Straforel.

PERCINET (*with a start*): This is too much!

STRAFOREL (*smiling*): Then you know, young man?

PERCINET (*throwing the bill in* STRAFOREL's *face*): Wretch! It was you!

STRAFOREL: It was, per Bacco!

PERCINET: I have you at last.

STRAFOREL: The people you kill, you see, are in the best of health.

PERCINET (*drawing his sword and making a pass at* STRAFOREL): You will see!

STRAFOREL (*parrying with his arm, like a fencing master giving a lesson*): Hand high! Foot out! Monsieur, at your age, you should know better than that! (*He takes the sword from* PERCINET *with his naked hand, and returns it as he bows.*) What, are you stopping your fencing lesson so soon?

PERCINET (*exasperated, as he takes back the sword*): I'm going away. Here I am treated like a child. I shall have my revenge. I am going to seek my romance—true romance: love affairs, duels, and—ah, Don Juan, I will scandalize your ghost! I will elope with actresses! (*He dashes out, brandishing his sword.*)

STRAFOREL: Very well, but who is going to pay me? (*Looking in the distance.*) Stop there! Here's someone else.

(*Enter* BERGAMIN *and* PASQUINOT, *their hair and clothes ruffled, as if they had been fighting.*)

PASQUINOT (*readjusting his clothes and holding* BERGAMIN's *wig*): Here's your wig!

BERGAMIN: And here's yours!

PASQUINOT: After this, you can't imagine I'll—?

BERGAMIN: I would no more live with you now than—

(*Enter* SYLVETTE.)

PASQUINOT: My daughter!—Say nothing about this!

SYLVETTE (*throwing her arms about her father's neck*): Papa, I can't marry Percinet!

(*Enter the* NOTARY *and four witnesses.*)

BERGAMIN: The witnesses!
WITNESSES: What—?
STRAFOREL (*in the midst of the tumult*):   My bill! Who is going to pay me? Ninety pistoles!

(*Enter the* GUESTS *and three* FIDDLERS, *who play.*)

BERGAMIN: What's all this? The guests? Music?

(*The* FIDDLERS *continue their minuet.*)

STRAFOREL (*to* BERGAMIN):   Well?
BERGAMIN: See Pasquinot.
STRAFOREL (*reading*):   "For the purpose of bringing about a marriage—"
BERGAMIN: Well, there is to be no marriage! Therefore I owe you nothing!

(*Enter* BLAISE.)

STRAFOREL (*to* PASQUINOT):   But, monsieur—
PASQUINOT: What? Pay you now that it is broken off!
BERGAMIN (*to whom* BLAISE *has just whispered*):   My son —run away?
SYLVETTE: Run away?
STRAFOREL: Well! Well!
BERGAMIN: Quick, follow him! (*He runs out, followed by the* NOTARY *and the witnesses.*)
SYLVETTE: Gone!
STRAFOREL (*coming downstage*):   Why can't I straighten all this out?
SYLVETTE: This is too much! (*She goes out, followed by* PASQUINOT.)
STRAFOREL: Straforel, my son, if you want your ninety pistoles, you must patch up this marriage! (*He goes out. The three* FIDDLERS, *left alone, continue their minuet.*)

ACT III

(*Scene: The scene is the same except that the wall is being rebuilt. Bricks and sacks of plaster lie about.*

As the curtain rises, the BRICKLAYER *is seen at work with his trowel. His back is turned to the audience.* BERGAMIN *and* PASQUINOT, *each on his own side of the wall, watch the progress of the work.*)

THE BRICKLAYER (*singing at his work*): Tra la la—
BERGAMIN: These masons are so slow!
PASQUINOT: Good! It's getting higher.
BERGAMIN: How he slaps the mortar!
PASQUINOT: There goes another brick!

(THE BRICKLAYER *sings a number of trills.*)

PASQUINOT: Sings well, but works very slowly! By to-morrow the wall will be at least two feet high!
BERGAMIN: I'm impatient to see it higher!
PASQUINOT: What is that you say, monsieur?
BERGAMIN: I was not addressing you. (*A pause.*) What do you do evenings after dinner?
PASQUINOT: Nothing—and you?
BERGAMIN: Nothing. (*Another pause. They bow and walk about again.*)
PASQUINOT (*stopping*): Any news from your son?
BERGAMIN: No—he is still away.
PASQUINOT: He will return soon: his money will surely give out.
BERGAMIN: Thank you. (*They bow again, and walk.*)
PASQUINOT: Now that the wall is being built again, monsieur, I should be glad to see you from time to time.
BERGAMIN: Thank you. Perhaps I shall come. (*They bow.*)
PASQUINOT: Tell me, now, will you play piquet?
BERGAMIN: I beg your pardon—I don't know—
PASQUINOT: I invite you!
BERGAMIN: To tell the truth, I prefer *bésigue*—
PASQUINOT: Then come at once.

BERGAMIN (*following* PASQUINOT, *who goes out*):   You owe me ten sous from the last time. (*Turning round.*) Work hard, bricklayer!

THE BRICKLAYER: Tra la la la la!

PASQUINOT: Beautiful voice! (*They disappear.*)

(*When they are gone, the* BRICKLAYER *turns round, and takes off his hat: he is* STRAFOREL.)

STRAFOREL: Now for the work of reconstruction! (*He sits down on the row or two of bricks.*) The young man is still off on his quest for adventure and romance. Life must be washing away his illusions and simplicity. I can see him as he returns, his tail between his legs. Now I am working on Sylvette—she, too, will soon be cured. (*He takes a letter from his pocket and puts it in the hollow of a tree trunk.* SYLVETTE *appears at the back.*) Here she is. Now to work!

SYLVETTE (*looking anxiously about*):   Not a soul. (*She lays her muslin scarf on the bench to the left.*) Will the letter be there today as usual? (*She goes toward the tree.*) Every day a certain gallant gentleman leaves one for me. (*She thrusts her hand into the hollow.*) Ah, here is my mail! (*She takes the letter, opens it, and reads.*) "Sylvette, heart of marble, this is the last letter you will find in this tree. Why have you not answered me?" Ah, what style! "The love that gnaws at my vitals!" Monsieur Percinet has gone forth into the great romantic world, and he is right. I shall do as he has done. How can I possibly stay here and die of boredom? Now let this man who writes me such beautiful letters appear. I am ready to fly with him! I almost love him already!

STRAFOREL (*rising from his work, and in a voice of thunder*):   Here I am!

SYLVETTE (*screaming*):   Help! Percinet! Man, not another step!

STRAFOREL (*gallantly*):   Why this hostile attitude? I am the man whose letters you love, whose words have had the honor of pleasing you, and upon whose love you just called. Come, fly with me!

SYLVETTE (*not knowing what to do*):   A man!

STRAFOREL: You think I am a bricklayer? Charming! Know, then, that I am the Marquis D'Astafiorquercita. My heart is languishing for you. I seek to color my drab existence with a few pigments from your own. I must travel— but with you. That is why I have penetrated into your garden, disguised as a workman! (*He throws off his workman's clothes and hat, and appears in a dazzling costume. His wig is powdered and his mustache bristles.*)

SYLVETTE: Monsieur!

STRAFOREL: I learned your story from a man named Straforel. I felt at once a mad, unreasoning love for the victim of that unfortunate affair.

SYLVETTE: Marquis!

STRAFOREL: Don't be afraid of me. That fellow who played the trick on you—I killed him!

SYLVETTE: Killed him!

STRAFOREL: With a single blow!

SYLVETTE: Monsieur!

STRAFOREL: I understand you, you who have never been understood. You want romance, do you not? Romance at any price?

SYLVETTE: But, Marquis—

STRAFOREL: Tonight we elope!

SYLVETTE: Monsieur!

STRAFOREL: We shall go away, never to return.

SYLVETTE: Monsieur!

STRAFOREL: My dream is realized. You consent! Tonight! If your father objects, so much the worse for him!

SYLVETTE: Monsieur!

STRAFOREL: Let them follow us—I know how to deal with pursuers. In some far land, at last, we shall live happily in a little cottage!

SYLVETTE: But I—

STRAFOREL: For I am poor. I have nothing. We shall live on bread soaked in sweet tears!

SYLVETTE: But, I tell you—

STRAFOREL: We shall thrive on misfortune—with you I shan't care for anything else. A tent, perhaps—

SYLVETTE: A tent?

STRAFOREL: Or nothing at all—just the stars!

SYLVETTE: Oh, I—

STRAFOREL: Why, you're trembling—possibly you don't want to go so far away? Then we shall hide somewhere—

SYLVETTE: But, monsieur, you are mistaken!

STRAFOREL: Let people say what they will!

SYLVETTE: Good heavens!

STRAFOREL: I shall spend every moment of my time telling you how I love you!

SYLVETTE: Monsieur—

STRAFOREL: Ours shall be a long life of poetry. And I shall be furiously jealous!

SYLVETTE: Monsieur—

STRAFOREL: Are you afraid now?

SYLVETTE: Heavens, what a lesson for me!

STRAFOREL: Ha, now you look like a little boarding-school miss. Tell me, shall we fly together, or shall I go alone?

SYLVETTE: Monsieur—

STRAFOREL: I understand. I see you are strong: we shall go together. I shall throw you across my saddle. No sedan chair—they are used only in make-believe abductions! I return soon! (*He goes upstage.*)

SYLVETTE: Monsieur, let me tell you—

STRAFOREL: I must get my horse and my mantle!

SYLVETTE (*deeply distressed*):   Monsieur!!

STRAFOREL (*with a sweeping gesture*):   We shall travel from land to land. My dream at last. I shall return and take you away, never to return!

SYLVETTE (*gasping*):   Never to return!

STRAFOREL: You shall live by the side of your adored one, by the side of him who loved you before he set eyes on you. (*As he is about to leave, she falls onto the bench, and he says aside.*) It's now time for you, Percinet! (*He goes out.*)

SYLVETTE (*opening her eyes after a moment*):   Monsieur le marquis—no, not across the saddle, please. I couldn't do that! Please, please let me stay home. I *am* a little boarding-school miss! Why—he's gone! Marquis! Heavens, what an awful dream! (*Another pause, then she rises.*) Romance? Was it not romance that you craved not so long ago? It has come, and are you afraid? Love, stars, a cottage. Yes, I did want it—but only a little—like seasoning in a stew! This is too much—I couldn't stand it. (*The sun is setting.* SYLVETTE *takes up her scarf, which she had left on the bench, and puts it over her head.*) Who knows whether—?

(PERCINET *appears. He is in rags, and his arm is in a sling. He looks ill, and can scarcely walk.*)

PERCINET (*not seeing* SYLVETTE):   I have had nothing to eat since yesterday—I can hardly walk. I'm not proud now! I want no more adventures. (*He sits down on the wall. His hat falls from his eyes, and reveals his identity.* SYLVETTE *sees him.*)

SYLVETTE: You?! (*He rises, and stands looking at her.*) What has happened to you? Can it be—?

PERCINET (*piteously*):   It can!

SYLVETTE (*wringing her hands*):   Heavens!

PERCINET: I resemble the prodigal son, do I not? (*He totters.*)

SYLVETTE: You can't stand up!

PERCINET: I am so tired.

SYLVETTE (*looking at his arm—with a cry*):   Wounded!

PERCINET: Can you pity the ungrateful?

SYLVETTE (*severely*):   Only fathers kill fatted calves. Still, that wounded arm?

PERCINET: Oh, I assure you it's not serious.

SYLVETTE: But what have you been doing, Monsieur Vagabond, all this while!

PERCINET: Nothing very creditable, Sylvette. (*He coughs.*)

SYLVETTE: You are coughing?

PERCINET: Walking the damp roads at night.

SYLVETTE: What strange clothes you have!

PERCINET: Mine were stolen, and the thieves left me these.

SYLVETTE (*ironically*):   How many fortunes did you find?

PERCINET: Sylvette, please say nothing about that.

SYLVETTE: You must have scaled many a balcony?

PERCINET (*aside*):   I nearly broke my neck once!

SYLVETTE: Guitar in hand! And what nocturnes and serenades you must have sung!

PERCINET: Which earned for me more than one bucket of water!

SYLVETTE: But I see you have been wounded in a real duel?

PERCINET: It came near being mortal.

SYLVETTE: And now you return to us—?

PERCINET: Thoroughly worn out.

SYLVETTE: Yes, but you have at least found romance and poetry?

PERCINET: No—I was looking into the distance for what was here all the time. Don't make fun of me: I adore you!

SYLVETTE: Even after our disillusion?

PERCINET: What difference does that make?

SYLVETTE: But our fathers played an abominable trick on us.

PERCINET: What of it? What I feel in my heart is real.

SYLVETTE: They pretended to hate each other.

PERCINET: Did we pretend that we loved?

SYLVETTE: The wall was a Punch-and-Judy theater—you said so yourself.

PERCINET: I did, Sylvette, but it was blasphemy. Ah, wall, you gave us a divine setting, with moonlight and stars, flowers and vines, the four winds for music, and Shakespeare for prompter! Yes, our fathers made us go through the motions, but it was Love that made us speak: *it* pulled the strings.

SYLVETTE (*sighing*): That's true, but we loved because we believed it was wicked.

PERCINET: And it was! Only the intention counts, and thinking we were guilty, we were.

SYLVETTE: Really?

PERCINET: Really. It was wrong of us to love.

SYLVETTE (*seating herself beside him*): Very wrong? (*She changes her tone, as she rises and goes away.*) Still, I wish the danger had been a little more real.

PERCINET: It *was* real, because we believed it so.

SYLVETTE: No: my abduction, like your duel, was false.

PERCINET: Was your fear false? If you were afraid then, it was as if you were really being abducted.

SYLVETTE: No, the dear remembrance is gone. All those masks and torches, the soft music, the duel; it is too cruel to think that Straforel prepared it all.

PERCINET: But who prepared the spring night? Was that Straforel? Did he also sprinkle the sky with stars? Did he plant roses, did he create the gray of evening and the blue mists of night? Did he have anything to do with the rising of that huge pink star?

SYLVETTE: No, of course—

PERCINET: Was it his doing that we were two children of twenty, on a spring night, and that we loved each other? We loved, that was the charm—all the charm!

SYLVETTE: All the—? That's true, yet—

PERCINET: A tear? Am I—forgiven?

SYLVETTE: I have always loved you, my poor dear.

PERCINET: At last I have you again! (*He takes* SYLVETTE's *scarf and plays with it.*) What beautiful shades and lights in this gorgeous satin.

SYLVETTE: What satin?

PERCINET: Oh, nothing! Nothing!

SYLVETTE: But it's only muslin!

PERCINET (*kneeling and kissing her hand*): I love it and I'm afraid to soil it with a kiss. It's a breath of air, the flutter of a wing, a snowflake, a thought—it is you.

SYLVETTE (*falling into his arms*): See? I know now that poetry and romance are in the hearts of lovers; they have nothing to do with other things.

PERCINET: That is true, Sylvette. I have seen what ought to be poetry and romance, but it wasn't—to me!

SYLVETTE: And what was prepared for and arranged be
forehand was real, though it was contrived for us by others
PERCINET: We can weave realities on a false frame.
SYLVETTE: How foolish we were to seek elsewhere for
romance, when it was our own hearts!

(STRAFOREL *appears, followed by the two fathers, and*
shows them SYLVETTE *and* PERCINET *in each other's arms.*)

STRAFOREL: Ah!
BERGAMIN: My son! (*He embraces* PERCINET.)
STRAFOREL: Now do I get my money?
PASQUINOT (*to his daughter*):   Do you love him?
SYLVETTE: Yes.
STRAFOREL (*to* BERGAMIN):   Shall I have my money?
BERGAMIN: You shall.
SYLVETTE (*trembling as she hears* STRAFOREL's *voice and*
recognizes it):   But—that—voice—the Marquis D'Asta—
fior—
STRAFOREL (*bowing*):   —quercita. Yes, my dear mademoi-
selle. 'Tis Straforel. Pardon my excessive zeal. I have at least
taught you how tiresome and hollow and useless real ad-
ventures are. You might, like this young man, have had your
share, but I allowed you to see them in prospect through the
magic lantern of my imagination.
PERCINET: What is this?
SYLVETTE (*quickly*):   Nothing, nothing. I love you!
BERGAMIN (*pointing to the wall*):   And tomorrow we shall
knock down these few rows of bricks!
PASQUINOT: Yes, away with the cement, the bricks, and
the sand.
STRAFOREL: No, let us finish our explanation.
SYLVETTE (*gathering them all about her*):   Better still, let's
all dance. (*They dance.*)

GIRAUDOUX: *Song of Songs*

JEAN GIRAUDOUX (1882–1944)

With a curious mixture of defiance and reverence, Giraudoux often wrote about Bellac, the tiny town in the Haute-Vienne where he was born, although he lived there for only two years. His father was a minor civil servant, who worked under an engineer on the construction and upkeep of bridges and dams in that area, and when Giraudoux Senior was moved from one job to another his wife and two sons (Hippolyte-Jean was the younger) naturally went with him. Jean attended a number of different schools, culminating in the Lycée de Châteauroux, where he won prizes for Latin, Greek, French, and history, and for running, his favorite sport. (Later, at college, he would win the four-hundred-meter dash in the record time of fifty seconds.)

He left Châteauroux, having passed his *baccalauréat*, in 1900, prepared himself for college by studying at the Lycée Lakanal (named after the great French scholar Joseph Lakanal) in Paris, where he became interested in German literature; then went into military training for the statutory year, in the 298th Infantry Regiment. He was released with the rank of reserve sergeant. In 1902 he passed the difficult entrance examination for the highly reputed École Normale Supérieure, which he later called "the true Academy, the Academy of Plato, the Academy of life's beginning." After studying at the Normale Supérieure for two years (1903–05), he traveled to Germany, Italy, and southeastern Europe on a summer scholarship, staying for a long spell in Munich, reading and writing fitfully in German, preparing a thesis, and covering small assignments for the newspaper *Le Figaro*.

Once the thesis was written, in Paris, he went to Germany for another summer sojourn, which gave him a chance to see Prague—then part of Bohemia; there was no Czechoslovakia yet—and Dresden.

Giraudoux's next move was a distant one. He was appointed junior lecturer at Harvard University. He crossed the Atlantic eagerly, taught for nine leisurely months, became fluent in English, learned to bid at bridge, visited cities beyond the edges of New England (Montreal, Ottawa, Quebec, New York, Niagara Falls), and spent great quantities of money on clothes and luggage.

Back in Paris in 1907, he wrote a number of articles and stories and worked as an editor, but was fired from the literary page of *Le Matin* after publishing stories that annoyed the readers. His own first collection of stories was published by Grasset under the title *Provinciales* and sold thirty copies in the four years after publication but was favorably reviewed by André Gide. Giraudoux, who was not earning enough to support his stylish apartment on the Rue de Condé, took more entrance examinations, this time for the diplomatic service, and came out at the head of the list, just as he had done on his graduation from the Normale Supérieure. He was appointed to the foreign press section on the Quai d'Orsay, where he stayed, with minor promotions, until he was called back into his regiment in August 1914, on the outbreak of World War I.

During combat he was injured by a small piece of shrapnel and sent to a hospital in Bordeaux, where he was decorated. Soon after he had recovered, he went to the Dardanelles, was wounded a second time, in the leg, and had to undergo two operations. In July 1915, Giraudoux became the first French writer to win the Legion of Honor for wartime courage. He saw no more action during the war. He was sent by the Quai d'Orsay first to Portugal, in 1916, and from April to August of 1917 back to Harvard with an officer contingent, to train American boys.

He was discharged early in 1918 and promptly married Suzanne Boland. In the early postwar years Giraudoux rejoined the diplomatic service and rose to become head of his department by 1922, the year in which he also published *Siegfried et le Limousin*, the second (and most complex) in a burst of five novels (1921–27). This book, a deft compound of word- and idea-punning, allusions, satire, lyricism, and comparisons between postwar France and Germany, won Giraudoux a Balzac Prize and recognition as a major—if controversial—literary figure. It also served six years later to propel him to the front rank of French dramatists.

For this was the plot that Giraudoux chose, at the age of forty-five, to adapt into *Siegfried*, his first play. In the years that separated *Siegfried et le Limousin*, novel, from *Siegfried*, play, Giraudoux wrote three more novels and served in the French embassy in Berlin and as a commissioner of Allied war reparations in Turkey.

In 1928 he met Louis Jouvet. He had just completed the play of *Siegfried* which, according to a friend, was long enough to provide three continuous evenings of theater. Jouvet seized on the play, worked intensively on it with the author and, after six rewrites, staged it at his theater, the Comédie des Champs Élysées, on May 3, 1928, with four great performers in the leading roles: himself, Michel Simon, Valentine Tessier, and Pierre Renoir. *Siegfried* exploded during a lull in French theater activity. It paled the commercial efforts of Henri Bernstein, the watery naturalism of Jean-Jacques Bernard, the psycho-philosophical melodramas of Gabriel Marcel, and the odds and ends by Sacha Guitry and others.

Eighteen months later, in the same theater, Giraudoux and Jouvet surpassed *Siegfried*, both artistically and in public and critical acclaim, with their production of *Amphitryon 38*, a new version of the old myth, according to which Jupiter descends from Olympus disguised as the general Amphitryon and shares the latter's bed for a night with his wife, Alcmena. (The result of the union was the demigod Hercules.) Molière wrote a broad comedy in verse on the same theme in 1668. The treatment by Giraudoux, 261 years later, was lighter, perhaps flimsier, but with a great deal more surface glitter, sharper speculative discourse, and more verbal trickery.

And so down through the Thirties, Giraudoux established and reasserted himself as far and away the most talented playwright in France. Serious dramas (*Judith, Tessa, Tiger at the Gates, Electra*) and comedies (*Intermezzo, The Improvisation in Paris*) followed one another to theater after theater: the Pigalle, the Comédie des Champs Élysées, the Athénée and, in October 1938, with *Song of Songs*, to the Comédie-Française, (He had been offered the directorship of the Comédie two years earlier but had refused it.) He traveled widely during these years, holding increasingly higher diplomatic ranks.

In 1939, after war was declared, Giraudoux became minister of information under Daladier. He left this post the following year when France was defeated, and retired to Cusset. Two of his plays were produced during the war, *The Apollo of Bellac*, directed by Jouvet (who had taken his troupe to South America) and staged in Rio de Janeiro, and *Sodom and Gomorrha*. In January 1944, three months after the opening of *Sodom*, his only bitter play, Giraudoux died of uremia, in Paris. His two last plays were produced posthumously: *The Madwoman of Chaillot*, ironically the most successful of his dramas both in Paris and abroad, and *For*

Lucrezia (Duel of Angels), which Mme. Giraudoux would not release for production before 1953; *For Lucrezia* was directed by Jean-Louis Barrault (Jouvet had died fifteen months earlier) and starred Edwige Feuillère, Madeleine Renaud, and Yvonne de Bray.

A LIST OF GIRADOUX'S PLAYS:

Siegfried (1928); *Amphitryon 38* (1929); *Judith* (1931); *Intermezzo,* translated as *The Enchanted* (1933); *Tessa,* an adaptation of Margaret Kennedy's novel *The Constant Nymph* (1934); *End of Siegfried* (1934); *The Trojan War Will Not Take Place,* translated as *Tiger at the Gates* (1935); *Supplement to Cook's Voyage* (1937); *Electra* (1937); *The Improvisation in Paris* (also 1937); *Song of Songs* (1938); *Ondine* (1939); *The Apollo of Bellac* (1942); *Sodom and Gomorrha* (1943); *The Madwoman of Chaillot* (performed and published in 1945); *For Lucrezia,* translated as *Duel of Angels* (performed and published in 1953).

SUGGESTIONS FOR FURTHER READING ON GIRAUDOUX:

Inskip, Donald. *Jean Giraudoux; the Making of a Dramatist.* New York: Oxford University Press, 1958.

LeSage, Laurent. *Jean Giraudoux, His Life and Works.* University Park, Pa.: Pennsylvania State University Press, 1959.

The Tulane Drama Review, Giraudoux issue, Summer 1959.

IN FRENCH ONLY:

Cocteau, Jean. *Souvenir de Giraudoux.* Haumont, 1946.

Jouvet, Louis. "Dans les yeux de Giraudoux," in *Pages Françaises,* No. 2, 1945.

Marker, Chris. *Giraudoux par lui-même.* Editions du Seuil, 1959.

NOTE: A critical essay on Giraudoux, "Thoughts on *Song of Songs,*" by Robert Kemp, will be found on p. 558.

SONG OF SONGS

By Jean Giraudoux

First performed at the Comédie-Française in 1938

Translated by John Raikes

CHARACTERS

PRESIDENT
VICTOR, *a waiter*
CASHIER
JEROME, *a young man*
FLORENCE, *a young woman*
CHAUFFEUR
PAGE
THE JEWEL SPIRIT
TWO GIPSIES

(Fine open-air terrace of a luxury café beside the Seine or in the Bois de Boulogne at four o'clock on a beautiful October afternoon. The waiter, VICTOR, and the girl from the cash desk are looking out. Enter the PRESIDENT.)

PRESIDENT: Which table do you recommend, waiter?

VICTOR: Whichever you like.

PRESIDENT: Is the tea good here?

VICTOR: No idea. I drink beer.

PRESIDENT: When you see a young lady, show her to my table, please. The most charming of young ladies.

VICTOR: Charming young ladies find their own way about here quite well by themselves. . . . *(Going away.)*

PRESIDENT: Waiter! (VICTOR *turns round.*) Come here. *(The waiter approaches. The PRESIDENT speaks quietly.)* You know you have no right to speak to customers like that!

VICTOR: I speak to them as they speak to me.

PRESIDENT: I have come here today, because I need an hour away from the world, above the world; a balcony of calm and peace to look down from, a terrace of well-being. And look at the terrace you're offering me!

VICTOR: I sprinkled the sawdust. That's as far as my job goes.

PRESIDENT: But listen, my friend, are all you waiters as narrow-minded as that? . . . No! You won't shut me up. I'm well-known to be the most obstinate orator in Europe! . . . Must you all go on misunderstanding what your customers are to you and you to them? Will your union realize in the end that the finest café—yours if you like—is in the last resort no more than a meeting place—let me speak!—a meeting place between the waiter and the customer? What do you think customers look for in a café? It isn't your coffee, which is always filthy—I insist upon silence!—it's you! . . . The sight of their regular waiter—yet God knows you're not handsome. . . .

VICTOR: Sir!

PRESIDENT: No! I'm speaking!

CASHIER *(who, during this scene, has been climbing into a high cash desk with all the care of an old lady on the steps of a bus)*: The gentleman is speaking. Let him go on. He is speaking in general terms. And anyway you in particular, you're no Apollo. The sight of their waiter . . .

PRESIDENT: Thank you. A glimpse of their regular waiter can more easily drag them from their homes than all the stars in the cinema. Bankers, novelists, colonels—they all say to themselves: "I've dined enough with gentlemen, with politicians, with industrialists; I'll go to my own café. There at least I shall be alone, alone with Isidore, or René, or Gustave. . . ." What is your name?

VICTOR: Victor . . . . But . . . my dear sir . . .

CASHIER: His name is really Charles. But the manager's name is Charles too. Every time Victor—when he was called Charles—got an order, the manager turned round too. That was bad for his prestige. . . . So we called him Victor.

PRESIDENT: It's a good name. It means victorious. And they all come, Victor!

CASHIER: The real Victor was run over six months ago. . . . Just after his villa at Maisons-Laffitte was burned down. . . . Excuse me, sir: and they all come, Victor. . . .

PRESIDENT: Thank you. . . . Yes, they come, Victor! And at last they achieve their minute of happiness, of peace, of interlude before they go back to their various duties—their careers, their homes, perhaps the cares of the nation. Yet God knows you serve them badly. You wipe your foreheads with the napkin you have for wiping the glasses. Coffee is always slopped into the saucer. Cups of chocolate swim with tea leaves. You give the chessboard to those who want to play bridge, the checkerboard arrives when they want a game of belote. And yet they love you. All the reserve of good humor cunningly stolen from their families, all the inner kindliness which they have managed to preserve after all the world's crises and disasters—they keep all of this for this meeting with you, a meeting as speechless but as passionate as that of Tristan and Yseult—(turning to the CASHIER) am I not right?—in which their only words are your Christian names and the name of whatever potion you give them to drink.

CASHIER: Not everything you say is quite accurate, sir. The glasses are wiped in the kitchen. If the waiter wipes them again, it is on his own responsibility and with his own linen. But the comparison with Tristan and Yseult is inevitable and right. It is the truth itself.

VICTOR: My dear sir, there must be a misunderstanding then. Speaking for us, the waiters, I can only say that we do not love our customers—I mean our regular customers—we adore them! How else do you think we manage to stick it all our lives giving out drinks when we're not thirsty and sandwiches when we're not hungry? We have as many talents as the rest of you, sir. There's a waiters' academy. Some of us have degrees. I should have made an excellent life-saver. I can't swim, but in life-saving it's coolness which counts, not swimming. No, instead of painting or life-saving we stay down among the crowd, the screaming, swearing, sweating crowd, because we know we shall see the faces of our regular customers, each in its turn, at its proper time and in its proper place, seeming to come out of the walls. . . .

CASHIER: They aren't always so handsome either, M. le Président, sir. Thanks to them we know what baldness looks like above the face we love, or a sallow complexion, or spots, or pockmarks.

VICTOR: But they are really there! . . . They revive the taste in all these concoctions that are so stale for us. *They* are our refreshing draught at dawn, our midday brandy, our cooling drink at evening. When we meet, our exchange is only little words, looks, smiles, but we love them, M. le Président, we love them, and a café without regular customers —the cashier will confirm this—is like a church without chapels.

CASHIER: Without saints, he means. His simile is less exact than yours, sir.

VICTOR: I mean without its saints, do I? Of course I do! But they are saints who never tell us their first names, sir, and often, on the days when we are sad for some reason, we long to know them!

CASHIER: I know only one or two.

VICTOR: So all I can do is call you M. le Président—at a guess, just from what you look like. You are a president or chairman or director—there can be no mistake. But whether you're director of a company, chairman of a council or president of the Republic I have no idea! If I am wrong, remember it was only meant as a compliment.

PRESIDENT: You are quite right, Victor—that is just what I am called. . . . Well, why wouldn't you speak to me just now?

VICTOR: Because you weren't a regular, M. le Président. Now you are. Put your three questions again. You'll see if we don't make you a balcony of well-being!

PRESIDENT: Which table do you recommend, Victor?

VICTOR: Not the one where you are, sir. That's the quarreling table. Take number two.

CASHIER: Especially if you're expecting a woman. At number two they are gentle and kind. The auditor explained to me once that it's a question of the light there. At that table the light strikes aslant on their cheeks. So they're gentle.

PRESIDENT: Why not the table under the lime?

VICTOR: Number nine? I shouldn't advise number nine, sir. That one we call the accursed table.

CASHIER: When there's a suicide in the neighborhood, you always find he came and had his last drink at number nine.

VICTOR: He usually pays for it.

CASHIER: Come now, M. le Président. I can see quite well what you're looking for. We have it too sometimes, your state of mind, poor as we are. You want a table where everything will be easy, simple, don't you?

VICTOR: And extraordinary?

PRESIDENT: Yes, just that.

CASHIER: Where nature will be on your side, from its leaves to its roots, where vulgarity, from its hair to its toes, will have no place?

VICTOR: Where life will be a game and a blessing—as it ought to be, sir, and too often is not?

CASHIER: Where you will feel young and handsome?

PRESIDENT: Yes, if possible.

VICTOR: Take number two, M. le Président.

CASHIER: Take number two.

VICTOR: I promise you the only place for you here is number two.

CASHIER: I often sit down myself during slack hours at number two; just to wait. And yet I have nothing to wait for. (*The* PRESIDENT *sits down at number two.*)

PRESIDENT: All right, let's take number two! . . . Is the tea good here, Victor?

VICTOR: Not so good as in China, better than across the road.

PRESIDENT: If you see the most charming of young ladies, Victor, show her at once to my table!

VICTOR: She won't get lost, M. le Président. I'll carry her if necessary.

PRESIDENT: Carry her gently. . . . She is all my joy.

(*Enter* JEROME.)

JEROME: Are you waiting for Florence, sir?

PRESIDENT: Yes, I am waiting for Florence.

JEROME: Allow me to introduce myself. I am Jerome.

PRESIDENT: Delighted   to   make   your   acquaintance. Though I don't quite see the connection between those two Christian names.

JEROME: You'll soon see it. It's an intimate one—the most intimate. Only a hyphen separates them. I'm her fiancé.

PRESIDENT: Florence is to be married!

JEROME: The banns are already up.

PRESIDENT: I congratulate you. . . . You are to marry the most charming lady alive.

JEROME: Thank you. Yes, Florence did tell me you thought a lot of her.

PRESIDENT: Ah, so it was Florence who sent you?

JEROME: She said she was going to meet you. She sent me on in advance. I suppose she wanted you to know me.

PRESIDENT: She is always thoughtful.

JEROME: Yes, always, for you. You don't realize how true that is. She adores you, Florence does. She talks of no one but you. She scarcely remembers anyone but you. All her opinions are formed after yours. "Adore" is a stupid word: Florence loves you.

PRESIDENT: I am duly sensible of the happiness of being loved by Florence.

JEROME: Why, her only subject of conversation is how kind you were to her, how you helped her to be happy, how you encouraged her to live. She was afraid of nothing, thanks to you. Even now you're the only certain support she can count on.

PRESIDENT: A good man deserves a sensitive woman, they say.

JEROME: Florence is proud of you. She told me you were the finest orator in the world. She only goes to the cinema, even for a program of cartoons, if you are to appear in the newsreel. When you appear, I feel her hand tighten on my arm. I had to switch off the radio the day before yesterday, when you were speaking about the exchange rates—I thought she was going to cry. In fact, for Florence there's no one in the world but you!

PRESIDENT: I am enchanted to hear it.

JEROME: It's just the same with her dresses. I know quite well that, when she goes out, she chooses the clothes which you would have chosen. It's you who make the weather for her, who put the color into her world. In the evening, when I'm in bed already, I see her take off her dress, hang it up, admire it. It's plain she's thinking of you. Florence dresses for you!

PRESIDENT: I am indeed honored.

JEROME: That's why she's late too. She wants to be perfect. You'll see her in a moment. She's wearing the blue dress with the silver fox stole. I believe you were specially fond of the blue, weren't you?

PRESIDENT: Yes, most particularly.

JEROME: Then her choice of food . . . I used to wonder why, in a restaurant, Florence always had such exact, unchanging habits. It's because she eats what you eat, and drinks the same wines as you. I always make mistakes. When I choose the menu, I always manage to make her irritable, to annoy her. . . . With one of your menus she's calm and gentle at once.

PRESIDENT: Well, is she coming? Did she choose her birthday to tell me of her marriage? As you say, she is very thoughtful for me!

JEROME: Her birthday? Is it Florence's birthday today?

PRESIDENT: You don't seem to be very well informed about the life of Florence.

JEROME: Yes, I confess it. Our conversation hasn't yet touched on the subject. . . . Florence. . . . Her birthday?

PRESIDENT: Florence was actually born on the 8th of January. At midnight. They had to rub her all night to keep her alive. She was quite black.

JEROME: They must have rubbed her very hard. There's scarcely anything left of her.

PRESIDENT: She has a special birthday on October the 10th. It's not Saint Florence's day, but Saint John of the Golden Tongue. It's a tradition in her family. Her mother insisted on it when she was alive.

JEROME: Ah! So her mother is dead? What a pity! Did she die in Paris?

PRESIDENT: No, at Mayenne, where her father lives.

JEROME: Ah! Her father is alive? How nice! And he lives in Mayenne? How interesting!

PRESIDENT: Yes, he is alive. She goes to see him every month, on the 15th. She takes the 10:33 at Montparnasse. She travels in the third coach from the barrier. Above the seat where she usually sits there is a photograph of the prehistoric stone at Gisors. Her brother goes with her every second month.

JEROME: She has a brother too? Good! She isn't alone then. And today is her birthday? What does she drink on her birthday?

PRESIDENT: I have no recollection at all.

JEROME: What kind of birthday present would she like?

PRESIDENT: I have completely forgotten that too.

JEROME: An azalea perhaps?

PRESIDENT: Does she like azaleas? Are hydrangeas her flowers? Or orchids? Does the zinnia soften her? Can mignonette excite her? It's all suddenly gone from my memory.

I sometimes have failings like that. (*Getting up.*) Excuse me, I had forgotten I have a meeting at five o'clock. An important meeting. I've just got time to get there.

JEROME: Florence will be heartbroken she was late.

PRESIDENT: Make her my excuses, please. Give her my regards. Victor, a taxi!

VICTOR: There are no taxis here, sir. The next taxi will certainly be the one bringing Florence—Madame Florence—excuse me, I mean Mademoiselle Florence. I think the best thing you can do is to wait, sir.

CASHIER: Stay here, M. le Président, please. Put your trust in table number two.

JEROME: Besides, I think I can hear her now. . . .

CASHIER: No doubt of it. If, as the President says, she is really the most charming of young ladies, here she is!

JEROME: The President is here, Florence!

CASHIER: The President is at number two, Mlle. Florence!

VICTOR (*to the* CASHIER): I don't think I shall have to carry her.

CASHIER: That's lucky. You drop everything. (*Enter FLORENCE.*)

PRESIDENT: Good afternoon, Florence.

FLORENCE: Good afternoon, M. le Président.

JEROME: You can speak freely, Florence. I've told the President all he is to you. I told him the story of his talk on the rates of exchange. . . . Good-by! I'll leave you now. . . .

PRESIDENT: Why run away?

JEROME: Florence will be talking about me. I prefer not to be there. Besides, I don't talk like you. She does, exactly like you. You've scarcely spoken three words to me, but that was enough to show me she speaks like you. Just the same tone of voice, the same accent. She has your tongue, your palate. On her teeth, her charming tongue . . .

FLORENCE: All right. Leave us, please.

JEROME: How long will you be?

PRESIDENT: Five minutes, I should think.

JEROME: You're joking! You don't know Florence. She likes to talk and talk, when it's about you. How long, Florence?

FLORENCE: Ten minutes.

JEROME: Right! I'll be back in half an hour. (*Exit.*)

PRESIDENT: Good afternoon, Florence. . . .

FLORENCE: Good afternoon, Claude. . . .

PRESIDENT: Good-by, Florence. . . .

FLORENCE: Why are you called Claude? It's no name for a separation, Claude!

PRESIDENT: I'm sorry. They called me Claude, because they knew I should meet you one day. But they never thought I might lose you. They didn't call me Alfred.

FLORENCE: It's a pity. It would have helped.

PRESIDENT: You were better supplied. Florence serves two purposes. "Good-by, Florence!"—that sounds all right. It hurts. It kills. But it is possible. . . .

FLORENCE: Why good-by? Surely one can meet again in Paris?

PRESIDENT: One can meet in the Sahara, or in the goods station at Mont-de-Marsan. In Paris it happens less often.

FLORENCE: We met.

PRESIDENT: We met because a friend, to make us meet, bribed dressmakers, theatre managers, members of parliament, the fine weather, the rain. This friend was friendship, love itself. We were driven towards each other every moment of our lives, every minute, night and day. So we met about once a fortnight for an hour.

FLORENCE: You are always so busy. I never dared to distract you. I saw no one else.

PRESIDENT: I am sure of that.

FLORENCE: I don't need to teach you who and what you are—to tell you your life isn't confined in space and time. It's not the whole of you that's there when *you* are; what I had left of you in your absence too, that was a lot.

PRESIDENT: Much too much. It was enough for you.

FLORENCE: Your absence was a kind, a full one; it wasn't a real absence at all. It was to you I devoted all my daily tasks, even those which had nothing at all to do with you. It was for you I used to knit pullovers for my brother, for you I lined drawers and cupboards. I know them all well now, the materials of absence—horsehair, organdy, cotton. If I gave something to the man with the barrel organ in the street, it was really for you. It was the same with wait ng, with sickness, with happiness. They were all for you, when you weren't there

PRESIDENT: But with him it isn't the same?

FLORENCE: No. With him it's terrible.

PRESIDENT: It's because you weren't jealous, Florence. Now you are.

FLORENCE: Jealous of Jerome? Why should you think I'm jealous of Jerome? What is Jerome? You've seen him. . . . What can be left of him when he isn't there? Absence doesn't even change him, it dissolves him. He's gone entirely, Jerome, when he isn't there. I always wonder what I still have of him when he's ten yards away, except a memory of his name.

PRESIDENT: He doesn't leave you often, I hope?

FLORENCE: In three weeks he's left me for one afternoon.

PRESIDENT: That was very bad. Where did he go?

FLORENCE: He had his medical exam for the army.

PRESIDENT: Did they accept him? Will he have to leave you for the wars, Florence?

FLORENCE: They accepted him. He's blind to everything I can see, deaf to everything I can hear, but they took him. He could scarcely be more simpleminded, more fragile, more hopeless. But *they* saw nothing wrong.

PRESIDENT: War will show them.

FLORENCE: If there's anything hot about, he'll burn himself on it. If there's anything to stumble over, he'll stumble and hurt himself. In every doorway he pinches his fingers. Whenever there's an umbrella open, the points stick into his eyes. In the last month I've got to know every variety of massage and dressing and embrocation. In the middle of the night warts grow on his fingers. I spend my life anointing him, mending the holes he's made in himself. What with splinters, with nails on his car, I have to suck his blood ten times a day. If a serpent had been given the special mission of biting him endlessly, I should have no more to do than I have. He's the god of little accidents.

PRESIDENT: A modest little god. You should be thankful.

FLORENCE: But you—you never had a cold, never a snuffle. You had in you, on you, something immortal, invulnerable. . . .

PRESIDENT: That was for one hour every fortnight. For the rest of the time I might have been one aching sore.

FLORENCE: You never got hot ashes in both eyes at once. You never let an aching tooth get chilled. Even when you were carving, or shutting doors, or opening packing cases, the serpent of the home never bit you, the vulture never pecked at you, the panther on the staircase drew back his claws. Your heart went on beating gently, quietly, endlessly. . . .

PRESIDENT: Of course. You have heard my heart beating. . . .

FLORENCE: His gallops, trots, stops altogether. Stops for seconds, for centuries. It resounds ominously right through his body, from his head to his feet. . . . It's impossible to find anywhere to rest one's head. . . .

PRESIDENT: Hearts that stay in one place have great advantages.

FLORENCE: What's he like, Jerome? Is he handsome?

PRESIDENT: Haven't you seen him?

FLORENCE: I caught sight of him once for a second, I noticed him once. I have a memory of that. Since then, no.

PRESIDENT: He seems a nice fellow.

FLORENCE: I wonder. . . . He may be handsome. But he isn't nice. You, you're nice. Each time one sees you, one can take it all in. It's impossible not to. You have a fine stern face with a smile. Your forehead is straight and high, but it shows tenderness too. Your mouth is firm, but kind. You have all that I admire most—a royal carriage, calm demeanor, straight limbs. But he—if he isn't knock-kneed, he only just escaped. I can see that.

PRESIDENT: Then how did he capture you? Does he sing?

FLORENCE: He sings more out of tune than anyone has ever sung before. You never sang in front of me. I never expected one of the great ones of the earth to sing in front of me anyhow. But I know what it would be like if you did sing. I know, because I've often heard you singing Don Giovanni or Otello at the Opera—just by closing my eyes during some of your long journeys away. He whistles. Or rather he used to whistle. Since a quarter to one he's had a crack on his lip.

PRESIDENT: Where did you find him?

FLORENCE: We ran full tilt into each other on the boulevards. He was running as hard as he could. . . . He hurt me.

PRESIDENT: He was coming from a long way away. They sent him off twenty years ago. . . .

FLORENCE: Twenty-one. . . . He hurt me. . . . Even now I can't make up my mind whether my exhaustion is really love or stiffness. With you. . . .

PRESIDENT: With me?

FLORENCE: Nothing. . . . It's the refrain. . . . Let's leave it out. . . . What is he like, Jerome? Is he intelligent?

PRESIDENT: His eye is clear. His words come easily.

FLORENCE: His brow is empty. . . .

PRESIDENT: What does he do with that brow?

FLORENCE: Nothing. A lawyer pays him a rotten salary. He manages somehow.

PRESIDENT: But, in his life, what does he do?

FLORENCE: Nothing. He's there: that's his profession. He never leaves the flat. He makes the greatest possible use of the furniture. With him, you can easily understand why men thought of pegs and drawers and curtain rails. A cuff link is a mystery to him, a mystery he'll spend the whole day solving. With a window fastening, or the castor on a bed he can have an affair which will keep him awake till midnight. He loves toys too. If I put a rubber duck into the bathroom, he never comes out. I'm going to get him a little blowing whale. He never has any plans. He's always studying the weather with anxious care, at the window, at the barometer, at the thermometer, but he never goes out, never takes flight, his feet never leave the ground. He's like a pilot in the days when there were no airplanes.

CASHIER (*who has caught* FLORENCE'*s eye*): A kind of archangel. . . .

FLORENCE: With you I was only aware of great professions and great undertakings. I used to know about and follow world struggles, world needs, world treasures. With you it was oil, gold, iron. With him it's celluloid, chromium plate, tin, aluminum. He has a pocket workshop. He knows all about mending watch chains, all the alloys used for clasps. He's the god of little metals.

PRESIDENT: The days must go by quickly.

FLORENCE: Yes, like years. My week's composed of seven years. It wasn't because I hadn't time I didn't warn you about today. It was because our past life, after my first day with him, was much too far away already.

PRESIDENT: Is he jealous of this past?

FLORENCE: He refuses to know anything of the past. He's never asked me one question about it. He must be ignorant of his own too. He never speaks of it. I think he believes I was born the day he met me. He's made me forget I was ever small, that I ever had another bed or lived in another house. I was born this size, with these curls, wearing these stockings. This actual pair, no other. He has put a stamp of inevitability even on my toothbrush.

PRESIDENT: Is he jealous of the present?

FLORENCE: He has no imagination. He has the open frankness of a monster. He's without suspicion of any kind. He's ignorant of good and bad. He doesn't know that the most faithful fiancée may write love letters to a third person, that the woman who is bound by the strongest of ties to her lover may still be making signs to the man across the road, that a true wife may deceive her sleeping husband even in the bed he is sleeping in. He's ignorant of conquest and defeat. He knows nothing.

PRESIDENT: Surely he knows something about me?

FLORENCE: He does not know that friendship may be love, an understanding an intrigue; that affinity may mean complicity. He knows nothing and guesses nothing about you, or me. . . . At this moment he is thinking, naïvely, that we're talking about him.

PRESIDENT: What presumption!

FLORENCE: He's so little jealous he's made me forget how careful I was of myself. With you I belonged to you and no one else, and yet I always felt guilty. You were everything to me and I shuddered when any other man was near me. It was only you who existed, and if a hand touched me in the Métro I almost fainted. I can walk without my veil across the Place de la Concorde, now. . . . I shouldn't even fold my arms. . . . When the bell rings at home, I go to the door without my dressing gown.

PRESIDENT: He is sometimes passionate, angry?

FLORENCE: No. Usually good-humored, an even smile, ready to help with anything. I can feel him close to me like one of these fake companions they're supposed to put in the cells of suspects to make them confess. He sits there just like them, indifferent, friendly. He eats the food I give him. He washes himself in my basin. He sleeps in my bed. He doesn't even trouble to talk. He just waits for me to confess.

PRESIDENT: To confess what?

FLORENCE: My happiness before I knew him. My guilty knowledge of so many beautiful things, so many kind people, so much that one values and loves. I scarcely even dare to pass my hand over my furs, to look at the birds, or the statues in the streets—I should confess! I daren't even look at Jerome when he is asleep, breathing softly, when he has become a different person, as you did. I should wake him up and confess. All my former happiness, my unfathomable happiness would be swallowed up and vanish in our room. . . . I should be lost.

PRESIDENT: Is it always like that?

FLORENCE: No. Often it's just the opposite. Then his humor is a little less sunny, his smile a little less ready. But there can be no mistake. . . . This time they've put him in my room to stop me confessing.

PRESIDENT: To stop you confessing what?

FLORENCE: I don't know. I was counting on you to tell me. To judge from my conscience it must be something between receiving, forgery, and issuing false money. At any rate I belong to a gang whose vengeance is sure if you give them away. . . . Do I surprise you, Claude? Does this hurt you?

PRESIDENT: I'm learning about love, Florence. Such lessons are always expensive.

FLORENCE: That's what I wanted you to say. Because it is love, isn't it? It's only that, but it *is* that?

PRESIDENT: Not a doubt of it.

FLORENCE: I don't really love him. That's obvious. But it *is* love?

PRESIDENT: It isn't your love. Your love is quite different. Your love's like you. It's an agreement, a harmony, a comfort. This love is exactly the opposite. But it *is* love. You love Jerome with the love of someone else.

FLORENCE: Strange person whose love I have taken. I hope I never meet her. How far away from her I feel!

PRESIDENT: You'd grow mean in time.

FLORENCE: In time? No, there's no more time, Claude! That's the worst part of it. With you time passed normally. There were weeks and months. One wanted new dresses, new coats, for the season still came and went. There was travel, because there was still space. The earth went on turning—I could even feel it turning. We had found a way to feel it when we were together. We could even see with the naked eye that it was round. With him the world itself hardly realizes it. With him the minutes don't pass—I am living in a time which has stopped. Stopped at the supreme moment, as they say in the guidebooks, but that doesn't make it any the less terrible. A poor modest little affair like ours doesn't warrant such an end of the universe. It's all he can do, little soul that he is, with his pocket workshop: hand out eternity, stop the world. . . . So, Claude, often. . . . Are you sure no one is listening?

CASHIER: No, no one.

PRESIDENT: So?

(*Two fortune-tellers in gipsy clothes come in suddenly. With a quick gesture each snatches one of* FLORENCE'S *hands.*)

FIRST GIPSY (*to the* PRESIDENT): You've got a treasure in your pocket, a big treasure.

SECOND GIPSY (*to the* PRESIDENT): And you've got one in your bag. So big it burns my eyes to see it.

PRESIDENT: Victor!

CASHIER: Victor! Turn these gipsies out!

SECOND GIPSY (*to* FLORENCE): There are three men in your life. (*As if she were reading something dreadful.*) Oh dear me! Oh dear me!

CASHIER: Victor!

FIRST GIPSY (*to the* PRESIDENT): Fifty francs and I'll tell you if she loves you.

SECOND GIPSY (*to* FLORENCE): I can see a marriage. ... Two bodies. ...

FIRST GIPSY: Twenty francs and I'll tell you how long you have to live.

VICTOR (*appearing*):   Come on now, get away!

FIRST GIPSY: Loiaichti Victor and carra President betcha.

SECOND GIPSY: Baiana Florence betcha Cashier.

CASHIER: Yes, my love, it's like that. . . . (*The gipsies go off, chased by* VICTOR.) I congratulate you, Victor. As a terrace of well-being it was a success.

VICTOR: There, M. le Président sir, everything is in order now.

PRESIDENT (*to* VICTOR, *and pointing to a woman who has sat down to write a letter at the accursed table*):   Do you think so? Are you going to leave that woman at the suicides' table?

VICTOR: She's so plain! . . . Shall I really move her?

PRESIDENT: I should be very grateful. (*The* PRESIDENT *comes closer to* FLORENCE *again, and takes her hand.*) So, often . . . ?

FLORENCE: What did you say?

CASHIER (*with deep feeling*):   So, often. . . .

PRESIDENT: You had just got to "So, often . . ."

FLORENCE: So nothing. So it's all over.

PRESIDENT: What is over?

FLORENCE: My little dirge. I sang it rather well, didn't I? It wasn't really too bad either in itself, but rather too long even when I stopped. It's finished.

PRESIDENT: So, often . . . ?

FLORENCE: No, it's finished. What I said I said. But you mustn't take an unfair advantage of me.

PRESIDENT: As you will.

FLORENCE: You know what women are. I was suddenly seized with a desire to complain, to air my grievances, my most secret grievances. It was just like an urge to stretch, to shout, to sing. Yes, that's what it was—the need to sing. I had a theme in my head, a pathetic theme. I tried it out in all its possible forms, I treated it like a fugue. It was my fugue with you. But it's of no importance, and it had no sense either. The gayest woman in the world has to proclaim her despair at some time in her life. It's a physical reaction, nothing to do with the soul. It wasn't my fault—I had to do it.

PRESIDENT: As you please. I agree entirely. You were singing. . . . I shall remember nothing but the tune.

FLORENCE: Yes. Let's talk now. This is why I came, Claude: I'm getting married.

PRESIDENT: You have all my best wishes, Florence.

FLORENCE: I'm going to marry this young man, Jerome. We understand each other. We like each other. We shall be happy.

PRESIDENT: That is quite possible.

FLORENCE: Do you want to know why I like him? Because he shot straight into my life—into my body on that boulevard, like a meteorite. He stayed there. In fact he's stuck there. I can't see any reason to take him out. Why, there are cavalry colonels going around now with a shell splinter in their hearts. If they can avoid bending down to draw off their wine in the cellar, they live to be a hundred. I promise you I won't be too energetic. And anyhow Jerome is charming.

PRESIDENT: Yes, he is.

FLORENCE: You ask what he does in life? He certainly won't run into any trouble. He's clever with his hands, ingenious, hard-working. He'll solve the problems of existence just as you solve a Chinese puzzle—with his hands. As a mechanic or an electrician he has his future. You don't know him well enough. Ignorant as I am, I can feel there are flashes, short circuits, blown fuses which rely on *him* to deal with them. He's nothing, but he's one of those who would have invented fire.

PRESIDENT: We'll help him, if it's necessary. . . .

FLORENCE: You ask how he won me? It wasn't because he was young. Anybody can be young, all the young people in the world. But he has the gift of giving his own age to a whole row of things which were older than you before—grief, appetite, pleasure. For instance death with a fresh, smooth skin is rather nice. . . .

PRESIDENT: Less than that would be enough for a conquest. . . . So?

FLORENCE: So, I want to face this marriage worthy of him. . . . He's a being without stain—without stain of worry or memory, or of age. He has all his goods in one shop window. He has only one word to tell you it's raining or that he's in love with you. Perhaps it would be going a little far to call him Parsifal. But he is someone who has gathered no crystal, no deposit from the past. I mustn't bring him a dowry from there either. I don't mean thoughts and feelings. Those you have to take with you. Though he hasn't. And I don't mean physical marks, scars, mortal illnesses either. Though he has none. . . . But things. . . .

PRESIDENT: Yes, Florence?

FLORENCE: I owe it to him to get rid of everything which

might be equivocal, everything I couldn't explain without lying to him.

PRESIDENT: You don't want ever to lie to him?

FLORENCE: Life lies to him for me—in everything which concerns me. I mustn't join in.

PRESIDENT: In other words you are jealous for him because he isn't for himself—or just until he becomes so?

FLORENCE: Yes, if you like. . . . So I am getting rid of all the concrete things from my past. I'm giving them back to those they came from. . . . There they are. . . .

PRESIDENT: There are what?

FLORENCE: Your jewels. . . . I mean . . . my jewels.

PRESIDENT: The jewels I gave you?

FLORENCE: No one else ever gave me any.

PRESIDENT: Wonderful! The gipsy was right. . . . Now I can see you as you were when I first saw you, Florence—your hands bare.

FLORENCE: Yes, everything is bare now—neck, wrists, breast.

PRESIDENT: What am I to do with them?

FLORENCE: There are plenty of bare hands in this poor world.

PRESIDENT: I had always supposed that women's jewels became flesh of their flesh, sinews, grew on to them. . . . Doesn't it hurt?

FLORENCE: Tearing away the flesh of my flesh? No, it doesn't matter now.

PRESIDENT: Wonderful! . . . I shall certainly lose them.

FLORENCE: They are insured.

PRESIDENT: Is this a sort of ransom you're paying to fate? How do you know fate will accept it? If you find your rings again in a piece of fish, you'll know what that means.

FLORENCE: With Jerome lobster always comes out of a tin.

PRESIDENT: Surely it would have been enough to have got rid of them? You could have thrown them into the river.

FLORENCE: What would happen to the world if women forgot their duties to jewelry?

PRESIDENT: You could have given them away. . . .

FLORENCE: Then I should have been deceiving you.

PRESIDENT: It's embarrassing to meet so many birthdays again all at once, so many special occasions.

FLORENCE: I used to meet them again every evening. With my back to Jerome I used to gaze at them in a corner of the drawer. I mayn't do that any longer.

PRESIDENT: All those in one bag. Just one little bag. It makes a noise of rattling bones.

FLORENCE: Don't shake it about. I heard it.

PRESIDENT: And yet you could bear to say to yourself: "He'll be going home with all my jewels in his right pocket"?

FLORENCE: If I'd been dead, of course I'd have taken them without scruple. But I'm not dead. And Jerome is alive.

PRESIDENT: It's hard. And it's heavy. I shall have to carry something insoluble in my body from now on. There's no mineral water you can drink strong enough to dissolve diamonds. . . . It's going to be painful. . . . Do you know what you're going to do, Florence, now you've given them to me? You're going to take them back.

FLORENCE: You haven't understood.

PRESIDENT: I understand you very well. You've been taking vows. You think you're going into an order where there's no place for the will, for freedom. So jewels are given up at the doors. Precious stones have a way of taking the light out here in the open, and it's obviously a treacherous way for the one one loves. . . . But I can't agree with you.

FLORENCE: I want to be strong when I am with Jerome.

PRESIDENT: You've chosen the wrong way. You're laying down your arms. The only shield left to your sex is the brooch; the only battle-ax the ring; the only lie the opal. Women have lost all hope of victory over men if they try to fight with their hands bare.

FLORENCE: I've lost already.

PRESIDENT: Where is your perception, Florence? Let's leave your body out of it for the moment. Just to exist before Jerome you need a secret within yourself, a treasure.

FLORENCE: I've got one. I love you.

PRESIDENT: You can see where that secret is taking you. That's the one you must get rid of. Give me back everything I made sensitive in you if you like; give me back my way of speaking—as Jerome says; give me back the music I gave you. Give me back myself. I don't quite know what I shall do with it, but that's my affair. I've managed to deal with stupider problems. The only thing I and my seraphs can do for you now is weaken you, make you a powerless slave in front of Jerome. You must say good-by to us. But there *are* these few little ways of escape from him, of preserving your independence, of not suffering—your jewels. Don't give them back to me.

FLORENCE: But they don't like Jerome. They deceive him.

PRESIDENT: Obviously they do. They're the only things that do. They're the only part of you that faces him, and betrays him. Look at them. They won't surrender, even inside this little bag. . . . They're as lovely there as they were on you. Oh Florence, why are you trying to be sentimental about these stones? They are the indifferent, the scornful, the insensitive part of you. And you've none of that to spare. Don't let what you have of it escape with them! . . . Look at this clasp. Tht's a diamond. Indifference itself.

FLORENCE: If there is anything that rivals Jerome in my thoughts, I suppose it is diamonds.

PRESIDENT: Very well, then. . . . I shall lock them up in my safe. Perhaps you'll want to wear them again in your thoughts sometimes. You'll be able to wear them all.

FLORENCE: Forgive me. . . . There's one I shall always wear in my thoughts.

PRESIDENT: The pearl?

FLORENCE: Yes, the first.

PRESIDENT: There it is.

FLORENCE: You gave it to me in Aix. There was a great lime tree there, I remember. It was autumn.

PRESIDENT: We didn't know each other yet then. There was a chestnut too.

FLORENCE: For ten days you came and sat down politely at my table on the terrace. On the second day, as soon as you appeared, you took my hand. You turned it over, palm upwards. You made a shell of it; I thought you were going to put a penny into it. No . . . the pearl was born.

PRESIDENT: The hotel manager was furious.

FLORENCE: He was quite right. His name was François. He was watching over me. He adored me. And suddenly he saw this pearl on my left hand. He was certain it hadn't been there five minutes earlier. When he brought the bottle he called me Mademoiselle. When he poured it out he called me Madame.

PRESIDENT: I was so nervous I had to sit opposite you to calculate which was your right hand and which your left.

FLORENCE: And we didn't say anything. It was the perfect gift. The present from unknown to unknown, given and taken without speech.

PRESIDENT: And you left almost at once. But you modestly put on your left glove as you crossed the hall of the hotel. No one but François and I saw the little lump under the leather. My heart was bursting as I watched you disappear —it was as though you had become pregnant when you left me—pregnant with a pearl.

FLORENCE: I must keep this one. . . . Poor François. Poor Jerome. So much the worse for them. May I? . . .

PRESIDENT: Sweet lady, to whom one can offer the same pearl twice.

FLORENCE: Why did you cover me with jewels like that, Claude?

PRESIDENT: Idle vanity. We all show off our wealth in our own way.

FLORENCE: That was the time when you had so many conferences to go to. I used to wait in agony for your return to know what was happening to the country, to the world. You brought me back an emerald.

PRESIDENT: An emerald which had been fortifying me all day, helping me against my passions and my rages—just as it will help you against Jerome. I had it in my pocket all through the meetings. There it is! How many attacks I beat off with its help! I was accused of being too broadminded, too generous. "What is behind his generosity?" said our enemies. "Why is he so weak?" the French asked. "What's making him so just?" said the neutrals. They didn't know I had your emerald with me. The rest of them had a core of hatred, of national pride, of self-interest. I didn't even need to have an idea—I had a talisman. I was what I was, because *it* was pure, true, unyielding. I could feel it in my pocket. It was like a rosary with one bead. I could face my friends and my enemies with my whole weight, measured in carats of precious stone. . . . "The man's a rock!" they all said in the general assembly. . . . That was the rock. . . .

FLORENCE: Wouldn't the thought of me have been enough?

PRESIDENT: Love is no weapon of defense. You can't resist in your own person. The statesman who puts *himself* into the battle is as stupid as the novelist who thinks he can wrestle or suffer or love for his characters in his own person. He's either a fool or he's being arrogant. You can't know real suffering any more than you can defend your country except as a mercenary, except by rejecting your own heart inside you and using another one without feeling, a token. I wasn't the only one there. My neighbor, the German, rolled around in his hand a kind of egg made of boxwood. That was what helped him to stitch up the wounds of his country. And how happy are those who can recover their human memories *from* that impersonal token when the struggle is over! I have no idea where the German went with his egg after the meeting. But I ran off to my happiness—I ran off to you. . . . It goes on the right hand, doesn't it?

FLORENCE: That's where you put it that evening.

PRESIDENT: Then here's the ruby I had on the day of my greatest defeat. You're not going to refuse that one. Look, it wants its revenge. I can remember looking at it in my room

before the meeting. I opened the case from time to time during the debate, like a cigarette case. I don't smoke or take
snuff—surely I can open jewel cases during a meeting.
How fine the Dutch setting looked in the sun of Versailles
or Geneva! The bracelet goes with the ring, Florence. So
does the clasp.

(*A young and pretty woman enters during the last few
remarks without being seen. Now she has come forward,
and is standing near them, gently swaying to and fro.*)

FLORENCE: What do you suppose *she* wants?
PRESIDENT: A pretty woman always appears when jewels
are being handled in the open air. I think she's their spirit.
She's quite harmless.
FLORENCE: She's very pretty.
PRESIDENT: Of course. The sapphire goes on the third
finger?
FLORENCE: No, Claude, don't go on. I don't want the
sapphire. That's the one I love best of all!
PRESIDENT: Its spirit is watching you. You're not going to
insult her publicly! Which finger?
FLORENCE: The middle finger. . . . She's smiling. . . . She
understands. . . . She's laughing at me.
PRESIDENT: What about the turquoise?
FLORENCE: I don't want the turquoise.
PRESIDENT: That goes on the little finger, I think? . . .
JEWEL SPIRIT: Everyone knows it's the little fingers which
carry heavy loads the best.
FLORENCE: It isn't right, what you're doing, Claude. You
don't respect me. You don't want me to respect myself. I
should have thought someone who could get our defense
bonds accepted by Sweden, or the Stresa agreement by Germany, might have found something better to do than force
precious stones on a woman. You want to prove I'm a coward,
to prove it to yourself and to me. I suppose you think that
will console you. Or perhaps you don't even need consolation. It's just the male reflex, the desire to decorate a woman
even with what she doesn't want.
PRESIDENT: You know I'm right really.
FLORENCE: All right then. I'll take them back. I'll take
them all back. You don't want me to swallow them to make
them even more part of myself? They'll protect me against
Jerome. At least I'll be able to keep from him everything in
me which isn't me. . . . They'll protect me against you too. Yes
especially against you. They'll remind me how much you pre-

fer my wedding day to me. Innocence, living with a lie. I'll wear white to show them off.

PRESIDENT: Very well then, give them back to me.

FLORENCE: No, no, I'm keeping them now! I suppose you haven't got any more on you?

PRESIDENT: As a matter of fact, Florence, I have. My gipsy's sight was good too. Today is Saint John of the Golden Tongue.

FLORENCE: My birthday! I thought there was something. There's been an air of celebration all round me ever since this morning.

PRESIDENT: I didn't know you were going to marry Jerome. I never gave you your necklace. . . . I brought it with me.

FLORENCE: Oh, how lovely it is!

(*She puts the necklace on. The* JEWEL SPIRIT *comes near.*)

PRESIDENT: Did you want something, madame?

JEWEL SPIRIT: I? Oh, nothing. The weather is lovely, isn't it? I was just enjoying the air. . . .

VICTOR: The young man is on the way, M. le Président.

CASHIER: He is crossing the lawns. Tiger and Bismarck, our terrible wolfhounds, leap around his feet. How gentle is his look; he has killed a bee. How lightly he runs; he is trampling the flowers.

FLORENCE: Off with the armor again.

(*She puts all the jewels in the little bag.*)

JEWEL SPIRIT (*to the* PRESIDENT): This whisper of a breeze is delightful too. . . .

PRESIDENT: Delightful. You could also say "delicious." Both words are used.

(*The* JEWEL SPIRIT *moves away.*)

FLORENCE: So you're giving up?

PRESIDENT: Yes, Florence. I haven't the strength.

FLORENCE: You can see what I'm suffering, how I've suffered. . . .

PRESIDENT: And what you're going to suffer.

FLORENCE: You loved me! You still love me!

PRESIDENT: I meant to tell you how much today. But I seem to have chosen a bad day.

FLORENCE: You won't even try?

PRESIDENT: Do you really want me to?

FLORENCE: Yes, oh, yes!

PRESIDENT: Shall Jerome arrive in a moment and not find you?

FLORENCE: We'll go miles away. He'll never make up his mind. He needs two days to catch a train. Let's just go away with no destination, no luggage. We'll live as we can. I've got my jewels.

PRESIDENT: No. I'm unlucky: I'm the only man in Europe who can recognize conquerors.

CASHIER: He is striding over the streams. His lips are like a thread of purple. He is breathing the scent of the roses. Oh! He has pricked himself!

FLORENCE: He may be beautiful, but I can't see it. He may be good, but his goodness escapes me. He may be generous, but from him I receive no gift. Take me away, Claude!

VICTOR: One word from his lips, and the dogs are calm. One gesture, and the birds fly to his command!

FLORENCE: All I ask is bread, and his pockets hold nothing but crumbs. Why don't you believe me, Claude? Why?

PRESIDENT: Because now it isn't you who are speaking. It is your complaint beginning again.

FLORENCE: My dirge, do you mean?

PRESIDENT: Yes, your song. I can hear it. It is beautiful. And it is true—in itself. You came here today only to sing. Never think anything else.

FLORENCE: Don't you believe me?

PRESIDENT: How am I to know whether this is a song of sadness or a cry for help?

FLORENCE: So you're not jealous? You're like him?

CASHIER: He glideth around the turning spray on the lawn and the fountains spring forth.

FLORENCE: The establishment is lucky. For me whenever he passes the grass is dead. He touches me and everything within me is dry. My jewels? You'll see what he'll do with them. Though he won't even see them! I could have gone on wearing them. He wouldn't see the arrows on Saint Sebastian. He'd barge into them as he went by, without a thought of apology as they quivered. He'll find a phrase for my jewels, something to express a cheap idea which will ruin them for me, make them false, take their luster from them.

PRESIDENT: Be calm! He is coming.

CASHIER: He is coming.

FLORENCE: Yes, I can hear you. His lips are like a thread of purple. His mouth is a garden of charm. He comes.

The hills gambol around him like wolfhounds. He'll ask me
whether I'm ready. He never says anything else. Every time
it gives me a start. One day I shall have to ask him for what.
. . . Am I ready for the night without sleep, whose minutes
are soldered together in his pocket workshop; for my eternal
toothbrush; thanks to you, for shame! Take me in your arms,
Claude! Let him find me in your arms!

PRESIDENT: Do you want that?
VICTOR: Here he is!
FLORENCE: Leave me alone, Claude.
CASHIER: Here he is. He's whistling.
FLORENCE: Wonderful. His cracked lip is better.

(*Enter* JEROME.)

JEROME: Are you ready, Florence?
FLORENCE: Yes, I'm ready.
JEROME: Has Florence told you everything she wanted
to tell you, sir?
PRESIDENT: Yes, absolutely everything.
JEROME: You mustn't mind me. You can go on in front
of me. I shall be delighted. I should be able to hear Florence
talking in her real language at last. I'm sure of that, even if
you only talked about fine weather and rain.
PRESIDENT: We have exhausted that subject too.
FLORENCE: The President hasn't much time, Jerome.
JEROME: But I must ask him for a moment all the same.
He won't deny me, since he told me the news. . . .
FLORENCE: What news?
JEROME: That today is your birthday. I dashed off to
Saint-Cloud. I managed to find this ring.
FLORENCE: A ring?
JEROME: It's a jacinth. Not a very big one. In fact it's
minute. But, as it's only paste, it doesn't matter. In fact its
all the better.
JEWEL SPIRIT: Yes, all the better.

(*She pointedly withdraws.*)

JEROME: It would have been a joke in rather poor taste
to have given you a big artificial jacinth. Wouldn't it, sir?
PRESIDENT: It's the intention that matters.
JEROME: Intention is the word. A true intention with a
false jacinth.
JEWEL SPIRIT: She wins on the deal. (*Exit.*)
JEROME: It's solid anyhow. And very light. The jeweler

assured me you can wear it night and day, wash your hands without taking it off—even with English soap, which is made with very strong potassium. The only disadvantage is that it rings rather. If you knock it against the banisters, or glasses or plates, as the jeweler explained. Lucky it's quite small, darling. If it had been a big one, we should hardly have been able to hear ourselves speak.

FLORENCE: Thank you, Jerome.

JEROME: You must thank the President. I shouldn't ever have thought of it but for him. Well, are you ready, Florence?

FLORENCE: For what, Jerome?

JEROME: I asked you if you were ready.

FLORENCE: Yes, I'm ready.

JEROME: Well then, say good-by.

FLORENCE: Good-by.

PRESIDENT: Good-by, Florence. (*She comes back again.*)

FLORENCE: I'm so sorry, I was just going off with this bag of yours. (*She gives it back to the* PRESIDENT.)

JEROME: Absent-minded as ever! (*Exit* JEROME *and* FLORENCE.)

VICTOR: If I were you, I'd have a try, M. le Président.

PRESIDENT: A try at what, Victor?

VICTOR: To get her back from Jerome. It's not impossible.

PRESIDENT: Ah! So you heard?

VICTOR: Everyone heard. I forgot to tell you table two is like a sounding board. It corresponds acoustically to number eleven on the other side. You could have put Mlle. Florence at number eleven, and she wouldn't have missed a word.

PRESIDENT: It was quite all right as it was.

VICTOR: Everyone here is on your side. Even the manager. Of course with him it's because of your title.

MANAGER (*coming forward*): Pardon me! Of course I know what is due from me to the President. But if I wasn't on his side, I should take refuge in silence: silence is the real defense of managers. But I am on his side. If I were a woman, I should abandon Jerome on the spot. I should throw myself into the President's arms. I should fasten myself there and hang on in spite of him. No one should dislodge me.

PRESIDENT: Unhappily, manager, you are not.

CASHIER: You're like all managers: you believe in possession, but in love the only thing that counts is presence.

PRESIDENT: And strength, manager. Jerome is the stronger.

MANAGER: Intelligence, power, kindliness—what about them? Aren't they arms?

PRESIDENT: Alas, no, manager! They're no more than the baggage train. There's only one arm weaker—genius.

CASHIER: He has caught his feet in the roots of the trees, and has not fallen. The sun shines straight in his eyes; but he frowns not.

MANAGER: Is he kissing her?

VICTOR: No. . . .

MANAGER: Then she is kissing him.

CASHIER: Why do you say that? She has taken his head in her two hands, she has put her mouth close to his—that could quite well not be to kiss him.

PRESIDENT: It could quite well be to take something out of his eye.

CASHIER: The air in the country is full of smuts. . . . (*To the* PAGE *who enters with a* CHAUFFEUR.) What do *you* want?

PAGE: It's the Prime Minister's chauffeur looking for you, M. le Président.

PRESIDENT: Ah, it's you, Lawrence? What have you come for?

CHAUFFEUR: For you, M. le Président. The Prime Minister told me to find you wherever you might be, and to bring you back. As fast as I could make the car move. He said laughingly that it was a matter of saving the Republic.

PRESIDENT: He has come in the nick of time. I will come at once.

ANOUILH: The Lark

JEAN ANOUILH (born 1910?)

Most of Anouilh's biographers give his birth date as 1910, although one, Jean Didier, puts it at 1902. Anouilh himself is reticent about his private life, but it seems fairly certain that he was born on June 23, 1910, in Bordeaux; his mother was a violinist who played in a Casino orchestra; his father was a tailor. He has told Hubert Gignoux that as a child he wrote verse plays, went to the Colbert School and Chaptal College, and studied at the Law University in Paris, which he left after one year. For a time he worked as a copywriter in an advertising firm on automobile, underwear, and other accounts, which "for me took the place of studies in literature." He wrote and acted in several publicity films, the kind that are shown in French theaters before the main movie and are, today at least, on a much more adult level than American and British television commercials. He also wrote gags and jokes for French film comedies.

His first known play, *Humulus the Dumb*, about a young man who could utter only one word a day, was written in 1929, and so was his second play, a skit called *Mandarine*. In 1931 he took a job as Louis Jouvet's secretary, which brought him right into the heart of Paris theater life. He met a number of important stars, and also Jean Giraudoux, who was then working on *Judith*—Anouilh has since been a great admirer of Giraudoux—and a young actress, Monelle Valentin, who later became his wife. One story has it that the Anouilhs were so poor at first that they borrowed stage furniture from Jouvet's production of *Siegfried* in order to set up a home, and had to return it when the play reopened.

For several years Anouilh lived and worked in great poverty. He gave up his position with Jouvet, who did not seem impressed by his playwriting talent, and wrote copiously to try to support his wife, his baby daughter and himself. He did not align himself with any movement or group—he was not an *avant-gardiste*—and had few influential friends, although Pierre Fresnay the actor did help him to get *Mandarine* staged in 1933. Anouilh persisted, without recognition, until 1935 when his play, *There Was a Prisoner*, found a production. It did not bring him fame, but it did

438

bring a nice advance from Hollywood for the film rights,
and, thus encouraged, he continued to turn out at least one
play a year and to manage a new production almost every
season. He also wrote film scripts, and has continued to do
so, two of the best-known being the postwar *Caroline
Chérie* and *Monsieur Vincent*. *Monsieur Vincent* may be
regarded as a generous repayment of Anouilh's debt to Pierre
Fresnay; it has been one of that powerful actor's finest movie
roles.

Anouilh had a minor success with *Traveler With No Baggage*, but it was not until his association with the director
André Barsacq that he acquired his wide and loyal following
among French audiences. In 1940 Barsacq directed *Thieves'
Carnival*, which had been written in 1932. The play ran for
412 performances, and the following year Barsacq staged
two more Anouilh plays, *The Rendezvous at Senlis* and
Eurydice (translated as either *Legend of Lovers* or *Point of
Departure*).

Anouilh's greatest success in the years that followed was
Antigone, also in a Barsacq *mise-en-scène*, which ran for 641
performances and stirred up a violent discussion among
French intellectuals. Was it communist or fascist (pro-
Vichy)? The truth probably is that it was neither; Anouilh
does not usually make political points in his plays; he is concerned with personal and emotional issues.

Since the war Barsacq has staged four more plays by
Anouilh: *Romeo and Jeannette, Invitation to the Castle*
(translated as *Ring Round the Moon*), *Mademoiselle Colombe*,
and *Medea*. Various other leading French directors have
worked with Anouilh, including Marguérite Jamois, who
directed the original production of *The Lark* in 1953,
and Jean-Louis Barrault. During the 1959–60 season in Paris,
Anouilh had three of his plays going at once: *Becket, or The
Honor of God*, directed by Roland Pietri and Anouilh himself; *La Petite Molière* at the Odéon, under Barrault, and
starring Anouilh's daughter, Catherine, a beautiful and accomplished actress; and *L'Hurluberlu*, which later showed up
on Broadway with the title *The Fighting Cock*.

Anouilh's plays have drawn big audiences in theaters all
over the world. He is unquestionably the most successful
playwright alive, and publishers, particularly in the United
States, compete fiercely for the right to print his next play.
He does not write very much about his work, except to dis-
claim research and historical validity in his plays based on
real people (Molière, Becket, Joan of Arc), although he has
subdivided his work into four main classifications: Dark

Plays, Pink (i.e., rosy) Plays, Grating Plays, and Glittering
Plays. Most of them are acutely pessimistic and are concerned
with the influence of the evil world and evil people on "pure
souls."

A LIST OF ANOUILH'S PLAYS TO DATE:

Humulus the Dumb (1929), *Mandarine* (1929), *Attila the
Magnificent* (1930), *Hermine* (1931), *Jezabel* (1932),
Thieves' Carnival (1932), *The Savage* (1934), *There Was a
Prisoner* (1934), *The Small Happiness* (1935), *Traveler with
No Baggage* (1936), *The Rendezvous at Senlis* (1937),
Léocadia (1939), *Eurydice* (also known as *Legend of Lovers*
or *Point of Departure* in English, 1941), *Antigone* (1942),
Romeo and Jeannette (1945), *Medea* (1946), *Invitation to
the Castle* (*Ring Round the Moon*, 1947), *Ardèle* (1948),
Episode in an Author's Life (1948), *The School for Fathers*
(1949), *The Rehearsal* (1950), *Colombe* (1950), *Waltz of
the Toreadors* (1951), *The Lark* (1952), *Ornifle or The
Current of Air* (1954), *Poor Bitos or The Dinner of Heads*
(1956), *L'Hurluberlu* (*The Fighting Cock*, 1958), *Becket*
(1958), *La Petite Molière* (1959), *The Grotto* (1961).

SUGGESTIONS FOR FURTHER READING
ON ANOUILH:

Guicharnaud, J., and Beckelman, J. *The Modern French
   Theatre.* New Haven: Yale University Press, 1961.
Marsh, Edward Owen. *Jean Anouilh; Poet of Pierrot and
   Pantaloon.* London: W. H. Allen & Co., Ltd., 1953.
Many recent and current reviews of Anouilh plays in news-
papers and magazines, too numerous to list.

IN FRENCH ONLY:

Didier, Jean. *À la rencontre de Jean Anouilh.* Paris: Les
   Editions la Sixaine, 1946.
Gignoux, Hubert. *Jean Anouilh.* Paris: Editions du Temps
   Présent, 1946.
Lassalle, Jean Pierre. *Jean Anouilh, ou La vaine révolte.*
   Editions Subervie Rodez, 1956.

NOTE: A critical essay in which reference is made to
Anouilh, "A Brief Survey of Modern French Drama," by
Joseph Chiari, will be found on p. 563.

THE LARK

by Jean Anouilh

FIRST PERFORMED IN PARIS IN 1953

Translated by Christopher Fry

CHARACTERS

BEAUCHAMP, *Earl of Warwick*
CAUCHON, *Bishop of Beauvais*
JOAN
HER FATHER
HER MOTHER
HER BROTHER
THE PROMOTER
THE INQUISITOR
BROTHER LADVENU
ROBERT DE BEAUDRICOURT, *Squire of Vaucouleurs*
BOUDOUSSE, *a guard*
AGNES SOREL
THE YOUNG QUEEN
CHARLES, *the Dauphin*
QUEEN YOLANDE
ARCHBISHOP OF RHEIMS
M. DE LA TREMOUILLE
PAGE TO THE DAUPHIN
CAPTAIN LA HIRE
THE HANGMAN
AN ENGLISH SOLDIER

NOTE

The following note by Jean Anouilh appeared in the program of the French production of The Lark:

The play that follows makes no attempt to explain the mystery of Joan.

The persistent effort of so-called modern minds to explain mysteries is, in any case, one of the most naïve and foolish activities indulged in by the puny human brain since it became overstocked with shallow political and scientific notions, and can yield nothing, in the long run, but the nostalgic satisfaction of the small boy who discovers at last that his mechanical duck was made up of two wheels, three springs and a screw. The little boy holds in his hands three springs, two wheels and a screw, objects which are doubtless reassuring, but he has lost his mechanical duck, and he has usually not found an explanation.

For my own part I always refuse to tell children how things work, even when I know; and in the case of Joan I must confess that I did not know.

Some nights, when I am feeling depressed, I try to be rational and I say: the situation—social, political and military —was ripe for the phenomenon of Joan; a little shepherdess, one of the countless little shepherdesses who had seen the Virgin or heard voices, and who happened to be called Joan, came to fill a gap in the works, and then everything began turning. If it hadn't been this one, another would have been found—there were candidates before and after her. When she was burnt, her place was taken by a little shepherd from the Landes, who led his countrymen to a few incomplete victories and was in his turn taken prisoner and burnt, without anyone thinking of making him into a hero or a saint. (As regards the hypothesis familiar to Catholics, at least in France, that God had begun to worry about France and sent Joan to save her, I must point out as a matter of general interest and without drawing any conclusion therefrom that Joan was officially recognized as a saint and not as a martyr. She was canonized for "the excellence of her theological virtues" and not because she died for her faith—her faith being identical with the cause of France, which, even in 1920, was hardly acceptable from the Vatican's point of view. Joan was thus a saint who died as a result of a political intrigue, and God did not necessarily take sides against Henry VI of Lancaster. It's a pity, but it's true.)

Be that as it may, all this is typical of that reassuring sort of explanation which explains nothing, but which allows Monsieur Homais to go to sleep in peace after his cup of camomile tea.

And, supported by accurate texts and irrefutable evidence, it affords the same peaceful slumbers to Professor Homais, an academic bigwig. For a couple of generations, matter-of-fact people sleep thus, reassured, and then one day, by chance, in Michelet or in an illustrated paper, somebody reads one of Joan's answers at the trial, an authentic answer, a single, simple little answer, and the whole of Professor Homais' work collapses, as did the dialectic of the seventy judges in their stiff robes who spent long months harassing that weary, undernourished little girl, haggard and thin (yes, I know she was a big healthy girl, but I couldn't care less), and so strangely stubborn.

You cannot explain Joan, any more than you can explain the tiniest flower growing by the wayside. There's just a little living flower that has always known, ever since it was a microscopic seed, how many petals it would have and how big they would grow, exactly how blue its blue would be and how its delicate scent would be compounded. There's just the phenomenon of Joan, as there is the phenomenon of a daisy or of the sky or of a bird. What pretentious creatures men are, if that's not enough for them.

Children, even when they are growing older, are allowed to make a bunch of daisies or play at imitating bird-song, even if they know nothing about botany or ornithology. That is just about what I have done.

ACT I

(A simple, neutral setting. The stage is empty at first; then the characters enter by twos and threes. The costumes are plain. JOAN wears man's clothes throughout the play. WARWICK is the last to enter.)

WARWICK: Well, now; is everyone here? If so, let's have the trial and be done with it. The sooner she is found guilty and burned the better for all concerned.

CAUCHON: But, my lord, before we do that we have the whole story to play: Domremy, the Voices, Vaucouleurs, Chinon, the Coronation.

WARWICK: Theatrical poppycock! You can tell that story to the children: the beautiful white armour, the fluttering standard, the gentle and implacable warrior maid. The statues of her can tell that story, later on, when policies have changed. We might even put up a statue ourselves in London, though I know at the moment that sounds wildly improbable: but you never know, in a few hundred years it might suit His Majesty's Government for some reason or other. But, as for now, I am Beauchamp, Earl of Warwick; and I've got my grubby little witch lying on the straw in the dungeon at Rouen, and a fine packet of trouble she has been, and a pretty sum she has cost us; but the money's been paid, and the next thing is to put her on trial and burn her.

CAUCHON: Not immediately. Before we come to that, there's the whole of her life to go through. It won't take very long, my lord.

WARWICK (*going to a corner resignedly*): Well, if you insist. An Englishman knows how to wait. (*Anxiously.*) I hope you're not expecting me to stand by while you go through that monstrous farce of a coronation again. And all the battles as well—Orleans, Patay, Beaugency?—I may as well tell you now, I should find that in very poor taste.

CAUCHON (*singing*): Put your mind at rest, my lord. There are too few of us here to stage the battles.

WARWICK: Good.

CAUCHON: Joan. (*She looks up.*) You may begin.

JOAN: May I begin wherever I like?

CAUCHON: Yes.

JOAN: I like remembering the beginning: at home, in the fields, when I was still a little girl looking after the sheep, the first time I heard the Voices, that is what I like to remember. . . . It is after the evening Angelus. I am very small and my hair is still in pigtails. I am sitting in the field, thinking of nothing at all. God is good and keeps me safe and happy, close to my mother and my father and my brother, in the quiet countryside of Domremy, while the English soldiers are looting and burning villages up and down the land. My big sheep-dog is lying with his head in my lap; and suddenly I feel his body ripple and tremble, and a hand seems to have touched my shoulder, though I know no one has touched me, and the voice says—

SOMEONE IN THE CROWD: Who is going to be the voice?

JOAN: I am, of course. I turned to look. A great light was filling the shadows behind me. The voice was gentle and grave. I had never heard it before, and all it said to me was: "Be a good and sensible child, and go often to church." But I *was* good, and I *did* go to church often, and I showed I was sensible by running away to safety. That was all that happened the first time. And I didn't say anything about it when I got home; but after supper I went back. The moon was rising; it shone on the white sheep; and that was all the light there was. And then came the second time; the bells were ringing for the noonday Angelus. The light came again, in bright sunlight, but brighter than the sun, and that time I saw him.

CAUCHON: You saw whom?

JOAN: A man in a white robe, with two white wings reaching from the sky to the ground. He didn't tell me his name that day, but later on I found out that he was the blessed St. Michael.

WARWICK: Is it absolutely necessary to have her telling these absurdities all over again?

CAUCHON: Absolutely necessary, my lord.

(WARWICK *goes back to his corner in silence, and smells the rose he has in his hand.*)

JOAN (*in the deep voice of the Archangel*): —Joan, go to the help of the King of France, and give him back his kingdom. (*She replies in her own voice.*) Oh sir, you haven't looked at me; I am only a young peasant girl, not a great

captain who can lead an army.—You will go and search
out Robert de Beaudricourt, the Governor of Vaucouleurs.
He will give you a suit of clothes to dress you like a man,
and he will take you to the Dauphin. St. Catherine and St.
Margaret will protect you. (*She suddenly drops to the floor
sobbing with fear.*)—Please, please pity me, holy sir! I'm
happy here alone in the fields. I've never had to be responsible
for anything, except my sheep. The Kingdom of France is
far beyond anything I can do. If you will only look at me
you will see I am small, and ignorant. The realm of France is
too heavy, sir. But the King of France has famous Captains,
as strong as you could need and they're used to doing these
things. If they lose a battle they sleep as soundly as ever.
They simply say the snow or the wind was against them; and
they just cross all the dead men off their roll. But I should always remember I had killed them. Please have pity on me!
. . . No such thing. No pity. He had gone already, and
there I was, with France on my shoulders. Not to mention
the work on the farm, and my father, who wasn't easy.

(*Her* FATHER, *who has been wandering around her*
MOTHER, *suddenly speaks.*)

FATHER: Where has that girl got to?
MOTHER (*going on with her knitting*): She is out in the
fields.
FATHER: Well, I was out in the fields, and I'm back home
again. It's six o'clock. She's no business to be out in the
fields.
BROTHER: She's sitting under the Fairy Tree, staring at
nothing. I saw her when I went to fetch in the bull.
PROMOTER (*from among the crowd*): The Fairy Tree!
Note that, gentlemen, if you will. Note the superstition. The
beginning of witchcraft already. The Fairy Tree! I ask you
to note that!
CAUCHON: There are Fairy Trees all over France, my Lord
Promoter. It's in our own interest not to refuse the fairies to
these little girls.
PROMOTER (*primly*): We have our saints. That should be
sufficient.
CAUCHON (*conciliating him*): Later on, certainly. But I
mean while they are still very young; as Joan was; not yet
fifteen.
PROMOTER: By fifteen they know everything: they're as
old as Eve.

CAUCHON: Not Joan: Joan at that time was very simple and innocent. It will be another matter when we come to the trial; I shan't spare her Voices then. But a little girl shall keep her fairies. (*Firmly.*) And these discussions are under my charge.

(*The* PROMOTER *bows, and retires, unmollified.*)

FATHER (*bursting out afresh, to the* BROTHER): So that's where you say she is? And what does she think she's doing there, sitting under the tree?

BROTHER: Try and find out! She's just staring in front of her as if she was expecting something. And it isn't the first time either.

FATHER: Well, why didn't you tell me when you saw her before, then? Aren't you old enough to know what trouble there is with girls of her age, you little fool? What do you think she was expecting, eh? Somebody, not something, idiot! She's got a lover, and you know it! Give me my stick!

MOTHER (*gently, still knitting*): You know quite well, Joan's as innocent as a baby.

FATHER: Maybe she is. And girls as innocent as babies can come to you one evening and hold up their faces to be kissed, and the next morning, though you've kept them locked in their room all night, what has happened? You can't see into their eyes at all: they're avoiding you, and lying to you. They're the devil, all at once.

PROMOTER (*raising a finger*): The word has been said, my lords, and by her father!

MOTHER: How do you know that? The day I married you I was as innocent as Joan, and I daresay you could look into my eyes just as well next morning.

FATHER (*muttering*): That's nothing to do with it.

MOTHER: Who are these other girls you've known, then, that you've never told me about?

FATHER (*thundering to cover his embarrassment*): I tell you it's got nothing to do with it! We're not talking about other girls, we're talking about Joan! Hand me that stick. I'm going to look for her, and if she's been meeting somebody on the quiet I'll skin them alive!

JOAN (*smiling gently*): I was meeting someone on the quiet, and his solemn voice was saying: "Joan! Joan! What are you waiting for? There's a great sorrow in the realm of France."—"Holy Sir of Heaven, I'm so afraid; I'm only a young village girl; surely you've made a mistake?"—"Does

God make mistakes, Joan?" (*She turns to her Judges.*) How could I have answered Yes?

PROMOTER (*shrugging*):   You should have made the sign of the cross.

JOAN: I did, and the Archangel made it, too, all the time keeping his eyes carefully on mine, and the church clock sounded.

PROMOTER: You should have cried: Vade retro Satanus!

JOAN: I don't know Latin, my Lord.

PROMOTER: Don't be an idiot! The devil understands French. You should have cried: Get thee behind me, foul Satan, and don't tempt me again.

JOAN: But, my Lord, it was St. Michael.

PROMOTER (*sneering*):   So he told you. And you were fool enough to believe him.

JOAN: Yes, I believed him. He couldn't have been the devil. He shone with light; he was beautiful.

PROMOTER (*losing his temper*):   So is the devil, so is the devil. He shone with light; he was beautiful.

JOAN (*scandalised*):   Oh, my Lord!

CAUCHON (*calming the* PROMOTER *with a gesture*):   These subtle theological points, my lord Promoter, are proper for debating between ourselves, but they're beyond the understanding of this poor girl. No good is served by shocking her.

JOAN (*to the* PROMOTER):   You're telling a lie, Canon! I haven't any of your learning, but I know the devil is ugly, and all that's beautiful is the work of God.

PROMOTER (*sneering*):   Very charming, simple and stupid! Do you think the devil is stupid? He's a thousand times more intelligent than you and I put together. Do you think when he comes to snare a soul he would come like a horror of the flesh, with black ploughed skin and a snouting tusk like a rhinoceros? If he did, souls would fly to virtue at the sight of him. I tell you he chooses a moonlit summer night, and comes with coaxing hands, with eyes that receive you into them like water that drowns you, with naked women's flesh, transparent, white . . . beautiful—

CAUCHON (*stopping him sternly*):   Canon! You are losing your way! This is very far from Joan's devil, if she has seen one. I beg you not to confuse your devil with hers.

PROMOTER (*flushed and confused in front of the smiling crowd*):   I beg your pardon, my lord; there is only one devil.

CAUCHON: Go on, Joan.

JOAN (*still troubled*):   If the devil is beautiful, how can we know him?

PROMOTER: By asking your parish priest.

JOAN: Can we never know by ourselves?

PROMOTER: No. That is why there is no salvation out-side the church.

JOAN: Only rich people have a parish priest always at hand. It's hard for the poor.

PROMOTER: It is hard for everyone to escape damnation.

CAUCHON: My lord Promoter, let her talk with her Voices in peace and quiet. It is the beginning of the story. We mustn't reproach her with them yet.

JOAN (*continuing*):   Another time it was St. Catherine and St. Margaret who came to me. (*She turns to the* PROMOTER *with a slightly mischievous defiance.*) They were beautiful, too.

PROMOTER (*blushing, but unable to prevent himself*):   Did they appear to you naked?

JOAN (*smiling*):   Oh, my Lord! Do you imagine that God can't afford clothes for the saints in heaven?

(*The* CROWD *chuckles at this answer, and the* PROMOTER *sits down confused.*)

CAUCHON: You see, you make us all smile with your questions, my lord Promoter. Be wise enough to keep your interruptions until we come to the serious heart of this busi-ness. And when we do so, particularly when we come to judge her, remember that the soul in this little arrogant body is in our care. Aren't you risking very much confusion in her mind, to suggest to her that good and evil are no more than a ques-tion of clothes? It is true certainly, that our saints are tradi-tionally represented as clothed; yet, on the other hand—

JOAN (*to the* PROMOTER):   Our Lord is naked on the cross.

CAUCHON (*turning to her*):   I was going to say so, Joan, if you had not prevented me. It isn't for you to correct the reverend Canon. You forget who you are; you forget that we are your priests, your masters and your judges. Beware of your pride, Joan. If the devil one day wins you for his own, that is the way he will come to you.

JOAN: I know I am proud. But if God didn't mean me to be proud, why did He send an Archangel to see me, and saints with the light of heaven on them to speak to me? Why did He promise I should persuade all the people I have persuaded—men as learned and as wise as you—and say I should ride in white armour, with a bright sword given me by the King, to lead France into battle: and it has been so. He had only to leave me looking after the sheep, and I don't think pride would ever have entered my head.

CAUCHON: Weigh your words, Joan; weigh your thoughts. It is your Saviour you are accusing now.

JOAN (*crossing herself*): God guide me. His will be done, if His will is to make me proud and damned. That is His right, as well.

PROMOTER (*unable to contain himself*): Terrible! What she says is terrible! God's will to damn a soul? And you all listen to this without a murmur, my lords? I see here the seed of a fearful heresy which will one day tear the Church apart.

(*The* INQUISITOR *has risen. He is an intelligent-looking man, spare and hard, speaking with great quietness.*)

INQUISITOR: Listen carefully to what I am going to ask you, Joan. Do you think you are in a state of grace at this moment?

JOAN (*firmly*): At what moment, my lord? Is it the beginning, when I hear my Voices, or the end, when my King and all my friends have deserted me, when I doubt and recant and the Church receives me again?

INQUISITOR: Don't evade my question. Do you think you are in a state of grace?

(*All the* PRIESTS *are watching her in silence; it seems a dangerous question.*)

LADVENU (*rising*): My lord Inquisitor, it is a formidable question for a simple girl who believes in all sincerity that God has called her. I ask that her reply shall not be held against her: she is risking quite unwittingly—

INQUISITOR: Quiet, Brother Ladvenu! I ask what I consider good to ask. Let her answer my question. Do you think you are in a state of grace, Joan?

JOAN: If I am not, may God in His goodness set me there. If I am, may God in His goodness keep me so.

(*The* PRIESTS *murmur. The* INQUISITOR *sits again, inscrutable.*)

LADVENU (*quietly*): Well answered, Joan.

PROMOTER (*muttering, annoyed by* JOAN's *success*): What of it? The devil has cunning, or he wouldn't be the devil. It isn't the first time he has been asked that question. We know what he is; he has his answers all ready.

WARWICK (*bored, to* CAUCHON): No doubt this is all very interesting, my lord, but if you go on at this rate we shall never get to the trial, never have her burnt, never get anywhere. I said she could take us over the old ground again, if you thought it so necessary, but let her get on with it. And let us come to the essentials. His Majesty's Government have to discredit this wretched little Charles Valois, at once; it's imperative that we should let Christendom know that the Coronation was all a humbug, the performance of a witch, a heretic, an army's whore.

CAUCHON: My lord, we're trying her only for heresy.

WARWICK: I know that; but I have to make more of it for the sake of the troops. The findings of your trial, I'm afraid, will be too rarefied for my soldiers. Propaganda, my lord Archbishop, is black or white. The main thing is to say something pretty staggering, and repeat it often enough until you turn it into a truth. It's a new idea, but, believe me, it will make its way. The essential thing, so far as I am concerned, is that the girl should be a nonentity, whatever she is in fact. And what she is in fact is of no particular importance to His Majesty's Government. Personally, I must admit, I find the girl attractive. The way she takes the wind out of your sails gives me a lot of pleasure; and her seat on a horse is very good: that's rare in a woman. If the circumstances had been different, and she had belonged to my own set, I should have enjoyed a day's hunting with her. But unfortunately there's been this damned Coronation, and that was nobody's notion but hers in the first place. Really, my lords, what impudence! To have himself crowned King of France right under our noses: a Valois, King of France! and to do it at Rheims, our territory! To dare to pick France out of our pockets, and pilfer the English heritage! Luckily, God is on the side of England, as he satisfactorily proved at Agincourt. God and our right. Two ideas completely synonymous. And moreover, inscribed on our coat-of-arms. So rattle her through the rest of it, and have her burned, and not so much talk. Earlier on I was joking. I give it ten years, and this whole incident will have been forgotten.

CAUCHON (*sighing*): God grant so, my lord.

WARWICK: Where had we got to?

FATHER (*coming forward with his stick*): To where I was going out to find her, sitting under her tree, waiting to get herself into trouble, the little bitch. And I can tell you she'll be sorry she ever began it! (*He drags* JOAN *up by the wrists.*) What are you doing here, eh? Tell me what you're waiting about here for, when you know you ought to be indoors, eating your supper!

JOAN (*stammering, shy at being surprised, raising her arm to protect her face*):   I didn't know it was so late. I had lost count of the time.

FATHER: That's it, you lost count of the time! And what else have you lost that you daren't tell me? (*He shakes her abominably.*) Who made you forget it was so late? I heard you as I came along, calling out goodbye to somebody. Well, who was it?

JOAN: St. Michael, father.

FATHER (*giving her a resounding slap on the face*):   You make fun at your father, you'll be sorry! I won't have any girl of mine sitting out in the fields waiting for any man who wants to find her. You'll marry the decent fellow we choose for you, or I'll break every bone in your body!

JOAN: I've done nothing wrong, father: truthfully it was the blessed St. Michael who spoke to me.

FATHER: And when you can't hide your sinning any longer, and every day it grows bigger in you for all to see, and you've killed your mother with grief, and your brothers have to join the army to get away from the scandal in the village, it will be the Holy Ghost who brought it on us, I suppose? I'll tell the priest: not content with whoring, you have to blaspheme: and you'll be shut up in a convent on bread and water, my girl.

JOAN (*kneeling before him*):   Father, stop shouting, you can't hear what I say. I promise you, by our Saviour, I'm telling you the truth. They've been coming for a long time now to ask things of me. It is always at the mid-day Angelus or the evening Angelus; always when I'm praying, when I am least sinful and nearest to God. Above all doubt, surely it must be true. St. Michael has appeared to me, and St. Margaret, and St. Catherine. They speak to me, and they answer when I question them, and each one says the same as the others.

FATHER (*pulling her about*):   Why should St. Michael speak to you, you little idiot? Does he speak to me? Natural enough, if he had something to say to us, he'd say it to me, the head of the family. Does he speak to our priest?

JOAN: Father, as well as shaking me and shouting at me, try to understand what I'm saying. I'm so alone, and they want me to do so much. For three years I've been trying not to believe them, but all that time they've been saying the same thing. These voices I hear: I can't go on fighting them all by myself. I've got to do what they say.

FATHER: The voices you hear? Do you want to drive me mad?

JOAN: They say it can't wait any longer; the time has come when I have to say yes.

FATHER: What can't wait any longer, idiot? What are they telling you to do, what you call these Voices? Voices! Well, it's better than being deaf!

JOAN: They tell me to go and save the realm of France which is in grave danger of being destroyed. Is it true?

FATHER: Heavens above! Of course the realm of France is in danger of being destroyed. It isn't the first time, and it won't be the last: and she always gets out of it. Leave it in God's hands; there's nothing you can do about it, you poor girl. Even a man can't do anything about it, unless he's a soldier.

JOAN: But I can. My voices have said so.

FATHER (laughing): Oh, you can, can you? Dear me! You're sharper than all our great captains, of course, who can't do anything these days except be beaten every time they fight?

JOAN: Yes, father.

FATHER: Yes, father! Perhaps you're not a bad girl, but worse. You're a mad, idiot girl. What do you think you can do then, poor idiot?

JOAN: What my Voices tell me. I can ask the Squire of Beaudricourt for an armed escort. And when I've got my escort, I can go straight to the Dauphin at Chinon, to tell him that he's the rightful King; and I can lead him out at the head of the soldiers to save Orleans; and then I can persuade him to be consecrated with holy oil by the Archbishop, and then we can hurl the English into the sea.

FATHER (suddenly understanding): Now you're explaining yourself, at last, you filthy little slut! You want to go off with the soldiers, like the lowest of the low?

JOAN (smiling mysteriously): No, father, like the highest under God, riding first into the battle, and not looking back until I have saved France. (Suddenly sad.) And after that is done, what happens is God's will.

FATHER: I've heard enough shameless lying! I won't stand any more of it! I'll teach you what happens to girls who go chasing after soldiers, pretending to save France!

(He savagely and unmercifully beats and kicks her.)

JOAN (crying): Stop, father, stop! stop!

(*The* FATHER *has taken off his belt, and starts to leather her, gasping with effort.*)

LADVENU (*rising, very pale*):   This must be stopped! He means to injure her.

CAUCHON (*gently*):   We can do nothing, Brother Ladvenu. At this part of the story we have never met Joan; we don't get to know her until the trial. We can only act our parts, each his own, good or bad, as they are written, and in his turn. And later on, you know, we shall do worse things than this to her. (*He turns to* WARWICK.) This domestic scene is not very pleasant to witness, my lord?

WARWICK (*with a gesture*):   Why not? We're firm believers in corporal punishment in England; it forms the character. I myself have been flogged many times as a boy; and I took it extremely well.

(*The* FATHER, *at last too exhausted to go on, wipes the sweat off his forehead, and shouts at* JOAN, *lying crumpled at his feet.*)

FATHER: There! you carrion! Do you still want to save France? (*He turns to the others, rather ashamed of himself.*) Well, sirs, what would you have done in my place if your daughter had said that to you?

MOTHER (*coming forward*):   Have you killed her?

FATHER: Not this time. But if she talks any more about going off with the soldiers, I'll drown that girl of yours in the river with my own hands, do you hear me? And if I'm nowhere about, I give her brother full permission to do it for me. (*He strides off.*)

(*The* MOTHER *bends over* JOAN *and dries her face.*)

MOTHER: Joan, my little Joan, my little Joan. Did he hurt you?

JOAN (*giving a pathetic smile when she recognises her* MOTHER):   Yes. He meant me to feel it.

MOTHER: He's your father, Joan; you must bear it patiently.

JOAN (*in a small voice*):   I do bear it, mother, I prayed while he beat me: prayed that our heavenly Father would forgive him.

MOTHER (*shocked*):   Our heavenly Father doesn't have to forgive fathers for beating their daughters. It's their right.

JOAN: And I prayed for him to understand.

MOTHER (*fondling her*):   Understand what, my silly one? Why did you have to tell him all this nonsense?

JOAN (*in agony*):   Someone has to understand; otherwise I'm by myself, and I have to face them alone!

MOTHER (*rocking her in her arms*):   Now, now, now, you don't have to upset yourself. You remember when you were little, we would rock away your nightmares together. But now you're nearly a woman: nearly too big to hold in my arms any more, and I can tell you it's no good breaking your heart to make men understand anything. All you can do is say "yes" to whatever they think, and wait till they've gone out to the fields. Then you can be mistress in your own house again. Your father's a good man; but if I didn't trick him sometimes for his own good I don't know where we should be. Who is it, Joan? You can tell your mother. Don't you even know his name, perhaps? And yet I don't know but it must be someone in the village. Why, your father might even agree to him; he's not against a good marriage for you. We might even be able to persuade him he chose the boy himself, the poor old stupid. You know what men are: roar a lot, and lay down the law, and bang you about: but, the same as with a bull, you can lead them by the nose.

JOAN: It isn't marriage that I have to think of, mother. The blessed St. Michael has told me I should leave the village, put on a man's clothes, and go and find his highness the Dauphin, to save the realm of France.

MOTHER (*severely*):   Joan, I speak nicely and gently to you, but I won't have you talking wickedness. And I won't have you put on a man's clothes, not if you beg at my grave. Have my daughter a man! You let me catch you, my goodness!

JOAN: But, mother, I should have to, if I'm to ride on horseback with the soldiers. It's the blessed St. Michael who says so.

MOTHER: I don't care what the blessed St. Michael says, you shall never go off on a horse. Joan of Arc on a horse! It would be the talk of the village.

JOAN: But the lady of Vaucouleurs rides a horse to hawking.

MOTHER: You will not ride a horse, never! It isn't the station of life you were born to. Such grand ideas, indeed!

JOAN: But if I don't ride a horse, how can I lead the soldiers?

MOTHER: And you won't go with the soldiers, either, you wicked girl! I'd rather see you cold and dead. You see, how you make me talk the same as your father. There are some things we feel the same about. A daughter spins, and scrubs, and stays at home. Your grandmother never left this village, and neither have I, and neither will you, and when you have a daughter of your own, neither will she. (*She suddenly bursts into tears.*) Going off with the soldiers! Do you want to kill me?

JOAN (*throwing herself into her mother's arms, crying too*): No, mother!

MOTHER: You do: I can see you do. And you'll destroy yourself in the end if you don't soon get these thoughts out of your head. (*Exit.*)

(JOAN straightens herself up, still in tears, while her MOTHER goes back to the CROWD.)

JOAN: You see, holy St. Michael, it isn't possible; they won't ever understand. No one will. It is better that I should give up at once. Our Lord has said that we have to obey our father and mother. (*She speaks with the voice of the Archangel.*)

—But first, Joan, you have to obey God.

—But if God commands the impossible?

—Then you have to attempt the impossible, calmly and quietly. It is a cause for pride, Joan, that God gives you something of His burden to carry.

(*After a pause.*)

—My Lord, do you think our Saviour can want a daughter to make her parents weep, and leave them alone to break their hearts, perhaps to die? That's hard to understand.

—He has said, I come to bring not peace, but a sword. I am come to set the brother against the sister and the son against the father. God came to bring struggle, Joan; not to make the way easy, but to make the way harder. He doesn't ask the impossible of everybody, but He does ask it of you. That is all. (JOAN *looks up, and says simply.*)—Well, I will go.

A VOICE (*from somewhere out of the shadows behind*): Proud and arrogant!

JOAN (*disturbed*): Who is calling me proud and arrogant?

(*After a pause, in the voice of the Archangel.*)

—It was you, Joan. And when you begin to do what God is asking, it will be what the world calls you. But if you give yourself humbly into the hands of God, you can bear this blame of pride.

—It is heavy to bear, my Lord!

—Yes, it is heavy. But God knows that you are strong.

(*A silence. She looks straight in front of her, and suddenly becomes a little girl again, happy and decided.*)

All right, then. It's all decided. I shall go and find my Uncle Durand. With him I always get my own way. He's as easy to manage as a tame sparrow. I shall kiss him on both cheeks, and on the top of his head, and sit on his lap, and he will say "Oh Lord, Oh Lord," and take me to Vaucouleurs!

BROTHER: You're a silly donkey! Why did you have to go and tell the old people all that stuff? Next time, if you give me a ha'penny, I won't say a word about where I saw you.

JOAN (*leaping cheerfully at him*): Oh, so it was you who told them, you beastly little pig? Sneak, sneak, I'll give you a tweak! Tell tales out of school, duck him in a muddy pool! There's your halfpenny, lardy-head. Tell-tale-tit, your tongue shall be split, and all the children in the town shall have a little bit!

(*They fight like urchins. She chases straight across the stage towards* BEAUDRICOURT *who has come forward to take the centre of the stage.*)

BEAUDRICOURT: Well, what is it? What does she want? What is it you want, you infernal nuisance? What's this nonsensical story I hear—

(JOAN *collides head first with* BEAUDRICOURT's *great paunch. He is half winded, gives a yell of pain, grabs her by the arm and lifts her level with his nose, apoplectic with rage.*)

What the devil do you want, you horrible mosquito? What the devil do you mean, playing the fool outside my gates for three days on end? What the devil are these tales you've been telling the guards until their eyes pop out as far as their noses?

JOAN (*breathless with her running and poised on tip-toe in the arms of the giant*): I want a horse, my lord, a man's clothes, and an escort, to go to Chinon to see his highness the Dauphin.

BEAUDRICOURT: And my boot, you want that, too, of course?

JOAN: If you like, my lord, and a good clout, as long as I get the horse as well.

BEAUDRICOURT (*still holding her*): You know about me and you know what I want; the village girls have told you all about it, haven't they? They come along to see me, usually to beg for the life of a brother, or their old father who's been caught poaching on my lands. If the girl is pretty, I always hook him down off the gallows, being amiable at heart. If she's ugly, I hang the old chap, to make an example of him. But it's always the pretty ones who come; they manage to dig up one in the family somehow; with the admirable result that I have a fine reputation for benevolence in the neighbourhood. So now you know the rate of exchange, and we can come to terms.

JOAN (*simply*): I don't know what you're trying to say, my lord. The blessed St. Michael sent me to you.

BEAUDRICOURT (*crossing himself anxiously with his free hand*): You don't have to bring the saints into this. That was all right for the guards, to get you in to see me. But now you're here, and you can leave the saints in their proper places. And I wouldn't be surprised if you get your horse. An old jade for a young maid; it's a reasonable bargain. Are you a virgin?

JOAN: Yes, my lord.

BEAUDRICOURT (*looking at her all the time*): I agree to the horse.

JOAN: That isn't all I want, my lord.

BEAUDRICOURT: A greedy child, I see! Well, go on; you're amusing me. If I pay well for my pleasures it helps me to believe I really want them. You understand where this conversation is leading?

JOAN (*frankly*): No, my lord.

BEAUDRICOURT: Splendid. The bed's no place for brains. What else do you want beside the horse? The taxes are coming in very well this autumn; I don't mind being generous.

JOAN: An escort of men-at-arms, my lord, to accompany me to Chinon.

BEAUDRICOURT (*freeing her, changing his tone*): Now listen to me, if we're to get on together: I may be easygoing, but I won't stand any impudence. I'm the master here and you're using up my patience fast. I can just as well have you whipped for forcing your way in here, and send you home with nothing except the marks on your backside. So behave yourself. Why do you want to go to Chinon?

JOAN: To find his highness the Dauphin.

BEAUDRICOURT: Well, well, you mean to get on! Why not the Duke of Burgundy while you're about it? In theory, you might have a sporting chance with him: the Duke's as hot as a buck rabbit. Whereas, as you probably know, the Dauphin when it comes to war and women . . . I don't know what you expect to get from him.

JOAN: An army, my lord, which I can lead to Orleans.

BEAUDRICOURT: Ah: if you're mad it's another thing altogether. I'm not getting involved in any scandal. (*He turns to the crowd upstage.*) Hey, there, Boudousse!

(*A GUARD comes forward.*) Take her away and give her a ducking, and then lock her up. You can send her back to her father tomorrow evening. But no beating, I don't want any trouble; the girl's mad.

JOAN (*calmly, held by the GUARD*):   You can lock me up, my lord: I don't mind that; but when they let me out tomorrow evening I shall come back again. So it would be simpler if you let me talk to you now.

BEAUDRICOURT: Ten million thunders! Don't I frighten you?

JOAN: No, my lord. Not at all.

BEAUDRICOURT (*to the GUARD*):   Get back to your post! you don't need to stand about, listening to this.

(*The GUARD goes, and when he has gone BEAUDRICOURT asks uneasily.*) And why don't I frighten you? I frighten everybody.

JOAN (*quietly*):   You are very good, my lord.

BEAUDRICOURT: Good? Good? I've told you, that depends on the price.

JOAN: And what's more, very intelligent. There are many people I will have to convince before I can do everything my Voices want; so it's lucky the first pèrson I have to deal with, the one everything really depends on, should turn out to be the most intelligent.

BEAUDRICOURT (*slightly puzzled, asks in a casual voice while he pours himself some wine*):   You're an odd girl, in your way. How did you come to notice that I'm intelligent?

JOAN: Because you're very handsome, my lord.

BEAUDRICOURT (*with a furtive glance into the metal mirror beside him*):   Oh, tush! I suppose, twenty years ago, I might say that I pleased the ladies; and I've taken care of myself, not let myself get too old too soon; that's all it is.—It's quite peculiar and unsettling to have a conversation like this with a farm girl I've never heard of, who happens to drop in like a stray kitten. (*He sighs.*) On the whole I vegetate here. My lieutenants are a poor bunch: hardly a brain between them. And while we're on the subject, what's this connection you find between intellect and beauty! I've usually heard quite the opposite: handsome people are always stupid; that's the general opinion.

JOAN: That's the opinion of the plain people, who like to believe God can't manage both things at once.

BEAUDRICOURT (*flattered*): Ah, well, you've made a point there. But then, take myself for example. I know, as you so kindly say, I'm not one of the plain people; but I wonder sometimes, am I, after all, very intelligent? No, no, don't protest. It's a question I have to ask now and again. I can tell you this, between ourselves, as you're not anyone in particular. Obviously I'm more intelligent than my lieutenants, that's only natural, being officer in command. If that wasn't an established fact there wouldn't be an army at all. But even so, I sometimes meet with problems which I find very troublesome. They ask me to decide something, some tactical or administrative point, and quite suddenly, I don't know why, my mind is a blank. There it is, nothing but a sort of fog. Mark you, nobody knows that. I get out of it, without my face showing any change of expression; I make a decision all right. And that's the essential thing when you're in command, of course: make a decision, whatever it is. Until you've had some experience you're apt to get flustered: but you realise after a bit, it all amounts to the same thing, whatever you decide. Still, I should like to see myself doing better. Vaucouleurs, as you see, is of no great size. I'm looking forward to the day when I make a really important decision: one of those momentous decisions, of great consequence to the nation: not a question of somebody who hasn't paid his taxes, or half a dozen prisoners to be hanged: but something a bit exceptional, which would get me noticed and talked about higher up. (*He stops dreaming, and looks at her.*) I don't know what in the world I'm doing telling you all this. You can't do anything about it, and God help you, you're half crazy into the bargain.

JOAN (*smiling gently*): I know why. I knew it would happen, because they told me so. Listen, Robert—

BEAUDRICOURT (*startled*): What are you doing calling me by my Christian name?

JOAN: It's God's name for you, Robert. Now listen, Robert, and don't bluster again, because it isn't any use. What is the important decision, which will get you noticed and talked about higher up? I can tell you, Robert. It's me.

BEAUDRICOURT: What are you talking about?

JOAN (*coming to him*):   I'll tell you, if you'll listen. First of all, you have to stop thinking of me as a girl, that's what is getting you confused. And I don't mean much to you anyway, do I? (*He hesitates, afraid of being cheated; she flares up.*) Robert, if you want to help yourself, you have to help me, too! When I tell you the truth, acknowledge it and say Yes: otherwise we shall never get anywhere.

BEAUDRICOURT (*muttering, rather shamefaced*):   Well, no . . .

JOAN (*severely*):   What do you mean, no?

BEAUDRICOURT: I mean, yes, it's true. I'm not particular about you. (*Adding politely.*) Though, mind you, you're a pretty enough little thing. . . .

JOAN: All right, you don't have to think you've upset me. I'm very happy the point is cleared up. And now you can imagine you have already given me the suit of clothes I asked for, and we can discuss things together, sensibly and calmly, as man to man.

BEAUDRICOURT (*still suspicious*):   Discuss what?

JOAN (*sitting on the edge of the table, finishing the dregs in the wine glass*):   Your own important decision, my splendid Robert. Your great achievement which will make everyone take notice of you. Think of all of them, there at Bourges. They don't know whether they're praying or cursing, or which saint to turn to next. The English are everywhere. And you know the French army. Good boys, who have still got fight in them, but they're discouraged. They've got it into their heads that the English will always be the strongest, and there's nothing to be done. Dunois the Bastard; he's a good captain; intelligent, which is rare in the army, but no one listens to him any more, and he's getting tired of it. So he spends his days having a high old time with the women in the camp (and that's something else I shall have to deal with): and he's far too cock-a-hoop, like all bastards. "The affairs of France aren't his concern: let that milksop Charles get his country out of the tangle for himself." Then there's La Hire, and there's Xantrailles: prize angry bulls: they always want to charge in head first, slashing and thrusting like old heroes in the chronicles. They belong among the champions of single combat, who don't understand how to use their cannons, and always get killed to no purpose whatever, the way they did at Agincourt. They're wonderful at getting killed, but it isn't any help. That's true, isn't it, Robert. You can't treat war like a tournament. You have to win. You have to be cunning. (*She touches her forehead.*) You have to wage it here. With all your intelligence, Robert, you know that better than I do.

BEAUDRICOURT: I've always said so. Nowadays we don't think enough. Take my lieutenants: always spoiling for a fight, and that's all they can think of. And the men who know how to think get overlooked; nobody dreams of using them.

JOAN: Nobody. So they have to think for themselves. It's a lucky thing you have had such a tremendous idea. It's certain to alter everything.

BEAUDRICOURT (*uneasily*): I have an idea?

JOAN: Don't question it, Robert; be very proud of it. Your brain is working at great speed, clearly and concisely. It's a sad thing to think that, in the whole of France at this moment, no one sees things clearly, except you.

BEAUDRICOURT: You believe so?

JOAN: I tell you so.

BEAUDRICOURT: And what is it I see?

JOAN: You see simply that the people of France have to be given a spirit and a faith. And it so happens that you have with you at this moment a young country girl. St. Michael has appeared to her, and St. Catherine and St. Margaret, or at least she says they have. You are not so sure about it, but for the time being it's not important. And this is where you show yourself to be so remarkable. You say to yourself: Here's a little peasant girl, of no consequence at all; all right. If by any chance she really has been sent by God, then nothing could stop her, and it can't be proved one way or the other whether God sent her or not. She certainly got in to see me, without my permission, and I've been listening to her for half an hour; nobody could deny that. And then, like a sword of lightning, the idea strikes home to you. You say to yourself: If she has the power to convince me, why shouldn't she convince the Dauphin and Dunois and the Archbishop? They're men, just as I'm a man; as a matter of fact, between ourselves, rather less intelligent. Moreover, why shouldn't she convince our soldiers that the English in the main are exactly like themselves, half courage and half a wish to save their skins; pummel them hard enough at the right moment, and you send them staggering out of Orleans. It's magnificent how you marshal the whole situation in your mind. What our fellows need, you are saying to yourself: what they need is someone to rouse their spirit and prove to them that God is still with them. This is where you show yourself a born leader, Robert.

BEAUDRICOURT (*pitifully*):   You think that?

JOAN: I know it. And very soon so will everyone else. Like all great politicians, you're a realist, Robert. You say to yourself: I, Beaudricourt, have my doubts about her coming from God, but I'll send her off to them, and if they think she is, it will have the same effect whether it's true or false. By a stroke of good luck my courier is leaving for Bourges tomorrow morning—

BEAUDRICOURT: Who told you that? It's a secret.

JOAN: I found it out. (*She continues.*) I pick half a dozen strong men for an escort, give her a horse and send her off with the courier. At Chinon, as far as I can see, she will work things out for herself. (*She looks at him admiringly.*) My word, my word, Robert!

BEAUDRICOURT: What?

JOAN: You have a marvellous intelligence to think of all that.

BEAUDRICOURT (*wiping his forehead, worn out*):   Yes.

JOAN: Only, please give me a quiet horse, because I don't know how to ride one yet.

BEAUDRICOURT (*delighted*):   You're going to break your neck, my girl!

JOAN: I don't think so. St. Michael will hold me on. I tell you what, Robert: I'll have a wager with you. I'll bet you a suit of clothes—the man's clothes which you still haven't said you'll give me—against a punch on the nose. Bring two horses into the courtyard and we'll gallop them together. If I fall off, you can lose faith in me. Is that fair? (*She offers him her hand.*) Agreed? And whoever doesn't pay up is a man of mud!

BEAUDRICOURT (*getting up*):   Agreed! I need to move about a bit. I wouldn't have believed how tiring it is to think so much. (*He calls.*) Boudousse!

(*Enter the* GUARD.)

GUARD: Do I take her away and give her a ducking, sir?

BEAUDRICOURT: No, you idiot! You fetch her some breeches, and bring us a couple of horses. We're taking a gallop together.

GUARD: What about the Council, sir? It's four o'clock.

BEAUDRICOURT: It can wait till tomorrow. Today I've used my brains quite enough.

(*He goes.* JOAN *passes the astonished* GUARD *and sticks out her tongue. They lose themselves in the crowd up stage.*)

WARWICK (*to* CAUCHON): I can see this girl had quality. Very entertaining, to watch her playing the old fish, didn't you think so?

CAUCHON: Rather too crude for my taste, my lord. Something subtler than that will be needed when she comes to deal with Charles.

WARWICK: My lord Bishop, the tricks that you and I use in our way of business aren't so remarkably different from hers. Whether we're ruling the world with a mace or a crozier, in the long run, we do it by persuading fools that what we make them think is their own opinion. No need for any intervention of God in that. Which is why I found it so entertaining. (*He bows politely towards the* BISHOP.) Entertaining, at least, if one isn't professionally concerned, of course, as you are. Have you faith yourself, my lord Bishop? Forgive my bluntness; but between ourselves. I'm interested to know.

CAUCHON (*simply*): A child's faith, my lord. And that is why I shall make problems for you during the trial, and why we shall go as far as ever we can to save Joan, even though we have been sincere collaborators with the English rule, which seemed to us then the only reasonable solution to chaos. It was very easy for those who were at Bourges to call us traitors, when they had the protection of the French army. We were in occupied Rouen.

WARWICK: I don't like the word "occupied": You forget the Treaty of Troyes. You were quite simply on His Majesty's territory.

CAUCHON: In the midst of His Majesty's army, and the execution of His Majesty's hostages; submitting to the curfew, and the condescension of His Majesty's food-supplies. We were men, with the frailty of men, who wanted to go on living, and yet at the same time to save Joan if we could. It was not in any way a happy part that we were called upon to fill.

WARWICK (*smiling*): There was nothing to stop you becoming martyrs, my dear fellow, if that would have made it more inspiring for you. My eight hundred soldiers were quite ready.

CAUCHON: We knew it. They took great pleasure in shouting their insults at us, hammering on the door with the butts of their halberds, to remind us they were there. We temporised for nine months before we would deliver Joan up to you; this little girl, forsaken by everyone; nine months to make her say Yes. Future times will be pleased to say we were barbarous. But I fancy, for all their fine principles, they will take to expediency faster than we did; in every camp.

WARWICK: Nine months, that's quite true. What a difficult confinement this trial has been. Our Holy Mother Church takes her time, when she's asked to give birth to a small matter of policy. But the nightmare is over. The mother and child are both doing well.

CAUCHON: I have pondered deeply over these things, my lord. The health of the mother, as you put it, is our one concern. And that is why, when we saw there could be no alternative, we sacrificed the child in good faith. Ever since that day of Joan's arrest, God has been dead to us. Neither she, whatever she may imagine, nor we, certainly, have heard Him any more. We have gone on, following our daily custom; our pre-eminent duty, to defend the old house, this great and wise human building which is all that remains to us in the absence of God. From the time we were fifteen years old, we were taught how to defend it. Joan had no such help, and yet, though her faith fell on dreadful days, when she was left alone by men and by God, she also has gone on, recovering at once after the single moment when she weakened, bearing herself with her curious mixture of humility and insolence, of grandeur and good sense, even up to execution and death. We weren't able to understand it then; we had our eyes buried in our mother's skirts, like children grown old. And yet, precisely in this loneliness, in the desert of a vanished God, in the privation and misery of the animal, the man is indeed great who continues to lift his head. Greatly alone.

WARWICK: Yes, well, no doubt. But if our business is politics we can't afford to brood about such men. We seem fated, as a rule, to meet them among the people we condemn to execution.

CAUCHON (*quietly, after a pause*): It is a consolation to me sometimes to think of those old priests who, though they were deeply offended by her insolent answers, nevertheless, even with English swords at their back, tried for nine months not to commit the irreparable.

WARWICK: Enough of fine phrases, Bishop. Nothing is irreparable in politics. I tell you we shall raise a handsome statue to her in London one day, when the right time comes. (*He turns towards the people of Chinon, who have been putting up a small palace set during this conversation.*) But now let's come to Chinon, my lord. I've got a profound disrespect for that lounging little idler, Charles, but he's a character who never fails to amuse me.

(CHARLES *is with the two* QUEENS *and* AGNES SOREL.)

AGNES: But Charles, it's impossible! You can't let me appear at the ball looking such a frump. Your mistress in one of last year's steeple-hats.

QUEEN: And your Queen, Charles! The Queen of France! What would they say?

CHARLES (*playing cup-and-ball, dropping into his throne*): They would say the King of France isn't worth a farthing. Which is quite right.

QUEEN: And think how the English court would laugh! The Duchess of Bedford, and Gloucester's wife, to say nothing of the Cardinal of Winchester's mistress! Now there's someone who knows how to dress.

AGNES: Imagine, Charles, if they're wearing our newest fashions over there before we are!

CHARLES: At least they pay for them. Fashion is practically the only thing we can sell them: our fashions and our cooking. They are the only things which still give us some prestige with the foreigners.

YOLANDE: We have to defend this prestige. The girls aren't altogether wrong, Charles. It's most important there should be no question at this ball that ladies of the court of France are the best dressed women in the world. No one has ever been able to decide, remember, exactly where triviality begins. A steeple-hat the English have never seen before might be as good as a great victory.

CHARLES (*with a dry laugh*):   A victory which isn't going to stop them making off with Orleans, mother-in-law! According to the latest reports, Orleans is lost. And you think we should counter-attack with a new fashion.

AGNES: Certainly. You've no idea what a dangerous blow it will be to their confidence. If you want a victory, Charles, here is one you can have for nothing.

CHARLES: For nothing? You make me laugh! How much did you say these steeple-hats would come to?

AGNES: Six thousand francs, my darling. That's next to nothing, when you remember they're completely embroidered with pearls. And the pearls are a good investment. When the steeple-hat isn't fashionable any more you can always sell the pearls at a profit and put it towards the army's back pay.

CHARLES: Six thousand francs! But where do you think I can find six thousand francs, you poor little fool?

QUEEN (*softly*):   Twelve thousand francs, Charles, because there are two of us, remember. You wouldn't want your mistress to be better dressed than your wife.

CHARLES (*raising his hands to heaven*): Twelve thousand francs! They've gone out of their minds!

AGNES: Of course there's a simpler model, but I wouldn' advise it. You would forfeit the moral effect we should have on the stupid English. And that, after all, is the effect we're after.

CHARLES: Twelve thousand francs! Enough to pay three quarters of Dunois's army. I don't understand how you can encourage them, mother-in-law, a woman of your good judgment.

YOLANDE: It's because I'm a woman of good judgment that I support them, Charles. Have you ever found me opposing anything that might be for your good or the dignity of the throne? I am the mother of your Queen, and yet it was I who introduced you to Agnes when I saw clearly how it might help you.

QUEEN: Please, mother, don't brag about it!

YOLANDE: Daughter, Agnes is a very charming girl who perfectly knows her place. It was quite as important to you as to me, that Charles should decide to become a man. And the kingdom had even more need of it than we had. A little more pride, dear girl; at the moment you have thoughts like a tradesman's wife! Before Charles could become a man he had to be given a woman.

QUEEN (*acidly*): I was a woman, it seems to me, and his wife, what is more.

YOLANDE: I don't want to wound you, my dearest girl: but only slightly a woman. I can say this to you, because I was very much the same. Good sense, intelligence—more than you have—but that was all. Which is why I was always willing that the King, your father, should have his mistresses. Be his Queen, run his house, give him a son and heir, and leave the rest to other people. We can't do everything. And anyway, love is scarcely an honest woman's concern. We don't do well at it. Besides, you will thank me later on: one sleeps so much better alone. And Charles is far more manly since he knew Agnes. You are more manly, aren't you, Charles?

CHARLES: Yesterday I said "No" to the Archbishop. He tried to scare me, he sent La Tremouille in first to roar at me, and then he threatened to excommunicate me. All the old tricks. But I held firm.

AGNES: And thanks to whom?

CHARLES: Thanks to Agnes! We had rehearsed the whole scene in bed.

YOLANDE: What did the Archbishop want? You didn't tell me.

CHARLES (*caressing* AGNES *absent-mindedly*): I can't remember. To give up Paris to the Duke of Burgundy, or something of the sort, in return for a year's truce. I might say it wouldn't really have meant anything at all. The Duke's in Paris already. But it was a matter of principle: Paris is France, and France is mine. At least I encourage myself to believe it is. So I said "No." The Archbishop made such a great fuss about it, the Duke must have promised him a pretty good sum.

AGNES: And what would have happened, Charles dear, if you had said "yes" in spite of me?

CHARLES: You would have had a headache for a week, and although, I suppose, if I had to, I could do without Paris, I couldn't do without you.

AGNES: Well, then, my darling, if I have helped you to save Paris, you can surely buy me the new steeple-hat, and one for your little Queen, too, because you have said some very hurtful things to her, without noticing it, as usual, you bad boy. You don't want me to be ill for a whole week, do you? You wouldn't know what to do with yourself.

CHARLES: All right, then, order your steeple-hats. I always have to say "yes" to somebody, if it isn't the Archbishop, it's you. But I may as well tell you, I haven't the least idea how I'm going to pay for them.

AGNES: You're going to sign a draft on the Treasury, Charles, and we will see what happens later. Come along, little Majesty, we will try them on together. Would you rather have this rose-coloured one, or the sky-blue? I think myself the rose is the one which will suit you best.

CHARLES: What do you mean? Have you got them already?

AGNES: You're very slow at understanding, my dearest! Surely you can see, if we were to have them in time for the ball we had to order them a month ago? But we were so sure you would say "yes," weren't we, Your Majesty? You shall see what a sensation this causes in London! It's a great victory for France, you know, Charles!

(*They take to their heels.*)

CHARLES (*sitting back on his throne again*): There's nothing you can do but laugh, the way they harp on victories. La Tremouille, Dunois, they're all the same! There is always going to be a great victory. But everything has to be paid for, including great victories, these days. And suppose I can't afford a great victory? Suppose France is above my means? (*He takes his writing desk, muttering.*) Ah well, we shall see! I can always sign a draft on the Treasury. Let's hope it will please the tradesmen. The Treasury is empty, but there's nothing on this paper to say so. (*He turns towards the* QUEEN YOLANDE.) You wouldn't like a steeple-hat too, while I'm doing it? You needn't mind saying so. My signature isn't worth the ink it's written in.

YOLANDE (*coming to him*): I'm past the age for steeple hats, Charles. I want something else.

CHARLES (*wearily*): To make me a great King, I know! It gets very boring in the end, everybody wants to make me a great King. Even Agnes. Even in bed. Imagine how jolly that is. I wish you would all try and get it into your heads I'm an unimportant, insignificant Valois, and to make a King of me would need a miracle. I know my grandfather Charles was a great king; but he lived before the war when everything was much cheaper. Besides, he was rich. But my father and mother spent it all, so whether you like it or not, I can't afford to be a great king; I haven't got the money, and I haven't got the courage; you all know I haven't. Courage is far too dangerous in a world full of bullying brutes. That fat pig La Tremouille was in a raging temper the other day, and drew his sword on me. We were alone together: nobody there to defend me. He was quite prepared to give me a jab with it, the beastly hooligan! I only just had time to dodge behind the throne. So you see what we've come to. Drawing his sword on the King! I should have sent for the constable to arrest him, except that unfortunately he is the constable, and I'm not sure that I am the King. That's why they treat me like this; they know that I may be only a bastard.

YOLANDE: It's nobody but yourself, Charles, who is always saying so.

CHARLES: When I look at the legitimate faces all round me I hope I am a bastard. It's a charming day and age to live in, when a man isn't considered anybody unless he can brandish an eight-pound sword, and stroll about in a suit of armour which would sink a galleon. When they put it on me, I'm welded into the ground; a great help to my dignity. And I don't like fighting. I don't like hitting, and I don't like being hit. And what's more, if you want to know, I'm frightened of it. (*He turns towards her crossly.*) What other impossibilities do you want me to do?

YOLANDE: I want you to receive this girl from Vaucouleurs. She says God sent her; and furthermore she says she has come to deliver Orleans. The people can think and talk of nothing else, and they're only waiting now to hear that you agree to receive her.

CHARLES: Then they're going to find I'm not as ridiculous as they think I am. Give audience to an eccentric peasant girl? Really, mother-in-law, for a woman of good sense you disappoint me.

YOLANDE: I've given you Agnes, because I thought it was for your good, Charles, though against my interest as a mother. Now I tell you to accept this girl from Domremy. She seems to possess some exceptional power, or so everybody says, which is a point to be considered.

CHARLES (*bored*): I don't like virgins. I know, you're going to tell me again that I'm not virile enough. But they frighten me. And, anyway, I have Agnes, who still pleases me quite well enough. Don't think I'm reproaching you, but for someone who is a queen and my mother-in-law, you have a very remarkable vocation.

YOLANDE (*smiles*): You don't understand me, Charles, or else you're pretending not to. I'm asking you to take this peasant girl into your council, not into your bed.

CHARLES: In that case, in spite of all the respect I owe you, I have to tell you you're absolutely mad. Into my council, with the Archbishop, and La Tremouille, who believes that he sprang from Jupiter's thigh? Do you want them to knock my head off?

YOLANDE (*gently*): I think apeasant in your council is exactly what you all need. The nobility governs the kingdom, which is as it should be; God has entrusted it into their hands. But, without presuming to criticise the wisdom of providence, I wonder sometimes that he hasn't given them what he gives so generously to humbler men, a better measure of simplicity and common sense.

CHARLES (*ironically*): And courage!

YOLANDE (*gently*): And courage, Charles.

CHARLES: As far as I can understand you, you recommend turning the government over to the people? To the good people who have all the virtues. You've read the history of tyrants, I suppose?

YOLANDE: No, Charles. In my day, knowledge was not encouraged in young women.

CHARLES: But I've read it: the endless procession of horrors and scandals; and I amuse myself sometimes by imagining how the procession will go on in the future. They will certainly try what you recommend. They'll try everything.

Men of the people will become masters of the kingdoms, maybe for centuries, the time it takes for a meteor to cross the sky; and that will be the time for massacres and the most monstrous errors. And what will they find, at the great account, when all is done? They'll find that not even the most vile, capricious, and cruel of the princes have cost the world as much as one of these virtuous men. Give France a powerful man of action, born of the people, whose ambition is to make the people happy, whatever it may entail, and see how they'll come to wish to God they had their poor lazy Charles back again, with his everlasting game of cup-and-ball. At least I've no theories about organizing the happy life. A negative virtue, perhaps, but more valuable than they realise yet.

YOLANDE: You should give up this cup-and-ball game, Charles, and this habit of sitting upside down on your throne. It's no behaviour for a king.

CHARLES: You would be sensible to let me be as I am. When the ball misses the cup, it drops on to my nose and nobody else's. But sit me on the throne the right way up, with the orb in one hand and the sceptre in the other, then whenever I make a mistake the ball will drop on everybody's nose.

(*Enter the* ARCHBISHOP *and* LA TREMOUILLE. *He sits like a king on his throne.*)

CHARLES: Archbishop, Constable, you've come at the perfect moment. I am starting to govern. You see I have here the orb and the sceptre.

ARCHBISHOP (*taking his eye-glass*): It's a cup-and-ball!

CHARLES: Unimportant, Archbishop; symbolism, after all. That isn't something I have to teach a prince of the Church. Your announced visit to me, my lord, must mean you wish for an audience.

ARCHBISHOP: I haven't come to be playful, Sire. I know very well the minority opinion, which cares to intrigue and agitate on every possible occasion, is trying to persuade you to see this notorious peasant girl you have heard of. The Constable and I are here, Sire, to say it is not our intention to admit her.

CHARLES (*to* QUEEN YOLANDE): What did I tell you?— I have taken note of what you recommend, my lord, and I shall consider what course to follow. Now you may go; the audience is over.

ARCHBISHOP: I will remind you, Sire, we are not here for your amusement.

CHARLES: Whenever I talk like a king for a moment, they always think I'm amusing myself. (*He lies back on his throne with the cup and ball.*) Very well, then; leave me to amuse myself in peace.

ARCHBISHOP: This girl's miraculous reputation is spreading across the country ahead of her; it was here before she arrived; it's already causing excitement in besieged Orleans. God has taken her by the hand and leads her: this is the story. God has decided that she shall save France and drive the English back across the sea; and other such nonsense. God will expect you to receive her into the royal presence, and nothing is going to prevent her. I don't know why they're so anxious that God should concern Himself in their affairs. And naturally she has performed miracles; it would have surprised me more if she hadn't. A soldier called her I don't know what when she arrived at Chinon. She told him that he was wrong to swear, because soon he would be standing before his Redeemer. And an hour later this boorish fellow missed his footing, and fell into the well in the servants' yard, and drowned himself. That blundering step of a drunkard has done more for the girl's reputation than a great victory ever did for Dunois. Apparently the opinion is unanimous, from the lowest kennel-boy to the highest lady in your court: only this wretched girl can save us. A preposterous infatuation!—I speak to you, sir, of the gravest matters of the realm, and you play at cup-and-ball.

CHARLES: My lord, let us be clear about this. Do you want me to play at cup-and-ball, or do you want me to govern? (*He sits up.*) Do you want me to govern?

ARCHBISHOP (*disturbed*):   Sire, we don't ask you to go as far as that. We wish you to notice and appreciate the efforts we are making. . . .

CHARLES: I assure you, I notice them; I appreciate them; and I find them quite useless, my lord. Everyone expects me to see this girl, isn't it so?

ARCHBISHOP: I haven't said that!

CHARLES: Well, I'm not at all curious to see her. I'm not fond of new faces; we have to know too many people as it is. And messengers from God aren't usually very enlivening. But I want to be a good king, and content my people. I shall see this peasant girl, if only to take the wind out of her sails. Have you spoken to her yourself, Archbishop?

ARCHBISHOP: I have other things to do, sir, when you consider that I carry the whole burden of the kingdom's affairs.

CHARLES: Quite so. And I have nothing else to do except play at cup-and-ball. So I shall see her to save you the trouble: and I shall tell you frankly what I think of her. You can trust me to do that, my lord. I know you don't easily credit me with any qualities worth having, but at least you will agree that I'm a frivolous man: a quite useful condition for this interview. I'm very soon bored by anyone who takes himself seriously. I am going to receive this girl, and if she can make me want to listen to her talking about the welfare of the kingdom, which no one has ever done yet without making me yawn, then there's no doubt about her performing miracles.

ARCHBISHOP (*muttering*): A peasant girl in the presence of the king!

CHARLES (*simply*): You will remember, I think, that some of all kinds have been admitted to my presence. I don't mean M. de La Tremouille, who springs, of course, direct from Jupiter's thigh. But, for instance, yourself, my lord:—I think I remember being told you were the grandson of a wine merchant. There is no reproach in that. What could be more natural? You have carried the wine from your cellars to the altar. And as for myself, as you frequently have told me, it's a moot point whether I'm the son of a king. So we'd better not play the ancestry game, my lord, or we shall be making ourselves altogether ridiculous. (*To* QUEEN YOLANDE.) Come with me, and help me get ready for her. I've thought of a very amusing joke. We can disguise one of the pages in a royal doublet, if we can find one that isn't too shabby; sit him on the throne, which I am sure he will manage better than I can, and I shall hide myself in the crowd. Then we can listen to a solemn harangue from the messenger of God to a page-boy! It ought to be irresistible, don't you think so?

(*They go out.*)

ARCHBISHOP (*to* LA TREMOUILLE): Do we let him do it? It's a game to him, like everything else. It shouldn't be dangerous. And once he has seen her, the people may very well calm down again. In a fortnight they will have found some other messenger of God to infatuate them, and the girl will be forgotten.

LA TREMOUILLE: I command the army, Archbishop, and I can only tell you, the official doctor of the nation has nothing more to say. We're now entirely in the hands of the bonesetters, the faith-healers, the quacks. In other words, what you call messengers from God. What do we risk?

ARCHBISHOP (*anxiously*):   Constable, wherever God concerns himself everything is a risk. If the unlikely should be true, and He really has sent this girl to us: if, in fact, He means to take our part, then our troubles are only beginning. We shall be shaken out of all custom and orthodoxy, contrive to win four or five battles, and then will come the problems, the complications. Long experience as a man, both in the church and in government, teaches me that never, never must we draw God's attention to us. It is better to remain very small, Constable, very small and unnoticed.

(*The* COURTIERS *take their places with the* QUEENS; *a* PAGE *sits on the throne;* CHARLES *slips into the crowd. The* ARCHBISHOP *concludes in an undertone. Everybody is grouped round the throne where the little* PAGE *sits;* CHARLES *is in the crowd.* JOAN *enters alone, looking very small and simple among the armour and the court fashions. They make a way for her to pass to the throne. She is about kneel, hesitates, blushes, looking at the* PAGE.)

YOLANDE (*whispering in her ear*):   You must kneel, child, before the king.

(JOAN *turns towards her, puzzled; then suddenly she looks at all the silent people who are watching her, and advances silently in the crowd, who make way for her. She goes towards* CHARLES, *who tries to hide from her. When he sees that she is about to reach him, he almost runs to hide behind the others, but she follows him, almost running, too. She finds him in a corner and falls on her knees.*)

CHARLES (*embarrassed in the silence*):   What do you want with me?

JOAN: Gentle Dauphin, I am called Joan the Maid. God has brought me to you, to tell you that you will be anointed and crowned in the city of Rheims. You will be viceroy of the King of Heaven, who is King of France.

CHARLES (*awkwardly*):   Well, that is very nice. But Rheims belongs to the English, I understand. How would I get there?

JOAN (*still on her knees*):   By your own strength, gentle Dauphin; by beating them. We will start with Orleans, and then we can go to Rheims.

LA TREMOUILLE (*coming up*):   Little lunatic! Isn't that

what all the army commanders have been trying to do for months? I am the head of them; I know something about it. And they haven't got there.

JOAN (*getting up*): I will get there.

LA TREMOUILLE: Will you indeed? And how will you get there?

JOAN: With the help of God Who sends me.

LA TREMOUILLE: I see. So God has arranged for us to re-take Orleans?

JOAN: Yes, my lord; and to hunt the English out of France.

LA TREMOUILLE (*jeering*): A very beautiful thought! But God can't convey His own messages Himself? He has to have you to do it for Him?

JOAN: Yes, my lord.

ARCHBISHOP (*approaching her*): Young woman ... (JOAN *sees him, kneels and kisses the hem of his robe. He gives her his ring to kiss, and motions her to rise.*) You say that God wishes to deliver the kingdom of France. If such is indeed His will, He has no need of àrmies, or you to lead them.

JOAN: Oh, my lord, does God care for those who have no care? First the soldiers must fight, and then He will give the victory.

CHARLES: How did you recognize me without my crown?

JOAN: Gentle Dauphin, it was a good joke to put your crown on this boy, it doesn't take much to see that he's really a little nobody.

CHARLES: You're mistaken. The boy is the son of a great lord.

JOAN: Great lords are not the king.

CHARLES (*troubled*): Who told you I was the king? I don't look like a king.

JOAN: God told me, gentle Dauphin: Who appointed you from the beginning of time, through your father and your grandfather and all the line of kings, to be viceroy of His kingdom.

(*The* ARCHBISHIP *and* LA TREMOUILLE *exchange a look of annoyance.*)

ARCHBISHOP: Sire. The girl's answers are interesting: they show a remarkable good sense. But in a matter as delicate as this you cannot surround yourself with precautions too strict or thorough. A commission of learned theologians must question and examine her very closely. We will then discuss their report in Council, and decide if it is timely for you to give this girl a longer hearing. There's no need for her to importune you any further today. First of all I shall interrogate her myself. Come here, my daughter.

CHARLES: Not at all.(*He stops* JOAN.) Stay where you are. (*He turns to the* ARCHBISHOP, *taking* JOAN's *hand to give himself courage.*) I was the one she recognised. I was the one she spoke to. I wish you to leave me alone with her: all of you.

ARCHBISHOP: This blunt dismissal, sir: it is quite extraordinary, it is improper! Apart from all else, you should at least think of your own security. . . .

CHARLES (*fearful for a moment, but he looks at* JOAN *and pulls himself together*):   I am the only judge of that. (*He recites:*) Through my father, my grandfather, and all the line of kings . . . (*He winks at* JOAN.) Isn't that right? (*He turns to the others, imperturbable.*) Leave us, my lords, when the king commands it. (*They all bow, and go.* CHARLES *keeps his regal pose for a moment, and then explodes with laughter.*) They've gone, they've gone! Did I do that, or did you? It's the first time in my life I have ever made myself obeyed. (*He looks at her, suddenly anxious.*) I hope there is nothing in what the Archbishop was trying to suggest. You haven't come here to kill me? There isn't a knife hidden about you somewhere? (*He looks at her, and she smiles gravely.*) No. You reassure me. I had forgotten, among all these pirates in my court, how reassuring a smile could be. Are there many of you in my kingdom with such honest faces?

JOAN (*still smiling gravely*):   Yes, sir, very many.

CHARLES: But I never see you. Only ruffians, hypocrites, and whores: my entourage. Though of course there's my little queen, who has a certain amount of charm but not many brains. (*He goes back to his throne, his feet on the rail, and sighs.*) Well, there you are. I suppose now you have to start boring me. You're going to tell me to become a great king.

JOAN (*gently*):   Yes, Charles.

CHARLES: Don't let's bother. We shall have to stay shut up here together for an hour at least, to impress them. If you talk to me about God and the kingdom of France for an hour, I shall never last out. I propose instead we talk about something quite different. Do you play cards?

JOAN (*opening her eyes wide*):   I don't know what it is.

CHARLES: It's an amusing game they invented for Papa, to distract him during his illness. You'll see, I shall teach you. I've played so often now I've got tired of it, but I think you may like it if you've never played before. (*He goes to rummage about in a chest.*) I hope they haven't stolen them from me. They steal everything here. And a pack of cards, you know, costs a lot of money. Only the royal princes have them. Mine were left to me by my father. I shall never have enough money to buy myself another pack. If those devils have stolen them . . . No, here they are. (*He returns with the cards.*) You knew Papa was mad, did you? Sometimes I hope I'm really his son, so that I can be sure I'm the true king; and then, at other times I hope I'm a bastard, so that I don't have to dread going mad before I'm thirty.

JOAN (*gently*):   And which of the two would you prefer, Charles?

CHARLES (*turning in surprise*):   Good heavens, are you calling me Charles? This is turning out to be a most surprising day. I believe I'm not going to be bored, for once; it's marvellous.

JOAN: Not now, Charles, or ever again.

CHARLES: Extraordinary.—Which of the two would I prefer? Well, I suppose on the days when I have some courage I would rather take the risk of going mad, and be the true king; and on the day when I haven't I would rather let everything go, and retire on my twopence-ha'penny to somewhere abroad, and live in peace. Have you met Agnes?

JOAN: No.

CHARLES (*shuffling the cards*):   No, of course you haven't. Retiring wouldn't do for her. And I couldn't afford her then. She is always wanting me to buy her things.

JOAN (*suddenly grave*):   And today: are you feeling brave today, Charles?

CHARLES: Today? (*He ponders a moment.*) Yes, it seems to me I feel fairly brave. Not very, but fairly. Well, you saw how I packed off the Archbishop.

JOAN: How would you like to be brave all the time, from today onwards?

CHARLES (*leaning forward, interested*):   Do you mean you know the secret?

JOAN: Yes.

CHARLES: Are you some sort of a witch? You needn't be afraid to tell me; it isn't something I object to. I promise you I won't repeat it. Those executions horrify me. I was taken once to see them burn a heretic. I was sick all night.

JOAN (*smiling*):   No, I'm not a witch, Charles. But I know the secret.

CHARLES: Would you sell it to me, without letting the others know about it? I'm not very well off, but I could make you a draft on the Treasury.

JOAN: I will give it to you, Charles.

CHARLES (*suspiciously*):   For nothing?

JOAN: Yes.

CHARLES: Then I'm not interested. A secret is either no good, or far beyond my means. Disinterested people are too rare, at any price. (*He shuffles the cards.*) I've taken to behaving like a fool, so that I shall be left in peace, but I know more than you think I know. I'm not so easily gulled.

JOAN: You know too much.

CHARLES: Too much? You can never know too much.

JOAN: Sometimes; it is possible.

CHARLES: I have to defend myself. You would soon see, if you were here in my position! If you were alone, among a lot of brutes whose one idea is to stab you when you are least expecting it, and if you've been born a weak sort of fellow, as I was, you would soon realise the only way to steer safely through it is by being more clever than they are. And I am; much more clever. Which is why I more or less hang on to my throne.

JOAN (*puts her hand on his arm*):   I shall be with you now, defending you.

CHARLES: Do you think you will?

JOAN: And I'm strong. I'm not afraid of anything.

CHARLES (*sighing*):   You're very lucky! (*He deals the cards.*) Sit down on the cushion; I'm going to teach you to play cards.

JOAN (*smiling, sitting close to the throne*):   All right. And then I'll teach you something.

CHARLES: What?

JOAN: Not to be afraid. And not to know too much.

CHARLES: Now pay attention. You see the cards, and these pictures on them? There's something of everything here: knaves, queens, kings: the same as in the world: and here are the commoners: spades, hearts, clubs, diamonds. Those are the troops. There are plenty of them, you can lose as many as you like. You deal the cards without looking at them, and fate either gives you a good hand, or a bad hand, and then the battle begins. The higher cards can capture the lower cards. Which do you think is the strongest?

JOAN: The king is.

CHARLES: Well, he is almost the strongest, but there's one stronger still. This card here, for instance, the single heart. Do you know what it's called?

JOAN: God, of course: because He's the only one who commands kings.

CHARLES (*annoyed*):   No, it isn't at all. For goodness sake let God alone for five minutes. For the time being we're playing cards. It's called the ace.

JOAN: Then the game of cards is ridiculous. What can be stronger than a king, except God?

CHARLES: The ace, in fact. The ace, or God if you like; but there's one in each camp. You see: ace of hearts, ace of spades, ace of clubs, ace of diamonds. One for each of them. You're not so intelligent as I thought you were. Do you think the English don't say their prayers, as well as us? And, what's more, to a God who protects them, and gives them victories over us. And my cousin, the Duke of Burgundy, he has a God for Burgundy, in just the same way: a smallish one, maybe, but a bold one, a cunning one, who gets my cousin out of difficulties very well. God is with everybody, my girl. He marks the points, and keeps the score. But, in the long run, He plumps for the people who have the most money and the biggest armies. So why do you imagine He should be with France, now that France has got nothing at all?

JOAN: Perhaps for that reason: because she has nothing at all, Charles.

CHARLES (shrugging his shoulders):   You don't know Him!

JOAN: I do. God isn't with the strongest; He is with the bravest. There's the difference. God hasn't any love for cowards.

CHARLES: Then He doesn't love me. And if He doesn't love me, why do you expect me to love Him? All He had to do was to give me some courage. I don't ask for anything better.

JOAN (severely):   Do you think He's your nurse, with no one else to think about but you? Why can't you make the best of what you have got; I know He has made you weak in the legs. . . .

CHARLES: You've noticed that? He ought to have managed better than that. Particularly with the present fashions. It's because of my legs that Agnes can't bring herself to love me. If He had only an eye for proportion, and hadn't given me my big knees as well . . .

JOAN: Well, I grant you that. He didn't go to much trouble over your knees. But there was something else that more concerned Him; His eye was on your head and your heart, Charles, where you most resemble Him. And there it is He makes you free, to be whatever you will. You can use them to play cards, or to outmanœuvre the Archbishop for a time, though in the end you have to pay for it; or else you can use them to make the house of Valois glorious again, and remake the kingdom. Your little queen gave you a son,

Charles. What are you going to leave the boy when you die?
This wretched scrap of France, nibbled by the English? If
so, when he grows up, the boy will be able to say, as you
did just now, that God hasn't any interest in him. You are
God, Charles, to your little son; and you have to take care of
him.

CHARLES (*groans*):   But I keep telling you, everything
frightens me.

JOAN (*coming nearer to him*):   You shall have the secret
now, Charles. But don't give me away when I tell you first
that everything frightens me, too. Do you know why M. de
la Tremouille isn't afraid of anything?

CHARLES: Because he is strong.

JOAN: No. Because he is stupid. He never imagines anything. Wild boars, and bulls, and barrel-headed oxen are
never afraid of anything, either. And I tell you this: it has
been even more complicated for me to get to you than it
will be for you to get to Orleans and refashion your kingdom. I had to explain to my father, and that was a bad
enough beginning. He wouldn't believe I wanted anything,
except to go dragging off after the soldiers; and so he beat
me, and, my goodness, the English don't hit any harder than
he does. And then I had to make my mother cry; there
was nothing worse than that; and then to convince Beaudricourt, who didn't want to think of anything except adding
one more to his list of sins. Don't think I haven't been afraid.
I was afraid all the time, from the very beginning.

CHARLES: Then how have you done it?

JOAN: Just as I should have done without the fear. That's
all the difficulty there is, Charles. Try it once and see. You
say: one thing is obvious, I'm frightened, which is nobody's
business but mine, and now on I go. And on you go. And if
you see something ahead which nothing can overcome . . .

CHARLES: Like Tremouille enjoying one of his rages—

JOAN: Yes, if you like. Or the unshakeable English facing
Orleans in their fortress built like rocks. You say: Here it is
—they outnumber us, their walls are as thick as the length of
a giant's arm, their cannons out-thunder thunder, their arrows out-rain the rain. So be it. I'm frightened. Now I've
realised how frightening it is, on we go.—And the English
are so astonished, they begin to be frightened themselves,
and you get through! You get through because you think
deeper, imagine more, and get your fear over first. That's
the secret of it.

CHARLES: But is it always so successful?

JOAN: Always. As long as you turn and face what frightens you. But the first step has to be yours; He waits for that

CHARLES (*after a pause*): You think we could try your secret?

JOAN: We have to try it.

CHARLES (*suddenly frightened by his temerity*): Tomorrow, perhaps. By tomorrow I shall have had time to prepare for it.

JOAN: No, Charles; now; you're ready now.

CHARLES: Do you mean that I'm ready to call the Archbishop and La Tremouille? That I'm ready to tell them that I've given you command of the army, and then sit calmly back and watch their faces?

JOAN: Absolutely ready.

CHARLES: I'm scared out of my life.

JOAN: Then the worst is over. One thing is essential: you mustn't be still frightened after you've called them. Are you sure you are as frightened as you possibly can be?

CHARLES (*his hand on his belly*): Oh yes, I agree with you.

JOAN: Wonderful! That's an enormous advantage. When they start to be frightened, you will have got over it already. The whole scheme is to be afraid first, before the battle begins. You'll soon see. I'll call them. (*She calls offstage.*) My Lord Archbishop, M. de la Tremouille! M. le Dauphin wishes to speak to you.

CHARLES (*taken by panic*): Oh dear, I'm so frightened! Goodness, goodness, I'm so frightened.

JOAN: That's it, that's right, Charles; more frightened still!

CHARLES (*his teeth chattering*): I can't be more frightened: it's impossible!

JOAN: Then we have the victory! God has joined you; He says "Charles is afraid, but still he calls them." In eight hours we shall hold Orleans!

(*Enter the* ARCHBISHOP *and* LA TREMOUILLE, *surprised.*)

ARCHBISHOP: You called us, your Highness?

CHARLES (*suddenly, after a last look at* JOAN): Yes: I've come to a decision, my lord, and it also concerns you, M. de la Tremouille. I am giving the command of my royal army to this Maid here. (*He suddenly shouts.*) If you don't agree, M. de la Tremouille, I must ask you to surrender your sword to me. You are under arrest!

(LA TREMOUILLE *and the* ARCHBISHOP *stand petrified.*)

JOAN (*clapping her hands*): Well done! Now you know

how simple it is! Do you see their faces, Charles? Look at them: do look at them! Who is frightened now, Charles? (*She bursts out laughing;* CHARLES *begins to laugh as well: they rock with laughter, unable to stop; and the* ARCHBISHOP *and* LA TREMOUILLE *seem turned to stone.* JOAN *drops suddenly on to her knees, crying*):   Thank you, God!

CHARLES (*also kneeling*):   On your knees, M. de la Tremouille, on to your knees! And give us your blessing, Archbishop: no hesitating: give us your blessing! Now that we've all been thoroughly frightened, we must make straight for Orleans!

(LA TREMOUILLE *is on his knees, stupefied by the blow. The* ARCHBISHOP, *bewildered, mechanically gives his blessing.*)

ACT II

WARWICK (*laughing and coming forward with* CAUCHON): In point of fact, that wasn't exactly how it happened. They called a meeting of the Council, and discussed the matter for hours. In the end they agreed to use Joan as a sort of flag-pole to nail their colours to: an attractive little mascot, well qualified to charm the general public into letting themselves be killed. The best we could do to restore the balance was to treble the men's drink ration before they went into action, though it had nothing like as good an effect. We started being beaten from that time on, against all the laws of strategy. I know some people have said there was nothing miraculous about that. They maintain that our system of isolated forts around Orleans was ludicrous, and all the enemy had to do was attack: which is what Joan made them agree to try. But that's not true. Sir John Talbot was no fool. He knew his job thoroughly well; as he has proved again and again, both before this regrettable business, and since. His system of for-tification was theoretically impregnable. No: we must have the grace to admit there was more in it than that: a strong ele-ment of the imponderable—or God, as you might say, my Lord Bishop—which the rules of strategy don't provide for. Without question, it was Joan: singing like a lark in the sky over the heads of your French armies on the march. I am very fond of France, my Lord: which is why I should be most unhappy if we lost her. This lark singing in the sky, while we all take aim to shoot her down: that seems very like France to me. Or at least like the best of her. In her time she has had plenty of fools, rogues and blunderers; but every now and then a lark sings in her sky, and the fools and the rogues can be forgotten. I am very fond of France.

CAUCHON (*gently*): But still you take aim and shoot her down.

WARWICK: A man is a mass of contradictions, my lord Bishop. It isn't unusual in him to kill what he loves. I love animals, but I hunt them, too. (*He suddenly gets up, look-ing stern. He raps with his stick on his boot, and makes a sign*

484

to Two Soldiers *who come forward.*) Come along now: the lark has been caught. The cage of Compiègne has shut her in. The singing is over; and Charles and his court are leaving her there, without a second glance. They're going back to their old political methods, now that their little mascot isn't bringing them luck any more.

(*Indeed,* Charles, La Tremouille, *and the* Archbishop *have slyly got up and edged away from* Joan, *who is on her knees, praying. She starts up astonished to be alone, and sees* Charles *deserting her. The* Guards *begin to drag her away.*)

Cauchon: Your king has left you, Joan! There's no reason now to go on defending him. Yesterday we read you the letter he has sent to every town, telling them to say he repudiates you.

Joan (*after a pause, quietly*): He is my king.

Charles (*in a low voice to the* Archbishop): That letter is going to be thrown in our teeth for a long time yet.

Archbishop (*also aside*): It had to be, sir: it was absolutely necessary. At this juncture, the cause of France cannot be linked in any way with Joan's.

Cauchon: Joan: listen carefully, and try to understand what I'm saying. Your king is not our king. A treaty in rightful and due form has made Henry the Sixth of Lancaster King of France and England. Your trial is not a political trial. We are simply trying with all our power and with all our faith to lead a lost sheep back into the fold of our Holy Mother Church. But as men, Joan, we consider ourselves to be faithful subjects of His Majesty King Henry. We have as great and sincere a love of France as you: and because of that we recognise him as our sovereign: so that France can rise up again out of her ruins, dress her wounds, and be free of this appalling, interminable war which has drained all her strength. The useless resistance of the man you call your king, and his absurd pretensions to a throne which isn't his, appear to us to be acts of rebellion and terrorism against a peace which was almost assured. The puppet whom you served is not our master, be certain of that.

Joan: Say what you like, you can't alter the truth. This is the king God gave you. Thin as he is, with his long legs and his big, bony knees.

Charles (*to the* Archbishop): This is really most disagreeable.

Archbishop: For a little while we have to have patience;

but they mean to hurry through the trial and burn her, and after that we shall not be disturbed. You must surely admit sir, the English have done us a good turn, making themselves responsible for her arrest and execution. If they hadn't done it, we ourselves should have had to, some day or other. She was becoming impossible!

(*They withdraw, unnoticed.*)

CAUCHON: We know by many of your answers, insolent though they were, that you're not slow of understanding, Joan. Put yourself for a moment in our place. How can you suppose that we, men with most earnest human convictions, can agree that God has sent you to oppose the cause you defend? How can you think, only because you say voices have spoken to you, that we should believe God to be against us?

JOAN: You will know when we have beaten you.

CAUCHON (*shrugging*): You are answering like a self-willed, obstinate child. Considering the question now as priests and defenders of our Holy Mother Church, have we any better reason to put faith in what you tell us? Do you think you are the first who has heard Voices?

JOAN: No, of course not.

CAUCHON: Neither the first, nor the last, Joan. Now, do you believe that each time a little girl goes to her village priest and says: I have seen some saint, or the Blessed Virgin, I have heard Voices which have told me to do one thing or another—that her priest should believe and encourage her: and how long then would the Church still remain?

JOAN: I don't know.

CAUCHON: You don't know; but you are full of good sense, and that is why I am trying to lead you to reason with me. Have you not been in command in battle, Joan?

JOAN: Yes, I was in command of hundreds of good soldiers who followed me, and believed me.

CAUCHON: You were in command. And if on the morning of some attack one of your soldiers had heard voices persuading him to attack by another gate than the one you had chosen, or not to attack at all, what would you have done?

JOAN (*speechless for a moment, before she suddenly bursts out laughing*): My lord Bishop, it's easy to see you're a priest! It's clear you don't know much about our men. They can drink and swear and fight, but they're not ones for hearing Voices!

CAUCHON: A joke is no answer, Joan. But you gave your answer before you spoke, in the second of hesitation when you were held and disarmed by what I said to you. And you see it is true: that the Church militant is an army in a world still overrun by infidels and the powers of evil. The Church owes obedience to our Holy Father the Pope and his bishops, as your soldiers owed obedience to you and your lieutenants. If a soldier says on the morning of attack that Voices have told him not to advance, in yours or any army in the world he would be silenced. And far more brutally than this effort of ours to reason with you.

JOAN (*gathering herself together, on the defensive*): You have a right to hit at me with all your power. And my right is to say No, and go on believing.

CAUCHON: Don't make yourself a prisoner of your own pride, Joan. You can surely see that we have no possible reason, either as men or as priests, to believe that your mission is divinely inspired. You alone have a reason to believe so; encouraged by the fiend who means to damn you, and also, as long as you were useful to them, by those whom you served. You served them; and yet the way they behaved before your capture, and their explicit repudiation since, certainly proves that the most intelligent of them never believed you. No one believes you, Joan, any longer, except the common people, who believe everything, and tomorrow they will believe half a dozen others. You are quite alone. (JOAN *makes no reply, sitting small and quiet among them all.*) I beg you not to imagine that your strong will and your stubborn resistance to us is a sign that God is upholding you. The devil has also got intelligence and a tough hide. His mind had the flash of a star among the angels before he rebelled.

JOAN (*after a pause*): I am not intelligent, my lord. I am a peasant girl, the same as any other in my village. But when something is black I cannot say it is white, that is all.

(*Another pause.*)

PROMOTER (*suddenly rising up behind her*): What was the sign you gave to the man you are calling your king, to make him trust you with his army?

JOAN: I don't know what you mean: what sign I gave.

PROMOTER: Did you make him sip mandragora, to be a protection against harm?

JOAN: I don't know what you mean by mandragora.

PROMOTER: Your secret has a name, whether it's a potion or a formula, and we mean to know it. What did you give him at Chinon to make him so heroic all of a sudden? A Hebrew name? The devil speaks all languages, but he delights in Hebrew.

JOAN (*smiling*):   No, my lord: it has a French name. I gave him courage.

CAUCHON: And so you think that God, or at least the power you believe to be God, took no part in this.

JOAN: He always takes part, my lord Bishop. When a girl speaks two words of good sense and someone listens, there He is. But He is thrifty; when those two words of good sense will do, He isn't likely to throw away a miracle.

LADVENU (*quietly*):   The answer's a good one, in all humility, my lord: it can't be held against her.

PROMOTER (*with venom, to* JOAN):   I see, I see! So you don't believe in such miracles as we are shown in the gospels? You deny what was done by Our Lord Jesus at the marriage of Cana? You deny that He raised Lazarus from the dead?

JOAN: No, my lord. What is written in Holy Scripture was surely done. He changed the water into wine just as easily as He created them. And it was not more extraordinary for Him, the Master of life and death, to make Lazarus live again, than for me to thread a needle.

PROMOTER (*yelping*):   Listen to that! Listen to that! She says there is no such thing as a miracle!

JOAN: No, my lord. I say that a true miracle is not done with a magic wand or incantation. The gypsies on our village green can do miracles of that sort. The true miracle is done by men themselves, with the mind and the courage which God has given to them.

CAUCHON: Are you measuring the gravity of your words, Joan? You seem to be telling us quite calmly that God's true miracle on earth is man, who is nothing but sin and error, blindness and futility. . . .

JOAN: And strength, too, and courage, and light sometimes when he is deepest in sin. I have seen men during the battles. . . .

LADVENU: My lord, Joan is talking to us in her rough and ready language about things which come instinctively from her heart, which may be wrong but are surely simple and genuine. Her thoughts are not so schooled that she can shape them to our way of argument. Perhaps by pressing her with questions we run the risk of making her say more than she meant, or something different from her belief.

CAUCHON: Brother Ladvenu, we shall try and estimate as fairly as we can what part lack of skill plays in her answers. But our duty is to question her to the last point of doubt. We are not perfectly sure, remember, that our concern now is *only* the question of Joan. So then, Joan, you excuse man all his faults, and think him one of God's greatest miracles, even the only one?

JOAN: Yes, my lord.

PROMOTER (*yelping, beside himself*): It's blasphemy! Man is filth, lust, a nightmare of obscenity!

JOAN: Yes, my lord. He sins; he is evil enough. And then something happens: it may be he is coming out of a brothel, roaring out his bawdy songs in praise of a good time, and suddenly he has thrown himself at the reins of a runaway horse to save some child he has never seen before; his bones broken, he dies at peace.

PROMOTER: But he dies like an animal, without a priest, in the full damnation of sin.

JOAN: No, my lord; he dies in the light which was lighted within him when the world began. He behaved as a man, both in doing evil and doing good, and God created him in that contradiction to make his difficult way.

(*A storm of indignation from the* PRIESTS *when they hear this said. The* INQUISITOR *quietens them, and suddenly rises.*)

INQUISITOR (*calmly*): Joan. I have let you speak throughout this trial, with scarcely a question to you. I wanted you to find your way clearly to your position. It has taken some time. The Promoter could see only the Devil, the Bishop only the pride of a young girl intoxicated with success; I waited for something else to show itself. Now it has happened—I represent the Holy Inquisition. My Lord the Bishop told you just now, with great humanity, how his human feelings linked him with the English cause, which he considers just; and how they were confounded by his sentiments as priest and bishop, charged with the defence of our Mother Church. But I have come from the heart of Spain. This is the first time I have been sent to France. I know nothing of either the Armagnac faction, or of the English. It is indifferent to me who shall rule France, whether your prince or Henry of Lancaster. As for that strict discipline of our Mother Church which will not tolerate those who play a lone hand, however well-intentioned, but directs them back into the fold: I'll not say that is indifferent to me; but it is perhaps a secondary task, which the Inquisition leaves to the Bishops and the parish priests. The Holy Inquisition has something higher and more secret to defend than the temporal integrity of the Church. She wrestles on an invisible ground, inwardly, with an enemy only she knows how to detect, of whom only she can estimate the danger. It has been her care sometimes to take up arms against an Emperor; at other times the same solemnity, the same vigilance, the same fixity of purpose have been deployed against some old apparently inoffensive scholar, or a herdsman buried away in a mountain village, or a young girl. The princes of the earth laugh very heartily to see the Inquisition give itself such endless care, when for them a piece of rope or a sergeant's signature on a death warrant would be enough. The Inquisition lets them laugh. It knows how to recognise the enemy; it knows better than to under-estimate him wherever he may be found. And its enemy is not the devil, not the devil with the cloven hooves, the chastener of troublesome children, whom my lord Promoter sees on every side. His enemy, you yourself spoke his name, when at last you came into the open: his only enemy, is man. Stand up, Joan, and answer me. I am your interrogator now. (JOAN *rises and turns towards him. He asks in an expressionless voice.*) Are you a Christian?

JOAN: Yes, my lord.

INQUISITOR: You were baptized, and in your earliest years you lived in the shadow of the church whose walls touched the walls of your home. The church bells ruled over your day, your playtime, your work, and your prayers. The emissaries we sent to your village have all come back with the same story: you were a little girl full of piety. Sometimes, instead of playing and running about with other children, though you were not a solemn child, you delighted to play, yet you would slip away into the church, and for a long time you would be there alone, kneeling, not even praying, but gazing at the coloured glass of the window.

JOAN: Yes. I was happy.

INQUISITOR: You had a friend you loved very dearly, a little girl called Haumette.

JOAN: Yes, my lord.

INQUISITOR: And when you made up your mind to leave for Vaucouleurs, already believing that you would never go back, you said goodbye to all your other friends, but you passed her house by.

JOAN: Yes. I was afraid to be too unhappy.

INQUISITOR: But you cared for more than only those you loved most. You cared for old people in sickness, children in poverty. And later on, when you fought in your first battle, you stood among the wounded and cried very bitterly.

JOAN: French blood was being shed; it was hard to bear.

INQUISITOR: Not only because it was French blood. A bully who had captured two English soldiers in a skirmish outside Orleans, knocked one of them down because he didn't move fast enough for him. You jumped off your horse, took the man's head on your knee, wiped the blood from his mouth, and helped him in his dying, calling him your little son, and promising him Heaven.

JOAN: How is it you can know that, my lord?

INQUISITOR: The Holy Inquisition knows everything, Joan. It weighed your human tenderness in the scales before it sent me to judge you.

LADVENU (*rising*): My Lord Inquisitor, I am happy to hear you recalling all these details which until now have been passed over in silence. Yes, indeed, everything we know of Joan since her earliest years has been gentleness, humility, and Christian charity.

INQUISITOR (*turning upon him, suddenly stern*): Silence, Brother Ladvenu! I ask you to remember that I stand here for the Holy Inquisition, alone qualified to make the distinction between Charity, the theological virtue, and the uncommendable, graceless, cloudy drink of the milk of human kindness. (*He passes his eye over them all.*) Ah, my Masters! How quickly your hearts can be melted. The accused has only to be a little girl, looking at you with a pair of wide-open eyes, and with a ha'porth of simple kindness, and you're all ready to fall over yourselves to absolve her. Very good guardians of the faith we have here! I see that the Holy Inquisition has enough to occupy it still: and still so much has to be cut away, cut, cut, always the dead wood to be cut away: and after us, others will go on, still pruning, hacking away without mercy, clearing the ranks of unruliness, so that the forest will be sound from root to branch.

(*A pause, and then* LADVENU *replies.*)

LADVENU: Our Saviour also loved with this loving-kindness, my lord. He said: Suffer the little children to come unto me. He put His hand on the shoulder of the woman taken in adultery, and said to her: Go in peace.

INQUISITOR: I tell you to be silent, Brother Ladvenu! Otherwise I shall have to investigate your case as well as Joan's. Lessons from the Gospels are read to the congregations, and we ask the parish priests to explain them. But we have not translated them into the vulgar tongue, or put them into every hand to make of them what they will. How mischievous that would be, to leave untutored souls to let their imaginations play with the texts which only we should interpret. (*He quietens down.*) You are young, Brother Ladvenu, and you have a young man's generosity. But you must not suppose that youth and generosity find grace in the eyes of the faith's defenders. Those are transitory ills which experience will cure. I see that we should have considered your age, and not your learning which I believe is remarkable, before we invited you to join us here. Experience will soon make plain to you that youth, generosity, human tenderness are names of the enemy. At least, I trust it may. Surely you can see, if we were so unwise as to put these words you have spoken into the hands of simple people, they would draw from them a love of Man. And love of Man excludes the love of God.

LADVENU (*quietly*): And yet He chose to become a man . . .

INQUISITOR (*turning suddenly to* CAUCHON, *curtly*): My lord Bishop, in virtue of your discretionary power as president of these debates, I ask you to dispense for today with the collaboration of your young assessor. I shall inform you, when the session is over, what conclusions will be entered against him, if needs be. (*He suddenly thunders.*) Against him or against whomsoever! For no one is of too great importance to be put out of our care: understand so! I would denounce myself, if God should allow me to be misled. (*He gravely crosses himself and ends.*) May He mercifully watch over me!

(*A breath of fear whispers through the tribunal.* CAUCHON *says simply, with a gesture of distress to* BROTHER LADVENU.)

CAUCHON: Leave us, Brother Ladvenu.

LADVENU (*before he moves off*):   My Lord Inquisitor, I owe you obedience, as I do my Reverend Lord Bishop. I will go, saying no more: except that my prayers must be to our Lord Jesus that He shall lead you to remember the fragility of your small enemy who faces you now.

INQUISITOR (*not answering until he has gone, and then speaking quietly*):   Small, fragile, tender, pure: and therefore formidable. (*He turns to* JOAN *and says in his neutral tone.*) The first time you heard your Voices you were not yet fifteen. On that occasion they simply said to you: "Be a good and sensible child, and go often to church." In fact you were a happy and contented little girl. And the unhappiness of France was only old men's talk. And yet one day you felt you should leave the village.

JOAN: My Voices told me that I must.

INQUISITOR: One day you felt that you must take upon

yourself the unhappiness of others around you. And you knew even then everything that would come of it: how glorious your ride would be, how soon it would come to an end, and once your King had been anointed, how you would find yourself where you are now, surrounded and alone, the faggots heaped up in the market place, waiting to be set alight. You know this is—

JOAN: My Voices told me that I should be captured, and then delivered.

INQUISITOR: Delivered! They very well might use that word: and you guessed in what way it might be taken, how ambiguously as a word from heaven. Death is a deliverance, certainly. And you set off all the same, in spite of your father and mother, and in spite of all the grave difficulties ahead of you.

JOAN: Yes, my lord; it had to be. If I had been the daughter of a hundred mothers and a hundred fathers: still it would have had to be.

INQUISITOR: So that you could help your fellow men to keep possession of the soil where they were born, which they fondly imagine belongs to them.

JOAN: Our Lord couldn't want the English to pillage, and kill and overrule us in our own country. When they have gone back across the sea, they can be God's children then in their own land. I shall pick no quarrel with them then.

PROMOTER: Presumption! Pride! Don't you think you would have done better to go on with your sewing and spinning beside your mother?

JOAN: I had something else to do, my lord. There have always been plenty of women to do women's work.

INQUISITOR: When you found yourself in such direct communication with heaven did it never occur to you to consecrate your life to prayer, supplicating that heaven itself should expel the English from France?

JOAN: God likes to see action first, my lord. Prayer is extra. It was simpler to explain to Charles that he ought to attack, and he believed me, and gentle Dunois believed me, too. And so did La Hire and Xantrailles, my fine couple of angry bulls! We had some joyful battles, all of us together. It was good to face every new day with friends, ready to turn on the English, ready to rescue France, ready to—

PROMOTER: Kill, Joan? Ready to kill? And does Our Lord tell us to kill for what we want, as though we had fangs and claws?

(JOAN *does not reply*.)

CAUCHON (*gently*):   You loved the war, Joan . . .

JOAN (*simply*):   Yes. It is one of the sins which I have most
need of God's forgiveness for. Though in the evening I would
look across the battlefield and cry to see that the joyous beginning to the morning had gone down in a heap of dead.

PROMOTER: And the next day, you began again?

JOAN: God wished it. While there remained one Englishman in France. It isn't difficult to understand. There was
work to be done first, that was all. You are learned, and you
think too much. You can't understand the simple things, but
the dullest of my soldiers understands them. Isn't that true,
La Hire?

(LA HIRE *strides forward, in huge armour, gay and alarm-
ing.*)

LA HIRE: You bet it's true.

(*Everybody finds himself pushed into the shade: this
one figure is clear. A vague music of the fife is heard.* JOAN
*goes quietly up to him, incredulous, and touches him with
her finger.*)

JOAN: La Hire . . .

LA HIRE (*taking up again the comradeship of the battle
mornings*):   Well, Miss, we've had the bit of praying we agreed
to have: what's the next thing? Do we take a bash at them
this morning?

JOAN (*throwing herself into his arms*):   It is La Hire, my
dear, fat La Hire! You smell so good!

LA HIRE (*embarrassed*):   A glass of wine and an onion. It's
my usual morning meal. Excuse me, Miss: I know you don't
like it, but I did my praying beforehand so that God shouldn't
take against my breath. Don't come too near: I know I stink
in a way.

JOAN (*pressed against him*):   No: it's good.

LA HIRE: You don't want to make me feel awkward. Usually you tell me I stink and it's a shame for a Christian.
Usually you say that if the wind carries in that direction I
shall give us away to the goddams, I stink so much; and we
shall ruin our ambush because of me. One quite small onion
and two tots of red wine, no more. Of course, let's be honest, no water with it.

JOAN: Well, I was a fool if I said so. If an onion has a
right to stink why shouldn't you?

LA HIRE: It's what war does for you. Be a clerk, or a

priest, or a linen draper: no smell. But be a captain, you're bound to sweat. As for washing, up in the line: a man doesn't see the interest in it. There was no need to add the onion, I suppose: I ought to do with a bit of garlic sausage like the other fellows: it's better behaved when you come to conversation. But, look here, you wouldn't call it a sin, would you, eating the onion?

JOAN (*smiling*):   No, La Hire: not a sin.

LA HIRE: You never know with you, you know.

JOAN: Have I pestered you with sins, La Hire? I was silly to tease you so much: it's odd, but there you are, a great bear smelling of sweat and onions and red wine, and you kill, and swear, and think of nothing except the girls. . . .

LA HIRE (*very astonished*):   Who, me?

JOAN: You. Yes. Look astonished, you old rogue. And yet you shine in the hand of God as bright as a new penny.

LA HIRE: Is that a fact? I should have thought I'd bitched my chance of paradise years ago. But you think if I keep on praying as arranged, a bit every day, I might still get there?

JOAN: They're expecting you. I know that God's paradise must be full of ruffians like you.

LA HIRE: Is that a fact? It would make all the difference to feel that there were a few kindred spirits around. I wasn't much looking forward to being in a crowd of saints and bishops looking like Heaven's village idiot.

JOAN (*gaily thumping him*):   Great jackass! Of course Heaven's full of dunces. Hasn't our Lord said so? It may even be they're the only ones who get in: the others have had so many brains to sin with, they never get past the door.

LA HIRE (*uneasily*):   You don't think, between ourselves, we'll get bored to death, do you, always on our best behaviour? Any fighting at all, do you imagine?

JOAN: All the day long.

LA HIRE (*respectfully*):   Wait, now. Only when God isn't looking at us.

JOAN: But He's looking at you all the time, crackpot! He sees everything. And what's more, He is going to enjoy watching you at it. "Go it, La Hire," He'll say: "Bash the stuffing out of old Xantrailles! Pitch into him, now! Show him what you're made of!"

LA HIRE: Is that a fact?

JOAN: Not in those words perhaps, but in His own way.

LA HIRE: By God Almighty. (*Enthusiastically.*)

JOAN (*suddenly stern*):   La Hire!

LA HIRE (*hanging his head*):   Sorry, Miss.

JOAN (*pitilessly*):   If you swear He will throw you out.

LA HIRE (*stammering*):   I was feeling pleased, you see: had to thank Him somehow.

JOAN: So He thought. But don't do it again! We've talked quite enough for one morning. Let's get up on horseback and take a look at the day.

LA HIRE: It's dead country this morning. Not a soul to see.

(*They ride imaginary horses side by side.*)

JOAN: Look, we've got France all to ourselves—shall we ever see the world to better advantage? Here on horseback side by side: this is how it will be, La Hire, when the English have gone. Smell the wet grass, La Hire, isn't this why men go fighting? To ride out together smelling the world when the light of day is just beginning to discover it.

LA HIRE: So anyone can who likes to take a walk in his garden.

JOAN: No. I think death has to be somewhere near before God will show us the world like this.

LA HIRE: Suppose we should meet some English, who might also be liking the good smells of the morning?

JOAN: We attack them, we smite them, and send them flying. That's what we're here for! (*A little pause. She suddenly cries.*) Stop! (*They draw in their horses.*) There are three English over there. They've seen us. They're running away! No! Now they've turned back again: they've seen there are only two of us. They're attacking. You're not afraid, La Hire? No use counting on me; I'm only a girl, and I've got no sword. Will you fight them alone?

LA HIRE (*brandishing his sword with a delighted roar*): Hell, yes, by God I will! (*Shouting to the sky as he charges.*) I didn't say anything, God, I didn't say anything. Pay no attention. . . .

(*He charges into the middle of the Tribunal: they scatter as he swings his sword to left and right. He disappears still fighting.*)

JOAN: He didn't say anything, God. He didn't say anything! He is as good as a French loaf. So all my soldiers are, though they kill, and loot, and swear: good as your wolves are, God, whom you created innocent. I will answer for all of them! (JOAN *is deep in prayer. The Tribunal has re-formed round her: the light has come back.* JOAN *raises her head, sees them, seems to shake herself free of a dream.*) La Hire and Xantrailles! Oh, we're not at the end of things yet. You can be sure they will come and deliver me with two or three or four hundred men. . . .

CAUCHON (*quietly*): They came, Joan: right up to the gates of Rouen to find out how many of the English were in the town, and then they went away again.

JOAN (*dashed*): Oh, they went away? Without fighting? (*A silence; she looks up.*) Why, they have gone to find reinforcements, of course. I myself taught them, it is no good to attack willynilly, as they did at Agincourt.

CAUCHON: They withdrew to the South of the Loire; Charles is down there, disbanding his armies. He is tired of the war, and if he can he will make a treaty, to secure at least his own small portion of France. They will never come back again, Joan.

JOAN: That isn't true! La Hire will come back, even if he hasn't a chance.

CAUCHON: La Hire is only the captain of an army of mercenaries, who sold himself and his men to another Prince as soon as he found that yours was out to make peace. He is marching at this moment towards Germany, to find another country to plunder; simply that.

JOAN: It isn't true!

CAUCHON (*rising*): Have I ever lied to you, Joan? It is true. Then why will you sacrifice yourself to defend those who have deserted you? The only men on earth who are trying to save you—paradoxical though it may seem—are ourselves, your old enemies and now your judges. Recant, Joan: your resistance helps no one now; your friends are betraying you. Return to the arms of your Mother Church. Humble yourself, she will lift you up again. I am convinced that deep in your heart you have never ceased to be one of her daughters.

JOAN: Yes, I am a daughter of the Church!

CAUCHON: Then give yourself into the care of your mother, Joan, without question. She will weigh your burden of error, and so release you from the anguish of judging it for yourself. You needn't think of anything any more: you will do your penance, whether it be heavy or light, and at last you will be at peace. Surely you have a great need of peace.

JOAN (*after a pause*): In what concerns the Faith, I trust myself to the Church. But what I have done I shall never wish to undo.

(*A stir among the priests. The* INQUISITOR *breaks in.*)

INQUISITOR: Do you hear, my masters? Do you see Man raising up his head, like a serpent ready to strike us dead? Do you understand now what it is you have to judge? These heavenly voices have deafened you as well as the girl, on my word they have! You have been labouring to discover what devil has been behind her actions. Would it were only a question of the devil. His trial would soon be over. The devil speaks our language. In his time he was an angel, and we understand him. The sum of his blasphemies, his insults, even his hatred of God, is an act of faith. But man, calm and transparent as he seems, frightens me infinitely more. Look at him: in chains, disarmed, deserted, no longer sure even in himself (isn't that so, Joan?) that the Voices which have been silent for so long have ever truly spoken. Does he throw himself down, supplicating God to hold him again in His Hand? Does he at least implore his Voices to come back and give light to his path? No. He turns away, suffers the torture, suffers humiliation and beatings, suffers like a dumb animal, while his eyes fasten on the invincible image of himself; (*he thunders.*) himself, his only true God! That is what I fear! And he replies—repeat it, Joan; you are longing to say it again; "But what I have done . . ."

JOAN (*quietly*):   . . . I shall never wish to undo.

INQUISITOR (*repeats*):   "But what I have done I shall never wish to undo!" You hear those words? And you will hear them said on the scaffold, at the stake, in the torture chamber, wherever they come to suffer for the errors they commit. And centuries hence they will be saying it; the hunting down of Man will go on endlessly. However powerful we become one day in one shape or another, however inexorably the Idea shall dominate the world, however rigorous, precise and subtle its organisation and its police, there will always be a man who has escaped, a man to hunt, who will presently be caught, presently be killed: a man who, even so, will humiliate the Idea at the highest point of its Power, simply because he will say "No" without lowering his eyes. (*He hisses through his teeth, looking at* JOAN *with hatred.*) An insolent breed! (*He turns again towards the Tribunal.*) Do you need to question her any more? Do you need to ask her why she threw herself from the heights of the tower where she was imprisoned, whether to escape, or to destroy herself against the commandments of God? Why she has left her father and mother, put on the clothes of a man, and wears them still, against the commandments of the Church? She will give you the same reply, the reply of Man: What I have done, I have done. It is mine, and my doing. No one can take it from me;

no one can make me disown it. All that you can do is kill me, to make me cry out no matter what under the torture, but make me say "Yes," you cannot do. (*He cries to them.*) Ah well: by some means or other he must be taught to say Yes, whatever it may cost the world. As long as one man remains who will not be broken, the Idea, even if it dominates and pervades all the rest of mankind, will be in danger of perishing. That is why I require Joan's excommunication, her rejection from the bosom of the Church and that she should be given over to the secular arm for punishment. (*He adds neutrally, reciting a formula.*) Beseeching it nevertheless to limit its sentence on this side of death and the mutilation of the limbs. (*He turns to* JOAN.) This will be a paltry victory against you, Joan, but at least it will silence you. And, up to now, we have not thought of a better. (*He sits down again in silence.*)

CAUCHON (*gently*): My Lord Inquisitor is the first to ask for your excommunication, Joan. In a moment I am afraid my Lord Promoter will ask for the same thing. Each one of us will speak his mind and then I shall have to give my decision. Before lopping the dead branch, which you have become, and casting it far from her, your Holy Mother Church, to whom the one lost sheep is more dear than all the others, remember that, entreats you now for the last time. (CAUCHON *makes a sign, and a man comes forward.*) Do you know this man, Joan? (*She turns to look and gives a little shudder of fear.*) It is the master hangman of Rouen. In a short time from now you will belong to him, unless you give your soul into our keeping so that we can save it. Is the stake ready, Master Hangman?

HANGMAN: Quite ready, my lord. Higher than the regulation stake, such was the orders: so that the girl can be got a good view of from all sides. The nuisance of it for her is that I shan't be able to help her at all, she will be too high up.

CAUCHON: What do you call helping her, Master Hangman?

HANGMAN: A trick of the trade, my lord: it's the custom, when there aren't any special instructions. You wait till the first flames get up, and then I climb up behind, under cover of the smoke, and strangle the party. Then it's only the corpse that burns, and it isn't so bad. But with the instructions I've had, it's too high, and I won't be able to get up there. (*He adds simply:*) So, naturally, it will take longer.

CAUCHON: Do you hear that, Joan?

JOAN (*softly*): Yes.

CAUCHON: I am going to offer you once more the hand of your Mother, the great hand which opens towards you to take you back and save you. But the delay can't be for long. You hear the noise outside, as though the sea had come up to the door? That is the sound of the crowd, who already have been waiting for you since daybreak. They came early to get good places: and there they are still, eating the food they brought with them, grumbling at their children, joking and singing, and asking the soldier how long it will be before things begin to happen. They are not bad people. They are the same men and women who would have cheered you if you had captured Rouen. But things have turned out differently, that's all, and so instead they come to see you burned. As nothing very much ever happens to them, they make their adventures out of the triumphs or the deaths of the world's great ones. You will have to forgive them, Joan. All their lives long they pay dearly for being the common people; they deserve these little distractions.

JOAN (*quietly*): I do forgive them. And I forgive you, as well, my lord.

PROMOTER: Appalling, abominable pride! My lord the Bishop troubles to talk to you like a father, in the hope of saving your miserable soul, and you have the effrontery to say that you forgive him!

JOAN: My lord talks to me gently, but I don't know whether it is to save me or to overthrow me. And since in a little while he will have to burn me anyway, I forgive him.

CAUCHON: Joan: try to understand that there is something absurd in your refusal. You are not an unbeliever. The God you claim as your own is ours also. And we are, in fact, those whom God has ordained to guide you, through the apostle Peter upon whom His Church is built. God did not say to His creatures: You will understand My will from Me. He said "Thou art Peter, and upon this rock I will build My church . . . and its priests will be your shepherds . . . ." Do you think us unworthy priests, Joan?

JOAN (*quietly*): No.

CAUCHON: Then why will you not do as God has said? Why will you not resign your fault to the Church, as you did when you were a small girl, at home in your village? Has your faith so changed?

JOAN (*crying out in anguish*): I want to submit to the Church. I want to receive the Holy Sacrament, but you won't let me!

CAUCHON: We will give it to you after your confession, and when your penance has begun; we only wait for you to say "Yes." You are brave, we know that indeed: but your flesh is still frail: you are surely afraid of dying?

JOAN (*quietly*):   Yes. I'm afraid. But what else can I do?

CAUCHON: I think well enough of you, Joan, to know that fear in itself is not enough to make you draw back. But you should have another, greater fear: the fear of being deceived, and of laying yourself open to eternal damnation. Now, what risk do you run, even if your Voices are from God, if you perform the act of submission to the priests of His church? If we do not believe in your Voices, and if nevertheless God has really spoken to you, then it is we who have committed the monstrous sin of ignorance, presumption and pride, and we who will have to make expiation through all eternity. We will take this risk for you, Joan, and you risk nothing. Say to us: "I submit to you," say simply, "Yes," and you will be at peace, blameless, and safe in your redemption.

JOAN (*suddenly exhausted*):   Why will you torture me so gently, my lord? I would far rather you beat me.

CAUCHON (*smiling*):   If I beat you, Joan, I should only add to your pride: your pride which wishes to see you persecuted and killed. I reason with you because God gifted you with reason and good sense. I beseech you, because I know you have gentle feeling. I am an old man, Joan; I have no more ambitions in this world, and, like each of us here, I have put many to death in defence of the Church, as you have put many to death in defence of your Voices. It is enough. I am tired. I wish to die without adding to those deaths the death of a little girl. Help me.

JOAN (*after a pause*):   What do I have to say?

CAUCHON: First of all you must understand that by insisting that God sent you, you no longer help anything or anyone. It is only playing into the hands of the English and the Executioner. Your king himself has declared in his letters that he doesn't in any way wish to owe the possession of his crown to a divine intervention of which you were the instrument.

(JOAN *turns towards* CHARLES *in distress*.)

CHARLES: Put yourself in my place, Joan! If there had to be a miracle to crown me King of France, it means I wasn't naturally king at all. It means I wasn't the true son of my father, or else my coronation would have followed of its own accord. All the other kings in my family have been crowned without needing a miracle. Divine help is all very well in its way, but suspect. And it's even more suspect when it stops Since that unhappy Paris business, we've been beaten at ever step; and then you let yourself be captured at Compiègne They've got a little verdict up their sleeve for you, to de nounce you as a witch, a heretic, the devil's intermediary, a in one. I prefer people to think you were never sent by any one, God or devil. In that way, God has neither helped me nor thrown me over. I won because I was the strongest at th time; I am being beaten now because I am the weakest, fo the moment. That is healthy politics, if you understand?

JOAN (*softly*): Yes, I understand.

CAUCHON: I'm thankful to see you're wiser at last. We have put so many questions to you, you became confused. I am going to ask you three more, three essential ones. If you answer "Yes" three times, we shall all of us be saved, you who are going to die, and we who are putting you to death.

JOAN (*quietly, after a pause*): Ask them. I will see whether I can answer them.

CAUCHON: The first question is the really important one. If you answer "Yes," the other answers will take care of themselves. Listen carefully, weighing each word: "Do you humbly put yourself into the hands of the Holy Apostolic Church of Rome; of our Holy Father the Pope and his bishops, that they shall estimate your deeds and judge you? Do you surrender yourself entirely and undoubtedly, and do you ask to be received again into the bosom of the Church?" It is enough for you to answer "Yes."

(JOAN *after a pause, looks around her without moving. At last she speaks.*)

JOAN: Yes, but . . .

INQUISITOR (*in a level voice*): With no "but."

JOAN: I do not wish to be made to deny what my Voices have said to me. I do not wish to be made to bear witness against my king, or to say anything which will dim the glory of his coronation which is his, irrevocably, now and for ever.

(The INQUISITOR *shrugs his shoulders.*)

INQUISITOR: Such is the voice of man. There is only one way of bringing him to silence.

CAUCHON (*becoming angry*): Joan, Joan, Joan, are you mad? Do you not see this man in red who is waiting for you? Realise, understand, this is my last effort to save you, after this there is nothing more I can do. The Church still wishes to believe that you are one of her daughters. She has weighed with care the form her question should take, to help you on the path, and you cavil and try to bargain. There is no bargaining with your Mother, you impudent girl! You should beg her on your knees to wrap you in her cloak of love and protect you. Our Lord suffered far more than you in the humiliation and injustice of His Passion. Did He bargain or cavil when He came to die for you? Your suffering bears no comparison with His: scourged, mocked, spat upon: crowned with thorns, and nailed in a long agony between two thieves; you can never hope to rival His suffering! And He asks, through us, only one thing of you, that you submit to the judgment of His Church, and you hesitate.

JOAN (*after a pause, tears in her eyes*):   Forgive me, my lord. I hadn't thought that Our Saviour might wish it. It is true that He has surely suffered more than I. (*A short pause, again, and she says*:) I submit.

CAUCHON: Do you humbly and without any restriction supplicate the Holy Catholic Church to receive you again into her bosom, and do you defer to her judgment?

JOAN: I humbly supplicate my Mother Church to receive me again into her bosom, and I surrender myself to her judgment.

CAUCHON (*with a sigh of relief*):   Good, Joan; well done. The rest will be simple enough now. Do you promise never again to take up arms?

JOAN: There is still work to be done . . .

CAUCHON: The work, as you call it, will be done by others. Don't be foolish, Joan. You are in chains, a prisoner, and in great danger of being burned. So whether you say yes or no the work will not be done by you. Your part is played out. The English have you in their grasp, and they'll not let you fight again. You said to us just now that when a girl has two words of good sense God is there performing His miracle. If God is protecting you, this is the time for Him to bring you the two words of good sense. So you promise never again to take up arms?

JOAN (*groaning*):   But if my King still needs me?

CHARLES (*hastily*):   Oh, goodness me! If it's me you're thinking about you can say yes at once. I don't need you any more.

JOAN (*heavily*):   Then, yes; yes.

CAUCHON: Do you promise never to wear again these

man's clothes, which is contrary to all the rules of decency and Christian modesty?

JOAN (*tired of the question*):   You have asked me that ten times. The clothes are nothing. My Voices told me to wear them.

PROMOTER: The devil told you! Who except the devil would incite a girl to overthrow decency?

JOAN (*quietly*):   Common sense, my lord.

PROMOTER (*sneering*):   Common sense? Common sense is your strong card! Are breeches on a girl common sense?

JOAN: Of course, my lord. I had to ride horseback with the soldiers; I had to wear what they wore so that they wouldn't think of me as a girl, but as a soldier like themselves.

PROMOTER: A worthless reply! A girl who isn't damned to begin with wouldn't wish to ride with the soldiers!

CAUCHON: Even though it may be that these clothes had their purpose during the war, why do you still refuse to dress as a woman? The fighting's over, you are in our hands; yet you still refuse.

JOAN: It is necessary.

CAUCHON: Why?

JOAN (*hesitating for a moment, blushing*):   If I were in a Church prison, I wouldn't refuse then.

PROMOTER: You hear this nonsense, my lord? What hair splitting: what deliberate prevarication! Why should she agree to modesty in a Church prison, and not where she is? I don't understand it, and I don't wish to!

JOAN (*smiling sadly*):   And yet it is very easy to understand, my lord. You don't have to be very wise to see it.

PROMOTER: It is very easy to understand, and I don't understand because I'm a fool, I suppose? Will you note that, my lord? She insults me, in the exercise of my public office. She treats her indecency as something to glory in, boasts of it, in fact, takes a gross delight in it, I've no doubt! If she submits to the Church, as she apparently wants to, I may have to give up my chief accusation of heresy; but as long as she refuses to put off this diabolical dress, I shall persist in my charge of witchcraft, even though pressure is put upon me by the conspiracy to shield her which I see presides over this debate. I shall appeal, if necessary, to the Council of Basle! The devil is in this, my lord, the devil is in it! I can feel his terrible presence! He it is who is making her refuse to give up these clothes of immodesty and vice, no doubt of that.

JOAN: Put me in a Church prison, and I shall give them up.

PROMOTER: You shall not make your bargains with the Church: my lord has already told you so. You will give up this dress altogether, or you will be condemned as a witch and burnt!

CAUCHON: If you accept the principle, Joan, why don't you wish to obey us now, in the prison where you are?

JOAN: I'm not alone there.

PROMOTER: Well? you're not alone there. Well? What of that?

JOAN: The English soldiers are on guard in the cell, all through the day, and through the night.

PROMOTER: Well? (*A pause.*) Do you mean to go on? Your powers of invention have failed you already, is that it? I should have thought the devil was more ingenious! You feel that you've been caught out, my girl, and it makes you blush.

CAUCHON (*quietly*): You must answer him, Joan. I think I understand but it must be you who tells us so.

JOAN (*after a moment of hesitation*): The nights are long, my lord. I am in chains. I do my best to keep awake, but sleep sometimes is too strong for me. (*She stops.*)

PROMOTER (*more and more obtuse*): Well, what then? The nights are long, you are in chains, you want to sleep. What then?

JOAN (*quietly*): I can defend myself better if I wear these clothes.

CAUCHON (*heavily*): Has this been so all the time of the trial?

JOAN: Ever since I was captured, my lord, each night; and when you send me back there in the evening, it begins again. I've got into the way of not sleeping now, which is why my answers are so sleepy and muddled when I'm brought before you in the mornings. But each night seems longer; and the soldiers are strong, and full of tricks. I should as soon wear a woman's dress on the battlefield.

CAUCHON: Why don't you call the officer, and he would defend you?

JOAN (*after a pause*): They told me they would be hanged if I called for help.

WARWICK (*to* CAUCHON): Incredible. I never heard of such a thing! Quite possible in the French army. But in the English army, no, quite ridiculous. I shall inquire into this.

CAUCHON: If you would return, Joan, back to your Mother the Church who is waiting for you: promise to change from these clothes to the dress of a girl: the Church from now on would see you had no such fears.

JOAN: Then I do promise.

CAUCHON (*giving a deep sigh*): Good. Thank you, Joan, you have helped me. I was afraid for a time we should have no power to save you. We shall read your promise to adjure your sins: the document is all ready, you have only to sign it.

JOAN: I don't know how to write.

CAUCHON: You will make a cross. My Lord Inquisitor, allow me to recall Brother Ladvenu so that he may read this to the prisoner. It is Brother Ladvenu who is responsible, at my request, for drawing up this paper. And, moreover, we have all to be here now, to pronounce sentence, now that Joan has returned to us. (*He leans towards him.*) You should be gratified, my lord: Man has said "yes."

INQUISITOR (*a pallid smile on his thin lips*): I am waiting until the conclusion; until the conclusion.

(CAUCHON *calls to the* GUARD.)

CAUCHON: Recall Brother Ladvenu!

PROMOTER (*whispering*): My Lord Inquisitor, you won't allow them to do this?

INQUISITOR (*with a vague gesture*): If she has said "Yes" . . .

PROMOTER: My Lord Bishop has conducted the enquiry with an indulgence towards the girl which I can't begin to understand! And yet I have reliable information that he feeds well from the English manger. Does he feed even more rapaciously from the French? That is what I ask myself.

INQUISITOR (*smiling*): It is not what I ask myself, my Lord Promoter. It is not of eating, well or better, that I am thinking, but of something graver. (*He falls on to his knees, oblivious of all around him.*) O Lord! It has pleased You to grant that Man should humble himself at the eleventh hour in the person of this young girl. It has been Your will that this time he shall say "Yes." But why has it also pleased You to let an evident and earthly tenderness be born in the heart of this old man who was judging her? Will you never grant, O Lord, that this world should be unburdened of every trace of humanity, so that at last we may in peace consecrate it to Thy glory alone?

(BROTHER LADVENU *has come forward.*)

CAUCHON: She is saved, Brother Ladvenu, Joan is saved.

She has agreed to return to us, and to Holy Mother Church. Read her the Act of Abjuration, and she will sign it.

LADVENU: Thank you, Joan. I was praying for you, I prayed that this might be possible. (*He reads.*) "I, Joan, known as the Maid, confess to having sinned, by pride, obstinacy, and wrong-doing, in pretending to receive revelation from Our Lord God, Father of all Men, through the means of His angels and His blessed Saints. I confess to having blasphemed by wearing immodest clothing, contrary to the ruling of our Holy Mother Church; and to having, by persuasion, incited men to kill one another. I foreswear and abjure all these sins; I vow upon the Holy Gospels no more to wear these clothes or to bear arms. I promise to surrender myself in humility to our Holy Mother Church, and to our Holy Father the Pope of Rome, and to his Bishops, that they shall weigh and estimate my sins and wickedness. I beseech the Church to receive me again into her bosom; and I declare myself ready to suffer the sentence which it will please her to inflict upon me. In token of which I have signed my name to this Act of Abjuration which I profess I have understood."

JOAN (*who seems now like a shy and awkward girl*): Do I make a circle or a cross? I can't write my name.

LADVENU: I will guide your hand. (*He helps her to sign.*)

CAUCHON: There; it is done, Joan; and the Church rejoices to see her daughter safely returned: and you know she rejoices more for the one lost sheep than for the ninety-and-nine safely enfolded. Your soul is saved, and your body will not be delivered up to the executioner. We condemn you only, through the mercy and the grace of God, to live the rest of your days a prisoner, in penitence of these errors, eating the bread of sorrow, drinking the water of anguish, so that in solitary contemplation you may repent; and by these means we shall admit you free of the danger of excommunication into which you were fallen. You may go in peace. (*He makes the sign of the cross over her.*) Take her away.

(*The SOLDIERS lead JOAN away. The assembly breaks up into groups, conversing among themselves.*)

WARWICK (*coming up to CAUCHON*): Good enough, my lord; good enough. I was wondering for a moment or so what irresponsible whim was urging you to save the girl, and whether you hadn't a slight inclination to betray your king.

CAUCHON: Which king, my lord?

WARWICK (*with a touch of frigidity*): I said your king. I imagine you have only one? Yes; very uncertain for a time whether His Majesty was going to get his money's worth, owing to this fancy of yours. But then, when I thought about it, I could see this method would discredit young Charles equally well, without the disadvantages of martyrdom, which are unpredictable, when you think of the sort of sentimental reactions we get from the public. The resolute, unshakeable girl, tied to the stake and burning in the flames, would have seemed, even so, something of a triumph for the French cause. This admission of guilt, on the other hand, is properly disgraceful. Perfect.

(*The characters move away. The lighting changes.* JOAN *is brought on by a* GUARD. AGNES SOREL *and* QUEEN YOLANDE *slip in beside her.*)

AGNES (*coming forward*): Joan, Joan, my dear; we're so very happy it has all turned out well for you. Congratulations!

YOLANDE: Dying is quite useless, my little Joan: and whatever we do in life should have a use of some kind. People may have different opinions about the way my life has been lived, but at least I've never done anything absolutely useless.

AGNES: It was all so very stupid. Usually I adore political trials, and I particularly begged Charles to get me a seat; to watch someone fighting for his life is desperately exciting, as a rule. But really I didn't feel in the least happy when I was there. All the time I kept saying to myself: This is so very stupid: this poor little tomboy: she is going to get herself killed, and all for nothing. (*She takes* CHARLES's *arm.*) Being alive is much better, you know, in every way.

CHARLES: Yes, of course it is; and when you practically ruined your chances, just because of me—well, I was very touched, naturally, but I didn't know how to make you understand that you were getting everything quite wrong. In the first place, as you might expect, I had taken the precaution to disown you, on the advice of that old fox of an Archbishop; but, more than that, I don't like people being devoted to me. I don't like being loved. It creates obligations, and obligations are detestable.

(JOAN *does not look at them; she hears their prattle without seeming to hear it. Then suddenly she speaks quietly.*)

JOAN: Take care of Charles. I hope he keeps his courage.

AGNES: Of course he will; why shouldn't he? My way with him is not so different from yours. I don't want him to be a poor little king who is always being beaten, any more than you do; and you shall see, I shall make our Charles a great King yet, and without getting myself burnt, either. (*She adds in a low voice.*) I suppose it may be rather disillusioning to say so, Joan (though, of course, the two sexes are presumably what God wanted): but I do seem to get as much out of Charles by my little campaigns in the bedroom as ever you did with swords and angels.

JOAN (*murmuring*):   Poor Charles . . .

AGNES: Why poor? He is perfectly happy, like all egoists: and one of these days he is going to be a great king into the bargain.

YOLANDE: We shall see that done, Joan: not your way, but ours, and effectively enough.

AGNES (*with a gesture to the little* QUEEN):   Even her little Majesty will help. She has just given him a second son. It is all she can do, but she does it very well. So if the first son dies there is no feverish worry. The succession is assured. You can be quite happy, Joan, that you're leaving everything in good order at the Court of France.

CHARLES (*after a sneeze*):   Are you coming, my dear? This prison atmosphere is deadly, so damp it would really be healthier to sit in the river. Goodbye, Joan, for the moment; we'll come and visit you from time to time.

JOAN: Goodbye, Charles.

CHARLES: Goodbye, goodbye . . . I might say, if ever you come back to Court, you will have to call me Sire, like anybody else. I've seen to that, since my coronation. Even La Tremouille does it. It's a great victory.

(*They go off, rustling their robes.*)

JOAN (*murmuring*):   Goodbye, Sire. I am glad I got you that privilege at least. (*The light changes again, as the* GUARD *leads her to a three-legged stool; she is alone now in her cell.*) Blessed St. Michael, blessed ladies Catherine and Margaret, are you never going to come again and speak to me? Why have you left me alone since the English captured me? You were there to see me safely to victory: but it's now, in the suffering time, that I need you most. I know it would be too simple, too easy, if God always held me by the hand: where would the merit be? I know He took my hand at the beginning because I was still too small to be alone, and later

He thought I could make my own way. But I am not very big yet, God. It was very difficult to follow clearly everything the Bishop said to me. With the Canon it was easy: I could see where he was wrong, and where he was wicked, and I was ready to give him any answer which would make him furious. But the Bishop spoke so gently, and it often seemed to me he was right. Are you sure that you meant that, God? Did you mean me to feel so afraid of suffering, when the man said he would have no chance to strangle me before the flames could reach me? Are you sure that you want me to live? (*A pause. She seems to be waiting for an answer, her eyes on the sky.*) No word for me? I shall have to answer that question for myself, as well. (*A pause. She nods.*) Perhaps I am only proud and self-willed after all? Perhaps after all, I did imagine everything?

(*Another pause. She suddenly bursts into tears, her head on the stool.* WARWICK *comes quickly on to the stage, preceded by a* GUARD *who leaves them at once.* WARWICK *stops and looks at* JOAN, *surprised.*)

WARWICK: Are you crying?

JOAN: Yes, my lord.

WARWICK: And I came here to congratulate you! That was a very happy solution to it all, I thought, the outcome of the trial, very. I told Cauchon, I was delighted you managed to avoid an execution. Quite apart from my own personal sympathy for you, the suffering is really frightful, you know, and quite useless, and most unpleasant to watch. I'm perfectly convinced you've done right to steer clear of martyrdom; better for us all. I congratulate you most sincerely. It was astonishing, considering the peasant stock you come from, that you should behave with such distinction. A gentleman is always ready, when he must, to die for his honour or his king, but it's only the riff-raff who get themselves killed for nothing. And then I was very entertained to see you queen the Inquisitor's pawn. A sinister character, that Inquisitor fellow! I detest intellectuals more than anybody. These fleshless people, what unpleasant fossils they are!— Are you really a virgin?

JOAN: Yes.

WARWICK: Well, yes, of course you are. No woman would have spoken quite in the way you did. My fiancée in England, who's a very innocent girl, reasons exactly like a boy herself, and, like you, there's no gainsaying her. There's an Indian proverb—I don't know whether you may have heard it—which says it takes a virgin to walk on water. (*He gives a little laugh.*) We shall see how long she manages that, once she becomes Lady Warwick! Being a virgin is a state of grace. We adore them, and revere them, and yet, the sad thing is, as soon as we meet one we're in the greatest possible hurry to make a woman of her: and we expect the miracle to go on as if nothing had happened. Madmen! Just as soon as ever this campaign is over—it won't be long now, I hope: your little Charles is tottering to a fall—but as soon as it is, back I go to England, to do that very same idiotic thing. Warwick Castle is a very beautiful place, a bit big, a bit severe, but very beautiful. I breed superb horses—and my fiancée rides rather well, not as well as you do, but rather well. So she ought to be very happy there. We shall go fox-hunting, of course, and entertain fairly lavishly from time to time. I'm only sorry the circumstances make it so difficult to invite you over. (*An awkward pause.*) Well, there it is, I thought I'd pay you this visit, rather like shaking hands after a match, if you know what I mean. I hope I haven't disturbed you. Are my men behaving themselves now?

JOAN: Yes.

WARWICK: I should think they will certainly transfer you to a Church prison. But in any case, until they do, if there's any sign of a lapse, don't hesitate to report it to me. I'll have the blackguard hung. It's not really possible to have a whole army of gentlemen, but we can try. (*He bows.*) Madam.

(*He starts to go.* JOAN *calls him back.*)

JOAN: My lord!

WARWICK (*returning*): Yes?

JOAN (*without looking at him*): It would have been better, wouldn't it, if I had been burned?

WARWICK: I told you, for His Majesty's Government, the admission of guilt was just as good.

JOAN: But for me?

WARWICK: Unprofitable suffering. An ugly business. No, really, it wouldn't have been better. It would have been, as I told you just now, slightly plebeian, and ill-bred, and more than slightly stupid, to insist on dying just to embarrass everybody and make a demonstration.

JOAN (*as though to herself*): But I am ill-bred, I am stupid. And then, remember, my lord, my life isn't prepared and perfected like yours, running so orderly and smoothly between war, hunting, and your beautiful bride waiting for you in England. What is left of me when I am not Joan any longer?

WARWICK: Life isn't going to be very gay for you, I agree, not at first, anyway. But things will adjust themselves in time, I don't think you need have any doubt of that.

JOAN: But I don't want things to adjust themselves. I don't want to live through however long this "in time" of yours will be. (*She gets up like a sleepwalker, and stares blindly ahead.*) Do you see Joan after living through it, when things have adjusted themselves: Joan, set free, perhaps, and vegetating at the French Court on her small pension?

WARWICK (*impatient*): My dear girl, I can tell you, in six months there won't be a French Court!

JOAN (*almost laughing, though sadly*): Joan accepting everything, Joan fat and complacent, Joan doing nothing but eat. Can you see me painted and powdered, trying to look fashionable, getting entangled in her skirts, fussing over her little dog, or trailing a man at her heels: who knows, perhaps with a husband?

WARWICK: Why not? Everything has to come to an end sometime. I'm going to be married myself.

JOAN (*suddenly cries out in another voice*): But I don't want everything to come to an end! Or at least not an end like that, an end which is no end at all. Blessed St. Michael: St. Margaret: St. Catherine! You may be silent now, but I wasn't born until you first spoke to me, that day in the fields: my life truly began when I did what you told me to do, riding horseback with a sword in my hand. And that is Joan, and no other one. Certainly not one sitting placid in her convent, pasty-faced and going to pieces in comfort: continuing to live as a tolerable habit: set free, they would call it! You kept yourself silent, God, while all the priests were trying to speak at once, and everything became a confusion of words. But You told St. Michael to make it clear to me in the very beginning, that when You're silent You have then the most certain trust in us. It is the time when You let us take on everything alone. (*She draws herself up.*) Well, I take it on, O God: I take it upon myself! I give Joan back to You: true to what she is, now and forever! Call your soldiers, Warwick; call them, call them, quickly now: for I tell you I withdraw my admission of guilt: I take back my promises: they can pile their faggots, and set up their stake: they can have their holiday after all!

WARWICK (*bored*): Now for God's sake don't let's have

ny such nonsense, I do implore you. I told you, I'm very
atisfied with things as they are. And besides, I loathe exe-
utions. I couldn't bear to watch you going through any-
ning of the kind.

JOAN: You have to have courage, that's all; I shall have
ourage. (*She looks at his pale face and puts a hand on his
houlder.*) You're a good dear fellow, in spite of your gen-
lemanly poker-face; but there isn't anything you can do:
ve belong, as you say, to different ways of life. (*She unex-
ectedly gives him a little kiss on the cheeks, and runs off,
alling.*) Soldiers, goddams! Hey there, goddams! Fetch me
he clothes I wore to fight in, and when I'm back in my
reeches tell all my judges Joan is herself again!

(WARWICK *remains alone, wiping his cheek.*)

WARWICK: How out of place this all is. What bad form.
t's impossible to get on well with these French for long.

(*A great clamour.*)

CROWD: Death to the witch! Burn the heretic! Kill her,
ill her, kill her!

(*All the actors return quickly, grasping faggots: the* EXE-
UTIONER *dragging* JOAN *with the help of* TWO ENGLISH
SOLDIERS. LADVENU *follows, very pale. The movement is rapid
and brutal. The* EXECUTIONER, *with someone's help, perhaps
he* PROMOTER's, *makes a stake with the benches from the
trial scene. They make* JOAN *climb up, they tie her to the
stake, and nail a defamatory inscription over her head. The*
CROWD *yells.*)

CROWD: To the stake with the witch! To the stake! Shave
her head, the soldier's bitch! To the stake! To the stake!
Burn her!

WARWICK: Stupidity! Absurd stupidity! This is something
we could have done without, perfectly well.

JOAN: A cross! Let me have a cross, a cross to hold: pity
me!

PROMOTER: No, no! No cross for a witch!

JOAN: Give me a cross, a cross to hold, a crucifix!

CAUCHON: Ladvenu! To the parish church! Run, Ladvenu!

(LADVENU *runs off.*)

PROMOTER (*to the* INQUISITOR): This is most irregular Aren't you going to protest, my lord?

INQUISITOR (*staring at* JOAN): With or without a cross, she has to be silenced, and quickly! Look at her, defying us Are we never going to be able to master this flaunting spirit of man?

JOAN: A cross!

(*An* ENGLISH SOLDIER *has taken two sticks, ties them together and calls to* JOAN.)

SOLDIER: Hold on, wait a bit, my girl: here you are! What are they talking about, these two priests? They make me vomit. She's got a right to a cross, like anybody else.

PROMOTER (*rushing forward*): She is a heretic! I forbid you to give it to her!

SOLDIER (*jostling him off*): You choke yourself.

(*He offers the improvised cross to* JOAN, *who clasps it against her, and kisses it.*)

PROMOTER (*rushing to* WARWICK): My lord! This man ought to be arrested as a heretic. I insist that you arrest him immediately!

WARWICK: You make me tired, sir. I have eight hundred men like that, each one more heretical than the others. They are what I use to fight the wars with.

INQUISITOR (*to the* EXECUTIONER): Will you hurry and light the fire? Let the smoke cover her quickly, and hide her away out of our sight! (*To* WARWICK.) We must make haste! In five minutes everybody will have swung to her side, they will all be for her!

WARWICK: I'm very much afraid that has already happened.

(LADVENU *runs in with a cross.*)

PROMOTER (*yelling*): Don't dare to give her the cross, Brother Ladvenu!

CAUCHON: Let him alone, Canon: I order you to let him alone.

PROMOTER: I shall refer this matter to the court of Rome!

CAUCHON: You can refer it to the devil, if you like: for the present moment, the orders to be obeyed here are mine.

(*All this is rapid, hurly-burly, improvised, like a police operation.*)

INQUISITOR (*running from one to the other nervously*): We must be quick! We must be quick! We must be quick!

LADVENU (*who has climbed up to the stake*): Courage, Joan. We are all praying for you.

JOAN: Thank you, little brother. But get down: the flames will catch you: you will be burnt as well.

INQUISITOR (*who can't bear it any more, to the EXECUTIONER*): Well, man, have you done it yet, have you done it?

EXECUTIONER (*climbing down*): Yes, it's done, my lord, it's alight. In two minutes, you'll see, the flames will have reached her.

INQUISITOR (*with a sigh of relief*): At last!

CAUCHON (*falling on his knees*): O God, forgive us! (*They all kneel, and start the prayers for the dead. The PROMOTER, in a fury of hatred, remains standing.*) Get down on your knees, Canon! (*The PROMOTER looks like a cornered animal: he kneels.*)

INQUISITOR (*who dares not look, to LADVENU who is near him and holding the cross for JOAN*): Is she looking straight in front of her?

LADVENU: Yes, my lord.

INQUISITOR: Without flinching?

LADVENU: Yes, my lord.

INQUISITOR (*almost sorrowfully*): And there is almost a smile on her lips, is there not?

LADVENU: Yes, my lord.

INQUISITOR (*with bowed head, overwhelmed, heavily*): I shall never be able to master him.

LADVENU (*radiant with confidence and joy*): No, my lord!

JOAN (*murmuring, already twisted with pain*): Blessed Michael, Margaret, and Catherine, you were brighter than these flames: let your voices burn me. O Lord Jesus, let them speak to me. Speak to me. In the fields, in the heat of the sun. Noon.

AGNES (*kneeling in a corner with CHARLES and the QUEEN*): Poor little Joan. It is monstrous and stupid. Do you think she is suffering already?

CHARLES (*wiping his forehead and looking away*): There is still the agony to come.

(*The murmur of the prayers for the dead drowns the voices. Suddenly BEAUDRICOURT bursts on to the stage breathless from running.*)

BEAUDRICOURT: Stop! Stop! Stop! (*Everyone is startled; a moment of uncertainty. To* CAUCHON.) This can't be the way it goes! Grant a stay of execution, and let me have time to think! For, as I said to her when she first came to me, I don't think clearly when suddenly put to it. But one thing I do see: we haven't done what we said we'd do. We haven't performed the coronation! We said that we were going to play everything! And we haven't at all. It isn't justice to her. And she has a right to see the coronation performed: it's a part of her story.

CAUCHON (*struck by this*): We did say so, indeed; you are right to remind us. You remember, gentlemen: the whole of her life to go through, was what we said. We were in too great a hurry to bring her to an end. We were committing an injustice!

CHARLES: You see! I knew they would forget my coronation. No one ever remembers my coronation. And look what it cost me.

WARWICK: Well, really! The coronation, now! And at this time of the day, as though their little victory came last. It would be most improper for me to attend any such ceremony; I shall go away. As far as I'm concerned it is all over, and Joan is burnt. His Majesty's Government has obtained its political objective. (*He goes.*)

CAUCHON: Unchain her! Drag away the faggots! Give her the sword and the standard again!

(*He goes. Everyone joyously drags down the stake and faggots.*)

CAUCHON: This man is quite right. The real end of Joan's story, the end which will never come to an end, which they will always tell, long after they have forgotten our names or confused them all together: it isn't the painful and miserable end of the cornered animal caught at Rouen: but the lark singing in the open sky. Joan at Rheims in all her glory. The true end of the story is a kind of joy. Joan of Arc: a story which ends happily.

(*They have quickly set up an altar where the stake was standing. Bells suddenly ring out proudly. A procession forms with* CHARLES, JOAN *a little behind him, then the* QUEENS, LA TREMOUILLE, *etc. The procession moves towards the altar. Everyone kneels. Only* JOAN *remains standing, leaning on her standard, smiling upward, like a statue of her. The* ARCHBISHOP *puts the crown on* CHARLES's *head. Bells, a salute of cannon, a flight of doves, a play of light perhaps, which throws the reflection of the cathedral stained glass across the scene, transforming it. The Curtain falls slowly on this beautiful illustration from a school prize.)*

PART TWO ❧ THE ESSAYS

ANDRÉ GIDE: Classicism[1]

I have been interviewed. The *Renaissance* wanted my opinion on the question of classicism.

Since I believe that those who talk most are often those who produce least, I began by declaring that I had nothing to say. But Emile Henriot, who came to get my answer, brings so much intelligence, courtesy, and persuasiveness to his interviews that it is not enough to say that it is easy to talk with him; with him one cannot keep from talking. You may already have seen my answer in print.

Having identified modesty as the essence of classicism, I can now tell you that I see myself as the best representative of classicism today. I was about to say the only one; but I was forgetting MM. Gonzague Truc and Benda.

And now if you will allow me a few supplementary remarks, I will note down my ideas as they come.

The triumph of individualism and the triumph of classicism merge. But the triumph of individualism resides in the renunciation of individuality. There is no single quality of the classical style that has not been bought at the sacrifice of some self-indulgence. The painters and writers we most praise today have a manner; the great classical artist makes an effort not to have a manner—he strives for the commonplace. If he achieves this banality without effort, he is manifestly not a great artist. The classical work will be strong and beautiful only by virtue of a romanticism brought under control. Twenty years ago I wrote:

A great artist[2] has but one concern: to become as human as possible—or, to put it better, to become *commonplace*. . . . The wonderful thing is that he thus becomes more personal. But he who flees humanity for himself alone, succeeds only in becoming special, bizarre, incomplete. It is perhaps appropriate to

[1] From "Notes to Angèle," in *Pretexts*. First published in *Nouvelle Revue Française* in 1921. *Ed.*

[2] Gide misquotes himself: the original reads "great man." *Ed.*

ᵗᵉᶜᵃ11 the words of the Gospel here—I do not think I am distorting the sense: "Whosoever shall seek to save his life [his personal life] shall lose it; and whosoever shall lose his life shall preserve it." (Or, to translate more faithfully the Greek text: "...shall make it truly alive.")

I judge that the successful work of art will be that which will first pass unnoticed, which will not even be singled out; in which the most unlike qualities, apparently the most contradictory, strength and softness, erectness and grace, logic and impulse, exactness and poetry, will breathe so easily, that they will seem natural and not at all surprising. Accordingly, the first sacrifice to require of oneself is that of startling one's contemporaries: Baudelaire, Blake, Keats, Browning, Stendhal wrote only for future generations. On this matter Proust has said some very sound things.

And yet I do not believe that the classical work is necessarily first misunderstood. Boileau, Racine, La Fontaine, Molière himself, were at once appreciated; and if we see in their writings many qualities that were not those to which their contemporaries were most responsive, those whom we recognize today as supreme were from the first celebrated. Despite the rather unintelligent attempt of Gautier to turn up neglected geniuses among the *"grotesques"* of the seventeenth century, their position is in no way comparable to that of Baudelaire with respect to a Ponsard or a Baour-Lormian. The public itself was classical and demanded of the work of art those very qualities that make us today judge it classical.

The word "classical" is today in such honor and carries such weight that we incline to call classical every great and beautiful work. This is absurd. There are giant works that are not in the least classical. This does not mean that they are romantic. The classification is meaningless except in France, and even in France what could be less classical often than Pascal, Rabelais, Villon? Neither Shakespeare nor Michelangelo, neither Beethoven nor Dostoevsky, not Rembrandt—not even Dante (I cite only the greatest) is a classicist. *Don Quixote* and Calderón's plays are not classical— they are not romantic—they are purely Spanish.

Indeed, since antiquity I know of no other classicists but the French (with the exception of Goethe—and he is classical only by imitation of the ancients). Classicism seems to me so completely a French invention, that I would almost make the two synonymous—classical and French—if the first could lay claim to exhausting the French genius and had romanticism not succeeded in making itself French; at least it is in its classical art that the French genius has been most fully manifested. But among other peoples every attempt at classicism will remain artificial, as, say, in the case of Pope. Moreover in France and in France alone intelligence tends always to win out over feeling and instinct. This does not mean (as some foreigners are likely to believe) that feeling or instinct is absent. One has only to go through the recently reopened Louvre galleries, both sculpture and painting. To what a degree all those works are dominated by reason! What balance, what moderation! It is necessary to examine them at length before they yield up their profound meaning, so secret is their vibration. Sensuality overflows in Rubens; is it the less powerful in Poussin for being completely inward?

Classicism—and by that I mean French classicism—tends wholly toward litotes. It is the art of expressing the more by saying the less. It is an art of restraint and of modesty. Each of our classicists is more moved than he lets first appear. The romanticist, because of the splendor of his expression, appears always to be more moved than he really is, so that among our romantic authors the word continually precedes and overstates the emotion and the thought; it corresponded to a certain blunting of taste as a result of an inferior culture, which allowed them to doubt the reality of what was so modestly expressed by our classicists. For lack of knowing how to penetrate them and catch their allusions, they found our classicists cold, and judged as a shortcoming their most exquisite quality—reserve.

The romantic author remains always this side of his words; but one must seek the classical author over and beyond his words. A certain faculty for passing too rapidly, too easily, from emotion to word is characteristic of all French romanticists; hence their lack of effort to seize emotion other than by words, their lack of effort to master it. The essential for them is no longer to be moved, but to *seem* to be moved. In all Greek literature, in the best English poetry, in Racine, in Pascal, in Baudelaire, you sense that the word, while revealing emotion, does not contain it entire, and that, once the word is uttered, the emotion that preceded it continues. In Ronsard, Corneille, Hugo, to cite only great names, it seems that the emotion ends with the word and is held within it; it is verbal and the word exhausts it; the only overtones to be found in it are supplied by the voice.

Translated by JEFFREY J. CARRE

GEORGE MEREDITH:
From *An Essay on Comedy* [1]

The French have a school of stately comedy to which they can fly for renovation whenever they have fallen away from it; and their having such a school is mainly the reason why, as John Stuart Mill pointed out, they know men and women more accurately than we do. Molière followed the Horatian precept, to observe the manners of his age, and give his characters the color befitting them at the time. He did not paint in raw realism. He seized his characters firmly for the central purpose of the play, stamped them in the idea, and, by slightly raising and softening the object of study (as in the case of the ex-Huguenot, Duc de Montausier, for the study of the Misanthrope, and, according to Saint-Simon, the Abbé Roquette for Tartuffe),. generalized upon it so as to make it permanently human. Concede that it is natural for human creatures to live in society, and Alceste is an imperishable mark of one, though he is drawn in light outline, without any forcible human coloring.

Our English school has not clearly imagined society; and of the mind hovering above congregated men and women it has imagined nothing. The critics who praise it for its downrightness, and for bringing the situations home to us, as they admiringly say, cannot but disapprove of Molière's comedy, which appeals to the individual mind to perceive and participate in the social. We have splendid tragedies, we have the most beautiful of poetic plays, and we have literary comedies passingly pleasant to read, and occasionally to see acted. By literary comedies, I mean comedies of classic inspiration, drawn chiefly from Menander and the Greek New Comedy through Terence; or else comedies of the poet's personal conception, that have had no model in life, and are humorous exaggerations, happy or otherwise. These are the comedies of Ben Jonson, Massinger, and Fletcher. Massinger's Justice Greedy we can all of us refer to a type, "with good capon lined," that has been, and will be; and he would be comic, as Panurge is comic, but only a Rabelais could set him moving

[1] First published in 1897. *Ed.*

with real animation. Probably Justice Greedy would be comic to the audience of a country booth, and to some of our friends. If we have lost our youthful relish for the presentation of characters put together to fit a type, we find it hard to put together the mechanism of a civil smile at his enumeration of his dishes. Something of the same is to be said of Bobadill, swearing "by the foot of Pharaoh"; with a reservation, for he is made to move faster, and to act. The comic of Jonson is a scholar's excogitation of the comic; that of Massinger a moralist's.

Shakespeare is a well-spring of characters which are saturated with the comic spirit; with more of what we will call blood-life than is to be found anywhere out of Shakespeare; and they are of this world, but they are of the world enlarged to our embrace by imagination, and by great poetic imagination. They are, as it were—I put it to suit my present comparison—creatures of the woods and wilds, not in walled towns, not grouped and toned to pursue a comic exhibition of the narrower world of society. Jaques, Falstaff and his regiment, the varied troop of clowns, Malvolio, Sir Hugh Evans and Fluellen (marvelous Welshmen!), Benedick and Beatrice, Dogberry, and the rest, are subjects of a special study in the poetically comic.

His comedy of incredible imbroglio belongs to the literary section. One may conceive that there was a natural resemblance between him and Menander, both in the scheme and style of his lighter plays. Had Shakespeare lived in a later and less emotional, less heroical, period of our history, he might have turned to the painting of manners as well as humanity. Euripides would probably, in the time of Menander, when Athens was enslaved but prosperous, have lent his hand to the composition of romantic comedy. He certainly inspired that fine genius.

Politically, it is accounted a misfortune for France that her nobles thronged to the Court of Louis Quatorze. It was a boon to the comic poet. He had that lively quicksilver world of the animalcule passions, the huge pretensions, the placid absurdities, under his eyes in full activity; vociferous quacks and snapping dupes, hypocrites, posturers, extravagants, pedants, rose-pink ladies and mad grammarians, sonneteering marquises, highflying mistresses, plain-minded maids, interthreading as in a loom, noisy as at a fair. A simply bourgeois circle will not furnish it, for the middle class must have the brilliant, flippant, independent upper for a spur and a pattern; otherwise it is likely to be inwardly dull, as well as outwardly correct. Yet, though the King was benevolent toward Molière, it is not to the French Court that we are indebted for his unrivaled studies of mankind in society. For the amusement of the Court the ballets and farces were written, which are dearer to the rabble upper, as to the rabble lower, class than intellectual comedy. The French bourgeoisie of Paris were sufficiently quick-witted and enlightened by education to welcome great works like *Le Tartuffe*, *Les Femmes Savantes*, and *Le Misanthrope*, works that were perilous ventures on the popular intelligence, big vessels to launch on streams running to shallows. The *Tartuffe* hove into view as an enemy's vessel; it offended, not "*Dieu, mais . . . les dévots,*" as the Prince de Condé explained the cabal raised against it to the King.

The *Femmes Savantes* is a capital instance of the uses of comedy in teaching the world to understand what ails it. The farce of the *Précieuses* ridiculed, and put a stop to, the monstrous romantic jargon made popular by certain famous novels. The comedy of the *Femmes Savantes* exposed the later and less apparent, but more finely comic, absurdity of an excessive purism in grammar and diction, and the tendency to be idiotic in precision. The French had felt the burden of this new nonsense; but they had to see the comedy several times before they were consoled in their suffering by seeing the cause of it exposed.

The *Misanthrope* was yet more frigidly received. Molière thought it dead. "I can not improve on it, and assuredly never shall," he said. It is one of the French titles to honor that this quintessential comedy of the opposition of Alceste and Célimène was ultimately understood and applauded. In all countries the middle class presents the public which, fighting the world, and with a good footing in the fight, knows the world best. It may be the most selfish, but that is a question leading us into sophistries. Cultivated men and women who do not skim the cream of life, and are attached to the duties, yet escape the harsher blows, make acute and balanced observers. Molière is their poet.

Of this class in England, a large body, neither Puritan nor Bacchanalian, have a sentimental objection to face the study of the actual world. They take up disdain of it, when its truths appear humiliating; when the facts are not immediately forced on them, they take up the pride of incredulity. They live in a hazy atmosphere that they suppose an ideal one. Humorous writing they will endure, perhaps approve, if it mingles with pathos to shake and elevate the feelings. They approve of satire, because, like the beak of the vulture, it smells of carrion, which they are not. But of comedy they have a shivering dread, for comedy enfolds them with the wretched host of the world, huddles them with us all in an ignoble assimilation, and cannot be used by any exalted variety as a scourge and a broom. Nay, to be an exalted variety is to come under the calm, curious eye of the Comic Spirit, and be probed for what you are. Men are seen among them, and very many cultivated women. You may distinguish them by a favorite phrase: "Surely we are not so bad!" and the remark: "If that is human nature, save us from it!"— as if it could be done; but in the peculiar paradise of the wilful people who will not see, the exclamation assumes the saving grace.

Yet, should you ask them whether they dislike sound sense, they vow they do not. And question cultivated women whether it pleases them to be shown moving on an intellectual level with men, they will answer that it does; numbers of them claim the situation. Now comedy is the fountain of sound sense; not the less perfectly sound on account of the sparkle; and comedy lifts women to a station offering them free play for their wit, as they usually show it, when they have it, on the side of sound sense. The higher the comedy, the more prominent the part they enjoy in it. Dorine in the *Tartuffe* is common sense incarnate, though palpably a waiting-maid. Célimène is undisputed mistress of the same attribute in the *Misanthrope;* wiser as a woman than Alceste as man. In Congreve's *Way of the World,* Millamant overshadows Mirabell, the sprightliest male figure of English comedy.

But those two ravishing women, so copious and so choice of speech, who fence with men and pass their guard, are heartless! Is it not preferable to be the pretty idiot, the passive beauty, the adorable bundle of caprices, very feminine, very sympathetic, of romantic and sentimental fiction? Our women are taught to think so. The Agnès of the *École des Femmes* should be a lesson for men. The heroines of comedy are like women of the world, not necessarily heartless from being clear-sighted; they seem so to the sentimentally reared, only for the reason that they use their wits, and are not wandering vessels crying for a captain or a pilot. Comedy is an exhibition of their battle with men, and that of men with them; and as the two, however divergent, both look on one object, namely, life, the gradual similarity of their impressions must bring them to some resemblance. The comic poet dares to show us men and women coming to this mutual likeness; he is for saying that when they draw together in social life their minds grow liker; just as the philosopher discerns the similarity of boy and girl, until the girl is marched away to the nursery. Philosopher and comic poet are of a cousinship in the eye they cast on life; and they are equally unpopular with our wilful English of the hazy region and the ideal that is not to be disturbed.

Thus, for want of instruction in the comic idea, we lose a large audience among our cultivated middle class that we should expect to support comedy. The sentimentalist is as averse as the Puritan and as the Bacchanalian.

Our traditions are unfortunate. The public taste is with the idle laughers, and still inclines to follow them. It may be shown by an analysis of Wycherley's *Plain Dealer*, a coarse prose adaption of the *Misanthrope*, stuffed with lumps of realism in a vulgarized theme to hit the mark of English appetite, that we have in it the key-note of the comedy of our stage. It is Molière travestied, with the hoof to his foot, and hair on the pointed tip of his ear. And how difficult it is for writers to disentangle themselves from bad traditions is noticeable when we find Goldsmith, who had grave command of the comic in narrative, producing an elegant farce for a comedy; and Fielding, who was a master of the comic both in narrative and in dialogue, not even approaching to the presentable in farce.

These bad traditions of comedy affect us, not only on the stage, but in our literature, and may be tracked into our social life. They are the ground of the heavy moralizings by which we are outwearied, about life as a comedy, and comedy as a jade, when popular writers, conscious of fatigue in creativeness, desire to be cogent in a modish cynicism; perversions of the idea of life, and of the proper esteem for the society we have wrested from brutishness, and would carry higher. Stock images of this description are accepted by the timid and the sensitive, as well as by the saturnine, quite seriously; for not many look abroad with their own eyes—fewer still have the habit of thinking for themselves. Life, we know too well, is not a comedy, but something strangely mixed; nor is comedy a vile mask. The corrupted importation from France was noxious, a noble entertainment spoilt to suit the wretched taste of a villainous age; and the later imitations of it, partly drained of its poison and made decorous, became tiresome, notwithstanding their fun, in the perpetual recurring of the same situations, owing to the absence of original study and vigor of conception. Scene 5, Act 2, of the *Misanthrope*, owing, no doubt, to the fact of our not producing matter for original study, is repeated in succession by Wycherley, Congreve, and Sheridan, and, as it is at second hand, we have it done cynically—or such is the tone—in the manner of "below stairs." Comedy thus treated may be accepted as a version of the ordinary worldly understanding of our social life; at least, in accord with the current dicta concerning it. The epigrams can be made; but it is uninstructive, rather tending to do disservice. Comedy justly treated, as you find it in Molière, whom we so clownishly mishandled—the comedy of Molière throws no infamous reflection upon life. It is deeply conceived, in the first place, and therefore it cannot be impure. Meditate on that statement. Never did man wield so shrieking a scourge upon vice; but his consummate self-mastery is not shaken while administering it. Tartuffe and Harpagon, in fact, are made each to whip himself and his class—the false pietists, and the insanely covetous. Molière has only set them in motion. He strips Folly to the skin, displays the imposture of the creature, and is content to offer her better clothing, with the lesson Chrysale reads to Philaminte and Bélise. He conceives purely, and he writes purely, in the simplest language, the simplest of French verse. The source of his wit is clear reason; it is a fountain of that soil, and it springs to vindicate reason, common sense, rightness, and justice—for no vain purpose ever. The wit is of such pervading spirit that it inspires a pun with meaning and interest. His moral does not hang like a tail, or preach from one character incessantly cocking an eye at the audience, as in recent [2] realistic French plays, but is in the heart of his work, throbbing with every pulsation of an organic structure. If life is likened to the comedy of Molière, there is no scandal in the comparison.

2 Late nineteenth century. *Ed.*

ROBERT KEMP: The Return of Andromache[1]

According to M. Maurice Donnaud himself, the leading idea for the new production of *Andromache* which he has just created for the stage of the Richelieu is that this is "a tragedy of inevitability." He sees in it the continual intervention of the gods, whose sovereign will Racine allows to be "mistress of the plot's resolution." I consider it very fortunate that, except in the last episode, this thought remains imperceptible to the spectator, because I do not believe in it, and from it arise the rare, regrettable errors. Isn't it to show this divine fury that he has caused storm clouds to gather in the skies of Epirus at the moment when Orestes loses his reason? And hurled bolts of lightning and rolled great cavernous thunder claps? Thus Zeus seems to converse with the murderer of Pyrrhus. "I have become a parricide . . ." ("Brroum," answers Zeus), "a murderer . . ." ("Brroum") "traitor!" ("Brroum!") The text, however, does not even indicate that night is falling. Nothing suggests that the wedding celebration of Pyrrhus was held by torchlight. . . . Pylades wants to set sail immediately. He does not say that it will be dangerous to go by sea because of bad weather. Actually, the storm is in the soul of Orestes, not in the heavens. Racine did not dream up this romantic accord between human passions and atmospheric electricity. . . . And he had good reason not to. In my opinion a beautiful evening will settle on the frenzied Orestes. And I find the serenity of the gods—who are indifferent to the disputes of Andromache and Pyrrhus and to the grievous miseries of Hermione and Orestes—more majestic and moving than the introduction of thunder into a purely human tragedy.

No, Ananke[2] does not govern Racine's *Andromache*. Not any more than she governs *Britannicus* or *Bajazet*. It is true that a goddess and a god overwhelm the unhappy Phaedra and Hippolytus. And the god of the Jews is on the side of Joad.[3] But although I may have been too simulated at

[1] First appeared in *Le Monde*, March 21, 1947. *Ed.*

[2] Necessity or Fate personified. *Ed.*

[3] In *Athaliah*. *Ed.*

the time to protest, I now maintain that *Andromache* is a godless tragedy; it is pure love-psychology. Orestes' madness is Racine's concession to the legend, a convenient way of concluding; but it appears disproportionate to the disappointment, cruel though it may have been, experienced by that pathetic lover. The Ancients reserved madness for the parricide who was pursued by the Furies. Racine has "adapted" it to the event. But that brilliant pastiche certainly does not provide the key to the tragedy, a tragedy of love in which the gods do not act on their "personal whim," in Renan's admirable phrase; it is enough for them to have laid down the law of love. Eros, not Ananke, has determined the fate of the four protagonists—as far back as the origin of humanity. And in order to abide by the conflict between the two couples who play their frightening four-cornered game, the "mistress of the resolution" must be, not Fate, but Andromache. The fluctuations of her will are transmitted—with increasing intensity—to Orestes, Hermione, Pyrrhus. She dreams beneath her veils; she means no one harm, she believes she can glide from memory to memory, a solitary figure; but once her melodious musings are freed, they turn into a terrifying groundswell. It is Andromache who is responsible for a triple death.

To be sure, we are dealing with the loves of heroes, epic heroes and heroines. And I will be the last to allow their grandeur to be diminished or the force of their interplaying passions weakened. But in the end *Andromache* is Marivaux on a mortal level; it is Marivaux among the monsters. The joy of this play is in perceiving the impulses behind free choice. The "four" do not submit; they shape their own destiny. And Cleone states it explicitly in speaking of Orestes: "I pity him the more since he himself brought about his own undoing. . . ." Everyone says, "I will it." Hermione proclaims the absolute liberty of Pyrrhus: "He does only what he wants; and if he marries me, he loves me." We are in the presence of four tacticians who reveal their plans, their intentions, and their hopes to us. The game is played in broad daylight, like chess. Chance is excluded. Aside from the love passion, which is "given," the pieces are man's freedom to choose, that is, four free wills.

This is how the first four acts are played. I even admired the clarity that the actors have brought to the production. Their diction—intelligent rather than musical, illuminating rather than passionate—permits us to follow with ease the blows, counterblows, preparations for attack, and defensive dodges. And my highest praise goes to this regard for subtle, reasoned diction, which opens up each verse and turns a searchlight on it. This was already striking in *Berenice,* and in spite of the disputes caused by Baty's[4] inventions, one is forced to admit the rightness of the whole vocal side of his recent productions. Although they have less music and poetry in their voices than Yonnel and Annie Ducaux, the current interpreters of *Andromache* have the same intellectual qualities. I stress this because people are bent on weighing down today's interpreters under the memory of their predecessors. I know that they do not possess the great, tragic projection of a Mounet or of a Segon-Weber. How I remember the *Andromache* of my childhood! There was Mounet, with his roars and his miraculous gulpings; and the flapping wings of his gigantic cloak. . . . Sometimes there was Bartet, opening her violet eyes under her turtledove veils, and her divine, magisterial, didactic accents. But you had to listen to Mme. Dudlay, lisping her lines: *"Non, cheigneur, demeurons. . . . Mais Cheigneur, ch'il le faut, chi le chiel en colère. . . ."*[5] and the beloved Paul Mounet, pitching out the words of Racine like pebbles from a wagon; or Sylvain, biting, admirable, but big-bellied—Pyrrhus at fifty; and, most often, in *Andromache,* Mme. du Minil. . . . They circled between the dusty columns which were barely noticeable in those days before Copeau and Le Cartel.[6] How we would protest if those feats were performed in front of us today! I deplore the excesses of our set designers; I would like to see moderation. But the river does not flow back to its source. We would no longer tolerate the settings of 1900.

And so, this one is sumptuous. You see first a wonderful sham, a curtain which imitates a tapestry, muted with delicate hues, which the reds and yellows have managed to resist. It depicts the taking of Troy, as Andromache described it to Cephise: "Imagine the cries of the victors; imagine the cries of the dying." It deserves more bravos than it received. . . . M. Roland Oudot's setting is enclosed by two wings of the palace at Buthrotum. In the background a view of the violet sea and the reddish and gray rocks of Greece's shore which make your heart beat when you first see them. The architecture appears to be inspired by the Pelasgians; I have no objection. But the concern for primitive archaeology does annoy me. It has already given us a Minoan Phaedra who

---

4 Gaston Baty, an eminent French director. *Ed.*

5 *"Mais, Seigneur, s'il le faut, si le ciel en colère. . . ." Ed.*

6 A twentieth-century theater movement which was a reaction against extreme naturalism and emphasized the play rather than the stage trappings. *Ed.*

would have scared the wits out of Racine and Euripides; a palace of Theseus, striped like bathing trunks, and a frightful Casino—a cross between the Peloponnese and the Archipelago—which gave me nightmares. The Pelasgian style is less painful. In the end, there are two choices in this "inner theater" in which Racine saw his characters evolve: either the groves of Versailles, the setting and splendors of the Hôtel de Bourgogne, the screens for performances at court, and plumed, corseted princesses lost in folds of velvet and silk; or else a conventional Greece, drawn from what he had seen in the way of statues, engravings, and mythological frontispieces, a fifth-century Greece that he had learned from his masters at Port-Royal. The first version would be intolerable to us, in spite of Taine.[7] It is therefore to Euripides' classic Greece that we must turn. And don't speak to me of "Pelasgians!" They create jarring discords! The abominable costume of Pyrrhus seems like a pedant's idea of Pelasgian to me. It would be about as suitable in *Renaud and Armide.* And what are gray, beaded tights doing on the legs of the conqueror of Troy? They make me pine for Flaxman and Louis David. They belong on Faust, on Hamlet, on the baritone in an opera. M. Eyser's too-lush voice brings the resemblance even closer; he tries commendably to make the text comprehensible—but overacts beyond belief. And that gives rise to unexpected smiles all the way through *Andromache.* On the other hand, Andromache's costume, with its Phrygian coloring, looks sumptuous among the splendors of Troy and contrasts, as satisfyingly to the mind as to the eye, with Hermione's simple, Hellenic dress. And do you think I like the bronze statue of Achilles, primitive and weird, an insect in tight armor, a gigantic ant, a praying mantis with a terrifying profile, a "black crustacean" like the Samurai of Heredia? It gets in the way! It gets in the way!

Let us pass on to the actors. Mme. Vera Korène was making her comeback. She was brilliant and original. I don't know why a tradition of hysterical Hermiones has been established: perhaps because of her "Aimless in this palace, I cannot now tell love from hate"—and her cries at the end. But Hermione knows how to keep secrets: her silences frighten Cleone. Mme. Korène—very young in appearance, her hair drawn down to cover her forehead (this immediately makes her look stubborn), sparing of gesture and voice—has created a more interesting Hermione than her predecessors. She is a creature obsessed by love; lost for months past in

7 Hippolyte Taine, French philosopher and historian (1828-1893). *Ed.*

morose delights which Pyrrhus' infidelity has rudely shattered and made hopeless. A Racinian heroine, with touches of Mauriac . . . a sort of Thérèse Desqueyroux,[8] given to somber dreaming and capable of anything. Her little head is stuffed with lascivious images and thoughts of murder. Hermione the viper; Hermione rejected and ready to explode like an atomic bomb. A virgin exasperated with waiting, frozen with jealousy.

Here and there, punctuating her flow of clever ideas, are obvious bits of artificiality. There is too striking a contrast from pianissimo to forte, between the two halves of her scene with Pyrrhus. And an exit that I do not like. She says: *"Va, cours! Mais crains encor d'y trouver* . . . (a pause, a gulp of air; and then a cry) *Hermione!"* It is not natural, or genuine. It is theatrical, reminiscent of the Conservatoire. But the general effect is very fine, except for two or three vulgarities of gesture and tone that suddenly whisk away the daughter of the Atrides and replace her by a girl of the people—haughty under her golden crown but in the end an idol of the streets over whom the boys sharpen their switchblades. Or perhaps Zola's proud Gervaise who knows how to thrash her rivals in the laundry with a washing stick. . . . You think that I am exaggerating. But that was the picture that came to me. And it should not have.

M. Donnaud too has interpreted his role of Orestes with wisdom. One would never guess that madness could overtake such a well-balanced diplomat. The very Racinian exalted tones which he and Mme. Korène have adopted in the early scenes do not foretell the furies. But Racine is certainly to blame for that too.

Mme. Rouer had one very beautiful moment: that was the report to Cephise. The rest of the time, she seemed a little too agitated to me, breaking that image of detached dreaming, of thought suspended between the past and the present, of preparation for death, which is the enigma and the magic of the role. The male and female confidants took great pains with their small roles. One only has to think back to M. Hamel as Pylades to appreciate M. Eymond.

Naturally, there are a prologue and epilogue in dumbshow. In the prologue Pylades paces back and forth, like a wild animal in his lair until the trumpet sounds the disembarkation. I expected him to take his Pelasgic watch from his belt. . . . He runs to meet Orestes, disappears, comes back. The opening line begins. *"Oui, puisque je retrouve. . . ."*

---

[8] Mauriac's heroine. *Ed.*

Confidentially, all that business is worth nothing. The epilogue is better. Pylades takes Orestes, who is unconscious and foaming at the lips, on his back, like a wounded comrade in the trenches, and carries him slowly toward his ship. Some have found this too "Shakespearean." Well, that is not so disgraceful. This "reminder of the theme," the theme of friendship, coming after all the horrors of love, may be an "addition" to Racine, but I find it noble and moving.

Translated by Joyce Bermel

ALGERNON CHARLES SWINBURNE:
The Work of Victor Hugo [1]

Poet, dramatist, novelist, historian, philosopher, and patriot, the spiritual sovereign of the nineteenth century was before all things and above all things a poet. Throughout all the various and ambitious attempts of his marvellous boyhood—criticism, drama, satire, elegy, epigram, and romance —the dominant vein is poetic. His example will stand for ever as the crowning disproof of the doubtless more than plausible opinion that the most amazing precocity of power is a sign of ensuing impotence and premature decay. There was never a more brilliant boy than Victor Hugo: but there has never been a greater man. At any other than a time of mourning it might be neither unseasonable nor unprofitable to observe that the boy's early verse, moulded on the models of the eighteenth century, is an arsenal of satire on revolutionary principles or notions which might suffice to furnish forth with more than their natural equipment of epigram a whole army of reactionary rhymesters and pamphleteers. But from the first, without knowing it, he was on the road to Damascus: if not to be struck down by sudden miracle, yet by no less inevitable a process to undergo a no less unquestionable conversion. At sixteen he wrote for a wager in the space of a fortnight the chivalrous and heroic story of *Bug-Jargal*; afterwards recast and reinformed with fresh vigour of vitality, when the author had attained the maturer age of twenty-three. His tenderness and manliness of spirit were here made nobly manifest: his originality and ardour of imagination, wild as yet and crude and violent, found vent two years later in *Han d'Islande*. But no boyish work on record ever showed more singular force of hand, more brilliant variety of power: though the author's criticism ten years later admits that "il n'y a dans *Han d' Islande* qu'une chose sentie, l'amour du jeune homme; qu'une chose observée, l'amour de la jeune fille." [2] But as the work of a

[1] From *A Study of Victor Hugo*, 1886. *Ed.*

[2] ". . . In *Han d'Islande*, there is only one thing felt: the love of a young man; only one thing observed: the love of a young woman." *Ed.*

boy's fancy or invention, touched here and there with genuine humour, terror, and pathos, it is not less wonderful
than are the author's first odes for ease and force and
freshness and fluency of verse imbued with simple and
sincere feeling, with cordial and candid faith. And in
both these boyish stories the hand of a soldier's son, a child
of the camp, reared in the lap of war and cradled in traditions
of daring, is evident whenever an episode of martial adventure comes in among the more fantastic excursions of adolescent inventiveness. But it is in the ballads written between his
twenty-second and his twenty-seventh year that Victor Hugo
first showed himself, beyond all question and above all cavil,
an original and a great poet. *La Chasse du Burgrave* and
Le Pas d'Armes du Roi Jean would suffice of themselves to
establish that. The fire, the music, the force, the tenderness,
the spirit of these glorious little poems must needs, one
would think, impress even such readers as might be im-
pervious to the charm of their exquisitely vigorous and
dexterous execution. . . .

It will of course, I should hope, be understood once for
all that when I venture to select for special mention any
special poem of Hugo's I do not dream of venturing to suggest
that others are not or may not be fully as worthy of homage,
or that anything of this incomparable master's work will
not requite our study or does not demand our admiration;
I do but take leave to indicate in passing some of those which
have been to me especially fruitful of enduring delight, and
still are cherished in consequence with a peculiar gratitude.

At twenty-five the already celebrated lyric poet published
his magnificent historic drama of *Cromwell*: a work sufficient of itself to establish the author's fame for all ages in
which poetry and thought, passion and humour, subtle truth
of character, stately perfection of structure, facile force of
dialogue and splendid eloquence of style, continue to be
admired and enjoyed. That the author has apparently confounded one earl of Rochester with another more famous
bearer of the same title must not be allowed to interfere
with the credit due to him for wide and various research.
Any dullard can point the finger at a slip here and there
in the history, a change or an error of detail or of date: it
needs more care to appreciate the painstaking and ardent
industry which has collected and fused together a great mass
of historic and legendary material, the fervent energy of
inspiration which has given life, order and harmony to the
vast and versatile design. As to the executive part of the
poem, the least that can be said by any competent judge of

that matter is that Molière was already equalled and Corneille was already excelled in their respective provinces of verse by the young conqueror whose rule was equal and imperial over every realm of song. The comic interludes or episodes of the second and third acts, so admirably welded into the structure or woven into the thread of the action, would suffice to prove this when collated with the seventeenth scene of the third act and the great speech of Cromwell in the fifth. . . .

The subtlety and variety of power displayed in the treatment of the chief character should be evident alike to those who look only on the upright side of it and those who can see only its more oblique aspect. The Cromwell of Hugo is as far from the faultless monster of Carlyle's creation and adoration as from the all but unredeemed villain of royalist and Hibernian tradition: he is a great and terrible poetic figure, imbued throughout with active life and harmonized throughout by imaginative intuition: a patriot and a tyrant, a dissembler and a believer, a practical humourist and a national hero.

The famous preface in which the batteries of pseudo-classic tradition were stormed and shattered at a charge has itself long since become a classic. That the greatest poet was also the greatest prose-writer of his generation there could no longer be any doubt among men of any intelligence: but not even yet was more than half the greatness of his multitudinous force revealed. Two years later, at the age of twenty-seven, he published the superb and entrancing *Orientales*: the most musical and many-coloured volume of verse that ever had glorified the language. From *Le Feu du Ciel* to *Sara la Baigneuse,* from the thunder-peals of exterminating judgment to the flute-notes of innocent girlish luxury in the sense of loveliness and life, the inexhaustible range of his triumph expands and culminates and extends. Shelley has left us no more exquisite and miraculous piece of lyrical craftsmanship than *Les Djinns*; none perhaps so rich in variety of modulation, so perfect in rise and growth and relapse and reiterance of music.

Murs, ville,	[Walls, city,
Et port,	And port,
Asile	Shelter
De mort,	Of death,
Mer grise	Gray sea
Où brise	Where breaks
La brise,	The breeze,

Tout dort.	Everything sleeps.

Dans la plaine	On the plain
Naît un bruit.	A sound is born.
C'est l'haleine	It is the breath
De la nuit.	Of the night.
Elle brame	And it cries out
Comme une âme	Like a soul
Qu'une flamme	That a flame
Toujours suit.	Always pursues.] [3]

Then the terrible music of the flight of evil spirits—"troupeau lourd et rapide" [4]—grows as it were note by note and minute by minute up to its full height of tempest, and again relapses and recedes into the subsiding whisper of the corresponsive close.

Ce bruit vague	[This vague sound
Qui s'endort,	That is falling into sleep,
C'est la vague	Is the wave
Sur le bord;	On the shore;
C'est la plainte	It is the plaint
Presque éteinte	Almost quenched
D'une sainte	Of a saint
Pour un mort.	For a dead man.

On doute	One suspects
La nuit ...	The night ...
J'écoute:—	I listen:—
Tout fuit,	Everything flees,
Tout passe;	Everything passes;
L'espace	Space
Efface	Effaces
Le bruit.	The sound.] [5]

And here, like Shelley, was Hugo already the poet of freedom, a champion of the sacred right and the holy duty of resistance. The husk of a royalist education, the crust of reactionary misconceptions, had already begun to drop off: not yet a pure republican, he was now ripe to receive and to understand the doctrine of human right, the conception of the common weal, as distinguished from imaginary duties and opposed to hereditary claims.

[3] Literal translation. The triple rhymes and verbal dexterity of the French must have intoxicated Swinburne. *Ed.*

[4] "Swift and heavy flock." *Ed.*

[5] Literal translation. See note [3]. *Ed.*

The twenty-eighth year of his life, which was illuminated by the issue of these passionate and radiant poems, witnessed also the opening of his generous and lifelong campaign or crusade against the principle of capital punishment. With all possible reverence and all possible reluctance, but remembering that without perfect straightforwardness and absolute sincerity I should be even unworthier than I am to speak of Victor Hugo at all, I must say that his reasoning on this subject seems to me insufficient and inconclusive: that his own radical principle, the absolute inviolability of human life, the absolute sinfulness of retributive bloodshedding, if not utterly illogical and untenable, is tenable or logical only on the ground assumed by those quaintest though not least pathetic among fanatics and heroes, the early disciples of George Fox. If a man tells you that supernatural revelation has forbidden him to take another man's life under all and any circumstances, he is above or beyond refutation; if he says that self-defense is justifiable, and that righteous warfare is a patriotic duty, but that to exact from the very worst of murderers, a parricide or a poisoner, a Philip the Second or a Napoleon the Third, the payment of a life for a life—or even of one infamous existence for whole hecatombs of innocent lives—is an offence against civilization and a sin against humanity, I am not merely unable to accept but incompetent to understand his argument. We may most heartily agree with him that France is degraded by the guillotine, and that England is disgraced by the gallows, and yet our abhorrence of these barbarous and nauseous brutalities may not preclude us from feeling that a dealer (for example) in professional infanticide by starvation might very properly be subjected to vivisection without anaesthetics, and that all manly and womanly minds not distorted or distracted by prepossessions or assumptions might rationally and laudably rejoice in the prospect of this legal and equitable process. "The senseless old law of retaliation" (la vieille et inepte loi du talion) is inept or senseless only when the application of it is false to the principle: when justice in theory becomes unjust in practice. Another stale old principle or proverb—"abusus non tollit usum"—suffices to confute some of the arguments—I am very far from saying, all—adduced or alleged by the ardent eloquence of Victor Hugo in his admirable masterpiece of terrible and pathetic invention, Le dernier jour d'un condamné, and subsequently in the impressive little history of Claude Gueux, in the famous speech on behalf of Charles Hugo when impeached on a charge of insult to the laws in an article on the punishment of death, and in the fervent eloquence of his appeal in the case of a criminal executed in Guernsey, and of his protest addressed to Lord Palmerston against the horrible result of its rejection. That certain surviving methods of execution are execrable scandals to the country which maintains them, he has proved beyond all humane or reasonable question: and that all murderers are not alike inexcusable is no less indisputable a proposition: but beyond these two points the most earnest and exuberant advocacy can advance nothing likely to convince any but those already converted to the principle that human life must never be taken in punishment of crime—that there are not criminals whose existence insults humanity, and cries aloud on justice for mercy's very sake to cut it off.

The next year (1830) is famous for ever beyond all others in the history of French literature: it was the year of *Hernani,* the date of liberation and transfiguration for the tragic stage of France. The battle which raged round the first acted play of Hugo's and the triumph which crowned the struggles of its champions, are not these things written in too many chronicles to be for the thousandth time related here? And of its dramatic and poetic quality what praise could be uttered that must not before this have been repeated at least some myriads of times? But if there be any mortal to whom the heroic scene of the portraits, the majestic and august monologue of Charles the Fifth at the tomb of Charles the Great, the terrible beauty, the vivid pathos, the bitter sweetness of the close, convey no sense of genius and utter no message of delight, we can only say that it would simply be natural, consistent, and proper for such a critic to recognize in Shakespeare a barbarian, and a Philistine in Milton. . . .

ERIC BENTLEY:
The Psychology of Farce [1]

"Be friends, be lovers, be what you will, but
as for being husband and wife, God in heaven!"

Count Almaviva

Ideally a compendium of exact information and intelligent
opinion, an encyclopedia addresses itself, in fact, to the
codification of current prejudices. The article on farce in
the only encyclopedia of theatre in our language starts out
this way:

Farce, an extreme form of comedy in which laughter is raised
at the expense of probability, particularly by horseplay and
bodily assault. It must, however, retain its hold on humanity,
even if only in depicting the grosser faults of mankind; otherwise it degenerates into travesty and burlesque.

After remarking, *en passant,* that farce died out before
Molière, the writer winds round to this conclusion:

In modern usage, the word farce is applied to a full-length
play dealing with some absurd situation hingeing generally
on extra-marital relations—hence the term bedroom farce.
Farce has small literary merit, but great entertainment value,
and owing to its lack of subtlety can be translated from one
language to another more easily than comedy.

An extreme form. The tone is patronizing. Why? Is extremity bad? And if farce is already an extremity, how can
it further *degenerate into travesty and burlesque?* And why
does the writer have it in for travesty and burlesque? Or is it
just that everything is a degenerate something else: burlesque
is degenerate farce, farce is degenerate comedy, comedy is
degenerate tragedy . . . ? *At the expense of probability.*
And why not? Why should not probability have its price?

[1] First published in 1958, as an introduction to a book of French farces,
Let's Get a Divorce and Other Plays (Hill & Wang, New York.) *Ed.*

Even if only in depicting the grosser faults of mankind.
Why "even if only"? Is this such a contemptible or easy
thing to do? Why be hoity-toity about gross faults? *Owing
to its lack of subtlety it can be translated . . . more easily.*
Not "its lack of subtlety of language," please note, but its
"lack of subtlety," *tout court.* That farce has subtlety in
other spheres than dialogue is nowhere intimated, and that
even its dialogue often has subtlety of a kind (I am thinking
not only of the obvious case of Wilde but of the more orthodox farceurs like Labiche and Feydeau) is completely overlooked. *Small literary merit but great entertainment value.*
In the middle of this phrase the subject switches abruptly
from the inherent qualities of the work to the response of an
audience. And are we to understand that a work pleases an
audience by its lack of merit? Merit apart, it would seem
psychologically necessary to attribute pleasure to the presence,
not the absence, of something. But, of course, the whole article
is based on the opposite assumption—that farce consists of
defects without qualities.

What we uncover, then, in this guide to theatre is a massive prejudice against one of the most honorable and remarkable forms of dramatic art. It is not a new prejudice.
The comment was made on Labiche's admission to the
Academy that it was farce, the first of theatre arts in France,
that was now being honored—last. The "literature" of the subject is, accordingly, very slender, and in fact the only thorough descriptions of farce are to be found in works on
comedy or laughter. There is, for example, no better account
of the mechanisms of farcical plot than Bergson's famous
essay; references to Labiche abound in it; but Bergson's subject is laughter, and even life, in general. Most dramatic
critics assume that the farcical bag of tricks was easy to
amass and is even easier to use. Once there is a bed on stage,
and some confusion as to its proper occupancy, no difference is noted between the clumsiness of a tyro and the
virtuosity of a master. The craftsmanship of Feydeau is
as complex and, yes, as subtle as any in the whole history of
drama, yet when one of his plays is done in Anglo-Saxon
countries we inevitably have to hear it talked down to as a
quaint period piece.

If farce is more readily acknowledged as an ingredient in
higher comedy, it has not always been welcome even there.
Molière has been scolded for using farce by generations of
critics, beginning with his own generation. He would certainly
have roused more enthusiasm in Anglo-Saxon countries had
he left farce entirely alone. Confronted with Molière, the

young American asks: "If he wants to be taken seriously, why isn't he serious?" Conversely, a playwright of half Molière's talent could secure a reputation for twice as much by replacing the farcical elements with what might be called certified seriousness, that is, currently fashionable psychology and sociology.

Melodrama—the counterpart of farce on the tragic side—is in similar disrepute. The term, like the term farce, is used to show contempt for something admirable or admiration for something contemptible. Yet just as the supreme master of comedy, Molière, was an incorrigible farceur, the supreme master of tragedy, Shakespeare, was an incorrigible melodramatist. Explaining this away has provided employment for generations of scholars. They have advanced such arguments as these: Shakespeare wasn't as great as he is cracked up to be, and melodrama is one of his many Gothic mistakes of taste; Shakespeare was so great he could get away with anything, even melodrama; Shakespeare may have been melodramatic, but he wasn't as melodramatic as Marlowe or Webster; Shakespeare wasn't melodramatic, there's a consistent and naturalistic psychology to him, once you find out how many children Lady Macbeth had. . . . And to this day, it is impossible to stage a Shakespearean tragedy without inviting, from the press in general and The New Yorker in particular, a lot of heavy irony on the subject of stage villains, the pile of corpses in the last scene, or some other melodramatic item. If a bit of melodrama actually takes a critic's fancy, he will hasten to assure you that this is not Shakespeare at his best: it is a case of *small literary merit but great entertainment value.*

The words farce and melodrama are now so devalued that one would wish them discarded like farthings and one-lira bills, were it not that they would then have to be speedily replaced because what they refer to—in Elizabethan tragedy, the comedy of Molière, or even the classic American novel—is central to literature and drama. And it is not a defect but a quality. The "absurd" plots of tragedies from *Oedipus Rex* to *King Lear* represent, not a failure of primitive man to be mature, but the refusal of tragic man to limit himself to naturalism. The feeling one had as a child that the "absurd" opening scene in *Lear* was supremely right is justified. The "absurdity" expresses the real absurdity of life, of which our encyclopedist's "probability" is a misleading mask. If art imitates life, it should be added that while naturalistic art imitates the surfaces, "melodramatic" art imitates what is beneath the surface. It is a matter, then, of finding external representation—symbol—for what cannot be photographed or described. As such symbols, the plots of the masters are apt, expressive, economic, and amazing. Aristotle, who has more often been thought too rational than not rational enough, put the plots of the Greek tragedies before all their other attributes, and made a special favorite of *Oedipus Rex,* which has the "absurdest" plot of any.

It may be that the principle of the primacy of plot holds for all drama. It certainly holds for melodrama and farce. Here in the action lies that subtlety which is sometimes and notoriously absent from dialogue and even character. The enacted story is itself a language. And this is to say that it is symbolic. Like dreams, farces show the disguised fulfillment of repressed wishes. That is a Freudian formula, but not, surely, one that only Freudians can accept. For one thing, the comparison between farce and dream is a matter, up to a point, not of analogy but identity. Examining my own dreams, I have been not a little surprised to discover how many affinities they show with Chaplin films—in ideas for a whole sequence of action (chases in automobiles, "routines" of dressing or moving furniture) or in characterization (heroes and villains, "chickens" and bullies) or even in style of performance (large grimaces and gesticulation being very much in order).

The word *repressed* brings us back to our encyclopedist's remarks about grossness. Repressed wishes find an outlet, surely, in all drama; many repressed wishes are gross ones; and if we take the family to be the very center of culture, we should not be surprised that gross wishes are mainly, if not exclusively, desires to damage the family, to desecrate the household gods. Consider the Greeks, who had just created the patriarchal family. They naturally found the supreme virtue in the pious and loyal relation of husband to wife, of child to parent, of sibling to sibling. The subject of tragedy is the violation of this piety. What, then, would be the worst conceivable violation of both the marital and filial pieties? Why, the double crime of Oedipus. And the phrase "some absurd situation hingeing on extra-marital relations" is richly suggestive of tragic plot—the plot of *Othello,* for example.

But what situation "hingeing on extra-marital relations" is not full of absurdities and therefore potentially melodramatic or farcical, tragic or comic, according to the temperament, state of mind, and view of life of the witness? Outrage to family piety and propriety is certainly at the heart of farce—"hence," as the book says, "the term bedroom farce." Indeed, the fearsomeness of the enterprise might explain

why people prefer either to brush farce off as totally meaningless or assign it a meaning that could never explain its
prodigious energy. For example, the great dramatic critic
Sarcey, noting that serious plays about adultery were un-
savory, concluded that playwrights should get a little fun out
of the subject instead: he justified farce on grounds of its
triviality, and one is surprised, perhaps, to find Labiche
agreeing with him.[2]

If Sarcey's view—though preferable to the Anglo-Saxon
notion that adultery should be banished from the drama altogether—is one that skims the surface, there is a more
widely current view that is merely an error—the idea that
"wicked" comedy, farce or otherwise, French or English-Res-
toration, is amoral. It is hard to imagine what true indifference to morals could produce, if anything at all. Comedy
and farce presuppose accepted standards, and when the playwrights don't respect those standards, they resent them. If
English Puritanism were ever totally forgotten, it could still
be deduced from Restoration comedy, which was born under
the sign of Oliver Cromwell. And it is interesting that the
word we today apply to bawdy farces is "naughty"—a word
that belongs essentially to the vocabulary of mothers and
nursemaids, the appointed deputies of the Censorship. Where
there is no established virtue, there can be no sense of outrage, and farce, as we have seen, is no less "outrageous" than
tragedy.

The marriage joke, then, exists only for a culture that
knows itself committed to marriage. But is the joke necessary or even salutary? There is a growing tendency in

---

[2] Sarcey's own curious discussion of the theme, as mentioned
above, is to be found in his review of another Labiche play, *The
Happiest of the Three*. Here is an extract:
"I had often complained that they bored us constantly with this
question of adultery, which nowadays is the subject of three-
quarters of the plays. Why, I asked, take pleasure in painting its
dark and sad sides, enlarging on the dreadful consequences which it
brings with it in reality? Our fathers took the thing more lightheartedly in the theatre, and even called adultery by a name which
awoke in the mind only ideas of the ridiculous and a sprightly light-
heartedness. . . . Chance brought it about that I met Labiche. 'I was
very struck,' he said to me, 'with your observations on adultery and
on what one could derive from it—even with a present-day audience—for farce. You think one would find lots of material for
laughter in that area; I agree. You want the play; I shall try to do
it for you.' I had all but forgotten this conversation when I saw the
title posted outside the Palais Royal: *The Happiest of the Three*.
It was my play; it was adultery treated lightheartedly. . . ."

modern civilization to think that it is neither. Only the other day, I happened upon a magazine headline: "Don't Let Them Scoff at Marriage," which turned out to be the title of an article blaming "the moral crisis of today" on the marriage joke and attributing that joke to the post–1945 generation as if it had not been told through the centuries.[3]

It is true, however, that the marriage joke could be abolished if the family were the unmixed blessing that many of our contemporaries take it for. In another recent article, the chief of the Division of Social Medicine at an important American hospital writes as follows:

The family is central to the development of humanity not only for the perpetuation of the race but because the proper psychological development of an individual can only occur within the warm circle of the nuclear family. Social and psychological studies indicate quite clearly that a strong family structure helps to develop and maintain a personality free of dangerous (to self and society) characteristics.

The author draws the conclusion that sexual deviation and juvenile delinquency can be prevented by closer, warmer family relations, and no doubt there is some truth in this. Unhappily there is evident truth in precisely the opposite proposition. The close, warm family is also a seedbed of neurosis, vice, and crime. About the same time as this article appeared,[4] a newspaper picture caught my eye. It showed a beaming public relations executive with his good-looking wife and three attractive children. They seemed a model American family in a model American home, and one could imagine the picture passing in triumph around the public relations office. The caption underneath, however, reported that the mildest and most candid-looking of the boys had just killed the mother and sister and told the police that he had planned to kill the rest of the family as well. It would be comforting to think that such a shocking event could be declared irrelevant to the experience of normal folk. But, however psychotic that poor lad's behavior, the fact remains that neurosis and psychosis are extensions of patterns present in us all. The understanding attitude to Hitler's mas-

[3] The author does not use the *term* "marriage joke" but does describe the *thing*: "The gross libel on marriage is the notion that the chase, the allure is the goal. Marriage is seen as a dull aftermath." Gross libel may be; it is certainly a perennial fantasy of mankind, and therefore no good pretext for a gross libel on the present generation. The article, by Howard Whitman, appeared in *Better Homes and Gardens*, August, 1957.

[4] May 25th, 1957, in *The Nation*.

sacres is not: "How could he ever dream of such a thing?"
but: "How could he ever have done what others only dream
of?"

The cruelty of sick behavior and healthy fantasy is found
also in farce. In Charlie Chaplin's film farces, for instance.
Though what we consciously remember from them may be
Chaplin's incomparable delicacy, they are for the most part
taken up with violent pursuit and violent combat. Fantasy
multiplies movements and blows by a thousand. The villain
is a giant whose strength passes the limits of nature. He can
bend lampposts with his bare hands. Since the "little man's"
revenges have to be more than proportionate to the provocation (as with Brecht's Jenny the Pirate's Bride), he can drop
a cast-iron stove on the villain's head and ram that head inside
a street lamp with the gas turned on. Another symptom of
cruelty is the abstractness of the violence. Prongs of a rake
in the backside are received as pin pricks. Bullets seem to
pass right through people, sledge-hammer blows to produce
only momentary irritation. The speeding up of movement
contributes to the abstract effect. So, even more, does the
silence proper to the screen of those days, many of the effects being lost when a sound track is superimposed. The
cops shoot, but there is no noise. Heavy objects fall, but there
is no crash. Gruesome infighting has the air of shadowbox-
ing. . . . All of which signifies that, in farce, as in dreams,
one is permitted the outrage but is spared the consequences.
Chaplin's delicacy of style is actually part of the pattern: he
parades an air of nonchalance when acting in a manner that,
in real life, would land him in Bellevue or Sing Sing.

But while dreams are ignored or forgotten, farces incur
the censure of professional moralists and amateur psychol-
ogists. The thought arises: "The theatre is inciting my children to hate the home, if not to commit murder and arson.
We must have more censorship!" It is overlooked that such
fantasies are kept for dreams and pictures and plays just
because each of us already has within him so strong a Censorship, and it is wrongly inferred from the power of the
fantasies that people are likely to fail to distinguish between fantasy and reality. On a person who could not distinguish between fantasy and reality, Chaplin movies might
well have a disastrous effect *except that such a person is already too far gone to go much further*. Though, from the
devil's standpoint, Hitler excels the rest of us in having the
courage to do what we all dream of doing, from the standpoint of mental hygiene, the Satanic superman must simply
be adjudged a lunatic, while those who refuse to act out

their morbid fantasies are, in that respect at least, sensible and sane.

The function of "farcical" fantasies, in dreams or in plays, is not as provocation but as compensation. The violent release is comparable to the sudden relieving hiss of steam through a safety valve. Certainly, the mental energies involved are destructive, and in all comedy there remains something of destructive orgy, farce being the kind of comedy which disguises that fact least thoroughly. But the function of orgies is also that of a safety valve. An orgy—as still practiced in the Munich Carnival, for example—is an essentially temporary truancy from the family pieties, and, like farces, if it has any appreciable effect at all, it helps those pieties to go on existing. The main point of Freud's *Civilization and Its Discontents* is pertinent here: when we buy civilization, as we do, at the price of frustration, the frustrated impulses become a potential source of trouble. The pressures are enormous and perpetual. We ought to welcome any relief from them, however slight or trivial, provided it is harmless. Dreams are the commonest relief but are usually unpleasant. The most pleasurable relief is to be found in the arts, for one of which I am staking out a claim in this essay.

In his book on jokes, Freud explains in effect that he would "let them scoff at marriage" not only because he would never be able to prevent them but also because a safety valve is a good thing. It is a sort of open secret, he says on one page,[5] that marriage does not satisfy the sexual demands of men and that this secret is half-kept, half-told in marriage jokes. I would add that the classic form of the marriage joke takes a couple of hours to tell and has a cast of three characters known as *le mari, la femme, et l'amant,*—"hence," again, "the term bedroom farce." Just as Restoration comedy was provoked by the Puritans and is, so to speak, forever dedicated to them, the farce of adultery has been provoked by married men and is dedicated to them. Farce in general enables us, seated in dark security, to enjoy the delights of complete passivity while watching on stage the most violently

---

[5] The exact words are: *"Dass die Ehe nicht die Veranstaltung ist, die Sexualität des Mannes zu befriedigen, getraut man nicht laut und öffentlich zu sagen . . ."* The familiar English title of the book is *Wit and Its Relation to the Unconscious,* but *Der Witz,* here translated as wit, is also the ordinary German word for a joke; and Freud's book is all about jokes, though it has implications for wit and humor in general. Incidentally, *Civilization and Its Discontents* is another misleading title, though there may be no perfect substitute for it. "Discontents" suggest political grievances ("Thoughts on the Present Discontents") whereas the original title, *Das Unbehagen in der Kultur,* connotes stress and strain, discomfort, uneasiness, malaise.

active creatures ever imagined by man. In that particular application of the general formula which is bedroom farce, we enjoy the adventure of adultery, ingeniously exaggerated to the nth degree, without incurring the responsibilities or suffering the guilt, without even the hint of an affront to the wife at our side.[6]

In speaking of exaggeration, it is important to see what is exaggerated in a farce and what is not. While, certainly, the external facts are distorted, the inner experience is so wild and preposterous that it would probably be impossible to exaggerate it. To the inner experience, the farceur tries to be utterly faithful. This fact raises the question whether farce is as indirect a form of literature as it is commonly assumed to be.

What kind of literature is direct? I have addressed the question to well-read persons, and have sometimes received the answer: Jane Austen's novels. For they are straightforward in style and crystal clear in tenor. But is not this limpidity the last effect of indirectness? It is Jane Austen's strategy, surely, to pretend to accept the surfaces of life at what is well called face value, then, in highly indirect ways, to enable us to sense how much happens beneath those surfaces. An open breach of the surface would be an unthinkable breach of decorum.

Farce, on the other hand, while it begins by accepting the bland, placid, imposing façade of life, proceeds to become farcical by knocking the façade down. The farceur, like the lunatic and the unruly child, flies in the face of decorum. Harpo Marx is the supreme case in point. For him, there is nothing to do with clothes but take the scissors to them, nothing to do with a façade but throw a bomb at it. Many other comedians destroy things. Few manage so impressively as Harpo to convey the idea of human nature as in itself de-

---

[6] I refer those who find Freudianism newfangled to Gilbert Murray's Norton lectures of 1925 (reprinted as *The Classical Tradition in Poetry*) for some fine remarks, albeit not always fair to psychoanalysis, about the "close similarity . . . between . . . Aristotle and Freud." Murray applies to the whole of comedy a theory which I have not dared to extend beyond the frontiers of farce: "The anarchist and the polygamist, close-prisoned and chained in ordinary life, enjoy their release in comedy. . . . As for the polygamist . . . comedy provides him with an atmosphere in which . . . husbands are recognized as ridiculous and wives as a nuisance, where Captain Macheath and Don Juan and Célimare find a world that exactly suits them." One cannot but enjoy the contrast in mentality between the "other-directed" modernists of *The Nation* or *Better Homes and Gardens* and Professor Murray, last of the great Victorian gentlemen-scholars, when we find the latter saying: "Comedy . . . must . . . not be spoilt by any tiresome temperance or prudential considerations of the morrow."

ructive. It is the impishness, the quasi innocence, the compli-
ation of aggression with bizarre fantasy; and the dumbness
elps, both as a psychological trait (suggestive of a general
eficiency) and as a physical fact (for nothing is so econom-
cally expressive as silence).

In one of Noel Coward's short farces, a man knocks his
nother-in-law out with, if I remember rightly, a straight
eft to the jaw.[7] As the only form of literature or theatre in
rhich such an incident could occur, farce may reasonably
laim to be the most direct of all the forms. Such are the ag-
ressions which are rampant in human beings all day and, as
e are increasingly aware, all night. In a sense, Coward's trifle
s more realistic than all the realisms. For that—"crudely
xpressed," as the encyclopedias will have it—is what life is
ke.

But the most direct form is still not in all ways direct.
ince, as we have seen, the wishes expressed in farce often
ppear there in disguised forms, there is still the duality in
hese fantasies, as in others, of manifest and latent content,
f mask and face. Failure to render either the directness or
he duality (with its indirectness) is usually very marked in
nodern stage productions. When a character knocks out his
nother-in-law, he is acting out[8] the fantasies of millions,
et a bad actor is able to suggest that he is acting out pre-
isely nothing—he didn't mean to hurt the old lady and the
olay is just a "romp," destined to elicit from newspaper re-
riewers epithets like "delicious" and "cute."

There are two wrong ways of playing the indirectness of
arce: the amateur way and the professional way. The ama-
eur's failure is more or less total. He lacks the art to create
a mask of actuality (normality, gravity, sophistication) and,
as for the life beneath, he hasn't an inkling how to get at it or,
oerhaps even, that it is there to be got at. He concludes
hat, since farce is very energetic, he should bound about, and
hat, since it is very funny, he should be facetious; and so his
urious efforts end in vacuity.

The professional is wiser. He knows he has no such weapon

[7] What I am remembering (and, I believe, rightly) is one particular
performance. The published script of *Fumed Oak* testifies only to a
light slap on the cheek, followed by a moment in which the audience
thinks the mother-in-law has fallen unconscious. In not quite daring to
deliver a real knock-out to the lady, Mr. Coward might be said to have
been a ... coward.

[8] "Acting out" is another psychoanalytic term of considerable pertin-
ency in this field. Unconscious conflicts find release and relief in the
famous physical exertions of farcical fantasy (our encyclopedist's "horse-
olay and bodily assault"). Freud quotes the proverb: *"Was man nicht
m Kopfe hat, muss man in den Beinen haben."*

in his armory as funniness. He knows that being funny is a result, and that what God gave him is fantasy; and he uses this fantasy to create a mask. Professional productions of farce tend to be plausible, even elegant, but it is the habit of the professional to neglect the face beneath the mask. Though smooth, his work is hollow. There have been productions of *The Importance of Being Earnest* in which the manner of an upper class was very accurately rendered in voice and gesture but in which one had no feeling of the inordinate aggression of Wilde against Victorian civilization, if not against all civilization.

Not all professional productions take this "naturalistic line" with a farce. On the contrary, more of them nowadays overlook the naturalistic mask entirely and try to give direct expression to the author's fantasy. In this case, the work of the designer and the director, as well as the actor, is concentrated on announcing: This is fantasy, this is artifice, this is unreal. Everyone wears fantastic costumes and gesticulates in a curious manner that the director calls "stylized." The decor seems to be by Toulouse-Lautrec and probably is by Mr. Cecil Beaton or Mr. Oliver Messel.

There are two things wrong with such a procedure. This *kind* of fantasy is far too superficial and sophisticated for true farce; and, in any case, it is not an advantage to dispense with the façade, because the dynamic of farce proper derives from the interplay between the mask (of actuality) and the real face (of primitive instinct). Even an amateur who could impart a sense of primitive life would fail to communicate farce if he could compose no mask, while the professional who creates the most elaborate "style" is giving us scarcely anything if primitive energy is lacking.

It is, of course, only the professional that one has the right to complain of, and even he might plead that he cannot by himself counteract a trend of the times, this trend being the decline of farce. Compared with the five-course banquet that was served on the Paris boulevards half a century ago—1850 to 1920 was the heyday of modern farce—the fey pleasantries of Roussin and Husson are mere hors d'oeuvres.

But need productions of Labiche and Feydeau have fallen off quite so much as they have? I am not thinking of productions in which a director's intention was not carried out or even of productions that failed to have any sort of appeal. I have in mind shows which could not fail to amuse people who came to the theatre without special preparation or expectation but which did not realize the full potentiality of the script because they deviated too widely from the original conception. Two such productions that many Americans have seen and of which many photographs have been published [9] are Gaston Baty's staging of *An Italian Straw Hat* and Jean Meyer's of *A Trip Abroad*. Both were exquisite; and, by that token, neither was Labiche. Consider the visual side alone. For scenery, bright colors were painted on obviously two-dimensional materials, and, just as objects were reduced to pictures by losing a dimension, clothes were reduced to operetta costumes by bright contrasting colors, heavy stripes, checks, and evident flimsiness of texture.

Now look at a drawing of *An Italian Straw Hat* made shortly after the first production.[10] The clothes are clothes —a little drab, perhaps, as is proper to the period and the milieu, yet, with their high collars, their bulgy trousers, their bulbous bodices, full of drama. Here the associations would not be operetta, period charm, "stylization," but realistic plays, immediacy, forthrightness. The caricature is not delicious but manly, not cute but cutting. We are not far from Daumier, and distinctly close to Cruikshank and Dickens. Such is the world of Labiche. One can only get at it by fighting one's way through a jungle of misinterpretation that has had nearly a century to grow.

With Feydeau, though he has been dead less than forty years, there is already a similar tale to tell. Produced in England or America, his plays seem like bad Oscar Wilde or Brandon Thomas turned scabrous. Even the superbly acted Barrault production of *Keep an Eye on Amélie!* in Paris was weakened by the work of a designer who tended to substitute *chichi* decoration for robustness.[11] Recent book illustrations of either Labiche or Feydeau can be relied on to give the latter-day, effete notion of them—and of farce.

In making a certain claim for farce I have stressed that it has more in common with melodrama and even tragedy than with naturalistic drama. In doing so I have understressed the differences, for most of them are obvious. They amount to the fact that tragedy presents a nobler, more profound image of man. Struck with the thought of man's weakness, Pascal, a tragic mind if there ever was one, called him a reed, a thinking reed. Farce confronts the cruder

[9] In, for example, the Appleton-Century-Crofts edition of *Un Chapeau de paille d'Italie* and the Parisian compilation *Masques: Théâtre 1944-46.*

[10] And reproduced in Lucien Dubech's *Histoire générale illustrée du théâtre*, Volume V, p. 119.

[11] A sketch of his, reproduced in Barrault's *Reflections on the Theatre*, opposite p. 140, will satisfy anyone on this point. Its demonstrative delicacy suggests a Bonwit Teller store window rather than the milieu of an Amélie or the mental world of a Feydeau.

kinds of man's strength, all of which he misuses. Man, says farce, may or may not be one of the more intelligent animals; he is certainly an animal, and not one of the least violent; and one of the chief uses to which he puts his intelligence, such as it is, is to think aggression when he is not committing it. (Mona Lisa's civilized smile might mean that she was plotting murder, but is more likely to signify that she was imagining murders she would never plot.)

The people who act out his fantasies for the farceur—his characters—are what are commonly stigmatized as "not individuals but types": human nature in the abstract, in the mass, in the rough, in the raw, in anything but fine personal flower. Our encyclopedist remarks that they are stupid, which is an understatement. They are monuments to stupidity, disturbing yet, surely, deliberate reminders that God lavished stupidity on the human race with a recklessly prodigal hand. They put us in mind of our own stupidities. They even teach us (if we are not too stupid to learn) what stupidity is. For one thing, it is being absent in mind: the *distrait*, as Bergson showed, is a comic archetype . . .

Like Hitler, who acted out farcical fantasies, farce characters pass beyond stupidity into craziness, and the farceur must have the gift of some lunatics (such as paranoiacs) to build a large, intricate, and self-consistent structure of "improbabilities." *Charley's Aunt* is a loosely organized example. Any Feydeau play is an instance of the tightest and most complex organization possible, and, as a result, Feydeau has been praised by the few who appreciate such things for his superlative craftsmanship. In this department, a Labiche or a Feydeau is not excelled even by a Shakespeare, and it is fair enough to distinguish them from Shakespeare as "merely" craftsmen, and to assert that the art of farce is "all technique," provided we also see that such craftsmanship and technique arise from a certain mentality and communicate a particular vision (if not exactly a view) of life. When we praise the famous three- and five-act structures of Labiche and Feydeau, what are we praising? At the least, the efficiency with which the playwrights take a piece of life and box it up; at the most, their invention of new kinds of boxes and the virtuosity which they lavish upon packing paper, string, hammer, and nails. Dramatic critics—whose argot can also be "all technique"—speak of the "well-made play" or the closed type of structure (as against the open), which is a good beginning if we then observe that the result is a closed *mental* system, a world of its own, lit by its own lurid and unnatural sun. There is something frightening about such worlds because there is something maniacal about them. Danger is omnipresent. One touch, we feel, and we shall be sent spinning in space. The farceur's structure of scenes presents points for comparison with systems of delusion.

An example of a feature that has nearly always been considered a merely technical, literary, or theatrical fact is the swift tempo of farce. Men of the theatre encourage actors in farce to "get a move on" for the sake of slick showmanship, that is, to avoid boring the audience. In my passing comments on Chaplin, I have suggested that the speeding up of movements has a psychological and moral—or rather, immoral—effect, namely, that of making actions seem abstract and automatic when in real life they would be concrete and subject to free will. This effect being of the essence, rapidity is not merely a technical asset, it is a psychological necessity. No wonder "slow" productions are dull! No wonder expert critics of the genre, like Sarcey, describe the *verve* of farce as *endiablé!* The devil is in farce rhythm. Although the great farceurs drive with a very firm rein, they are trick artists and like to give the impression of being behind a runaway horse. This being one of the farcical "facts of life," one sees what a *trouvaille* was the plot of *An Italian Straw Hat*. Later, the chase was to be the pride and glory of the Keystone Cops. . . .

It is not my purpose, however, to provide a catalogue of devices and effects, but only, by showing how farce functions, to prove that it deserves a more positive definition and could, with the aid of a little psychology, be given one.

CLEVELAND MOFFETT:
The Essence of Rostand's Greatness [1]

It is good to know that from the outset of his career as poet and dramatist, M. Edmond Rostand has professed the loftiest literary principles and has been strong enough to live up to them, which, we may be sure, in these commercial days, argues a strength of character and a moral courage that stand out in marked contrast to the man's rather effeminate manner and physical unrobustness.

It seems natural enough after a writer has produced *Cyrano* and *L'Aiglon* that he should have been willing to work hard and wait long for such success, but is very different when these plays exist nowhere but as fancies in the author's brain or as pages in his table drawer.

It is hard to look, year after year, at a manuscript that nobody knows about or cares about and never waver in the conviction that it is good and that the world *must* one day pronounce it good. And it is hard to go on bravely, quietly working at another thing that may also have to wait. And then at another thing—for years. The man who can do that without compromise or surrender of his ideals must have in him something akin to inspiration; and Rostand did this practically for seven years, for his plays between 1891 and 1898 were either failures like *La Princesse Lointaine,* or but modest successes like *La Samaritaine.*

The chief virtue, then, in Rostand's method lies in his absolute unwillingness to be diverted from his serious purposes by anything in the nature of hackwork or anything that might have brought a quick but ephemeral popularity. He was always true to the finest that was in him; he would do his best or nothing. Money pressure could not move him, partly, no doubt, because he never felt money need. Yet, let us not forget how easy it is for a rich man to fall into habits of literary indolence or carelessness. Rostand was master of himself before he became master of his art.

As to what he has written or purposes to write Rostand

[1] From *The Theatre*, July 1901. *Ed.*

relies absolutely on his own judgment, will have nothing o. any other man's judgment, will sink or swim on his own ship, under his own flag, in his own way. In private life he is a charming and modest French gentleman; in dramatic and literary matters he is an absolute autocrat, to whose will even the imperious Sarah must yield; and, oddly enough, she yields gladly.

As to habits of composition, Rostand writes only when he can write best; he scorns the machine methods of some authors—so many words a day, so many lines a week. A play of his will be finished when it *is* finished, never before, and the date is never specified in any literary time-table. If his third act is not ready when people want it, then so much the worse for the people; the third act will *not* hurry.

Rostand feels tremendously what he is writing; he lives with his characters, he suffers with them. For days he will be lifted into such a frenzy of creation that food and sleep and time and the world are brushed aside as vain things. The blood of his heart, the tears of his soul, must get themselves somehow put down on paper at any cost to himself or others. He conceives of the poet's passion for his work as the intensest of all passions.

All of which makes it clear that he is a very extraordinary man, to whom ordinary rules scarcely apply.

EDWARD CHILDS CARPENTER:
Les Romanesques *in Philadelphia*[1]

The recent production in the Quaker City of Rostand's dainty and picturesque comedy, *Les Romanesques,* by the Browning Society of Philadelphia, was a dramatic event of rather more than usual interest, inasmuch that it was the first production of the play in English in this country. The piece has been performed in Boston in French, and in England it has been acted by Mrs. Patrick Campbell. The English actress used the Fletcher translation in English verse, published here by R. H. Russell under the title of *The Fantasticks,*[2] which is obviously a better title than that of *The Romancers,* of the Mary Hendee version, which the Society used. It would be indeed difficult to find the exact equivalent of the French title in English. *The Romantic Lovers* or *The Absurdly Romantic Lovers* would be about the author's meaning, and as his clever and gracefully written play is intended to be nothing more than a fantasy and satire, the title is perhaps happily rendered as *The Fantasticks. ...*

[A detailed plot synopsis is now given by Mr. Carpenter, ending as follows:] . . . Wounded, tattered and torn and weary with his struggle with the world, Percinet returns, finds Sylvette in the park and tells her of his woes. The lovers are reunited, Straforel's bill is paid, the fathers raze the wall once more and this most charming little play is ended.

That the members of the Browning Society did little more than suggest the fine possibilities in the piece goes without saying. For amateurs their performance was, on the whole, satisfactory. Some committed the blunder of mistaking satire for burlesque and overplayed their parts, and Miss Helen Baldwin, while she acted the part of Sylvette with intelligence, did not quite enter into the spirit of the character. Mr. H. S.

---

[1] As reviewed in *The Theatre,* July 1901. *Ed.*

[2] The title used for an Off-Broadway, musical version of the play. *Ed.*

Richardson looked well as Percinet, but his acting was colorless. Mr. William M. Price made an excellent Bergamin. The stage settings showed the exercise of both care and taste, and the piece was carefully and elaborately costumed, reflecting much credit on the stage management which was in the hands of Mr. H. S. Richardson.

ROBERT KEMP:
Thoughts on Song of Songs

Scarcely ten years separate the premiere of *Song of Songs* from its revival at the Comédie-Française this spring. And although the audience was reverent toward the death and the brilliant and fresh genius of Jean Giraudoux, I was annoyed to sense a barrenness and apathy—a lack of sensitivity. An explanation immediately comes to mind, but it is banal. Trying times have hardened our skins; the intelligence and the heart have turned into pachyderms. There is something more serious, though: we are growing less and less familiar with the Song of Solomon which Bossuet and Voltaire knew by heart. Other, more recent men, knew it too. Verlaine ("*J'arrive tout couvert encore de rosée—que le vent du matin vient glacer à mon front. . . .*") [1], brought to perfection the impetuous cry of the shepherd as he approached the Shulamite maiden: *Caput meum plenum est rore—Ma tête est pleine de rosée, et mes boucles des gouttes de la nuit.* [2] In [his novel] *Aphrodite*, Pierre Louÿs translates *Le Chant des Chants;* [3] and Chrysis inundates Demetrios' dream with it. Before talking to you about this perfect act, this poem by Giraudoux, I thought of studying what the most recent exegetes said about the great Jewish eclogue—by consulting the multiple dictionary which you find to your left as you enter the Bibliothèque Nationale. Here patient, well-informed men of God give orthodox replies to whatever is asked them concerning the Bible, Christian antiquities, and problems of theology.

But as I was opening volume CA-, I saw my pretty young neighbor, who was waiting for books in the next armchair, take a photograph from her bag and tenderly examine a face, a uniform, and a lieutenant's insignia. And I thought to myself that Giraudoux had perhaps never leafed through that dictionary—possibly the only one he mistrusted—and

---

[1] Literally: "I come still covered with dew—which the morning wind turns to ice on my forehead. . . ." *Ed.*

[2] "For my head is filled with dew, my locks with the mist of the night." *Ed.*

[3] Variation on the more common *Cantique des Cantiques. Ed.*

that what had set his thought in motion was the pure text of the Song of Songs, the version that is the most fluent, popular and therefore most poetically rich of them all. No poet is more bookish, more spontaneous, and more personal all at once than Giraudoux. He confirms President Herriot's definition of an Oriental sage in *Jadis*:[4] "Culture is what remains when one has forgotten everything. . . ." Well, not everything. But the minute details, the scholarly part. Whether it is a question of Judith putting Holofernes to death, of the burning of Gomorrha, or of the origins of the Trojan War,[5] he has retained only the essential: the rough legend in its most simple and traditional form. He immediately chose Solomon as the source of the *Song;* the Shulamite maiden leaving the harem where she was going to be the favorite; renouncing perfumes, jewels, servants, the daughters of Jerusalem; to share her small farm with the shepherd who offers her only his youth. . . . After all, that is how M. Renan ended, after careful meditation.[6]

The little shock, the impulse which provoked Giraudoux to write his own *Song* must have been a *rapprochement* in an affair which he himself was observing; the misfortune of some high official of the Quai d'Orsay, suddenly deprived of a tenderly loved young thing by some passing "attaché" aged twenty—an attaché, or a notary's clerk; that is Jerome's modest title in the play—or some other fresh-complexioned youngster. Since at that very moment Giraudoux could feel sixty approaching, the confidences moved him. "Wait a minute," he said to himself, "here, in all its glory, is Solomon's love affair, for which all the daughters of Israel wove and embroidered; and when it ended, it faded like the lily of the fields—that is, the anemone—which neither toils nor spins." He kept the subject, the title. . . . And like many diplomats who retreat into their self-made haven of dreams, goodness, and poetry to compensate for their positions, he would go into his private corner of melancholy and regret for the passage of time. He put himself in the position of the jilted "President" who is reminiscent of King Solomon, Aristide Briand, Philippe Berthelot.[7]

He delicately blended his personal treasure with the bucolic verses of the son of David. How he does it is his

[4] His autobiograhy. *Ed.*

[5] In *Judith, Sodom and Gomorrha,* and *The Trojan War Will Not Take Place,* respectively. *Ed.*

[6] Nineteenth-century French philosopher.

[7] Briand and Berthelot were Giraudoux's superiors in the diplomatic service. *Ed.*

technique, his secret. He makes new flowers grow in old books. And they are real flowers. Whereas when you touch the *En Marge* of Jules Lemaître,[8] you distinctly feel the silk, the imitation velvet, and the wire.

Here there are no big ideas. No question of the inevitability of wars, of injustice being preferable to disorder, of the disastrous meddling of the gods in the affairs of men. The injustice dealt with here is the natural order of things. "Intelligence, power, kindliness—what about them?" the manager of the café asks the President after Florence leaves. "Aren't they arms?" "Alas, no, manager. They're no more than the baggage train. There's only one arm weaker—genius." Goethe and Faust knew that; and knew it better than the ancient Greeks whose hearts grew old almost as quickly as their bodies. But civilization and cultivated living have succeeded in prolonging the youth of the heart without slowing down the decline of the body. We no longer laugh when Arnolphe is cast off in favor of insignificant young Horace. *The School for Wives* is a Song of Songs; and the Shulamite maiden is named Agnes.[9]

Giraudoux's scenario follows the same undulating line as the Jewish song. Like the Shulamite, Florence has been the prisoner of a good, generous man, whom she could not help admiring. But what can she do against the shepherd of the mountain? *Ecce iste venit saliens in montibus, transiliens colles. . . .* "Here he comes, leaping over the mountains, skipping over the hills." Translating into Giraudoux's words: "He is crossing the lawns. Tiger and Bismarck, our terrible wolfhounds, leap around his feet. How gentle is his look; he has killed a bee. How lightly he runs; he is trampling the flowers. . . . He is striding over the streams. His lips are like a thread of purple. He is breathing the scent of the roses." Do you see how the old song and the new follow and accompany each other? The new one is sonorous. The ear takes it in. The other is mute, and memory must reconstruct the counter-melody. "You are asking a great deal of us," say those who like the theater to lull their imaginations to sleep. What pleasure they are missing!

And the transposition of regions . . . the cedars of Lebanon becoming lime trees and chestnuts. It was under a lime tree that Florence received her first pearl from the President. She

---

[8] *En Marge des vieux livres*, stories by Jules Lemaître based on the classics of world literature. *Ed.*

[9] Heroine of Molière's *School for Wives*, who spurns her guardian, Arnolphe, because she is in love with a boy of her own age, Horace. *Ed.*

loves, not the anemones sown on Israel's soil, but azaleas, hydrangeas, zinnias. Oh, too-learned Giraudoux! How he loves magic, mysterious words like "Sesame" or "Abracadabra." He moves comfortably among horticultural labels. "Now enter my garden," the Shulamite said. Like Colette and Paul Claudel, Giraudoux knows vegetable language. It is one of his accomplishments, which Anatole France lacked, although he did strive from time to time to wither flowers in their vases.

Now, put together the moralist's reflections that occur throughout the *Song*. Solomon is the one who is made to comment on the instinct of the Shulamite maiden. With discretion and exquisite forbearance, the President says all there is to say. "I'm learning about love, Florence. Such lessons are always expensive." Florence is intelligent too, after the manner, I admit, of Roxane, if not of Cathos.[10] "What I had left of you in your absence, that too was a lot," she tells the President.

She is infinitely more complex than the little peasant Agnes, or than that passionate Oriental, the Shulamite. She knows the value of what she is losing, and the little worth of her choice. "A poor modest little affair like ours doesn't warrant such an end of the universe." For desire has wiped out everything. I grant that these delicate little thoughts are burned away and vanish as they cross the blazing footlights. But if we learn them by heart, they will not vanish again. And another delightful moment: with Jerome far away, Florence is on the point of allowing herself to be won back. One by one, the President returns the jewels she no longer wanted. "Take me away . . . !" The Shulamite did not say that. The President answers as if he himself were the author of *La Sagesse*:[11] "Be calm. He is coming." But once Jerome has returned, magic is indeed at work. "In love, the only thing that counts is presence," says the Cashier of the café. That dear old Cashier! It is possible to guess at everything in her past. Here we are in France. The money-taker and the tray-carrier know all about love. It is like that from birth, north and south of the Loire. Compared with these "lessons in love," what does the count have to compete with in *Tannhäuser*? A cave, in place of Versailles. Are there renegades who think there is too much wit in Giraudoux's *Song*, and that a simple little woman talks about love as eloquently as a Lafayette or a Stendhal? But that is what I

---

10 Roxane: heroine of Rostand's *Cyrano de Bergerac*. Cathos: in Molière's *Les Précieuses Ridicules (The Precious Young Women)*. *Ed.*

11 Luke 14:16-24, and Claudel's play, *La Sagesse*, based upon it. *Ed.*

am proud of: because it is almost true. Lisette spoke of love too. And as cleverly as her mistress.[12]

I am very fond of this precious *Song of Songs*. I see its honest success as a good sign. The playing is not undistinguished, but neither is it ideal. What would I want to change? The setting is still Jouvet's, and countersigned by Giraudoux himself. I ought therefore to keep quiet about it. But remembering the vines, cedar forests, flocks, and little fawns which are in the original poem, I would prefer a more pastoral café. More trees ought to be seen through the openings; the roses, the bees, and the grass of which the Cashier speaks should be near at hand. The scent of the Bois de Boulogne ought to pass from the courtyard into the garden. What else? That M. Debucourt—that perfect actor—consent to be less diplomatic and more presidential, now that Giraudoux, Briand, and Berthelot are no longer watching him. A trifle aged, a little neglected. . . . Watching him, I would never believe that this is his final affair. And it *must* be the last if the play is to end with an "amen." But these are meager quibblings—to relieve my conscience.

Translated by Joyce Bermel

[12] Lisette is the servant girl in Molière's *Love, the Doctor.* Ed.

JOSEPH CHIARI:
A Brief Survey of Modern French Drama [1]

The artistic sensibility which underlies the arts of our time
acquired its most distinctive traits at the end of the nineteenth
century, and, in spite of the ups and downs of two world wars
and the great progress of scientific discoveries, it still retains
them. Science has added to its failure to bring about the expected millennium a greater and greater anxiety brought
about by its potentially lethal discoveries. Nature and anything
pertaining to it have proved uncontrollable and murderous,
therefore artists tend to feel that the best is to abstract Nature, that is to say phenomenal reality, or to transmute it.
Such is not of course the point of view of Marxists or of true
Christians. The Marxists trust in scientific materialism and they
believe that the determinism of history works in their favour.
There is, and there has been, no Marxist theatre in France.
Sartre is the only important playwright who has shown affinities with Marxism, and his play *Les Mains sales* which
deals with Marxist ideology, was not received with applause
by the party. Brecht has been a success in Paris, not because
of his rather unorthodox Marxism, but because he has written good plays. His theatre is the opposite of naturalism, his
characters are no photographs of reality; they embody it in a
magnified way which makes every trait perceptible from the
auditorium. The actors keep at a distance from the part they
are playing, and the audience is kept at a distance from the
actors, so that there is no possible room here for any identification of actors with parts, or actors with audience. The
cleavage between nature and art is rigorously maintained.

Christianity from Thomas Aquinas onwards has regained
some of the materialism of Jewish thought and has reasserted
the Augustinian aspect of realism and existentialism, which
is the true foundation of Christianity shorn of Platonic and
neo-Platonic accretions. For true Christianity, the real actual-
izes the analogical diversities of being reflecting the imma-

1 From *The Contemporary French Theatre*, London, 1959. *Ed.*

nence and transcendence of the subsistent Being. What we call the real, in everyday life, is the world of phenomenal appearances which are used in art by the imagination as means to compose organic entities which symbolize or stand for experiences of perceptual apprehensions or of emotions which have been imaginatively lived. Imagination is not anti-realistic; on the contrary, it works directly from perceptual reality towards the revelation of the essential structures of reality which it apprehends in moments of apperception and which it represents in symbols. Great art is always realistic, not in the sense that it is perceptually the same for all, something which is not possible, but in the sense that the phenomenal appearances used, are perceptually recognizable as in Rembrandt's paintings, or imaginatively recognizable as embodiments of truth, in Milton, Shakespeare or Dante. They are not unreal shapes from the world of fantasy, they are imaginative representations of relationships between existents themselves and also between them and the transcendent Being which informs existence. The realism of Rembrandt or of Breughel is precise and without any intellectual distortions; the imagery of Dante and Shakespeare always conforms to perceptual reality, even when it purports to suggest the impression of fleeting emotions or visions. The best poetry of Yeats is that of his later years and it is taut, precise and realistic. It is the same for Eliot and Claudel, who although they are described as post-Symbolists, convey their experiences through precise images or symbolizations of the phenomenal world.

[My] examination of the work of Sartre, Anouilh, Montherlant, and Claudel has shown that these writers displayed at times, taut, stark realism, fully integrated by the imagination. As a staunch Catholic convinced that creation was God's work, Claudel had the greatest regard for reality and, together with other Catholic artists like Ghéon and Copeau, he played an important part in the flight from naturalism, and in restoring drama to its pristine function of religious art without ever confusing it with religion itself.

Naturalism in art is not the copying or the mirroring of nature, for every copy or reflection distorts and is not the real thing, but the lifting up of lumps of nature through senses as mechanical as cameras or tele-recorders, and their use without any imaginative transmutation. This is plain reporting and functionalism, but not art, and it can only be the refuge of the small talent, for none of the important originators of the naturalistic movement at the end of the nineteenth century applied his preachings to the letter. Flaubert used to spend days in rolling his phrases through his *gueuloir*, and his dialogue was certainly not the kind that could be obtained by tele-recording from everyday life the characters he sought to portray. Yet this is the kind of naturalism, which some critics, as intent on discovering genius as Columbus's sailors were in discovering land, have hailed as the new theatre. They say that this is the age of the plain man and therefore the setting of plays must be a plain man's home, so that when he goes to the theatre and looks at such a setting from the other side of the proscenium, he will feel in his own climate while the characters on the stage will behave and talk in a way which will enable him to think that it is he himself who is on the stage. Copeau's dream of communion between actor and audience in a religious theatre is in this case fully realized, and it enables the audience not to worship God but to worship itself. The aim of this kind of naturalistic theatre is not aesthetic pleasure, but satisfaction of the craving for sensationalism for the political and sociological topicality which one finds in the daily Press; it is a kind of naturalism which, much as its authors profess to despise it, rejoins the naturalism of the bedroom farce and kitchen comedy which are the usual post-prandial forms of entertainment or jollifications of the commercial theatre. The names of these playwrights are not worth mentioning at this juncture, but there is one playwright who sails very close to naturalism which he mingles with abstractionism and who has also been hailed as a new light by professional discoverers of talents and snobs intent in being "cultured": Ionesco. In some of his plays he uses a form of flat naturalism made up of dull iterations of platitudes and banalities, which Flaubert had already listed in his "dictionnaire des idées reçues." The result is unbearable banality and dullness, and characters who sound like mechanical parrots. In other plays he uses surrealistic fantasy, expressionism and explorations of the subconscious in a manner which could be exploited in novels or films, but which is totally unsuited to drama. The result is that none of his full-length plays are worth a serious examination and his success, which is entirely out of proportion with his achievement, rests for the moment on two or three moderately good one-act plays.

In the same line of country we find Beckett whose reputation has also been much inflated, but with far more reason and evidence of talent than in the case of Ionesco. *Waiting for Godot* is not, in my view, a masterpiece, but it is in parts an original play and quite an achievement. The first act is truly brilliant and the author has sustained throughout a masterly dialogue laden with suggestiveness and conveying admirably the boredom and hopelessness of the two tramps, representative of the human condition, and whose plight draws our sympathy. Unfortunately the second act labours the first, is fully repetitious and overstresses a very obvious symbolism. This play is technically a dead end, but it is also a commendable *tour de force* and it is interesting to watch and see what Beckett will do next.

There are no such doubts about Montherlant who is now with T. S. Eliot, the only writer in the world who could write a tragedy, that is to say who has proved that he is capable of approaching the highest summits of drama. Anouilh remains the most versatile and accomplished playwright of our time. His last plays, which have not been discussed, continue to show him as a master of wry pathos—which is not of course, the pathos of tragedy, which must remain pure of any Chaplinesque or little man's comedy which dilutes it, and must be only shot through with the grotesque and irony which heighten it. In spite of certain failings, such as lack of unity of style and the absence of a truly tragic character, I am inclined to think that O'Casey's masterly play *Juno and the Paycock* comes closer to tragedy than any of Anouilh's plays, and for that matter, than those of Arthur Miller. My previous restrictive remark about one of his plays, should not be construed as a lack of admiration for his achievements which are, in my opinion, unsurpassed in the American theatre of to-day. Yet in spite of his praiseworthy intentions to write what he calls a tragedy of the common man, I am not convinced that he has as yet fully succeeded. Reading or watching the performance of his best plays, one is brought face to face with aspects of characters, events, situations which partially shatter the atmosphere of tragedy. The melodramatic flaunting of the dead airman's letter, at the end of *All My Sons,* is such an event and the paltriness, sentimentality and mushy suicide of Willy Loman, together with the sociologico-psychological ambiguities inherent to the theme, mar the tragic atmosphere of *Death of a Salesman.* On the contrary, Eddie Carbone, in *A View from the Bridge,* shows none of these defects. He is like a dumb animal consumed by elemental force which he does not understand, but which leads him to destruction. He is, all in all, the most accomplished tragic character Miller has created. Tragic emotions whatever they are, must not be flawed by self-consciousness or compromises which could suggest vulgarity, sensationalism or insignificance. The tragic hero need not necessarily be cast in a heroic mould, but he must not be stained by any of the petty defects that have been mentioned above, or anything similar, for, if so, the pity which he draws from the audience will lack terror and could well induce in it conscious or subconscious strains of contempt and condescension. Similarly the speech of tragedy, whether prose or verse, and whatever its level, must always be concise, avoiding throughout, pseudo-poetical vagueness suggestive of sentimentality or incoherence of vision, and baroque adornments which are empty rhetoric. One could never stress enough the fact that imagination is not day-dreaming but creativity, and that poetry, whether direct or indirect, is, when it is good, an art of rigorous precision.

Sartre is only in his middle life and he has shown that he can compensate by mind and psychological insight what he lacks in dramatic skill. There is no doubt that he still has plenty to say. The name of Sartre has often been linked with that of a man who shares some of his philosophical beliefs, and this man is Albert Camus.[2] To date, he has written four plays—*Le Malentendu, Caligula, Les Justes* and *l'Etat de Siège*. It seems to me that Camus has not yet resolved the problem of giving dramatic reality to the ideas and problems which preoccupy him, and I have too great an admiration for his other imaginative works to take up what still seems to me a secondary aspect of his creative activities and to submit it to a rigorous analysis and evaluation. This seems to me both unreasonable and unwise. On the one hand Camus's dramatic works do not yet warrant a full assessment of his dramatic abilities, on the other he is still young; in fact he has not yet reached the age when for instance both Giraudoux and Montherlant produced their first dramatic successes, therefore it seems wise to postpone judgment.

Sartre is well-known as an existentialist; up to a point, Montherlant and Anouilh have a similar attitude. For them as for Sartre, man is alone; he is the sum of his actions; he makes his life and its meaning (as we have seen for Ferrante) can only be known once he is dead. These writers are part of a climate which includes Camus, who believes with them that life is absurd and does not imply any essence, and also writers like Bernanos, who was a believer, or Malraux and Montherlant who have a religious attitude. All these writers accept the notion of some kind of plight or despair which, whether it is called original sin or the absurdity of the human

---

[2] Mr. Chiari's book was published two years before the death of Albert Camus, but Camus wrote no subsequent original plays, only a dramatization of Dostoyevsky's *The Possessed. Ed.*

condition in a hostile, timeless world, can elicit only one response from man: a noble stoicism which refuses to be deluded by pharisaism or false values, and which seeks refuge, not in passivity or in the ivory tower, but in action towards all those who endure the same plight and who accept all—death and even wars—with a noble dispassionateness. Leaving out questions about the Primal cause and the meaning of evil, the Promethean revolt of all these atheists against suffering and despair meets Christ's love and accepted suffering for his fellow beings.

Together with these playwrights, there are excellent producers who have maintained in Paris a style of production which is both inspired and free from sensationalism. Foremost among these producers is Jean-Louis Barrault, who has had the courage to produce plays which no commercial management would have undertaken. With him there are Pierre Dux, and Jean Meyer, who produces regularly at the Comédie Française. The dowager of the theatre has not been unwilling to open its doors to living playwrights, and there is no doubt that Paris remains the town which can still claim the most lively theatre in the world.

FRANCIS FERGUSSON:
Sartre as Playwright

Perhaps it is not too soon to offer a few observations on Sartre's dramaturgy, and on his sudden career in the American Theater. I take as my text three of his plays: *No Exit*, as produced by the *Theatre Intime* in Princeton, *The Victors*, produced by New Stages in their Bleecker Street theater, and *Red Gloves*, the Jed Harris production, late of the Mansfield.

No Exit was the first of Sartre's plays to attract wide attention in this country. Garcin, a pacifist who subtly betrayed his cause, his comrades and his wife; Inez, a lesbian who drove a man and a woman to their deaths; and Estelle, a faithless wife who drove her lover to suicide, have died and meet in Hell. Hell consists for them in the fact that they are confined together in an ugly second empire parlor. They are literally everything to each other, for they can see themselves, confirm their own existences, only in each other's eyes. They begin to hate each other after the first five minutes; for they discover that they can get no satisfaction from each other, not even that of lust. Estelle is not a lesbian, and she and Garcin cannot get together because Garcin suffers from a kind of guilty *pudeur*, he loses his enthusiasm when Inez, watching his advances to the willing Estelle, makes scornful comments. Garcin puts their plight succinctly: "Hell is other people." When this little trap has been explained with great dialectical ingenuity and with mounting suspense, the three see that their punishment is to consist of an eternity of each other's murderous scrutiny; and the curtain falls.

The Victors was adapted by Thornton Wilder from Sartre's *Morts Sans Sépulture*. I think Mr. Wilder did a competent and faithful job of translation, but I am judging on the basis of the performance which seemed to me to preserve the intent of the original. The acting (which was in

1 From *Partisan Review*, April 1949.

general good, and sometimes superb) may account for a good deal of the vitality of the play. The story is that of a group of Maquis captured by the Vichy police, at about the time of the early Allied victories in Normandy. The police torture the captives, to make them reveal the whereabouts of their leader. The Maquis are a varied group, illustrating every possible attitude to torture, from an experienced revolutionary who takes it calmly, to a fifteen-year-old boy who collapses at the mere thought, and including one woman. The leader himself is added to this group when the police arrest him, not knowing who he is; and though he is in no physical danger, he is soon morally "engaged" in the ordeal, and suffers a more painful case of *Angst* than the actual victims. Upon this situation Sartre plays many ingenious variations. One of the men murders the boy, and then engages in some painful casuistry to justify the murder. The woman is raped, and the physical coward commits suicide. In the final scene, when the leader has been released, the captives can reveal his former hiding place without betraying the cause; and this produces a new *cas de conscience* for them to debate: is it better to go free, or to stay, for the sake of thwarting their tormentors? They finally decide for freedom, but one of the policemen shoots them anyway to indulge a purely personal appetite for cruelty.

Jed Harris's production of *Red Gloves*, adapted by Daniel Taradash from *Les Mains Sales*, was a skillful job of denaturing Sartre for the Broadway market. *Les Mains Sales*, as Sartre wrote it, is a grim contemporary parable of *Existenz*, illustrating the same metaphysical extremity as all his other plays. Hugo, a young man from a well-to-do family in a central European country, has joined the Communist Party because he feels the need to prove himself in action, and has an idealistic faith (which Sartre does not share) in the redemptive destiny of the proletariat. The Russians are beginning to drive the German armies back; soon they will arrive. Hoederer (the local Communist chief) wants to make a coalition with the liberals and conservatives in order to take power as bloodlessly as possible, but the comrades think this a betrayal of the Party line, and they decree that Hoederer must be liquidated. Hugo volunteers for this job, is made Hoederer's secretary, and, with his nice young wife Jessica, moves into the old palace where the Party has its headquarters. But when he actually sees Hoederer, and hears his side of the story, he doesn't want to kill him. Thus he is caught in an impossible situation: he does not recognize his moral freedom either in murdering or not murdering: it is the familiar existential mixture of pride and self-hatred, intensified by an obsessive need to make a crucial decision. His wife unwittingly helps him out of this blind alley: bored with his indecision, she makes love to Hoederer. Hoederer demurs at first; an affair with Jessica would ruin a good secretary; but at last (candidly explaining that he hasn't had a woman in six months) he sighs and kisses her. This little vacation from Party matters is his undoing: Hugo catches them and shoots Hoederer. This, however, solves nothing for Hugo. He is sent to prison for the murder, but released with the other political prisoners when the Russians arrive, and he carries his existential problem right along with him. Was the murder heroism—the gesture of a big man of action such as he had always wanted to be—or was it a mere bourgeois crime of passion? He also finds, when he is released, and looks up his tough Party mistress, Olga, that the Party line has changed: Hoederer's policy of boring from within has been adopted, and Hoederer is canonized as a martyr to the orthodox cause. Hugo's crucial choice now appears in other terms, closer to what Sartre thinks of as the one reality of the human situation: He may either rejoin the party in another country under another name, or keep his name, together with the blame or credit for the murder. Since the murder is all he has to call his own, the only sign of his existence, he chooses the latter alternative, and cheerfully marches off with the comrades to be liquidated.

Mr. Taradash's *Red Gloves* keeps the main facts of this typical and very skillful Sartre plot. His changes were chiefly cuts, in the role of Olga, Hugo's communist mistress (reduced in his version to a perfunctory lay figure who merely gives information) and in the scenes between Hugo and Jessica. But the effect of these cuts was to make a very different play, in which Hugo is no longer the protagonist, and the existential theme is almost lost to sight. In *Les Mains Sales* we learn (mostly by way of Hugo's relation to Olga) that he identifies himself with Raskolnikov, and even took the name of this hero to use in the Party. Thus he inherits the sterile willfulness of that long line of lost young highbrows who are Sartre's own ancestors—Julien Sorel, Ivan Karamazov, Gide's immoralist, and the rest; and so we understand more richly the absurd incommensurability between his platonic infatuation with the idea of action, and the Realpolitik of the comrades themselves. In *Les Mains Sales* the relation between Hugo and Jessica is also much more developed than it is in *Red Gloves*; and Sartre completely understands their childish eroticism, so abstract and irresponsible that it is hardly sexual at all. In the economy of his play, this relationship establishes the background of futility, emptiness and moral anarchy which we must have if we are to accept Hugo's compulsion to murder. When Mr. Taradash drastically reduced these elements, he cut most of the crazy intensity out of the role of Hugo, leaving Hoederer the center of interest. In the performance, Boyer's authority and intelligence also helped to make that role overshadow all the rest, and to turn the play into a study of a saintly commissar (Yogi and thug in one) who is martyrized by his myopic associates.

I have remarked that Messrs Harris and Taradash between them did a skillful job of transforming Sartre's sardonic parable into the sleek suburban terms of serious, or "better," Broadway. The production was handsome, and granted that version of the play, the acting was good. John Dall, for instance, as Hugo, was certainly not acting the role which Sartre wrote, but he offered a shrewd and humorous portrait of a mildly leftish young American with horn-rimmed spectacles, a BA in Social Studies, and a minor job in the New Deal. One could not believe that such a young man would be that kind of a martyr to a theory of himself; the American analogue of Hugo would be Leopold or Loeb, rather than our bachelors of arts who take up government work and get into messes with Communism. In the same way, Joan Tetzel was charming as a nice young wife who is bored with her husband; but she was far from presenting the amoral little kitten Sartre had in mind.

These three plays, though the productions they received were different, and also the audiences they met, all proved to have great theatrical viability. There is no doubt that Sartre has found a way to make himself heard, even in our jaded and confused theaters. He has the authentic playwright's gift for living speech, and for characters with the immediate impact of newsreel closeups. He is also an extremely resourceful plot-maker in the French tradition—the French word for plot is "intrigue." It would be a mistake to dismiss his plays merely because his existentialism is so feeble as ethics or epistemology. But his philosophy did lead him to his dramaturgic formula. He writes a "drama of crisis" on the analogy of Barth's "theology of crisis"; and it is this existentialist slant that gives the new look to his moral casuistry and his gripping well-made plots.

Each of his plays illustrates the extreme, or existential situation, but his style has changed and grown a good deal. In his first plays he tried to put his metaphysical point unrealistically, in *The Flies* by means of the Orestes myth, in *No Exit* by the metaphor of Hell. But his didacticism is too violent and literal for this style (which he may have learned from Giraudoux) and the photographic realism of *The Respectful Prostitute*, *The Victors*, and *Red Gloves* serves his purposes better. Contemporary life offers plenty of extreme situations, with all the authority of the headline and all the fascination of the street-accident. He found one in this country also—that of the Negro unjustly accused of murder. I can think of another which he has overlooked: a visit to the dentist. Here too we have an inescapable ordeal with an obsessive power; a form of torment which threatens the very basis of human freedom, and which only the heroic can survive with dignity:

> *Beneath the bludgeoning of fate*
> *My head is bloody but unbowed.*

And this situation is more austerely existential than most of the ones he has used: it is more abstract, and may the more easily be considered apart from ultimate values.

I think that all three audiences which I observed at his plays, though unquestionably held during the performance, were in the long run somewhat let down by this abstract nature of his basic situation—the moral crisis considered apart from ultimate common values. "I have suppressed God the Father," he tells us; and he adds that there is no such thing as human nature. He is consistent enough to suppress also all the up-to-date versions of a common end: he is not interested in the Communism of his characters in *Red Gloves*, nor in the Cause of his Maquis in *The Victors*, nor in the actual problem of racial justice in the South—these issues merely precipitate extreme situations which illustrate his peculiar moral athleticism in a meaningless world. The *Red Gloves* production softened this metaphysical anarchism, inviting the rather puzzled audience to interpret the play in a long-suffering liberal sense. The productions of *No Exit* and of *The Victors*, by the Princeton undergraduates and New Stages respectively, were true to the plays he wrote, and both had the honesty and disinterested pleasure in the theater which Broadway seldom offers; I am sorry I lack the space to do justice to these performances. But there too the audiences seemed slightly puzzled and unsatisfied, and for the same reason. The highbrow, socially-conscious Bleecker Street audience would seem to be the right one for Sartre, if we have it at all; but I thought they were first piqued, and then disappointed, to discover that *The Victors* was not an anti-Vichy tract.

The American Theater, trying to be up-to-date, groping about for material with some life in it, has received Sartre with enthusiasm and treated him as handsomely as it could, both on and off Broadway. But on the whole this encounter does not look very auspicious. As for Sartre himself, probably it would be necessary to see him in the livelier theatrical life of Paris, where he is only one voice in an animated, but not too serious discussion which has been going on for a long time, in order to place him in the proper perspective. Our dispersed, spasmodic and undernourished theater has nothing to digest him with. Until and unless we develop some sort of continuous theatrical life of our own, we shall be in the position of eavesdropping upon a conversation in the next flat, trying to make sense out of the fragments we get, and usually mistaking the most emphatic remarks for the most pregnant.

SIGNET CLASSICS by French Authors

ADOLPHE and THE RED NOTEBOOK
$\qquad$ **by Benjamin Constant**
By the close friend of Mme. de Stael, this 18th-century French novel is the story of a young man's passion for a woman with whom he can never be happy. *Adolphe* translated by Carl Wildman, *The Red Notebook* translated by Norman Cameron. Introduction by Harold Nicolson. (#CD1—50¢)

CANDIDE, ZADIG and Selected Stories $\qquad$ **by Voltaire**
The master of social commentary employs his ruthless wit to dissect science and spiritual faith, ethics and legal systems, love and human vanity. Newly translated with an Introduction by Donald Frame. (#CD35—50¢)

THE DEATH OF A NOBODY $\qquad$ **by Jules Romains**
This noted modern classic, by a novelist considered "the French Dos Passos," tells how the memory of an unimportant nobody survives in the minds of all who knew him. Translated by Desmond MacCarthy and Sidney Waterlow. Afterword by Maurice Natanson.
$\qquad$ (#CD54—50¢)

MANON LESCAUT $\qquad$ **by Abbé Prevost**
The first modern "novel of passion" on which the operas of Massenet and Puccini are based. Newly translated and with an introduction by Donald Frame.
$\qquad$ (#CP96—60¢)

NIGHT FLIGHT $\qquad$ **by Antoine de St.-Exupéry**
A novel of beauty and power about the intrepid flyers of the early, heroic age of aviation. Translated by Stuart Gilbert. Foreword by André Gide. (#CD46—50¢)

THE PRINCESS OF CLEVES $\qquad$ **by Mme. de Lafayette**
A profound and delicate psychological novel about a woman involved in a triangle. Newly translated with a Foreword by Walter J. Cobb. (#CD89—50¢)

To Our Readers: We welcome your request for our free catalog of Signet and Mentor books. If your dealer does not have the books you want, you may order them by mail enclosing the list price plus 5¢ a copy to cover mailing. The New American Library of World Literature, Inc., P. O. Box 2310, Grand Central Station, New York 17, N. Y.

How To Build
A Low-Cost Library

You can build a personal library of the best books for as little as 35 or 50 cents a volume. Choose from thousands of the classics and best sellers in literature, biography, poetry, art, history, religion, reference, and science as listed in a new catalog:

Paperbound books in print

If you've often had trouble finding the paperbacks you want—here are over 13,000—with information on how and where to get them. Here you can locate all the low-priced paper books available either by checking the thousands of titles listed alphabetically by author and by title, or by looking under any of the 90 categories where selected titles are grouped under helpful subject classification.

Order your copy of this unique buying guide today—either from your dealer or direct from RRB, New American Library of World Literature, 501 Madison Avenue, New York 22, N. Y.

Make checks payable to: R. R. Bowker Company. Single copies are $2 prepaid, or you can subscribe to the 4 quarterly issues for just $6 a year and automatically be kept up to date on available paperbacks.